The World We Have Gained

Peter Laslett

The World We Have Gained
Histories of Population and Social Structure

Essays presented to Peter Laslett
on his Seventieth Birthday

Edited by
Lloyd Bonfield, Richard M. Smith
and Keith Wrightson

Basil Blackwell

First published 1986

Basil Blackwell Ltd
108 Cowley Road, Oxford OX4 1JF, UK

Basil Blackwell Inc.
432 Park Avenue South, Suite 1505,
New York, NY 10016, USA

British Library Cataloguing in Publication Data

The world we have gained: histories of population
and social structure: essays presented to Peter
Laslett on his seventieth birthday.
1. Great Britain—Social conditions
I. Bonfield, Lloyd   II. Smith, Richard M.
(Richard Michael)   III. Wrightson, Keith
IV. Laslett, Peter
941   HN385

ISBN 0–631–13871–4

Library of Congress Cataloging in Publication Data
Main entry under title:

The World we have gained.

Includes index.
1. Social structure—England—History—Addresses,
essays, lectures. 2. England—Population—History—
Addresses, essays, lectures. 3. England—Economic
conditions—Addresses, essays, lectures. 4. Marriage—
England—History—Addresses, essays, lectures.
I. Bonfield, Lloyd, 1949– . II. Smith,
Richard (Richard M.) III. Wrightson, Keith.
HN385.W67 1986   305'.0942   85–25466
ISBN 0–631–13871–4

Typeset in 10 on 11½pt Linotron Baskerville
by Photographics Ltd, Honiton, Devon
Printed in Great Britain by T.J. Press Ltd, Padstow, Cornwall

Contents

Preface

For Peter Laslett, retirement has been a concept to be studied rather than a condition to be experienced. Although over two years have passed since Peter relinquished his Readership in Politics and the History of Social Structure in the University of Cambridge, his friends and colleagues have observed little change in his way of life. Visitors continue to call frequently at 27 Trumpington Street and E-2 Bishop's Hostel, Trinity College, in search of advice, discussion or simply an audience with one of the internationally most influential social historians of our time. Ideas, papers and controversy are still generated by him at an almost alarming rate. If anything, freedom from university and college responsibilities has enabled Peter to indulge his intellectual passions, proselytizing energies and creative influence to an even greater extent. He is even more conspicuously a historian on the move physically as well as intellectually. His interests, and their geographical limits, have expanded: the former extending from a continued preoccupation with household structures, the processes generating them and the transfer incomes sustaining them, to the microsimulation of kin sets and the history of ageing; and the latter from Europe to China. In the University of the Third Age he has made a further institutional contribution to British educational life not unlike that he made in the planning stage of the Open University, and one which creates yet again a new arena for participation and a new agenda for study.

Our purpose cannot therefore be to observe the rites of passage into the twilight of an academic career. Rather, we celebrate the onset of an eighth decade of continued vigour. Teaching, research and writing have characterized Peter Laslett's past 40 years, and there are no signs that a man who was never bounded by the parochialism of academe is about to change his ways as a result of a shift in employment status. Peter is no academic patriarch to be shuffled off with appropriate decencies by his heirs and successors anxious to get their hands on his land. He remains a Young Turk in an age of Young Fogeys, an enthusiast in a world of trimmers, a pathfinder at a time when too many are content to retreat defensively into their shells. What we wish to acknowledge between these covers is his continued commitment to the task of 'understanding ourselves in time' – incomprehensible and unseemly to his detractors, but inspirational to his students, his colleagues and above all his readers.

It is shared respect for that vital concern which unites the contributors to this volume. We vary in our institutional affiliations, our disciplines, our preoccupations and our relationships to Peter Laslett. We are of diverse nationality. We are demographers, lapsed geographers, anthropologists, statisticians, historians and lawyers. We are former students, colleagues, friends and visitors. We do not necessarily agree with one another, or with Peter Laslett himself. Our link is the influence of a man, and more specifically the seminars and countless discussions over tea at the Cambridge Group at which Peter shared his insights, his criticisms, his wit, his delight in provocation, and most of all his sheer enthusiasm and intellectual excitement. We have all been enriched intellectually – and indeed emotionally – by our contacts with Peter, be they at a reading desk, across a seminar room or around a table.

The year 1985 marked not only the seventieth birthday of a man for whom we have a profound respect, but the coming of age of his most influential work. *The World We Have Lost* was a book full of questions. Still more, it was pregnant with the hope that those questions could be answered. It appalled some of Peter's peers and contemporaries, wedded as they were to their certainties and comfortable assertions. To far more it was a revelation, an inspiration, a promise. It announced an agenda. It introduced a methodology. It offered a perspective. Above all, it established connections between national historiographies, between the past and the present. A survey of the references to *The World We Have Lost* in the *Social Science Citation Index* serves to demonstrate its enormous influence. No other work ostensibly devoted to the history of early modern England has been cited (often repeatedly) not only in every one of the familiar historical journals of the English-speaking world but also in publications as diverse as *New Society, Daedalus, The Journal of Biosocial Science, Human Relations, African Affairs, Psychiatry, Central European History, World Affairs* and *Western Political Quarterly*, to name but a few. The establishment of such a wide-ranging sphere of relevance and influence is not to be ignored.

Many whose backgrounds are in the 'harder' social sciences and who cite or encounter Peter's work for the first time are not always cognizant of the fact that he has another distinguished career in the history of political theory, to which his contribution in the 20 years after the Second World War might be regarded in most quarters as more than sufficient for any mere mortal. Peter now rather disparagingly refers to these years as a phase when he 'fretted about where to place and how to interpret the meaning of the commas in the writings of Locke and

Filmer'. We suspect, however, that he remains proud, and justifiably so, of his contribution in this area. In fact, in a more reflective mood he would most likely insist that no obvious redirection of his career occurred in the early 1960s, preferring rather to see his subsequent research and writing as a logical outgrowth of his earlier preoccupations. Indeed, although *The World We Have Lost* was eventually published in 1965, it had begun life in Cambridge in 1954. At that time, in addition to teaching the history of political theory, Peter delivered a series of lectures on the history of English social structure which, in the context of Cambridge and British history at that time, were decidedly avant-garde. Out of these lectures emerged a radio talk given on his beloved Third Programme in the late 1950s under the title of 'The world we have lost'. It is amusing to note – although a telling reminder of his flexibility and willingness to admit mistakes – that in this talk he provided an account of the early modern family and household as extended and multi-generational in form and with domestic work undertaken by a large group of related persons. Of course the sources he employed for this interpretation were largely literary, in particular the work of Sir Robert Filmer, on whom Peter had earlier published a number of studies. His suspicion of belletristic evidence, of which his critics might be surprised to discover he is very much the master, and of those scholars who use it in their so-called re-creation of past societies, has ever since remained prominent in Peter's approach as a social historian.

Peter had intended to publish those Cambridge lectures in 1959, but for various reasons he did not then complete the task. In the autumn of that year he was very firmly stopped in his tracks by what he found in *The Rector's Book of Clayworth, Nottinghamshire*, a copy of which (appropriately perhaps, given the peripatetic nature of his work patterns) he came to consult in the Folger Shakespeare Library in Washington. That source, containing two village listings taken within 12 years of each other in the seventeenth century, proved a revelation to Peter. Their contents, when analysed and later published in a Festschrift, might be seen as inaugurating a new kind of English social history that eventually received a much clearer definition with the appearance of *The World We Have Lost* some two years later. The latter book coincided with Peter's fiftieth birthday, and the subsequent decade witnessed a phase of ceaseless activity, including much writing, travelling and discussion. In particular that period saw a great achievement, one that must never be underestimated in view of the practical difficulties that had to be overcome and the research paradigm shift in history it entailed – the formal establishment of what came to be known as the 'Group'. This eventually crystallized physically around 20 Silver Street, where two of us retain vivid memories of postgraduate supervisions and the tangible excitement that accompanied coffee and tea breaks when everyone's findings were announced and debated *in commune*. In that atmosphere, very largely because of the example set by Peter, history ceased to be the concern of the researcher contemplating his or her own navel in glorious isolation.

The events of the 15 or 20 years that followed are much better known. We do not wish to pursue them here, as we suspect that they and Peter and the Group's work during them, will warrant an important place in a full account of the history of the social sciences in the last third of the twentieth century. A remarkable momentum has been sustained during this 'second career' as Peter's energy has driven him from issue to issue: from the problems of classifying domestic group structure, to illegitimacy, to the history of ageing, to the family's relations with the collectivity, to the daunting but so fundamental question of stochastic influences on social processes.

In our title we have chosen to echo that of Peter's seminal intervention, the flag-bearer of that second academic career which we honour for its achievement and celebrate in its continuance. To do so is an affectionate joke. It is an acknowledgement. Perhaps it may also seem a pretension. This is not a volume which attempts to resolve the myriad issues which exercised Peter when he set out to urge the recovery of *The World We Have Lost*. Far from it. The agenda which he proposed has not been exhausted in the 21 years of active research and debate which have ensued. Neither do we lodge any claim to the further definition of the 'new' social history, or 'historical sociology' as Peter is wont to call it. We hope, however, that there may be embedded in this collection an essay that will prove to be as portentous in its implications as that which Peter himself wrote in that Festschrift in 1963 for David Ogg. We have drawn together a varied array of scholars who have in common a concern for the themes announced by Peter Laslett in a new way, and elaborated by him and by those who have trodden in and around his footsteps in the years that separated the first and the third editions of *The World We Have Lost*. If these essays add successfully to the accumulating pool of knowledge on the history of western society for which he called so effectively, then we have repaid part of our debt to Peter Laslett. Peter always urged those around him to break ground, to discover, to count and to weigh, to compare, to conceptualize, to think afresh. He still does. We still try.

Lloyd Bonfield
Richard M. Smith
Keith Wrightson

1

Population Turnover in Medieval Essex: The Evidence of some Early-Fourteenth-Century Tithing Lists

L. R. Poos

In 1963, as he was increasingly turning his attention toward the historical sociology of pre-industrial England, Peter Laslett published a paper which he later described as 'that first exercise in the historical analysis of familial and social structure'.[1] 'Clayworth and Cogenhoe' dealt with two seventeenth-century English parishes, each of which possesses two comprehensive listings of inhabitants compiled within a short time-span.[2] Laslett's discovery (then startling) that more than half the dwellers in a seemingly ordinary English village would disappear within a decade, some by death but most through migration, was an early milestone in our understanding of 'the world we have lost'. 'Clayworth and Cogenhoe' is also notable as a precursor of much subsequent research, since community or parochial listings of this kind, collected and analysed by members of the Cambridge Group over succeeding years, were crucial for establishing many features of household size and composition in the English past.[3]

1 The author is grateful to Richard Smith and Lloyd Bonfield for advice and comments; to Christopher Dyer, for information relating to the Margaret Roding documents discussed; and to the British Academy and the managers of the Ellen McArthur Fund at the University of Cambridge History Faculty, whose financial assistance helped partially to defray research expenses.

2 P. Laslett and J. Harrison, 'Clayworth and Cogenhoe', in H.E. Bell and R.L. Ollard (eds), *Historical essays presented to David Ogg* (London, 1963), pp. 157–84, reprinted in revised and expanded form in P. Laslett, *Family life and illicit love in earlier generations: essays in historical sociology* (Cambridge, 1977), pp. 50–101. The quotation is cited from the latter, p. 50, and all subsequent citations of this paper will be from the later version also.

3 For example, P. Laslett, 'The study of social structure from listings of inhabitants', in E.A. Wrigley (ed.), *An introduction to English historical demography* (London, 1966), pp. 160–208; P. Laslett, 'Mean household size in England since the sixteenth century', in P. Laslett and R. Wall (eds), *Household and family in past time* (Cambridge, 1972), pp. 125–58; R. Wall, 'Regional and temporal variations in English household structure from 1650', in J. Hobcraft and P. Rees (eds), *Regional demographic development* (London, 1977), pp. 89–113; P. Laslett, K.W. Wachter and R. Laslett, 'The English evidence on household structure compared with the outcomes of microsimulation', in K.W. Wachter, E.A. Hammel and P. Laslett, *Statistical studies of historical social structure* (London, 1978), pp. 65–87.

The objective demographic measure whose calculation is allowed by rare documentary survivals such as those from Clayworth and Cogenhoe is population turnover: that is, proportions of original inhabitants removed either by death or by migration, and of newcomers taking their places, over specific intervals. The paucity of empirical population turnover measures is of course hardly peculiar to England, or even to the pre-industrial period, although comparable series of sequential listings have been scrutinized from continental Europe, Russia and colonial New England.[4] But Laslett was able to go further than simple turnover calculations, and by combining listings with parish register data he demonstrated that geographical mobility accounted for nearly two-thirds of recorded turnover in these two villages. He was careful to emphasize, however, that one should not equate rapid turnover of *individuals* with instability of larger social *institutions* such as households, neighbourhoods and communities, or the norms which governed their configurations. Indeed, certain attributes of England's long-persisting familial and household formation structures were crucial determinants of population turnover. Most notably, movements of adolescents circulating as servants among households, together with moves by isolated individuals (doubtless including many other young persons departing their parental households), formed the single largest component of migration at Clayworth and Cogenhoe, followed by movements of entire households and movements coincident upon marriages.[5] Thus one might envision relatively high degrees of mobility, and therefore turnover, as in one sense a corollary of the household formation pattern characteristic of pre-industrial north-western Europe.

During the past 20 years the geographical mobility of early modern English men and women has become a commonplace among demographic and social historians, and subsequent research has confirmed the relatively circumscribed spatial dimensions of such movements and their strong association with particular stages of the individual's life cycle.[6] None the less, migration remains one of the least-understood

4 W.R. Prest, 'Stability and change in Old and New England: Clayworth and Dedham', *Journal of Interdisciplinary History* 6 (1976), pp. 359–74; M.W. Flinn, *The European demographic system 1500–1820* (Brighton, 1981), pp. 65–75 and sources cited therein; P. Czap, '"A large family: the peasant's greatest wealth": serf households in Mishino, Russia, 1814–1858', in R. Wall (ed.), *Family forms in historic Europe* (Cambridge, 1983), pp. 141–3; L.A. Kosinski, 'Data and measures in migration research', in L.A. Kosinski and R.M. Prothero (eds), *People on the move: studies in internal migration* (London, 1975), pp. 107–19; A. Rogers and L.J. Castro, 'Model migration schedules', in A.J. Boyce (ed.), *Migration and mobility: biosocial aspects of human movement* (London, 1984), pp. 1–48.

5 Laslett and Harrison, 'Clayworth and Cogenhoe', pp. 68–75. By far the fullest study of servanthood in its economic and demographic contexts is A.S. Kussmaul, *Servants in husbandry in early modern England* (Cambridge, 1981).

6 P. Laslett, *The world we have lost, further explored* (New York, 1984), pp. 74–7; K. Wrightson, *English society 1580–1680* (London, 1982), pp. 40–4.

areas of English historical demography, in part because few available documentary sources are capable of yielding precise community turnover rates comparable with those from Clayworth and Cogenhoe. In some circumstances it is possible to compile collections of individual migration 'histories', for example from details of depositions recorded in ecclesiastical courts, settlement examinations and statute sessions.[7] Parish register reconstitution data have been used to isolate proportions of persons appearing in some, but not all, vital events in a given parish and so to identify 'movers' and 'stayers'.[8] But most of this evidence is partial in one way or another, typically because the exact chronology of movements cannot be reconstructed or because the experiences of persons known to have been migrants in particular contexts are not readily assimilated into the larger pattern of entire populations. Thus however tentative or preliminary Laslett's 1963 remarks may have seemed at the time, in retrospect Clayworth and Cogenhoe still stand as rare examples of empirical population turnover rates.

Many of these inadequacies apply with even greater force to the problem of medieval English turnover. There have been some remarkable parallels between the growing appreciation that early modern English people were very mobile and a similar realization that the medieval community also witnessed constant comings and goings. Perhaps most significant among early empirical studies in this area were those by J.A. Raftis, charting the destinations of villeins whose legal and illegal movements away from their home manors were recorded in medieval manorial court proceedings.[9] It has been possible to augment this information with other medieval sources, such as criminal proceedings in the royal courts,[10] ecclesiastical court depositions, which in some instances provide data similar to those of their early modern counterparts,[11] and rare documents recording servile populations of

7 P. Clark, 'Migration in England during the late seventeenth and early eighteenth centuries', *Past and Present* 83 (1979), pp. 57–90; K. Wrightson and D. Levine, *Poverty and piety in an English village: Terling 1525–1700* (London, 1979), pp. 74–82; A.S. Kussmaul, 'The ambiguous mobility of farm servants', *Economic History Review* 2nd series, 34 (1981), pp. 222–35.

8 David Souden, 'Movers and stayers in family reconstitution populations', *Local Population Studies*, 33 (1984), pp. 11–28.

9 J.A. Raftis, *Tenure and mobility: studies in the social history of the medieval English village* (Toronto, 1964), pp. 129–82; J.A. Raftis, *Warboys: two hundred years in the life of an English medieval village* (Toronto, 1974), pp. 13–152, 264–5; cf. E. Britton, *The community of the vill: a study in the history of the family and village life in fourteenth-century England* (Toronto, 1977), pp. 179–90.

10 For example, B.A. Hanawalt, *Crime and conflict in English communities 1300–1348* (Cambridge, Massachusetts, 1979), pp. 168–71; L.R. Poos, 'Population and resources in two fourteenth-century Essex communities: Great Waltham and High Easter 1327–1389' (unpublished Ph.D. dissertation, University of Cambridge, 1984), pp. 45–50.

11 Pre-1500 sources in this category await systematic analysis of this issue, although work is currently being done with the documents from York diocese by Jeremy Goldberg and from

particular manors together with notations of places of eventual settlement if outside the home village.[12] Surnames incorporating place-name
elements have also provided some measure of the 'catchment area'
furnishing immigrants into urban settlements, although here there are
especially serious difficulties in specifying the time over which migration may be presumed to have taken place.[13]

In certain respects the medieval evidence, tantalizingly sketchy as it
is at present, suggests continuity rather than discontinuity in migration
patterns between the Middle Ages and the early modern period. Most
notably, the spatial dimensions of local migration fields which have
been plotted for the respective periods often seem almost identical, with
high density of moves within a radius of ten miles or so but longer-
distance moves rather more rare.[14] There would also appear to be
strong continuities in status-specific propensity to move: in both periods
the middling to upper status groups at the village level, whose families
tended to remain in residence (typically in association with substantial
agricultural tenements) for at least two or three generations, have been
contrasted with the relatively transient smallholders, landless, and
labourers and servants whose appearances in local records tended to be
fleeting and peripheral if not non-existent.[15]

Medieval social historians have in fact become increasingly aware of
the implications of turnover, occasioned both by mobility and by intrin-

---

London diocese by the present author. A taste of the circumstantial details sometimes
provided in these sources is given by D.M. Owen, 'White Annays and others', in D. Baker
(ed.), *Medieval women* (Oxford, 1978), pp. 331–46.

12 For example, R.M. Smith, 'Hypothèses sur la nuptialité en Angleterre aux XIIIe–XIVe
siècles', *Annales, économies, sociétés, civilisations* (1983), pp. 120–4, 128–9; R.K. Field, 'Migration in the later Middle Ages: the case of the Hampton Lovett villeins', *Midland History* 8
(1983), pp. 29–48.

13 For example, P. McClure, 'Patterns of migration in the late Middle Ages: the evidence
of English place-name surnames', *Economic History Review* 2nd series, 32 (1979), pp. 167–82.

14 Compare, for example, the 'social area' mapped for residents of early modern Terling
(Essex) by Wrightson and Levine, *Poverty and piety*, p. 78, with distributions of extralocal
contacts reconstructed for fourteenth-century Great Waltham and High Easter (Essex) in
Poos, 'Population and resources', pp. 45–50, or known emigrations from medieval Warboys
(Huntingdonshire) in Raftis, *Warboys*, pp. 264–5, or distances between home villages of
victim and accused in early-fourteenth-century Northamptonshire and Norfolk criminal
proceedings in Hanawalt, *Crime and conflict*, p. 169.

15 For general remarks on this subject for early modern England, see Wrightson, *English
society*, pp. 41–4. This differential in migration behaviour has become axiomatic among
medieval social historians, although medieval sources render it rather more difficult to
distinguish actual movement in or out of communities from spurious 'appearances' and
'disappearances' stemming from different degrees of representation in local records: cf. J.A.
Raftis, 'Social structures in five East Midland villages', *Economic History Review* 2nd series, 18
(1965), pp. 90–3; Z. Razi, *Life, marriage and death in a medieval parish: economy, society and
demography in Halesowen 1270–1400* (Cambridge, 1980), pp. 74–9. Some reflections on the social
implications of this enduring feature of village structure have been offered by K. Wrightson,
'Medieval villagers in perspective', *Peasant Studies* 7 (1978), pp. 203–17.

sic factors of mortality and fertility, for such issues as family structure, property transmission, and social networks within and between village groups. Attempts to demonstrate turnover in the medieval village have usually entailed analysis of generational succession to property or of composition of successive tenantry cohorts, and such inferences concerning migration as can be attempted from appearance patterns in manor court rolls and related local records.[16] Such procedures, however, necessarily deal disproportionately with higher social and economic strata within the village who bulk largest in manorial documentation but whose experience cannot be taken at face value as fully representative of all of a community's residents. Since there survive no medieval English household enumerations (comparable for example with the fifteenth-century Tuscan *catasto*[17]), there has appeared to be little prospect of directly measuring turnover rates for any medieval English community which might be compared with Clayworth and Cogenhoe.

But an opportunity to do so is afforded by an unusual series of nominative lists from four small rural communities in Essex from the early fourteenth century. Although these sources are by no means so comprehensive as the early modern English listings in terms of information provided or the range of questions they can answer, nevertheless they allow calculation of crude population turnover rates for these communities on the eve of the Black Death. The lists are administrative byproducts of the medieval institution of frankpledge, and some description of this institution is necessary background to analysis of the lists themselves.[18]

I

Legal and administrative outlines of the frankpledge system have long been known to medieval historians. In origin a rudimentary organ for policing and for providing surety for good conduct, frankpledge was

16 For example, R.M. Smith, 'Some issues concerning families and their properties in England, 1250–1800', in R.M. Smith (ed.), *Land, kinship and life-cycle* (Cambridge, 1984) pp. 38–55, and other studies contained therein; C.C. Dyer, *Lords and peasants in a changing society: the estates of the Bishopric of Worcester 680–1540* (Cambridge, 1980), p. 366. For reservations concerning the completeness and biases inherent in appearances in tenurial contexts or in manorial court transactions, see L.R. Poos and R.M. Smith, '"Legal windows onto historical populations?" Recent research on demography and the manor court in medieval England', *Law and History Review* 2 (1984), pp. 128–52.

17 D. Herlihy and C. Klapisch-Zuber, *Les Toscans et leurs familles: une étude du catasto florentin de 1427* (Paris, 1978).

18 The following outline is derived chiefly from: W.A. Morris, *The frankpledge system* (Cambridge, Massachusetts, 1910); D.A. Crowley, 'Frankpledge and leet jurisdiction in later medieval Essex' (unpublished Ph.D. dissertation, University of Sheffield, 1971); D.A. Crowley, 'The later history of frankpledge', *Bulletin of the Institute of Historical Research* 48 (1975), pp. 1–15; F.W. Maitland, 'Leet and tourn', in H.M. Cam (ed.), *Selected historical essays of F.W. Maitland* (Cambridge, 1957), pp. 41–51; Poos, 'Population and resources', pp. 65–75.

one of a number of local legal franchises appropriated by many land-lords in the generations after the Norman Conquest. As such it became linked with jurisdiction over minor criminal offences, public nuisances, and the like which was exercised in local leet courts. Although arrangements varied among different regions of England and indeed from community to community within each region, the most important aspect of this system for present purposes is that all males aged 12 and older (except clerics and members of high economic or social status, probably to be understood as meaning gentry standing or higher), and resident within the franchise's purview for at least a year and a day, were required to be enrolled by oath into groups called 'tithings'. In Essex during the later Middle Ages a frankpledge jurisdiction typically comprised several tithings, each consisting of one or two 'chief pledges' and a number of 'tithingmen'; a tithing's total membership usually averaged between eight and fifteen. At the annual leet court and 'view of frankpledge', tithings' memberships were reviewed and new members enrolled, while the jurisdiction's chief pledges together constituted the jury who presented and determined offences and in some circumstances rendered evidence or verdicts to higher judicial bodies. The tithing was collectively responsible for ensuring court attendance by its members, and especially for producing delinquents from among its ranks, in default of which its tithingmen and chief pledges might be amerced or otherwise penalized.

Apart from presentments and amercements, the frankpledge system's functions were recorded among leet court proceedings in several ways. Most sessions of these courts included admissions of new members into tithings. either because a newcomer had resided within the community for a year or because the son of a local resident had reached the age of 12. An individual would be recorded as sworn in, or else would be named as eligible for membership and a chief pledge ordered to swear him in at a subsequent time.[19] In some Essex communities all tithing-men and chief pledges were liable to render an annual payment to the franchise's lordship at the annual leet, amounting to a penny or half-penny per head, and series of these payments surviving among leet court transactions provide an index of aggregate population change in this region over the later Middle Ages.[20] At other places a collective

19 For example, Essex Record Office (hereafter ERO) D/DTu M257 (Chatham Hall leet, 9 April 1314): ...'[chief pledges] presentant quod Adam le Rat recepit Johannem Starteleheg et non in decennia ... postea juratus fuit'. University College, Oxford (hereafter UCO) Pyx G-H (Margaret Roding leet, 7 June 1435): '[chief pledges] presentant quod Johannes Cosyn Thomas Cosyn et Willemus Cosyn sunt etatis xij annorum et amplius ac residentes infra pertinitium visi et extra decenniam ideo etc. et preceptum est ipsos distringere contra proximam curiam ad recipiendum onus decennari.' The Margaret Roding material is cited by kind permission of the Master and Fellows of University College.

20 L.R. Poos, 'The rural population of Essex in the later Middle Ages', *Economic History Review* 38 (1985), pp. 515–30.

payment of fixed amount was paid by all tithings annually. Finally, from some places there survive occasional lists of all chief pledges and tithingmen within the local tithings at the time of the list's compilation. These lists were drawn up, apparently at irregular intervals, in order (as will be shown later) to assist chief pledges and other curial officials in keeping track of tithing membership, assigning responsibility for offenders, and ensuring full payment of the annual monetary obligations.[21]

Ostensibly, then, the tithing lists record names of all males (with the exceptions already noted) aged 12 and older and resident within their communities for at least a year and a day on the date of the leet court at which the list was drawn up. As such, they permit scrutiny of at least the great majority of residents in the pertinent age and sex groups, and so obviate dependence upon information drawn from tenurial or other sources less fully representative of all inhabitants within a given community. There are of course shortcomings in the material, as is obvious from the description given, and these will need to be considered in due course. The lists are, for example, clearly unsatisfactory by many of the criteria demanded of the early modern community listings.[22] But as nominative lists of inhabitants of defined age and sex categories and resident at known dates, with due allowance for their inherent limitations they afford the prospect (probably as rare for their period as the Clayworth and Cogenhoe listings for the seventeenth century) for deriving crude population turnover rates.

II

There are only four known instances of 'sequential' tithing lists from Essex – that is, two or more listings drawn up for the same community within a short timespan – although isolated, single lists do survive from other places.[23] As map 1.1 indicates, these four communities are located within 20 miles or so of each other; although few in number and

21 A. Clark 'Tithing lists from Essex, 1329–1343', *English Historical Review* 19 (1904), pp. 715–19; Crowley, 'Later history of frankpledge', pp. 2–3.

22 Laslett, 'Social structure from listings of inhabitants'. For instance, apart from their being limited to adolescent and adult males and lacking any information regarding household structure, these lists fail to meet the 'census-like' quality of many later listings in that they undoubtedly resulted not from house-to-house surveys but from enrolment at a central gathering. They should also, under Laslett's terms, probably be classed as 'ideal' lists (in the sense of being lists of all tithing members, whether actually present at court or not, although of course their initial admission into tithing depended upon court attendance): cf. Poos, 'Population and resources', p. 65.

23 For example, from Essex: ERO D/DP M832 m. 70 (East Hanningfield leet, 17 May 1339); ERO D/DU 565/5 m. 1v (Berden leet, 30 June 1377). Cf. J.C. Russell, *British medieval population* (Albuquerque, 1948), pp. 67–8, referring to frankpledge lists from early-fourteenth-century Surrey.

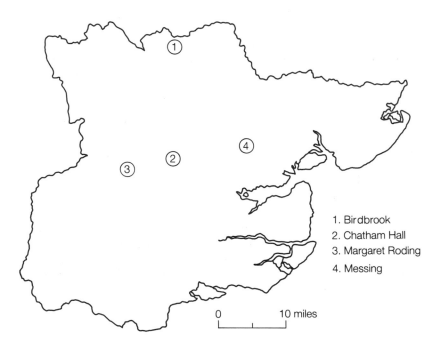

Map 1.1   Sources of tithing lists in medieval Essex

small in size, then, taken together they may perhaps be regarded as representative of patterns in communities of this size within a fairly circumscribed region. The richest material comes from Margaret Roding, for which tithing lists are available from three consecutive years (1322, 1323, 1324) and another 15 years later (1339)[24]. From Chatham Hall, a small settlement within the large township of Great Waltham, are two lists separated by eight years (1329, 1337).[25] The other two cases are less satisfactory: Birdbrook possesses two lists which, unfortunately, can be dated only approximately (*c.*1325, *c.*1340),[26] and two

24 UCO Pyx G-H (Margaret Roding leets, 1 June 1322, 17 May 1323, 5 June 1324, 15 May 1339). There were two frankpledge franchises in Margaret Roding township (Roding Marcy alias Marcys Fee and Margaret Roding alias Helys Fee), each with its own set of tithings. All of these lists include the tithings of both franchises, and for the present analysis the two franchises have been treated as one.

25 ERO D/DTu M257 mm. 18, 25 (Chatham Hall leets, 13 June 1329, 10 June 1337).

26 ERO D/DU 267/85; D/DU 267/86. The lists have been dated thus by the record office cataloguers, apparently by cross-referencing of names from other Birdbrook documents. There is a third, much later Birdbrook frankpledge list also: ERO D/DU 267/87 (*c.*1425).

lists from Messing are separated by 29 years (1293, 1322) and therefore present somewhat greater uncertainties in nominal linkage from list to list.[27]

It is essential that these communities' experiences be understood also in the contexts of their local geography and economy and of the historical period involved. During the fourteenth century this region of central and northern Essex was among the most densely populated areas of the country, with large proportions of smallholders or landless persons and widespread employment of wage labour, a fairly dense concentration of small market centres, and a nascent rural cloth industry already in evidence in the earlier 1300s.[28] Moreover, these tithing lists come from the the decades immediately following a serious agrarian crisis, with famine mortality during the second decade of the century amounting to between 10 and 15 per cent in this region of Essex.[29] It is difficult to gauge *a priori* how these circumstances might have affected either geographical mobility or longer-term mortality patterns during the period covered by these sources, or to demonstrate how in this context Essex in the early fourteenth century might have contrasted with other regions or periods. But although these circumstances might if anything be expected to heighten turnover it is unlikely that the experiences of this region's inhabitants could have been of a grossly different order of magnitude from the bulk of their contemporaries.

It may be useful at this point to provide an excerpt from one of these lists, in order to give a clearer impression of the format and content of information contained. All these lists have essentially similar form; the following extract contains the heading and first tithing listed in the earlier Birdbrook list:[30]

Birdbrook: roll of chief pledges and tithingmen

Chief pledges:	John Dreye William Osbern	who have in their tithing: Roger Salemon junior, Henry son of Adam del Banleye, William son of Edmund, Matthew atte Parkegate, John son of William Osebern, Michael de Brydebrok, Matthew Penyford

There then follow 12 more tithings listed in the same form, a total of 133 names being recorded in all.

27 ERO D/DH X1 m. 14v (Messing leet, 19 May 1293); D/DH X2 m. 16 (Messing leet, 1 June 1322).

28 Cf. Poos, 'Population and resources'.

29 Poos, 'Rural population of Essex'.

30 ERO D/DU 267/85: 'Bridebrok: Rotulus capitalum plegiorum ac decenniorum suorum ... ; ... Capitales ... qui habent in decennia sua ... [etc.].'

Six sequential 'pairings' of consecutive tithing lists are possible with the available material: three among the four surviving lists from Margaret Roding, and one each from the other three communities. Table 1.1 presents the bald data resulting from comparisons of names recorded in these six pairings. Each list tabulates the presumed date of its compilation (in fact, the date of the leet court session among whose proceedings the list is enrolled) and the total number of tithing members listed. A range of plausible estimates for the total size of the community in question is also given for each list, calculated on the basis of Princeton model West life tables' ratios of males aged 12 and older to total population including women and children, under a wide range of assumptions regarding underlying mortality levels.[31] Then for each pairing the table presents total numbers of 'exits' and 'entries': respectively, numbers of names present in the earlier list but absent from the later (and therefore presumed to represent males either dying or emigrating in the meantime), and names present in the later list but not in the earlier (accounting for males either unborn or present in the community as under-12s at the time of the earlier list but having attained the age of 12 years by the time of the later list, or else having entered the community as adolescent or adult newcomers during the interval). The 'exits' and 'entries' are also expressed as percentages of earlier and later tithing membership size, respectively, over the interval in question and as annual percentage rates of change.

Some preliminary comments may be made here concerning the implications of these raw data. Most obviously, they cannot be compared directly as yet to Laslett's calculated rates of turnover from Clayworth and Cogenhoe, because to do so will not compare like with like. For example, apart from immigration, 'entries' in Laslett's seventeenth-century villages represented births (since the entire population of all ages and both sexes was included in the listings with which he was dealing), whereas the cognate component of 'entries' among turnover incorporated in the tithing lists' evidence is represented by males born years before the lists' compilation and surviving to attain age 12. It will therefore be necessary to attempt an estimate of the dimensions of this

31 A.J. Coale and P. Demeny, *Regional model life tables and stable populations* (Princeton, 1966), pp. 123, 136. The ratios have been calculated from model West, with population declining at 0.5 per cent per annum and with the extreme assumptions of mortality levels 1 and 8. Model West is used here because it appears to fit most closely the characteristics of infant and child mortality (one important factor determining proportions of those under 12 to total population) observable in the earliest English parish registers: R.S. Schofield and E.A. Wrigley, 'Infant and child mortality in the late Tudor and early Stuart period', in C. Webster (ed.), *Health, medicine and mortality in the sixteenth century* (Cambridge, 1979), pp. 61–95. This rate of population decline has been employed because it fits the aggregate population trends implied by the Essex tithingpenny series during the early fourteenth century: Poos, 'Rural population of Essex'. See later for comments on these choices for mortality levels.

Table 1.1 Crude rates of turnover, tithing membership in four Essex communities

Community	Date of list	Number in tithing	Estimated community population	Exits (no.)	Exits (%)	Exits (annual %)	Entries (no.)	Entries (%)	Entries (annual %)
Margaret Roding	1 June 1322	57	141–169						
	17 May 1323	60	148–178	2	3.5	3.5	5	8.3	8.3
	5 June 1324	62	153–184	8	13.3	13.3	10	16.1	16.1
	15 May 1339	43	106–127	20	46.5	3.1	11	25.6	1.7
Chatham Hall	13 June 1329	59	146–175						
	10 June 1337	60	148–178	16	27.1	3.4	17	28.3	3.5
Birdbrook	c. 1325	133	329–394						
	c. 1340	122	302–362	31	23.3	1.6	20	16.4	1.1
Messing	19 May 1293	83	205–246						
	1 June 1322	60	148–178	77	92.8	3.2	54	90.0	3.1

'Exits' refers to males present in the earlier list but absent from the later; 'entries' vice versa. Percentages are the ratios of 'exits' to the number recorded in the earlier list, or 'entries' to the number recorded in the later list. The annual percentage is simply the total percentage change divided by the number of years elapsed between the lists to nearest whole year.

difference, before the tithing turnover rates can be placed into a meaningful comparative demographic context. Moreover, it remains to be shown that the units under observation – parishes in the case of Clayworth and Cogenhoe, frankpledge jurisdictions in the case of four-teenth-century Essex – are indeed comparable.

As is shown in table 1.1, with the exception of Birdbrook these Essex communities' total population sizes are rather smaller than that of seventeenth-century Clayworth (where slightly more than 400 people dwelt at the time of their enumeration), although all are at least roughly comparable in size to Cogenhoe (where residents numbered between about 150 and 180 in the early 1600s).[32] The smaller the base population involved, the greater would be the variability of turnover rates one might expect simply as a product of stochastic variation, particularly for single-year comparisons. In fact the calculated annual rates of tithing membership turnover implied by the consecutive lists from Margaret Roding do vary considerably. It is perhaps better, then, to consider an aggregated mean of annual tithing membership turnover rates, weighted in proportion to community size; this amounts to 4.1 'exits' per cent per annum, and 5.2 'entries'.[33] These means include the data from Birdbrook, which appear low in comparison with the other figures and so may imply that the approximate dating of the Birdbrook lists is suspect.

Even so, and before the necessary qualifications are made, the tithing evidence appears to imply rates of population turnover which are at least roughly equivalent to Clayworth and Cogenhoe's seventeenth-century patterns, and also comparable with (if not greater than) the later-eighteenth-century French parishes of Hallines and Longueness, while indicating a population considerably more volatile than the early-nineteenth-century servile inhabitants of Krasnoe Sabakino in Russia.[34] In fact, it will be argued later that the figures presented in table 1.1 if anything understate the actual level of turnover among all males in these fourteenth-century communities. But an array of factors must be taken into account before such an assertion can be substantiated and the general comparative significance of the tithing data can become apparent. These considerations may be classed as factors arising from textual problems posed by the documents themselves, from limitations inherent in analysis of recorded tithing membership as opposed to actual residents in the pertinent age and sex groups, and from the broader demographic characteristics of these groups in relation to the entire base populations from which they are drawn.

32 Laslett and Harrison, 'Clayworth and Cogenhoe', p. 78.
33 Aggregated means of annual rates, weighted in proportion to initial number in tithing (for 'exits') and final number in tithing (for 'entries').
34 This will be discussed in more detail later; see table 1.3.

III

The tithing lists in their extant form are by no means so pristine or unambiguous as the extract given earlier might imply. At the time a list was drawn up it was no doubt a straightforward detailing of chief pledges' and tithingmen's names in the form described. But the lists appear to have been intended for use in court for some time after their compilation, as reference guides against which to review tithings' memberships, and so to check that all were present who were required to be or to determine responsibility for delinquents, and upon which 'exits' and 'entries' could be recorded. Thirteenth- and fourteenth-century formularies recommending exemplary procedures in leet courts hint at oral testimony by each chief pledge concerning his own tithing's members, with reference by himself or other curial officials to written lists for confirmation.[35] Oblique glimpses of this practice sometimes appear in recorded leet court proceedings.[36]

For this reason many of the extant Essex tithing lists contain not only the original tithing membership but also names added later, as new members were sworn in. In such circumstances it is necessary to infer their later addition from their different handwriting or ink, or from their physical position in the list as clearly later insertions. Conversely, names originally listed were often struck through, occasionally with a note added above the name indicating that the man had died (*quia mortuus*), had been removed from tithing by paying a fine, presumably because he had migrated elsewhere (*remotus quia fecit finem*),[37] or had been promoted to the status of chief pledge and so now appeared in a different section of the list (*quia capitalis*). The Messing lists are especially heavily amended in this way, the Chatham Hall and Birdbrook lists somewhat less so, and most of the Margaret Roding lists are relatively unaffected. These notations themselves are not without interest, but because few deletions are thus annotated they are unlikely to

35 For example, F.W. Maitland and W.P. Baildon (eds), *The court baron*, Selden Society 4 (1891), p. 72: 'Item quesitum fuit de capitali plegio utrum sciret quot et quos haberet in thewinga sua et testatum fuit quod sic lectis [previous word doubtful, read thus by editors] nominibus singulorum inventum est R. Fabrum concellasse N. et N. qui transtulerunt se.' Cf. J.S. Beckerman, 'The articles of presentment of a court leet and court baron, in English, c.1400', *Bulletin of the Institute of Historical Research* 47 (1974), pp. 231, 233.

36 For example, Public Record Office (hereafter PRO) DL30.64.811 (Great Waltham leet, 28 May 1355): a man was presented as being resident and out of tithing, but was 'pardoned because he is in the roll of tithingmen' ('condonatur quia in rotulo decennariorum').

37 Fines were occasionally recorded in medieval Essex leet courts for removal from tithing. When reasons for removal are given, they typically result from tithingmen's moving out of the vicinity: e.g. PRO DL30.64.823 (High Easter leet, 10 June 1367): fines paid for removal because the men in question were 'resident elsewhere' ('alibi residens'). On a very few occasions fines were paid for removal because the man in question was 'elderly' ('senex'): e.g. PRO DL30.65.824 (High Easter leet, 1 June 1368).

serve as reliable indications of the relative importance of migration or
mortality as causes for 'exit'. It is also impossible to know over how
many years these changes in tithing membership actually took place
after the list was originally written down.[38] Since for present purposes
it is necessary to possess a profile of tithing membership at a specific
time, in order to gain a measure of temporal rates of change, the lists
must be reconstructed as originally written by disregarding deletions
and later additions. In practice, with paleographical diligence this is
not difficult, and is unlikely to be the source of significant error in
nominative comparisons.

A potentially more serious source of error is posed by basic problems
of nominal linkage. Simply put, how may one be reasonably certain
that the 'A. B.' of one list is identical to the 'A. B.' of another?
Although of course inherent in any exercise of this kind,[39] the difficulty
is undoubtedly especially pertinent in dealing with sources from an era
when surnames were only beginning to stabilize and when the same
man might be denoted at different times by an occupational, a place-
name, and a patronymic designation. Cognizance of this point has
undermined some early research in community reconstruction from
medieval records,[40] but in most of the Essex cases considered here the
surviving manorial records are too skeletal to warrant attempting linkage confirmation from them. Informal, frankly intuitive rules have
however been adopted here, in order to minimize the chances of identifying one man as two and so overstating imputed turnover.[41] A
special case arises in the 'A. son of B.' name form, of which the earlier
Messing list in particular contains many; nevertheless it can be shown
that names recorded in this form do not significantly raise the probabil-

38 Two previous discussions of the tithing lists have attempted to set 'terminal' dates for
such annotations, but it is unclear upon what basis this was done, and attempts to do so will
be eschewed here: Clark, 'Tithing lists'; Crowley, 'Later history of frankpledge', p. 3.

39 Cf. E.A. Wrigley, 'Introduction', in E.A. Wrigley (ed.), *Identifying people in the past*
(Cambridge, 1973), pp. 1–16.

40 For example, Z. Razi, 'The Toronto school's reconstitution of medieval peasant society:
a critical view', *Past and Present* 85 (1980), pp. 142–9; Wrightson, 'Medieval villagers in
perspective', pp. 210–13.

41 For example, maximum latitude has been given in making potentially doubtful linkages
on etymological grounds (e.g. the 'John Dilset' listed at Margaret Roding in 1323 has been
linked to the 'John Denleset' of the following year); similarly, where an 'A. son of B. C.' has
been linked to an 'A. C.' (e.g. the 'William son of Nicholas le Hoppere' at Margaret Roding
in 1322 has been regarded as identical to the 'William le Hoppere' of the following year). The
intention here has been, as stated, to minimize the double counting potentially resulting from
doubtful nominal linkage, and so to minimize the imputed turnover rates. Nevertheless it
should be noted that doubtful nominal linkage need not necessarily serve to overstate
imputed turnover; indeed it could work in the opposite direction (e.g. the Messing lists,
separated by 29 years, each contain a 'John Bard', which have been tabulated as the same
man; there is no *prima facie* reason to regard this, over such an interval, as more likely to be
one man than two).

ity of double counting.[42] Moreover, an additional factor aiding identification is the lists' arrangement of names into tithings; in most
'pairings' there is sufficient continuity of membership in individual
tithings to aid linkage of some names from list to list where this might
not be otherwise obvious.[43] Still, nominal linkage doubtless remains the
factor most likely to result in overstating turnover rates from the tithing
lists.

Even if it is possible to reconstruct tithing membership changes with
reasonable accuracy from these lists, it is still necessary to consider
certain limitations posed by the nature of this information. Lists of
tithing members are still not equivalent to comprehensive census-like
enumerations, even (necessarily) of all adolescent and adult males
resident within the community in question. Clerics and wealthy freemen are excluded, and there is no scope for conjectures about household size and structure from these sources, as was possible in the cases
of Clayworth and Cogenhoe. But there are less obvious qualities of the
tithing evidence which further limit its direct comparability with the
early modern listings. One of these factors is the nature of the geographical area serving as the unit of observation for turnover.

Throughout this discussion the term 'community' has been employed
to describe this unit. But in reality the geographical basis upon which
calculations of resident turnover from these sources must be based was
delimited by the purviews of the leet court's jurisdiction. Although in
origin such jurisdiction probably centred upon the township, in practice
historical idiosyncrasy, division of lordship, and evolving custom might
conspire to fragment frankpledge jurisdiction in unpredictable ways. In
Essex, a region of dispersed settlement where lordship tended to be
more markedly fragmented than elsewhere, by the fourteenth century a
township might possess two or more frankpledge jurisdictions demar-
cated along manorial bounds, or jurisdiction might extend into portions
of adjacent townships, or certain lordships might exercise authority

---

42 The earlier Messing list contains twelve names (out of a total of 83) in the form of, for
example, 'Lucas son of Stephen.' The second list was checked for all possible linkages, on the
possibility that an earlier 'A. son of B.' might masquerade as a later 'A. C.', and all such
names from the earlier lists as could be eliminated (either because, as in the example given,
no 'Lucas' appears at all, with or without any surname, in the later list, or because persons
appearing in the later list bearing the appropriate first name had otherwise been accounted
for) were regarded as 'exits'. Only eight possible linkages remained in addition to those
already tabulated, raising the maximum conceivable number of names persisting from
earlier to later listing from six (7.2 per cent of initial number in tithing) to 14 (16.9 per cent)
and so lowering the annual rate of 'exit' thus derived from 3.2 to 2.9 per cent of the initial
number in tithing.

43 For example, in one tithing at Margaret Roding there appeared, in successive years
1322, 1323 and 1324, 'William le Finch', 'William le Fycchett', and 'William Vinch', who
have been judged to be identical, mainly because of their persistence in this tithing.

over sub-manors or neighbouring manors.[44] Thus the frankpledge purview need not necessarily have corresponded with a physical village or settlement, and the exact circumstances must be reconstructed as closely as possible for any given place.

Of the four 'communities' whose tithing lists are considered here, only in the case of Margaret Roding do frankpledge purview and township appear to have been essentially coterminous. At Birdbrook and Messing, the tithings described in surviving lists apparently accounted for the majority of their townships' geographical areas and resident adolescent and adult male populations, although other small jurisdictions are known to have been present. Chatham Hall is perhaps at the opposite extreme, being limited to a sub-manor and associated small settlement within the large township of Great Waltham.[45] One might argue that this would qualify somewhat the tithing turnover data's direct comparability with other historical cases like Clayworth, Cogenhoe, Hallines or Longueness where parochial registration is involved, because in migration research the smaller the unit that is taken as the basis for studying inward and outward movement, the higher will be the rate of turnover registered from a given pattern of actual migration behaviour. Movements involving quite miniscule distances, that is, might nevertheless register as 'migrations', whereas if a larger area serves as the basis of observation this might not be so.[46] But in all these Essex examples the term 'community' would appear to be justified and comparison with Laslett's seventeenth-century villages permissible, because these units are closely related to defined physical settlements and their populations in the early fourteenth century were approximately as large as Cogenhoe's in the 1600s.

A more obvious question bearing upon the tithing lists' ability to reflect population turnover credibly is whether all males subject, under the rubrics of the frankpledge system, to compulsory tithing membership actually were recruited efficiently; that is, can the tithing members as recorded essentially be equated with the resident population of males aged 12 and older (with the exceptions noted), or was there widespread evasion? There are no means by which this can be answered conclusively for the early fourteenth century, although it has been possible to compare numbers in tithing in several Essex communities with populations reconstructed from slightly later poll-tax returns

44 Crowley, 'Frankpledge and leet jurisdiction', pp. 23–103; Poos, 'Population and resources', pp. 79–80.

45 Crowley, 'Frankpledge and leet jurisdiction', p. 44; Poos, 'Rural population of Essex'; P. Morant, *The history and antiquities of the county of Essex* 2nd edn, vol. 2 (London, 1978), pp. 344–5.

46 Cf. Roland Pressat, *Statistical demography* (London, 1978), p. 112; Kosinski, 'Data and measures in migration research'.

and even parish registers.[47] There comparisons strongly indicate that in most places evasion was probably minimal on the part of those eligible for membership, even well into the sixteenth century when other aspects of the tithing system were moribund in many places.

None the less, even under the formal rules of frankpledge authority, short-term residents (living in the vicinity for less than a year) were not required to be enrolled in the local tithings, while one can readily envisage highly migratory males temporarily settled within the community, even if for a year or longer, as the most obvious candidates for evasion from tithing (and thus from the tithing lists). Especially germane in this context would be the situation of males in their teens or early twenties, employed as migratory agricultural or unskilled craft workers, and especially as servants, who in the fourteenth century (as later) typically entered employment under annual hiring terms and might change place of employment yearly. [48] As has already been noted, in seventeenth-century Clayworth and Cogenhoe circulation of servants was the single largest component of migration, amounting to nearly one-quarter of all turnover.[49] Circumstantial evidence arising in Essex leet court proceedings throughout the Middle Ages implies a similar pattern, even though the available evidence permits no systematic assessment of its dimensions. Males explicitly denoted as servants of local residents or as having been 'received' into local households are prominent among the individuals ordered into tithing at these courts,[50] and in the (admittedly rare) known instances where ages are recorded for new tithing members the males in question were almost invariably teenagers.[51] Therefore turnover rates derived from tithing evidence undoubtedly exclude some quantity of short-term migration, indeterminate but potentially substantial, and thus understate actual turnover among all males in this age group.

Finally, even if all these foregoing qualifications are for the moment disregarded, and if it is presumed that the turnover exhibited by tithing

47 Poos, 'Rural population of Essex'; pp. 525–9.

48 The evidence for this is discussed in Poos, 'Population and resources', pp. 256–86, and L.R. Poos, 'The social context of Statute of Labourers enforcement', *Law and History Review* 1 (1983), pp. 27–52. For early modern patterns of servants' employment-related mobility, cf. Kussmaul, 'Mobility of farm servants'.

49 Laslett and Harrison, 'Clayworth and Cogenhoe', p. 98.

50 For example, UCO Pyx G-H (Margaret Roding leet, 22 May 1464): 'Johannes Mayford serviens Rectoris ecclesie de Rothyng Margarete' ordered into tithing; cf. note 19 in this chapter.

51 For example, Maitland and Baildon, *The court baron*, p. 140 (from Littleport, Cambridgeshire, 1324): ...'compertum est quod Henricus filius Walteri etatis xvj annorum est extra decennam et concelatur per capitales plegios'. A rather later Essex example is found in British Library Add. Roll 65939 (Stebbing leet, 6 April 1551): 'Ad hanc curiam venerunt Johannes Hacche modo etatis xviij annorum et Edwardus Hacche modo etatis quindecim annorum Johannes Portwey modo etatis xvij annorum et David Portwey modo etatis xv annorum et jurati sunt in decenniam domini Regis.'

members can essentially be equated with that of all adolescent and adult males resident in these early-fourteenth-century Essex communities, it remains to place this pattern into a broader demographic context. Two separate yet interrelated features of the tithing evidence further affect its ultimate comparability with previous studies of pre-industrial population turnover. The evidence in itself does not permit any conclusions about the relative importance of migration and of biological or intrinsic demographic factors – death among 'exits', birth and eventual attainment of age 12 among 'entries' – contributing to turnover among tithing members. A simple exercise involving Princeton model West life tables can however permit some tentative inferences on this point. But such an exercise in turn prompts recognition that intrinsic demographic factors within the group whom the tithing evidence makes it possible to observe (males aged 12 and older) will differ considerably from those of the entire population (i.e. births and deaths among males and females of all ages) of which they were members.

In Laslett's study of Clayworth and Cogenhoe, combining listings with parish registers made it possible to demonstrate that intrinsic demographic factors accounted for only a minority of turnover in the two parishes during the seventeenth century. The historian of the medieval English village has no recourse to corresponding vital data. The available medieval information approaching nearest to such data for levels of society beneath the gentry are notices of deaths of manorial tenants coupled with admissions of their heirs to their tenements, which are recorded among manorial court proceedings. These notices, when used in conjunction with estimates of total tenantry numbers, have served as the basis for attempts by some historians to construct medieval mortality schedules.[52] But such a procedure entails drawbacks unfortunately rendering it unsatisfactory,[53] and in any event the tenurial records needed to estimate tenantry numbers have not survived from these particular Essex places.

Reference to Princeton model West life tables reveals how different intrinsic demographic rates may be expected when the 'universe' of people under observation comprises only adolescent and adult males, as opposed to entire populations. High infant and child mortality rates typical of pre-industrial populations remove large numbers of successive birth cohorts in their early years of life. For instance, a recent study of infant and child mortality in late Tudor and early Stuart England suggests at a rough estimate that deaths of children aged nine and younger might typically make up between one-third and nearly one-half

52 For example, Razi, *Life, marriage and death in a medieval parish*, pp. 34–45, 124–31; M.M. Postan and J. Titow, 'Heriots and prices on Winchester manors', in M.M. Postan, *Essays on medieval agriculture and general problems of the medieval economy* (Cambridge, 1973), pp. 150–85.
53 Poos and Smith, 'Legal windows onto historical populations', pp. 137–42.

of all deaths occurring among the entire population.[54] Therefore the intrinsic rates of 'exits' and 'entries' relevant to the tithing evidence (numbers annually dying and annually attaining the age of 12, expressed as percentages of all males aged 12 and older) will be considerably lower than those which are pertinent when all people in the village can be observed (i.e. death and birth rates, respectively, expressed as percentages of total population). At Princeton mortality level 8 (corresponding to life expectancy at birth for males of 39.2 years, fairly high in the range of experiences calculated for early modern rural England), intrinsic 'exit' rates as defined above will be fully one-fifth lower for males aged 12 and older than for all males. At mortality level 1 (representing an expectation of life at birth for males of just under 21 years, practically as low as conceivably sustainable for any length of time), the disparity becomes much greater.[55] Table 1.2 summarizes these differences.

It is highly likely that the actual structures of the fourteenth-century populations of these four Essex communities fell somewhere between the two extreme scenarios. Variations inherent in small populations might alter these age structures considerably for individual communities over short periods, however, and although the weighted mean of four communities over a number of years may help to minimize stochastic variations of this kind the use of life tables can indicate the likely intrinsic component of turnover only approximately. When these projected intrinsic rates are compared with mean turnover among Essex tithing members (4.1 per cent 'exits' per annum, 5.2 per cent 'entries'), this would indicate that deaths might be expected to account for between about three-fifths and three-quarters of 'exits' and coming of age roughly half of the 'entries' among the Essex tithings. This is, however, rather misleading in comparison with Clayworth and Cogenhoe. In Laslett's seventeenth-century communities only persons whose deaths were registered within their home parish could be counted among the intrinsic component of 'exits', whereas people emigrating but dying elsewhere before the date of the later listing qualified as migrants.[56] Since the intrinsic rates exhibited in table 1.2 predict proportions who would under reasonable demographic projections be expected to die regardless of whether they did so 'at home' or after moving elsewhere, the actual intrinsic component of 'exits' for the four Essex communities (when expressed in terms comparable with Laslett's study) would be somewhat lower, perhaps closer to one-half.

A further consideration is raised by table 1.2. It is clearly unwarranted to attempt to project turnover rates in a deterministic manner from tithing

---

54 Schofield and Wrigley, 'Infant and child mortality', p. 61.
55 Coale and Demeny, *Regional model life tables*, pp. 2, 9, 123, 136. The rates of 'exit' and 'entry' exhibited in table 1.2 are also taken from here.
56 Laslett and Harrison, 'Clayworth and Cogenhoe', pp. 68–70.

Table 1.2 Princeton model West populations: intrinsic annual exit and entry rates, males aged 12+ and all males

	Males 12+		Males, all ages	
	Exits (deaths)	Entries (numbers attaining age 12)	Exits (deaths)	Entries (births)
Mortality level 1 (e_0 (male) = 20.96)	3.32	2.81	5.39	4.89
Mortality level 8 (e_0 (male) = 39.16)	2.62	2.11	2.96	2.46

All rates are calculated from model West, $r = -0.5$ per cent per annum. Rates are expressed as percentages (of total males 12+ and of all males) per annum.
e_0 (male) is life expectancy at birth for males.

members to total population, in part because female inhabitants' experiences cannot be recovered from this evidence. But even if males under 12 were completely immobile, adding their intrinsic 'exits' and 'entries' (i.e. deaths and births) to the comings and goings of tithing members would result in an estimated turnover rate for the entire male population at least one-tenth higher, if not more, than the rates shown in table 1.1. Thus when the unknown component of short-term migration is taken into account, it would appear overwhelmingly likely that these Essex communities' real underlying turnover patterns were virtually indistinguishable from Laslett's figures for Clayworth and Cogenhoe.

IV

With this array of qualifications in mind, the medieval Essex turnover patterns can be placed alongside the results of previous studies conducted with sequential listings of inhabitants in earlier societies. Table 1.3 summarizes these comparisons.[57]

As the table makes clear, the groups under observation and upon whom measures of turnover must be based differ somewhat in the various studies. But recorded turnover among tithing members in fourteenth-century Essex (which, it has already been argued, probably understates

57 Sources: (Clayworth, Cogenhoe, Hallines, Longueness) Laslett and Harrison, 'Clayworth and Cogenhoe', p. 79; (Dedham) Prest, 'Stability and change in Old and New England', p. 371, citing from K. Lockridge, 'The population of Dedham, Massachusetts, 1636–1736', *Economic History Review* 2nd series, 19 (1966), pp. 319–44; (Krasnoe Sabakino) Czap, 'Serf households in Mishino', pp. 141–3.

Table 1.3 Annual population turnover rates: medieval Essex compared with six other pre-industrial communities

Place and dates	Group under observation	Exits	Entries
Weighted mean of four Essex communities, early fourteenth century	Males aged 12+	4.1	5.2
Clayworth, 1676–88	Entire population	5.1	5.3
Cogenhoe, 1618–28	Entire population	5.2	5.3
Hallines, 1761–73	Entire population	3.8	4.3
Longueness, 1778–90	Entire population	3.8	3.0
Dedham (Massachusetts), 1640/48–1700	Males aged 21+	2.7	3.8
Krasnoe Sabakino (Russia), 1814–34	Servile males, all ages	1.9	–

significantly actual underlying population turnover rates) not only places these medieval communities squarely beside the Clayworth and Cogenhoe of three centuries later, but also implies a quite fundamentally different social order from that of servile Russian males on the Mishino estate 500 years after the tithing lists were written down. This polar contrast between Essex and Krasnoe Sabakino can be taken further: although it is impossible to obtain empirical confirmation, use of model life tables has suggested that intrinsic demographic factors probably accounted for no more than one-half of total turnover in fourteenth-century Essex, whereas at Krasnoe Sabakino migration accounted for only 7.7. per cent of 'exits' between 1814 and 1834.[58] It would appear, then, that geographical mobility played by far the greater role in determining overall turnover between these two historical environments. In the broad comparison between seventeenth-century England and nineteenth-century Russia, mobility in turn derived at least partly from household formation norms: very large, complex households and youthful marriage at Krasnoe Sabakino,[59] and the 'north-western European' marriage regime with its inbuilt component of adolescent mobility at Clayworth and Cogenhoe.

It would perhaps be unwarranted to extend this argument back to fourteenth-century Essex as well, on the basis of turnover patterns alone, but one might speculate that it was similar social-structural factors concerning household formation and associated economic and geographical features that allowed medieval Essex to exhibit population turnover essentially identical to that of Laslett's later communities, and

58 Czap, 'Serf households in Mishino', p. 142. An additional 11.5 per cent of 'exits' from Krasnoe Sabakino were caused by recruitment into the army.
59 Ibid., pp. 132–41.

(though less clearly) with similar contributions from geographical mobility toward this pattern. An accumulating body of evidence has suggested that medieval England did indeed possess a marriage regime more like than unlike its early modern counterpart. Later-fourteenth-century poll-tax returns, for example, now appear to support such an assertion,[60] as does other, more peripheral, evidence relating to marriage [61] and (as already noted) to medieval servanthood.

It may well be that the differences displayed among various historical settings in table 1.3 do not reflect a progression from medieval through early modern to modern times. Rather, they may illustrate divergences, measurable here in one particular index of historical demography, between particular social-structural regimes characteristic of different cultural regions of the West and long enduring within their own societies.[62] But the broader significance of these patterns in a comparative context will follow only a closer elucidation of other aspects of medieval social structure. The distinctive conjunction of features which comprised the social structure of England during the era of parish registers and listings, and which has been explicated over the past two decades by Peter Laslett and others working under his inspiration, may ultimately be found to have played a cognate role for several centuries before Clayworth's parson decided to set down his flock with pen and ink. Until then, the Essex evidence speaks strongly for another aspect of the long-term continuities of rural communities in the English past.

60 Smith, Hypothèses sur la nuptialité; R.M. Smith, 'Some reflections on the evidence for the origins of the "European marriage pattern" in England', in C. Harris (ed.), *The sociology of the family: new directions for Britain, Sociological Review* monograph 28 (1979), pp. 74–112; Poos, 'Population and resources', pp. 137–89. A comprehensive analysis of all surviving poll-tax returns is currently under way, under the direction of Richard Smith with contributions from the present author.

61 J. Bennett, 'Medieval peasant marriage: an examination of marriage licence fines in the *Liber Gersumarum*', in J.A. Raftis (ed.), *Pathways to medieval peasants* (Toronto, 1981), pp. 193–246.

62 Cf. Laslett and Harrison, 'Clayworth and Cogenhoe', pp. 71–4; P. Laslett, 'Characteristics of the Western family considered over time', in Laslett, *Family life and illicit love*, pp. 12–49; P. Laslett, 'Family and household as work group and kin group: areas of traditional Europe compared', and J. Hajnal, 'Two kinds of pre-industrial household formation system', in Wall, *Family forms in historic Europe*, pp. 65–104, 513–63.

2

Family Patterns and Relations of Bishop's Lynn Will-makers in the Fourteenth Century

Jacques Beauroy

Certain aspects of the family patterns of sections of medieval English urban society can be approached via the study of those wills that were enrolled in the rolls or registries of the borough courts. The 125 wills of Bishop's Lynn burgesses, on which the following analysis is based, enable us to define some of the characteristics of the urban family and relationships between its members from the end of the thirteenth century to the first quarter of the fifteenth century.[1] Most of the testators belonged to the upper layer of urban society: a good number of them could be found among the richer section of the list of Lynn's lay subsidy taxpayers of 1332.[2] Almost all had the status of 'Burgenses Lenne', but their occupations or professional activities were rarely mentioned.[3] There is no doubt, when one looks at the number of messuages and tenements with wharves and shops which are bequeathed, that their owners belonged to the merchant elite, that group of the *potentiores* who dominated Lynn's government at a time of relative prosperity in the history of the port and town, in spite of the four-

1 H. Ingleby (ed.), *The red register of King's Lynn*, 2 vols (King's Lynn, 1919/1922), p. 255 and p. 227, *passim*, 104 wills. (Abbreviations to the two volumes are RRI and RRII throughout). NRO, King's Lynn muniments, KL C/12/Ae, 1, 2, 3, 4, 5, 6, 7, 8, Ae 34, Ae 37, Ae 37a, Ae 38, Ae 39, Ae 40, Ae 41, Be 33, Be 38. NRO, Bradfer Lawrence Coll.: v y (m), P. de Melchebourne, 1350. NRO, NCC wills, Heydon 128, 133. PRO, PCC, 7 Rous, 13 March. CLRO, Cust. 15, 'Liber Lynne', fos. Vr et Vv, XXIv–XXIIIr. Seventy per cent of the wills (87) date from the first half of the fourteenth century.

2 PRO, E 179, 149/9, m. 5, Lynn, 1332–3. Among the 21 will-makers whose names appeared as taxpayers on the 1332 tax list, 17 belonged to the upper third paying the highest taxes.

3 The only will-makers whose professional status is known: Alexander de Cornere, faber (1308); Mathew le Taillour (1309); Thomas de Bauseye, apotecarius (1326); Philip Trubbok, Carnifex (1328); Adam de Walsoken, Mercator (1349); John de Wigenhale, Carpentarius (1349); Richard de Wottone, Tabennarius (1349); Giles Grym, Carnifex (1361); John de Lynn, mercerus (1371). Twenty-two will-makers were mayors of Lynn in the fourteenth century.

teenth-century crises. The total population of Bishop's Lynn *c.*1340 has been estimated at 9000. Owing to the Black Death of 1349 and to later visitations of plague, it seems that the population in 1380 had been reduced to 5500.[4] Thus it can be considered that this set of 125 wills, spread from 1276 to 1429, represents a useful sample for a specific and restricted social category of Lynn's population.

The probate of urban wills depended on the proceedings of two different courts. The episcopal court acted immediately after the testator's death. Its specific role was to confirm the executors named in the will by releasing to them the administration of all the movable and immovable property of the deceased will-maker. Also, the episcopal court dealt with the funeral itself and the distribution of pious bequests. The borough court, on the other hand, was concerned with the bequests of burgage tenures, 'approbatio quoad tenementa legata'.[5] The wills were presented for examination before a committee of jurors specially elected for that purpose. In the name of the mayor and the commonalty, the jurors confirmed the legatees in their seisin of the burgage tenements bequeathed to them. The seal of the commonalty was appended to the document, and an official enrolment of the will 'in papiro aule' could be approved.[6]

My particular concern here is the study of devolutionary practice as it revealed family patterns in fourteenth-century urban society. In considering the will-makers in this study, the majority of whom (83 per cent) were men, the following questions were asked: Was there a difference in the number and type of bequests according to the sex of the will-makers? Was there a difference in the number and type of bequests according to the sex of the heirs and legatees? How different were the inheritance shares of the sons and of the daughters of the will-makers? To what extent did the bequests of immovable and movable property go to the surviving spouse and the children constituting the nuclear family? Which individuals beyond the circle of the nuclear

4 H. Clarke and A. Carter, 'Excavations in King's Lynn, 1963–1970', *Soc. for Med. Arch. Monograph Series,* 7 (1977), p. 429.

5 RRII, fo. 153, p. 107, 3 November 1372: 'communitas ville Lenne congregata elegerunt Thomam de Botekesham, Johannem de Brunham, Johannem de Dockingge et Henricum de Betele pro examinacionibus testamentorum omnium que de cetero debent irrotulari in papiro aule Gilde Lenne et sine examinacione eorumdem nullum testamentum debet in dicto papiro irrotulari.' (pp. 148–9).

6 RRI, fo. 76 d, testament of John Burghard 5 April 1339, proved in the Borough Court 18 August 1344: 'Approbatum fuit testamentum quoad tenementa et redditus legata et contenta in prescripto testamento coram nobis Adam de Walsoken tunc maiore Lenne, Johanne de Swerdestone tunc aldermanno, et coram tota communitate burgi tunc in aula existente. ... Et adjudicata est execucio dicti testamenti quoad infrascripta tenementa et redditus, per ballivum faciendum legatoriis, in dicto testamento contenta et infrascripta, secundum consuetudinem ville de Lenna hactenus usitatam et approbatam. Et dictum testamentum consignatum est sigillo maioratus Lennensis ad hoc pendente et patente.'

family were the recipients of the remaining bequests? I have put aside, for consideration at a later date, the portion of the patrimony devoted to the 'purchase of paradise', or to 'la comptabilité de l'au-delà', as it was called in a recent study. Lastly I was interested in discerning, through an analysis of the distribution bequests, the quality of the feelings and attitudes which bound together the English urban family in the fourteenth century.[7]

Will-makers, Heirs and Legatees

Most of our will-makers were men (104, 83 per cent). As in the aristocracy, the making of a will in burgess society was predominantly a male practice. The testators generally designated, in their wills, the succeeding beneficiaries of the properties bequeathed in usufruct to their wives, 'ad totam vitam suam'. Thus widows without personal property of their own had little power on the choices regarding the next generation which had been made by their husbands. Among our 104 male testators, 70 per cent were married and made bequests to their surviving wives; 30 per cent were without wives, dying either as widowers or apparently unmarried (table 2.1).

Table 2.1   Marital status of the testators

Status	Men (no.)	(%)	Women (no.)	(%)
With spouse	73	70	5	24
Without spouse	31	30	16	76
Total	104	100	21	100

Women testators numbered only 21; most of them (16, 76 per cent) were without spouse, either widows or, in two cases, unmarried women. Helen atte Churche of Godwyck made her last will on 10 February 1348 and died some time before 19 April 1350. She had been the servant (famula) of Nicholas Page who bequeathed her a messuage in Lynn, and she in turn bequeathed it to her son Stephen Hervy.[8] Agnes

---

7 J.T. Rosenthal, *The purchase of paradise: gift giving and the aristocracy, 1307–1485* (London, 1972); J. Chiffoleau, *La Comptabilité de l'au-delà: les hommes, la mort et la religion dans la région Comtadine à la fin du moyen âge* (v. 1330–1480) (Rome, 1981); N.P. Tanner, *The Church in late medieval Norwich, 1370–1532* (Toronto, 1984); M.T. Lorcin, *Vivre et mourir en Lyonnais à la fin du moyen âge* (Paris, 1981).

8 RRI, fo. 81, pp. 164–8, testamentum Nicholai Page (1340); ibid., fo. 101 d., pp. 213–14.

de Sutton, who was clearly a spinster, made her will on 22 May 1349 and she died sometime before 5 June 1349, victim of the plague. She designated her mother Katherine de Sutton as her only legatee and her testamentary executor, bequeathing to her two tenements ('tenementa') in Lynn.[9] All the remaining 14 female testators were widows, mentioned as 'relicta' or 'quondam uxor'. Their sons and daughters were the main beneficiaries of their bequests, and for nine of them the wills of their husbands who preceded them in death are extant.[10]

Among the 21 female testators, only five women were married at the time they made their wills. Agnes, wife of John de Walpole, on 1 May 1307 bequeathed her two tenements, one to her husband and the other for sale by her executors to pay her debts.[11] Alice de Aldeby, married to Philip de Werthorp, bequeathed to her husband on 20 November 1319 the tenement which belonged to her father, 'quod quondam fuit Ricardi de Aldeby', and left another tenement to be sold by her executors who were named as her husband assisted by 'two capellani'.[12] Margeria de Sutton, who was remarried, bequeathed in 1318 to her four sons and two daughters of her first marriage with Richard Hopman all the tenements she held in an use, on the condition that the heirs paid £20 owed in debts by their father.[13] Alice Chappe bequeathed to her elder son John on 20 February 1348 a tenement on Tynereslane for the payment of 20 marks, if he wanted it. If he did not want it, it was to be sold to the highest bidder by her executors with another tenement in Northirne.[14] Emma de Toftes, on 26 May 1349, as the epidemic was raging, bequeathed three tenements to her dying husband 'ad totam vitam suam'. After her death, ten days later, the commissaries of the episcopal court had to appoint two new executors to replace the executors she had named in her will, her husband and John de Frenge, who had died in the interval.[15]

---

9 NRO, KL/C 12/4, Be 33, 22 May 1349.

10 Margeria Hopman (1319), RRI, fo. 64 d., pp. 119–20; Richard Hopman (1315), ibid., fo. 64 d., p. 119. Theophania de Swerdestone (1316), RRI, fo. 41, pp. 75–6; Alan de Swerdestone (before 1316), ibid., fo. 41, pp. 74–5. John de Thornegge (1340), RRI, fo. 79, pp. 159–61; John de Thornegge (1329), ibid., fo. 78 d.–79, pp. 157–9. Agnes de Rigges (1333), RRI, fo. 44, pp. 83–4; Thomas de Rigges (1330), ibid., fo. 30, pp. 55–6. Margareta de Frenge (1352), NRO, KL/C 12/ 1, Ae 2; John de Frenge (1338), ibid., Ae 1. Agnes de Biteringe (1341), RRI, fo. 66 d., pp. 124–5; Walter de Biteringe (1340), ibid., fo. 66, pp. 122–3. Matilda de Keteliston (1344), RRI, fo. 80 d., pp. 162–3; Geoffrey de Keteliston (1341), ibid., fo. 79 d.–80, pp. 161–2. Margeria de Betele (1349), RRI, fo. 95, pp. 194–5; Hugh de Betele (1348), ibid., fo.92, pp. 186–9. Margareta Grym (1375), NRO, KL/C 12/ 7; Egidius Grym (1361), ibid., KL/C 12/ 5.

11 RRI, fo. 6, pp. 11–12.

12 Ibid., fo. 23, pp. 42–3.

13 Ibid., fo. 64 d., pp. 119–20.

14 Ibid., fo. 99, p. 207.

15 Ibid., fo. 99 d., p. 208.

The total number of the children of the testators mentioned as heirs, sons and daughters, was 183. Considering all our wills (125) (table 2.2) but leaving out the two clerics who were among our testators, Reginald de Est-Walton and John de Acre, the average number of children named as beneficiaries per family at the death of the testator was 1.49.[16] However, children were sometimes mentioned collectively, as 'filii et filiae' or simply 'pueri', or wholly omitted in the wills which are not complete. Such a low figure of 1.49 children acknowledged by testator at his death seriously under-represents the reality of family size. Children, especially daughters who may have been the recipients of ante-mortem gifts as dowries at their marriages, may have been ignored. We have potentially useful informtion for only 76 families, as

Table 2.2 Testators mentioning and not mentioning children

Children	Men	Women	Total (no.)	(%)
Mentioned	63	13	76	61
Not mentioned	41	8	49	39
Total	104	21	125	100

there were 76 will-makers leaving property to their children. On this basis, an average of 2.41 children were specified at the death of the testator. This figure is likely to be more complete, although it too underestimates reality owing to collective designations of children. In Lyonnais, Marie-Thérèse Lorcin, in one of the most comprehensive analyses of late medieval European will-makers so far published, found a figure of 2.7 children per testator among commoners between 1340 and 1500, although the average figures fell to 2.6 children per testator between 1340 and 1380, quite close to our figures relating to the urban will-makers of West Norfolk.[17]

The effect of the demographic crisis of the fourteenth century can be seen through the fact that more than 14 per cent of our wills (18) were concentrated into a single six-month period between the end of March 1349 and the end of September 1349.[18]

16 Reginaldus de Est-Walton (1333), RRI, fo. 29, pp. 54–5; Johannes de Acra (1374), rector of All Saints, Lynn, NRO, NCC wills, Heydon, 128–33.

17 Lorcin, *Vivre et mourir en Lyonnais*, p. 18.

18 Henry de Betele (25 March 1349), RRI, fo. 94 d.–95, pp. 191–4; Philip Wythe (9 April 1349), ibid., fo. 97 d., pp. 202–6; Margeria de Betele (16 April 1349), ibid., fo. 95, pp. 194–5;

There were 97 sons and 86 daughters among the 183 heirs (table 2.3). This over-representation of sons could be the first index suggesting an unequal inheritance practice in favour of sons or the effect of previous gifts to daughters. Also, four posthumous children were mentioned in the wills of their fathers. Eustach de Toftes in 1309 asserted that he would make no difference according to the sex of the child to be 'sive masculi sexus feurit sive femini' and he bequeathed him an annual rent of 4s to be received on a capital messuage in Dampgate. Peter de Melchebourne bequeathed in 1350 to his future child, 'puero in utero Alicie uxoris mee, deo dante, nascituro', £5 and a tenement on Briggegate. As an expression of his hopes of finally having a boy, William de Swanton prescribed in 1361 to his wife to give the expected child, 'si masculus fuerit', two messuages and one wharf. Male heirs, as this last example shows, were distinguished by receiving real estate in the borough.[19]

Table 2.3 Testators mentioning children and the sex of those children

Testators		Sons	Daughters	Total
Men	63	81	71	152
Women	13	16	15	31
Total	76	97	86	183

Legatees belonging to the close kin group of relatives, beyond the nuclear family circle, could only be counted in 48 wills (41 men testators, 7 women). Table 2.4 shows the importance of the siblings, brothers and sisters among the family relations of the testators: 36 brothers and sisters, and also 60 nephews and nieces, were mentioned

---

Adam de Walsoken (28 April 1349), ibid., fo. 87 d–89, pp. 172–82; William de Rughton (1 May 1349), ibid., fo. 93 d., pp. 190–1; Richard de Wottone (13 May 1349), ibid., fo. 96 d., pp. 199–202; John de Wigenhale (15 May 1349), ibid., fo. 96, pp. 198–9; John de Walsingham (20 May 1349), ibid., fo. 93, pp. 189–90; Agnes de Sutton (22 May 1349), NRO, KL/C 12/4, Be 33; Thomas de Melchebourne (26 May 1349), RRI, fo. 101, pp. 212–13; Emma de Toftes (26 May 1349), ibid., fo. 99 d., p. 208; William Erl (9 June 1349), ibid., fo. 85, pp. 174–6; Simon de Biteringe (16 June 1349), ibid., fo. 95 d., pp. 195–7; John de Swerdstone senior (17 June 1349), ibid., fo. 90, pp. 182–5; Lambert d'Alemaigne (21 June 1349), ibid., fo. 103 d., pp. 218–19; Robert de Quetacre (28 June 1349), ibid., fo. 96, p. 197; Robert de Docking (4 July 1349), ibid., fo. 100, pp. 209–11; William de Massingham (30 September 1349), ibid., fo. 98 d., p. 206.

19 Posthumous children: Eustach de Toftes (1309), RRI, fo. 8, p. 17; Philip Trubbok (1328), ibid., fo. 65, p. 120; Richard de Wottone (1349), ibid., fo. 96, p. 200; Peter de Melchebourne (1350), NRO, Bradfer Lawrence Coll., v y (m); William de Swanton (1361), RRI, fo. 108 d., p. 235.

Table 2.4   Legatees and close kin group

Relationship or status	No.
Brother	26
Sister	10
Father	1
Mother	3
Uncle	1
Niece	30
Nephew	30
Son-in-law	5
Daughter-in-law	2
Grandson	7
Granddaughter	10
Godchildren	2
Cousin	4
Servant (sex unknown)	9
Servant (female)	27
Servant (male)	23

as legatees, representing the main beneficiaries of bequests in the close kin group.

Seventeen grandchildren received bequests, as well as two godchildren of the same godfather (Peter de Melchebourne, 1350). More than 59 servants were gratified by their master in their wills. Figures for nephews and nieces and the servants must be regarded as slight underestimates, for they were occasionally mentioned collectively.

Besides the clearly identified close kin group and the members of the domestic group there were, in 33 wills, 199 named legatees, whose precise relationship with the will-makers was not defined. Some of them could be friends or partners. A good number were evidently close relatives bearing the same family name. Only three will-makers were thinking, in this final hour, of a wider kin group, designating it by a general formula – 'parentes et consanguinei' (Robert Lambert, 1322) or, as Thomas de Sedgeford in 1326, bequeathing 20s 'ad distribuendos inter pauperem parentelam meam in villa de Sedgeford'. John Burghard in 1339 bequeathed all his clothes to his poor relatives, 'item lego pauperibus de parentela mea omnia indumenta corpori meo spectantia'.[20] The average number of legatees named but not identified precisely as to their relationship with the will-maker amounted to six per will, and they could reach 19 as in the will of John Burghard in

20 Robert Lambert (1322), RRI, fo. 43, pp. 80–2; Thomas de Sedgeford senior (1326), ibid., fo. 64, p. 116.

1339, or the 23 in the will of John Wace (1399) who received bequests amounting to £89.[21] The bequests made to this particular group of 'unidentified' relatives (or friends and partners) were mostly bequests of cash or objects. There were for this group only two cases of bequests of annual rent and five cases of bequests of immovable property.

The will-makers usually appointed three or four testamentary executors. There were at least two executors and at most seven per will. It was possible to count 261 of them and it was clear that, in general, they were 'burgenses Lenne' and belonged to the peer group of the merchant families, relatives or partners of the will-makers. Very often they were members of the nuclear family of the will-maker: firstly, wives and adult sons were appointed executors. Brothers and servants were also appointed. Thomas de Melchebourne in 1349 appointed three testamentary executors: his wife, his brother and his son.[22] Many will-makers appointed among their executors a member of the secular clergy (chaplain, vicar, rector etc.) who assisted in the writing of the will. These clerics were experts who, after having guided and oriented the testamentary dispositions, also knew how to organize their implementation. Some executors combined family membership and clerical status.[23] Table 2.5 shows the family relationship or status of 108 executors.

Table 2.5   Testamentary executors and
relationship with testators

Relationship or status	No.
Wife	33
Husband	2
Son	19
Mother	2
Father	1
Brother	9
Son-in-law	3
Nephew	2
Cousin	1
Servant	5
Apprentice	2
Cleric	29
Total	108

21 John Burghard (1339), RRI, fo. 75, p. 141; John Wace (1399), NRO, KL/C 12/8.
22 Thomas de Melchebourne (1349), RRI, fo. 101, p. 213: 'Hujus autem testamenti mei executores constituo meos videlicet Johannam uxorem meam, Willelmum de Melchebourne fratrem meum et Petrum de Melchebourne filium meum.'
23 RRI, fo. 81, pp. 166–7, Nicholas Page (1340): 'istos constituo executores meos videlicet. ... Henricum rectorem ecclesie de Bixley fratrem meum predictum.'

Some testators also appointed an adviser, generally a cleric, who would oversee the operations of the testamentary executors, as Nicholas Page in 1340, who stated in his will: 'Volo eciam quod omnia et singula que in hoc testamento continentur facienda fiant per consilium, visum et auxilium domini Ricardi de Godewyck, vicarii ecclesia ominum sanctorum de South Lenna'.[24]

Testamentary executors had an essential role as main legatees and distributors and sellers of the legacies. They had to separate and attribute the 'lay' and the 'pious' bequests, ensure that the heirs, legatees and other beneficiaries received their legacies, settle the debts and pay for the masses requested by the will-makers. In the event of the failure of their appointees the will-makers relied as a last resort on the mayor and the 'aldermanni' of the guild of Lynn to guarantee the bequests of their immovable property in the town.[25]

Thus beyond the nuclear family, which was paramount in the concerns of the will-makers, it appears that the close circle constituted by the brothers and sisters of the will-makers and their children, nephews and nieces received numerous legacies, reflecting the relatively narrow circle of organized family relationships and feelings. Frequently also in his last thoughts and acts the will-maker singled out his servants. Executors were mostly members of the nuclear family and the close kin group, but included a large number of clerics. Secular clerics were, in fact, the necessary intermediaries for entry into the Christian afterlife.

Patrimony and Bequests

In order to analyse the number and types of bequests contained in the wills, they were divided into four main categories: bequests in cash, bequests of immovable property, bequests in annual rent and bequests of objects and movables.[26] The wills, in all, leave a record of 1,432 bequests.

Our enrolled wills were particularly concerned with immovable property in the town. Burgage tenures were described either as 'messuagia cum edificiis et pertinenciis' or as 'tenementa cum edificiis'.[27] Although they were counted apart, they represented the same types of property

24 RRI, fo. 80, p. 166, Nicholas Page (1340).

25 For example, Cecilia de Conteshale (1387), NRO, KL/C 12/1: 'et si ad hoc illi autem hujus testamenti complendum decederint tunc volo et ordino quod maior et aldermannus ville Lenne predicte qui pro tempore fuerint in omnibus istius testamenti adimplendum compleant et exequantur.'

26 For the eight categories of immovables, cf. caption of table 2.10. Bequests of movables: (1) grain, malt, bread, herring, etc.; (2) clothes, wool, linen, furs, shoes; (3) household furniture, pots, iron, copper, lead, wood, others; (4) precious objects, cups, spoons, jewels, boxes; (5) bed, sheets, blankets, cushions, others; (6) others.

27 The messuage was a complex of residential and work unit including a courtyard ('curtilagium') and several buildings with shops and even wharves.

bequeathed. There were a few capital messuages which constituted a superior variety of the same type of urban immovable property. Larger in size, they were the main residence and seat of activity of the will-makers, who generally owned several messuages in the town. Wharves and shops were often attached to the messuages or tenements.

The types of movable goods bequeathed did not display a great diversity. They included objects made of metal or other matter such as precious clothes, furniture, household equipment and utensils designated by the word 'camera', and beds. Bequests in cash were sometimes attributed to an undefined group of heirs or legatees, children, nephews and nieces, and servants. They varied between 1s and £2 when given to executors, close kin or servants. The larger cash bequests, which could amount to £200, formed gifts to sons, dowries to daughters, and particularly dowers to surviving wives. Finally, bequests of annual rents were sums payable at the four usual terms of Lynn from the income of messuages, tenements and shops.

Table 2.6   Proportion of bequests of each sort (per cent)

Legatees	Cash	Immovable	Annual rent	Movable	Total
Spouse	2.0	49.0	8.0	41.0	100
Sons	14.1	44.2	13.3	28.4	100
Daughters	22.2	35.4	17.2	25.2	100
Kin	42.3	12.1	4.6	41.0	100
Servants	38.2	2.3	–	59.5	100
Executors	35.6	49.5	2.4	12.5	100

Table 2.6 shows the distribution of all types of bequests, which enables us to have an overview of the relative position of the legatees. The largest proportion of bequests within the respective shares of the members of the nuclear family was made up of real estate bequests: 49 per cent for the surviving spouses, 44.2 per cent for the sons, 35.4 per cent for the daughters. Within the executors' share, the bequests of immovable property represented 49.5 per cent. By contrast, the close kin's share of bequests included only a small proportion of bequests of immovable property (12.6 per cent) and a very large proportion of cash bequests (42.3 per cent). The servants also received in their share a large proportion of cash bequests (38.2 per cent).

Movables (objects, clothes etc.) comprised the largest proportion of bequests to servants (59.5 per cent). The close kin group had in its share a large proportion of movable goods (41 per cent) as did the surviving spouse (41 per cent).

By contrast with the other groups of legatees, sons and daughters received, in their shares, a relatively even proportion of each of the four categories of bequests.

A comparison of the devolutionary practices of male and female will-makers shows that women testators reproduced the same bias in the devolution of property as men testators in favouring their male heirs. In table 2.7 the comparison between male and female testators is based upon 981 bequests including the three categories of cash bequests, of immovable property and of annual rent bequests. These three categories constituted, largely owing to bequests of real estate, the most valuable part of the patrimony. Most women testators were widows and had thus no surviving spouses to whom they could make bequests: 19 per cent of their bequests went to their sons as against 13 per cent to their daughters. In both cases of men and women testators there was a difference of at least six percentage points to the disadvantage of daughters.

Table 2.7   Number of bequests (cash, immovable, annual rent) according to types of legatees and sex of testators

Testators		Legatees						
		Spouse	Sons	Daughters	Kin	Servants	Executors	Total
Men	(no.)	162	178	118	122	54	247	881
	(%)	18.4	20.2	13.4	14.0	6.0	28.0	100
Women	(no.)	5	19	13	5	3	55	100
	(%)	5.0	19.0	13.0	5.0	3.0	55.0	100
Total (no.)								981

Women will-makers gave to their executors twice as many bequests (55 per cent) as did their male counterparts. One might ask whether they were more in debt or whether they increased, in this manner, the number of pious bequests for whom the executors were responsible. Furthermore, in the absence of a surviving spouse, was his share transferred to the executor?

Women bequeathed their movables – clothes, household effects, jewels and other precious objects – primarily to their daughters and close kin rather than their sons (table 2.8). Men gave a great deal more of their movable goods to their sons, although the greater proportion of their bequests of movables went to their surviving wives. Men and women behaved in a similar fashion with regard to the bequests in clothes and objects to their servants.

Table 2.8   Number of bequests of movable goods according to types of legatees and sex of testators

Testators		Spouse	Sons	Daughters	Kin	Servants	Executors	Total
						Legatees		
Men	(no.)	114	78	16	64	74	43	389
	(%)	30	20	4	16	19	11	100
Women	(no.)	–	–	28	24	10	–	62
	(%)	–	–	45	39	16	–	100

Table 2.9 shows from another angle the total number of bequests distributed to the nuclear family, to close kin and to servants. Half of the total number of bequests went to the nuclear family. Executors received three times as many cash, immovable and annual rent bequests to be paid out or sold than they received bequests of movables. The surviving spouse, close kin and servants received the larger number of bequests of movables. And, once again, one can observe greater recognition of sons than daughters by the Lynn testators.

Table 2.9   Number and types of bequests and types of legatees. Group 1: cash, immovables, annual rent. Group 2: movables

Types of bequests		Spouse	Sons	Daughters	Kin	Servants	Executors	Total
						Legatees		
Group 1	(no.)	167	197	131	127	57	302	981
	(%)	17.0	20.0	13.0	13.0	6.0	31.0	100
Group 2	(no.)	114	78	44	88	84	43	451
	(%)	25.3	17.2	10.0	19.5	18.5	9.5	100

The bequests of immovable property, the central component in the patrimony of Lynn's burgesses, deserves a particular study. In the wills the terms used to describe the most valuable urban properties were: 'capitale messuagium', 'messuagium' and 'tenementum'. In all, 308 messuages and tenements were identified, representing 59 per cent of all the bequests of immovable property (by table 2.10). These messuages were the residential units for the urban nuclear family and domestic group, while they also sheltered its craft and mercantile activities.

Table 2.10 Number and types of immovable property and types of legatees

Types of immovables	Legatees							
	Spouse	Sons	Daugh-ters	Kin	Ser-vants	Executors	Total	%
Capitale messuagium	5	2	1	–	–	3	11	2.1
Messuagium	31	14	13	7	1	30	96	18.4
Tenementum	48	50	17	10	–	76	201	38.5
Cayum (quay)	8	6	3	2	–	10	29	5.6
Selda	35	38	22	4	–	22	121	23.2
Solarium	4	6	–	–	–	15	25	4.8
Placea	–	–	–	–	–	4	4	0.8
Terra	2	1	2	2	1	3	11	2.1
Others	4	5	4	1	1	8	23	4.5
Total	137	122	62	26	3	171	521	100

Given that Lynn was an important port, it might be expected that the wills would reveal relatively numerous bequests of wharves, and it seems surprising that only 29 of them were mentioned in 125 wills of burgesses of Lynn from 1276 to 1425. It can only be supposed that they must have been included generally in the appurtenances of the messuages and were consequently not mentioned individually.[28] It is also rather surprising to find only two wills mentioning bequests of ships.[29]

Table 2.10 shows that bequests of capital messuages, messuages, tenements and wharves represented 65 per cent of all the bequests of immovable property. The nuclear family received 58.8 per cent of the bequests and the executors received 35.3 per cent for sale and payments of the debts of the deceased will-maker. Sons received twice as many bequests of these immovable properties – 21.4 per cent as opposed to the 10.1 per cent that went to daughters.

Shops (constituting 23.2 per cent) were numerous among the bequests of immovables. Almost 80 per cent of them were bequeathed to members of the nuclear family, confirming the importance of the retail trade

28 Wharves could be mentioned in the appurtenances of a tenement: Peter de Thorndene (1309), RRI, fo. 2, p. 3; 'Lego et assigno Ele filie Johannis de Spaldinge terram meam cum edificiis et cayis et alii pertinenciis suis quam adquisisi de Roberto C.'

29 RRI, fo. 78 d., p. 156, Nicholas de Fakenham (1332): 'Et ad istud testamentum meam adimplendum et debita mea persolvenda lego omnia bona mea et catalla, ac naves seu batillos.' And ibid., fo. 104, p. 129: 'Dispono, do et lego quod ... duo feriebots, navis quoque mea vocata "Le Thomas" cum toto apparati ejusdem ac armaturis in eadem existentibus necnon totum meremeum [timber wood] super Bishopestathe in dicta villa Lenne.'

in the borough for our group of will-makers.[30] They invested in the building of shops attached to their messuages, and they rented them out. Some of these shops (25) were described as having a room above called a 'solarium' (solar) so that goods might be stocked in a dry place. Of the rather imprecise categories of property including 'placea', 'terra', houses, 'curtilagia' and pasture, 53 per cent went to the nuclear family.

Another way of assessing the devolutionary practice of Lynn's burgesses is to examine the value of bequests, although this can be done only for cash bequests, annual rent bequests and the bequests of immovable property. Surviving spouse, sons and daughters received an equal amount of bequests in cash. Seventy-seven per cent of the value of bequests in annual rent went to the nuclear family; sons received the largest amount (30.2 per cent). This type of bequest was often used to maintain, during their lifetime, children who entered religious orders.[31] The total value of immovable properties, based on the average price of a messuage, indicates that the bequests of immovable properties left to the surviving spouses amounted to £5,880 (27.3 per cent).[32] Sons received bequests of immovable property valued £5,620 (21.4 per cent) and daughters only £2,170 (10.1 per cent). The difference of inheritance shares between sons and daughters was caused primarily by the larger number of bequests of immovable properties which the sons received.[33] Preoccupied with the problem of family continuity, the burgesses of Lynn sought to buttress the masculine line by bequeathing a much larger proportion of their immovable property in the town, the base of their wealth, to their sons. They also made sure that their surviving wives enjoyed a firm material security and welfare 'ad totam vitam suam'.

Aspects of Family Solidarity

Considering in more detail the examples of the wills of John Ode (1307) and of John Lambert (1312), we may be able to gain a more personalized view of family relationships and sentiments than could be achieved from the statistical analysis we have so far pursued.

30 Shops were attached to messuages and constituted an important investment for our group of will-makers. They were undoubtedly rented out.

31 As in the cases of the wills of John Ode (1307) and John Lambert (1312) (analysed later): annual rents were bequeathed to sons who were Dominicans for their needs.

32 The average price of a tenement or messuage in Lynn, in the fourteenth century, was calculated on the basis of three prices mentioned in the wills: (1) £33 6s (1308), RRI, fo. 6, p. 12; (2) £90 (1333), RRI, fo. 44, p. 84; (3) £100 (1429), KL/C/12/11, Ae 41.

33 The value of cash bequests was equal for sons and for daughters. The value of annual rent bequests was superior by 5.5 per cent in favour of sons by comparison with the daughters' share, and the value of immovable property bequests was superior by 11.3 per cent in favour of sons (21.4 per cent for sons against 10.1 per cent for daughters).

John Ode in 1307 bequeathed all his immovable property and his annual rents to his three sons and four daughters, but he decided that his children would have possession of them only after the death of their mother Alice. Two of his sons, John and Michael, were to inherit his two messuages: John would have his capital messuage of Wyngate, and Michael his messuage close to Meyrisflete, called Duffecoteyard. James, the third son, who was a Dominican, received 10s of annual rent 'pro habitu suo', paid on his capital messuage of Wyngate. This would be paid by his mother, and after her death by John, the heir of the Wyngate property. His four daughters, Margaret, Muriel, Etheldreda and Agnes, each received an annual rent payable on several messuages in the town, which varied between 20s and 33s. John Ode specified that, if need be, his wife could sell four shops that he had bequeathed to her. Finally, John Ode gave a plot of land and three other, unoccupied, tenements to his executors for sale in order to pay his debts and implement his will.[34] John Ode's will showed clearly how the surviving wife was treated. The widow, as head of the family, had the use rights of all the immovable property up to her death. It emphasizes, also, the unequal inheritance share of sons and daughters.

The will of John Lambert (1312) contained dispositions which were somewhat different. The will-maker had four children who were adult – Robert, Alexander, Nicholas and the daughter Matilda, married with two children. He had as principal heir his eldest son Robert, and he appointed him and his wife Matilda to act jointly as executors. Robert received, with immediate seisin, a messuage on Wyngate, five annual rents and three new shops with their solars. The second son Alexander received only an annual rent of 40s to be paid on the tenements and shops only after the death of his mother Matilda. To his third son Nicholas a Dominican, John Lambert bequeathed an annual rent of 20s for life, which Robert, his principal heir, had to start to pay from the first Michaelmas after his death, 'pro habitu suo et aliis necessariis suis'. To his married daughter Matilda and his two grandchildren, Margaret and John, he bequeathed a messuage and three shops on Briggegate. He also gave her his diamond 'petram meam vocatam diamaunt'. He did not omit to mention his wife's use rights on his properties by the following clause: 'Item volo quod predicta Matildis uxor mea habeat omnia tenementa predicta in tota vita sua pro plena dote sua tam bonorum mobilium quam immobilium'. The will-maker endowed his surviving wife with parental authority and established the rules of conduct which his elder son Robert should follow in his relations with his mother: 'Quandocumque dictus Robertus accessum habeat ad matrem suam honorifice, reverenter et obedienter, prout filius matris sue debet parere teneatur'.[35]

34 RRI, fo. 5, pp. 9–11, John Ode (1307).
35 Ibid., fo. 42, pp. 76–80, John Lambert (1312).

The dower of widows consisted of an use of the whole patrimony in the case of minor children, or of a part of the family movable and immovable property according to the decision of the will-maker and the agreement of adult children. In the case of the richer families, the widow could have her use rights limited to a charge of a capital sum on the common goods which might amount to £200. John Burghard, on 5 April 1339, made his will in favour of his wife Alice, his three sons, Geoffrey (his main heir), Nicholas and Peter, and his two daughters, Alice (who was a nun) and Margaret (a minor). He bequeathed 18 messuages in Lynn, of which at least two had wharves, 33 shops, 20 annual rents and numerous bequests in cash. To his minor daughter he bequeathed £60. He bequeathed to his wife Alice a tenement and the custody of his minor children, Peter and Margaret, with the properties bequeathed to them, until their majority or the marriage of Margaret. In his codicil, John Burghard added that his wife should receive £200 on the common goods as dower, a cash sum which could constitute her definitive portion of the inheritance. Likewise, in 1368 William de Biteringe bequeathed to his wife Juliana two messuages, one annual rent, 'ad totam vitam suam', and £200 for her portion on all the rest of his property.[36]

The conditions of the custody of their children was a major preoccupation of the will-makers. The surviving wife, mother of the children, or close relatives generally took on this burden. Richard de Geyton in 1276 appointed Richard de Gerneston, his son-in-law and executor, custodian of his four minor daughters in the event of the death of his wife.[37] William de Roughton, widower, gave the custody of his younger son to Simon, his elder son.[38] But Ralph Wake, in 1339, divided the custody of his three minor children: he gave the custody of his younger son William to his elder son John, who was married, but decided that his two minor daughters, Catherina and Joan, to whom he gave good dowries, would be placed in the care of custodians outside the family, 'in custodia aliquorum proborum hominum'.[39] There was, undoubtedly, a good market for the custody of daughters who were endowed.

The will-makers defined different custody dispositions according to the sex of their children. In respect of their sons they showed concern about family continuity and about their professional future. They appointed alongside their wife a custodian, a male executor who could

36 Ibid., fo. 75, pp. 140–8, John Burghard (1339); and ibid., fo. 110–11 d., pp. 238–40, William de Biteringe (1368).

37 NRO, KL/C 12/ 2, Richard de Geyton (1276).

38 RRI, fo. 55, pp. 97–9, William de Roughton (1328): 'Item volo quod Simon filius meus custodiat domum meam, videlicet capitale messuagium unacum tota familia mea et pueris meis.' Furthermore he appointed his second son William as the tutor of his third son Roger until his majority.

39 RRI fo. 73 d., p. 139, Ralph Wace (1339).

replace her and assist in the education of their son and his professional apprenticeship. Peter of Melchebourne (29 September 1350) decided that his wife would keep the custody of their son Thomas if she did not remarry. But, if she remarried, the custody of Thomas and of all the properties bequeathed to him would be given to Robert de Cokesford, friend and testamentary executor, until Thomas's majority.[40] The same reasons must have inspired Geoffrey Drew in 1361 when he gave the custody of his two sons, William and Thomas, to his executors, while his wife Goldithe retained the custody of their daughter Caterina.[41] The surviving wife, who had custody of minor daughters, had the power of consent over their marriage. So John de Docking stated in his will on 4 August 1380: 'Item lego et assigno Margarete uxori mee alimentacionem et custodiam Margarete filie mee predicte quousque ad legitimam etatem pervenerit vel per assensum et voluntatem eiusdem Margarete uxoris mee desponsata fuerit'.[42] For boys, custody dispositions sometimes included provisions for their schooling and studies.[43]

Will-makers expressed the feelings which had sustained their family relationship by the bequests of their movable goods. Normally the surviving wife was the beneficiary of the household furniture, linen, bedding and utensils: 'Omnia et singula utensilia et necessaria pertinentia domui mee et camere mee cujuscumque generii fuerint vel speciei'.[44] There must have been, however, some specific sentimental attention from John Burghard towards his sister when he bequeathed her in 1339 his death-bed: 'Volo quod lectum meum in quo me mori, Deo disponente, contingat, tradatur et liberetur Matildi sorori mee'.[45] Bequests of precious objects might well be assumed to reflect the psychological ties formed by the will-makers. There was a large number of bequests of clothes of a formal nature, like coats and gowns ('cloke', 'roba', 'gunna'), which were given to brothers, sons, sons-in-law or servants. A special value seemed to have been attached to clothes ornamented or lined with fur. John Lambert (1312) bequeathed

---

40 NRO, Bradfer Lawrence Coll., v y (m), Peter de Melchebourne (1350). RRI, fo. 105 d., p. 225, 1361: Thomas atte Beke, in the event of the remarriage or death of his wife, gave the custody of his son Lawrence to his executors John Urry and Thomas de Glaundford until the age of 21.

41 RRI, fo. 106 d., p. 227, Geoffrey Drew (1361).

42 NRO, KL/C 12/1, John de Docking (1380).

43 NRO, KL/C 12/8, Ae 38, John Wace, 16 August 1399: 'Volo et ordino quod Isabella uxor mea et executores mei habeat gubernariotem et custodiam de Johanne filio Nicholai Wace consanguineo meo et ipsum omnino ad scolas inveniant cum honis meis propriis et catallis. Si scolas ex cetero voluerit quousque pervenerit ad etatem XXIIII annorum.' And NRO KL Bb4, William Lok, 16 October 1408: 'Hoc videlicet quod predicti executores mei inveniant dictum Thomam filium meum ad scolas et in omnibus aliis suo statu competenter et decenter.'

44 NRO, KL/C 12/5, Giles Grym (1361).

45 RRI, fo. 75, p. 146, John Burghard (1339).

to Joan, his servant, 'tabardum meam furratum'.[46] Thomas Rightwys bequeathed to his servant Richard in 1365 one 'curta gunna cum vulpeo', and to his chaplain Geoffrey a 'longa gunna furrure'.[47] Also, arms and pieces of armour, which were expensive objects and associated with burgess status, were bequeathed to sons or executors.[48]

Jewels and objects made of precious metal and other precious materials were mainly bequeathed to wives, daughters and sons. As we noted previously, John Lambert (1312) gave his diamond to his daughter Matilda.[49] To his wife in 1322 Robert Lambert bequeathed the jewels contained in his safe.[50] Thomas de Sedgeford left to his wife in 1326 some silver cups and silver spoons.[51] Cups and spoons were often bequeathed to wives and sons. Perhaps the most numerous bequest of precious objects were those mounted maplewood cups ('ciphum de murno') or 'masers' with metal stands, or plain silver and gilded cups. They were often closed by a lid, 'pecia argenti cum cooperculo'.[52] The most remarkable object of this kind was bequeathed in 1350 by Peter de Melchebourne to his wife: 'Unum ovum gryphonis meam optimum cum cooperculo argenti ligato et pede argenti deaurati et in pleribus locis inamelatis'.[53]

Women will-makers bequeathed their precious objects and jewels to their daughters or their close kin. Alice de Aldeby (1319) bequeathed to her sister a 'roba de murra cum furruris'.[54] The will of Joan de Thornegge, a widow, written on 23 February 1340, is particularly full of details about her bequests of precious objects. She bequeathed to her daughter Agnes two rings, one with a sapphire and the other with a 'peridot', and two belts, one of pearls and the other of silk. To her sister she gave 'unum magnum par bedes argenti cum firmaculo et anulo auri eisdem annexis', and to her niece a belt of green silk decorated with images of animals. She did not forget her son-in-law, John of Massingham, to whom she bequeathed 'I firmaculum de auro, I par bedes de cural, VI cruces argenti deauratas', or her cousin the chaplain Master

---

46 Ibid., fo. 42, p. 80, John Lambert (1312): 'Lego Alexandro filio meo, meam supertunicam et tabardum et tunicam de russeto, Benedicto le Fitheler meam tunicam stragulatam, Johanni Leverich lego robam meam et tabardum de raye et meam robam perticem, Johanne servienti mee lego XL d., tabardum meam furratum.'

47 Ibid., fo. 114 d., pp. 253–4, Thomas Tyghtwys junior (1365).

48 Ibid., fo. 43, p. 81, Robert Lambert (1322); ibid., fo. 64, p. 118, Thomas de Sedgeford senior (1326); ibid., fo. 77, p. 149, Robert de Gousele (1341); NRO KL/C 12/1, John de Grantham (1384).

49 RRI, fo. 42, p. 79, John Lambert (1312).

50 Ibid., fo. 43, p. 81, Robert Lambert (1322).

51 Ibid., fo. 64, p. 118, Thomas de Sedgeford (1326).

52 NRO, KL/C 12/8. John Wace (1399).

53 Ibid., Bradfer Lawrence Coll. v y (m), Peter de Melchebourne (1350).

54 RRI, fo. 23, p. 42, Alice de Aldeby (1319).

Thomas Beek, to whom she gave a chalice, a prayer book and everything he needed to set up his altar to say mass in a dignified way.[55]

The wish to be interred close to their relatives, parents, wives or children was another way for some testators to express the strength of their feelings and family ties. John of Cranewych in 1338, and William Lok in 1408, wished to be buried next to the tombs of their fathers, the former in the choir of the Church of the Friar Preachers of Lynn, the latter in Saint Margaret's Church.[56] Nicholas Page in 1340, and John de Lynn in 1371, wished to be buried next to their wives.[57] Widows like Joan de Thornegge in 1340, and Margaret de Frenge in 1382, wanted their bodies to rest next to their husbands' tombs in Saint Margaret's.[58] To rest next to his sons ('juxta filios meos') in the Friar Preachers' Church of Lynn was the last wish of Philip Wyth in 1405.[59] Was it friendship or social vanity which inspired Adam Clerk in 1390, when he asked to be buried in the choir of Saint Margaret's 'juxta tumulum Roberti Braunche'?[60]

Conclusion

Peter Laslett has taught us to look at family forms in England and Northern Europe as enduring structures. Some of their characteristics, conventionally presented as the results of modernization or industrialization, existed already, it seems, in certain 'social groups' in the medieval period: the nuclear family; late and low incidence of marriage, especially for women; and a small age gap between husband and wife, indicative perhaps of a companionate relationship.[61]

The study of the wills of Lynn's burgesses of the fourteenth century brings vivid confirmation to some aspects of these hypotheses. Wills as a source are most useful in identifying certain salient familial relationships, and in particular those given highest priority within the larger kin group. The analysis of the distribution of bequests verified the existence of a nuclear family firmly based on the transmission of

55 Ibid., fo. 79, pp. 159–61, Joan de Thornegge.

56 Ibid., fo. 95–7 (1338); NRO, KL/Bb4 (1408). Among the 61 wills complete enough to mention burial place (church or cemetery), eight indicated the tomb next to which they wished to be buried.

57 RRI, fo. 81, p. 164, Nicholas Page (1340); NRO, KL/C 12/6, Ae 37, John de Lynn (1371).

58 RRI, fo. 79, p. 159, Joan de Thornegge (1340); NRO, KL/C 12/1, 2 Margareta de Frenge (1352).

59 CLRO, Cust. 15, 'Liber Lynne', to xxi v, Philip Wyth (1405).

60 NRO, KL/C 12/1, Adam Clerk (1390). Robert Braunche was mayor of Lynn in 1350 and 1360.

61 Cf. P. Laslett, 'Characteristics of the Western family over time', *Journal of Family History* (1977), pp. 89–115, and R.M. Smith, 'Hypothèses sur la nuptialité en Angleterre aux XIIIe–XIVe siècles', *Annales, économies, sociétés, civilisation* (1983), pp. 107–36.

paternal and maternal property, often acquired during the lifetime of the will-maker. The devolutionary practice of Lynn's burgesses emphasized that family relationships, beyond the nuclear circle, concerned mainly the sibling group of the will-makers, their brothers and sisters, with their children, nephews and nieces. Relations with a larger kin group were not numerous – on average six relatives or friends per will. Pious bequests seldom left evidence of links with an extended and anonymous kin group in the original village or small town from which the will-makers had emigrated to Lynn. The coresidential group around the nuclear family included apparently unrelated servants and apprentices who were given numerous bequests.

At the level of the ties within the nuclear family itself, the evidence in these late medieval wills could be interpreted as showing a model of marriage of the 'companionate' type, where the conjugal bond was of central importance. Perhaps the notion of a common outlook linking both spouses could be deduced from the very fact that woman will-makers practised the same devolutionary 'sexism' of the male will-makers in favouring their sons with a larger share of bequests of immovable property. In addition, male will-makers paid great attention to the material security of their surviving wives, whose extensive rights were guaranteed with great care.

Some features of the close relationship between parents and children were underlined by the numerous bequests of objects, and especially of precious objects. Closeness was also indicated by the paternal recommendation about obedience due by sons to their mothers or by the control of mothers over their daughter's marriage. In spite of the larger portion of immovables bequeathed to sons, the very extensive share held in use of the patrimony and the authority invested in widows by their husbands' wills defined a family type far removed from the patriarchal model.

3

Marriage Processes in the English Past: Some Continuities

R. M. Smith

Introduction

It would be hard to deny that, after almost two decades of committed research into the demographic and social-structural history of early modern England, marriage has emerged as the most – indeed the principal – institutional determinant of both aggregate demographic trends and the tempo of household formation.[1] It is perhaps ironic that the precision given in much of this recent research to the measurement of the age and incidence of marriage and their combined impact upon levels of total fertility should not have been matched by the establishment of a clearer understanding of the phenomenon itself.[2] In the discussion which follows an attempt will be made to relate certain of the approaches to marriage that have developed on the one hand among demographic historians and on the other legal historians, considering, in particular, analytical difficulties that arise from the use of too narrowly specified a time frame and introspective rather than comparative geographical perspectives. In an era when increasing specialization within the sub-disciplines of history proceeds apace, resulting doubtlessly in more sophisticated and incisive comprehension of the complex phenomena of the past, there is none the less an ever present danger that compartmentalization can create barriers that promote rather than thwart the emergence of fundamental misunderstandings.

1 E.A. Wrigley and R.S. Schofield, *The population history of England 1540–1871: a reconstruction* (London, 1981). R.M. Smith, 'Fertility, economy and household formation in England over three centuries', *Population and Development Review* 7 (1981), pp. 595–622.
2 Some valuable suggestions concerning research priorities in this area are to be found in E.A. Wrigley, 'The growth of population in eighteenth century England: a conundrum resolved', *Past and Present* 98 (1983), pp. 135–6, 148–9. For the value of a comparative approach to these issues see the endorsement of R.S. Schofield and E.A. Wrigley in their 'Introduction' to *Journal of Interdisciplinary History* 15 (1985), p. 568 where they refer to 'important differences in marriage characteristics among different parts of western Europe, not simply in the timing and incidence of marriage, but in other aspects of marriage as a social and demographic phenomenon'.

Demographers in their analysis of nuptiality ideally prefer to treat marriage as if it were a discrete, readily identifiable *event* and easily allocated to a precise moment. By so doing, they confidently expect to be able to depict the marital characteristics of whole societies in terms of their average ages at marriage and their proportions never marrying; in other words they assume that it is feasible statistically to compare societies in terms of the *timing* and *prevalence* of marriages as *events*.[3] Such is their concern because marriage is conventionally regarded as legitimating cohabitation and regular sexual intercourse between two adults (or more in polygamous societies) and to sanction a context for socially approved reproduction, where the offspring enjoy full rights and privileges in relation to their parents and the larger society.[4] But exposure to intercourse is a continuous rather than discrete variable, and societies vary greatly in the extent to which it is possible to identify a 'gradient' of situations ranging from celibacy (in which there may be considerable promiscuity), through free union and consensual union, to customary, religious and civil marriage.[5] In practice, something approaching the following categorization has become commonplace.

We may firstly identify unions involving some element of duration and stability, social recognition, and cohabitation (or at least more or less continual exposure to intercourse). Such a category could be differentiated still further as follows: on the one hand, legal marriages constituting unions formed as the result of a ceremony having full legal effect in civil law (in some societies this may include 'customary marriages', based on traditional ceremonies, as well as marriages based on

3 The classic paper concerned with large-scale comparisons of this kind and of enormous influence among both historians and demographers is by J. Hajnal, 'European marriage patterns in perspective', in D.V. Glass and D.E.C. Eversley (eds), *Population and history* (London, 1965), pp. 101–43. See too, the essays in L.T. Rusicka (ed.), *Nuptiality and fertility* (Liege, 1981). An important article, exemplary for its concern with the impact of marriage timing and prevalence on fertility and intrinsic growth rates, is R. Lesthaeghe, 'Nuptiality and population growth', *Population Studies* 25 (1971), pp. 415–32. It has influenced, for example, studies that do attempt to take into account behaviour other than that within a strictly defined marital context upon total fertility; see D. Weir, 'Rather never than late: celibacy and age at marriage in English cohort fertility', *Journal of Family History* 9 (1984), pp. 340–54 and R.S. Schofield, 'English marriage patterns revisited', *Journal of Family History* 10 (1985), pp. 2–20.

4 L. Mair, *Marriage* (London, 1977), pp. 7–17. J. Goody has been notable in drawing attention to the relatively restricted distribution of monogamous societies, concentrated in fact in the advanced agricultural societies of Europe and Asia where the institution of dowry was important as a form of ante-mortem inheritance by women. Although in theory in such societies additional wives would bring additional dowries, the management of several conjugal funds is thought difficult; see J. Goody, 'Inheritance, property and marriage in Africa and Eurasia', *Sociology* 3 (1969), pp. 55–76 and his *Production and reproduction: a comparative study of the domestic domain* (Cambridge, 1976).

5 For a particularly useful discussion with relevance for many other contexts see E. van de Walle, 'Marriage in African censuses and inquiries', in W. Brass et al. (eds), *The demography of tropical Africa* (Princeton, NJ, 1968).

civil or religious ceremonies); on the other, consensual (or *de facto*) unions that would be socially recognized and stable but with little or no legal standing.

In the second category, we may encounter casual unions of various types, characterized by the absence of continuous cohabitation, often temporary or unstable. 'Free unions', 'visiting unions' and 'keeper unions' are terms frequently encountered to describe such relationships.[6]

Peter Laslett, as a historical commentator upon these issues, has perhaps been the most outspoken in suggesting that we jettison our preoccupation with marriage as an event *per se* and focus instead upon what he has termed the 'procreative career' which 'can begin before marriage, persist between marriages and continue beyond the death of the last spouse'.[7] Although marriage is still characterized in these remarks as an event, Laslett is helpfully proposing that by distinguishing between the onset of procreative union and first marriage it is no longer necessary to regard nuptiality as a strictly demographic phenomenon at all. It is understandable that Laslett should have adopted this position given his familiarity with the highly distinctive 'inverse' interrelationship in early modern England between illegitimacy and pre-nuptial pregnancy on the one hand, and marriage age and the proportions never marrying on the other – the latter based, it should however be stressed, on measuring the ecclesiastical celebration of events.[8] Indeed, on the basis of research published over the last five years it could be claimed that, in England from at least the middle of the sixteenth century to the early nineteenth century, whatever sanctions operated to delay or inhibit the ecclesiastical celebration of marriage were also effective in reducing fertility outside of, or prior to, the solemnized marriage event, and conversely an earlier age and greater incidence of ecclesiastical celebration and registration of marriage was accompanied by a relaxation of constraints upon pre-marital sexual relations and illegitimate fertility.[9] What is more, these dynamic relationships were apparently cyclical rather than linear in form, showing

6 T.W. Birch, 'The impact of forms of families and sexual unions and dissolution of unions on fertility', in R.A. Bulatao, R.D. Lee, P.E. Hollerbach and J. Bongaarts (eds), *Determinants of fertility in developing countries* (London, 1983), pp. 532–61.

7 'Illegitimate fertility and the matrimonial market', in J. Dupâquier et al. (eds), *Marriage and remarriage in populations of the past* (London, 1981), p. 461.

8 P. Laslett, 'Introduction: comparing illegitimacy over time and between cultures', in P. Laslett, K. Oosterveen and R.M. Smith (eds), *Bastardy and its comparative history* (London, 1980), especially pp. 19–21. For this inverse relationship in what has been termed the 'long eighteenth century' see E.A. Wrigley, 'Marriage, fertility and population growth in eighteenth century England', in R.B. Outhwaite (ed.), *Marriage and society: studies in the social history of marriage* (London, 1981), especially pp. 155–67.

9 For evidence bearing upon the tenacity of this relationship and its persistence into the early twentieth century see N.R. Crafts, 'Illegitimacy in England and Wales in 1911', *Population Studies* 36 (1982), pp. 327–31.

levels or intensities, but not trends, that varied (yet persisted) geo-graphically through time.[10] Certainly, the evidence suggests that the history of English marriage should not concern itself solely with matters to do with changes in the age and incidence of 'legally' approved nuptials but should also incorporate the study of unions that never or only belatedly found such a formal seal of approval.

We have noted that in the English case we cannot recognize any obviously progressive, unilineal tendencies for one type of union to become the 'norm' during the period when our data derive very largely from recordings of events by parochial incumbents. None the less, as in the English case, at a societal level it is frequently difficult to observe a monotonic trend to these patterns. It is in fact commonly encountered in the demographic and sociological literature relating to a wide variety of contexts, both in the past and in the present, that from the perspec-tive of the couple the type of union which they experience is closely related to their ages or life-cycle stage.[11] The proportion in stable unions tends to rise steadily with age, as does the proportion in legal marriages among those in stable unions. The orthodox interpretation of these patterns is that consensual unions (as well as other forms of non-legal union) represent 'a transitional stage in conjugal status'.[12] Most men and women are seen as moving towards formal and stable unions during their lifetimes, rather than opting permanently or initial-ly for one particular type. Viewed in this light, marriage may be more appropriately considered as a *process* rather than a status.[13]

Demographic and sociological writings on these matters are replete, therefore, with accounts of perdurable patterns of resistance to elite ideologies by sizeable minorities or indeed notable majorities of popula-tions, with indications of peaceful and not-so-peaceful coexistence be-tween customary or unofficial and official secular or religious definitions of 'marriage'.[14] Spatial continuities and processes indicative of shifting

10 Laslett et al., *Bastardy and its comparative history*, pp. 29–41 and C. Wilson, 'Marital fertility in pre-industrial England, 1550–1849 (unpublished Ph.D. thesis, University of Cambridge, 1983), chapter 3.
11 E.H. Denton, 'Economic determinants of fertility in Jamaica', *Population Studies* 33 (1979), p. 296; van de Walle, 'Marriage in African censuses', p. 213.
12 van de Walle, 'Marriage in African censuses', p. 213.
13 H.J. Page, 'Fertility levels, patterns and trends', in J.C. Caldwell (ed.), *Population growth and socio-economic change in West Africa* (New York, 1975), p. 47.
14 See P. Viazzo, 'Illegitimacy and the European marriage pattern', chapter 4 in this book; P. Laslett, 'The bastardy-prone sub-society', in Laslett et al. *Bastardy*, pp. 217–39; B.J. O'Neill, 'Social hierarchy in a northern Portuguese hamlet 1870–1978' (unpublished Ph.D. thesis, University of London, 1982), published in Portuguese as *Proprietarios, lavradores e jornaleiras* (Lisbon, 1984), and 'Nuptiality and illegitimacy in twentieth-century northern Portugal', paper presented at International Union for the Scientific Study of Population seminar on micro-approaches to demographic research, Australian National University, Canberra, 3–7 September 1984; J.M. Phayer, 'Sub-communal bastardy and regional religion: micro- and macro-aspects of the debate on the sexual revolution', *Journal of Sex*

allegiances from unofficial to official definitions of formal marriage over the couple's life course rather than wholescale societal evolution are consistently emphasized.[15]

Inducing Conformity: the Role of the Church

However (surprisingly perhaps), European historians who have approached these matters have, with only a few notable exceptions, been much more readily disposed to downplay the possible persistence of geographical differences and to emphasize in their arguments convergence towards a ubiquitously encountered mode of behaviour.[16] None seems more inclined to this position than those historians who, especially in the last 15 years or

Research 17 (1981), pp. 204–23; G.N. Gandy, 'Illegitimacy in a handloom weaving community: fertility patterns in Culcheth, Lancashire 1781–1860' (unpublished D.Phil. thesis, Oxford University, 1978); J. Gillis, 'Conjugal settlements: resort to clandestine common law marriage in England and Wales 1650–1850', in J. Bossy (ed.), *Disputes and settlements* (Cambridge, 1983); J. Dupâquier, *La Population rurale du bassin parisien 1670–1720* (Paris, 1979), p. 367.

15 For instance, although the 'living together' form of union has increased markedly in most western European countries since the mid 1970s, it is largely a 'child-free transitional phase preceding a legal marriage' according to K.E. Kiernan, 'The structure of families today: continuity or change?', in Office of Population Censuses and Surveys Occasional Papers 3, British Society for Population Studies Conference on the Family, Exeter, 1983, p. 34; and A. Brown and K.E. Kiernan, 'Cohabitation in Great Britain: evidence from the General Household Survey', *Population Trends* 25 (1981), pp. 4–10. Cohabitation is also a 'normal' precedent of remarriage; see D. Coleman, 'The contemporary pattern of remarriage in England and Wales', International Union for the Scientific Study of Population seminar on the later phases of the family life cycle, Berlin 3–7 September 1984. Recent trends observable in Sweden may suggest that there are exceptions to these patterns where more muted tendencies to convert consensual to legal unions are clearly evident. See J.M. Hoen and B. Rennermalm, 'Cohabitation, marriage and first birth among never-married Swedish women in cohorts born 1936–1960', in *Demography* 8 (University of Stockholm, 1982). See too, L. Roussel, Le cycle de la vie familiale dans la société post-industrielle', paper given in session F13, demographic and other factors of the family life cycle, International Union for the Scientific Study of Population General Conference, Florence, 5–12 June 1985.

16 For instance, the emphasis in Hajnal's paper, 'European marriage patterns in perspective' on the 'European' character of marital behaviour (defined, it should be stressed, in terms of certain conventional demographic parameters, west of a notional line drawn from Trieste to Leningrad) has fostered among certain scholars a tendency to see that nuptiality pattern as a phenomenon that either spread in the form of a social diffusion process associated with religious and/or economic changes that are first identified in north-west Europe or emerged as a response to pressures that built up on available resources as mortality declined following the ravages of the plague-infested later Middle Ages. For example, Pierre Chaunu considers the English situation as reflected in the poll-tax returns of 1377 as occupying a midpoint in a slow 'transition' from marriage at puberty in the twelfth century to the patterns encountered in the seventeenth century when female ages at first marriage had reached 25 to 30 years. See P. Chaunu, *Histoire, science sociale. La durée, l'espace et l'homme à l'époque moderne* (Paris, 1974),pp. 321–3. A similar interpretation, but in terms of a cultural diffusion from west to east, is to be found in A. Sharlin, 'Historical demography as

so, have sought to identify those institutions that might be seen as having induced some common elements in the form of the European family. One such institution that has attracted a great deal of attention by scholars from, at times, quite different backgrounds is the Christian Church. A pervasive theme in the writings of students of canon law and its operation in ecclesiastical courts, or through the evidence in synodal rulings and manuals for the priesthood outlining forms of 'best practice', concerns the influence of the Church in the realm of ideas and moral guidance.[17] Broadly speaking, a significant corps of medievalists see the eleventh and twelfth centuries as a critical period during which a major change of emphasis is detectable, while early modernists look to the later sixteenth century as initiating major reorientations, whether they are to be discovered in the wake of the Council of Trent in Catholic Europe or as a central preoccupation of the reformed Churches of the emerging Protestant regions of the continent.[18] Furthermore, the social anthropologist Jack Goody, while accepting the significance of both of these periods of intensified activity on the part of the Church, believes that the seeds for major changes in the body of its marriage laws and doctrines had been sown even earlier.[19] In the fourth century in the matter of its marital practices he claims European society diverged from the remainder of the world very largely because of influences stemming from a new set of ideas and laws relating to marriage fostered by the early Christian Church.

Professor Michael Sheehan, one of the more active contributors to this field and one who is convinced of the significance of the late eleventh and twelfth centuries as the era of really fundamental developments, writes

If family ... is examined from the point of view of one of its procedures for recruiting new members, namely marriage, there is a special place for the role

---

history and demography', *American Behavioural Scientist* 21 (1977), pp. 258–9. Other scholars have constructed quite elaborate theories on the basis of Chaunu's remarks. See, for example, E.W. Monter, 'Historical demography and religious history in sixteenth century Geneva', *Journal of Interdisciplinary History* 9 (1979), pp. 418–24 and the prologue by J. Nadal to V. Perez Moreda, *Las crisis de mortalidad en la Espana interior siglis XVI–XIX* (Madrid, 1980), pp. 6–8, where Spain is regarded as an anachronism for showing persistent regional differences in marriage age with no tendency towards a convergence between the sixteenth and nineteenth century.

17 A seminal paper is M. Sheehan, 'Choice of marriage partner in the Middle Ages: development and mode of application of a theory of marriage', *Studies in Medieval and Renaissance History* (new series) 1 (1978), pp. 3–33.

18 See, as examples of this particular chronological emphasis, the essays of J.-L. Flandrin collected in *Le Sexe et l'occident. Évolution des attitudes et des comportements* (Paris, 1981) and S. Ozment, *When fathers ruled: family life in reformation Europe* (Cambridge, Mass., 1983), where it is argued (p. 41) that 'concubinage and sexual promiscuity were widespread in the later Middle Ages' and (p. 37) 'that, beginning in the late fourteenth century, western Europeans generally married at progressively later ages, creating by the sixteenth century what has been described as a distinctive, widespread "late marriage pattern".'

19 J. Goody, *The development of the family and marriage in Europe* (Cambridge, 1983).

of ideas. This is true not only in the sense that spouses often developed through different processes of socialization, but also because the very notion of marriage, its mode of establishment and its purpose were capable of analysis and development. Furthermore, whilst it *was* [my emphasis] characteristic of Europe to consist of many areas with different family customs and different marriage usages, matrimony came to an ever greater extent under the control of the religion that was common to Europe. In that situation a common ideology of marriage was developed. However that ideology may have been refracted in the practical order, it is important to realize that, along with the variety of customs touching the family and marriage, there was to appear a common set of ideas that concerned an essential mode of family recruitment, and that, we may theorize, was an important influence on the family itself.[20]

Those who share a view such as Sheehan's would argue that at its beginnings Christianity had no special or highly distinctive position on the family, or on marriage. Indeed they would point to the absence of any clearly codified official position on these matters through the first millenium after Christ. However, a powerful case has been made by canon law historians to suggest that some of the most profound successes of the Gregorian reform movement were the specification and subsequent promotion of a new model of binding, consensual Christian marriage.[21] Stress in these arguments is given to the fact that the 1150s sees the first canonical synthesis in the *Decretum Gratianii* and a major theological statement in Peter Lombard's *Libri IV Sententiarum*, and that, between the advent of Alexander III in 1159 and the death of Innocent III in 1216, papal judgements in marriage cases gradually reduced teaching of the schools to consistency and set off a process whereby these ideas were applied throughout the western Church.[22] Consequently Lombard's position that the marriage bond was formed by the simple exchange of consent of bride and groom whose role was thereby emphasized became firmly rooted.[23] During these same years, it is

---

20 Sheehan, 'Choice of marriage partner', p. 5.

21 Ibid., p. 7; J. Noonan, 'Power to choose', *Viator* 4 (1973), pp. 419–34; C.N.L. Brooke, *Marriage in Christian history* (Cambridge, 1978) and his 'Aspects of marriage law in the eleventh and twelfth centuries', *Proceedings of the 5th International Congress of Medieval Canon Law* (Vatican City, 1980), pp. 333–44, and 'Marriage and society in the central Middle Ages', in R.B. Outhwaite (ed.), *Marriage and society* (London, 1981), pp. 17–34; C. Vogel, 'Les rites de la célébration du mariage: leur signification dans la formation du lien durant le haut moyen âge', in *Il matrimonio nella societa altomedievale* (settimani di studio del centro italiano di studi sull' alto mediaevo xxiv, Spoleto, 1977), pp. 397–465.

22 Sheehan, 'Choice of marriage partner', pp. 8–14; G. Fransen, 'La formation du lien matrimonial au moyen âge', in *Le Lien matrimonial colloque de Cerdic* (Strasbourg, 1970), pp. 106–26; C. Duggan, 'Equity and compassion in papal marriage decretals to England', in W. van Hoecke and A. Welkenhuysen (eds), *Love and marriage in the twelfth century* (Leuven, 1981), pp. 59–87.

23 C. Donahue Jr., 'The policy of Alexander the Third's consent theory of marriage', *Proceedings of the Fourth International Congress of Medieval Canon Law* (Vatican City, 1976), pp. 251–81.

argued, demands grew for marriage to take place publicly within a religious ceremony – a development connected with the increased emphasis upon the sacramental nature of matrimony while, so the 'consensualists' suggest, protecting the rights of the couple whose subsequent freedom to act might be jeopardized when private exchanges without witnesses formed the sole basis of the union.[24]

To facilitate maximum publicity, so the evidence is believed to indicate, a system of banns – public announcements of the intention to marry made at mass in the parish some days and/or weeks before the formal marriage ceremony – was developed in northern France and England early in the thirteenth century and diffused more broadly throughout the western Church after its adoption by the Fourth Lateran Council and its promulgation in the Decretals of Gregory IX in 1234.[25] Not only were the new marriage laws diffused broadly, but the evidence left in the synodal legislation is assumed to mean that the Church was intent upon hammering home the need for consent which, if liturgies and contemporary confessor's manuals are a reasonable guide to actual practice, implies a complete Alexandrine view of marriage being advocated, demonstrated and enforced at the grass roots levels in society.[26] Furthermore, a coercive machinery in the form of episcopal and archidiaconal courts was set in train by the early thirteenth century and provided, it is believed, the means whereby clergy could foster among the peasantry a deepening sense that formal Church solemnized marriage should be the desirable norm.[27] Although these tribunals have left little in the way of evidence for their early years they show in Sheehan's reading of them that the 'revolutionary ideas touching matrimonial consent in the Decretum were known even by the young.'[28] Furthermore, if some sources are treated as reliable testimony, the only arbiter concerning impediments to this freedom of

24 Noonan, 'Power to choose', pp. 427–34; Donahue, 'The policy of Alexander the Third', pp. 271–2.

25 Sheehan, 'Choice of marriage partner', pp. 16–19, and his 'Marriage theory and practice in the conciliar legislation and diocesan statutes of medieval England', *Medieval Studies* 40 (1978), pp. 408–60, and 'Marriage and family in English conciliar and synodal legislation', in J.R. O'Donnell (ed.), *Essays in honour of Anton Charles Pegis* (Toronto, 1974).

26 Sheehan, 'Choice of marriage partner', pp. 20–32; K. Ritzer, *Le Mariage dans les églises chrétiennes du Ier au XIe siècle* (Paris, 1970); J.-B. Molin and P. Mutembe, *Le rituel du mariage en France du XIIe au XVIe siècle* (Paris, 1974).

27 J. Scammel, 'The rural chapter in England from the eleventh to the fourteenth century', *English Historical Review* 86 (1971), pp. 1–21, and 'Freedom and marriage in medieval England', *Economic History Review* 27 (1974), p. 535; A. Gransden, 'Some late thirteenth century records of an ecclesiastical court in the Archdeaconry of Sudbury', *Bulletin of the Institute of Historical Research* 32 (1959), pp. 62–9; R.M. Hill, *The labourer in the vineyard*, Borthwick Papers, 35 (York, 1968); N. Adams and C. Donahue Jr. (eds), *Select cases from the ecclesiastical courts of the province of Canterbury c.1200–1301* Selden Society, vol. 95 (London, 1978–9), pp. 57–9.

28 Sheehan, 'Choice of marriage partner', p. 18.

choice had become, so it is claimed, not the family or the seigneur but the local community through the medium of the parish priest.[29] In other words, the marriage event was increasingly supposed to be taking on a religious dimension in which the inquiry as to the suitability of a marriage, the endowment and conferment of the bride and the exchange of consent were completed *in facie ecclesiae* to be followed immediately by the mass and priestly blessing.

Such an interpretation would imply considerable truncation in the period over which the marriage was completed in so far as we might expect to observe an increasing adherence to the 'proper' formalities: that the couple should initially betroth themselves only by means of a promise to marry (i.e. spousals *per verba de futuro*) preferably in the presence of witnesses and indeed of a priest. The next step would be the threefold publication of the banns of marriage in the parish church of each of the parties on three Sundays or major feast days, to facilitate the discovery of any possible impediments, such as close kin relations or prior contracts, which might invalidate the marriage. Assuming no such impediment was discovered the couple would *ad hostium ecclesiae* take each other as man and wife by an exchange of present consent (*per verba de praesenti*) in a solemn act before the priest and assembled witnesses to be accompanied by the giving of the ring and other rituals. Finally the couple were to participate in a nuptial mass.

Any unions which involved substantial deviation from the prescribed regulations were irregular and referred to as clandestine.[30] However, very considerable problems were created by the fact that the ecclesiastical law, having set up an idealized procedure or sequence of steps to create a valid marriage and indeed proscribed unsolemnized unions or irregularly solemnized unions, did at the same time continue to regard them as constituting a valid marriage if they were made in the form of either *de praesenti* promises or *de futuro* promises followed by sexual intercourse and if, of course, no impediments could be found to invalidate them. As Martin Ingram notes in reviewing spousals litigation in English ecclesiastical courts in the three centuries from 1370, this situation was highly anomalous and was bound to lead to confusion. In fact, he suggests that the Church would have done better if it had at the outset made the due solemnization of marriage in church a necessary condition for the recognition of a valid union.[31] Thus throughout

---

29 M. Sheehan, 'Marriage theory and practice; the medieval peasant', *Medieval Studies* (forthcoming).

30 The definitive discussion is in R.H. Helmholz, *Marriage litigation in medieval England* (Cambridge, 1974), pp. 26–57; and M. Sheehan, 'The formation and stability of marriage in the fourteenth-century England: evidence of an Ely register', *Medieval Studies* 33 (1971), pp. 228–63.

31 M. Ingram, 'Spousals litigation in the English ecclesiastical courts *c.*1350–1640', in Outhwaite, *Marriage and society*, p. 40.

these centuries we can observe in the proceedings of these courts a considerable proportion of their business concerned with adjudicating the status of unsolemnized marriage contracts.

'Informality' in Marital Behaviour in Medieval England

Michael Sheehan's investigation, in particular, of the marital litigation in the register of Thomas Arundel's consistory court of Ely between 1374 and 1382 has had a profound influence upon recent studies of popular marriage practice in later medieval England.[32] Because he finds very considerable evidence that almost all the disputed contracts that came before the court were clandestine and furthermore because a little more than one-third of those cases displayed a hint of 'bigamy' (in other words were multi-party cases), we encounter frequent references in recent writing to the 'flexibility', 'fluidity', 'uncertainty' or indeed 'instability' of popular marriage. These are all terms used to treat marriage as a developing or more specifically an evolving social ideal and practice which had still to attain complete equilibrium at this date.[33] Such arguments appear to suggest an implicit pre-Alexandrine world of casual unions, often of a temporary kind in which continuous cohabitation was absent, as still detectable in the 'unreformed' behaviour of the peasant population of the fourteenth century.

Here we undertake an assessment of this literature, attempting to evaluate those arguments that have made claims for a muted or only partial adherence to 'legally' constituted unions, especially within the broad mass of the rural population in thirteenth- and fourteenth-century England. Our remarks in this portion of the essay concentrate upon three approaches which would in certain important respects appear to be interconnected.

The first such study is an investigation of illegitimacy among customary tenants on a west midlands manor which has much to say on the incidence of this phenomenon and its implications for the demography and social meaning of marriage in the late thirteenth and early fourteenth centuries.[34] In this study of the north Worcestershire manor of

32 Sheehan, 'Formation and stability of marriage'.

33 R.H. Hilton, *The English peasantry in the later Middle Ages* (Oxford, 1975), pp. 107–8 writes of 'a certain lack of rigidity in the lower-class marriage patterns', and Barbara Hanawalt notes that 'the marriage contract was fairly loose' in her *Crime and conflict in English communities, 1300–1348* (Princeton, NJ, 1979), p. 165, n. 44. It is worth mentioning that J.A. Raftis in his study of a Huntingdonshire village between 1290 and 1458, *Warboys: two hundred years in the life of an English medieval village* (Toronto, 1974), p. 256 notes that given 'the great activity recently discovered for ecclesiastical courts of this region (referring to Sheehan's work on the nearby area over which the Bishop of Ely had jurisdiction) ... it is surprising to find so few references to marital problems in the village court.'

34 Z. Razi, *Life, marriage and death in a medieval parish: economy, society and demography in Halesowen 1270–1400* (Cambridge, 1980).

Halesowen, Zvi Razi employs a particular definition in his consideration of the serf due of *leyrwite* that led R.H. Hilton, when referring to
this work and its findings, to state that 'in Halesowen from 1270–1348
the manor court rolls leave evidence of 117 leyrwite payments and
about 220 merchets, and show just how widespread and lacking in
social stigma pregnancy outside of wedlock could be.'[35] To understand
Professor Hilton's reasons for this statement it should be noted that
Razi had adopted the view that payments by serf women of leyrwite
occurred when they had become pregnant outside of marriage.[36] In this
case it is far from evident that Razi is justified in his interpretation of
leyrwite, but he, in a similar vein to Professor Hilton, is inclined to
perceive formally recognized matrimony as somewhat devalued in this
period, entered or violated without much consequence, in the popular
culture of rural society of the late thirteenth and early fourteenth
centuries.[37]

Razi notes that on some manors, specifically certain of those of
Ramsey Abbey, women paid leyrwite when discovered to have fornicated and *childwite* when they actually bore a child out of wedlock. In
Halesowen, however, only leyrwite was levied. The form of entry
appearing in the record was 'A. filia B. in misericordia pro leyrwite';
more rarely, the form was 'A. filia B. deflorata est ideo leyrwite'; very
infrequently, the entry was further embellished to read 'A. filia B.
deflorata est impregnata ideo in misericordia.' This terminological elaboration leads Razi to believe that, in all or most of the cases, leyrwite
implied an actual extramarital conception and birth.[38] Furthermore, he
argues that it is difficult to see how it could have been proved that a
woman had fornicated without the visible evidence of pregnancy. This
is certainly questionable logic, in view of comparable situations revealed by fifteenth-, sixteenth- or seventeenth-century archdeaconry
court books. For instance, in the Norwich archdeaconry during the
sixteenth century, only approximately one-third of all sexual delicts
recorded in the commissary's court records came to the knowledge of

35 R.H. Hilton, 'Freedom and villeinage in England', in R.H. Hilton (ed.), *Peasants, knights
and heretics in medieval English social history* (Cambridge, 1976), p. 191.

36 Razi, *Life, marriage and death*, pp. 64–71.

37 Ibid., p. 69, citing M. Sheehan's work as justification for such a view and suggesting
that the Church's reluctant acceptance of private or clandestine marriages and the lack of
firm proof concerning the words actually spoken by the parties made 'it quite easy for a man
to have sex with a single woman or widow under false pretence and get away with it'. Such a
view had, of course, been advanced much earlier by F.W. Maitland when he commented
that in the Middle Ages marriages or what looked like marriages were exceedingly insecure
and that 'of all people in the world lovers are the least likely to distinguish precisely between
the present and future tenses'; F. Pollock and F.W. Maitland, *The history of English law before
the time of Edward I* vol. 2 (Cambridge, 1968), pp. 368–9.

38 Razi, *Life, marriage and death*, p. 64.

the court because a woman had actually become pregnant.[39] In the village community, one might speculate that such tangible evidence would have been even less necessary to have secured a presentment.

Recent research in a variety of English thirteenth- and fourteenth-century court proceedings suggests that the evidence relating to *merchet* greatly underestimates the likely incidence of marriage. In this Halesowen is no exception, with an implied marriage rate (based on recorded merchets alone) of no more that 6 per 1000.[40] Such a rate suggests that at best only half of the marriages are recorded in the court proceedings. Such an under-recording of marriages, combined with the exaggerated impression of extramarital pregnancy obtained under Razi's assumptions, leads to a highly inflated measure of illegitimacy (as expressed in terms of the ratios of presumed extramarital pregnancies to recorded marriages). Whatever interpretation is placed upon leyrwite, unlike the payers of merchet it relates to a fairly broad spectrum of the Halesowen tenantry.[41] Presentment juries may also have been more zealous in exposing and punishing the actions of girls of lower status levels than those from which the jurors themselves came.[42] Consequently as a measure of social conformity leyrwite may

39 R.H. Houlbrooke, *Church courts and the people during the English Reformation 1520–70* (Oxford, 1979), p. 76. For rather higher numbers of pregnancies relative to 'incontinents' and adulterers that did not involve pregnancies, see K. Wrightson and D. Levine, *Poverty and piety in an English village: Terling 1525–1700* (London, 1979), pp. 125–7. However, in the presentments in an Archdeaconry of Colchester act book for the period 1600–42 relating to the Essex parish of Kelvedon, cases concerning fornication and adultery were much more frequent than bastard births and extramarital pregnancies: J.A. Sharpe, 'Crime and delinquency in an Essex parish, 1600–1640', in J.S. Cockburn (ed.), *Crime in England 1550–1800* (London, 1977), p. 109. Martin Ingram none the less, in his examination of cases of sexual incontinencies in the ecclesiastical courts of early-seventeenth-century Wiltshire, states that 'acts of sexual intercourse which did not lead to a visible state of illicit pregnancy were relatively speaking unlikely to lead to prosecution': 'Ecclesiastical justice in Wiltshire 1600–1640, with special reference to cases concerning sex and marriage' (unpublished D.Phil. thesis, University of Oxford, 1976), p. 374. In the two Wiltshire villages of Wyle (1600–40) and Keevil (1600–29) Ingram found that in 33 of the 47 cases of sexual incontinence known to have involved unmarried women, bastardy or illicit pregnancy was certainly at issue: 'Ecclesiastical justice in Wiltshire', pp. 222–3. The high proportion (70 per cent) in these communities of female incontinencies identified through a pregnancy may, however, reflect the evidently active campaigns against bastard-bearers that seem to have characterized this period in many villages, and the wider implications of these findings is at present very uncertain. It is interesting to note that Razi has subsequently agreed that 'leyrwite payment does not necessarily mean that the woman involved was pregnant and gave birth out of wedlock': 'The use of manorial court rolls in demographic analysis: a reconsideration', *Law and History Review* 3 (1984), p. 199.

40 See L.R. Poos and R.M. Smith, '"Legal windows on to historical populations"? Recent research in demography and the manor court in medieval England', *Law and History Review* 2 (1984), pp. 144–8, and '"Shades still on those windows": a reply to Zvi Razi', *Law and History Review* 3 (1985).

41 Razi, *Life, marriage and death*, p. 64. See too, Raftis, *Warboys*, pp. 255–6.

42 The evidence in E. Britton, *The community of the vill: a study in the history of the family and village life in fourteenth-century England* (Toronto, 1977), pp. 53–4 is somewhat equivocal on the matter of this bias, although almost half of the fines paid for illegitimacy and sexual

have been broadly inclusive, and thus the 'population at risk' to pay it may have been considerably larger than the segment of the tenantry which paid marriage fines or merchets.

From evidence in the manorial court rolls that survive from 1260 for the Suffolk manors of Redgrave and Rickinghall we know that a servile woman paid childwite 'quia peperit extra matermonium.'[43] Such an explicit reference to extramarital childbearing among daughters of customary tenants might therefore be expected to render a more reliable measure of actual illegitimacy than that provided by simple, unembellished reference to leyrwite such as the Halesowen courts give. Yet these fines should not be related as a simple ratio to recorded servile marriages, as if the two measures were comparable with the records of marriage and bastard births in any early modern English parish register.[44] Between 1260 and 1319, for instance, 263 merchet payments are recorded in the extant Redgrave court rolls, and these can be shown to relate disproportionately to the daughters of tenants with landed properties above average size. Childwite, perhaps like leyrwite, appears to have been paid by a wider social and economic spectrum of the servile population. For instance, only 12.6 per cent of the 263 marriages can be linked to customary families whose individual members did not also appear definitively as landholders (either through an appearance as a tenant in an extent of 1289 or as payers of heriot in the court rolls). Twenty-one (almost 30 per cent) of the 72 childwite payers recorded for the same period were for women whose families left no evidence of customary land tenure. This strongly suggests that, as merchet payers were disproportionately drawn from the upper social and economic strata of village society, so childwite payers were more likely to have come from the lower strata, although far from exclusively. It is apparent therefore that the two 'populations at risk' (the one likely to pay childwite and the other to pay merchet) were far from identical; it would appear highly questionable to match them in order to estimate simple illegitimacy levels in this particular manor, as it was also to relate leyrwite payers to merchet payers in Halesowen. The net effect is seriously to overestimate the degree both of implied sexual activity outside of wedlock and of births of bastard status.[45]

---

misconduct are shown as having been paid by women from what Professor Raftis and his pupils have defined as B- and C-type families who rarely or never held positions in the manorial or village administration.

43 Manorial court rolls of Redgrave, University of Chicago, Joseph Regenstein Library **Bacon MSS 1–15 and Rickinghall, British Library Add. 62771–63594.**

44 As, for example, could be done with the evidence presented by P. Laslett in *Family life and illicit love in earlier generations* (Cambridge, 1977), pp. 116–17. In a sample of 24 parishes the decadal ratios of recorded marriages to illegitimacies varied between 5.7 and 8.2 from 1580 to 1640. The ratio implied in the merchets and childwites in the Redgrave evidence from 1260 to 1319 is 3.4.

45 I made this unfortunate error in 'English peasant life-cycles and socio-economic networks (unpublished Ph.D. thesis, University of Cambridge, 1974), pp. 456–7. These

In questioning Razi's interpretation of leyrwite and in noting the difficulties of crude comparisons of childwites and merchets for the study of medieval illegitimacy, it is not intended to deny the existence in medieval English society, whether in that of Halesowen or elsewhere, of sexual activity outside of marriage. Rather it is meant to consider to what extent such activities could have coexisted with marriage or cohabitational patterns that were inherently stable although based on behaviour involving, in the first instance, the bride and the groom acting not necessarily with specific reference to a formal, community- or Church-monitored marriage ceremony.[46] Of course, every student of medieval English manor courts or ecclesiastical court act books has found his equivalent of Ladurie's (or more precisely Fournier's) cele- brated Pierre Clergue of Montaillou (if not always as picturesque).[47] For instance, we can mention the case of William Parson, reeve of the Bishop of Ely's manor of Little Downham, who had abused his pri- vileges by wintering his livestock on the lord's forage, having used the lord's oxen and horses for carting timber, sedges and turves, and peas and wheat; had misused his allowances, by seeking more in sheaves to reimburse himself for travelling expenses, for using the lord's labourers for his own purposes and for absconding with fines and amercements from the manorial court; and had colluded with the wife of Robert Morris in allowing her to carry hay and forage away from the manor in return for her sexual services.[48]

---

results were cited with approval by Razi, *Life, marriage and death*, p. 70, as evidence of high levels of illegitimacy in communities other than Halesowen. An even higher level of implied 'bastardy' using Razi's criteria would have applied on the Abbot of Crowland's manor of Cottenham between 1303 and 1379, where only 83 marriage fines were recorded and 40 leyrwites were registered; see J. Ravensdale, 'Population changes and the transfer of customary land on a Cambridgeshire manor in the fourteenth century', in R.M. Smith (ed.), *Land, kinship and life-cycle* (Cambridge, 1984), pp. 220–2, table 4.3.

46 For a very sensitive consideration of these issues in early-seventeenth-century Wiltshire and raising matters of far wider relevance, see Ingram, 'Ecclesiastical justice in Wiltshire', pp. 229–37. It is interesting to note the implied association between pre-marital sexual relations and eventual marriage in a statement of services owed by the holders of half yardlands in the Bishop of Ely's Cambridgeshire manor of Horningsea in 1277, British Museum Cotton MS Claudius C.XI, f.117v; 'Item si filia istius fornicata fuerit cum aliquo et inde sit accitata tunc dabit triginta et duos denarios pro leyrwite. Et si idem cum quo ipsa prius fornicata fuerit eam postea desponsaverit tunc quietus erit de gersuma'. English medievalists would do well to familiarize themselves with Beryl Rawson's article 'Roman concubinage and other *de facto* marriages', *Transactions of the American Philological Association* 104 (1974), pp. 279–310, in which she exposes the value-laden prejudices of certain classical historians who misguidedly have quite evidently assumed the informal and *de facto* unions were necessarily unstable.

47 E. Le Roy Ladurie, *Montaillou, village occitan de 1294 à 1324* (Paris, 1975), chapter ix.

48 M.C. Coleman, *Downham-in-the-Isle: a study of an ecclesiastical manor in the thirteenth and fourteenth centuries* (Woodbridge, 1984), pp. 89–90. Page relates the story of Simon Warlock, a chief pledge on the Abbot of Crowland's manor of Cottenham who, in spite of fines from the Church court and a fine of £5 from the manorial court, an enormous total, concerning his

Yet it is doubtful if the vast bulk of citations for fornication, whether in the manorial or ecclesiastical courts, were of this sensational character. Indeed, a good many of the citations for fornication in these courts must fall into that twilight area between supposed, disputed or misunderstood trothplight (an essentially secular matter in so far as it, in theory, concerned just bride and groom, and often although not invariably their friends and kin) and formal solemnization at church, which of course would have been, in the eyes of canon law, the desired culmination of the very act of marriage.

We can perhaps understand this better if we proceed to a second approach to marriage that has concerned itself with concepts of 'legitimacy' under customary law. When we encounter references to marriage in the matter of bastardy cases in the customary law courts of English manors we are obliged to ask whether they are to trothplight or to an act performed publicly *in facie ecclesiae*. In doing this we seem invariably to discover that in the eyes of the hallmote, trothplight was the act that 'established' the marriage. Our information on this comes primarily from inheritance cases in which the bastard status of a claimant is a principal plank in the argument of the plaintiff barring the defendant's entry or seeking his or her dispossession. In the court book of Park, a manor of St Albans, Hertfordshire, in 1271 we can observe a dispute between two brothers on the matter of whether one or the other was the nearest heir to the deceased. The inquest said that X was the nearer than Y since X was the first born and 'pater suus matrem suam affideverat antequam idem Willelmus genitus fuit'.[49] Likewise, in Wakefield in 1285 two brothers came and sought admittance to their father's land after his death, each claiming to be the right heir. A, the younger, said that B, the elder, ought not to be heir for he was born before the parent's marriage was solemnized at the church door. B answered that it was the custom on the lord's land in these parts for the eldest brother born after trothplight to be heir. B won his case.[50]

Some idea of the gap in terms of both meaning and time between trothplight and solemnization is suggested by two interesting cases from the manorial courts of Drayton and Cottenham in 1346.[51] These two

---

alleged adultery with his niece, refused to eject her from his house: F.M. Page, *The estates of Crowland Abbey: a study in manorial organisation* (Cambridge, 1934), p. 59 and pp. 373–4.

49 British Museum Add. MS 40625 fo. 17: 'Simon filius Willelmi atte Leye dat domino xijd ad habendum inquisitionem si ipse sit propinquior heres quam Willelmus (frater) suis. Et idem Willelmus dat xviijd pro eadem. Et inquisitio dicit quod idem Willelmus propinquior heres est quam dictus Simon frater eius quia idem Willelmus primogenitus fuit et pater suus matrem suam affideverat antequam idem Willelmus genitus fuit, ideo etc. Et idem Willelmus venit et gersumavit terram predicti Willelmi patris sui faciendo inde etc.'.

50 W.P. Baildon and J. Lister (eds), *Court rolls of the manor of Wakefield* I, Yorkshire Archaeological Society Record Series, p. 212.

51 University of Cambridge Queens' College 3 Dd. 1 m. 5r. It was claimed in the case of Johanna Sped that she 'nata fuit ante matrimonium solempnizationem per unum annum ante'.

communities, in which serfs of the Abbot of Crowland held land, were close to the town of Cambridge. In 1346 Johanna, daughter of Robert Sped of Drayton, was presented by a jury for leyrwite because she had fornicated. Her mother came to court claiming her daughter to possess free status contingent upon a bastardy deriving from her supposed procreation before matrimony was solemnized. Furthermore, Johanna's mother claimed she had lived with her 'husband' Robert for a year in this state. Annicia, wife of Henry Gilbert of Cottenham, pleaded a similar case for her daughter and that she had cohabited with her husband for three years after her daughter's birth before the marriage was solemnized. These two cases were not won by the contestants as the daughters were considered by the inquisition jury to be the legitimate offspring under customary law. As such they did not possess 'bastard' status and therefore were not deemed free, thereby remaining eligible leyrwite payers.[52]

In a different approach to 'legitimacy', concerned for the most part with the severe restraints imposed on villeins in the matter of their tenure of land, given what she believes to be the essentially arbitrary nature of customary law under seigneurial influences in customary tribunals, Eleanor Searle has suggested that bastardy rarely appears to have mattered. Indeed she seems to doubt whether rural society, certainly at the levels of the customary tenantry, had any clear sense of 'legitimacy'.[53] She writes: 'Juries recognized the rights of sons, but legitimacy is mentioned only in exceedingly rare instances.'[54] Her argument places great emphasis on what she terms 'the ability of a villein father to make an heir'. In developing her views concerning the great rarity of disputed claims to inheritance based on illegitimacy of a claimant she cites what she terms a 'virtually unique case' from among the confiscated charters of Peterborough Abbey villeins. In this the lord allows a displacement of the bastard occupant on the grounds that the bastard nephew's 'legitimate' aunt and her husband were prepared to quitclaim the land to the lord and receive it back at an increased rent. In fact it is clear that the land in this case, like the bulk of the free land in the *Carte Nativorum*, had been regranted to villein 'holders' for increased rents (the charters for which had been confiscated).[55] The suggestion of a conspiratorial negotiation

52 In the courts of the Cambridge manors of Crowland Abbey it is expressly laid down in two cases that bastards were not to pay merchet (Queens' College 3 Ad 35, m. 17d.), though Alice Warlock 'que nata fuit extra matrimonium' was made to pay a merchet of 5s.

53 E. Searle, 'Seigneurial control of women's marriage: the antecedents and function of merchet in England', *Past and Present* 82 (1979), p. 36.

54 Ibid., p. 36.

55 This interpretation seems to have been offered with a disregard for Edmund King's emphasis that the *Carte Nativorum* exists principally because the Abbey insisted that villein transactions in free land be enrolled and that on entry into such land the tenant paid a fine in addition to an 'increment of rent' or 'new rent'. It was because this land was outside the customary framework that the rent could be increased: *Peterborough Abbey, 1086–1310; a study in the land market* (Cambridge, 1973), p. 100.

between lord and another relative to displace a suggested or fabricated 'bastard' cannot be proven. The other instance employed to support the idea that common law bastardy had no meaning in the customary courts is, contrary to Searle's interpretation, perfectly compatible with the common law principle that a bastard had the same legal rights as anyone else with the single exception that he or she could not be heir to his or her parents or have any collateral heir.[56] The case under consideration comes from the Essex manor of Great Waltham at the turn of the third decade of the fourteenth century and involved a bastard girl who, contrary to common law (Professor Searle erroneously suggests), had been endowed with land by her father. In fact that land was held only for her lifetime, which was perfectly in order, and escheated at her death (as would have occurred under common law) because of her bastard status.[57]

As we have already seen in our discussion of trothplight from manors in Yorkshire, Hertfordshire and Cambridgeshire, Professor Searle's claim as to the 'exceedingly rare' occurrences of litigation disputing the rights of bastards to hold villein land is far from proven. A cursory search through manor court rolls will find such cases in relative abundance. For example, Hugh Fuller of Rickinghall in 1284 on the death of his brother William disputed the right of his niece Matilda to inherit on the grounds that she was conceived and born outside of wedlock (the phrase 'antequam matrimonium contractum erat inter eos' is ambiguous); winning his case, Hugh entered into his brother's land as lawful heir.[58] In the neighbouring manor of Redgrave we discover in 1300 an inquiry to establish who was the lawful heir to the holding of Thomas Terry who died that year. There

---

56 J.H. Baker, *An introduction to English legal history* 2nd edn (London, 1979), p. 400.

57 See Public Records Office DL30/63/790 and DL30/63/792. These are the two documentary citations given by Searle. The person involved was Juliana Aynolf, wife of John Aynolf who first appears when it was ordered in the court of 15 April 1327 that the land should escheat to the lord on account of her bastardy. A trial jury was summoned to consider this matter and reported on 5 January 1331. The evidence is not forthcoming on whether the land was a gift of her father, although this is irrelevant in so far as she was, as a bastard, able to hold land in her lifetime but (as the jury informed the court) not able to have heirs, so the land reverted to the lord at her death.

58 British Library Add. Ch. 63400: 'Hugo le Fuller venit in plena curia et petit totum tenementum in quo Willelmo le Fuller frater eius obiit seysitus quia heredes predicti Willelmi obierunt unde dictus Hugo dicit se esse propinquior heres de tenemento fratris sui et quod habet maius jus in eodem tenemento sicut petit quam Matilda filia predicti Willelmi quia non matrimonialiter procreata fuit eo quod procreata fuit prius quam predictus Willelmus duxit Tessamam matrem predicte Matilda in uxorem et quod ita est petit ut inquiratur. Et dicta Matilda defendit jus eiusdem Hugonis et dicit se esse matrimonialiter procreata et quod habet maius jus in eodem tenemento sicut propinquior heres petit sibi inquisitionem xiiij legalium hominum. Jurati dicunt per sacramentum suum quod predicta Matilda procreata fuit antequam nullum matrimonium contractum erat inter eos et ideo consideratum est quod dictus Hugo habet majus jus eiusdem tenementi quam dicta Matilda. Et dictus Hugo dat domino iiij solidos pro seysina habenda in eodem tenemento ten' sibi et heredibus suis faciendo inde per annum servicia etc. Plegii Johannes Yde et Martinus de Sugenhal.'

were two claimants; one was Philip, a son of Ingred, whose marriage to
Thomas Terry had been annulled after it was discovered that he had
pre-contracted with another named Cristina, whose son subsequently
entered the holding as legitimate heir. Here we have a definition of a
legitimate marriage which is in all respects consistent with the ecclesiastical rules, but again it emphasizes the trothplight or clandestine marriage
rather than its public celebration at church door.[59]

The last case provides a convenient means of considering certain areas
of potential conflict conventionally featuring in discussions of the
approaches of medieval secular and ecclesiastical authorities to bastardy
litigation. The common law took a pragmatic view of these matters and
refused to admit that a bastard could be legitimized by subsequent
marriage of his or her parents (which could be achieved under ecclesiastical law), and justified such a stance by arguing that any alternative
position would have had the effect of rendering inheritance precarious.
Furthermore, since inheritance was a matter of temporal law the judges of
the King's court felt their jurisdiction should be the sole one in the matter
of free land. The judges in 1236 under the Statute of Merton ensured that
when cases concerning illegitimacy required decisions from the bishops
the Church court should be asked only to state whether the birth had
occurred before or after the marriage. This was unacceptable to the
bishops. Subsequently small numbers of bastardy cases were referred to
the episcopal courts.[60] However, Richard Helmholz in a very comprehensive assessment of the apparent difference between Church and State has
shown that there were in practice quite large areas of agreement and
compromise between the two legal codes, although even before Merton
cases of alleged bastardy were dealt with by common law tribunals with
no request for a decision from the bishop's court.[61]

---

59 University of Chicago Bacon MS 9, court of 30 December 1300. (For other examples of
bastards barred from inheritance, see University of Chicago Bacon MS 10, court held on 6
February 1303 at Redgrave; British Library Add. Ch. 63407, a court held 4 November 1294
at Rickinghall; British Library Add. Ch. 63435, court held Saturday 30 October 1322.)
'Presentatum est per inquisitionem quod Edmundus filius Cristine le Redelestere obiit post
ultimam curiam et tenuit de domino in villenagio j pichtellum continentem medietatem j
rode terre per servicia et opera. Et dicunt quod dictus Edmundus bastardus fuit et obiit sine
herede de se. Ideo preceptum est seisire dictum tenementum in manus domini et respondere
de exitu.' More explicitly, in court held November 1331 at Rickinghall, British Library Add.
Ch. 63444: 'Item quod Radulphus Lappyng nativus domini diem clausit extremum et tenuit
de domino unum cotagium et unam acram terre per servicia etc. Et dicunt quod dicta terra
est escaeta domini eo quod dictus Radulphus fuit bastardus et obiit sine herede de se.' See
also Norfolk Record Office ING 8, court held 23 June 1287 at Gressenhall; Norfolk Record
Office ING 8, court held 8 July 1288 at Gressenhall. It should be noted that in certain
situations local custom recognized the right of the bastard to inherit. See J. Beckerman,
'Customary law in manorial courts in the thirteenth and fourteenth centuries' (unpublished
Ph.D. thesis, University of London, 1976), pp. 156–7.

60 See F.W. Maitland's introduction to *Bracton's Note Book* (London, 1887), pp. 14–17 and
his *Roman canon law in the Church of England* (London, 1898), p. 52 *et seq.*

61 R.H. Helmholz, 'Bastardy litigation in medieval England', *American Journal of Legal
History* 13 (1969), pp. 367–77.

It would appear that, on the question of legitimacy of heirs of parents whose marriages had not been formally solemnized *in facie ecclesiae*, both legal codes displayed a considerable degree of overlap. Bracton indicates that a marriage which was not contracted *in facie ecclesiae* would be good enough so far as regards the legitimacy of the children: 'et ita poterit esse matrimonium legitimum, quoad hereditatis successionem ubicumque contractum fuerit.'[62] Maitland comments on the case of William de Cardunville, tenant-in-chief of the crown, who died in 1254 when an inquisition *post mortem* was taken as to the rightful heir.[63] It was reported that William had married at the church door one Alice and they had lived together for 16 years, and that one Richard, aged four, was the surviving son and heir; but that after these 16 years one Joan came and claimed to be William's lawful wife as he had known her carnally subsequent to an affidation taking place. The case apparently went to Church court where the marriage to Alice was dissolved. William lived with Joan for a further year before his death. The jurors were unable to decide on the inheritance claims of the two sons and ruled that William's brother was to be heir. However, royal officials in Chancery ordered that Joan's son should have seisin, preferring therefore the unsolemnized to the solemnized marriage. Of course, the position adopted by the royal officials would have applied equally in the cases from the customary tribunals of Park, Wakefield and Rickinghall to which we have referred.

Canon law would not necessarily have regarded the offspring of William's marriage to Alice as illegitimate in so far as there were differences between it and common law on the legitimacy of children of divorced parents. The Church evolved a number of standards for judging the matters, the most important of which involved investigation of the formal correctness of the marriage and the good faith of the parents.[64] If they were innocent of wrongdoing and knowledge of any impediment which rendered their union unlawful, or at least if one of them was, their children were deemed legitimate; otherwise the children were not.[65] Early common law positions on this issue appear somewhat confusing. Bracton wrote that 'if a woman in good faith marries a man who is already married, believing him to be unmarried, and has children by him, such children are to be adjudged legitimate and capable of inheriting.'[66] Glanvill takes a harder-headed approach when he states that 'if the wife is separated from the husband on the ground that he previously contracted marriage with some other woman by words of the present tense, then her children cannot be legitimate, nor can they succeed to their father, nor to

---

62 *Bracton de legibus et consuetudines Angliae*, ed. G.E. Woodbine, trans. with revisions and notes by S.E. Thorne, vol. 3 (Cambridge, Mass., 1977), p. 377, f.304.
63 Pollock and Maitland, *History of English law* vol. 2, pp. 379–80.
64 Helmholz, 'Bastardy litigation', p. 371.
65 Ibid.
66 *Bracton de legibus*, vol. 2, p. 185, f.63.

their mother, according to the law of the realm.'[67] In this we observe a principle to a very large extent common to both secular and ecclesiastical legal codes; that is, the rationale of visiting the parents' faults on their children.[68] But the common law is more ready to accept that a person had been ignorant of the extent of his kinship than that he had forgotten previously contracting a marriage, thereby imposing the penalty of bastardy on potential heirs more strictly in the latter case. This principle seems certainly relevant to the common law ruling in the case of William de Cardunville's formally celebrated marriage to Alice (1254), as well as in the customary court judgement in the case considered earlier from Redgrave (1300) concerning the bastardization of Philip, son of Ingred, whose father Thomas Terry had pre-contracted with Cristina; both common and customary law codes are apparently in unison. It should nevertheless be stressed that the termination of the original marriage (if not the judgement of the legitimacy of its offspring) between Thomas Terry and Ingred was fully compatible with canon law and may have been achieved through a *causa matrimonialis divorcii*, although we have no surviving consistory court evidence explicitly proving this to have happened.[69] Cases such as these, furthermore, provide reason for doubting Searle's belief that customary and common law treatments of bastardy diverged seriously. Both contexts had clearly defined rules as to legitimacy and neither required celebration of the marriage at the church door for its validation as far as the rights of the heirs to such unions were concerned.

Although the views of both Bracton and Glanvill, taken in conjunction with decisions in certain common law court cases of the late twelfth and early thirteenth centuries, seem to indicate an acceptance of an unsolemnized marriage as lawful in so far as the inheritance of the offspring of such unions was concerned, the matter of the wife's property rights in such unions is far less certain. Maitland stated in highly categorical terms that in defining a wife's eligibility for dower the result is curious, 'for at first sight the lay tribunal seems to be rightly requiring a religious ceremony which in the eyes of the church is unessential.'[70] He accepted without question Bracton's rule on this subject and refers to certain case-law of the time in the *Note Book* that a woman was to have no dower if she was not endowed *ad hostium ecclesiae*.[71] Historians have readily accepted that such a position under common law would, for the property-owning classes at least, have created a powerful incentive towards according the solemnization of marriage in church the status of normal practice in this matter.[72]

---

67 F. W. Maitland, 'Glanvill Revisited', *Harvard Law Review* 6 (1982), p. 11.

68 Helmholz, 'Bastardy litigation', p. 371.

69 Helmholz, *Marriage litigation*, pp. 76–7.

70 Pollock and Maitland, *History of English law*, vol. 2, p. 374.

71 Ibid., p. 375.

72 For example, Ingram, 'Spousals litigation in England', p. 53; R. Houlbrooke, *The English family 1450–1700* (London, 1984), p. 79.

Of course, underpinning this incentive was a desire for publicity and not necessarily a desire to abide by the 'religious rite' or even to secure the presence of an ordained priest, as is apparent from Bracton's remarks that the endowment can and must be made at the church door even during an interdict when the bridal mass cannot be celebrated.[73]

Others have been less predisposed to accept the categorical tone of either Bracton or Maitland on this issue. Hooper speaks in rather more practical terms of the refusal to sanction marriages that were unvouched by evidence and unknown to any bar the widow – for in 'a death-bed marriage, or a marriage in camera or other secret place, very often none but the parties themselves would be present'.[74] He suggests, in effect, that marriage must not have been so clandestine as to be unwitnessed by third parties. If it were otherwise a concubine might find it possible to step forward and claim a reasonable part of her man's goods, and bastard issue defeat the lawful heir on her bare assertion of a secret marriage. It is perhaps no coincidence that the cases in the *Note Book* cited by Maitland involving disputed dower all concern so-called 'death-bed marriages' around which suspicions would inevitably have been very great and which by their very nature may have lacked the required publicity.[75] Maitland seems to be offering a much more feasible approach to this issue in stating that

When a question about a marriage arises in a possessory action, it must be dealt with in what we might call a possessory spirit, and, as we have to get our facts from juries, it is necessary that we should lay stress on those things, and those only, which are done formally and in public. If a man and woman have gone through the ceremony at the church door, we may say that we have a *de facto* marriage. ... A religious ceremony ... is *de facto* and public; we can trust the jurors to know all about it.[76]

---

73 *Bracton de legibus*, vol. 3, p. 377, f.304.

74 W. Hooper, *The law of illegitimacy* (London, 1911), p. 36. Hooper cites in support of this view the following passage from *Clerke's trial of bastardy* (1594), p. 40: 'Clandestine marriages we call them *quae clam contrahuntur*, that is to say, that be contracted so privily that they cannot be lawfully proved by witnesses, shall that be bastarded? I say not so without exception, but I counsell thee trust it not for I assure thee (howsoever the matrimonie holdeth before God and the world) if the parties shall both of them acknowledge it incurring only a corporal penance and the clerke that shall celebrate the same but three years suspension from his office, yet if the one confess it not or that which is more renounce the marriage, and the other prove it not ... verily proved, it holdeth "Coram deo and ecclesia" – otherwise "coram deo" only.'

75 Pollock and Maitland, *History of English Law* vol. 2, p. 374; *Bracton's Note Book*, pl. 891, 1669, 1718 and 1875. See too, *Curia Regis Rolls* vol. 2, p. 63. The publicity given to the wife's dower and its obvious importance as 'proof' is well attested in a 1220 case when witnesses were brought by the widow to establish that such a transfer had taken place: *Curia Regis Rolls* vol. 9, p. 58. See too Adams and Donahue (eds), *Select cases*, p. 86 and appendix II, pp. 18–24.

76 Pollock and Maitland, *History of English Law* vol. 2, p. 380. A recent study of dower tends to accept the position of Bracton and Glanvill as to the requirement that dower be given *ad hostium ecclesiae*. However, it does at the same time present evidence from the dower disputes in the King's courts of the late twelfth and early thirteenth centuries that can be interpreted

Here we would seem to have some justification for assuming that secular custom not only supported but may also have promoted the ecclesiastical marriage in question, at least among sectors of the freeholding populace, although there were certainly other contexts in which the marriage and indeed any property endowments associated with it could have been effectively publicized.[77]

We should not, however, be reluctant to confront the issue of whether in the matter of dower and freebench trothplight was regarded as a suspect or inadequate form of marriage. In the case of the wife's claims over and above collateral heirs or children by a previous marriage, quite clearly the stakes are higher in so far as, in contrast to a decision between brothers in an illegitimacy dispute, the rights of a 'stranger' as opposed to a blood relative are involved.[78]

---

as emphasizing the need for *publicity*, especially the need for witnesses 'qui interfuit desponsacioni' or for '*probos homines* who were there when she was therein dowered'. Other types of proof could also be essential, especially it appears in suits against a father-in-law in cases of dower *ex assensu patris* where plaintiffs might, in order to buttress their claim, bring the charter and 'put themselves' of the witness to it. See J.S. Loengard, '"Of the gift of her husband"': English dower and its consequences in the year 1200', in J. Kirschner and S.F. Wemple (eds), *Women of the medieval world* (Oxford, 1985), pp. 218–20, 227–8.

77 It may be worth while considering the admittedly limited but certainly tantalizing work on the liturgies of marriage in the early and central Middle Ages which has at least partially confronted the complex question of the relative weighting to be attached to secular and ecclesiastical influences on such practices. One scholar provides an account which involves a shift among the recently Christianized peoples of northern Europe from an essentially secular marriage rite following which a priest is invited to bless the couple and bridal chamber to a ceremony that took place largely at church. See Ritzer, *Le Mariage dans les églises*. Molin and Mutembe, *Le Rituel du mariage*, argue that by or over the course of the twelfth century in parts of north-west Europe under Norman influences the *ordines* reveal a redesigned ritual involving the questions regarding the suitability of the partners, the endowment of the bride and the exchange of consent before the church door, followed by the mass and blessing in church. Sheehan stresses in his evaluation of these arguments a positive, indeed catalytic, role for the church by the fact that the ritual had been removed 'from the family circle to a public forum, the place of meeting of the local community in its religious capacity' ('Choice of marriage partner', p. 28) and notes that Glanvill in his legal treatise of 1189 could refer to the transfer of dower during the marriage ceremony at the door of the church as an established practice: *Tractatus qui Glanvilla vocatur*, pp. 58–9. It is interesting to find a rather different emphasis in another assessment of the same liturgical sources; André Burgière, referring to liturgies pertaining to Normandy, proceeds to contrast them with practices decribed for more southern and eastern parts of France. Because, he suggests, the Norman ritual is described as taking place largely outside the sanctuary, the church 'n'entend y participer que de manière formelle et limitée', and in this role the priest acts rather as a guarantor, a representative of the law: 'Le rituel du mariage en France: pratiques ecclésiastiques et pratiques populaires (XVIe–XVIIIes siècles)', *Annales, économies, sociétés, civilisations* 33 (1978), pp. 637–49. It is important to note that in none of these liturgies, when describing the practice of gift giving with all of its attendant symbolism, is reference ever made to property endowment as part of a 'valid' transaction, and as such the latter remained apart from the formal ecclesiastical 'event'. I am grateful to Professor Sheehan for confirming this point. See, for instance, M. Sheehan, 'The influence of canon law on the property rights of married women in England', *Medieval Studies* 25 (1963), pp. 109–24 (p. 114).

78 I am grateful to Lloyd Bonfield, who has forced me to recognize the potential

Yet if the common law courts indicated a theoretical preference for protecting those rights when marriages were publicly celebrated, it is not at all clear how the customary tribunals handled this matter. When Homans considered this issue in his classic work on thirteenth-century English village society he was disposed to draw upon common law evidence relating to endowment practices, specifically that presented by Bracton and used by Maitland.[79] However, he did cite one dower plea in a manorial court that referred to land received by the wife from her husband *ad hostium ecclesiae*.[80] Such references are not at all common in manorial court rolls in so far as it would appear that husbands frequently made no specific endowment, perhaps because there was a tacit acceptance of the *consuetudines manerii* taking effect at the wife's widowhood. However, the case cited by Homans from the Abbot of St Albans's manor of Barnet in Hertfordshire raises many questions as to the crucial criteria determining the status of this transfer; for in that instance the wife's claim to dower, although it had been made at the church door, was nullified by the fact that it had not at that moment, through payment of the licence fee, gained the lord's approval. In the customary sector therefore seigneurial acceptance registered with the proceedings of the manorial court may well have superseded any public display *in facie ecclesiae* in the verification of the widow's claim. Such a view is perfectly consistent with Eleanor Searle's

---

importance of this distinction. Of course it is possible to observe in this issue certain rather different, indeed contradictory emphases. On the one hand, the stress on the public celebration of the marriage *in facie ecclesiae* may be viewed as an integral element in what some would see as the strengthening and indeed promotion of female property rights against the claims of the lineage's members, the latter being individuals to whom the women are related either by blood or by marriage. See Sheehan, 'The influences of canon law', and especially Goody, *The development of the family and marriage*, pp. 43–6 and chapter 6, where such developments are seen as performing a pivotal role in his general thesis. On the other, it might be seen as a means by which the bride's agnatic kin limited and effectively policed the potential erosion of their landed resources by female ante-mortem inheritance and, in addition, ensured that offspring from such a marriage were recognized on all sides as legitimate. Georges Duby has been notable among historians of eleventh-century north-west European society in stressing this as an era in which women were brought more closely into subjection, by diminishing the proportion both of their fathers' land which it was customary to offer as dowry, and of their husbands' as marriage portion, and by transferring its management (which women had hitherto been accustomed to exercise independently) to the husbands. An insistence upon a public celebration of marital property endowment might therefore be perceived as propounding a code of behaviour which, although increasing the role of women as the vessel through which the patrimony was transmitted, effectively conspired to diminish their overall freedom. See especially G. Duby, *Medieval marriage: two models from twelfth-century France* (London, 1978), and *Le Chevalier, la femme et le prêtre. Le mariage dans la France féodale* (Paris, 1981). See too R.I. Moore, 'Family, community and cult on the eve of the Gregorian Reform', *Transactions of the Royal Historical Society* 5th series, 30 (1980), pp. 66–9. It should be stressed that these arguments, whichever is favoured, relate very largely to society's uppermost echelons in the eleventh century, and their relevance outside that relatively self-contained area remains problematic.

79 G.C. Homans, *English villagers of the thirteenth century* (Cambridge, Mass., 1941), pp. 177–8. See note 63 in this chapter, and *Bracton's Note Book* no. 669.

80 Homans, *English villagers*, pp. 179–80.

argument that dower (as well as dowry) was taxed, and that it is the taxing of this dower right that we may be observing in many of the merchet payments which appear to relate disproportionately to the marriages of daughters from the wealthier echelons of the customary tenantry.[81]

None the less, it should not be thought that endowment of dower was the only or indeed the principal means whereby the widow's property resources could be secured by the husband. For instance, a husband as donor might surrender property into the lord's hand and receive it back again as a tenancy held jointly with his wife. If the wife survived the husband, this would not involve circumvention of the rules of customary succession for widows in any sense, because on certain manors a wife might receive her husband's entire tenement in freebench anyway; however, more importantly it would perhaps give her freedom of disposition of the land in her widowhood. Sometimes remainders could be attached so that a tenant could make provisions for sons and daughters in addition to the widow.[82] Such joint tenancies seem to have grown in importance in the later fourteenth and the fifteenth centuries on some estates, although on others they appear to have been firmly in place relatively early, being detectable among those court rolls that survive in reasonable quantities from the later thirteenth century.[83]

81 Searle, 'Seigneurial control of women's marriage'. See too Poos and Smith, 'Legal windows on to historical populations', pp. 144–8. For the validation of dower when the transfer did not have seigneurial approval, see *Curia Regis Rolls*, vol. 14, p. 185. References of a more explicit kind to endowment at church door do occasionally occur, as one might expect in dower disputes in customary law tribunals; for example, British Library Add. Ch. 63417, Rickinghall court held 1 December 1305: 'Inquisitionem venit recognitur si Galfridus del Hil inuiste detinuit Agnetem que fuit uxorem Thome del Hel quartam partem j messuagio et dimidian v acras terre ... de quibus idem Thomas ipsam dotavit ad hostium ecclesiae quando ipsam disponsavit sicut eadem Agnes dicit ul quod idem Thomas pro ij annos antequam predictam Agnetem disponsavit predictam terram ei concessit et per licentiam curiae ei reddidit sibi et heredibus suis tenendum soluendum eidem Thomae ad totam vitam suam v cumbas bladi per annum.' Much more frequently reference is made to the dower with no attempt to specify the place of endowment, such as in the dower plea of Maria widow of Adam son of Peter against Adam's sons, Ralph, Peter and Adam, where the property was claimed 'ut dotem suam de dotatione predicti Ade viri sui', Rickinghall court held 22 July 1299, British Library Add. Roll 63411.

82 Homans, *English villagers*, p. 179. L.R. Poos, 'Population and resources in two fourteenth-century Essex communities: Great Waltham and High Easter 1327–1389' (unpublished Ph.D. thesis, University of Cambridge, 1983), pp. 232–3; R. Faith, 'Berkshire, fourteenth and fifteenth centuries', in P.D.A. Harvey (ed.), *The peasant land market in medieval England* (Oxford, 1984), pp. 140–2.

83 B. Harvey, *Westminster Abbey and its estates in the middle ages* (Oxford, 1977), pp. 280–3, 296 and 298; C. Dyer, *Lords and peasants in a changing society: the estates of the Bishopric of Worcester 680–1540* (Cambridge, 1980), p. 303. The registration of property transfers from husband to wife, giving the latter for the remainder of her life rights in property independent of dower, are not at all uncommon in late-thirteenth- and early-fourteenth-century manorial court proceedings. See, for example, University of Chicago Bacon MS 2, Redgrave manorial court held 20 September 1270; 'Eodem die venit Willelmus de Botulesdale et sursum reddidit in

Recent investigations of certain freehold property agreements in association with marriage also suggest a wide variety of arrangements in the matter of property transfers at marriage that frequently involved complex negotiations at the moment of affidation, sometimes many months in advance of the church ceremony, through the use of regrants via third parties. In disputes arising from such negotiations that failed or from broken agreements, it would seem that there were no set rules on whether a woman could or could not alienate land received in this way after affidation, although juries apparently regarded the promise or contract rather than the solemnization at the church door as the crucial moment to or from which these 'rights' applied.[84]

Certainly in considering our evidence relating to the middling and petty landholders among the customary tenantry we would do well to think of a set of multilateral interests in what was essentially a social event. Moreover, we should be wary of subscribing too readily to the notion of a marriage process within which the 'freedom to choose' or indeed an individualistic approach to matrimony on the part of the bride and groom, and the sacrament given by the couple to each other through the medium of the priest, are given an overbearing primacy. The social nature of the act implies that there were contexts other than at the church door when the process in its various phases, which might not even have been regularly sequential, could have been effectively publicized.[85] What we

---

plena curia quedam domum propter pontem de Botulesdale. Et postea venit Agnes uxor dicti Willelmi et dedit domino vjd pro licentia intrandi in dicto domo. Ita quod si dicta Agnes supervixerit dictum Willelmum quod dictus domus reverteat predicte Agnetis omnibus diebus vite sue et post decessum dicte Agnetis predictus domus reverteat ad heredes predicti Willelmi sine molestia alicubi.' University of Chicago Bacon MS 3, court held 16 June 1277: 'Herveus Carpenter venit et sursum reddidit j acram terre ad opus Alicie filia Roberti Jop et dicta Alicia dat domino (xijd) pro licentia intrandi et pro licentia se maritandi predicto Herveo Carpenter. Plegii Walteri Clericus et prepositus.' Cambridge University Library MS D.D.7.22, Winslow (Buckinghamshire) court held 26 October 1334: 'Johannes de Norton reddidit sursum in manu domini quinque acras terre cum pertinenciis in Greneburgh. ... Item reddidit sursum in manu domini unum curtilagium vocatur le Newewyrk. Et dominus concessit dictum tenementum cum pertinenciis predicto Johanni de Norton et Isabella uxor eius tenendum sibi et heredibus inter eos procreatis. Et si decedeant sine herede de se tunc predicta terra cum pertinenciis rectis heredibus ipsius Johannis de Norton revertantur. Et dant de fine xs. Et dictus Johannes de Norton habet licentiam se maritandi secundam vicem per finem predictam.'

84 R.C. Palmer, 'Contexts of marriage in medieval England: evidence from the King's court circa 1300', *Speculum* 59 (1984), pp. 51–6. The following case from a seigneurial court suggests that transactions that were binding and pledged by leading manorial tenants may often have preceded the formalization of a marriage by many months. University of Chicago Bacon MS 2, court held 27 April 1266: 'Johannes filius Adam de Walsham dat vjd pro licentia habendi j seldam in mercato de Botulesdale de Edwardo Kat. Et idem Edwardus debit dicto Johannis xls, in maritagio cum Elyanora filia sua in octava Sancti Edwardi regis et mart proximo futuro et si infra temporem decesserit Adam filius et heres dicti Edwardi intrat ad dictam solutionem termino predicto faciendum plegius.'

85 Marriage contracts, or more precisely transfers of property in association with a marriage, could take on a bewildering variety of forms, many involving quite complex

know – and that is unfortunately very little – suggests that customs relating to the celebrations and feasts sometimes accompanying peasant weddings, as Rosamond Faith notes, saw the involvement of certain social groups who had a customary claim to participate. Neighbours, relatives and friends are the obvious participants, but other representatives of seigneurial authority, such as the Abbot of Ramsey on his manors in the guise of the servants of his curia or the *custos ville* who, so some Kentish custumals suggest, should be invited to the wedding, appear to have represented another set of interests apart from those of the Church.[86]

---

contingency clauses bearing upon the wife's support during the marriage, in widowhood and in the event of the marriage failing to produce legitimate children as heirs, ensuring that the property would return intact to the bride's family of birth. Arrangements for the latter contingency figured very frequently in such transfers. See for example, University of Chicago Bacon MS, Redgrave court held 24 November 1273: 'Walterus le Heyward dat domino iijs pro licentia maritandi Mabiliam filiam suam et pro licentia donandi cum eadem Roberto del Forthe in maritagio totam suam terram adquisitio tam liberam quam aliam faciendo inde dicto Waltero j summam frumenti j summam et dimidiam ordei et j summam fabarum et pisarum per annum. Et si contingat quod dicta Mabilia obierit sine heredibus de se quod totam predicte terre revertantur predicto Waltero et heredibus suis faciendo inde per annum ij feodotales, servicia et consuetudines inde debita plegius Benedictus prepositus.' See, too, an agreement involving a father, his wife, his son and daughter-in-law, in which the father in return for care from the younger generation agrees not to alienate any of his land during his lifetime, half of which if the father is pre-deceased by his son will go to the daughter-in-law as dower providing she continues, when widowed, to 'serve' her father-in-law. University of Chicago, Bacon MS 6, Redgrave court held 19 January 1291: 'Walterus Sictrich venit in plena curia et concessit per licentiam domini quod Henricus filius eius et heres accepiet Cristinam quondam filiam Roberti Jop in uxore. Ita videlicet quod predicti Henricus et Cristina deservient eidem Waltero et uxore sue ad totam vitam suam honorifice secundum tam exigente. Et predictus Willelmus inveniet predictus Henricum et Cristinam uxorem suam victu et vestitu rationabiliter sicut dicit custodiendum filium et filias etc. preterea concessit in plena curia quod alienabit terram suam nec terram aliam partem tenementi sine dicetero ab Henrico filio suo nec ab heredibus ipsius Henrici. Et si ita contingat quod predictus Henricus obierit ante predicto Willelmo patre suo predicta Cristina uxor eiusdem Henrici remanebat in custodia predicto Waltero habeat victu et vestitu modo predicto et ipsa Cristina deserviet eidem Waltero ad totam vitam ipsius Walteri rationabiliter ut prius dictum est etc. Et post decessum ipsi Walteri predicta Cristina haberet dotem suam scilicet medietatem totum tenementum cum pertinenciis predicti Walteri sine alia contradictione. Et sub tali conventione fideliter tenendi predictus Walterus recepit catalla que data fuerunt cum predicta Cristina predicto Henrico filio suo maritagio. Et dant domino pro licentia predictam conventionem faciendum et tenendum ut rate et stabile imperpetuum vjd. Predicta Cristina dat domino pro licentia se maritandi Henrico Sictrich.' Agreements were also made in which land was specifically earmarked for the support of the bride and her offspring; for example see R.M. Smith, 'Some thoughts on "hereditary" and "proprietary" rights in land under customary law in thirteenth and fourteenth century England', *Law and History Review* 1 (1983), p. 111, n. 70.

86 R. Faith, 'Seigneurial control of women's marriage', *Past and Present* 99 (1983), pp. 137–8. For an interesting attempt to look at the relationships between the parties to a peasant marriage and their families both before and after the contract was specified, see J.M. Bennett, 'The ties that bind: peasant marriages and families in late medieval England', *Journal of Interdisciplinary History* 15 (1984), pp. 111–29. For references to a dowry dispute following a marriage agreement witnessed by persons other than kin that reveals details of

Betrothal or trothplight might be regarded at least within the middling layers of the tenantry as the ritual embodying popular, collectivist theory in the traditional form and entailed, as John Bossy states, 'legal and effective marriage, acceptable in the customary law of manorial courts'.[87]

Ecclesiastical Courts and Marital Disputes in England and France *c.*1300–1650

But we should not forget that a contractual, collectivist view was forced to coexist with an ecclesiastical theory of marriage whose individualistic implications are regularly emphasized in the writings of a significant school of canon law historians. When observed in the cases of the ecclesiastical courts it appears, at least superficially, as a rather unstable mixture. Of course, many students of the records of those courts that survive in increasing quantities from the fourteenth century, and which dealt with marital disputes that arose because of that coexistence, would argue that customary procedures were still in the process of reform, with the Church still 'pushing men and women towards the more individualistic view of marriage'.[88] None the less, students of the later medieval English ecclesiastical courts feel confident of an eventual victory for the Church's ideals and rules, because they can observe in the proceedings of those courts an apparent overall decline in the quantity of matrimonial contract litigation as time passed from the relatively high proportions that such business constituted in the later fourteenth century.[89] The waning of multi-party cases (regarded by some interpreters as potentially bigamous unions), as well as a declining frequency with which court officials adjudicated in disputes, are developments perceived as confirming this growing willingness to conform among the populace at large.[90] A preferred interpretation is taken to this latter development: officials by refusing

---

various payments in the form of moveable goods to be made by the bride's father, including the provision of 'convivium die nuptiarum' valued at the relatively large sum of 20 shillings, see J.M. Bennett, 'Gender, family and community: a comparative study of the English peasantry 1287–1348', (unpublished Ph.D. thesis, University of Toronto, 1981), p. 100.

87 J. Bossy, 'Blood and baptism: kinship, community and Christianity in western Europe from the fourteenth to the seventeenth century', in D. Baker (ed.), *Sanctity and secularity: the church and the world* (Oxford, 1973), pp. 131–2.

88 Sheehan, 'The formation and stability of marriage', p. 263.

89 Ingram, 'Spousals litigation in England', pp. 52–3; Helmholz, *Marriage litigation*, pp. 166–8; Houlbrooke, *The English family*, p. 79 and his *Church courts and the people*, p. 67.

90 Helmholz, *Marriage litigation*, pp. 58–9 and 167–8. It has been recently suggested by P.J.P. Goldberg of Trinity Hall, Cambridge that the relatively high proportion of multi-party cases found in ecclesiastical courts of the later fourteenth and early fifteenth century may be connected with rather protracted courtships in an era when marriage was late for women who were, under the demographic conditions then prevailing, more deeply involved in economic activities that were in certain contexts an alternative to marriage. This view should be taken seriously, for multi-party cases are most likely characteristic of a marriage regime in which women and young persons more broadly defined were able to act with

to adjudicate are perceived as showing sufficient confidence in a a general commitment to ecclesiastical precepts that no longer required them to fulfil an 'active' role in these matters. The curial officials' passive response is also believed to imply a growing recognition of the irrelevance of the ecclesiastical law of spousals – especially in the seventeenth century – relating to the marriage process, giving rise thereby to a dwindling number of clandestine unions.[91]

It is none the less very difficult to measure the extent as well as the changing level of uncertainty or indeed resistance to formal or publicly celebrated marriage that the statistics from these court proceedings reveal. The overall annual number of cases is very small and the diocesan populations to which they relate are notoriously difficult to specify at these dates.[92] For example, taking the evidence analysed by Sheehan from the Bishop of Ely's court book covering the years 1374–82, and being generous in allowances made for cases in courts whose records have not survived and being conservative in estimating the diocesan population, it is difficult to see more than 1 or at the most 2 per cent of the marriages in dispute. In other diocesan courts the ratio of cases to projected marriages may have been even lower.[93] It should furthermore be stressed most emphatically that almost 80 per cent of the 122 cases for which records have survived in Thomas Arundel's court book related to disputes concerning the establishment of marriages that, if they had been formed, had come into existence clandestinely.[94] The multi-party character of so many of them most likely confirms that they were disputes surrounding a relatively early phase in the 'marriage' or more specifically courtship process, and cannot therefore be related in any strict sense to the number of reasonably firmly established stable unions. In part their existence as

---

relatively high levels of freedom. I am grateful to Mr Goldberg for allowing me to read his forthcoming paper, 'Some York cause paper evidence for service and marriage in the late medieval town'.

91 Ingram, 'Spousals litigation in England', pp. 54–5 and Houlbrooke, *The English family*, pp. 79–80. Confirmation of such views is sought in opinions of contemporaries such as William Gouge, *Of domesticall duties* (London, 1622), p. 202 or Henry Swinburne, *A treatise of spousals or matrimonial contracts* (London, 1686), sig. A2v where it is stated that spousals are 'now in great measure worn out of use'.

92 The two centuries after the English poll-taxes of 1377–81 lack sources that facilitate the creation of tolerably accurate population estimates for the areas of ecclesiastical jurisdiction, and the poll-taxes, although useful, grossly underestimate the population, especially among young adults and the 'marriageable' sections of society. See R.M. Smith, 'Hypothèses sur la nuptialité en Angleterre aux XIIIe–XIVe siècles', *Annales, économies, sociétés, civilisations* (1983), p. 93. See R.M. Smith, 'Some reflections on the evidence for the origins of the "European marriage pattern" in England', in C.C. Harris (ed.), *The sociology of the family: new directions for Britain*, Sociological Review Monograph 28 (Keele, 1979), pp. 88–9. Even the 39 cases coming before Canterbury's consistory court in 1373 could have related to at best only 1 per cent of the extant and recently formed marriages of that year. See B.L. Woodcock, *Medieval ecclesiastical courts in the diocese of Canterbury* (Oxford, 1952), p. 85.

94 Sheehan, 'The formation and stability of marriage', p. 250.

historical evidence owes as much to the equivocal and ambiguous definitions of marriage formulated under canon law as it does to a concrete set of behavioural practices. Of course, the doubts expressed here as to their significance as evidence might be countered by suggesting that the courts were only dealing with the iceberg's tip and that much conflict failed to reach the curial arena.

However, even if the disputed clandestine marriages bore a consistent relationship to the incidence of unsolemnized matrimony in society at large, there is no easy means of interpreting the changes displayed by the quantity of such disputes in the overall business of the Church courts. As matrimonial cases declined as a component of business of the courts in the Norwich and Winchester diocesan courts between 1519 and 1569 there appeared to have been a simultaneous burgeoning of cases to do with tithe and testamentary disputes which, because they were often protracted affairs, proved more lucrative for the officials.[95] Were such shifts the result or the cause of declining marital dispute business in the courts? Furthermore, a fuller consideration of the influences bearing upon these trends would need to pay attention to the impact on Church court business of new opportunities for settling such disputes in secular courts which were, as the sixteenth century progressed, taking on an increasingly important role. For instance, the common law courts began to offer the remedy of an action for breach of promise which enabled the successful plaintiff to recover damages.[96]

Other historians would wish to see a conjuncture of economic and social forces in the late sixteenth and early seventeenth centuries providing a further impetus to the supposedly growing recognition that a church wedding was the only satisfactory guarantee of a socially and legally acceptable marriage. A number of studies have stressed a reorientation in moral values over the course of this period. A pioneer case study conducted on the Essex village of Terling by Keith Wrightson and David Levine unearthed a steep rise in illegitimacy during and in the wake of the years of exceptionally bad harvests in the later 1590s and reaching a high point of over 9 per cent in the decade 1601–10. This period of rapid increase was followed by a sharp decline, so that by the decade 1631–40 under 2 per cent of the baptisms in the Terling parish register were of bastards.[97] Doubtlessly much of the fall in the bastardy ratio after 1610 was the product of conditions returning to 'normal'; Wrightson and Levine would not, however, view that as a wholly satisfactory explanation of these changes. They note that there were subsequent years of harvest

---

95 Houlbrooke, *Church courts and the people*, p. 87.
96 Houlbrooke, *The English family*, p. 80 and S.F.C. Milsom, *Historical foundations of the common law* (London, 1969), p. 289.
97 Wrightson and Levine, *Poverty and piety*, p. 127, and their 'The social context of illegitimacy in early modern England', in Laslett et al., *Bastardy*, pp. 158–75.

failures and associated high prices together with a major depression in the
textile trade during the first 40 years of the seventeenth century, admittedly less catastrophic than the 1590s but none the less severe. Yet these
interludes did not produce further surges in Terling's illegitimacy ratio.
Moreover, by the 1630s the incidence of bastardy was well below the level
prevailing before the peak at the turn of the century. In addition, there
occurred also over this period a decline in the proportion of brides
pregnant at marriage.[98] These facts seem to indicate to these two scholars
that from around 1600 to 1640 increased efforts were made to ensure that
sexual relations between couples were confined to the years following a
marriage ceremony in church. Wrightson and Levine argue that the
change was, in part, a spontaneous adjustment at all levels of village
society to the economic conditions of the early seventeenth century, and
represented one aspect of a broader pattern of increased restraint on
fertility observable in the demographic history of the period. But an
adjustment of attitudes on the part of the more substantial inhabitants
was particularly important. Bridal pregnancy was no longer tolerated in
ways that it had been. Women pregnant at marriage after 1620 were
increasingly reported to the Church courts by parish officers. Roughly
similar declines in illegitimacy and pre-nuptial pregnancy, accompanied
by increasingly harsh treatment of bastard-bearing mothers and intensified punishment of sexual misbehaviour, have been found in other parish
case studies such that, for instance, pre-nuptial pregnancy at a greatly
reduced level is thought to have become very largely confined to poorer
couples.[99] English historians are not as yet agreed upon the relative
weighting to be attached on the one hand to the actions of village elites or
'better sorts' imbued with strongly held Protestant (indeed Puritan)
ideals, or on the other to economic forces stemming from a concern to
minimize idleness and waste and the charge placed upon greatly stretched
resources by what might be termed 'unwanted fertility'.[100] Some advo-
cates of this more mundane interpretation of developments would no

98 Wrightson and Levine, *Poverty and piety*, p. 132.
99 Ibid., pp. 132–3; M. Ingram, 'Religion, communities and moral discipline in late
sixteenth and early seventeenth century England: case studies', in K. von Greyerz (ed.),
Religion and society in early modern Europe 1500–1800 (London, 1984), pp. 198–9.
100 Ingram, 'Religion, communities and moral discipline', pp. 188–90, and M. Spufford,
'Puritanism and social control?' in A. Fletcher and J. Stevenson (eds), *Order and disorder in
early modern England 1500–1750* (Cambridge, 1985)pp. 41–57, which attempts an intriguing
comparison of the period 1590–1640 with the conditions on certain English manors in the
late thirteenth and early fourteenth centuries when real incomes dipped and harvests were
frequently deficient. Although there are difficulties confronting the use of manorial evidence
bearing upon leyrwite, childwite and merchet, and treating such entries as if they were
equivalent to baptisms and marriages in parish registers (pp. 54–6), Spufford provides a
timely reminder that the willingness of the village rich and office-holders to present their
poorer neighbours in the courts for sexual offences was not a new development peculiar to
the early seventeenth century.

doubt point towards the scattering of instances that have so far been discovered of ministers in league with more substantial elements of village society, refusing to read the banns or conduct marriages between poor people who might upon marriage and the subsequent arrival of their wretched offspring burden the parish rates.[101] Of course Wrightson and Levine would not wish to distinguish too categorically between either influence in so far as they portray them as mutually reinforcing.[102]

Yet in a wider perspective in considering Terling's place in the broader history of England it becomes necessary to isolate the relative importance of various influences bringing about social change. In returning to issues that were raised at an earlier stage in this discussion, are we to see Terling's early-seventeenth-century experience and perhaps that of other communities, although possibly in a more muted form, as the final assault of what some historians would like to see as an ultimately triumphant Christian Church on traditional and extrasacramental espousals? The question is never posed in these terms by Wrightson and Levine, who were concerned somewhat introspectively with what they assumed to be more pressing issues to do with cultural differentiation in seventeenth-century England. But if the matter is considered in a wider context, no

---

101 Recent publications have insisted upon the 'important part' played by the restrictions on the poor's freedom to marry, enforced by overseers of the poor and the clergy in their roles as 'village leaders', in contributing to the 'reinforcement of the process of demographic stabilization'. The evidence is interpreted as displaying 'numerous examples' of ministers and 'notables' of their parishes refusing 'to read the banns or conduct marriages between poor people who might burden the poor rates'. See Houlbrooke, *The English family*, p. 68; Wrightson and Levine, *Poverty and piety*, pp. 80 and 133; Ingram, 'Spousals litigation in England', p. 56. Examples have certainly been found of attempts to restrain the poor in their matrimonial wishes but the extent of these actions is very difficult to gauge. Ingram cites three or possibly four instances from early-seventeenth-century Wiltshire (see his 'Ecclesiastical justice in Wiltshire', pp. 121–2), and Wrightson cites a case from Worcestershire and three from Essex (see K. Wrightson, *English society 1580–1680* (London, 1982), p. 85). One of the latter concerns the rector of North Ockendon who in 1636 on reading the banns of a poor couple 'signified to the parish that they would marry and go begging together' and invited objections, although he was disciplined in the Archdeacon's court for such behaviour. See W. Hunt, *The puritan moment. The coming of revolution in an English county* (London, 1983), p. 74, where it is also argued, in somewhat strained terms, that such actions were indeed responsible for the actual rise in the bastardy ratios in Essex parishes (pp. 75–6). Both Wrightson, *English society*, p. 78 and Hunt, *The puritan moment* cite the writings of late-seventeenth-century commentators such as Carew Reynel and Sir William Coventry as acknowledging that 'such interventionist policies had served to hinder poor people from marrying.' The texts of Reynel and Coventry are to be found in J. Thirsk and J.P. Cooper (eds), *Seventeenth century economic documents* (Oxford, 1972), pp. 80 and 759. See, too, Sir Dudley North's complaints (written in the late seventeenth century) about poor law officers 'hindring all they can possibly the matching of young ones together'. He goes on to remark that he 'cannot accuse the law of this, not finding anything therein justifying the practice. Nor is it done but by indirect means, however the occasion is given by the law, and when the consequence toucheth the pocket means will be found out right or wrong.' *Some notes concerning the laws for the poor*, British Library MS 32, 512, fos. 127v.

102 Wrightson and Levine, *Poverty and piety*, especially pp. 174–6.

doubt some historians would want to see the energy exercised by Protestant ministers and their devouter parishioners in seventeenth-century England as part of the same post-Tridentine continental European enthusiasm for enforcing a code of uniform parochial practice that, following enormous efforts and disciplinary rigour, the Catholic bishops and their clergy succeeded in imposing upon Catholic Europe by the end of that same century.[103] Is the attack on the *fiançailles* in seventeenth-century France another version of the campaign to eradicate pre-nuptial pregnancy in England at an approximately comparable period?[104] Can they in any sense be equated with what Bossy would see as the enactment of a code of practice running counter to the collectivist and contractual traditions of kinship morality, the removal of which he believes is at the heart of so much Counter-Reformation clerical activity and giving rise, in the words of Pierre Chaunu, to 'un système démographique élaboré par la chrétienté latine ... la substitution au choix lignager du conjoint du choix individuel' producing 'un système de valeurs formant un véritable système de civilisation'?[105] To pose the questions in these ways may seem to be unnecessarily dramatic, indeed crass, but they are in fact of central significance in our understanding of certain highly distinctive attributes of early modern western European society.

French population historians regularly write about what they believe to have been a distinctive kind of *ancien régime* demography.[106] We have noted the remarks of Pierre Chaunu. Jacques Dupâquier has characterized that regime by specifying three traits he believes it displayed: one married couple to each home; no marriage without a home; no babies outside of marriage. He believes that the rules regarding celibacy and marriage were never enforced so strictly, or so much respected by the population, as in the seventeenth century. He writes: 'In France, the Catholic Counter-Reformation insisted on the publication of the banns of marriage, reduced betrothal to a simple formality often celebrated on the

---

103 More generally, J. Bossy, 'The Counter-Reformation and the people of Catholic Europe', *Past and Present* 47 (1971), pp. 51–70 and his recently published *Christianity and the West 1400–1700* (Oxford, 1985). See too P. Burke, *Popular culture in early modern Europe* (London, 1978), especially pp. 205–43, and more specifically R. Muchembled, *Culture populaire et culture des élites dans la France moderne* (Paris, 1978).

104 For example, J.-L. Flandrin, *Les Amours paysannes: amour et sexualité dans les campagnes de l'ancienne France (XVI–XIX siècles)* (Paris, 1975), pp. 37–59; J.-L. Flandrin and B. Le Wita, 'Les créantailles troyennes: un rite populaire de formation du couple et sa disparation aux XVIIe et XVIIIe siècles', in Flandrin, *Le Sexe et l'occident*, pp. 61–82. A. Burgière, 'Le rituel du mariage', pp. 40–9; G. Cabourdin, *Terre et hommes en Lorraine (1550–1635)* vol. 1 (Nancy, 1977), pp. 185–91; A. Lottin, *Lille, citadelle de la contre-reforme? (1598–1668)* (Dunkerque, 1984), pp. 216–23.

105 Chaunu, *Histoire, science sociale*, p. 315.

106 See for example, J. Dupâquier, 'De l'animal à l'homme: le mécanisme autorégulateur des populations traditionelles', *Révue de l'institut de sociologie* 2 (1972), pp. 177–211, and A. Bideau, 'Les mécanismes autorégulateurs des popultions', *Annales, économies, sociétés, civilisations* 38 (1983), pp. 1040–57.

eve of the wedding ceremony, hunted down irregular liaisons and even preached continence within marriage. In England, Puritanism had the same effect.'[107]

Notwithstanding Dupâquier's preference for seeing a common role for religious influences in both Catholic and Protestant areas of seventeenth-century western Europe, the demographic evidence upon which such views are based needs rather more careful assessment than it has received heretofore. The generally higher levels of illegitimacy in seventeenth- and early-eighteenth-century England than in France would make it difficult for certain commentators to agree with Dupâquier's claim as to the similarity of the effects of the Counter-Reformation Catholic and Puritan clergies on their respective parishioners in the matter of their behaviour prior to and upon entry into marriage. Do the differences in the levels of illegitimacy and the level and age patterns of pre-nuptial pregnancy in the two societies stem from the fact that England was never subject to the stringent behavioural restraints that the Counter-Reformation episcopate imposed upon her continental neighbours? Or was it that the efforts of English Puritan equivalents were aborted too soon before having the effect that the sustained efforts of the French clergies brought about?

John Bossy clearly thinks it so when, in referring to the effect of the Counter-Reformation on assessing the social climate of the seventeenth century and noting the different levels of illegitimacy in later-seventeenth-century England and France, he writes:

I can see no way of finding out whether English and French habits had differed in this respect before the Reformation, but it seems unlikely that they had; if they had not, the disparity would testify to the work of the Counter-Reformation episcopate and help to illustrate their success in the field of parochial observance.[108]

Very little comparative research has been undertaken, and there is very limited knowledge of French customary practices as they related to populations comparable with those considered in this essay whose activities are recorded in the proceedings of English manorial courts. It is worth considering in this context, however, some tantalizing if rather speculative arguments proposed very recently by a legal historian with a penchant for comparative analysis of marital dispute cases in the ecclesiastical courts of England and France in the fourteenth and fifteenth centuries.[109] Charles Donahue proposes that, although the canonical principles operating in both French and English courts were basically identical, it appears that in the French courts matrimonial causes were for the most part not civil disputes but criminal cases, initiated by the court

---

107 J. Dupâquier, 'Population', in P. Burke (ed.), *The New Cambridge Modern History* vol. 13 (Cambridge, 1979), p. 97.

108 Bossy, 'The Counter-Reformation and the people', p. 54.

109 C. Donahue, 'The canon law on the formation of marriage and social practice in the later Middle Ages', *Journal of Family History* 8 (1983), pp. 144–58.

official as prosecutor; ex officio cases relating to marriage in the English courts always appeared to be in the minority, although a rather large minority in the late-fourteenth-century Ely register analysed by Sheehan.[110] Furthermore, he argues that there seems to be a heavy preponderance of cases in the French courts that seek to enforce a simple *de futuro* promise through the use of judicial means. Certainly disputes concerning promises made in the future tense appeared in the English courts, but they mostly concerned the use of such words which were followed by sexual intercourse.[111] Thirdly, cases seeking to enforce a *de praesenti* marriage or a clandestine marriage are quite rare in the French courts but they loom very large in the English marital disputes throughout the period of surviving records from the thirteenth to the seventeenth century.[112] It was noted earlier that although there appeared to have been a decline in the sheer quantity of matrimonial cases in the English courts of the sixteenth and seventeenth centuries, the overwhelming dominance of *de praesenti* contract cases within this category of business as a whole did not alter. While not denying the presence of a certain number of *de praesenti* cases in the French evidence, Donahue believes they were perceived differently and handled more harshly; for, unlike their English equivalents, the French officials consistently condemned those involved with excommunication.[113] Donahue considers that the contrasts he believes he has identified cannot be attributed solely to differences in procedure but may reflect real differences in social practices.[114]

Furthermore, he would appear to question whether the courts really had very much freedom to act independently of the social and economic

110 Ibid., pp. 148–9, 154. But note that Sheehan's analysis of the late-fourteenth-century Ely ecclesiastical court register reveals marital disputes evenly divided between instance cases and office inquiries, although even this appears as a low level of criminal business compared with the little that is known of French disputes of a similar period: 'The formation and stability of marriage', pp. 259–61.

111 Donahue, 'The canon law on the formation of marriage', p. 150.

112 Ibid., pp. 150–2. Based on the fact that, of the 101 marriages about which the Ely register provides relevant information, 89 can be shown to have been clandestine *de praesenti* cases (Sheehan, 'The formation and stability of marriage', p. 252) whereas in a register from the court of the Official of the Bishop of Paris only three of some 400 cases between 1384 and 1387 concèrned such clandestine unions (see J.-P. Levy, 'L'officialité de Paris et les questions familiales à la fin du XIVe siècle', in *Études d'histoire du droit canonique dediées à Gabriel le Bras* (Paris, 1965), pp. 1265–94).

113 Donahue, 'The canon law on the formation of marriage', p. 154. While it would appear that excommunication was a very restricted response in the Church courts of later medieval England, it seems that such sentences were imposed for proven clandestine marriages more commonly in the early seventeenth century if the sentencing pattern discovered by Ingram in Wiltshire is shown to be more widely applicable. Almost 60 per cent of principals in clandestine marriage cases were excommunicated between 1615 and 1629: Ingram, 'Ecclesiastical justice in Wiltshire', pp. 128–30.

114 Donahue, 'The canon law on the formation of marriage', p. 155 and his 'The case of the man who fell into the Tiber: the Roman law of marriage at the time of the glossators', *American Journal of Legal History* 22 (1978), pp. 41–53.

milieu. In fact he goes so far as to suggest that the later medieval Church court evidence provides reasonable support for the view that the French Church courts were co-opted by parents in the policing of their children's marriages.[115] France, unlike England, had a strong tradition of Roman law learning throughout the Middle Ages. The *coutume de Paris*, unlike the English common or indeed customary law, suggests in a number of places an institution akin to *patria potestas*;[116] French *coutumes* and accounts of similar practices show that marriage without consent of the family was punished by the loss of property rights, indeed by infamy in some places.[117]

Sometimes historians have not always been sufficiently precise in their handling of the practical realities of Tridentine rules. To be sure the Council of Trent in 1563 issued a set of decrees on marriage, including the one called *Tametsi*, which made the presence of a priest and two other witnesses necessary for a valid marriage.[118] Of course, it would be possible to assemble many reasons for the undesirability of clandestine marriages, but one which loomed large in the pre-Tridentine debates was that they permitted persons to escape from the complex of family, financial and social concerns which surrounded marriage by forming unions in an ostensibly 'anti-social' way.[119] The delegates of the King of France to the Council were instructed to press for a rule which would make the consent of the parents of the marriage parties (if the parties were under parental power) a necessary element for a valid marriage. The earlier drafts of the decree contains this *sine qua non*. Only in the final draft of *Tametsi* did the Council omit this requirement and return to the spirit of the Alexandrine rules by providing that promulgation of the banns might be dispensed

115 Donahue, 'The canon law on the formation of marriage', p. 156 and 'The case of the man who fell into the Tiber', pp. 50–1.

116 F.T.M. Olivier-Martin, *Histoire de la coutume de la prévoté et vicomté de Paris* vol. 1 (Paris, 1922), pp. 151–9.

117 The idea that the consent of French parents to the marriage of their children was of long standing; see J.M. Turlan, 'Récherches sur le mariage dans la pratique coutumière (XIIe–XVIe siècles)', *Révue historique du droit français et étranger* series 4, 35 (1957), pp. 478–501. However, it appears that the sixteenth century did see a growing demand for legislation that ensured the nullification of marriage and for disinheritance of those who acted without parental approval, which was codified in Henry II's edict of 1556. On Roman law influences that were being written into the regional laws in the sixteenth century, see J. Basdevant, *Des Rapports de l'Église et de l'État dans la legislation du mariage, du concile de Trente au code civil* (Paris, 1900), p. 3; L. Dugent, 'Étude historique sur le rapt de séduction', *Nouvelle Révue historique de droit français et étranger* series 3, 10 (1886), pp. 601–3. For a valuable study of these laws in practice, see B.B. Diefendorf, *Paris city councillors in the sixteenth century: the politics of patrimony* (Princeton, N.J., 1983), pp. 160–70.

118 See Donahue, 'The policy of Alexander the Third', pp. 259–60.

119 See Jean Coras, 'Paraphrase sur l'édict des mariages clandestinement contractez par les enfans de famille contre le gré et consentement de leurs pères et mères (Paris, 1572) cited in M.A. Screech, *The Rabelasian marriage* (London, 1958), p. 49. Charles Du Moulin in his *Conseil sur le faict du concile de Trente* (Lyons, 1564) criticized marriages lacking parental approval as 'contre les bonnes et anciennes loix civiles et honnesteté publique', fo. 19v.

with where there was reason to fear force.[120] The French representatives, having failed to ensure that marriages by children under 25 could not be made validly without the consent of their parents, were not to be thwarted, however, for the decrees of the Council of Trent concerning marriage were never promulgated in France. Their place was taken by royal legislation which restored the old parental rule.[121]

'Procreative Careers' in Early Modern France and England

Had Donahue proceeded to consider the evidence of historical demographers with the same comparative emphasis he had employed in his challenging and some would say contentious handling of ecclesiastical courts and their business, he might have felt more confident in his view of the pervasiveness and indeed ultimate triumph of Roman law traditions in these matters. To a certain extent such comparisons in the immediate pre- and post-Tridentine phases are difficult because French historical demography is really a 'science' of the later seventeenth and eighteenth centuries in so far as its earliest parish registers, although surviving in large numbers from the sixteenth century and in some places even earlier, have many deficiencies as to the quality of their recordings and display notable variability in the extent to which all three demographic 'events' are registered. These deficiencies are, however, greater in the matter of registration of deaths and marriages than of births, so certain comparisons can be made.[122] There are, however, relatively few sixteenth-century statistics currently available for this purpose. Alain Croix, in a notable study, presents illegitimacy ratios for 34 rural and eight urban Breton parishes between 1593 and 1600, suggesting that in the vast majority of places fewer than 2 per cent of births were registered as illegitimate.[123] From parish registers whose recordings have been analysed for the years between 1600 and 1670, it would be equally hard to find illegitimacy ratios above 2 per cent.[124] Through most of the Paris Basin rates were less

120 B. Diefendorf, *Paris city councillors*, pp. 166–9.

121 J. Ghestin, 'L'action des parlements contre les mésalliances aux XVIIe et XVIIIe siècles', *Révue historique de droit français et étranger*, series 4, 34 (1956), pp. 74–110, 196–224; A. Rouest, 'Le consentement des parents au mariage', in *Actes du congrès de droit canonique*, Paris 22–26 avril 1947 (Paris, 1949), pp. 386–92. See too A. Esmein, *Le mariage en droit canonique* 2nd edn, R. Genestal and J. Dauvillier (eds) (Paris, 1935), pp. 192–5, 279–86.

122 See, for example, the problems of sixteenth- and early-seventeenth-century French parish registers discussed in G. Cabourdin, 'Introduction aux problèmes de la démographie de la période 1500–1570', *Annales de démographie historique* (1980), pp. 13–18; J.N. Biraben, D. Blanchet and N. Brouard, 'Pour reconstituer le mouvement de la population aux XVIe et XVIIe siècles', *Annales de démographie historique* (1980), pp. 39–52, and J.N. Biraben, 'Le point de l'enquête sur le mouvement de la population en France avant 1670', *Population* 40 (1985), pp. 47–70.

123 A. Croix, *Nantes et le pays nantais au XVIe siècle: étude démographique* (Paris, 1974), pp. 94–5.

124 J. Dupâquier, *La Population française aux XVIIe et XVIIIe siècles* (Paris, 1979), p. 27.

than 1 per cent, although communities in parts of upper Normandy leave evidence of baptisms of illegitimate infants reaching between 3 and 4 per cent of all baptisms.[125] Jean-Louis Flandrin has suggested that the evidence reveals a steady decline in illegitimacy levels from the later sixteenth century onwards, although its patchy character suggests that it is hardly complete enough to confirm such an interpretation.[126] Certainly some parish statistics from various parts of northern France do display patterns of decline through the late seventeenth into the early eighteenth century in the proportional significance of bastard births. Flandrin believes that a drop in bastardy ratios is detectable, and attributes it to a decline in both clerical and lay concubinage as well as to an effective campaign waged by both priests and parents to ensure that births stemming from sexual activities by young couples with no expectation of eventual marriage were increasingly brought to term within a 'forced' but

125 R.C. Polton, 'Coulommiers et Chailly-en-Brie (1557–1715)', *Annales de démographie historique* (1969), p. 27; E. Gironnay and J.M. Baldner, 'Récherches sur la population d'Argenteuil au XVIIe siècle (1598–1670)' (unpublished mémoire de maîtrise, University of Paris, 1973–4); E. Brocaud, 'Villepreux et Rennemoulin: 1587–1680' (unpublished mémoire de maîtrise, University of Paris, 1973); C. Garnier and C. Ripert, 'La population de Marly-le-Roi aux XVIe et XVIIe siècles, 1595–1699' (unpublished mémoire de maîtrise, University of Paris, 1974); M. Caoudal, 'Récherches sur la population de la région de Cormeilles-en-Parisis aux XVIe et XVIIe siècles, (Cormeilles-en-Paris, Herblay, Montigny, La Frette) (unpublished mémoire de maîtrise, University of Paris, 1973–4); J.C. Bourdon, 'Villages de la vallée de l'Oise de la fin du XVIIe siècle au debut de XIXe siècle: étude de démographie historique' (unpublished thèse de 3e cycle, University of Paris, 1974); J. Rogues, 'Benerville (1697–1792), Blonville (1684–1792), Tourgeville (1640–1792;0 Étude d'histoire démographique' (unpublished mémoire de maîtrise, University of Caen, 1970); A. Lecarpentier, 'Trouville-sur-Mer et Hennequeville, XVIIe–XVIIIe siècles; étude de démographie historique' (unpublished mémoire de maîtrise, University of Caen, 1970); A.M. Baguelin, 'Étude d'histoire démographique: Dives et Beuzeval, 1618–1792' (unpublished mémoire de maîtrise, University of Caen, 1970); Mlle Stephan, 'Étude démographique à l'époque moderne: Gonneville-sur-Dives et Trousseauville, 1590–1792' (unpublished mémoire de maîtrise, University of Caen, 1969); M. Rossard, 'Étude de la population à Athis-de-l'Orne au XVIIe siècle' (unpublished mémoire de maîtrise, University of Caen, 1970); H. Charbonneau, *Tourouvre-au-Perche aux XVIIe et XVIIIe siècles: étude de démographie historique* (Paris, 1970); E. Gautier and L. Henry, *La Population de Crulai, paroisse normande: étude démographique* (Paris, 1958); M. el Kordi, *Bayeux aux XVIIe et XVIIIe siècles: contribution à l'histoire urbaine de la France* (Paris, 1970); P. Gouhier, 'Port-en-Bessin (1597–1792): étude d'histoire démographique', *Cahiers des annales de Normandie* 1 (1962).

126 Flandrin *Les Amours paysannes (XVIe–XIXe siècles)* (Paris, 1975) p. 238, where data relating to only three parishes are presented graphically. Only one (Pont de Vaux) possesses illegitimacy recordings for the sixteenth century, and this shows only a marginal decline in the illegitimacy ratio from 1.0 to 0.9 per cent. Of the remaining two parishes, Isbergues (Pas-de-Calais) oscillates from 0.9 to 1.2 per cent and falls again but shows no noticeable trend over the course of the seventeenth century. Tourouvre-au-Perche registers an illegitimacy ratio of 0.9 between 1640 and 1670, but this falls by 1700–30 to 0.35 per cent. It should be noted that evidence for these same parishes is presented in Flandrin, *Families in former times*, p. 183, figure 4B, where although the trends are similar the actual values are shown to be higher. For instance, between 1570–90 and 1670–80 the illegitimacy ratio in Pont de Vaux is shown as falling from 2.56 to 1.15 per cent.

solemnized union.[127] It is, however, possible that in certain contexts where higher illegitimacy ratios have been encountered they may have been the result of inherently stable but 'unofficial' unions; of the 1801 cases studied by Croix in his sample of Breton parishes between 1593 and 1600, approximately 50 per cent appear to have been the children of couples living in stable unions.[128] In other parts of northern France pockets of high 'illegitimacy' seem to have been associated with Protestant marriages whose offspring were baptized as bastards by Catholic clergy unwilling to sanction such unions.[129]

Studies of pre-nuptial pregnancy among seventeenth-century French brides show that rates rarely exceeded 10 per cent, and in almost one-third of the parishes for which data have so far been published rates were closer to 5 per cent.[130] Rates continued low and may well have fallen still further, in so far as the better-covered period after 1670 indicates pre-nuptial pregnancy levels rarely in excess of 7 per cent.[131] Furthermore, for systematically derived samples of French marriage cohorts

127 Flandrin, *Families in former times*, pp. 180–4 and his *Le Sexe et l'occident*, pp. 288–9, and *Amours paysannes*, p. 239.

128 Croix, *Nantes et le pays nantais*, p. 96.

129 Dupâquier, *La Population française*, p. 27 and *La Population rurale du bassin parisien*, p. 367.

130 For relevant studies see note 125 in this chapter, conveniently summarized in Dupâquier, *La Population rurale du bassin parisien*, table 151, pp. 369–70.

131 In addition to studies in note 125 in this chapter, see: B. Griet and D. Pierrot, 'Études démographiques: la population argenteillaise de 1670 à 1720' (unpublished mémoire de maîtrise, University of Paris, 1970); M. Lachiver, *La Population de Meulan du XVIIe au XIXe siècle (vers 1600–1870): étude de démographie historique* (Paris, 1969); A. Verbaere, 'Un village d'Ile-de-France sous l'ancien régime. Pommeuse, 1670–1799' (unpublished mémoire de maîtrise, University of Paris, 1975); D. Joly, 'Démographique d'Anet au XVIIIe siècle' (unpublished mémoire de maîtrise, University of Paris, 1970); C. Soudjian, 'Les crises démographiques dans la banlieue sud et sud-ouest de Paris entre 1690 et 1715' (unpublished mémoire de maîtrise, University of Paris, 1973–4); F. Desjardins, 'Étude démographique du pays d'Arthes', *Démographie historique (DH) bulletin d'information société de démographie historique* 11 (1971), pp. 5–11; A. Chance, D. Gallardo et M. Lerride, 'Honfleur 1684–1792', *DH bulletin d'information société de démographie historique* 15 (1975), pp. 2–10; N. Zens and J.Y. Delange, 'Lisieux aux XVIIe et XVIIIe siècles', *DH bulletin d'information société de démographie historique* 12 (1974), pp. 12–70; M.L.J. Jambou, 'Cricqueboeuf et Pennedepie, 1668–1792', *Annales de Normandie* 21 (1971), pp. 261–5; M. Mogensen, 'Aspects de la société augeronne aux XVIIe et XVIIIe siècles' (unpublished thèse de 3e cycle, University of Paris, 1971); A. Huet, 'Annebault et Bourgeauville aux XVIIe et XVIIIe siècles', *Annales de Normandie* 22 (1972), pp. 277–304; F. Becart, 'Saint-Andre-d'Hebertot au XVIIe et au XVIIIe siècle, 1644–1792' (unpublished mémoire de maîtrise, University of Caen, 1972); C. Quesnel, 'Deauville, Saint-Arnoult, Touques, Daubeuf: étude d'histoire démographique 1654–1792' (unpublished mémoire de maîtrise, University of Caen, 1971); J.L. Mutrelle, 'Une commune rurale de l'ouest du pays de Caux: la paroisse Saint-Martin d'Octeville: étude réligieuse et démographique d'après les registres paroissiaux (1680–1759)' (unpublished mémoire de maîtrise, University of Rouen, 1969); M.C. Bellanger, 'Une paroisse du Bas-Maine aux XVIIe et XVIIIe siècles: étude d'histoire démographique et sociale: Saint-Paul-le-Gaultier, 1646–1792', (unpublished mémoire de maîtrise, University of Caen, 1966); R. Toutain, 'Démographie d'un village normand: Saint-Maurice-du-Desert (1668–1770)', *Annales de Normandie* 26 (1976), pp. 67–78; D. Larose, 'Étude démographique de la paroisse de Millières, 1673–1790', *Annales de Normandie* 22 (1972).

between 1670 and 1720 from different regions, 'older' brides over 25 years of age were considerably more likely to have been pregnant at marriage than brides marrying between the ages of 15 and 25.[132] For some women, waiting to marry appeared to increase the likelihood of pregnancy. Indeed this remained a characteristic of French brides throughout the eighteenth and early nineteenth centuries, with a few apparent regional exceptions.[133]

132 In five parishes to the north and six to the west of the Seine 1.2 per cent and 3.6 per cent of births to brides aged under 25 and 6.7 and 5.3 per cent respectively of births to brides aged over 25 years were the result of pre-nuptial conceptions between 1690 and 1719; see J. Houdaille, 'Fécondité des mariages dans le quart nord-ouest de la France de 1670 à 1829', *Population* 28 (1973), p. 918. In a sample of parishes in N.E. France over the same period 7.0 per cent of births to young brides (i.e. under 25 years) and 10 per cent to older brides were pre-nuptially conceived: see J. Houdaille, Fécondité des mariages dans le quart nord-est de la France de 1670 à 1829', *Annales de démographie historique* (1976), p. 385. In seven parishes in south-east France 2.6 per cent and 5.8 per cent of births to brides under and over 25 years of age were pregnant when their marriages were solemnized: see L. Henry, 'Fécondité des mariages dan le quart sud-est de la France de 1670 à 1829', *Population* 33 (1978), p. 881. No data on pre-nuptial pregnancy by age at marriage of brides are available from villages of south-west France before 1720. By assuming that rates for the south-western region bore the same relation to the average of the other regional quarters in the earlier period as was the case in the next period, 1720–39, E.A. Wrigley has computed a French national estimate of births pre-nuptially conceived by mother's marriage age between 1690 and 1719 which is 4.4 per cent and 7.4 per cent for younger and older brides respectively: see Wrigley, 'Marriage, fertility and population growth', p. 181.

133 Bridal pregnancy rates by age of bride for French regions have been estimated at the following levels:

Ages	South-east <25	South-east 25>	North-east <25	North-east 25>	North-west[a] <25	North-west 25. 13	South-west <25	South-west 25>
1720–39	3.6	3.6	8.7	8.9	2.5	8.8	6.1	8.7
1740–69	2.9	5.9	11.2	9.8	10.1	6.6	3.6	8.7
1770–89	5.6	9.2	12.2	15.2	8.5	10.9	10.7	13.7
1790–1819	7.1	14.0	16.1	15.3	13.9	11.6	9.2	13.6

[a]It is important to note that the areas to the north and the west of the Seine that make up the north-west region present rather different patterns:

Ages	North <25	West <25	North 25>	West 25>
1690–1719	1.2	3.6	6.7	5.3
1720–39	0.0	3.2	17.7	5.1
1740–69	20.3	6.3	14.0	4.2
1770–89	17.9	3.7	13.2	9.8
1790–1819	20.9	8.9	19.8	7.8

The areas to the north of the Seine, throughout a considerable part of the period after 1740, show a pattern of pre-nuptial conceptions that in its overall incidence and its age patterns is much closer to that of England, and in that respect is distinctly aberrant in France as a whole. For the sources relating to these statistics see note 132 in this chapter.

Furthermore, the French evidence also seems to suggest that pregnant brides tended to fall disproportionately into two categories; 30 to 40 per cent of brides were visibly pregnant at marriage, giving birth within three months of the ceremony (the product of what Dupâquier has called 'les accidents'), and roughly similar proportions gave birth in the seventh and eighth months of the marriage, implying that sexual relations had only commenced just before or immediately after the formalization of the marriage. Very few pregnancies appeared to come to term in the fourth, fifth or sixth months following the marriage ceremony.[134]

English trends in illegitimacy throughout the sixteenth and seventeenth centuries can be charted with rather greater precision than in France, but too much weight should not be attached to their absolute values.[135] English illegitimacy ratios would, however, appear at all dates during these two centuries to be higher than those in France. Even at their low point in the latter half of the seventeenth century, English rates were twice as high as those found in the French registers of a similar date. It is important to stress that for the latter period we know relatively little about the age at marriage and proportions never marrying in France compared with England; thus small values of the kind presented by these 'statistics' could be ambiguous as to their meaning for the true incidence of illegitimacy among the unmarried female population, which only a measure of the illegitimacy rate could provide.[136] The true magnitude of

For estimates for the whole of France in the eighteenth and early nineteenth century, see Wrigley, 'Marriage, fertility and population growth', p. 181. Further case studies continue to verify the pattern found over the greater part of France: see J.C. Sangoi, 'Démographie de trois communes rurales du Bas-Quercy (1751–1872)', *DH bulletin d'information société de démographie historique* 37 (1983), p. 7, where the author in referring to the higher levels of pre-nuptial pregnancy among older brides and widows suggests that 'la chasteté leur paraissant plus contraignant'. However, in this community the pattern reverses in the 1842–72 marriage cohort, signifying, Sangoi suggests, 'une meilleure connaissance en matière de contraception'. An identical pattern is found in a village in the southern part of the Massif Central, with a shift to a higher probability of pre-nuptial pregnancy among younger brides after 1840. Here, however, the overall level of pre-nuptial conception never exceeded 10 per cent. See J. Houdaille and Y. Tugault, 'Un village des Cévennes (Les Aires Hérault)', *Population* 40 (1985), p. 176.

134 Flandrin, *Le Sexe et l'occident*, pp. 273–5, citing P. Wiel, 'Un grosse paroisse du Cotentin aux XVIIe et XVIIIe siècles: Tamerville', *Annales de démographie historique* (1969), pp. 162–3, especially table 17; Cabourdin, *Terre et hommes en Lorraine*, p. 119, where data on pregnancies coming to term within the first eight months of a formalized marriage are presented for the parishes of Vézelize, Goudreville, Vaucouleurs and Châtenois. See too, R. Deniel and L. Henry, 'La population d'un village du Nord de la France, Sainghin-en-Melantois de 1665 à 1851', *Population* (1965), pp. 503–602.

135 See the various estimates of the absolute level of the illegitimacy ratio in England in the parish register period (i.e. after 1538) in P. Laslett, *Family life*, chapter 3, especially figure 3.2. See too, the discussion of these measurse in Laslett, 'Introduction', in Laslett et al., *Bastardy*.

136 See the discussion highly relevant to this problem in M. Drake, 'Norway', in W.R. Lee (ed.), *European demography and economic growth* (London, 1979), pp. 299–306; and Wrigley,

the fall in the level of illegitimacy in the first half of the seventeenth century is most likely understated when, as very recent estimates seem to suggest, there was a rapid increase in the proportions never marrying, thereby placing increasing proportions of the potential child-bearing population at risk of giving birth outside of wedlock.[137] Furthermore, what often goes unnoticed (and possibly presents difficulties for the interpretation of a change, indeed a fundamental reorientation, in the early seventeenth century offered by Levine and Wrightson) is that the evidence, based unfortunately at present on a rather small sample of registers, tantalizingly suggests that illegitimacy may well have been dropping steadily in the period between 1540 and 1580 before rising rather sharply in the last decade of the sixteenth century.[138] Pre-nuptial

---

'Marriage, fertility and population growth', p. 156. See too the definition of illegitimacy rates and ratios in C. Wilson (ed.), *Dictionary of demography* (Oxford, 1985), pp. 101–2.

137 It has come to be assumed that the true low point in English illegitimacy ratios is to be located in the decade immediately after the Restoration. See K. Wrightson, 'The nadir of English illegitimacy in the seventeenth century', in Laslett et al., *Bastardy*. However, recent estimates of the proportions ever marrying suggest that the birth cohorts between 1616 and 1641 may have experienced 20 to 22 per cent of their survivors never marrying at age 40–44; consequently the illegitimacy rate, if not the ratio, might well suggest a minimal level of bastardy in the years encompassed by the Civil War and the Commonwealth. See Weir, 'Rather never than late', p. 347, and Schofield, 'English marriage patterns revisited', p. 9. It is possible, too, that the illegitimacy rate in parts of France may have declined in the seventeenth century, although ratios display no obvious trend, in so far as a scattering of studies seem to suggest a rise in female marriage age from the low to middle twenties in the seventeenth century; see Dupâquier, *La Population Française*, p. 26; J.-M. Moriceau, 'Les crises démographiques dans le sud de la région parisienne de 1560 à 1670', *Annales de démographie historique*, (1980), pp. 122–3; Cabourdin, 'Introduction aux problèmes de la démographie', pp. 16–17. Data on proportions never marrying, comparable to those derived from the larger-scale aggregative analysis of English registers, are currently lacking for France in so far as French estimates of this variable have been derived to date from information on age and marital status at death, which is rarely entered in registers before 1670.

138 English illegitimacy ratios and gross reproduction rates show a remarkable tendency to move together in the same direction over time, and the sixteenth century appears to be no exception to this rule. See 'News from the SSRC Cambridge Group for the History of Population and Social Structure', *Local Population Studies* 24 (1980), pp. 7–9. The gross reproduction rate appears to have dropped sharply before 1580 and illegitimacy ratios were relatively high at over 4 per cent in the 1540s. Unfortunately fewer than 13 parishes of the sample of 98 are regarded as reliable, and although by 1570 between 47 and 54 are contributing to the curve of the illegitimacy ratio the numbers are sufficiently small to require the exercise of some caution in accepting these figures at their face value. Obviously, this is a subject in need of more intensive research than it has received to date. It should be noted in support of these data that the marriage rate revived between 1560 and 1581 in response to a short-lived improvement in real incomes; see Houlbrooke, *The English family*, p. 67. Furthermore, a recent synthesis of English Tudor economic conditions notes the apparently healthy sign that between the 1560s and the 1590s industrial prices kept pace with agricultural ones. See D.M. Palliser, *The age of Elizabeth: England under the later Tudors 1547–1603* (London, 1983), p. 141 and p. 159.

pregnancy levels were consistently two to three times higher than those found in France in the period after 1550, falling to a low point in the marriage cohort of 1650–99 of 11.3 per cent and 17.3 per cent of first births occurring within eight and nine months respectively of the marriage.[139] At the turn of the sixteenth century almost one in four first births had been conceived before marriage in England compared with fewer than one in ten, or even one in twenty, in the French parishes for which evidence has been collected.[140]

Evidence on both the distribution of births in the eight or nine months following the marriage and the age patterns of pre-nuptial pregnancy among brides reveal further contrasts between the French and English populations. Births to pregnant English brides were much more evenly distributed over the months following the marriage and only a relatively small minority would have gone to church visibly with child, their pregnancies coming to term within two months of the marriage ceremony. The contrast with those French parishes for which detailed pre-nuptial pregnancy statistics have been published is striking.[141] In both the Normandy parish of Tamerville in the seventeenth century and the Lorraine parishes of Vézelize, Goudreville and Vaucouleurs in the later sixteenth and early seventeenth centuries, at least three-quarters of pregnant brides gave birth within the first three or the eighth and ninth months of their marriage. In 16 English parishes the pattern seems to have been markedly different, with between 50 and 60 per cent of pre-nuptially conceived births in months one to three and eight to nine of the marriage (table 3.1). What is more, the proportion of all first births coming to term within the eighth or ninth month of the marriage remained remarkably constant between 1550 and 1849, never more than 8.9 and never less than 6.8 per cent (table 3.2).

It has been argued by Flandrin that, in France during the eighteenth century, when the incidence of pre-nuptial pregnancy grew it did so very largely because of increasingly higher proportions of brides waiting until

---

139 Laslett, 'Introduction', in Laslett et al., *Bastardy*, p. 20. A fuller list relating to reconstitutions of 16 English parish registers is to be found in C. Wilson, 'Marital fertility in pre-industrial England 1550–1849' (unpublished Ph.D. thesis, University of Cambridge, 1982), chapter 3, table 3.3. Of these 16 parishes for the marriage cohort 1550–99 only one (Shepshed, Leicestershire) had fewer than 15 per cent of first births occurring within 240 days of the marriage, and six had proportions ranging from 20.5 to 32.3 per cent (ibid., table 3.3).

140 Evidence for the English 'sample' is to be found in Wilson, 'Marital fertility', table 3.1. The sixteen parishes are: Alcester (Warwickshire), Aldenham (Hertfordshire), Ash (Kent), Banbury (Oxfordshire), Bottesford (Leicestershire), Campton and Shefford (Bedfordshire), Colyton (Devon), Earsdon (Northumberland), Gainsborough (Lincolnshire), Gedling (Nottinghamshire), Hartland (Devon), Methley (West Riding), Shepshed (Leicestershire), Terling (Essex), Willingham (Cambridgeshire).

141 See note 125 in this chapter.

Table 3.1 Relative distribution of first births occurring within nine months of marriage by duration of marriage and marriage cohort, all women: English and French parishes 1550–1669

	Marriage cohort							
	Tamerville 1624–69		Lorraine[a] 1550–1635		16 English parishes			
Marriage duration (complete months)					1550–99		1650–49	
	(no.)	(%)	(no.)	(%)	(no.)	(%)	(no.)	(%)
0–2	25	30.9	8	28.6	172	24.5	186	19.5
3–6	16	19.8	7	25.0	293	41.7	410	42.9
7–8	40	49.3	13	46.4	238	33.8	359	37.6
Total	81	100.0	28	100.0	703	100.0	955	100.0

[a] Vezelize, Goudreville, Vaucouleurs and Chatenois.

the sixth, seventh and eighth months of their pregnancy before solemnizing their marriage.[142] There was correspondingly (and unlike the chronology among English brides) a steady decline in the relative importance of pregnancies that terminated in the eighth and ninth months of the marriage. For instance, Flandrin cites the case of Tamerville where only 3.1 per cent of first births were of the former type (births within the first three months of marriage) in the years 1624–69 but by the period 1741–90 they had grown fourfold to become 13.4 per cent. In the 16 English parishes such first births within the first three months of marriage fluctuated between a low in the marriage cohort of 1650–99 of 2.7 per cent to a high of 6.4 per cent of births to brides in the 1750–99 cohort (table 3.2).[143] What is even more distinct about the English pattern is that the proportion of first births that occurred in the fourth through seventh completed months of marriage were generally sizeable and undoubtedly appear to have displayed the greatest volatility over time. Wrigley has already drawn attention to this issue in contrasting the relative importance of such births to marriage cohorts of 1670–94 and 1770–94 in a sample of 12 English parishes.[144] The latter period shows a threefold to fourfold expansion over the intervening century in first births coming to

142 Flandrin, *Le Sexe et l'occident*, p. 274. A similar case has been argued based on evidence concerning an increasing proportion of pre-nuptially pregnant brides in eighteenth-century Rouen who were more than four months pregnant at their marriage. 'L'accroissement de la proportion des grossesses avancées laisse penser qu'au XVIIIème siècle, les scruples de purité se sont un peu atténués', writes J.-P. Bardet in his *Rouen aux XVIIe et XVIIIe siècles: les mutations d'un espace social* (Paris, 1983), p. 327.

143 Statistics based on Wilson, 'Marital fertility in pre-industrial England', table 3.2.

144 Wrigley, 'Marriage, fertility and population growth', pp. 158–60, especially figure VI.

Table 3.2 Relative distribution of first births occurring within nine months of marriage by duration of marriage and marriage cohort, all women: combined set of 16 English parishes

Marriage duration (complete months)	Marriage cohort									
	1550–99		1600–49		1650–99		1700–49		1750–99	
	(%TFB)[a]	(no.)	(%TFB)	(no.)	(%TFB)	(no.)	(%TFB)	(no.)	(%TFB)	(no.)
0	1.2	34	0.7	29	0.6	21	0.9	37	0.9	61
1	1.7	48	1.1	45	0.8	28	1.5	65	2.2	142
2	3.3	90	2.8	112	1.3	44	2.4	101	3.3	214
3	3.1	86	2.7	110	1.2	40	2.1	91	3.5	225
4	2.5	68	2.9	116	1.3	45	1.9	82	3.7	243
5	2.0	56	1.8	75	1.2	40	2.1	88	3.9	251
6	3.0	83	2.7	110	1.7	57	2.3	98	3.9	249
7	3.1	86	2.7	108	2.8	93	2.9	132	3.9	251
8	5.5	152	6.2	250	6.0	201	4.8	205	4.7	305
Total		703		955		569		889		1941
Total first births		2757		4036		3346		4275		6497

a TFB: total first births.

term in the third to sixth months of the marriage. But the novelty of the later eighteenth century would seem less if the parish-register-based evidence of the later sixteenth century is taken into account. In figure 3.1 we can observe considerable growth in the percentage of first births that came to term in the third to sixth months of the marriages from 16 English parishes between the marriage cohorts of 1650–99 and 1750–99. However, the marriage cohort of 1550–99 represents an intermediate situation with considerably more (almost twice as many) pregnancies terminating in the third through sixth completed months of marriage than in the 1650–99 cohort. Some doubts must exist concerning both the scale of the drop in pre-nuptial pregnancy and the representativeness of those whose events are recorded in the parish registers in the second half of the seventeenth century. For instance, observations are based on 4036 first births in the marriage cohort 1600–49, dropping to 3346 in the marriage cohort 1650–99 before returning to 4275 in that of 1700–49. We should not underestimate the possible effects of clandestine marriage, which is widely believed to have been growing in incidence in the second half of the

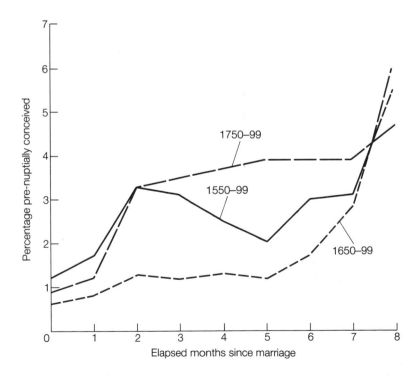

Figure 3.1   The changing level and character of pre-nuptial pregnancy: 16 English parishes 1550–1799

seventeenth century.[145] Such marriages may have enabled poorer elements in the populace to sidestep ratepayers' efforts to prevent their marriages and, by allowing them to marry at short notice, to shield the fact of the 'brides' ante-nuptial sexual relations from prying authorities'.[146]

We may observe other differences in the fact that 15 per cent of births to brides under 25 in later-seventeenth-century England appear to have resulted from conception before church solemnization of marriage compared with 5 per cent of births to French brides of comparable ages. Twelve per cent of births to brides over 25 years of age were the result of pre-marital conceptions compared with 8 per cent among their French counterparts.[147] It is interesting also to consider in rather more detail the age patterns of marital fertility of women in the five-year age groups between 20 and 39 for 16 English parishes (table 3.3) and the proportions of first births pre-nuptially conceived by women from the same parishes classified according to their age of marriage (table 3.4).[148] It is apparent that the former data when indexed against 100 for the age group 20–24 produce a curve whose shape is convex on its upper side (figure 3.2). Similar indexing of the latter data produces a curve reminiscent of the shape assumed by a curve of the age patterns of marital fertility in a population exhibiting 'natural fertility' (figure 3.3). Brides marrying between 35 and 39 tended to exhibit rates of pre-nuptial pregnancy of approximately half those found among brides marrying at ages 20 to 24 – a decline with age that is remarkably similar to that exhibited by the fertility of married women between the same ages. It would appear that this characteristic is strikingly identifiable among brides marrying after 1650. A less evident age decay pattern, although still detectable, is found among the pre-nuptially pregnant in marriage cohorts before 1650. Some of the apparent irregularities may, however, be due to the smaller

145 For instance it has been estimated that for most of the last 60 years of the seventeenth century at least 25 per cent of months displayed defective marriage entries in English parish registers. See Wrigley and Schofield, *The population history of England*, pp. 27–8. In a different context dealing with the supposed resort to 'family limitation' in late-seventeenth-century England, Wrigley has suggested that family reconstitutions in that period might be biased in exposing a disproportionate number of those who continued to formalize their marriages publicly: E.A. Wrigley, 'Marital fertility in seventeenth-century Colyton: a note', *Economic History Review* 31 (1978), pp. 433–4.

146 Houlbrooke, *The English family*, p. 86. Important research into this topic, with particular reference to Berkshire, is currently being undertaken by Stephen Taylor of the University of Reading.

147 See note 11 in this chapter, and Wilson, 'Marital fertility in pre-industrial England', table 3.5. Wilson's data relate to marriage cohorts 1550–1649 and 1650–1749 from 16 parishes, and should be contrasted with the figures for 12 parishes for the 1650–99 marriage cohort presented by Wrigley, 'Marriage, fertility and population growth', p. 181.

148 The data in table 3.3 and figure 3.3 are taken from Wilson, 'Marital fertility in pre-industrial England', table 2.1 and table 3.5.

Table 3.3 Age-specific and total marital fertility rates adjusted for the effect of pre-marital conceptions by marriage cohort: combined set of 16 English parishes

Marriage cohort	Woman's age							
	15–19	*20–24*	*25–29*	*30–34*	*35–39*	*40–44*	*45–49*	*TMFR[a]*
1550–99								
Rate,	381	351	344	300	248	139	18	7.00
'Woman' years	63	421	768	845	789	703	598	
1600–49								
Rate	290	357	348	303	241	129	24	7.01
'Woman' years	196	1435	3053	3790	3628	3140	2651	
1650–99								
Rate	325	363	333	297	239	121	26	6.90
'Woman' years	176	1249	2575	3091	3018	2715	2236	
1700–49								
Rate	278	365	358	305	242	131	25	7.13
'Woman' years	213	1762	3867	4850	4811	4425	3830	
1750–99								
Rate	360	367	345	308	246	144	33	7.22
'Woman' years	475	3328	6668	8068	8246	7769	7016	

[a]TMFR is the sum of the age-specific rate from 20 to 49 multiplied by five.

Table 3.4   Percentage of first births occurring within eight months of marriage by wife's age at marriage and marriage cohort: combined set of 16 English parishes

Marriage cohort	Age at marriage						
	15–19	*20–24*	*25–29*	*30–34*	*35–39*	*40–49*	*All ages*
1550–1649							
(%)	15.04	18.27	23.31	20.59	9.26	14.29	19.19
no. of cases	133	405	326	136	54	14	1068
1650–1749							
(%)	12.97	15.88	15.48	10.73	6.60	10.71	14.14
no. of cases	185	724	549	261	106	28	1883
1750–1849							
(%)	32.71	24.78	23.99	21.17	16.79	34.78	24.98
no. of cases	321	908	642	274	131	46	2292

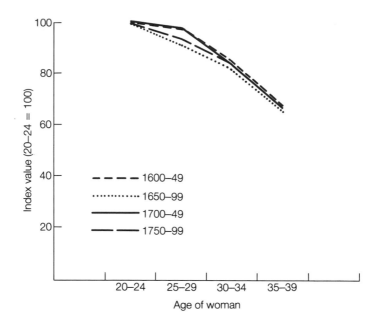

Figure 3.2 Index values of age-specific marital fertility rates: marriage cohorts for 16 English parishes 1600–1799

numbers of marriages upon which the earlier statistics are based. But what remains most significant is that the vast bulk of French data appear to show no such synchronism at *any* period before the middle of the nineteenth century[149]

Sexual relations seem therefore to have commenced in England in anticipation of eventual solemnization. Moreover, while there is little difference between the levels of pregnancy for young and old brides among those marrying in the late sixteenth and early seventeenth centuries, both groups having a one in six or one in seven chance of being pregnant, among the considerably smaller total number of occurrences in France older brides were two or three times more likely to have conceived pre-nuptially. Such a pattern among the French female population is consistent, one might suggest, with the view that marriage in certain cases may have been necessary 'to make good an increasing number of casual lapses' or even, but possibly far less frequently, to force a marriage as a *fait accompli* upon a reluctant family.[150]

149 Ideally, comparisons of the kind undertaken with the data in tables 3.3 and 3.4 should be made with identical sets of parishes and similar groupings of years. I hope to produce a more refined treatment of this matter in a future study, and any arguments based on the above presentation must be regarded as highly tentative.

150 Wrigley, 'Marriage, fertility and population growth', p. 182.

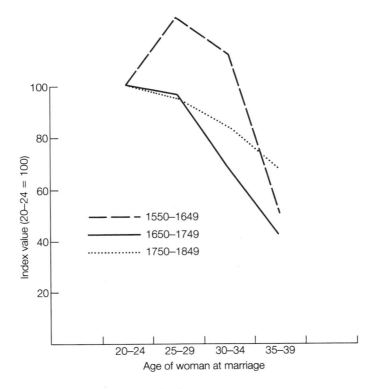

Figure 3.3   Index values of pre-nuptial pregnancy rates by bride's age at marriage: marriage cohorts for 16 English parishes 1550–1849

It would, on the basis of this evidence, be a strained interpretation that saw in these demographic statistics a warrant for claiming the existence in both early modern France and England of a common set of influences emanating from clerical efforts to impose an adherence to marriage rules more effectively administered at the parochial level by the clergy. Given the relative lack of comprehensive French studies for the last half of the sixteenth century, it is obviously dangerous to be too emphatic about these differences. However, taking account of the apparent irrelevance of *Tametsi* in France, the strikingly authoritative role proscribed in law for paternal decisions and reflected in ecclesiastical court business, and the markedly lower levels of both illegitimacy and pre-nuptial pregnancy observable in the few studies so far completed in France's earliest parish registers, it would seem that the English Channel separated two societies whose divergent patterns of behaviour were of long standing.

For a substantial proportion of the English population, from the 16 parishes that have formed the basis of our albeit brief discussion, 'procreative careers' were entered well in advance of the church ceremony. The significance of this fact can be readily appreciated by considering some salient features of the physiology of reproduction. Observations made upon women in a variety of cultural and economic contexts reveal that monthly probabilities of conception range from 15 to 50 per cent among ovulating women who have intercourse regularly – a probability significantly below 100 per cent because conception is possible only during a very brief period (probably two days) in the middle of a woman's cycle. As a consequence the average waiting time to conception is likely to be several months. But once an ovum has been fertilized it has about a 50 per cent chance of survival to the end of the nine months' pregnancy period to yield a live birth. Approximately one-third of fertilized ova are rejected during the first two weeks after conception so that, on average, about two fertilizations are needed to secure a live birth. A typical experience is about four months' waiting time to conception before an intra-uterine death, another four months' conception waiting time before a second conception and, finally, a nine-month full-term pregnancy.[151] It is possible, therefore, that periods of regular sexual relations or cohabitation of up to a year and a half could precede an eventual church marriage on the part of many of those who were pre-nuptially pregnant. The figures from the parish registers suggest that the proportions of sexual unions that began in advance of church solemnization could have been much higher than is suggested by the proportional totals of all women pregnant at that event.

Having taken account of these biological constraints it would doubtless be correct to suggest that even the very low levels of seventeenth-century French pre-nuptial pregnancy overestimate what Dupâquier refers to as 'la vertu de [ses] ancêtres'.[152] None the less, Dupâquier's forebears were less procreatively inclined in advance of the church ceremony formalizing marriage than were their early modern English counterparts.

The 'Autonomy' of Family Systems

One should not automatically conclude that the apparently widespread willingness to initiate the vast majority of unions in seventeenth-century France with a ceremony conducted by a priest in the presence of witnesses (which most likely included parents and kin) stemmed from a successful encounter on the part of the Church with what had been intransigent 'medieval' popular practices. Robin Briggs, in writing of seventeenth-century France, perceptively notes the mistrust displayed by clerics in their contacts with the family, whose networks of internal authority

---

151 The definitive study of these issues is J. Bongaarts and R.G. Potter, *Fertility, biology and behaviour* (London, 1983), especially chapter 2. A convenient and lucid presentation of the issues is to be found in J. Bongaarts, 'Why high birth rates are so low', *Population and Development Review* 1 (1975), pp. 289–96.

152 Dupâquier, *La Population rurale du bassin parisien*, p. 367.

weakened their influence compared with that which they could yield when dealing with society and its rituals at the level of the community.[153] Of course, clerical relations with the individual, where the asymmetry of power was more obviously apparent, could be conducted with higher hopes of success on the Church's part. This preference for working with the individual, as Briggs notes, was one 'that fitted well with the tendency to stress parental authority. The father could be asked to impose rules, mostly of a negative kind.'[154] Recent work on marriage customs and practices within areas of Reformed Germany in the sixteenth century might be interpreted as making very much the same point.[155] Luther's patriarchal view of the family inclined him to advocate the return of total authority over children's marriage to parents.[156] Furthermore, it would frequently appear that the marriage codes introduced in Lutheran principalities had older precedents in late medieval civil law codes. For example, in theory under Augsburg civic law (as in many other towns) parents could disinherit children who flaunted their parents' wishes. In the same city in 1450 the council had decreed that those who cited others before the bishop's court in matrimonial cases and whose pleas were rejected should be exiled and forfeit their citizenship – a direct attempt, so a recent student of these practices suggests, to discourage young persons from bringing cases of disputed marriage promises to court and, by implication, acting outside the sphere of parental authority.[157] In Augsburg the reformed churches effectively handed jurisdiction in matrimonial matters to secular authority which made parental consent a precondition of a valid marriage. Furthermore these authorities, in urban economies that were far from viable, increasingly limited the freedom of those

153 R. Briggs, 'The church and the family in seventeenth-century France', *The Newsletter of the Society for Seventeenth Century French Studies* 4 (1982), pp. 5–13.

154 Ibid., p. 7.

155 See, for instance, L. Roper, '"Going to church and street": weddings in reformation Augsburg', *Past and Present* 106 (1985), pp. 62–101; T.M. Safley, *Let no man put asunder. The control of marriage in the German southwest: a comparative study, 1550–1600* (Kirksville, Mo., 1984); T.M. Safley, 'Marital litigation in the diocese of Cologne', *Sixteenth Century Journal* 12 (1981), pp. 60–77; T.M. Safley, 'To preserve the marital state: The Basler Ehegericht, 1550–1592', *Journal of Family History* 7 (1982), pp. 162–79; T. Robisheaux, 'Peasants and pastors: rural youth control and the reformation in Hohenloe, 1540–1680', *Social History* 6 (1981), pp. 281–300; S. Ozment, *When fathers ruled*; J. Harvey, 'The influence of the reformation on Nuremberg marriage laws, 1520–1535' (unpublished Ph.D. thesis, Ohio State University, 1972).

156 See G. Strauss, *Luther's house of learning: indoctrination of the young in the German reformation* (Baltimore, 1978). Useful remarks on Luther's views are also to be found in B. Gottlieb, 'Getting married in pre-Reformation Europe: the doctrine of clandestine marriage and court cases in fifteenth century Champagne' (unpublished Ph.D. thesis, Columbia University, 1974), pp. 7–24.

157 Roper, 'Going to church and street', pp. 69–70. See too Ozment, *When fathers ruled*, pp. 35–6, and Harvey 'The influence of the reformation on Nuremberg marriage laws', pp. 195–219.

who were precariously placed in the matter of their economic independence and of immigrants to marry without official permission, which was evidently difficult to obtain.[158] Surviving proceedings from marriage courts reveal active parental involvement in bringing about the dissolution of their children's marriages entered without approval.[159] Similar patterns are revealed in rural areas of Germany in the later sixteenth century, where rapid population growth appears to have threatened the position of peasant households, whose head was forced to balance the needs of his family members against limited and shrinking resources.[160] Far from viewing the reformers' doctrines as an integrated body of thought which they could either accept or reject, the peasant patriarchs are presented in this recent writing as adopting only those ideas about marriage and paternal authority which were culturally deeply imbedded, and which in the specific economic circumstances were found to be particularly helpful as they manoeuvred to protect their family's resources.

One must, none the less, exercise caution in evaluating these ideas, for it is not always clear which status groups are being observed in, for

158 Roper, 'Going to church and street', pp. 85–7. It might be thought that, in handing marriage jurisdiction over to secular authority, parental influences would thereby be weakened. That is indeed a possible interpretation of developments, but the apparent effectiveness of civic policy would depend greatly on assistance from the older in imposing restrictions on younger generations. It is interesting to consider the long-standing tendency of German society to operate restrictions upon marriage by the use of local ordinances. A common feature of these restrictive laws was regulations requiring a couple to produce evidence of having sufficient wealth or property, a secure income, or assured stable employment opportunities in order to allay doubts about their ability to support their children. These issues are discussed in J. Knodel, 'Law, marriage and illegitimacy in nineteenth century Germany', *Population Studies* 20 (1967), pp. 279–94, and chapter 4 ('Marriage and remarriage') of his forthcoming book on the demography of German villages in the eighteenth and nineteenth centuries.

159 Roper, 'Going to church and street', where, according to the admittedly limited information in 16 cases brought before the marriage court of Augsburg between 1537 and 1546, marriages (or more precisely promises to marry) were dissolved because the parties had failed to gain parental approval. These would in the context of French ecclesiastical courts, which have been scrutinized by Donahue (see later) be *de futuro* cases which, he argues, reflect the force of parental involvement and disapproval of marriages negotiated without the latter's consent. See too, the striking evidence of overt parental challenges to marriage in the Zurich courts between 1525 and 1531 in W. Kohler, *Zurcher Ehegericht und Geufer Konsistorium, I. Das Zurcher Ehegericht une seine Auswirkung in der deutschen Schweiz zur Zeit Zwinglis* (Leipzig, 1932), pp. 76–7. Saffley notes in the Basel courts after 1570 a great increase in *ex officio* activity, emphasizing publicity rather than consent, and again, consistent with Donahue's general argument, much attention devoted to the legal aspects of marriage agreements: see his 'To preserve the marital state', pp. 168–77.

160 Robisheaux, 'Peasants and pastors', pp. 281–300, where in contested engagements or promises to marry (the principal issues brought before the courts of Hohenlohe-Langenburg between 1550 and 1679) parents constituted the most important group contesting (50 per cent) such arrangements, and pastors and officials accounted for a further 23 per cent. The young adults of marriageable ages were themselves of limited significance in initiating these procedures.

instance, the disputed marriages among the Church court proceedings (a worrying problem in Donahue's comparison of English and French case studies, where no attempt was made to see if approximately similar social and economic status groups were involved in both contexts).[161] Furthermore, in the French case to which we have drawn attention the insistence on the primacy of parental consent to children's marriages came from those echelons who were represented by the delegates of the King of France at the Council of Trent. The property interests of such groups had always led to a running conflict between the desire of the crown and the lawyers to dissolve clandestine or unauthorized unions and Catholic doctrine which held that the sacrament of marriage required only the solemn agreement of two individuals before God.[162]

Conclusion

If the emphasis in this chapter has been on a need to treat these problems comparatively rather than by adopting an insular or inward-looking preoccupation with one particular country, there has also been a stress upon the value to be derived from viewing the issues over the *longue durée*. Artificially bounded, chronological compartmentalizations, undertaken without reference to what Peter Laslett terms 'social-structural time', often fail to achieve this.[163] In the specifically English context within which we began this essay it might be suggested that part of the confusion that has possibly furthered the creation of a somewhat exaggerated claim for the growth in conformity to ecclesiastical ideals of the marriage 'event' stems from the fact that, by the second half of the sixteenth century, the English historian's principal sources become much more specifically concerned with recordings of solemnized marriages. By contrast, for those who work on these issues in earlier periods, whether concerned with customary, common or ecclesiastical laws and their courts, the evidence appears to be much more informative on the initial phase of this process, namely the customary ceremony of the espousal. There is an obvious danger that our partiality for asserting an evolution in matrimonial behaviour from 'process to event' may have something to do with the changing evidential bases for our research over time. It may be suggested

161 For a valuable summary of the views bearing upon the status attributes of parties in matrimonial suits in later medieval and early modern England, see Ingram, 'Spousals litigation', pp. 44–5. A study, heavily used by Donahue in his analysis of the later-fifteenth-century episcopal courts of the diocese of Troyes and Châlons-sur-Marne in southern Champagne, has argued that persons appearing in those courts were 'neither wealthy nor privileged': B. Gottlieb, 'The meaning of clandestine marriage', in R. Wheaton and T. Hareven (eds), *Family and sexuality in French history* (Philadelphia, 1980), p. 55.

162 For instance Diefendorf, *Paris city councillors*, and although its subtitle 'the politics of patrimony' is suggestive, it is concerned very largely with the city's governing elite.

163 P. Laslett, 'Social structural time' (unpublished typescript, ESRC Cambridge Group Library, 1979).

that a similar argument could be applied to the style of research in other European contexts.

None the less at a wider European level it cannot be too greatly emphasized that, in insisting on a public ceremony before witnesses, post-Tridentine ideas may well have overthrown the practice of non-sacramental union but did not thereby necessarily weaken kinship solidarities deeply rooted in secular customs and institutions. For such an argument, exemplified in particular in John Bossy's writing, ignores the fact that collective values, especially if embodied in an entrenched patriarchal authority sustained by other secular institutions, could just as easily attach themselves to the ceremony of solemnization before a priest in church. There may have been strains of these developments in happenings in England when, as an accumulating quantity of case studies appear to suggest, at the turn of the seventeenth century prodigious efforts were made to police the courtship and marriage practices of village populations whose economies were sorely stretched. However, there were, it would seem, important differences between the English population and certain of her continental neighbours that need to be given greater exposure and fuller attention. In recent French and German studies we begin to observe an emphasis upon an unholy alliance of Church and parental authority as that which was being imposed upon younger generations to induce a degree of uniformity to certain patriarchal norms.[164] In the English context, so startlingly presented in the seventeenth-century sources of Terling, it was more obviously a conflict between groups and strata, the village elite – the churchwardens and in certain contexts the poor law authorities – and the 'meaner sort'.[165]

---

164 There are perhaps other signs appearing in recent literature indicative of a reaction against the reification of ideas emanating from the 'Great Tradition' which subsequently proceed to penetrate the 'Little Tradition', the latter conventionally characterized as fundamentally autonomous and incapable of endogenous response. By far the most intellectually sustained attempt to question this approach to popular culture is that of D. Sabean, *Power in the blood: popular culture and village discourse in early modern Germany* (Cambridge, 1984), especially pp. 1–36. For an analysis of popular marriage ritual in early modern France which does not see it as an element in rural culture that acts as a filter for impulses from outside, see Burgière, 'Le rituel du mariage'. He writes wisely that 'le rituel religieux et le rituel populaire ne sont radicalement distincts ni dans leur histoire ni dans leur fonction' (p. 638) and that 'le rituel religieux qui s'est constitué par adaptations et rénouvellements successifs, a integré un grand nombre de ces rites populaires' (p. 638) and as such 'les deux pratiques ne sont ni totalement concurrentes ni totalement separées' (p. 648).

165 I have suggested elsewhere that the remarkable homeostasis exhibited by early modern French populations at all levels from village, through region to nation, in which fertility, very largely through marriage age and incidence until the later eighteenth century, reacted almost instantaneously to mortality shifts to ensure basically stationary demographic conditions, owed much to parental controls; whereas the sluggish, indeed at times perverse relationships between these two variables in early modern England suggest more flexible, less carefully synchronized 'community' control systems. See R.M. Smith, 'Pre-industrial European

Community constraints were, however, less direct and less effectively imposed upon a highly differentiated population within which geographical mobility and marital exogamy among adolescents and young adults were of long standing.[166]

As Wrigley has suggested when he wrote about eighteenth-century contrasts between England and France, and as we have tentatively suggested also seems to have existed in the two preceding centuries, it is tempting to see in France a 'peasant' variety of a marriage system within which demographic growth came quickly to place pressure on the viability of agricultural holdings and the populations that depended upon them.[167] English marriage with (relatively speaking) greater young adult freedom, not so strictly administered by the dictates of parents and kin, is then perceived as in tune with a 'wage' economy where more varied opportunities for earning power had reduced access to land or property as 'the decisive structural moment' in determining eligibility to marry. But while there is a great deal to recommend this view it would, given both the temporal depth and the contrasts in legal instruments and codes between, for instance, common and Roman law traditions underpinning these differences, be too overtly economically reductionist a position, with kinship patterns and certain of their non-material institutional correlates presented as induced rather than determining agencies. There would seem to be insufficient room in this interpretation for the kinship system's relative autonomy in its relationship with exogenous influences.

Of course, the persistent tendency for a sizeable component of the English population not to regard marriage as an event that was inaugurated by the formal approval of a parish priest, even if it cannot be directly explained by England's failure to be 'cleansed' by the impact of *Tametsi*, would most certainly require, in a fuller treatment of these issues, a more careful assessment of proletarian marriage practices that, as the eighteenth century advanced, quite clearly loomed larger in our evidence as an increasing proportion of the population fell into or reproduced themselves in that category.[168] But once again any simple resort to an argument that

---

demographic regimes', in S. Feld and R. Lesthaeghe (eds), *Population and societal outlook/ Population et prospective* (Brussels, 1985), pp. 41–3. An important paper that portrays demographic homeostasis generated by the 'nuptiality safety valve' maintained and administered by parental control in pre-industrial western Europe is R. Lesthaeghe, 'On the social control of human reproduction', *Population and Development Review*, 6 (1980), p. 533.

166 See the essays in Smith, *Land, kinship and life-cycle*, and 'Hypothèses sur la nuptialité en Angleterre aux XIIIe–XIVe siècles, *Annales, économies, sociétés, civilisations* (1983), pp. 107–36, and the polemical but fundamentally sound evaluation of social behaviour, if not its consequences, in Alan Macfarlane, *The origins of English individualism; the family, property and social transition* (Oxford, 1978), especially chapter 6.

167 Wrigley, 'Marriage, fertility and population growth', p. 183.

168 This is certainly the thesis in J.R. Gillis, 'Peasant, plebian and proletarian marriage in Britain, 1600–1900' in D. Levine (ed.), *Proletarianization and family history* (London, 1984), pp. 129–57 and reiterated in D. Levine, 'Industrialisation and the proletarian family in England', *Past and Present* 107 (1985), p. 180 and 184–5.

depended upon the relations of production as a means of explaining these patterns would need to take note of the fact that both the age patterns of illegitimacy and the timing of conceptions with respect to formalized marriages, when or if they came about among the pre-nuptially pregnant, showed variations among wage labourers whether agricultural or industrial and their brides in Germany, France and England which owed much to traditions that ran deep in their respective social structures.[169]

169 For instance, in France in the nineteenth century illegitimacy was closely and positively correlated with the urban population of certain *départements*, especially those with urban settlements of over 40,000 persons; see E. van de Walle, 'Illegitimacy in France during the nineteenth century', in Laslett et al., *Bastardy*, pp. 264–77. Similarly, the rural illegitimacy rates for nineteenth-century Bavaria and Prussia were considerably lower than for Munich and Berlin, respectively; see J. Knodel and S. Hochstadt, 'Urban and rural illegitimacy in Imperial Germany', in Laslett et al., *Bastardy*, pp. 287–8. In England in the nineteenth century and at earlier times there was no noticeable enhancement of illegitimacy rates in the larger urban conurbations. For instance, among the 44 English registration counties London was for the years 1870–72, 1880–2, 1890–2 and 1900–02 ranked with regard to its illegitimacy rate 41st, 41st, 38th and 38th respectively. Likewise, the more highly urbanized West Riding of Yorkshire was consistently below the more rural counties of the North and East Ridings. What is more, the predominantly agricultural county of Norfolk displayed the highest illegitimacy rate of all English counties in 1900–02; see Laslett, 'Introduction', in Laslett et al., *Bastardy*, p. 44. These nineteenth-century patterns, with no doubt some discrepancies, may have been of great age, for in the late sixteenth and early seventeenth centuries a study of eight London parishes has shown them to have had illegitimacy ratios much lower than those derived from a national sample of parishes for the same date; see R.A.P. Finlay, *Population and metropolis: the demography of London 1580–1650* (Cambridge, 1981), p. 149. Pre-nuptial pregnancy too was not in England, unlike in France, greatly increased within urban environments. In fact in a sample of 16 English parishes from 1550 to 1849 women in urban parishes were considerably less likely to have been pregnant at marriage than their rural contemporaries: see Wilson, 'Marital fertility in pre-industrial England', p. 46. In France the opposite appears to have applied consistently; see for instance, Bardet, *Rouen aux XVIIe et XVIIIe siècles*, pp. 324–5 and Lottin, *Lille, citadelle de la contre-réforme?*, p. 218. In Germany, unlike in England, there appears to have been no positive relationship between illegitimacy ratios and pre-nuptial pregnancy rates across space. Furthermore German trends in illegitimacy, pre-nuptial pregnancy and nuptiality in the eighteenth and nineteenth century indicate that if there was any association it was generally in the opposite direction than that found in England. Indeed statutory restrictions on marriage were imposed in early-nineteenth-century Germany and are believed to have increased the incidence of extramarital fertility, markedly. Furthermore, age patterns of illegitimacy, unlike those for England, indicate that it increased considerably with the age of the woman. Related to the latter feature were the facts that in the eighteenth and nineteenth centuries pre-nuptial pregnancy was not, as in England, most common among young brides, and that this category of pregnancy grew most among brides who had conceived six to eight months prior to the solemnization of their marriage. Such a pattern suggests that marriage was entered into somewhat reluctantly or that in the conditions of restrictions upon marriage a pre-nuptial pregnancy served to advance or force a marriage upon reluctant families or local authorities. A first-rate analysis of these issues is to be found in chapter 5, 'Illegitimacy, bridal pregnancy and pre-nuptial births' in J. Knodel's forthcoming book on the demographic history of German villages in the eighteenth and nineteenth centuries. Work on illegitimacy and pre-nuptial pregnancy in the community of Rothiemay in Banffshire, where illegitimacy was at the highest levels for any region in the British Isles, suggests a set of relationships between illegitimacy, pre-nuptial pregnancy and marriage that was not at all characteristic of England at the same date. I am grateful to Andrew Blaikie for allowing me

Postscript

This chapter was written before the recent publication of an important and very stimulating article by Martin Ingram.[170] Ingram presents an argument that differs from my own in so far as he is inclined to uphold the view of those who would regard the Church in the period from the twelfth to the seventeenth century as having succeeded in ensuring that 'by 1640 the need for marriage in church [seemed] to have been widely accepted at all levels'; he notes that 'it may be fairly said that the wedding service of the Church of England had been absorbed as part of popular culture'.[171] Such a view might be regarded as underestimating the extent of later-seventeenth-century nonconformity in the formalization of matrimony (see note 145 in this chapter). More significantly, I believe, this view is reluctant to confront difficulties that stem from a willingness to give a privileged position to the solemnized marriage event, which certainly does not rest well with the evidence that can be extracted, albeit painfully, from the post-1640 parish registers. It also implicitly accepts the view of marriage as evolving out of a more unstable medieval form. However, Ingram's paper is especially convincing in suggesting that it would seem more realistic to assume that the growing concern for the 'support costs' associated with illegitimacy and marriages that may have been hastened by the pregnant condition of the bride, especially in communities suffering from severe economic difficulties in the late sixteenth and early seventeenth centuries, brought forth a burst of activity on the part of elite groups against the poorer strata of society that reflected a growth in '*parochial* rather than parental control'.[172] Such a response, Ingram argues, was not in any fundamental sense inspired by religious reform, although he does not comment on the ultimate demographic implications of this remark; this is perhaps understandable given his principal concern with the popular culture of sex and marriage in early modern England. He does, however, cast some timely doubt on the scale of the so-called reform of popular culture that certain authorities, such as Muchembled, who writes from the perspective of sixteenth-century France, postulate as resulting in a notable sexual repression amounting in effect to a major cultural revolution. I agree wholeheartedly with Ingram when he writes that Muchembled's 'picture will not do for England'.[173]

---

to read chapter 4, 'Unmarried motherhood in demographic perspective', of his forthcoming University of London Ph.D. thesis on 'Illegitimacy in nineteenth-century northeast Scotland'.

170 M. Ingram, 'The reform of popular culture? Sex and marriage in early modern England', in B. Reay (ed.), *Popular culture in seventeenth-century England* (London, 1985), pp. 129–65.

171 Ibid., p. 143.

172 Ibid., p. 172.

173 Ibid., p. 159.

4

Illegitimacy and the European Marriage Pattern: Comparative Evidence from the Alpine Area

Pier Paolo Viazzo

Late marriage and high rates of celibacy have long been regarded as resulting in high levels of illegitimacy. It would therefore seem reasonable to expect illegitimacy to be associated with what Hajnal has termed the European marriage pattern.[1] The 'chastity of the Irish', however, provides a classic warning against easy generalizations;[2] and perhaps the most disconcerting finding to emerge from Peter Laslett's study of English illegitimacy is 'the direct contradiction of the natural expectation that when marriage is late, illegitimacy will be high'.[3] In pre-industrial England, age at marriage was in fact negatively correlated with illegitimacy, and the relationship between illegitimacy levels and celibacy rates was also problematic.[4]

The Irish and English examples demonstrate that a good deal of caution is required before one draws generalized explanations of illegitimacy trends. But it is remarkable that the 'sexual deprivation' theory, though unlikely to be universally applicable, appears to be supported by research conducted in a number of Alpine districts, where the European marriage pattern is at its most pronounced.

The view that mountain areas produced a pronounced tendency towards 'preventive checks' goes back to Malthus himself. In his *Summary View of the Principle of Population*, a pamphlet he published in 1830, Malthus argued that since 'there is no land so little capable of provid-

---

1 J. Hajnal, 'European marriage patterns in perspective', in D.V. Glass and D.E.C. Eversley (eds), *Population in history: essays in historical demography* (London, 1965), pp. 101–43.

2 K.H. Connell, 'Illegitimacy before the famine', in *Irish peasant society: four historical essays* (Oxford, 1968), pp. 51–86; S.J. Connolly, 'Illegitimacy and pre-nuptial pregnancy in Ireland before 1864: the evidence of some Catholic parish registers,' *Irish Economic and Social History* 4 (1979), pp. 5–23.

3 P. Laslett, *Family life and illicit love in earlier generations* (Cambridge, 1977), p. 106.

4 P. Laslett, 'Introduction: comparing illegitimacy over time and between cultures', in P. Laslett, K. Oosterveen and R.M. Smith (eds), *Bastardy and its comparative history* (London, 1980), pp. 20–4.

ing for an increasing population as mountainous pastures', in upland regions 'the necessity of the preventive check should be more strongly forced on the attention of the inhabitants, and should, in consequence, prevail to a greater degree'.[5] Malthus's reflections were prompted by data from the Alpine parish of Leyzin, in Switzerland. Our knowledge of the demography of the Alpine *ancien régime* has not progressed very far since Malthus's days. As Guichonnet acknowledged in 1975, and Bergier has repeated in 1980, the historical demography of the Alps is still in its infancy.[6] Nevertheless, the evidence we possess indicates that in the Alps a high frequency of permanent celibacy and a late marriage age were probably the norm.[7]

The existence of a link between this 'Alpine' marriage pattern and high levels of illegitimacy has been explicitly asserted by Shorter, who has recently stated that in the 'homogeneous region' comprising Southern Bavaria, Austria and German Switzerland 'marriage had always been late, high proportions of the population had always remained single, and illegitimacy had always been substantial compared with other parts of Europe.'[8] Much the same conclusion emerges from Mitterauer's major historical study of illegitimacy in rural Austria.[9] Weinberg, to quote an example from Alpine ethnography, also has no doubt that the high frequency of children conceived (and sometimes born) out of wedlock in the French-speaking Swiss village of Bruson is a by-product of late marriage.[10]

At first glance the connection between late marriage and high levels of illegitimacy in Alpine central Europe seems to be beyond dispute. On closer inspection, however, it becomes clear that the evidence from the area mentioned by Shorter – and from the very literature he cites – is rather conflicting. In nineteenth-century Tyrol and Vorarlberg, for instance, Mitterauer is forced to admit that illegitimacy was low.[11] Yet in these two regions the marriage pattern was the same as in the other

5 T.R. Malthus, *A summary view of the principle of population*, ed. A. Flew (Harmondsworth, 1970; 1st edn 1830), pp. 261–2.

6 P. Guichonnet, 'Le développement démographique et économique des régions alpines', in P. Guichonnet et al., *Le Alpi e l'Europa* vol. 2 (Bari, 1975), p. 143; J.-F. Bergier, 'Le cycle médiéval,' in P. Guichonnet, (ed.), *Histoire et civilisations des Alpes* vol. 1 (Toulouse/Lausanne, 1980), p. 166.

7 J. Friedl and W.S. Ellis, 'Celibacy, late marriage and potential mates in a Swiss isolate', in B. Kaplan (ed.), *Anthropological studies of human fertility* (Detroit, 1976); M. Livi Bacci, *A history of Italian fertility during the last two centuries* (Princeton, 1977), p. 153; P. Schmidtbauer, 'Daten zur historischen Demographie und Familienstruktur' (unpublished manuscript, 1977).

8 E. Shorter, 'Bastardy in South Germany: a comment', *Journal of Interdisciplinary History* 8 (1978), p. 460.

9 M. Mitterauer, 'Familienformen und Illegitimität in ländlichen Gebieten Oesterreichs', *Archiv für Sozialgeschichte* 19 (1979), pp. 179–81.

10 D. Weinberg, *Peasant wisdom: cultural adaptation in a Swiss village* (Berkeley, 1975), p. 116.

11 Mitterauer, 'Familienformen un Illegitimität', pp. 123–4.

Austrian mountain areas, and the much discussed *Ehekonsens* or 'marriage permit' had been required since 1820.[12] Moreover, Friedl and Ellis's work on the Lötchental (one of the studies quoted by Shorter) actually suggests that late marriage and a high rate of permanent celibacy did not result in high illegitimacy.[13]

As for Weinberg's statement, it should be observed that no quantitative data are provided to substantiate her contention; nor does she make any attempt to determine whether a correlation between illegitimacy and marriage age really existed in Bruson. Like most anthropological studies of Alpine communities published before 1980, Weinberg's work deals with illegitimacy only tangentially and is mainly concerned with present and 'traditional' attitudes towards unwed mothers and their children.[14] These anthropological reports are not without interest, but the underlying approach is highly impressionistic. As Macfarlane has observed, the failure of anthropologists to quantify bastardy levels has limited their contribution to the problems surrounding the topic of illegitimacy.[15]

In the last few years, greater familiarity with historical demography acquired by several anthropologists, coupled with a growing tendency to supplement conventional fieldwork by serious archival research, has considerably changed this state of affairs. An article by Khera on illegitimacy and the mode of land inheritance among Austrian peasants is especially worthy of note.[16] Besides being one of the first anthropological studies specifically devoted to illegitimacy, this paper is also unusual because of the wealth of quantitative data it provides. Furthermore, it is probably the first attempt to test, with respect to illegitimacy, Goody's intimation that inheritance should be treated as an independent variable crucially affecting a wide range of social and demographic phenomena.[17]

In order to test Goody's prediction that 'alternative social arrangements (e.g. greater or lesser migration, age of marriage, rates of illegitimacy) will be linked to differing modes of transmission',[18] Khera compares two Austrian villages taken as representative of two regions where contrasting inheritance systems were customary: St Georgen, in

12 M. Mitterauer and R. Sieder, *The European family* (Oxford, 1982), p. 123.

13 Friedl and Ellis, 'Celibacy, late marriage and potential mates', pp. 27–34.

14 Cf. e.g. J.J. Honigmann, 'Survival of a cultural focus', in W.H. Goodenough (ed.), *Explorations in cultural anthropology* (New York, 1964), p. 283; C. Macherel, 'La traversée du champ matrimonial: un exemple alpin', *Études rurales* 73 (1979), p. 12; P. Sibilla, *Una comunità walser delle Alpi* (Florence, 1980), pp. 105–6.

15 A. Macfarlane, 'Illegitimacy and illegitimates in English history', in Laslett et al., *Bastardy*, p. 72.

16 S. Khera, 'Illegitimacy and mode of land inheritance among Austrian peasants', *Ethnology* 20 (1981), pp. 307–23.

17 J. Goody, *Production and reproduction* (Cambridge, 1976).

18 J. Goody, 'Introduction' in J. Goody, J. Thirsk and E. P. Thompson (eds), *Family and inheritance* (Cambridge, 1976), p. 1.

mountainous Upper Austria, where undivided land inheritance was practised, and Tadten, in the flat Burgenland, one of the very few Austrian regions characterized by partibility. Her analysis of parish records spanning the period between the early nineteenth century and the Second World War convincingly shows that a broad association existed between inheritance systems, marriage patterns and levels of illegitimacy. Throughout the period under examination marriage ages for both men and women were much higher in St Georgen than in Tadten, and so were the proportions of illegitimate births.

Khera is less convincing, however, when she argues that the dramatic increase in illegitimacy recorded in both villages is correlated with rising age at marriage. In Tadten the rise in the illegitimacy ratio (from 2.1 per cent in the 1830s to 17.0 per cent in the 1930s) is hardly paralleled by any significant rise in marriage age. And even in St Georgen, where the frequency of illegitimate births increased from 17.6 per cent in the 1820s to 40.6 per cent a century later, the correlation is far from being perfect. Khera's single-cause model appears to be far too simple to account for variations in the absolute intensity of illegitimacy over time.

It should also be added that the dependence of marriage patterns on inheritance systems is not entirely unproblematic. It is particularly relevant to note that anthropological research carried out in the Alps has suggested that in mountain areas, where land scarcity is especially acute and environmental pressures are strongest, a marriage pattern is shaped more effectively by environmental constraints than by inheritance systems.[19] This hypothesis has been recently corroborated by Netting's detailed study of Törbel, a village in the Swiss Oberwallis. In Törbel the inheritance system has been for centuries one of strict partibility, yet marriage ages have always been very high: in the period 1700–1949 they hovered between 27 and 29 years for women and between 30 and 33 years for men. Illegitimacy rates, however, were very low.[20]

The contradictory indications offered by Khera's and Netting's studies suggest that the connection between age at marriage and illegitimacy is still open and that other studies are needed before we may hope to understand the strength of the link. On the other hand, it is necessary to do more than merely accumulate empirical evidence. The arguments put forward in the works discussed or referred to above are often inconclusive, or difficult to judge and compare, because of technical shortcomings or methodological inconsistencies. For example, most writers tend simply to rely on such an inferior measure as the

19 J.W. Cole and E.R. Wolf, *The hidden frontier: ecology and ethnicity in an Alpine valley* (New York, 1974); Friedl and Ellis, 'Celibacy, late marriage and potential mates'.
20 R.M. Netting, *Balancing on an alp: ecological change and continuity in a Swiss mountain community* (Cambridge, 1981), pp. 133–8.

illegitimacy ratio. This measure is easy to calculate, but is inadequate to answer several central questions and may even produce a seriously distorted picture. It is also common to compute aggregate indices referring to the whole population of a village or parish. As a consequence, differences between subgroups are frequently overlooked. If we want to go beyond the present impasse, we must therefore face squarely a number of technical and methodological problems. Further, we must rethink some of the assumptions that guide, and constrain, our theoretical efforts. In this chapter I intend first to present some new evidence on illegitimacy from Alagna, a German-speaking village in the Italian Western Alps.[21] I shall then consider some of the general issues raised in this introductory section in the light of my own research.

I

Located at the top of the Sesia Valley, Alagna is one of the German-speaking communities (usually designated by the term *Walser*) which occupy the high valleys at the foot of the southern face of Monte Rosa. The foundation of these settlements dates back to the second half of the thirteenth century, when these areas were colonized under manorial auspices by Germanic peoples coming from the upper Rhône Valley, the Oberwallis, which is today part of the Swiss canton Wallis/Valais. It must be recognized, however, that the ethnic composition of present-day Alagna is no longer homogeneous. The descendants of the original settlers have been joined by a large number of Italians; German is now a dying language, spoken only by some 80 elderly people out of a population of about 450 inhabitants.

Geographically, Alagna is not far (though, of course, situated on the other side of the mountains) from Törbel, the village studied by Netting, which lies in the homeland of the Walser. As we have observed, illegitimacy in Törbel was, and remains, quite rare. During the nineteenth century the proportion of illegitimate births ranged from 1.0 to 1.5 per cent. In the course of our century it has somewhat increased, but without exceeding a fairly modest 3.3 per cent.[22] Alagna offers a very different picture. In the last three or four decades the incidence of illegitimacy has been negligible, but even a limited degree of acquaintance with the village is sufficient to realize that before the Second World War the number and proportion of illegitimate births must have been extremely high.

Alagna provides further evidence that the relationship between illegitimacy and the rules that govern the transmission of property is less

21 My field work took place between April 1979 and September 1981. It was supported by grants from the Italian National Research Council, the Folklore Fund of University College London, and the Central Research Fund of the University of London.
22 Netting, *Balancing on an alp*, p. 138.

rigid than is implied by Khera's model. Older villagers agree that Alagna's traditional system of inheritance was one of complete partibility, each heir being entitled to an equal share of the estate regardless of sex and age. It was, in fact, similar to Oberwallis;[23] and indeed there is evidence suggesting that it was brought along by the Walser colonists from their homeland. Nevertheless, nuptiality apparently conformed, as in Törbel, to the expected 'Alpine' pattern. Partible inheritance should predictably result in high nuptiality,[24] but Alagnese informants assert that in the past many people – and in particular many women – failed to get married. The *muomi, the* maiden aunt, emerges as a prominent character in many old villagers' recollections of their family life.

Data for the period between the two world wars are available and confirm that in those years marriage was late and permanent celibacy very common. But it is also clear that in subsequent decades there has been substantial change. A comparison between my own census, taken in 1980, and a *status animarum* compiled by the parish priest in 1935, shows that Alagna accords with Hajnal's suggestion that in much of north-western Europe the rate of celibacy has been falling since the last war.[25] In 1980 the proportion of unmarried women over 60 years of age was still fairly high; 24.6 per cent compared with 30.4 per cent in 1935. The ratio was, however, quite low among women aged between 30 and 59. In 1980 only six women out of 73 belonging to this age group were spinsters (8.2 per cent), while in 1935 spinsters accounted for over one in three of the relevant age group (36 out of 107, or 33.6 per cent). The proportion of bachelors over 30 years of age was also very high in 1935: 24.1 per cent compared with 13.6 per cent in 1980. Age at married too has declined, though less markedly than the rate of celibacy. In the period between 1921 and 1950 the mean age at first marriage was 29.7 years for men and 26.4 for women. In the following three decades, from 1951 to 1980, it dropped respectively to 28.6 and 24.9 years.

It would appear that variation in nuptiality is the most likely factor in the decline of illegitimacy. It is worth noting that a no less impressive change has occurred in the sex ratio. The highly unbalanced sex ratio of 1935, when women outnumbered men in the ratio of 132 to 100 (total population 499), was replaced by one that was very balanced (or even with slightly higher numbers of men than women). In 1980 the population of Alagna consisted of 209 women and 219 men, which results in a ratio of 95 to 100.

23 J. Friedl, *Kippel: a changing village in the Alps* (New York, 1974), pp. 61–2; Netting, *Balancing on an alp*, pp. 172–3.

24 L.K. Berkner and F.F. Mendels, 'Inheritance systems, family structure, and demographic patterns in Western Europe, 1700–1900', in C. Tilly (ed.), *Historical studies of changing fertility* (Princeton, NJ, 1978), p. 213.

25 Hajnal, 'European marriage patterns', p. 104.

This alteration in the sex ratio is a change of great significance. It is not simply one of the factors behind the increase in nuptiality; it also indicates that the permanent male emigration so clearly reflected in the 1935 sex ratio is a thing of the past. As I have shown elsewhere, a steady flow of permanent emigration from Alagna can be detected as early as the sixteenth century.[26] Even more importantly, permanent emigration was only one facet of the rather complex pattern of movement in Alagna. A crucial feature of the social and economic life of the village was represented for over 350 years – from the late sixteenth century to the 1930s – by a massive seasonal emigration of men. Employed as skilled builders, most local men left the village towards the end of February and returned in late November or early December. What is more, Alagna was characterized not only by emigration but also by immigration. From the first decades of the eighteenth century onwards, Alagna witnessed a substantial flow of immigration caused by the growth of mining activities promoted by the government of the Piedmontese state, to which Alagna had been annexed in 1707. At first, many immigrant miners came from Saxony, Tyrol and other mining districts of central Europe. After 1750, however, most miners came from Piedmont and other Italian regions – a factor that greatly contributed to the shaping and acceleration of the process of ethnic change experienced by this Walser colony.

In areas affected by male emigration, be it the south of Italy[27] or central and east Africa,[28] it is apparently common for women who have to suffer the prolonged absence of husbands and fiancés to engage in irregular sexual relations. Thus the possibility cannot be ruled out that in Alagna illegitimacy may have been influenced by emigration. A further intriguing line of inquiry is suggested by the circumstance that until the Second World War immigrants of first or second generation, whether they worked as miners or labourers, were virtually the only men who remained in the village during the summer and, therefore, the obvious candidates to trigger sexual misbehaviour.

But there is still another factor which can be presumed to have played a role. In Alagna it was customary for women, and particularly for young unmarried women, to spend the summer alone in the high-altitude pastures known as 'alps'. Like her better-known Scandinavian

---

26 P.P. Viazzo, 'Ethnic change in a Walser community in the Italian Alps' (unpublished Ph.D. thesis, University College London, 1983); cf. P.P. Viazzo and M. Bodo, 'Emigrazione e immigrazione ad Alagna, 1618–1848', *Wir Walser: Halbjahresschrift für Walsertum* 18 (1980), pp. 9–15.

27 C. Levi, *Cristo si a fermato a Eboli*, 7th edn (Turin, 1981; 1st edn 1945), pp. 87–91; F. Piselli, *Parentela ed emigrazione: mutamenti e continuità in una comunità calabrese* (Turin, 1981), pp. 75–129.

28 R. Firth, *Elements of social organization*, 3rd edn (London, 1971), pp. 99–101.

and Scottish counterparts,[29] the Alagnese dairymaid enjoyed a privacy that can be plausibly related to illegitimacy. This is in many ways an attractive hypothesis, supported by comparative evidence from various parts of the Alpine crescent. In Styria and other neighbouring Austrian regions, where the same form of alp management was customary[30] and there were often high levels of illegitimacy,[31] the term for a baby conceived out of wedlock is the suggestive 'child of the alp'.[32] Conversely, in areas where a totally different system of *Alpwirtschaft* obtained – such as Tyrol or the Walliser village of Törbel – illegitimacy rates are rather lower.[33] Thus this custom may help explain illegitimacy in Alagna.

All three hypotheses that seek to explain shifts in bastardy levels consider illegitimacy a normal or 'endemic' feature of Alagna's traditional past. Its decline is seen as a concomitant of one of the major transformations of the last decades: the waning of agro-pastoral activities, the end of emigration, and the changes occurring in the marriage pattern. The first finding to emerge from an analysis of the parish records is, however, that in Alagna the history of illegitimacy was marked by quantitative discontinuity. The data contained in the birth registers show that in the 170 years from the late seventeenth century to the middle of the nineteenth century the proportion of illegitimate births had been low or very low. As figure 4.1 demonstrates, it was only in the 1850s that illegitimacy rocketed, to remain a pervasive phenomenon for nearly a century.

Since it is certain that the system of alp management remained basically the same from at least the seventeenth century until the Second World War, the importance of what we might call the '*Alpwirtschaft* theory' is weakened. To be sure, data on the seasonal distribution of births show that illegitimate conceptions were actually more frequent in the alp season than in the rest of the year.[34] This indicates that residential arrangements implied by the Alagnese agro-pastoral system may have been a contributory factor. The continuity through time of the pattern of seasonal distribution of illegitimate births is indeed considerable, and if future research should confirm that relative levels

29 O. Löfgren, 'Family and household among Scandinavian peasants: an exploratory essay', *Ethnologia Scandinavica* 2 (1974), p. 27; C. Smout, 'Aspects of sexual behaviour in nineteenth-century Scotland', in Laslett et al., *Bastardy*, p. 211.

30 J. Frödin, *Zentraleuropas Alpwirtschaft* vol. 2 (Oslo, 1941), pp. 441–50; cf. L. von Welden, *Der Monte-Rosa: eine topographische und naturhistorische Skizze* (Vienna, 1824), p. 81.

31 Mitterauer, 'Familienformen und Illegitimität'.

32 F.G. Bailey, 'The management of reputations and the process of change', in F.G. Bailey (ed.), *Gifts and poison* (Oxford, 1971), p. 300; cf. Honigmann, 'Survival'.

33 Frödin, *Zentraleuropas Alpwirtschaft*, pp. 442–3; Netting, *Balancing on an alp*, p. 64.

34 P.P. Viazzo, 'Tra antropologia e demografia storica: illegittimità, struttura sociale e mutamento etnico in un villaggio delle Alpi italiane', *L'Uomo* 8 (1984), pp. 163–96.

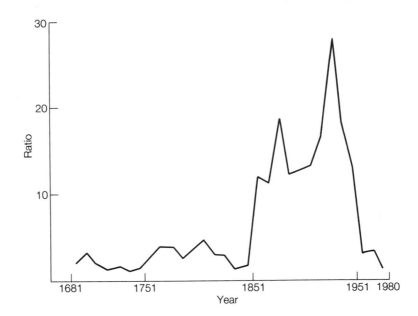

Figure 4.1   Illegitimacy ratio: Alagna 1681–1980

of illegitimacy in Alpine localities tended to be stable through time irrespective of variations in absolute intensity, then the *Alpwirtschaft* system might perhaps prove an important variable to account for this 'locality persistence'.[35] As far as Alagna is concerned, however, it is evident that the peculiar features of its agro-pastoral system cannot be regarded as always conducive to high absolute levels of illegitimacy. Nor can they explain the sudden rise of the 1850s, a decade which marked a transition to a different order of magnitude. Explanation must, therefore, be sought elsewhere.

The next hypothesis to be considered is the one linking illegitimacy to the marriage pattern. The essential information is summarized in tables 4.1 and 4.2 which reveal a number of interesting points. First, table 4.1 shows that age at marriage for both men and women peaked in the first half of the twentieth century. On the one hand, the data further confirm a primary finding of my research in Alagna, namely that the configuration of 'traditional' Alpine traits found in the period between the world wars was to a large extent the product of compara- tively recent changes.[36] On the other hand, it is remarkable that the

35 Cf. M. Mitterauer, *Ledige Mütter: zur Geschichte illegitimer Geburten in Europa* (Munich, 1983), p. 167.
36 Cf. Viazzo, 'Ethnic change in a Walser community', pp. 369–71.

Table 4.1 Mean age at first marriage in Alagna 1676–1980

| | Men | | Women | |
	No.	Age	No.	Age
1676–1700[a]	41	[29.23]	74	[26.19]
1701–1725	92	27.98	116	24.61
1726–1750	101	28.66	120	24.88
1751–1775	110	27.63	132	24.55
1776–1800	110	27.51	133	24.73
1801–1825	107	27.68	117	24.71
1826–1850	108	26.42	123	24.07
1851–1875	96	26.97	103	23.65
1876–1900	101	27.39	109	24.73
1901–1925	109	29.03	112	25.64
1926–1950	101	29.61	106	26.49
1951–1980	105	28.58	105	24.91

[a] The values for the period 1676–1700 must be treated with caution, since the ages of 40 grooms out of 41 and 68 brides out of 74 were established on the basis of entries in the death register and are therefore good approximations at best.
Sources: 1676–1865: Family Reconstitution Study. 1866–1980: Alagna Communal Archive, marriage registers

highest levels in the illegitimacy ratio broadly coincide with the highest marriage ages ever recorded in Alagna.

The coincidence of late age at marriage and high levels of illegitimacy, however, is not sufficient to demonstrate the existence of a correlation; nor can it explain the sudden upward surge of illegitimacy in the

Table 4.2 Illegitimacy ratio in Alagna 1678–1980

	All births	Illegitimate	%
1678–1700	523	14	2.68
1701–1725	525	9	1.71
1726–1750	558	9	1.61
1751–1775	769	25	3.25
1776–1800	669	26	3.89
1801–1825	461	17	3.69
1826–1850	381	8	2.10
1851–1875	396	56	14.14
1876–1900	407	51	12.53
1901–1925	348	55	15.80
1926–1950	211	39	18.48
1951–1980	208	6	2.88

Sources: 1678–1865: Alagna Parish Archive, *Liber baptizatorum*. 1866–1980: Alagna Communal Archive, birth registers

1850s. That marriage age in the second half of the nineteenth century was at its lowest indicates that a simple correlation between the two variables could not have existed. In fact, a linear regression of the illegitimacy ratios contained in table 4.2 on the mean ages for men and women contained in table 4.1 points to a complete lack of correlation, the values of the R-square coefficient being 0.0668 and 0.0952 respectively.

It should also be mentioned that tables 4.1 and 4.2 offer a very partial and imperfect picture of the relation between illegitimacy and the marriage pattern. On the one hand, the proportion of people never marrying does not always vary with age at marriage. Diverging trends were observed in seventeenth-century England[37] and seem to be present in Alagna in the eighteenth century.[38] Moreover, the illegitimacy ratio is a very crude measure. By simply expressing the number of illegitimate births per 100 live births, it is inevitably subject to the influence of outside factors, in particular changes in the number of unmarried women and changes in the number of legitimate births. Since in Alagna the First World War marked a sudden drop in crude birth rate from about 25 per 1000 to about 15 per 1000, it is clear that the illegitimacy ratio between the two world wars will be inflated by the decline of legitimate fertility.[39]

A much more reliable measure than the ratio is the illegitimacy rate (i.e. the number of illegitimate births per 1000 unmarried women aged 15–49), while a further refinement is represented by the index of illegitimate fertility (I_h) devised by Coale,[40] which removes the effect of differing age distributions of unmarried women by weighting age groups according to their presumed fecundity. Since both measures can be calculated only when a breakdown of the population by sex, age and marital status is available, it is often impossible to make use of them in village studies. In Alagna, however, these data can fortunately be derived from a number of surviving *status animarum*. Based on five selected listings spanning a period of two centuries, table 4.3 indicates that in the second half of the nineteenth century the increase in illegitimacy was very substantial indeed and that it was not due to changes in the demographic structure of the female population. Like marriage age, the number and proportion of unmarried women of procreative age (and more generally the rate of permanent celibacy) were, if anything, slightly lower in 1879 than in 1838, and much lower than in 1935.

37 E.A. Wrigley and R. Schofield, *The population history of England 1541–1871* (London, 1981), p. 264.

38 Viazzo, 'Ethnic change in a Walser community', p. 237.

39 Ibid., p. 100.

40 A.J. Coale, 'Factors associated with the development of low fertility: an historical summary', paper presented at World Population Conference, 1965.

Table 4.3 Illegitimacy in Alagna 1738–1935: comparison of illegitimacy ratio, illegitimacy rate, and index of illegitimate fertility

Year	N^a	Ratio^b	Rate^c	$I_h{}^d$
1738	0.27	1.18	1.96	0.005
1788	0.93	3.33	8.23	0.021
1838	0.33	2.24	3.44	0.011
1879	2.93	17.19	36.62	0.108
1935	1.60	19.67	16.67	0.042

[a] *N* is the mean annual number of illegitimate births in the 15-year period centred on the year in which the *status animarum* was compiled.
[b] The 'ratio' is the number of illegitimate births per 100 total births.
[c] The 'rate' is the number of illegitimate births per 1000 unmarried women aged 15–49.
[d] I_h is an index defined by the formula

$$I_h = \frac{\Sigma h_i u_i}{\Sigma F_i u_i}$$

where h_i is the number of illegitimate births per woman in each five-year age interval from 15 to 49, u_i is the number of unmarried women in each age interval, and F_i is the marital fertility in the corresponding age group of Hutterite women (chosen as standard population since the Hutterites, a religious sect in North America, had the highest marital fertility ever recorded). *Sources*: Alagna Parish Archive, *Libri status animarum et baptizatorum*. Alagna Communal Archive, birth registers

By confirming that there was a great increase in bearing illegitimate children in Alagna in the second half of the nineteenth century, table 4.3 restates the problem posed by the abrupt 'jump' of the 1850s, but is unable to resolve it. Admittedly, sudden explosions of illegitimacy cannot be easily accounted for by variables such as age at marriage or the proportion of celibates, because these rates tend to vary rather slowly. Nevertheless, it is surprising to see that even when the most refined measures are employed they shed little explanatory light.

Thus only one explanation remains: that illegitimacy is connected to migration. In the first half of the nineteenth century, and particularly in the 1830s and 1840s, mining in Alagna underwent a period of severe depression and immigration of miners greatly declined. In the early 1850s, however, the mines were reopened by a newly formed company, which resulted in a new wave of predominantly male immigration. A link between this event and the explosion of illegitimacy looks plausible, especially if we consider that the levels of illegitimacy had already gone up, though much less markedly, in coincidence with the intensification of the mining industry in the eighteenth century.

But this is a very crude way of solving the riddle. Moreover, the mining boom of the 1850s was shortlived, whereas the high wave of illegitimacy persisted for about 100 years. The partial failure of all the factors examined thus far to account for illegitimacy trends in Alagna suggests that a multidimensional explanation may be required. It should not be forgotten, after all, that the impact of the various factors affecting illegitimacy in Alagna may have changed through time. It would be conceivable to surmise, for example, that the immigration of miners in the 1850s provided the initial impetus, while the decline in marriage prospects reflected by the increase in both age at marriage and celibacy rate gradually came to play an important role in allowing high levels of illegitimacy to persist. If only aggregate data were available, this hypothesis would remain speculative. Nominal data, however, make it possible to go a step further and test its soundness.

Although complete family reconstitution was possible only for the period 1700–1865, I was able to collect nominal data which shed light on otherwise invisible, yet crucial, features of the wave of illegitimacy between 1850 and 1950. A first revealing test consists in comparing age at first marriage in the female population at large (the best proxy for the age of married women at the time of the birth of their first child) with the age of bastard-bearers at the time of the birth of their first illegitimate child. Table 4.4 shows a tendency for motherhood outside marriage to begin earlier than motherhood inside marriage – much earlier, indeed, in the case of 'repeaters', especially in the period 1901–50. This suggests on the one hand that the rise in the age of marriage had little to do with the dynamics of illegitimacy in Alagna, and on the other that the mothers of illegitimates may have belonged to, or even formed, a somewhat distinct group.

Table 4.4   Mean age of mothers of illegitimates at the time of the birth of their first illegitimate child in Alagna 1851–1950

Period	Singletons[a]		Repeaters		Total[b]		Mean age at first marriage
	Age	No.	Age	No.	Age	No.	
1851–1900	25.7	17	23.6	16	24.7	33	24.2
1901–1950	24.4	35	21.4	14	23.6	49	26.1
1851–1950	24.9	52	22.6	30	24.0	82	25.1

[a] 'Singletons' are women giving birth to only one illegitimate child in Alagna; 'repeaters' are those bearing at least two.
[b] The total number of women having illegitimates in Alagna between 1851 and 1950 and whose name is known in 104. (The name of the mothers of 8 illegitimates is unknown.) Of these 104, ten were widows, nine were of unknown age, two had their first illegitimate child outside Alagna, and one had her first illegitimate before 1851.
Sources: 1851–1865: Family Reconstitution Study. 1866–1950: Alagna Communal Archive, birth registers

Who were the members of this group? If we look at the surnames of the mothers of illegitimates (after 1810 the names of the fathers are recorded only in exceptional cases), it soon becomes apparent that they include a disproportionate number of surnames introduced into Alagna by recent immigration. In the second half of the nineteenth century there lived in Alagna a considerable number of people either born outside the village or born in the village to couples in which one or both partners were immigrants. Besides a non-Alagnese surname, these people shared the condition of poverty. Men were employed as miners or day labourers, two occupations on which most locals looked down. On the basis of the *status animarum* we may estimate that in the decades between 1850 and the First World War the female 'immigrant' population represented just one-fourth of the total female population, but accounted for over 80 per cent of all the illegitimates born in Alagna.

The importance of this finding hardly needs to be stressed. It demonstrates, first of all, that the link between immigration and illegitimacy was much more subtle than suggested in the preceding paragraphs. Moreover, it provides direct evidence that different sectors of the female population were differentially prone to illegitimacy. We may wonder, however, whether the immigrant sub-population contained within its numbers a core of individuals and families who tended to be involved in illegitimacy more frequently than others in spite of sharing a similar social and economic background. We may wonder, in other words, whether Alagna sheltered what Peter Laslett has called a 'bastardy-prone sub-society', that is a series of bastard-producing women, whose activities persisted over several generations and who tended to be related by kinship and marriage and to have borne more than one bastard.[41]

The simplest way to detect the presence of a bastardy-prone sub-society is to calculate the so-called 'repeater index', i.e. the number of bastards born by 100 women bearing bastards. In Alagna this index is astonishingly high. The 201 illegitimate births recorded from 1851 to 1950 are accounted for by only 112 mothers. The repeater index is therefore 179.5. The 'repeaters' (numbering 40) represented nearly 36 per cent of all mothers and accounted for over 63 per cent of all illegitimate births. If we add that at least 25 of the 72 'singletons' were either daughters or sisters of other women bearing illegitimates in Alagna, we see that well over one-half of the mothers of illegitimates comply with the two strictest criteria set by Laslett to define membership of the bastardy-prone sub-society.[42]

There can be little doubt that the Alagnese material offers an extreme example of a bastardy-prone sub-society. But there is more to the

---

41 P. Laslett, 'The bastardy prone sub-society', in Laslett et al., *Bastardy*, pp. 217–20.
42 Ibid., p. 220.

Alagnese bastardy-prone sub-society than merely figures. We have seen that after 1850 the great majority of illegitimates were born to a minority of women whose surnames had been recently introduced into Alagna by immigration. It would be simplistic, however, to conclude that illegitimacy was confined to women having no link whatsoever with members of the local population. Also unwarranted would be the conclusion that no element of continuity can be detected behind the drastic quantitative change of the 1850s.

Genealogical explorations are very helpful in correcting such mis-apprehensions. Let us consider one illuminating example. The genealogical exploration summarized in figure 4.2 commences with a set of four sisters (bottom right) born of a local woman married to an immigrant and all bearing at least one illegitimate child between 1910 and 1920. It goes back to an Alagnese matrilateral ancestor who turns out to be a certain Petrus Veber, one of the few Alagnese men known to have engaged in mining during the eighteenth century. What this genealogy provides is not simply an almost ideal-typical illustration of the definition of bastardy-prone sub-society proposed by Laslett. It also reveals a line of continuity crossing over the watershed of the 1850s as well as a strikingly persistent association between illegitimacy, mining and immigration.

Cases like that of Petrus Veber's daughters strongly suggest that a bastardy-prone sub-society was detectable well before the 1850s. In the early nineteenth century illegitimacy already tended to run in families – quite often, as illustrated by figure 4.2, in the same families as after 1850. If some elusive features of Alagnese illegitimacy are to be better understood, it is important to recognize that a core of bastardy-prone families not only existed but also had specific characteristics. In particular, it is easier to explain the sudden explosion of illegitimacy of the 1850s once it becomes clear that it was largely due to the activities of a limited number of outstanding repeaters (like Petrus Veber's granddaughter) who belonged to bastardy-prone families and whose potentialities appear to have been 'activated', as it were, by the arrival of new miners.

II

Although failing to do justice to the complexity of Alagnese illegitimacy, whose social and cultural dimensions have been discussed elsewhere,[43] our analysis of the extant demographic evidence is sufficient to demonstrate that in Alagna the history of illegitimacy was in no significant way determined by the characteristics of the marriage pattern. In the first half of the eighteenth century this Alpine village displayed a strongly marked version of Hajnal's European marriage pattern, epitomized by an index of

43 Viazzo, 'Tra antropologia e demografia storica'.

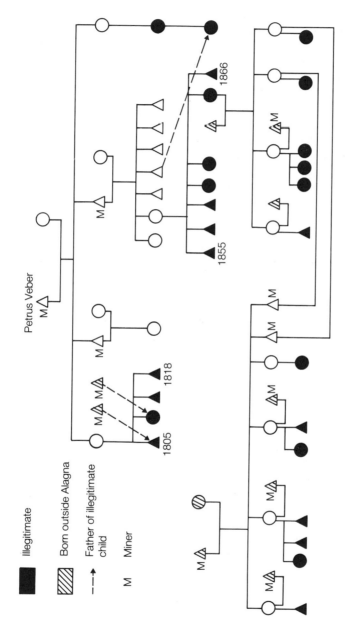

Petrus Veber

Illegitimate

Born outside Alagna

Father of illegitimate child

M   Miner

1866

1855

1818

1805

Figure 4.2   The bastardy-prone sub-society in Alagna: a genealogical case study

the proportion married (I_m) which in 1738 was well under 0.400, but illegitimate births were very infrequent. When the incidence of illegitimacy increased, it had little to do with variations in the age of marriage or in the rate of permanent celibacy.

Our analysis reveals, instead, a decisive connection between illegitimacy and mining. Such a link is all the more intriguing in the light of the data now emerging from rich Austrian sources recently studied by Mitterauer, where the 'infamous miners' (*ehrlosen Bergknappen*) are considered primarily responsible for sudden epidemics of illegitimacy.[44] That waves of immigration coincide with otherwise inexplicable explosions of illegitimacy is supported by the Alagnese case study, and Mitterauer is probably right in remarking that a big lacuna in all discussions of illegitimacy in historic Europe is the lack of attention paid to the role of soldiers and other highly mobile wage-earners such as miners and lumberjacks.

But the evidence presented in this paper also suggests that it would be simplistic to imagine that, in areas affected by predominantly male immigration, illegitimacy was merely a matter of itinerant workers seducing local girls and then moving on. What is impressive in Alagna is that most bastard-bearers were either daughters or sisters of miners or other immigrants. Virtually confined to a sub-community that included the families of the immigrants and the few locals engaged in mining (all living in the 'proletarianized' hamlets clustered around the church), illegitimacy was for two centuries a distinctive feature of this sub-community *vis-à-vis* the rest of the village population.[45]

In this connection it is interesting to mention the case of the Tyrolean village of Zell am Ziller. Listings from the middle of the eighteenth century make it clear that in addition to farmers and servants (the two usual social categories in rural Austria) there was in this village also a sizeable number of people descending from miners who had settled in the area in the sixteenth and seventeenth centuries. As in Alagna, it was these people – partly still engaged in the declining mining industry, partly working as muleteers and petty tradesmen – who prominently accounted for a level of illegitimacy which was considerably higher than in most other parts of Tyrol.[46]

In both Alagna and Zell am Ziller the social and occupational composition of the village population was, admittedly, the outcome of a very specific history. Nevertheless, given the diffusion of mining all over the Alps in the past centuries, these two villages are likely to be less atypical than one might at first glance think. Indeed, there are good reasons to believe that in pre-industrial Europe very similar situations were quite common. The German villages studied by Phayer,[47] for

44 Mitterauer, *Ledige Mütter*, p. 90.
45 Cf. Viazzo 'Ethnic change in a Walser community', pp. 265–76.
46 Mitterauer, 'Familienformen und Illegitimität', p. 159.
47 J.M. Phayer, *Sexual liberation and religion in nineteenth century Europe* (London, 1977), pp. 32–50.

instance, are in many ways strikingly reminiscent of Alagna and Zell am Ziller; nearly all bastards were produced by a minority separated from the rest of the village population by economic, occupational and spatial boundaries. It was fairly obvious that the rise of illegitimacy recorded in many parts of Europe in the late eighteenth century and in the course of the nineteenth century had affected some classes and strata more than others. However, the tiny village communities of which rural Europe was composed were assumed to be more homogeneous, in composition and behaviour, than they probable were.

Methodologically, this is a point of considerable significance. For it suggests that such measures as the illegitimacy rate or I_h, though generally superior to the illegitimacy ratio, may none the less prove not only incomplete but also positively misleading. One well-known limitation is that both the illegitimacy rate and I_h (being measures of fertility) take into account only the female unmarried population; it is becoming more and more evident – especially from anthropological studies[48] – that no correct understanding of illegitimacy can be achieved if we fail to consider the role of men, married and unmarried. But the tendency of both measures to take the female unmarried population as a socially indifferentiated whole, thus obscuring the differential proneness to illegitimacy of the various groups and categories of women, is certainly no less insidious. The case of Alagna provides a nice illustration of the danger of interpreting a sudden increase in the values of illegitimacy rate and I_h as evidence of changing sexual attitudes, instead of simply as a consequence of changes in the composition of the village population.

The realization that even at the village or parish level aggregate statistics may conceal a variety of sexual conduct raises a further, more general question. Are we entitled to argue, as Phayer has done,[49] that only by testing grand theories at the micro level can we expect decisive new departures in the study of illegitimacy? Although both community studies in anthropology and nominal methods of analysis in historical demography have, as this paper has tried to demonstrate, much to commend themselves, such a claim is not totally convincing.

Apart from the familiar methodological problems raised by this type of exercise (representativeness, comparison of data of different order, etc.), there are other reasons for scepticism. To judge from the present trend, a multiplication of local-level researches is likely to bring to light a large number of 'negative instances', partly because of the extreme variability which is so typical of local situations, partly because of the inadequacy of

48 Piselli, *Parentela ed emigrazionei*; B.J. O'Neill, *Social hierarchy in a northern Portuguese hamlet, 1870–1978* (unpublished Ph.D. thesis, London School of Economics, 1982); B.J. O'Neill, 'Dying and inheriting in rural Trás-os-Montes', *Journal of the Anthropological Society of Oxford* 14 (1983), pp. 44–74; cf. Viazzo, 'Tra antropologia e demografia storica'.
49 J.M. Phayer, 'Subcommunal bastardy and regional religion: micro and macro aspects of the debate on the sexual revolution', *Journal of Sex Research* 17 (1981), pp. 204–23.

many a grand generalization. Mitterauer has repeatedly remarked that most theories of illegitimacy are easy to falsify because they tend to be monocausal (or to be tested as such) and has suggested the necessity of multifactorial models.[50] Indeed, it is essential to recognize – as Laslett and Oosterveen had already stressed in their pioneering paper on English illegitimacy – that the figures for illegitimacy are 'the outcome of interplay of factors and circumstances rather than the result of one single "cause"'.[51] But it should also be recognized that any attempt to accommodate a growing number of exceptions to a pre-existing theoretical framework inevitably runs the risk of transforming even the most flexible of multifactorial models into a proliferation of *ad hoc* variables. Thus it seems dubious that the results of further detailed case studies will take us any closer to a new paradigm, to use Khun's term,[52] unless we are able to rethink some of the basic hypotheses that guide the collection of empirical data and their analysis.

One such major point of contention is the vexed question examined in this paper, namely the problem of ascertaining whether high illegitimacy levels are causally related to the European marriage pattern. In its cruder versions the 'sexual deprivation' theory has been definitely abandoned, but two recent and most authoritative books indicate that the connection between illegitimacy and the marriage pattern is still widely held. In his general work on illegitimacy in European history, Mitterauer explicitly argues a decisive link between high illegitimacy and the European marriage pattern,[53] while Goody, though acknowledging that the correlation is not perfect, nevertheless maintains that by and large late marriage and bastardy are closely connected.[54]

At the risk of restating the obvious, it seems useful to consider an ambiguity which is apparently still lurking in the debate. If we look at a map of Europe, we can easily see that all countries traditionally characterized by high illegitimacy ratios lie west of Hajnal's famous imaginary line running from Leningrad to Trieste. This means that whatever the causes of variations in illegitimacy through time (a related but somewhat different problem), the existence of a broad 'distributional' correlation between higher illegitimacy ratios and the European marriage pattern is beyond dispute.

On the other hand, it is hardly surprising that illegitimacy ratios tended to be higher in those countries where large proportions of the population were excluded from marriage, as opposed to Russia, the Balkans or the

50 Mitterauer, 'Familienformen und Illegitimität', p. 186; Mitterauer, *Ledige Mütter*, p. 30.

51 P. Laslett and K. Oosterveen, 'Long-term trends in bastardy in England', *Population Studies* 27 (1973), p. 258.

52 T.S. Kuhn, *The structure of scientific revolutions* (Chicago, 1962).

53 Mitterauer, *Ledige Mütter*, pp. 41–67, 112.

54 J. Goody, *The development of the family and marriage in Europe* (Cambridge, 1983), pp. 128–9, 192.

Mediterranean area, where women married at an early age and almost universally.[55] The really interesting question is to explain why social systems with largely similar demographic potential for illegitimacy had different levels. Around the year 1900, for example, in Austria the value of the index of illegitimate fertility I_h was over 0.100 compared with less than 0.020 for Ireland.[56] And we have seen that in Alagna the I_h was, in 1738, as low as 0.005.

Puzzled by this disparity, many students of the subject [57] have been inclined to regard the degree of penetration of religious movements into the masses as the crucial variable, but on the whole this thesis fails to be persuasive.[58] With reference to the Alpine area we may note, incidentally, that a religious explanation of low illegitimacy has some plausibility for Tyrol and perhaps also for Oberwallis, but can scarcely be applied to the case of Alagna, where the results of the Counter-Reformation were, from the point of view of the Church authorities, quite disappointing.[59]

In the latest edition of *The World We Have Lost*, Laslett has suggested that instead of resorting to religion we should admit that 'a force which is capable of keeping people from marrying at all must also be capable of preventing them from procreating outside marriage.'[60] This reasoning applies in pre-industrial England, where illegitimacy and nuptiality rose and fell together. Rather than solving the problem, however, this hypothesis actually turns it upside down: how can we explain that in most Austrian regions, for instance, such a 'force' was apparently unable to prevent people from having illegitimates?

Unfortunately, this question has always been approached in terms of prevention – in 'negative' terms, so to speak. The European marriage pattern has been praised for making possible a low-pressure demographic regime and, consequently, an efficient balance between resources and population.[61] But it is also usual to stress that this delicate demographic balance could be destroyed if extramarital fertility got out of hand: 'To prevent the inevitable nemesis of the Malthusian positive checks', writes Flinn, 'women must be generally discouraged from giving birth outside

55 Mitterauer, *Ledige Mütter*, p. 27.

56 E. Shorter, J. Knodel and E. van de Walle, 'The decline of non-marital fertility in Europe, 1880–1940', *Population Studies* 25 (1971), p. 387.

57 J. Bossy, 'The Counter-Reformation and the people of Catholic Europe', *Past and Present* 47 (1970), p. 54; P. Chaunu, *Histoire, science sociale* (Paris, 1974), pp. 326–7; Mitterauer, *Ledige Mütter*, pp. 30–41.

58 Cf. Laslett and Oosterveen, 'Long-term trends in bastardy', p. 256; K. Wrightson, 'The nadir of English illegitimacy in the seventeenth century', in Laslett et al., *Bastardy*, pp. 176–91; Phayer, 'Subcommunal bastardy', pp. 213–20.

59 Viazzo, 'Ethnic change in a Walser community', pp. 196–203.

60 P. Laslett, *The world we have lost, further explored* (London, 1983), p. 162.

61 R. Schofield, 'The relationship between demographic structure and environment in pre-industrial western Europe', in W. Conze (ed.), *Sozialgeschichte der Familie in der Neuzeit Europas* (Stuttgart, 1976), pp. 147–60.

wedlock'.[62] Rules forbidding the begetting of children outside marriage have thus been seen as 'part of that regulatory system which keeps the numbers of a society within its means of subsistence'.[63]

Yet the possibility cannot be ruled out that in a given social context illegitimacy may have 'positive' functions, at least from the point of view of the actors, or of *some* actors. In this sense, a suggestive contribution is O'Neill's anthropological study of the northern Portuguese hamlet of 'Fontelas' (a pseudonym), where in the period between the mid nineteenth century and the Second World War exceedingly high illegitimacy ratios were recorded. O'Neill's work is especially relevant because it concerns a mountain area displaying a pronounced version of the European marriage pattern: as the author himself notes, 'this region of Portugal provides some extremely unusual characteristics which suggest comparison with other regions of mountain Europe'.[64]

Interestingly enough, in this study two different explanatory strands appear to coexist. The first consists in simply relating illegitimacy to the marriage pattern and explaining its occurrence as the obvious consequence of sexual deprivation. This explanation, however, has no real connection with the central argument developed by O'Neill in the rest of his analysis, and looks like a tribute almost automatically paid by the author to the received wisdom in this field. Its weakness is demonstrated by the fact that in 'Fontelas' some categories of women, though destined to permanent celibacy, had a much lower propensity towards illegitimacy than others in the same condition.

The second strand is more promising. O'Neill's rich ethnography is most impressive in showing that the sphere of marriage was subject to very strong social control – low nuptiality being the outcome of family strategies that aimed, as in other mountain areas,[65] at the preservation of viable estates through the avoidance of partition. But illegitimacy, too, can hardly be seen as a failure of social control or as a dysfunctional element. The data furnish ample evidence of a persistent pattern of social reproduction of a 'bastard group' over time, which provided a key source of cheap labour for the wealthy and the landed without posing a threat to the bulk of the hamlet's patrimonies. Thus illegitimacy had at least two 'positive' functions: on the one hand it assured (biologically) the reproduction of the labour force without leading to land fragmentation; on the other it helped reproduce (socially) the pattern of stratification.[66]

The long-term demographic and ecological effects of 'unchecked' illegitimacy remain, of course, too important to be neglected, particularly in mountain areas where the balance between resources and population is

62 M.W. Flinn, *The European demographic system 1500–1820* (Brighton, 1981), p. 26.
63 Laslett, *Family life and illicit love*, p. 104.
64 O'Neill, 'Dying and inheriting', p. 73.
65 Cf. Cole and Wolf, *The hidden frontier*.
66 O'Neill, *Social hierarchy*, pp. 406–16; O'Neill, 'Dying and inheriting', pp. 68–72.

particularly delicate. But the processes whereby social structures are reproduced may well follow imperatives which are not fully consonant with the requirements of population control. If seen in terms of social reproduction, illegitimacy may prove dysfunctional in some contexts but functional and hardly a 'breach of the rules' in others. It may even provide, as O'Neill has contended for 'Fontelas', the only way in which a society's fundamental contradictions can be resolved.[67] This realization implies a theoretical reorientation, and might perhaps be the embryo of a unified generative approach capable of accounting for the presence or absence of illegitimacy (or for its variable intensity) on the basis of few structural principles and a limited number of permutations. A number of recent contributions, including O'Neill's study and, I believe, my own work on Alagna, have demonstrated the fruitfulness of Peter Laslett's intimation that the study of illegitimacy 'compels a searching analysis of the social structure, past and present'.[68] A better understanding of the logic that governs the reproduction of social structure will, in its turn, help us resolve some of the problems concerning illegitimacy which still await an explanation.

---

67 O'Neill, 'Dying and inheriting', p. 71.
68 Laslett, 'The bastardy-prone sub-society', p. 226.

5

Widows in Late Elizabethan London: Remarriage, Economic Opportunity and Family Orientations

Vivien Brodsky

Men and women are borne and come running into the world faster than coaches doe into Cheapside uppon Simon and Jude's day: and are eaten up by Death faster than mutton and porridge in a term time. Who would pin their hearts to any sleeve?

Thomas Dekker, *Westward Ho* (1607)

Most of the recent discoveries about marriage and its differing incidence for widows and widowers have derived from the family reconstitutions of principally rural settlements in England, western and eastern Europe.[1,2] An apparently constant differential has emerged: the higher incidence of male remarriage and the shorter intervals before remarriage of widowers compared with widows. For England, from the aggregated statistics of 14 parish reconstitutions, Wrigley and Schofield have demonstrated that between 1600 and 1799 the median interval to male remarriage was 12.6 months and to female 19.4 months.[3] On the separate issue of the incidence of lasting widowhood, with the exception of those women widowed in their early twenties, rates of female remarriage in France were half those for men in their thirties and forties. Widows in western European pre-industrial societies were apparently rarely able to attract a second spouse, especially after the age of 40. In her analysis of popular *mentalité* and remarriage, Martine Ségalen has reduced the pattern to two constants: at

1 I would like to express my gratitude to a number of people who read an earlier draft of this essay: Steve Rappaport, David Levine, Peter Laslett and Keith Wrightson.

2 J. Dupâquier, E. Hélin, P. Laslett, M. Livi-Bacci and S. Sognor (eds) *Marriage and remarriage in populations of the past* (London, 1981).

3 E.A. Wrigley and R.S. Schofield, 'Remarriage intervals and the effect of marriage order on fertility', in Dupâquier et al., *Marriage and remarriage*, p. 214.

all ages men remarry more often than women; and when they do remarry, they do so more rapidly than widowed women.[4]

This new research on remarriage, which has been undertaken from a primarily demographic perspective, raises a number of questions concerning the history of widows and the family in London. If such findings also applied to the early modern city, it would follow that in London, where marriages were interrupted more frequently by the earlier deaths of husbands, many children might anticipate growing up in single-parent households headed by their widowed mothers. Surprisingly, however, although it has not proved possible to recover firm estimates of the incidence of lasting widowhood, the records point to the existence of an active remarriage market, particularly for the widows of city craftsmen and tradesmen. Such women appear to have remarried quickly and to have often married single men younger than themselves.

Rapid remarriage, for at least some of London's widows, suggests that it may be timely to reconsider the commonly held view that widowhood afforded unique opportunities for independence, economic self-sufficiency and a 'social freedom' absent from the lives of both single and married women. Richard Vann, for one, has argued that 'given the patriarchal nature of pre-industrial Europe, a demographic situation that produced many widows was comparatively favourable to the position of women.'[5]

Through addressing the issue of economic opportunity and reviewing the evidence for widows who might be described as active in the city economy, my intention is to evoke the situation of those widows who were, to use that unlovely word, the 'relicts' of mainly craftsmen and tradesmen. Their apparent preference for a speedy remarriage must be contrasted with the low incidence of remarriage for those widows from the social elite of London aldermen, 56 per cent of whom remained widows. Nearly one-third of these women were involved in economic activity after the deaths of their husbands.[6] At the further reaches of the social hierarchy emerges yet another contrast: those widows of poor craftsmen, labourers and porters who could have rarely anticipated a second marriage in the inflationary decades of the 1580s, 1590s and 1600s in London and against whom the materialistic marriage market erected insuperable barriers. For such widows, survival itself was at stake. They appeared anonymously in a collective guise as 'poor widows' in receipt of parish charity. And they are to be identified in a

4 M. Ségalen, 'Mentalité populaire et remariage en Europe occidentale', in Dupâquier et al., *Marriage and remarriage*, pp. 68, 76.

5 R. Vann, 'Toward a new lifestyle: women in preindustrial capitalism', in R. Bridenthal and C. Koonz (eds), *Becoming visible: women in European history* (Boston, 1977), p. 195.

6 S. Rappaport, 'Social structure and mobility in sixteenth century London' (unpublished Ph.D. thesis, Columbia University, 1983), p. 97.

fledgeling economic capacity as the erstwhile keepers of the sick, as spinners, as unofficial weavers and even, at times, as servants. Their situations, so different from the more prosperous widows, are a necessary reminder of the diverse historical experiences of widowhood: of lessened status, limited autonomy and, one suspects, of attenuated family ties and too precarious a dependence on the goodwill of neighbours. They may indeed have lived in something of a poor widow subculture in the less wealthy London parishes.

Yet describing the varied experiences of widows in London may be an exercise of limited usefulness unless more is understood about the metropolitan family itself. Indirectly, this essay is concerned with promoting a fuller conception of the workings of the family and kinship in late Elizabethan London. For example, we need to set aside embryonic notions of widows burdened with large numbers of dependent children. High mortality reduced to modern dimensions the size of most urban families. Even the woman who had borne eight or nine children might bring to her remarriage two or three surviving children. Perhaps this may have been interpreted as an 'advantage' on the marriage market, but it is one which underscores sequential loss of infants and small children and which illustrates the frailty of the metropolitan family. We need, therefore, to set aside romanticized notions of the family and to recognize its profound limitations as a 'fundamental' social institution in the metropolis.

Keith Wrightson's recent assessment of the importance of the family in early modern England as a source of 'security' and 'identity' and 'the satisfaction of both physical and emotional needs not catered for by other social institutions' has a strictly limited application to the familial experiences of most Londoners, and has been explicitly called into question in my discussion of metropolitan families, admittedly comprising a small percentage of the overall population of England.[7] It is certainly of interest to sketch out an alternative view of shorter unions, rapid remarriages, parental loss, childless marriages and 'mixed' families which adumbrate the uncertain or precarious dimensions of familial life in London. The extent to which smaller market settlements, with their apparently higher levels of mortality than villages, may have shared such tendencies with London is suggestive and perhaps a topic worth further investigation. Certainly the levels of parental deprivation in Manchester in the 1650s, described by Peter Laslett, point to possible parallels between provincial towns and the metropolis.[8]

---

7 K. Wrightson, *English society 1580–1680*, (London, 1982), p. 66.

8 P. Laslett, 'Parental deprivation in the past', in P. Laslett, *Family life and illicit love in earlier generations* (Cambridge, 1977), p. 169.

In the interests of recovering the differing experiences of London widows, I have chosen to adopt a wide-ranging approach to many of these issues which belong, more properly, to the history of the London family. I begin with literary perceptions of widows, then introduce some statistics on the age structure of the marriage market and the intervals to remarriage for widows. This is supplemented with an analysis of families in aggregate from the reconstitution of 104 marriages of individuals and 494 commissary court wills for the period 1580 to 1600. Individual case studies, suggesting the obstacles in the way of stable family formation, are evinced to illustrate the overall tendencies towards transience and loss. The related issues of widowhood, economic opportunities and remarriage require a brief description of widows' participation in the London economy. And finally my discussion of widows' familial orientations marks a foray into the relatively unexplored world of urban social interaction, that is of kinship, friendship and neighbourliness – a foray which is, for the present, necessarily introductory.

I

How were widows perceived by their male contemporaries in late Elizabethan London? Certainly they attracted the attention of male playwrights with their allegedly manipulative and cynical behaviour, with their assumed sexual interest in younger men and their apparently rapid remarriages, tartly summarized by one commentator, Robert Greene: 'The call of the quail continues but one quarter, a widow's sorrow only two months, the one sad for her old mate, the other careful for a new match'.[9] Widows were seen as imperious in their chambers crowded with suitors, and lusty and demanding in their sexuality. Additionally, extreme discrepancies of age and wealth between widows and their opportunistic young suitors furnished the stuff of literary caricature.[10] Such plays form part of a subgenre of city comedy about city women and share common stereotypes about widows and women in general.

'Contemporary ideology, already stale and inadequate, now refracted on to stage.'[11] Such must be a necessary disclaimer to any attempt to equate literary prejudice with observed behaviour. Yet one must also agree with Theodore Leinwand that such plays remain indecipherable when removed from their social context.[12] The historian of London

9 Robert Greene, quoted in C. Carlton, 'The widow's tale', *Albion* 10 (1978), p. 120.
10 T. Dekker, 'Keep the widow waking' (1604), quoted in Carlton, 'The widow's tale', p. 118.
11 T.B. Leinwand, '"This gulph of marriage": Jacobean city wives and Jacobean city comedy', *Women's Studies* 10 (1984), p. 250.
12 Ibid., p. 257.

might be well placed to track down the genesis of such stereotypes while resisting a facile temptation, as Peter Laslett has often warned us, of taking deceptive literary evidence at face value. One might also contemplate the parallel dangers of prescriptive literature – conduct books and sermons – too often relied upon by the historian to describe ideals which might have been aired in lofty and didactic isolation from contemporary practices.

Demographic evidence may form a useful corrective to too heavy a dependence upon such literature, but it may be equally misleading when it is applied from an inappropriate geographic context: 'Widows rarely remarried, and if they did seldom chose younger men. ... The male stereotype [from literature] accused widows of rapidly remarrying younger single men, yet the demographic evidence shows the opposite to be the case. ... In Colyton, widowers were nine times more likely to marry younger single women than widows to wed unmarried youths.'[13] Colyton is Colyton and London is London. Remote villages with their patterns of higher life expectancy, enduring marriages, older widows and larger numbers of surviving children to burden an inheritance are manifestly inappropriate models to bring to bear on the social context of what was, quintessentially, city comedy about city women. From the evidence advanced here about remarriage in London, it could be argued that the literary obsession with lecherous widows, rapid remar-riage to younger men, and the lure of large dowries, while exaggerated and parodied, has at least some basis in historical reality.

A case study of one marriage, drawn from the autobiography of the London astrologer William Lilly, as one direct piece of evidence, fur-nishes an agreeable contrast to literary stereotypes about widows.[14]

Lilly, a migrant from Leicestershire, arrived in London at the tender age of 18 with 'seven shillings and sixpence left and no more; one suit of clothes upon my back, two shirts, three bands, one pair of shoes and as many stockings.'[15] Eight years later his fortunes changed abruptly as a consequence of his marriage with his master's third wife, Mistress Wright, the relict of Gilbert Wright, a rentier in London and one time Master of the Salters' Company. Widow Wright took for her third husband the 26-year-old William Lilly:

Of my marriage the first time. My mistress who had been twice married to old men was now resolved to be cozened no more. ... She was of a brown ruddy complexion, corpulent, of but mean stature, plain, no education. ... She had many suitors, old men whom she declined; some gentlemen of decayed fortunes whom she liked not. ... By my fellow servants she was observed frequently to say she cared not if she married a man that would love her so that he had never a penny. ... The disproportion of years and fortune being so great betwixt

13 Carlton, 'The widow's tale', pp. 119, 127.
14 W. Lilly, *History of his life and times. From the year 1602 to 1681* (London, 1822).
15 Ibid., p. 23.

us. ... However all her talk was of husbands, and in my presence saying one day after dinner she respected not wealth but desired an honest man ... I made no more ado but presently saluted her and told her myself was the man: she replied I was too young I sayd nay what I had not in wealth I would supply in love.[16]

The marriage of widow Wright and William Lilly lasted for six years, during which, according to Lilly, they 'lived very lovingly', he 'frequenting no Company at all'. At her death he was £1000 the richer, £530 of which he used to purchase the moiety of 13 houses in the Strand. His real estate and capital were further augmented with the £500 dowry he received from his second wife whom he married as a widower of eight months' standing.[17]

Marriage with an older wealthy widow was an indisputably vital ingredient in the rags-to-riches success of William Lilly. Such extreme contrasts of age and wealth were probably atypical, yet the recounting of William Lilly's courtship process suggests what may have been common tendencies: wealthy, apparently childless widows enjoying a measure of power from the importunings of suitors, and having a sexual and romantic interest in younger men; short intervals to remarriage for both men and women; and the widow's trump card of capital and property, the means by which she might translate, quite legitimately, her fantasies into realities. The union of older widows and younger men was a *common* pattern of city marriages in the period surveyed – marriages wherein the widow's interest in the younger man was complemented by the more practical reckonings of his past training as an apprentice and journeyman in the same or related trade or craft as that of her late husband. The arrangement could, after all, work both ways.

Some 60 per cent of widows remarried single men in the licence remarriages of 515 widows of craftsmen and tradesmen between 1598 and 1619.[18] Of the 327 widows who married bachelors, 80 per cent were older than their husbands. Widows were on average some 4.5 years older, although there are interesting variations between widows of craftsmen and those of tradesmen in this respect. Those widows whose husbands had been of higher-status occupations – goldsmiths, grocers, drapers, mercers, haberdashers, fishmongers and scriveners – were on average 2.2 years older than their single spouses. The difference climbs to 6.3 years for those widows of humble craftsmen, the wives of blacksmiths, carpenters, cutlers, tailors and weavers.[19] It cannot be doubted

---

16 Ibid., pp. 50–1.

17 Ibid., p. 78.

18 Bishop of London Marriage Allegations, 1598–1619. Guildhall Library (hereafter GL) MS 10, 091/1–6.

19 For an analysis of the social status of occupations in Tudor and Stuart London and the reconstruction of a social hierarchy of occupations using the technique of seriation and multidimensional scaling, see V.B. Elliott, 'Mobility and Marriage in pre-industrial England' (unpublished Ph.D. thesis, University of Cambridge, 1979), part I, pp. 21–133.

that such age inequalities must have given a bachelor–widow marriage a different character, providing greater opportunities for psychological and sexual dominance within marriage by the older woman.

Yet how common were such remarriages in the city? It is important to establish the overall proportion of marriages as remarriages, since I have suggested that remarriage may be a central issue in the history of the London family and, more tentatively, in the history of urban women. No figures can be cited for the overall rate of remarriage, and I have already implied that there may be significant differences between widows in this respect: the very rich and the very poor rarely remarrying, and those widows from craft and trade backgrounds having an apparently greater propensity to remarriage.

For women of middling status, frequent remarriage introduced elements of change and disruption into their lives: serial monogamy as against a single marriage partner, and a brief heading of the household in a shortlived phase of solitude followed by rapid re-entry into marriage and a possibly different role within the second or third marriage. Widowhood was to be counted in months, not years. For those from the elite and for many of the poor, widowhood, in contrast, was permanent and may have spanned several years of their lives.

To enumerate remarriages, we must turn to sources which are full of pitfalls and biases. Information is limited to the numbers and ages of men and women marrying and remarrying in London by licence, as distinct from the more common banns marriages. This introduces a bias of social selectivity into the calculations.[20]

Setting aside the unrecoverable aspect of the *order* of remarriage (second, third, fourth) there are four overall combinations of marriages: single men with single women; single women with widowers; single men with widows; and widows with widowers. At a given time the marriage market will comprise all four types of marriages in varying proportions. Figure 5.1 shows an example. Remarriages comprise some 45 per cent of all licence marriages. Of all women marrying by licence, some 35 per cent were widows. Nearly 19 per cent of widows were marrying bachelors and 16 per cent were marrying widowers. At 10 per cent of all marriages, widowers' marriages with single women were the least common combination.

It may be the case that proportionately more widows and widowers in London were attracted to the licence system because of the opportunities it afforded for a more private marriage. The extent to which banns marriages shared similar proportions of marriage 'types' cannot be resolved. Taking the bias of the licence process into account, the proportions of widows and widowers marrying by banns may have been lower, and of single men and women correspondingly higher. The

20 Ibid., pp. 14–17.

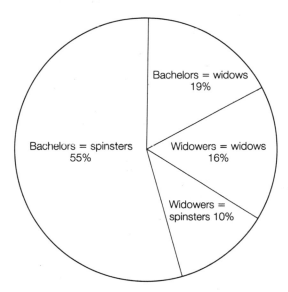

Figure 5.1   Marriage and remarriage by licence in London 1598–1619
Total marriages 2088

period 1598–1620 was marked by rapid inflation and sharp upswings in the cost of living, swelling the number of poor men and women in London's population.[21] On the other hand, high rates of remarriage were also determined by excess mortality, and the great plagues of 1593 and 1603 were the catalysts of an active remarriage market.

The licence system found favour among both the migrant and the native born, among the gentlemen (often self-styled), the tradesmen and the craftsmen. Certainly the cost of marrying by licence precluded the very poor. We might conjecture that, at least for those of high to middling status in the city, remarriage was a common occurrence.

While the age statements made by widows and widowers were of questionable accuracy,[22] ages have been analysed in a more refined measure – the breakdown of first and second marriages by each five-

21 S. Rappaport, 'Social structure and mobility in sixteenth century London, part 1, *London Journal* 9 (1983), p. 126.

22 The inaccuracy of age reporting can be tested using the Smith Index, which enumerates the number of stated ages ending in 1, 3, 7, 9 and expresses them as a percentage of 40 per cent of the total reported ages. Bachelors and spinsters scored highly on this index (87.3) which indicates quite accurate age reporting. Widows and widowers scored significantly lower (45.1, 44.6): both tended to round off their ages and favoured the ages 40, 45, 50 etc. For a fuller discussion of the Smith Index and the Whipple Index, see Elliott, 'Mobility and marriage', appendix B, pp. 374–86.

yearly age grouping (see table 5.1). This enables us to recover, firstly, the numbers of bachelors' marriages with widows and with single women, and secondly, widowers' remarriages with single women and widows, for each five-yearly age category. Some interesting tendencies are revealed.

The table is useful in demonstrating the radically different times at which young men and women entered the marriage market. In the age group 15–19 there were 272 women marrying, and mainly to bachelors, while only nine single men were marrying between the same ages. By ages 20–24 the difference had been partly rectified, although the ratio of women marrying to men was almost 2:1. By such ages, 31 women had already entered their second marriage.

Marriage entry for single men occurred most conspicuously in the next age category of 25–29. It was only at such ages that most crafts-men and tradesmen were technically free to marry since many had begun a seven- or eight-year apprenticeship in their late teens.[23] Of all single men in the age category 25–29, 21.8 per cent were marrying widows. Most young men aged 25–29 (74.6 per cent) were marrying single women. Yet by the ages 30–34, the proportion of bachelors marrying widows had risen sharply to nearly one third of all single men's marriages.

Widows aged 30–34 apparently preferred to marry bachelors rather than widowers (120:72), a tendency which was diminishing for widows aged 35–39 who had only a marginal preference for single men (57:42). Half the widows aged 40–44 were marrying bachelors, and by ages 45–49, widows were marrying proportionately more widowers than single men (33:18). The overall indication, perhaps predictable, is that widows aged between 45 and 65 – one-fifth of all widows – more commonly married widowers than single men (126:48). Thus the re-marriages of widows with bachelors, usually younger than themselves, were confined in the main to the more 'youthful' widows aged between 30 and 45.

To summarize the main tendencies for widows from table 5.1, it is convenient to divide widows into two categories – 'younger' (25–40) and 'older' (40–65) – and to contrast their two rather different styles of remarriage. The first was characterized by the widow's preference for the single man, usually younger than herself; the second by the more prosaic choice of a widower, the same age as and sometimes older than the widow.

From the distribution of ages in table 5.1 it would appear that there was a bias in favour of marriage and remarriage for men at more advanced ages than was the case for women. Comparatively few

23 V.B. Elliott, 'Single women in the London marriage market: age, status and mobility, 1598–1619', in R.B. Outhwaite (ed.), *Marriage and society* (London, 1981), p. 84.

Table 5.1 Age and marital status in the London licence marriages 1598–1619

Female

Age category	Single women = bachelors (no.)	(%)	Single women = widowers (no.)	(%)	Widows = bachelors (no.)	(%)	Widows = widowers (no.)	(%)	Total (no.)	(%)
15–19	245	90	24	8.8	2	0.8	1	0.4	272	100
20–24	484	82.3	76	12.9	23	3.9	5	0.9	588	100
25–29	220	61.6	44	12.3	67	18.8	26	7.3	357	100
30–34	110	31.4	48	13.7	120	34.3	72	20.6	350	100
35–39	15	12.1	10	8.1	57	45.9	42	33.9	124	100
40–44	13	8.0	9	5.5	71	43.6	70	42.9	163	100
45–49			1	1.9	18	34.6	33	63.5	52	100
50–54			3	3.4	25	28.1	61	68.5	89	100
55–59					3	21.4	11	78.6	14	100
60–64					2	8.7	21	91.3	23	100
65–69							1	100.0	1	100
70+										
All	1087	53.5	215	10.6	388	19.1	343	16.8	2033	100

Male

Age category	Bachelors = single women (no.)	(%)	Bachelors = widows (no.)	(%)	Widowers = single women (no.)	(%)	Widowers = widows (no.)	(%)	Total (no.)	(%)
15–19	8	88.9	1	11.1					9	100
20–24	304	85.6	48	13.5	1	0.3	2	0.6	355	100
25–29	496	74.7	145	21.8	18	2.7	5	0.8	664	100
30–34	260	56.8	123	26.8	47	10.3	28	6.1	458	100
35–39	56	32.2	39	22.4	48	27.6	31	17.8	174	100
40–44	37	20.3	31	17.1	39	21.4	75	41.2	182	100
45–49	4	5.5	9	12.3	17	23.3	43	58.9	73	100
50–54	2	1.7	4	3.5	29	25.2	80	69.6	115	100
55–59			1	2.3	9	20.4	34	77.3	44	100
60–64			3	6.1	9	13.4	37	75.5	49	100
65–69							5	100.0	5	100
70+					3	25.0	9	75.0	12	100
All	1167	54.5	404	18.9	220	10.3	349	16.3	2140	100

The different totals for males and females in each combination are the result of insufficient information being gained in some of the licences

widows married beyond the age of 50 (17 per cent of all widows), while widowers continued to remarry until the age of 70: 36 per cent of all widowers were aged from 50 to 69. Cultural imperatives rather than higher life expectancies for men must surely be the explanation, and we might infer that, for the widow of 55 and upwards, remarriage opportunities were very limited: her age was against her. The figures and proportions of table 5.1 obscure what may be interpreted as an unusual flexibility in marriage practices. The marriage process in late Elizabethan and early Stuart London accommodated many styles, including older men with much younger single women and young bachelors with older widows.

The final question of interest in the analysis of widows and remarriage is the speed at which they remarried. The conduct books and sermons of the age advocated a year of widowhood, and London dramatists caricatured the rapid remarriages of widows: reality lies somewhere between.[24] Certainly the clerical dispensers of marriage licences paid noticeably more attention to widows in this respect than they did to widowers, whose length of widowerhood was only occasionally recorded.

Again the possible inaccuracies of *reported* intervals of widowhood and the dates of the death of the late husband must be emphasized. Checking reported intervals against parish register entries of the date of the husband's burial indicates that fewer than half of 27 cases were accurately reported. The tendency appears to have been an overstatement of the actual period of widowhood rather than an understatement. Those whose husbands were said to have been 'deceased a year past' were often widows of only five months' standing, or 'deceased halfe a yeare' could be translated as two months' widowhood. This tendency to overstatement should be noted in reviewing the figures of table 5.2, which shows the distribution of reported intervals of widowhood prior to remarriage for those widows of craftsmen and tradesmen.

Nearly 47 per cent of all tradesmen's widows had remarried within six months or less – a significant difference from widows of craftsmen, only 28 per cent of whom had found a new partner in the same interval. Combining the two groups we find that some 67 per cent of all widows had remarried within a year. There were few widows who rivalled Cicely Swaine, a girdler's widow of three weeks' standing when she alleged marriage with Thomas Bond, a young girdler.[25] Nevertheless it is obvious that, especially for tradesmen's wives, Robert Greene's pointed remarks were not without substance. Nor was the useful

---

24 Carlton, 'The widow's tale', p. 20: 'Authorities as diverse as Sir Edward Coke, Bishop Latimer and Jeremy Taylor all expressed the widely held view that at least one year's delay was proper.'
25 GL MS 10, 091/3: 26 February 1606/7, Bond-Swaine.

Table 5.2 Reported intervals between the death of a husband and date of remarriage: widows of high-status tradesmen and of lower-status craftsmen

	Less than 1	1	2	3	4	5	6	7	8	9	10	11–12	15	18	2 yrs	3 yrs	4–5 yrs	
							Remarrying within (months)											
Widows of high-status tradesmen (n=161)	1	3	5	12	14	9	31	2	5	7	3	27	2	2	14	8	16	47% remarried within 6 months; 74% married within 1 year
Widows of middle-low-status craftsmen (n=229)	1	2	5	22	4	2	29	4	–	18	1	53	4	12	26	14	32	28% remarried within 6 months; 61% married within 1 year
All (n=390)	2	5	10	34	18	11	60	6	5	25	4	80	6	14	40	22	48	36% married within 6 months; 67% married within 1 year

advice of George Herbert unheeded: 'Marry a widow before she leaves mourning'.[26]

However we interpret the relatively speedy remarriage of widows, the contrast with widowhood outside London remains pronounced: the median interval to remarriage in 14 provincial parishes was 19.4 months, but for the wives of London craftsmen and tradesmen it was as low as nine months. In yet another aspect of its demography and culture, London reveals its uniqueness. There was no difference between widowers and widows in this respect within London. For 118 widowers, their median interval of widowerhood was also nine months. Men and women alike, in the city, wasted little time in finding a new partner.

II

Certain aspects of the remarriages of widows have been surveyed; it is now instructive to consider the demographic experience of women *within* marriage and to tabulate the number of children born to them. Two sources have been used for these aggregated statistics. The first consists of a reconstitution of 104 couples who married by both banns and licence and whose subsequent marital histories were followed up in the various registers of the parishes of their residence.[27] The 104 marriages were included in this analysis as, in virtually all cases, the dates of burial for one or both partners could be recovered even when there were two or more marriages involved.

As far as possible the conventions of family reconstitution were adhered to, which meant the exclusion of many individuals whose marital histories were less completely recorded. No attempt was made

---

26 *The Oxford Dictionary of English Proverbs* (Oxford, 1970), p. 515.
27 The reconstitution is hereafter referred to as 'London reconstitution'.

The registers consulted were mainly printed and indexed parish registers (ed. Harleian Society), e.g.

Register of St Helen's Bishopsgate (Harleian Society, London, 1929)
Registers of St James's Clerkenwell, vol. 1 (Harleian Society, London, 1932)
Registers of St Clement's Eastcheap (Harleian Society, London, 1933)
Registers of St Michael's Bassishaw (Harleian Society, London, 1934).

The following printed parish registers were consulted:

St Michael and St Peter Cornhill	St James's Clerkenwell
St Lawrence Old Jury	St Michael Bassishaw
St Botolph's without Bishopsgate	St Olave's Hart Street
St Mary Somerset	St Matthew Friday Street
St Martin's in the Fields	St Martin's Ludgate
St Antholin's	All Hallows Barking
St Thomas Apostles	St Dunstan's in the East
	St Mary Woolneth

to correct infant mortality figures, and it will be apparent that the figures provided probably understate both infant and child mortality.[28] The parishes comprised a cross-section of wealthy, middle-range and poor areas; where the occupations of the husbands were known, it appears that about half the sample were drawn from the various trades and half from the crafts. Information on the migratory origins of these men and women was only sporadically given.

The second source is more problematic.[29] It is doubtful that wills are a particularly reliable source for a complete record of surviving children. Since the wills sometimes indicate only a partial transfer of property and goods at the time of the testator's death, it is possible that children who had already been provided for with dowries and child 'partes' (a form of *inter vivos* inheritance) were not always mentioned.[30] There are additional difficulties in using nuncupative wills, which were usually although not always brief. Frequently all the goods and property were entrusted to one legatee only – the testator's wife. It is quite possible that these apparently childless marriages concealed unmentioned children. If the reconstituted parish marriages overstate the number of surviving children it would be fair to conclude that the wills understate the number of survivors – twin biases to be noted in assessing the statistics of tables 5.3 and 5.4.

The reconstituted marriages are, however, of interest in revealing a common pattern of serial monogamy and early orphanhood for children. Less than half of the marriages were between single men and women. Widows' marriages with bachelors account for over one-quarter of the reconstituted marriages (26 per cent) compared with 18 per cent of widows' marriages with widowers. Widowers' marriages with spinsters form 10 per cent of the total.

Of particular interest is the finding that widows had relatively few children in their remarriages with bachelors. Of the widows, 17 had no children and the remaining 12 marrying bachelors had a low average of 1.5 children per marriage. Their remarriages with widowers produced even fewer children. Widows rarely enjoyed long-lasting unions when they married either bachelors or widowers: the median length of all widows' marriages was as low as 2.1 years.[31] These findings are preliminary indications only, and many more families will have to be reconstituted before a characteristic pattern is established.

---

28 R.A. Finlay, *Population and metropolis. The demography of London 1580–1650* (Cambridge, 1981), p. 100.

29 GL Bishop of London Commissary Court MS 9172 reels 1–16. Microfilms of original wills, 1580–1600, University of Queensland Library.

30 L. Bonfield, 'Contrasting sources: court rolls and settlements as evidence of hereditary transmission of land among small land owners in early modern England', *University of Illinois Law Review* (1984), pp. 653–8.

31 London reconstitution, FRF 1–250, in author's possession.

The apparently low fertility of widows and their generally brief subsequent marriages have some influence on the aggregated statistics of table 5.3, which summarizes the marriage duration of all 104 marriages, the numbers of children born and the numbers surviving to age 12 as well as the proportions of childless marriages.

Despite the limitations of a small sample of marriages, it is clear from table 5.3 that the permanent residents of London had little likelihood of replacing themselves. Large families were confined to those atypical individuals who enjoyed unions of 15 years or more – about one-third of all the marriages. An average of 2.0 surviving children per marriage bears a spurious resemblance to the consciously reduced fertility of modern industrial societies. Such apparent 'modernity' for sixteenth- and seventeenth-century Londoners was an artefact of high death rates and short-lived marriages: more than half of all marriages lasted ten years or less.

The analysis in table 5.4 of 494 wills of married and widowed testators for the period 1580–97 parallels the findings of table 5.3. As many as 42 per cent of testators – married men, widowers and widows – appear to have had no surviving children. A further 24 per cent could name only one surviving son or daughter, while those who could boast of large families of five to nine surviving children account for only 3.6 per cent of testators. As I have suggested, it may be the case that these figures of survivorship are too pessimistic; yet one would not wish to err on the side of generosity. There are too many indications from the reconstituted marriages that London families were drastically affected by the prevailing high death rates.

Table 5.3   Duration of marriage, average numbers of children born per family and average numbers of children surviving per family, London 1580–1610

No. of marriages lasting (years)	No. of marriages	Total no. of children	Total surviving to age 12	Childless marriages	Average no. of children per marriage	Average no. surviving
0–2	13	4	0	8/13	0.3	0
2–4	7	7	5	2/7	1	0.7
4–6	6	14	11	1/6	2.3	1.8
6–8	10	21	14	3/10	2.1	1.4
8–10	19	15	6	5/19	0.8	0.3
10–12	9	36	26	0/9	4.0	2.9
12–15	7	16	11	3/7	2.3	1.6
15–20	17	126	72	0/17	7.4	4.2
20–30	9	56	32	1/9	6.2	3.6
30+	7	43	30	0/7	6.1	4.3
All	104	338	207	23/104	3.3	2.0

Table 5.4 Numbers of surviving children per will, percentages and
cumulative frequency distribution, London 1580–1596

No. of testators (n=494)	No. of surviving children per will	Cumulative %	% of sample
207	0	42	42
118	1	66	24
99	2	86	20
35	3	93	7
17	4	96.4	3.4
8	5	98	1.6
5	6	99	1.0
2	7	99.4	0.4
3	9	100	0.6

To conclude the discussion of aggregated statistics, tables 5.3 and 5.4 lend further support to those historians who have long inclined to the view that the birth surpluses of rural England were the population mainstay of London. Left to itself, for the period 1580–1680 at least, natural decrease in the city would have continued unabated.[32]

At the individual level, how men and women experienced their often short-lived unions and the deaths of their infants and children remains a matter for conjecture, but the evidence suggests it would be difficult to sustain a view of the metropolitan family as a particularly stable and secure institution. By citing the experiences of several individuals the precarious character of family formation will be obvious.

We begin with the marriage of a London draper, Richard Dodd, who resided in the wealthy parish of St Michael Cornhill. His first marriage, at 30, to the daughter of a Coventry innholder lasted four years and nine months, producing two sons, one of whom died within days of birth.[33] In 1587, at 34, he was a widower with a 19-day-old son, who very likely died. His second marriage, occurring nine months after the death of his first wife, was again to a single woman, originally from Guildford in Surrey.[34] This marriage lasted nine years and five months and was apparently childless. In 1598 he was widowed again, and eight months later he was married for the third time, at the age of 44; his new wife was the daughter of a barber surgeon of St Michael Cornhill.[35] Their marriage, of five years' duration, produced four chil-

32 Especially E.A. Wrigley, who made this point 20 years ago in 'A simple model of London's importance in changing English society', *Past and Present* no. 37 (1965), pp. 46–7.
33 London reconstitution, FRF 31.
34 Ibid., FRF 32.
35 Ibid., FRF 33.

dren, only two of whom, Lydia and Jeremy Dodd, appear to have been alive when their father died at the age of 53. Lydia was a child of two years eight months, her brother a baby of three months, and their mother Elizabeth a young widow of 29. Elizabeth remarried within eight months.[36] Her husband, a white baker of St Michael's, was a young widower of 33, whose first wife had died in childbirth. He was apparently childless, his first marriage having lasted four years.[37] The young widow and widower, both recently bereaved, had a short-lived marriage of only two years, Elizabeth dying at 31, leaving the now twice-widowed baker, John Cowdarye, with a five-year-old stepdaughter and a three-year-old stepson. The subsequent history of these three individuals remains unknown, but it is significant that there were six adults involved in this convoluted series of marriages and only two living children produced.

Moving to that poorer and ill-fated riverside parish of St Mary Somerset, for which Roger Finlay has postulated from the high infant and child mortality figures an overall life expectancy for the inhabitants of 21 years at birth,[38] we encounter the marriage in 1578 of Ellen Battison, a single woman, and William Pearson, an alebrewer.[39] Their marriage lasted 19 years. Ten children were born; seven of them died, two as young children of four and five years, and five in their first year of life. Widowed at the age of 44, Ellen Pearson remarried a merchant tailor and widower of the same parish within six months.[40] Her three surviving daughters were apparently aged 18, 16 and six at the time and no subsequent children were born. Ellen died in 1619, a widow at the comparatively old age of 65.

Thomas Ivie, a blacksmith of St Olave's Hart Street parish, suffered even more extreme losses: four of his children, Jane, Thomas, Miles and Anne were aged one year, one year seven months, two years four months, and two years six months at their respective deaths.[41] His daughter Marie, an 11-day-old baby at the death of her mother, miraculously survived to be accommodated within his second marriage six weeks later to the 20-year-old daughter of a London haberdasher.[42] Little Marie outlived her two half-sisters, Edith and Elizabeth, who died at one year eight months and at four years respectively. She subsequently died at the age of five. By 1610, at the age of 38, Thomas Ivie had buried two daughters and two sons from his first marriage; his first wife; the only surviving daughter of his first marriage; and two

36 Ibid., FRF 26.
37 Ibid., FRF 25.
38 Finlay, *Population and metropolis*, p. 108.
39 London reconstitution, FRF 124.
40 Ibid., FRF 160.
41 Ibid., FRF 54.
42 Ibid., FRF 55.

daughters from his second marriage. This was a total of eight individuals. His second marriage lasted close to 20 years and he was left a widower in 1610 with five young children – a 14-year-old daughter, an 11-year-old son, and eight-year-old daughter, a six-year-old daughter and a three-year-old son. Six months later, in 1625, all five children were fully orphaned with the death of their father.

The precarious family was also the pessimistic family. From the wills it is clear that two children were sometimes given the same name in the hope of one surviving: Richard Adams, a brown baker, referred to his two daughters as Elizabeth Adams and Elizabeth Adams *the younger*, and other instances could be cited.[43] Secondly, pessimism is indicated in the practice of testators who reserved their bequests to another legatee in the event of the death of all their children, even where four or five sons and daughters were named – an anticipated reality, not just a written formula or too scrupulous a concern for the ultimate destination of the testator's property.

Beyond these pathetic vignettes are instances of even more extreme serial monogamy. At the relatively late age of 29, Frances Medewell married by banns John Eastland, a householder of St James's Clerkenwell.[44] One month later she was a widow. Her second marriage occurred within 18 months, at the age of 31, to Thomas Chambers, a widower and a fishmonger, aged 46, also of St James's.[45] A son Francis was born six months later. For a second time Frances was left a widow at the age of 33 with a two-year-old son. Less than two years later she married at 35, and while the details of her third marriage to John Silson can not be recovered, the register notes in 1620 the marriage of Thomas Austen and Frances Silson, widow of John – Frances's fourth and perhaps not her last marriage, at 44.[46]

We have seen that widow Frances Eastland was pregnant when she married for the second time. There are, in addition, other cases which imply pre-marital sexual activity by widows. Widowed in 1598 at the age of 33, Agnes Broade, for example, was a resident of St Botolph's without Bishopsgate parish. Her husband Henry was variously described as a 'salter' in the marriage licence and as a 'sope boyler' in the parish register.[47] Twelve months after his death, widow Broade married

43 GL Commissary Court MS 9172 reel 3: 30 May 1587, will of Richarde Adam. The practice of giving two children the one name should be recognized, and runs counter to Dr Finlay's assumption 'that if two children in one family are given the same forename the first child would already have died when the second was christened. ... *Parents would not have called two children by the same name* even if one of them were not living at home.' Finlay, *Population and metropolis*, p. 95 (my emphasis).
44 London reconstitution, FRF 42.
45 Ibid., FRF 27.
46 Ibid., FRF 7.
47 Ibid., FRF 15.

a Thomas Ashby, a young serving man of 27.[48] Their son Joseph was baptized one month later. Her second marriage lasted less than one year; she died at the age of 36, leaving two daughters from her previous marriage, aged seven and four, and the son of her second marriage, who subsequently died at the age of five.

III

The evidence presented suggests that the biological family of London may have been an essentially tenuous institution. Without the buttresses of household organization, wider kinship networks, neighbourly sociability and the more formal company structures, this inherently fragile grouping of parents and children was inadequate for the satisfaction of physical and emotional needs. Its senior members were assailed by the loss of a spouse and the death of children, and its junior members by sudden orphanhood at early ages or by the bewilderingly rapid introduction of new stepfathers and stepmothers. The majority of London households were constantly changing in composition as apprentices died or ran away, never to finish their terms, as servant girls came and went, as children were put out to nurse and frequently did not return, as widowed parents remarried, as surviving children were sent out to service elsewhere, and as plague periodically raged, threatening many households with sudden and virtual extinction.

The Elizabethan penchant for rings with 'deathes heades' was perhaps unsurprising. Who, indeed, could pin their hearts to any sleeve, whether it was that of a child, a wife, a husband or an apprentice, and not anticipate loss? Such a demographic regime was perceived variously by testators as this 'vale of sorrows', as 'the fraile estate of this transitory life', as 'the fragilitie and short tyme of man's life ... and how certain and sure death is to mankind and the hour and time thereof most uncertain.'[49] In some respects the metropolitan family had a markedly different emotional coloration from its rural counterpart: *pessimistic*, regarding the survival of its children to adulthood; *kin oriented*, with a pronounced dependency on more distant kin especially noticeable among women; *unsentimental* in its rapid replacement of dead wives and husbands; and more *outwardly directed* towards kin and friends, neighbours, fellow goodwives and workers.

Where do widows fit into this picture? Apart from their problematic experiences of loss in burying children and husbands, how many chose a different option and struck out for themselves as the heads of an inherited craft or trade? In the current reclaiming of married and widowed women's contribution to the economy, in both the private and

---

48 Ibid., FRF 5.
49 GL Commissary Court MS 9172: 26 October 1592, will of Julyan Hurstwayte, widow; 4 March 1591, will of John Derry, merchant stranger and free denizen of London.

public sectors, much research effort has been expended in identifying active craftwomen and tradeswomen in sixteenth-century Lyons, Florence, Nuremberg and Calvinist Geneva.[50] In London, female economic activity was restricted by the combined forces of patriarchalism and fraternalism institutionalized in the household and, beyond, in about eighty London companies which held jurisdiction over virtually all trades and a myriad of craft specialities.[51] This was both a more organized and a more rigid system compared with the few sworn crafts of Lyons and the absence of guilds in Nuremberg, to name two examples.[52] The London companies provided an overarching structure for the thousands of male apprentices, journeymen and small masters, and were highly masculine in their identity and occupancy of positions of power – the masters, the wardens, the liverymen, the assistants and the yeomanry. Thanks to Mary Ann Clawson's incisive analysis of how institutionalized fraternalism joined forces with the patriarchalism of male-headed individual households, we are left in little doubt concerning the pre-eminently male occupational ordering of Tudor and early Stuart London.[53] Earlier research on the apprenticeship records of 15 London companies between 1570 and 1640 indicated an absence of female apprentices from the records of 8000 odd apprentices in the provisioning, textile, shoemaking and metal-working crafts and the retail trades.[54]

The weak occupational identity of married and widowed women, the only groups who were not formally debarred by company edicts from independent economic activity, is underscored in their infrequent appearances in both apprenticeship and freedom registers. Among the hundreds of individual male masters taking on apprentices are those few widows who appear sporadically in the records. Between 1597 and 1604 in the Cordwainers' Apprenticeship Register, wherein 450 youths were apprenticed to different masters, seven widows were mentioned.[55] In the Fishmongers' Company Register, for a similar timespan and roughly the same number of indentures, only four widows merit a mention.[56] The Grocers' Company, between the years 1629 and 1633,

50 See N.Z. Davis, 'Women in the crafts in sixteenth century Lyon', *Feminist Studies* 8 (Spring 1982), pp. 46–80. J.C. Brown and J. Goodman, 'Women and industry in Florence', *Journal of Economic History* 40 (1980), pp. 73–80; M.W. Wood, 'Paltry peddlers or essential merchants: women in the distributive trades in early modern Nuremberg', *Sixteenth Century Journal* 12 (Summer 1981), pp. 3–24; E.W. Monter, 'Women in Calvinist Geneva, 1500–1800', *Signs* 6 (Winter 1980), pp. 189–209.

51 Elliott, 'Mobility and marriage', chapter 3.

52 N.Z. Davis, 'The sacred and the body social in sixteenth century Lyon', *Past and Present* no. 90 (1981), p. 44; Wood, 'Paltry peddlers', p. 3.

53 M.A. Clawson, 'Early modern fraternalism and the patriarchal family', *Feminist Studies* 16 (Summer, 1980), pp. 370–1.

54 Elliott, 'Single women', p. 91.

55 GL MS 7351: Cordwainers' Audit Book, vol. 1.

56 GL MS 5576/1: Fishmongers' Apprenticeship Register, 1614–50.

discloses the names of the widows Swain, Foster, Godnett, Stamp and Dodd.[57] Only one woman, a widow taking on an apprentice, can be found in the Brewers' Register over a ten-year period,[58] while women are completely absent from the apprenticeship registers of the Carpenter's and Cutlers' Companies.[59]

From the formal company records, at least, the overall picture is an unimpressive one, and forms unconvincing evidence for an authoritative role in the urban economy by the widows of London craftsmen and tradesmen. There were, of course, those notable exceptions, women who pursued their trades and crafts and clung tenaciously to their guild privileges. Yet exceptions they surely must remain. As a consequence of there being virtually no formal apprenticeship opportunities for girls, women's labour in London might be described as unorganized, piecemeal, untrained and auxiliary in character. There are, moreover, indications that even the unskilled labour of women, of wives' assistance to their husbands, was under attack from the companies in the mid- and later sixteenth century. Additionally, it was ordered in 1590 that no more than 160 'persons being wives or widows of freemen could be granted licences as fish wives'. Such women had been described in 1584 as those 'who carry abroad any kind of task, fruit or such like things to be sold within the City'.[60]

Such formal obstacles and informal pressures emanating from well-organized male structures served to make rapid remarriage an attractive alternative to the independent exercising of a craft or trade as a widow. Some 50 per cent of craftsmen's widows married bachelors of the same or allied craft, and the figure is about the same for those widows of tradesmen. In widows' remarriages with widowers, 33 per cent made 'endogamous' marriages with men of the same or allied craft and trades.

In sixteenth-century Lyons we learn, from the work of Natalie Zemon Davis, that wives and widows played what might be described as a more active and visible role in the economy.[61] It is suggestive that the numbers of widows remarrying in Lyons was significantly lower than in London (25 per cent compared with 35 per cent).[62] Perhaps widowhood in Lyons offered more opportunities for economic independence.

While one cannot be too dogmatic on this point, it might be suggested that there were many negative influences at work discouraging trades-

57 GL MS 11, 593/1: Grocers' Register of Apprentice Bindings, 1629–65.
58 GL MS 5445/12/13/14: Brewers' Court Minutes, 1611–25.
59 GL MS 4329/2: Carpenters' Register, 1573–94; GL MS 7159/1,2: Cutlers' Registers.
60 Rappaport, 'Social structure and mobility', thesis, pp. 95–6.
61 Davis, 'Women in the crafts', pp. 49, 55, 65, 70.
62 Davis, 'The sacred and the body social', p. 43.

men's and craftsmen's widows from an active participation in the economy, particularly in those decades of economic distress in London. We do not find in London many English equivalents of the active *Unterkeuflin*, the *Zubringerinnen* and the *Keuflinnen* of Nuremberg – those women who, as wives and widows, dominated the victualling, appraising, second-hand goods and small provisions trades of Nuremberg.[63]

Denied formal office, often accommodated at separate tables at company dinners, widows would not have lacked suitors to guide them to a speedy remarriage and the taking over of the trade or craft of the widow's late husband. Certain exceptional widows did exercise considerable leverage and applied pressure in their own right, and were determined to preserve their standing within their company and to dictate the terms of their marriages, as Steve Rappaport has shown in his illuminating research on this point.[64] I cannot pretend to know how many women valued their economic independence. Yet it is clear that the work of married and widowed women in the London economy was always 'mediated through the men who dominated the economy and to whom they were married' (or widowed).[65] For many widows, remarriage, all things considered, was an appropriate proposition, and it could well be an anachronistically feminist conception to assume that most widows placed a desire for economic independence well beyond their conjugal and domestic aspirations. The reverse would be more likely.

Even those widows who had formal company rights and who also remained widows failed to exercise their right to take on apprentices or continue their late husbands' trades. It is not without significance that, of 70 widows left print shops by printers who died between 1553 and 1640, as many as fifty 'disposed of their shops – some almost immediately, some in a year or two, and a number in less than four years'.[66] Only ten of 200 London widows remembered apprentices in their wills – a figure that suggests that as few as 5 per cent of craftsmen's and tradesmen's widows were exercising their formal rights to take on apprentices. And it is significant that only *six* widows were known to have been practising a trade or craft from the large sample of masters that Rappaport investigated, a striking contrast with the older, more prosperous widows of aldermen, one-third of whom were involved directly in the economy.[67] It is possible that, in her influential study, Alice Clark gave undue prominence to the atypically independent, unusually wealthy widow in the late-sixteenth-century economy of London.[68]

63 Wood, 'Paltry peddlers', pp. 7–10.
64 Rappaport, 'Social structure and mobility', thesis, pp. 98–99.
65 Rappaport, 'Social structure and mobility', *London Journal*, p. 112.
66 P. Hogrefe, *Tudor Women* (Iowa, 1975), p. 87.
67 Rappaport, 'Social structure and mobility', thesis, p. 98.
68 A. Clark, *The working life of women in the seventeenth century* (London, 1919), chapter 5, pp. 150–235 (reprinted 1982).

There were, however, alternative means by which widows could support themselves in a sound, if less occupationally visible, way in the late Tudor economy of London. Widows might take in lodgers, for example, or they might function as rentiers in the urban economy. Certainly their role as money-lenders in rural communities has been well documented by historians,[69] and from a reading of their wills it is in their dual capacity as rentiers and as the facilitators of urban credit that the wealthier widows are conspicuous. The bills of hand, bonds and extra leases scattered throughout widows' wills suggest a more obvious means for the maintenance of the widow and her family. References to apprentices and the running of a business are rare by comparison.

Yet another influence restricting a woman's wider choices at widowhood was the determining hand of the husband himself. Theoretically a widow was empowered with a number of choices. In practice, choices were sometimes limited by the rival claims of sons and daughters, nephews and nieces, apprentices and servants. At this end of the spectrum is the situation of zero choice: the widow was straitjacketed by the provisions of her late husband's will, in which the endowing of leases and goods was made subject to her remaining a widow, bequests not lightly jettisoned for a penniless remarriage. Any notion of self-conscious 'strategies' or independent choices by widows concerning their futures must take into account the nature of the husband's predisposition to his widow.

The apparently unrelated issues of remarriage and economic independence are, in practice, bound up together. Husbands could clamp down on both possibilities by threatening the removal of bequests of leases and goods in the event of remarriage, reducing a woman to what she had personally brought to the marriage in goods and her lawful widows' thirds (see later). A husband could encumber his wife with the finding of sizeable portions and dowries for children at later ages, or he could alienate a shop and its equipment, the tools of the craft, and even pass on his apprentices to a son, brother or friend. Such acts would necessarily downgrade a widow's chances of remarriage and/or independent economic activity.

Images of 'clamps' and 'straitjackets' may be overly suggestive of patriarchal oppression. In certain wills, such a narrowing of choices could more readily be interpreted as indicating a man's protective and paternalistic attitude towards his wife. Thomas Field, a cordwainer of the parish of St Brides in Fleet Street, gave the executorship of his will and the residue of his goods to three men friends, 'in hope and truste yt they will kepte mayntaine find and releve Constance Field my wife with all things

---

69 R. Holderness, 'Credit in a rural community, 1660–1800', *Midland History* 3 (1975), pp. 101–2; K. Wrightson and D. Levine, *Poverty and piety in an English village: Terling 1525–1700* (New York and London, 1979), p. 101.

necessary for this life so far as the goods extend during her natural life'.[70] Clearly a new husband could not be included in 'all things necessary for this life'. He also forestalled his widow's right to bequeath her goods at her death by willing them to his daughter-in-law after the death of Constance; he relieved their apprentice of the rest of his apprenticeship (the end of unpaid labour); and he generously endowed Rose James, his maidservant, with his best gown faced with satin and 'the featherbed with the new tycke which lieth on my wife's bedde'.[71] Constance Field, we might infer, would probably be adequately maintained in her widowhood, but was denied the right to remarriage and to economic independence, control over her few goods, and even her new mattress to sleep on!

By drawing attention to those wills which limited the widow's future scenario and constrained her choices, it is noteworthy that children were usually involved as the rival claimants. Having dwelt on proscriptions, we can now acknowledge that such 'punitive' wills were a small minority (35 cases of a total of 315 wills). The mainstream attitude was an affirmative one, suggesting three elements: strong trust in a wife (80 per cent of married testators appointed their wives as sole executors of their wills); the absence of any constraints on remarriage beyond a cautionary safeguarding of their children's portions from the possible depredations of a future stepfather; and, finally, a high esteem and affection for wives among craftsmen and tradesmen alike. By the custom of the city of London, a widow was entitled to her 'thirds' (one-third of the property of her late husband), yet most widows were given a much higher proportion of their husbands' estates.

Keith Wrightson's emphasis on the conjugal, complementary bond between husband and wife can be underscored for most London testators.[72] Indeed, one can say that in familial relationships, at least from a man's viewpoint, this could be the deepest affective bond. Husbands and wives lived and worked together and shared the losses of their children. While there was concern for the adequate provisioning of surviving children, an engrained pessimism over their survival to legal age, coupled with mistrust and resentment over 'chargeable' children, quarrelling siblings, discontented daughters, and a concern lest their widows be 'vexed' or 'molested' by clamorous children, distanced fathers from their children. The subtle contrast between a man's attachment to his wife and a more distrustful attitude to his son is hinted at in the will of John Awdry, a citizen and painter stainer. He enjoined his son John not to 'in any wise by fayre speech ... deliver any thing or things, collers (colours) and pattens (patterns) without the consent of his mother who tenderly loves him and that he to doe his best to take paynes for her and to be her comfort as she hath always been to him'.[73]

70 GL MS 9172: 5 June 1581, will of Thomas Fielde.
71 Ibid.
72 Wrightson: *English Society*, pp. 92, 94.
73 GL MS 9172: undated will of John Awdrey, probated 24 April 1592.

There were many men who appear to have had no surviving children (42 per cent), and it is an indication of the narrowly male conception of kinship that wives were placed much higher than children, brothers, sibling, kinsmen and friends in affection (the conventional phrase 'well-beloved wife' is not devoid of meaning). Wives were appointed as executors and substantially endowed with goods, which facilitated their smooth re-entry into the remarriage market. In their high regard for their wives, many husbands, tradesmen and craftsmen alike, were exemplars of William Whateley's earnest injunction: 'For the first, a man must love his wife above all the creatures in the world besides. ... No neighbour, no kinsman, no friend, no parent, no child should be so near and dear'.[74]

The overall trust in wives and the absence of constraints upon them helps explain the rapid remarriage of craftsmen's and tradesmen's widows. Large sums of capital, shops and leases to 'dear' and 'well-beloved' wives all promoted a freedom of choice. Edward Pursell, a skinner, gave all his goods and leases to his 'well-beloved wife Margaret', only wishing (not ordering) 'she leave over the trade of victualling to William Allen and Rebecca his wife and she to dispose herself to gods service and go to Church and praie' – the only reference in the entire sample of wills to indicate a different occupation of the wife as a victualler from her husband's trade as a skinner.[75]

The property of a woman brought to marriage as a dowry, often comprising extensive amounts of furniture, household utensils and quantities of linen, was usually viewed by the husband as her own and returned to her at his death, further augmented by his own goods. Substantial dowries to a remarriage were thereby created. The material expectations of wives were, on occasion, forthrightly stated, as in the testamentary cause of a son disputing his dead father's bequest to his wife, the stepmother. In September 1593 the testator was sick of the plague. He made his will and signed it. Then his wife was called in and the will read to her. She did 'find fault that her husband had given her but £400 which was no more, as she then said, that she had brought with her to him, saying that she had deserved more than she had brought with her to him by reason. ... *they had lived about three years together*'.[76] Another witness testified that Ann 'was grieved that she had no more given unto her by the said testator saying that she seemed to be *accompted of by the testator her husband as a servant* because he had given her no more in value than she had brought with her'. Anne got her way: 'he asked what would content her and she asked for the lease of his house', a request he complied with.[77] Marriage was clearly seen, by widow Denwell, alias Vanderpost, as a

74 William Whateley, *A bride-bush or a direction for married persons* (1619), p. 38.

75 GL MS 9172: 8 June 1592, will of Edmond Pursell.

76 GL Deposition Book in the London Commissary Court, vol. 9065 A/C, fo. 234; my emphasis.

77 Ibid., fo. 237.

form of capital investment with yearly accruing rates of 'interest'. Yet it is also clear from the wills of single women that daughters expected, as a matter of course, to be provided with portions: the angry response of a young servant girl of Stepney was apparent 'and said that her father gave her nothinge and nothing she would give unto hym'.[78] Evidence of this nature intimates a self-conscious awareness among daughters and widows of their material rights. Many fathers and husbands were poor, however, and both their daughters and widows were correspondingly disadvantaged in the marriage market.

London wills are considerably more representative of the middle- and lower-status crafts than the marriage licences: only 35 per cent of married and widowed male testators were high-status tradesmen compared with 58 per cent of grooms in the marriage licence sample. Correspondingly, 65 per cent of will-makers were middle- and low-status London craftsmen (cf. 42 per cent of craftsmen marrying by licence). There were larger numbers of poorer men, tailors, porters, weavers, and blacksmiths who made wills in writing or, nuncupatively, by word of mouth. The lower we descend in the occupational hierarchy the more limited was the value of overall bequests.

A possible third of all married male testators consigned their wives to a future life of economic hardship and doubtful prospects of remarriage. For some testators, one detects sentiments of personal failure and a sadness that they had so little with which to endow their 'well-loved' wives. Thomas Salmon, a poor cutler, declared 'if he had a thousand pounds more he would give it all to his wife';[79] 'if there were more, I would give nothing from her', from a humble porter;[80] William Kempton, whose inventory was appraised at only £12 18s, said that 'if he had a great deal more his wife was worthy of it and she should have it'.[81] Who could doubt the strength of feeling in the will of Francis Bradshawe, a London grocer, for 'his dear and loving wife who I make my full and sole executrix beseeching God to give her much joy thereof being very sorrowful that I cannot leave her better'.[82] And John Lett, a seafaring man, 'in fight wounded to death', willed the 36s in his purse to his wife 'and all other goods whatsoever ... desiring her to take care of herself how she bestowed herself againe upon any seafaring man but that should take one that was able to keep her and like a man'.[83]

The strained material resources of such husbands are repeated in the wills of poorer widows, for whom widowhood was generally enduring. Agnes Fulgram made her only bequest of £5 to her son William 'to be

78 GL MS 9172: 2 April 1588, nuncupative will of Elizabeth Thomson, servant.
79 GL MS 9172: 2 November 1592, will of Thomas Salmon.
80 GL MS 9172: 2 July 1593 nuncupative will of Thomas Gee.
81 GL MS 9172: 12 May 1594, nuncupative will of Thomas Kempton.
82 GL MS 9172: 5 April 1592, will of Francis Bradshawe.
83 GL MS 9172: 7 August 1590, nuncupative will of John Lett.

raysed out of such poor implements and household stuffe as I shall leave behind'.[84] Even widows with greater resources had difficulties in maintaining themselves, especially where there were dependent children. Katherine Hollydaie, who kept an apprentice Toby Frank, confessed she owed her maidservant Jane Fenton £10. A widow with five children, she gave 20 shillings and the lease of her dwelling house to her brother so that he would bring up one daughter Susan, and asked her executor, her 'well-beloved friend' John Weiks, a merchant tailor, to see her sons John and Richard 'kept and brought up in the feare of God during their minoritie'. The debt to the loyal servant Jane was to be repaid, and in addition Widow Hollydaie bequeathed her 'a spining wheele, a fether bed with a bolster, a rugge, a platter, a dish, a sallet dish and an old kirtle'.[85] In the absence of brothers and 'well-beloved' friends, widows had to turn to the parish. Alice Garde of All Hallows Barking, a widow with three children, desired 'the maisters of the said parish to take my daughter Helen Garde ... and see her broughte up by their appointment'.[86]

IV

Many widows were well endowed with goods, property and often sizeable amounts of capital. The average number of bequests made in widows' wills was as high as 8.2, apart from their bequests to charities and London companies and their provision for sermons at their burials. The aggregated statistics from 131 wills provided in table 5.5 summarized an apparent variety of experiences. For about one-third of all widows, the few bequests made show a narrow concentration on their surviving children, and limited resources; for other widows, bequests extended to neighbours and their servants, distant kin and their many friends who were usually female.

This is not the first time a greater 'diffuseness' in widows' wills has been noted.[87] When the bequests are analysed more closely, two features are prominent: a recognition of distant kinship ties, and the significance of friends, neighbours and servants in the lives of widows.

The daily social interactions of most widows were determined principally through the locality of neighbourhood; their more intimate relationships centred on their surviving children, sons-in-law, brothers and sisters, grandchildren, cousins and fictive kin (godchildren and servants). And finally, for some widows, the London companies continued to structure their associations, friendships and sociability.

84 GL MS 9172: 31 August 1591, will of Agnes Fulgram, widow.
85 GL MS 9172: 15 November 1591, will of Katherine Hollydaie, widow.
86 GL MS 9172: 16 November 1596, will of Alice Garde, widow.
87 J.A. Johnston, 'The probate inventories and wills of a Worcestershire parish, 1676–1775', *Midland History* 1 (1971), p. 32; R.T. Vann, 'Wills and the family in an English town', *Journal of Family History* (Winter 1979), p. 366.

Table 5.5 Number of individual legatees named in widows' wills, London, 1580–1595 (excluding bequests to charities and companies and requests for sermons at burials)

Number of legatees per will	Number of wills (n=131)	% of total wills	Cumulative frequency (%)
1	16	12.2	12.2
2	14	10.7	22.9
3	14	10.7	33.6
4	9	6.8	40.4
5	11	8.4	48.8
6	12	9.2	58.0
7	6	4.6	62.6
7–10	14	10.7	73.3
10–15	16	12.2	85.5
15–20	4	3.1	88.6
20–30	10	7.6	96.2
30–40	4	3.1	99.3
40–50			
50–60	1	0.7	100

Since so little is known about kinship and neighbourly relations for London in this period, a few general remarks might be in order and might help provide an overall context within which the familial orientations of widows may be more fully understood. In a city of so many provincial migrants, it can hardly have been likely that kinship counted as a powerful force in social relationships for either men or women. We might anticipate *some* attenuation of wider kinship ties, where so many individuals residing in the city were born outside London, an attenuation further exacerbated by the prevailingly high death rates. For those women and men born *in* the city, however, the perils of high mortality notwithstanding, there are indications of well-developed kinship networks extending to secondary kin and cousins, noticeable at all social levels, yet most conspicuous for those of the middle and upper social strata. Such networks were constantly kept alive in the arranging of marriages, apprenticeships, and loans of capital for the setting up of a business. The instrumental strength of kinship, for native Londoners, provides some explanation of their advantageous position in trade, politics, business and marriage compared with the migrant newcomers.

I have discussed elsewhere how London kin could also render assistance to their provincial relatives – particularly for young apprentices and single girls arriving in London. For migrant girls, the presence or absence of kin in London spelled the difference between an upwardly mobile marriage to a London craftsman or tradesman and downward mobility.[88]

How these differences affected widows is less clear. Widows who had been born outside London had fewer brothers, sisters and cousins to turn to for aid and sociability. It is rarely possible to differentiate provincially born widows from Londoners in their wills: the origins of testators remain largely unrecoverable. Certainly the great emphasis placed on neighbours by many widows in their wills implies that neighbourhood replaced kinship as the key determinant of their social interactions. This is obvious in citing the will of Elizabeth Foulks, a widow of St Giles in the Fields. Her four female neighbours – Margarie Griffin, Averie Hankinson, Elizabeth Morgan and Ellen Cooke – witnessed her brief will. Hugh Hankinson and Richard Cooke, the husbands of Averie and Ellen, were appointed as the executors of her will. The overall value of widow Foulks's goods was assessed at £14 4s 2d, and her principal bequest, the sum of £5 was to her 'kinsman' Richard Younge.[89] He was also to receive 5s she had lent to her neighbour John Griffin. Goodwife Hankinson was to have all the 'shelves, boards and tables standing in my low room next the street'. In addition widow Foulks left to 'four of my neighbours' children a pewter platter. That is Isabell Hankinson, Phillip Cooke, John Griffin and Daniel Morgan'. Her executors were enjoined 'to make a drinking amongst my neighbours' as well as 'bestowing what they pleased on the poore of this parish'.[90]

When all legatees named in 200 widows' wills are analysed it is significant that some 55 per cent were unrelated friends, servants, goodwives, neighbours and their children. That so many interactions were acknowledged and recognized with gifts in wills indicates the subjective strength of neighbourly relationships for many widows. A high proportion of these unrelated legatees were women. Although of no apparent consanguineous or affinal connection, scores of such women were remembered in small bequests of clothing, money, household utensils and napery – often of trifling value yet carefully described in many wills. While male commentators made much of the 'gossip', 'tattle' and 'idle chatter' of city women in the streets together, at markets, at 'hot houses' (public baths) and elsewhere,[91] for many widows, within their informal networks of neighbourly associations, in what was pre-eminently an oral culture, the 'talk of women friends' found meaningful expression.[92]

Such interactions describe the majority of widows. In addition there was a sizeable minority of widows whose little worlds extended beyond the

88 Elliott, 'Single women', p. 93.

89 GL MS 9172: 14 April 1596, will of Elizabeth Foulks, widow.

90 Ibid.

91 1603 woodcut 'Tittle Tattle', reproduced in V. Pearl, 'Change and stability in seventeenth century London', *London Journal* 5 (1979), p. 24.

92 F.L. Johnson and E.J. Aries, 'The talk of women friends', *Women's Studies International Forum* 6 (1983), pp. 353–61.

parish to individual companies, wherein friendships and associations, formed through their late husbands, were maintained and relied upon until their own deaths. Why else would they have solicited the attendance of the liverymen or the fellows of this or that company at their burials? And who could ignore the sense of connexion many widows felt with the company? Craftsmen's and tradesmen's widows were certainly always excluded from formal office and power and they may have rarely exercised their formal privileges to enrol apprentices, yet they were the beneficiaries of low-interest company loans and, in times of hardship, the recipients of relief and occasional hand-outs.[93] More prosperous widows in their wills made generous bequests of money for 'drinkings', 'recreations' and 'dinners' to the companies, and appointed company men, their 'well-beloved' friends, as their executors and overseers. Some of their expensive silver plate and large goblets eventually garnished the company halls.

Some widows, like Ann Johnson, acknowledged fairly equally the claims of both the company and her neighbours: she gave £3 to 'the Livery of the Company of Vintners' to accompany her body to church and £4 'unto and among my neighbours which shall carry my body to the church for to be merry withall after my buriall'.[94] For widow Joyse Williamson, the Clothworkers' Company figured more prominently. She was one of the most wealthy widows to leave a will, bequeathing a 'free and franke gifte of £100' to the Clothworkers' Company, appointing two members of the company as the overseers of her will, and requesting that her bequest of £1000 to her grandson and granddaughter be invested in the Clothworkers' Company at 5 per cent per annum. Perhaps an active 'clothworker' herself, she had at least one apprentice, her god-daughter Joyse Ware, and remembered six godsons of no apparent kin relationship to her.[95] One is reminded that the institution of godparenthood might be a useful device in enlisting the patronage of such substantial widows as Mistress Williamson.

There is, indeed, much to uncover in the choice of godparents in London. In half the cases, it appears to have been utilized to reinforce or cement more distant kinship ties, where godchildren were the offspring of cousins and sometimes of siblings. In other cases it was a relationship between non-kin, a creation of fictive kinship ties for the primarily instrumental reason of sponsorship. Yet there are also those instances of godparenthood as examples of what Esther Goody has described as pro-parenthood[96] – not without appeal or emotional significance when as

93 S. Rappaport, 'Social structure and mobility in sixteenth century London, part 2', *London Journal* (forthcoming, 1985), pp. 11–15. I am indebted to Dr Rappaport for making available to me his forthcoming article and sections of his unpublished Ph.D. dissertation.
94 GL MS 9172: 7 October 1596, will of Ann Johnson, widow.
95 GL MS 9172: 17 February 1593, will of Joyse Williamson, widow.
96 E.N. Goody, 'Forms of pro-parenthood: the sharing and substitution of parental roles', in J. Goody (ed.), *Kinship*, pp. 337–41.

many as 40 per cent of widows appear to have had no surviving children. One in five widows remembered at least one godchild in their wills; all other groups of testators (unmarried men and women, married men) remembered significantly fewer godchildren. Widows also remembered proportionately more servants. In many cases, the apparently close relationships between widows and their servants provide further examples of the fostering and adoptive dimensions of pro-parenthood.

Widows had also the highest recognition of cousins (20 per cent), nieces and nephews (18 per cent) of all testators. They acknowledged proportionately more affines – brothers- and sisters-in-law, the spouses of cousins – than married men or widowers. Even the classic antagonism between mother and son-in-law was rarely evident. Sons-in-law were frequently appointed as executors, while only 6 per cent of widows left bequests to their daughters-in-law (20 per cent acknowledged sons-in-law). And, it would seem, our perception of widows as grandmothers might have to be confined to only 27 per cent of all widows, a consequence of low life expectancies for both men and women and few surviving children to produce grandsons and granddaughters. In terms of the *value* of bequests, it is certainly the case that widows' families and kin received the lion's share of their estates, the leases of their tenements and, in addition, large cash sums and their most valuable property. Neighbourly and non-kin relationships, while both numerous and frequently acknowledged in their wills, were of limited value in *material* terms.[97]

If I have succeeded in persuading historians of the family to unlock the household doors and contemplate the wider vistas beyond of neighbourhoods and companies, of particular relevance in understanding the experience of widows and, to a marginally lesser extent, of husbands and wives in the city, I might also reiterate David Herlihy's point that 'household members ... rarely live in total isolation in a spatial sense from other households. The relationships among the neighbouring households reverberate upon and affect the internal structure of each'.[98] The reduction of space in the urban context and the enhanced physical proximity of neighbours is self-evident. One might also extend Professor Herlihy's comment to the London companies, the central importance of which, in regulating the economy and society of early modern London, has been admirably demonstrated recently.[99] There are possibly wider ramifications to consider. I have only hinted at how the presence and organizational complexity of the pre-eminently masculine London companies might have curbed widows' participation in the crafts and trades of London. One might also conjecture that companies acted in informal,

97 A more detailed exploration of kinship and neighbourly ties will be included in a forthcoming book by the author on migration, marriage and the family in early modern London.
98 D. Herlihy, 'The making of the medieval family: structure, symmetry and sentiment', *Journal of Family History* (Spring 1983), p. 117.
99 Rappaport, 'Social structure and mobility, parts 1 and 2', *London Journal*.

unrecorded ways as clearing-houses of marriages and remarriages. At one symbolic level they provided models of hierarchically ordered rela- tionships – 'estates' of masters with journeymen and apprentices repli- cated in miniature in household relationships. In another related symbolic sense, the company itself might be perceived as a macrocosm of the family, with its master as 'father' at its head, in its manifest concern for the well-being of its lesser members and in its arbitrating of the conflicts and disputes of its 'children'. Yet here was an institution with a strength, perdurance and stability absent in the microcosm of the biological family of late Elizabethan London: hence the significance of the company as a reference point and a source of identity for many Londoners, men and women, husbands and wives, widowers and widows.

V

Having begun with what seemed an apposite metaphor from Thomas Dekker's *Westward Ho*, it now seems appropriate by way of conclusion to draw together the disparate themes of this essay and to express them in a symmetrical, if somewhat fanciful, metaphor of the workings of the London marriage market.

The 'market' itself is located within a small arena, fenced in protective- ly. The gates are attended by the dowry keepers and the company clerks, guardians of admission to the freedom of the city. The vast numbers of spectators and the young, the migrants, the apprentices and the servant girls sit patiently far back in the audience. The much smaller section of the front stalls is occupied by the surviving daughters and sons of Londoners. Two grim regulators, Death and Poverty, stalk the crowds of spectators, emptying seats or demanding removal to the fringes of the crowd. Death is also a frequent visitor to the arena, the population of which is constantly changing and reordering. Periodically the gates open, to allow in young men and women who have satisfied the gatekeepers, and to carry out some who have been within the arena. Poor widows will be quickly escorted to the distant outskirts of the crowd, where they will live aimlessly, certain never again to pass the gatekeepers; Death will eventually banish them altogether. Some of the spectators – the apprentices serving out their terms, and their girlfriends, usually migrant servants – will sit together, hand in hand, waiting for many years to move closer to the gates. Many in the crowd will tire of the long wait and, if they manage to evade Death, will wander disconsolately back to the countryside whence they came, leaving their unfinished apprenticeships behind them, only to have their seats rapidly taken by scores of other young hopefuls from the villages.

The wealthier widows and widowers will be courteously escorted to a convenient waiting area just outside the gate, where they will remain in comfortable seats for a short time; then they will triumphantly rejoin the privileged ranks within. Many will find a partner in the waiting area itself, while others will catch the eyes of attractive young servant girls in the crowd and well-endowered London daughters in the stalls. Widows will be suitably impressed with the youth, vigour and opportunism of young journeymen and will give them a free pass to the arena. Prosperous widows, as they make their final exit from the crowd, will scatter among the spectators large sums of money and goods, especially to their nieces, granddaughters and sometimes their maidservants; the last now have a better chance of satisfying the dowry keepers at the gate and of passing into the arena sooner than they might have expected.

All those entering the privileged area are priding themselves on their new authority and conjugal status. Anticipating a leisurely stroll in a pleasant and secure garden, their confidence subsides as they realize that they have instead entered a precarious ice-rink; in certain places the ice is not properly frozen, and sudden cracks and holes will swallow them up. When Death, in a particularly vindictive mood, unleashes plague, many skaters fall down, never to get up again, or disappear through the ice; and the vast numbers of spectators' seats in the immense auditorium are almost instantaneously emptied of younger people, who either flee when they realize what is happening in the arena and in the crowd, or succumb in greater numbers to the disease itself. In the aftermath of Death's vindictiveness, the gatekeepers are kept constantly busy with all the new faces seeking admission for the first time. The new partners of the suddenly widowed, who are standing in large numbers in the waiting area, are impatient to enter. At any time nearly half the people in the rink will have been skating there before; many can be said to have been repeated visitors. Some have cherished memories of previous skating partners.

6

Normative Rules and Property Transmission: Reflections on the Link between Marriage and Inheritance in Early Modern England

Lloyd Bonfield

Nearly two decades ago John Hajnal outlined the features of a distinctive pattern of marriage which he suggested was unique to northern and western Europe.[1] The geographical connection between this area, which exhibited postponed marriage coupled with a high level of celibacy and modern economic growth, did not escape Hajnal. Nevertheless he proffered the link between what is now referred to as the European marriage pattern and the Industrial Revolution with some reticence, preferring to analyse the causes of the pattern rather than its consequences.[2] According to Hajnal, the key distinction between European and non-European marriage behaviour dealt with the economics of household formation. In the north and west of Europe, marriage resulted in the creation of new, independent social units, whereas elsewhere 'the young couple could be incorporated in a larger economic unit, such as a joint family.'[3]

Crucial to Hajnal's sketch of the European marriage pattern and his subsequent discussions of typologies of household formation[4] is the assumption that it is more expensive to form an independent household than to extend a pre-existing unit. To marry in the north and west of Europe therefore required a more substantial economic base, and Hajnal

The walls of E-2 Bishop's Hostel, Trinity College, Cambridge witnessed (or more likely ignored) numerous discussions of the importance of law in understanding social structure between the author and Peter Laslett, without which this very preliminary essay could not have been written. My thanks to Peter for his inspiration and to my coeditors Richard Smith and Keith Wrightson for comments and suggestions.
1 J. Hajnal, 'European marriage patterns in perspective', in D.V. Glass and D.E.C. Eversley (eds), *Population in history: essays in historical demography* (London, 1965), pp. 101–43.
2 Ibid., pp. 130–5.
3 Ibid., p. 133.
4 J. Hajnal, 'Two kinds of pre-industrial household formation system', in R. Wall (ed.), *Family forms in historic Europe* (London, 1983), pp. 65–104.

suggested that late marriage provided a period when individuals were productive and unburdened by family responsibilities and during which savings could be accumulated.[5] More specifically, he argued that the interval between puberty and marriage in north-western Europe was spent in service in a household headed by an individual other than one's biological parent, during which the opportunity for independent capital accumulation occurred. Hajnal stressed the way that this uniquely European circulation of servants underpinned the crucial flexibility of the pattern: in less favourable economic times the period of service could be extended, leading to a later age at marriage.[6] Late marriage and peripatetic young people both characterized and distinguished the north-western European system of household formation.

However, Hajnal recognized that alternatively, or perhaps conjunctively, the requisite stake to enable household formation could be raised through inheritance of family wealth.[7] With characteristic perceptiveness he recognized that intergenerational transfers of property occurred throughout the life course and not exclusively at the father's death: 'The rate at which land became available for the founding of new families may have been controlled not so much by death as by social arrangements.'[8] These arrangements – what lawyers call inheritance practice, and what Jack Goody has referred to as 'devolution'[9] – are both linked with service as being integral to Hajnal's conception of the economic reality of household formulation, and are the concern of this chapter.

What is striking about the interconnection of these two factors of marriage and inheritance is that neither is controlled by positive law. In the Christian north and west of Europe, marriage could be entered into freely and (significantly) without parental consent;[10] and although there

5 Hajnal, 'European marriage patterns', p. 132.

6 Hajnal, 'Two kinds of household formation', p. 72. Hajnal does not, however, elaborate upon the economic rationale which would allow the unmarried to remain in service when economic conditions were unfavourable to family formation. In a more elaborate version of the paper, published in *Population and Development Review* 8 (1982), Hajnal suggests that servants could move to areas where labour was required. Ann Kussmaul, for example, sees a cyclical demand for service in early modern England. As population rose and the cost of living increased, day labour became more economical since food and lodging was a large component of the cost of a servant: *Servants in husbandry in early modern England* (Cambridge, 1981). More evidence for the proposition that demand for servants was rather elastic and varied regionally ought to be offered before this segment of Hajnal's hypothesis is accepted.

7 Hajnal, 'European marriage patterns', pp. 133–4.

8 Ibid., p. 134.

9 J. Goody, *Death, property and the ancestors* (Stanford, California, 1962), pp. 311–14, and also his *Production and reproduction: a comparative study of the domestic domain* (Cambridge, 1976), chapter 7.

10 M.M. Sheehan, 'The formation and stability of marriage in fourteenth century England: evidence of an Ely register', *Medieval Studies* 33 (1971), pp. 228–63; R.H. Helmholz, *Marriage litigation in medieval England* (Cambridge, 1974), especially chapter 2. For interesting speculations on why marriage formation cases differ in late medieval England and France, see C. Donahue Jr., 'The canon law on the formation of marriage and social practice in the later Middle Ages', *Journal of Family History* 8 (1983), pp. 144–57.

were laws and customs of inheritance, recent studies have suggested that peasants were not captives of law but were able to construct suitable inheritance strategies outside the strictures of customary law.[11] With respect to England, Alan Macfarlane has argued that the laws of descent might be circumvented by plenary powers of alienation *inter vivos* out of the kin group, and perhaps more importantly by exercising virtually unlimited powers of devise.[12] Indeed most studies of early modern English inheritance law focus largely if not exclusively upon wills to illuminate the 'social arrangements' which Hajnal saw as crucial to household formation.[13] Although Macfarlane provides few examples of actual disinheritance, he views the potential as significant in itself, arguing that it is a component of the 'individualism' which sets England apart from continental peasant societies.[14] That parents retain the capacity to disappoint their heirs until death would certainly allow them to intervene in, if not control outright, their children's behaviour, including the decision of when and with whom marriage should take place. Moreover, postponing intergenerational transmission until parental death would, if wealth transfer is required for family formation, likely result in delayed marriage.

By contrast, continental scholars, while recognizing the link between inheritance and household formation, look towards ante-mortem arrangements that govern property devolution.[15] Their studies indicate flexible strategies, governed by a myriad of social and economic forces. Peasants were able to circumvent inheritance customs by *inter vivos* intervention. In areas of single-heir inheritance, portions comprised of personal property given to daughters and younger sons (or elder sons in areas of ultimogeni-

11 See, for example, the following essays in J. Goody, J. Thirsk and E.P. Thompson (eds), *Family and inheritance: rural society in western Europe 1200–1800* (Cambridge, 1976), pp. 33–111: E. le Roy Ladurie, 'Family structures and inheritance customs in sixteenth-century France'; L.K. Berkner, 'Inheritance, land tenure and peasant family structure: a German regional comparison'; and D. Sabean, 'Aspects of kinship behaviour and property in rural western Europe before 1800'. In addition, see the studies in H. Medick and D.W. Sabean (eds), *Interest and emotion: essays on the study of family and kinship* (Cambridge, 1984), in particular: B. Vernier, 'Putting kin and kinship to good use: the circulation of goods, labour and names on Karpathos', pp. 28–76; M. Segalen, '"Avoir sa part": sibling relations in partible inheritance Brittany', pp. 129–44; A. Collomp, 'Tensions, dissensions, and ruptures inside the family in seventeenth- and eighteenth-century Haute Provence', pp. 145–70. See also L. Assier-Andrieu, 'Custom and law in the social order: some reflections upon French Catalan peasant communities', *Law and History Review* 1 (1983), pp. 86–94.

12 Alan Macfarlane, *The origins of English individualism: the family, property and social transition* (Oxford, 1978), especially chapter 4.

13 See, for example, M. Spufford, *Contrasting communities: English villagers in the sixteenth and seventeenth centuries* (Cambridge, 1974), chapters 3–5, and also her essay 'Peasant inheritance customs and land distribution in Cambridgeshire from the sixteenth to the eighteenth centuries', in Goody et al., *Family and inheritance*, pp. 156–76. See also C. Howell, 'Peasant inheritance customs in the Midlands, 1280–1700', in Goody et al., pp. 112–55.

14 Macfarlane, *Origins of English individualism*, pp. 84–90, 164, 175–203.

15 See the thoughtful discussion in L.K. Berkner and F.F. Mendels, 'Inheritance systems, family structure and demographic patterns in western Europe,' in C. Tilley (ed.), *Historical studies of changing fertility* (Princeton, N.J., 1978), pp. 209–23.

ture) often exceeded the share required by law.[16] Conversely, in areas
where partible inheritance was the rule, the father could, in order to
preserve the viability of the family farm, undervalue his successor's
inheritance, thereby requiring the heir to pay reduced amounts to his
siblings.[17] Moreover, siblings themselves often agreed to circumvent
partible inheritance for similar reasons.[18] Likewise community norms and
social pressure prompted particular modes of distribution; social status,
for example, might require generous ante-mortem endowment.[19] Finally,
certain forms of agricultural production required the elder generation to
withdraw from the holding and agree to a retirement contract to secure
from the heir support in old age.[20] Lurking behind the scenes were, of
course, demographic variables, in particular limited life expectancy and
childlessness, that might require the adaptation of customary rules of
inheritance.

The continental studies therefore demonstrate the flexibility of inheritance practice within the rather rigid framework of positive inheritance
law. This research sheds some doubt upon the argument that England
was set apart from her continental neighbours with respect to the latitude
allowed to landowners in constructing inheritance strategies by the early
modern period. Furthermore, and perhaps more significantly, such
findings undermine the conclusions of historians who would discern
behaviour by reference to the dictates of inheritance law rather than
actual practice, and who might argue that positive law comprehensively
embodies a shared ideology.[21]

Studies of actual practice regarding intergenerational studies, rather
than a focus upon legal texts, will help to illuminate Hajnal's 'social
arrangements'.[22] Two issues regarding the link between household formation and inheritance in England need to be confronted. First, we must

16 Collomp, 'Tensions, dissensions, and ruptures', pp. 157–64.

17 Segalen, 'Avoir sa part', pp. 135–9.

18 Assier-Andrieu, 'Custom and law', pp. 92–4; L. Berkner, 'The stem family and the
developmental cycle of the peasant household: an eighteenth century Austrian example',
American Historical Review 77 (1972), pp. 398–418.

19 Vernier, 'Putting kin and kinship to good use', pp. 28–31.

20 Berkner, 'Inheritance, land tenure and peasant family structure', pp. 77, 88; and
Berkner, 'The stem family'.

21 For a general discussion of this question, see L.R. Poos and L. Bonfield, 'Law and
"individualism" in pre-modern England' *Social History* (forthcoming, 1986).

22 The most significant aspect (in Hajnal's words the 'uniqueness') of the European
marriage pattern is the limitation of family size engendered by late age at first marriage for
woman. Hajnal's discussion of the 'social arrangements' seems to focus on the transmission
of land to males, and he comments: 'Even if we understand how the age at marriage of men
was determined at a given period, it would still need to be explained how women's age at
marriage was affected.' Hajnal, 'European marriage patterns', p. 134. This paper takes a
broader view of inheritance – that it consists of both real and personal property (though only
the former is actually discussed here) and the share in family property that women receive.
'Social arrangements', therefore, affect age at marriage for both spouses.

discern whether the timing of intergenerational transfer was appreciably different on our side of the Channel. If, as has been suggested by historians, the tendency was towards post-mortem transfer by will rather than ante-mortem endowment, the case for England's distinctiveness is in one respect bolstered, and this practice may contribute to postpone household formation in England. Secondly, if the 'social arrangements' which Hajnal perceived as crucial to household formation were not governed by positive law, historians must ponder the forces which shaped inheritance strategies and produced the means to enforce them.

While the first issue can be confronted and resolved by local studies of devolution, the second concern requires the historian to ponder the nature of law in pre-industrial England. In a recent essay, formidably entitled 'Demographic and microstructural history in relation to human adaptation', Peter Laslett has drawn a distinction between two types of law.[23] On the one hand there are 'ethical rules' enforceable by legal sanction; Laslett offers the example of illegitimacy in early modern England, where a number of ecclesiastical and civil penalties applied to those who bore bastards. Standing beside this positive law are noumenal normative rules defined by Laslett as 'programmatic principles embedded in collective attitudes'.[24] According to Laslett, this alternative form of law, though unenforceable in a legal forum, governs age at marriage and therefore household formation.

The concern of this paper is to reflect upon the link between inheritance and household formation and to consider the extent to which the concept of normative rules is useful in understanding inheritance practice. We shall begin by relating studies of inheritance in early modern England to the broader process of devolution employed by anthropologists. After concluding that these enquiries are flawed because the *inter vivos* element of transmission is largely ignored, we shall illuminate the extent of such transfers in one manor during the course of the late sixteenth and the seventeenth centuries. Finally, an attempt will be made to relate these transfers to household formation, and then to consider the forces which control property transmission.

I

The documentary focus of studies of inheritance in early modern England has been largely upon probate records. Heeding the exhortation of Joan Thirsk,[25] researchers interested in intergenerational transfers

23 P. Laslett, 'Demographic and microstructural history in relation to human adaptation: reflections on newly established evidence', in D.J. Ortner (ed.), *How humans adapt: a biocultural odyssey* (Washington, 1983), pp. 343–70.

24 Ibid., p. 358.

25 J. Thirsk, 'The family', *Past and Present* 27 (1964), pp. 117–23; and *Unexplored sources in local records* (Canterbury, 1965), p. 16.

among the ranks of landholders below gentry status have produced local studies based primarily upon wills and inventories.[26] Underlying their conclusions are the tacit assumptions that the reconstruction of post-mortem transfers by will represents an accurate (or at least the most complete) picture of inheritance practice, and that the universe of will-makers is not inherently biased so as to render problematical the patterns of distributions discerned. Because our purpose is to consider the link between 'social arrangements' and household formation, the issue of frequency of testation is significant because the will is the last possible moment to direct the transfer of property between generations (as has been suggested above). Postponed transfer of resources to the next generation may contribute in part to late age at marriage. Because the point at which property passes between generations may be controlled by a myriad of social and economic variables, it is therefore necessary, in order to illuminate the role of wills in the context of the broader process of property devolution in early modern England, to isolate other factors.

Devolution embraces the totality of transfer of resources from the senior generation to the junior. Anthropologists who have elaborated upon the concept are interested in social reproduction and have therefore focused upon the shares of familial wealth dispensed rather than the timing of passage.[27] Historians have likewise been concerned with what might be called the 'how much to whom' of transmission rather than the 'when'. For example, in an exhaustive study of three Cambridgeshire villages, Margaret Spufford wished to consider the role of inheritance customs in the fragmentation of landholdings and focused upon the distributions of property directed in wills.[28]

Yet it would be unwise to ignore the issue of timing in attempting to understand the process of devolution, because the passage of property from the senior generation to the junior takes place at various stages in the life course. Attention to the 'when' of devolution will require us to ponder the suitability of wills for analysing patterns of distribution. One must not attempt to discern a continuous process by focusing upon one event, albeit a crucial one. Ignoring the issue of timing may entice the historian into believing that he is observing the totality of transfer rather than a point on a continuum. After all, if our concern lies with the pattern of devolution because we wish to gauge the extent

---

26 Spufford, *Contrasting communities*, and her 'Peasant inheritance customs'; C. Howell, *Land, family and inheritance in transition: Kibworth Harcourt 1280–1700* (Cambridge, 1983), chapter 10; and her 'Peasant inheritance customs'; K. Wrightson and D. Levine, *Poverty and piety in an English village: Terling 1525–1700* (New York, 1979), chapter 4; R.T. Vann, 'Wills and the family in an English town: Banbury, 1550–1800', *Journal of Family History* 4 (1979), pp. 346–67.

27 For example, see Goody, *Death, property and ancestors*, pp. 311–14.

28 Spufford, *Contrasting communities*, chapters 3–5.

to which partition of resources within the family may have led to the fragmentation of holdings or, in our case, governed the timing of family formation, then *inter vivos* transfers and customs of inheritance must be viewed alongside testamentary provision to gain an accurate picture of this process. Ignoring other methods of transfer because they are too difficult, or perhaps even impossible, to ascertain might produce misleading results.

Devolution is therefore a process that extends throughout the life course; the will represents only one phase. Piecing together the totality of intergenerational transfer should assist in drawing conclusions regarding the connection between property and family formation; focus on the will alone cannot, unless it is demonstrated to be the exclusive mode of transmission.

Yet this was not the case; most men did not write wills. It is appropriate to ponder why they failed to execute them in trying to understand the function of testation.[29] Save for those whose death was sudden, the preponderance of men who did not execute wills must have done so out of conscious choice: they were content with the inheritance custom in force and saw no need to ratify it. Either they had already passed substantial portions of their property to selected individuals, or they were willing to allow inheritance customs to run their course for the bulk of their wealth. Those who had very little property, of course, had less incentive to write a will; but it would be misleading to assume that those who had small amounts were unconcerned with its passage. Because probate fees were in theory minimal for the poor, cost should not have been a deterrent.[30] If we can control for social status, we may attempt to determine why some wrote wills and others did not by considering the inheritance custom in effect, what happens to property not disposed of during life or by testament, and the extent of *inter vivos* transfer, that is, what remains to be passed at death.

Devolution may therefore be conceptualized spatially in three tiers: *inter vivos* transfer, testamentary disposition and customary inheritance. The quantum of property passing at each level will depend upon individual choice, influenced no doubt by family relationships but also by inheritance customs and perhaps the nature of property involved.

29 More men may have written wills than probate records indicate. Some wills may have been destroyed by disappointed heirs or remained undiscovered. If, however, the majority of wills were written on one's death-bed by the parish priest, they would have been more difficult to conceal or destroy.

30 Probate fees were a subject of complaint against the Church courts in the Commons' Supplication against the Ordinaries of 1532. Fees which had previously been regulated by a provincial scale were set by statute, 21 Henry VIII, c. 5; for estates under the value of £5 the fee was 6d exclusive of scribe's fees. But even before the statute, over 40 per cent of estates in the Norwich Archdeaconry between 1525 and 1527 were too small to attract fees. Ralph Houlbrooke, *Church courts and the people during the English reformation* (Oxford, 1979), p. 95.

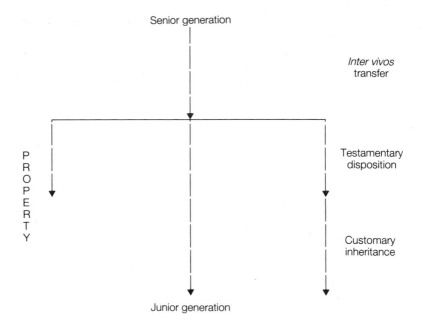

Figure 6.1　Model of devolution

Assuming that everyone makes some *inter vivos* transfer, we should find three permutations. The model might look like figure 6.1. This represents the pattern of devolution from the perspective of the senior generation. One might wish to view transmission from the opposite vantage point, that of heirs, in which a series of figures would be constructed, one for each heir, as in figure 6.2.[31]

What the figures illustrate is that concentration exclusively upon wills always results in the creation of an incomplete picture of devolution save in instances where *inter vivos* transfer is negligible. But the serious flaw from the perspective of the historian who wishes to observe the economic effects of patterns of distribution is the misleading picture that exclusive reliance on wills produces with regard to devolution. Failing to investigate the other two tiers might entice one into believing that daughters or younger sons or male heirs were excluded, when what has actually occurred is endowment by another means of

31 For the purpose of simplicity these figures only chart transmission of property from holder to heir. In reality property passed to others: relatives, servants, the poor etc. Moreover, intangibles such as status passed to the junior generation. I hope to undertake a more complete study of inheritance and to address these matters elsewhere. I owe this observation to Stephen White.

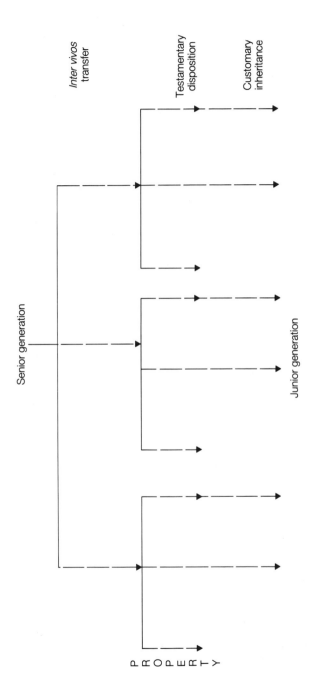

Figure 6.2   Model of devolution for multiple heirs

transfer.[32] For the historian who wishes to understand Hajnal's 'social arrangements', the frequency of will-making and the proportion of wealth passing through testation are crucial. If property passes generally at the death of the father, the transfer occurs at a later point in the life course of the junior generation, and perhaps helps explain late age at marriage in areas like north-western Europe where marriage requires the formation of a separate household.

Because alternative methods of intergeneration transmission existed, it is crucial to determine the percentage of men who wrote wills in order to consider the extent to which testation may have contributed to postponed household formation. Determining the percentage of men who wrote wills is helpful in understanding patterns of devolution, because our interest is also in isolating factors that led men to choose particular means of transfer. Furthermore it assists us in pinpointing the segment of society that wills-based studies of inheritance observe. After all, if will-makers are a small proportion of the population of the geographical area from which they are drawn, or if they are biased economically, or by age, the pattern ascertained reflects a particular group strategy or behaviour. While it is not inappropriate to focus upon a particular group rather than upon the community at large, most studies employing wills purport to deal with the latter without considering whether the sample is socially or economically biased.[33] Finally, such calculations may be helpful ultimately in ascertaining the reasons why men transmit property at particular stages in the life course.

Often it is difficult to ascertain the percentage of villagers who trouble themselves to make wills. To do so, one needs a parish register that has been the subject of a family reconstitution study or in which successive clerks have included age when noting burials. Without such information it is impossible to ascertain those dying over the age of testation. One study of inheritance considered this issue. Because the Banbury register was reconstituted, Richard Vann was able to calculate the rates of will-makers to intestates. He found that 25 per cent of males and 10 per cent of females buried in the parish who were 'potential testators' actually left wills.[34]

32 In discussing patterns of intergenerational transfer in particular families, Spufford is aware of the will's potential for creating a misleading picture of family size and wealth distribution. For example, Robert Tebbutt died in 1668. His will leaves all his goods valued at £258 19s 8d to his widow, 'and it sounds as if he was childless; in fact he left a son and daughter.' But his house and farm of at least 150 acres of leasehold was in the possession of his son Robert until the latter's death in 1682. Had Tebbutt been a copyholder, there would have been no evidence of his son's succession from the rental books she employs. We would conclude that Tebbutt either had no son, or that his son was disinherited. Spufford, *Contrasting communities*, pp. 72–4.

33 Spufford and Wrightson and Levine deal with resident villagers. Only Vann has separated the community into occupational groups.

34 Vann, 'Wills and the family', table 1, p. 352.

Because Banbury was a market town rather than an agricultural village, it would be useful to have similar calculations from villages studied by Spufford or from the Essex village of Terling, the subject of a detailed study by Keith Wrightson and David Levine. At the time Spufford's monograph was published the Cambridgeshire parishes had not been reconstituted, and the published indices of adult mortality in Terling cannot be used to ascertain deaths of men over the age of testation.[35] There is, however, an alternative method of estimating proportions of testators. Using a parish register with a reliable list of burials, we may make a crude calculation of 'potential testators' by employing model life tables.[36] First, appropriate model populations based upon assumptions of life expectancy and estimated rates of growth are selected. For the period 1550–1625, for example, West level 8 with a growth rate of 10 per 1000 is appropriate. If 29 is chosen as the age under which those buried will not be will-makers, about four deaths in ten were of persons over the age of testation (see table 6.1).[37] The proportion increases slightly over the period owing to the demographic trend. For purposes of simplicity, we can say that about half of the burials recorded in the parish register were persons over the age of testation. Assuming that burials were evenly distributed by sex, the

Table 6.1   Age distribution of deaths

	1550–1624[a]	1625–1674[b]	1675–1700[c]
Deaths age 29 and under (%)	58.37	55.26	54.69
Deaths age 30 and over (%)	41.63	44.74	45.31

The calculations were based upon:
[a]   Model West–Mortality Level 8; Population Growth Rate 10/1000
[b]   Model West–Mortality Level 7; Population Growth Rate 7/1000
[c]   Model North–Mortality Level 6; Population Growth Rate nil

35 A family reconstitution of the parish of Willingham has been completed and can be consulted at the Cambridge Group for the History of Population and Social Structure.

36 I have used the model life tables in A.J. Coale and P. Demeny, *Regional life tables and stable populations* (Princeton, 1966).

37 Admittedly the selection of 30 as the age of 'majority' for determining 'potential testators' is arbitrary. One might argue that the quinquennium 20–24 should be the dividing line because persons over 25 years might have enough property to warrant a will. However, marriage may be the event that creates need for a will because parents and spouse would be competing for the decedent's estate. During the course of the seventeenth century, the mean age at the first marriage for males was between 27 and 28. E.A. Wrigley and R.S. Schofield, *The population history of England, 1541–1871: a reconstruction* (London, 1981), table 10.1, p. 424. Because model life tables underestimate adult mortality, I think it justified to include the quinquennium 25–29 among those too young to write a will. Regardless, mortality between 25 and 30 is relatively low, and it is therefore unlikely that the conservative choice greatly alters the percentages in table 6.1.

figure must be further reduced by one-half. We may therefore posit that one-quarter of those buried in a parish should be males above the age of testation.

By employing this very crude indicator, the percentage of will-makers in Terling, Willingham and Orwell may be calculated. Table 6.2 indicates that Terling and Orwell suggest roughly the same incidence of will-making as Banbury, but there was a greater prevalence of testation in Willingham.

Table 6.2   Estimated proportions of testation in three English villages

	Orwell	Willingham	Terling
Time period observed	1543–1630	1575–1603	1550–1669
Number of wills	50	55	192
Total number of burials	616	369	3000
Mean number of burials per year	7	11	20
Estimated number of male deaths	308	184	1500
Estimated male descedents aged 30 and over	154	92	750
Percentage of testators to male descedents	32.5	59.8	25.6

These projections suggest a relatively low level of testation, leading us to conclude that in the villages observed, with the exception of Willingham, the practice of transmission by will does not explain high age at marriage. It would, however, be useful to determine whether age at first marriage for males was higher there than in the other villages. Other concerns must have led men to choose wills as a vehicle for property devolution. One might for example attribute their behaviour to the crisis which faced subsistence farmers from the mid 1580s. Increased mortality might lead to more men dying younger with family responsibilities to attend to. Yet Spufford argues that the existence of the fen common in Willingham provided a cushion against the effects of bad harvests,[38] and her notion that those with minor children tend to write wills in greater numbers has been disputed.[39] Besides, higher mortality might have been concentrated among infants and children,

38 With the exception of 1596 when the parish register records heavy mortality, Spufford argues that 'Willingham people were not vitally affected by bad harvests': *Contrasting communities*, p. 152.
39 Vann, 'Wills and the family', p. 350.

and would therefore have little effect upon the will-making population; and because we are concerned with the proportion of decedents who make wills rather than absolute numbers, it is unclear as to whether high mortality among adult males should have any effect upon proportions of testation. Although Banbury was a market town rather than an agricultural village, the proportion of will-makers to decedents does not increase greatly during periods of high mortality.[40]

Various other theories have been proffered to explain why some men were inclined to interfere with or to confirm the course of the laws of descent through the use of wills. Spufford and Cicely Howell suggest that family responsibilities, whether one has yet to provide for dependent children, are determinative.[41] Spufford finds that the largest group of will-makers in Willingham (34.7 per cent) probably had not advanced their children because they were minors or unmarried daughters. Another one-third had two or more adult sons alive at their death, and Spufford lumps these two groups together, suggesting that they 'were not yet independent'.[42] Admittedly a father would have to make a decision regarding apportionment if he left more than one child but, without evidence of their dependency, it is difficult to view the need to make a will in such situations in terms of 'responsibility'. The father could have, and likely already would have to some extent, advanced his child. Men with minor children would not have been able to advance and would therefore be concerned with a different matter: how can I arrange for my child's support during minority? Unlike men with adult children, the ultimate distribution would be less pressing. Men with adult children and no children face a common problem of apportionment. Besides, to argue that it is family responsibility that prompts men to write wills requires classification of decedents according to their stage in the life course and a subsequent calculation of the ratio of testators to intestates in each group, because it is the proportion of will-makers in each group rather than absolute numbers that is relevant.[43]

Another possible explanation offered by historians for will-making is wealth; the assumption is that those with substantial property are more

40 Ibid., figure 2, p. 350.

41 Spufford, 'Peasant inheritance customs', pp. 171–2; and Howell, 'Peasant inheritance customs', p. 141.

42 Spufford, 'Peasant inheritance customs', p. 171. Such a small number of childless men leaving wills is troubling. If the distribution of will-makers is a random sample of the community (which of course it is not), a 10 per cent childless rate is very low. R.M. Smith estimates childlessness at 20 per cent, given pre-industrial levels of fertility and mortality. This figure compares well with Wrightson/Levine's findings in Terling. R.M. Smith, 'Some issues regarding families and their land in England, 1250–1800', in R.M. Smith (ed.), *Land, kinship and life-cycle* (Cambridge, 1984), pp. 38–56; Wrightson and Levine, *Poverty and piety*, p. 96.

43 Vann, 'Wills and the family', p. 356.

concerned with its distribution. Although Spufford and Howell have argued that there is no correlation between wealth and propensity to make a will,[44] Vann has found a higher incidence of will-making among the wealthy by comparing probate and non-probate inventories.[45] Wrightson and Levine's findings in Terling, based upon hearth tax assessments, support Vann's view.[46] Ignoring the implication of ante-mortem transfers upon accurate estimations of wealth in Banbury, both Vann and Wrightson and Levine find poor men's wills in not inconsequential numbers.[47] Moreover, the experience in Banbury is not constant over time; there is a reversal in the first quarter of the eighteenth century.[48] These conflicting results suggest that wealth is not the sole determining factor in will-making. Even if more wealthy men make wills than the poor, their motivation in doing so may be independent of variable 'wealth'.

A further plausible explanation, and one that has yet to be considered, may be the nature of the property to be passed. Consideration of this variable may help to explain the greater incidence of testation in Willingham. Land use there differed markedly from Orwell and Terling. Spufford suggests that the economy of Willingham was dependent upon the fens.[49] Excerpts from wills she discusses in detail suggest that a major concern of testators was to distribute common rights and the animals with which one exercised them.[50] Spufford does not mention the inheritance custom with respect to common rights; nor does she discuss their transfer *inter vivos* in the court rolls. To dispose of them in a secure fashion may have prompted men to commit the distribution to paper. Such rights seem to be less susceptible to *inter vivos* transfer than the shillings or acres which constituted wealth in the uplands. Indeed, landholding did not render one more likely to write a will; and it would be interesting to know whether possession of common rights did.[51] Thus it may well be the incorporeal nature of the property to be transferred that governs the means selected for devolution.

More detailed comparisons of the substance of bequests embodied in wills and intestate succession to property must be undertaken before such a hypothesis can be accepted. But, as modern lawyers can attest, contemporary will-making is merely one event in a lifelong process of

44 Spufford, 'Peasant inheritance customs', table 2, p. 170; Howell, 'Peasant inheritance customs', p. 141.
45 Vann, 'Wills and the family', pp. 353–5.
46 Wrightson and Levine, *Poverty and piety*, p. 96.
47 Vann, 'Wills and the family', p. 353; Wrightson and Levine, *Poverty and piety*, p. 96.
48 Vann, 'Wills and the family', p. 353.
49 Spufford has found that most of her will-makers (64 per cent) were either cottagers with common rights, or men who held less than two acres of land. Spufford, 'Peasant inheritance customs', pp. 170–2.
50 Ibid., pp. 139–44, 159–61.
51 Ibid., p. 170.

transfer. The extent of the probate estate is directed by the nature of property, its suitability for *inter vivos* transfer, and the operation of the law of descent. In a cross-cultural comparison of hoe and plough societies, Goody argues that family structure and attitudes towards property (including inheritance) reflect peculiarities in the means of production.[52] There is no reason to believe that patterns of devolution in early modern England were ungoverned by such forces.

Linked with this notion that the nature of property may govern the manner of devolution is that use may have a bearing upon transmission. If a particular means of production requires heavy labour, the senior generation may pass the property associated with it to the junior earlier in the life course. Spufford has found evidence of what she calls 'retirement' in Willingham.[53] This pattern of *inter vivos* surrender in the manor court of arable copyhold by fathers to the use of their sons parallels Elaine Clark's 'social security' in medieval villages.[54] It may be that men working the fens were able to continue to exploit their property later in life than the half-yardlander, and therefore died in possession. This theory might help to explain relatively high levels of testation among those involved in food distribution and certain types of tradesmen like tailors, weavers and mercers in Banbury.[55]

Finally, levels of testation may reflect local peculiarities. Our discussion of motivation regarding will-making assumes that laws of inheritance were either unsatisfactory or improperly implemented. Levels of testation may reflect the nature not only of property or its use but also of an inheritance law whose sanctity may have varied locally. Early modern English inheritance law was complex because the course of descent and court supervising passage differed according to the type of property. Real property that was freehold passed according to common law; primogeniture applied except where the customs of gavelkind (partible inheritance) or borough English (ultimogeniture) were followed.[56] Copyhold passed according to manorial custom in the manor court. In the course of the sixteenth and seventeenth centuries, equity and then the common law came to protect the customary inheritance of copyhold.[57] Half-yardlanders in Willingham may not have written wills because they wished to follow customary descent and were certain of its implementation.[58] But those whose estates were largely

52 Goody, *Production and reproduction*, p. 97.
53 Spufford, 'Peasant inheritance customs', p. 173.
54 E. Clark, 'Some aspects of social security in medieval England', *Journal of Family History* 6 (1983), p. 335.
55 Vann, 'Wills and the family', p. 355.
56 F. Hargrave and C. Butler (eds), *The first part of the institutes of laws of England*, 2 vols (London, 1832), vol. 1, section 106.
57 C.M. Gray, *Copyhold, equity, and the common law* (Cambridge, Mass., 1963), pp. 4–21.
58 Spufford, *Contrasting communities*, p. 172.

comprised of personality or landowners with considerable personal property were subject to the probate process in the Church courts. The reliability of the Church courts in cases of intestacy is questionable. Before 'An Act for the Better Settling of Intestates' Estates' was passed in 1670 in the Statute of Distributions,[59] a contemporary commentator argued that 'there was no certain and positive law here to guide the Distribution of Intestates' Estates.'[60] Although this position may be extreme, the process of administration may not have been effectively supervised; in particular, once an administrator was appointed it was difficult for the ordinary to compel him to distribute the surplus after debts to the wife and children in accordance with custom.[61] By law administrations were to be granted to the deceased widow or next of kin,[62] and the ordinary required a bond in the amount of the surplus after debts.[63] However, relatives may not have always been honest, and calculations of estate assets were often difficult to make. The ordinary had no power to compel a distribution to heirs. Because clerical supervision of the administration of intestate estates was incomplete, some men might prefer to write wills to secure trusted executors rather than take court-appointed administrators. Moreover, because the probate jurisdiction was local, its efficacy and the security it offered may have varied. Persons living in a more efficient archdeaconry or peculiar may have had no reason to confirm the law of descent, while a person living in another jurisdiction, and desiring the customary descent of personal property, might be inclined to write a will. While this may not affect levels of testation in a particular village, it renders comparisons between local studies problematic.

Our discussion of devolution therefore suggests that historians may have placed too much importance on wills in charting patterns of transmission in early modern England. Most men must have relied upon other means of transfer and, perhaps more significant, levels of testation may have varied owing to a myriad of pecularities, institutional, economic and structural. Delayed household formation cannot be directly attributable to testation. Moreover, landholders may have used wills in conjunction with other forms of transmission, *inter vivos* or post mortem. If a substantial segment of the English peasantry did not, like their continental counterparts, rely upon wills to fashion strategies of inheritance, our attention must turn to a consideration of alternative 'social arrangements'.

---

59 22 and 23 Charles II, c. 10.

60 W. Nelson, *Lex testamentaria: or, a compendious system of all the laws of England concerning last wills and testaments* (London, 1714), p. 20.

61 Ibid., pp. 18–19.

62 21 Henry VIII, c. 5.

63 Nelson, *Lex testamentaria*, p. 19.

II

We have suggested that a focus upon intergenerational transmission by will may create an incomplete and distorted picture of property devolution. Because actual percentages of testation and projections derived from burials in parish registers indicate that methods of transmission other than testation must have been employed by many families to pass property between generations, studies focusing exclusively upon wills observe the distributions of rather a small minority of the community. Moreover, because testators may have passed property *inter vivos*, the pattern derived from an analysis of their wills alone is incomplete. The understanding of devolution as a process, with the will representing only one phase, limits the extent of Macfarlane's argument regarding the distinctiveness of English inheritance practice.[64] Perhaps more significantly, however, it raises the likelihood of alternative methods of transfer, rendering the search for Hajnal's 'social arrangements' all the more compelling. Admittedly, property may pass at death through intestate succession, but it may also during the lifetime of the senior generation. If it does, it is appropriate to consider at what juncture passage occurs, and the forces that govern the decision to transmit to ascertain if there is a link with household formation.

A study of intergenerational transmission of copyhold has been undertaken by analysing the court rolls of the manor of Preston[65] from the mid sixteenth century to the end of the seventeenth century as a preliminary to a wider study of inheritance in early modern England. Because a heriot was due at the death of each copyholder,[66] the court rolls yield a reasonably accurate listing of the deaths of copyhold tenants. By comparing these names with those listed in the index to wills probated in the Archdeaconry of Lewes,[67] the proportion of small landholders who wrote wills can be ascertained. In addition, because the court rolls indicate the course of descent of copyhold land, we can determine the mechanics selected to pass property between generations by linking these two sources. Further, by scanning parish registers for entries regarding marriages and baptisms for these families,[68] we may

---

64 Macfarlane, *Origins of English individualism*, pp. 84–90, 165–66.

65 C. Thomas-Stanford (ed.), *An abstract of the court rolls of the manor of Preston* (Sussex Records Society, 1921). Hereafter referred to as *Preston court rolls*.

66 *Preston court rolls*, p. xxv. According to a survey of the manor undertaken in 1608, the lord was entitled to 'the best quick Beast'.

67 The wills are located in the East Sussex Record Office (hereafter ESRO) in Lewes. An index to wills probated prior to 1640 was published by the British Record Society in 1901; wills proved after 1660 are indexed in a typescript volume in the Record Office.

68 I have used the parish registers and/or bishop's transcripts of the following surrounding parishes (in addition to Preston and Hove, printed in E.F. Salmon (ed.), *The parish registers of*

ascertain whether the *inter vivos* passage of property might have been linked to household formation.[69]

During the period 1562 to 1702, the court rolls record the deaths of 53 Preston copyholders; 21 (39.6 per cent) left wills that were probated in the court of the Archdeaconry of Lewes. Fourteen or slightly more than one-quarter (26.4 per cent) allowed the inheritance custom of borough English[70] with widow's right to free bench[71] to run its course. The court rolls also indicate a third approach to assuring intergenerational transfer: the *inter vivos* settlement.[72] Nearly half (26 tenants, 49.1 per cent)[73] of our copyholders effected ante-mortem transfers, often reserving a life interest in themselves, but directing the course of descent by remainder.[74]

Our findings have broad implications for studies of inheritance based exclusively on wills. The strategies adopted by individuals employing *inter vivos* settlements would be either omitted or misconceived in a wills-based analysis of inheritance. Why men chose to arrange intergenerational transfer of land prospectively is not always clear. Two-thirds of the settlors retained life estates, so the motive in most cases was not to transfer their entire interest immediately. Moreover, half the settlements merely confirm the customary order of succession. Other strategies are more complex: transferring land to heirs but retaining an annuity for themselves of spouses ('retirement') (two);[75] widows settling land on their husbands' children (two);[76] providing for succession to

---

Hove and Preston, 1538–1812 (Brighton, 1912): Brighton (printed in H.D. Roberts (ed.), *Brighton parish register* (1932): Falmer, Ovingdean, Patcham, Rottingdean and Telcome, which are located in the East Sussex Record Office.

69 Because there are gaps in each type of record, the researcher would expect to find a relatively low percentage of demonstrable links between *inter vivos* settlement and marriage.

70 *Preston court rolls*, pp. xxvi–xxvii.

71 'If a Copyholder die seized of a hereditary estate his widow shall have her widdows bench contynuing the same so long as she shall keep herself chast and unmarried': ibid., p. xxvi.

72 The mechanics of settlement was to surrender the copyhold to the lord and receive a regrant to oneself for life, with remainders over. Although it might be argued that the process was undertaken to avoid entry fines, they were paid at the time of surrender and regrant. Therefore the motive for settlement could not have been pecuniary.

73 The totals exceed 54 because some men who executed settlements also made wills.

74 For example in court (9 April 1575) John Boniface surrendered two cottages and a virgate 'to be regranted to him, Alice his wife and John Boniface his son and the heirs of his son John': *Preston court rolls*, p. 17. Although in legal form it would appear that they were holding in joint tenancy, their entrance is 'successively'. It is likely that the interests to wife and son were remainders. In the seventeenth century, conveyancing technique is refined. In the first settlement recorded after 1628, William Bowes surrendered a cottage under the cliff at Hove 'to the said William Bowes and Elizabeth his wife for the terms of their lives. And after their decease to the use of John Bowes and Hanna his wife for the term of their lives, remainder to their heirs lawfully begotten': ibid., p. 51.

75 Ibid.: Bartlee (5 March 1548), p. 57; Buckell (31 March 1657), p. 61.

76 Ibid.: Bradford (9 April 1575), pp. 16–17; Merchaunt (9 April 1575), p. 17.

children's spouse (two);[77] providing a fee interest for a spouse (presumably instead of her bench) (one);[78] and altering the course of succession (favouring the eldest son) (one).[79] Although these landholders, save those retaining annuities, could have employed wills to accomplish the same goal, they chose to settle their affairs during their lifetimes in the manor court. Moreover, more than one-third (eight of 21) of the landowners who made wills also settled land before death. Accordingly, the pattern derived from their wills alone would be an incomplete one. In most cases, the will merely supplements the pattern of transmission implemented by surrender and admittance in the manor court. Considering the will as a supplement is appropriate, because without exception those who used both means of intergenerational transfer passed most of their copyhold through *inter vivos* settlement.[80] Personalty – household items, farm implements, stock and money – passed by will; and two of the eight included bequests of lesser landholdings. In the main, settlements of land of these will-makers were to persons who would not have taken immediately by custom. Settlements, for example, deprived widows of all or part of their bench, and wills compensated them with personalty.[81] Land was also settled upon a child's spouse.[82]

Thus, nearly half (49.1 per cent) of copyholders whose deaths were recorded in the court rolls of the manor of Preston employed *inter vivos* settlements to pass land to their heirs. Some men executed wills as well; and some intergenerational transfers also embodied customary transmission. To hark back to figure 6.1, some copyholders availed themselves of the downward thrust of all three arrows! Because the will rarely confirmed the settlement, the researcher relying exclusively upon probate materials would draw a pattern of devolution that was serious-

---

77 Ibid.: Chapman (3 October 1562), p. 1; Avery (1 April 1577), p. 21.

78 Ibid.: Simons (8 April 1656), p. 60.

79 Ibid.: Prior (31 March 1569), p. 9.

80 To the extent that income-producing property (land) was more valuable to the copyholder than personal property, this position is defensible. For example, Robert Prior appeared in the court rolls (7 April 1565) purchasing a cottage, barn, half-virgate and half an acre. At the same court he surrendered the same and an additional virgate to himself and then to his younger son Robert: ibid., p. 4. Four years later, he appeared (31 March 1569) in court to surrender three virgates and receive the same 'to the said Robert and Joan his wife and William their son': ibid., p. 9. Upon his death (noted in the court rolls of 9 April 1575) Joan and Robert entered: ibid., p. 16. In his will, dated 8 October 1574, he divided 22 oxen, 220 sheep, and household items among his sons: ESRO A.6, 363–72. This pattern is also followed by the less wealthy copyholder. By the time of his death, recorded in the court rolls of 21 September 1587, George Blaker had surrendered and been readmitted to two half-virgates to himself and his son Henry: *Preston court rolls*, p. 33. His will divides personalty among his wife Alice and his daughters Anne and Joan: ESRO A.8, 105–6.

81 *Preston court rolls*, Chapman (3 October 1562), p. 1; ESRO A.6, 371. *Preston court rolls*, Blaker (21 September 1581), p. 32; ESRO A.8, 105–6.

82 *Preston court rolls*, Chapman (3 October 1562), p. 1; ESRO A.6, 371.

ly distorted. For many testators the will was a supplement, the means of correcting biases in lifetime transfers or creating them at death.

Having discerned the tendency in Preston towards *inter vivos* settlement,[83] we may attempt to determine whether these transfers were linked with household formation. Five of the 26 *inter vivos* settlements were eliminated either because they were multiple (i.e. father to son; then son to wife and heirs) or because no date of settlement could be derived from the entry in the court rolls. Of the remaining 21, seven could be linked with the formation of a household in that they occurred either one year before or one year after a child's marriage or the baptism of a child's first-born child in the parish register of Preston and its surrounding villages and towns.[84] Thus one-third of the settlements in the Preston court rolls were likely to have been the implementation of the 'social arrangements' which Hajnal believed may have been related to the formation of a new unit.

Some examples are useful in illustrating this nexus between property devolution and household formation. In the court held on 3 October 1562, Thomas Chapman surrendered a garden called Piers, a cottage and a half-virgate; the premises were then regranted to Thomas' wife Joan, and his daughter Joan, the wife of Thomas Towner and her heirs.[85] All three received seisin. It is likely that the transfer was linked to marriage, because the Preston parish register records the marriage of Joan Chapman and Thomas Towner on 26 July 1562.[86] The arrangement was implemented 13 years before the death of Thomas Chapman. Likewise, in 1575 Margaret Bradford surrendered a cottage and half-virgate and was readmitted with her son John and his heirs successively.[87] Although there is no entry of his marriage in Preston in the parish register examined, the first child of John Bradford was baptized the year before[88] and the marriage is recorded in the Brighton register.[89] Accordingly, it would

---

83 It should also be noted that some copyholders might also have some freehold. If so, they may have transmitted land by settlement; such a transfer would appear in neither court rolls nor wills. For some examples of settlements of freehold by small landowners, see L. Bonfield, 'Contrasting sources: court rolls and settlements as evidence of hereditary transmission of land among small landowners in early modern England', *University of Illinois Law Review* (1984), pp. 653–8.

84 Admittedly, the standard employed to determine whether a transfer was linked with marriage is a crude one. On the one hand, concerns other than marriage might have influenced the settlement; indeed the union could have been purely a coincidence. Motives are, however, often complex. Even if the father's primary purpose was other than allowing for a child's marriage, it seems reasonable to suppose that he recognized the possible implications of his action, and that the child would possibly respond.

85 *Preston court rolls*, p. 1.

86 Salmon, *Parish registers*, p. 50.

87 *Preston court rolls*, pp. 16–17.

88 Salmon, *Parish registers*, p. 34

appear that the settlement in the court rolls may also have been linked to the formation of a family.

Our attempt to relate *inter vivos* transfers in court rolls with household formation indicates that for some families the marriage of the child was the juncture at which commitments regarding inheritance were undertaken. Although a link can be assumed in only about one-third of the settlements, the number is not alarming small given probable levels of geographically exogamous marriages in early modern England.[90] Indeed, this factor as well as the rather low proportion of copyholders who might be expected to live to the marriage of a child[91] strengthens the proffered link between settlements and household formation.

III

The purpose of this chapter has been to consider the relationship between property transmission and household formation in early modern England. Our enquiry into patterns of devolution suggests that *inter vivos* settlement was a common method of arranging the hereditary transmission of property among copyholders in one English manor in early modern England. Although it would be rash to draw sweeping conclusions from a single local study, some light has been shed on inheritance practice which may allow us to speculate upon its relationship to household formation in early modern England.

In the first place, the study suggests a wide variety of options which copyholders might employ in fashioning inheritance strategies. Testamentary, customary and ante-mortem means were used; and at times they were even implemented in combination. Preston copyholders relied only very infrequently upon wills to pass land between generations, and rarely appear to have used their freedom of disposition to disinherit their children. Rather, they seem to have used their power to frame strategies that would distribute shares of family wealth to their children.[92] Our sketch of actual practice among these copyholders

89 Roberts, *Brighton parish register*, p. 113.

90 V.B. Elliott, 'Mobility and marriage in pre-industrial England' (unpublished Ph.D. dissertation, University of Cambridge, 1979).

91 See the discussion in Smith, 'Some issues', pp. 49–54; and a model of succession in the peerage in L. Bonfield, 'Marriage settlements and the "rise of great estates": the demographic aspect', *Economic History Review* 2nd series, 32 (1979), pp. 483–93, and 'Marriage, property and the "affective family"', *Law and History Review* 1 (1983), table 1, p. 300.

92 Length constraints do not allow a comprehensive discussion of the actual patterns of distribution. The impression from looking at the *inter vivos* and testamentary transfers confirms Keith Wrightson's view that the strategy was one of 'maximizing the opportunities of as many children as possible': Wrightson and Levine, *Poverty and piety*, p. 99.

would therefore appear to question Alan Macfarlane's position that English behaviour appreciably differed from that on the continent. Admittedly different legal techniques may have been employed, but the ultimate end was similar. In Preston, at least, much transfer was not by will, nor was the sword of disinheritance brandished. The objection of Keith Thomas, that Macfarlane's stress upon the possibility of will-making and disinheritance rather than actual occurrences may be misplaced, is vindicated.[93]

Secondly, we have observed a connection between the commitment of familial property to the junior generation and marriage, lending support to Hajnal's view that there is likely to have been a link between family formation and inheritance. What may be of interest is that practice in Preston suggests that admittance to a future rather than a present possessory interest in property was related to marriage. Thus it would appear that it was the assurance of resources rather than actual possessory transfer that was crucial, unless the economic basis of the arrangement was shared enjoyment of the land. Unfortunately, the evidence employed does not illuminate this reality, but one might wish to argue that it was senior generations' willingness to share their resources that promoted a union in the next generation. The extent to which parental concessions were crucial to the decision to marry no doubt varied from family to family. For those copyholders blessed with longevity, some control over the timing of marriage in the next generation may have been exercised by delaying the commitment to transmit land.

In order to link inheritance to Hajnal's marriage pattern, further studies comparing practice in non-European areas with those embracing the European pattern must be undertaken. It is therefore useful to highlight similarities as well as contrasts in inheritance practice between England and areas of Europe with similar marriage regimes. As the peasantry in both England and other regions of Europe is increasingly viewed as a group which could, within certain strictures, forge inheritance strategies which reflect their economic, demographic and cultural realities, attention must turn to internal or communitarian self-regulation. In this context, Peter Laslett's noumenal normative rules loom large as explanation of the means by which reproduction was governed.

---

93 Macfarlane, *Origins of English individualism*, p. 84. It should be noted that if post-mortem transfer by will was a primary means of wealth transmission between generations, and if that inheritance was related to household formation, mean age at first marriage and life expectancy should rise or fall together (unless the increase in life expectancy was due to a decline in infant or child mortality). Such was not the case in early modern England (Wrigley and Schofield, *Population history of England*, tables 7.15 and 10.1), although it may have occurred in France.

7

The Social Order of Early Modern England: Three Approaches

Keith Wrightson

The problem of the nature of the social order is one of the most familiar issues in the social and economic history of sixteenth- and seventeenth-century England. It is also one of the most uncertain. That English society in this period was highly stratified is universally acknowledged. Changes in the social distributions of land, wealth, status and power retain their place among the most persistent preoccupations of historical debate. Yet discussion of the social order is often curiously thin, fragmented or cloudy. A brief recitation of the conventional social hierarchy remains an obligatory exercise for the authors of textbooks, but few proceeed far beyond this genuflection at the altar of social context. Studies of particular social groups exist, some of them of great distinction, yet no single volume has been devoted to the problems posed by the social order in itself. Recent social history has been more than ever concerned to provide analysis which is 'socially specific'. The nature and significance of the overall structure of inequality, however, remain elusive. The terminology employed in the discussion of stratification is often imprecise and undefined. The relationships between social groups are rarely characterized. The broader implications of the

This essay is a formalized presentation of a discussion paper delivered to a number of seminars and conference sessions in Scotland, England, Canada and the USA in 1982–4. I must thank all those who commented on earlier versions of the arguments put forward here and suggested points which I have incorporated subsequently. Particular thanks are due to Richard de Lavigne, Rab Houston and Christopher Smout of the University of St Andrews, R.J. Morris of Edinburgh University and John Walter of the University of Essex. I must also acknowledge the influence of Michael Anderson's *Approaches to the history of the Western family, 1500–1914* (London, 1980) on the structure of this attempt to review a different field of study. In my title and on occasion in my text I have used the convenient shorthand term 'early modern'. As I hope will be clear, I have in mind the sixteenth and seventeenth centuries (and in particular the later sixteenth and earlier seventeenth centuries, since much of the evidence discussed relates to the latter period, which has been the focus of recent research). In discussing the 'social order' I have not attempted to include consideration of gender relations. This does not imply any failure to recognize their significance. My concern here, however, is with 'rank'.

patterns of stratification described are more commonly assumed, asserted or evaded than carefully explored.

All this is perhaps understandable. Social stratification is an uncertain, a demanding, even an uncomfortable subject for historians. It is at once a conceptual, methodological and ideological minefield. Nevertheless, the problem is ultimately inescapable. As Peter Laslett realized when he introduced his concept of a 'one-class society' in chapter 2 of *The World We Have Lost*, coming to grips with the structure of the social order is an essential prologue to any satisfactory discussion of the fortunes of individuals and groups, any meaningful approach to the nature and development of society at large.

In this chapter no pretence will be made of offering neat answers to the numerous outstanding problems in this field. Nor is my intention polemical. Rather, an attempt will be made to focus discussion by examining three broad approaches which can be distinguished in the handling of this subject by students of Tudor and Stuart England. Some have concentrated upon the exposition of *contemporary perceptions* of the social order, primarily through the analysis of contemporary social descriptions. Others have adopted what can be called a *social-distributional* approach, seeking to determine the relative size of the social groups distinguished by contemporaries, to establish the social distributions of land, income, status and power, or to observe social variations in myriad aspects of behaviour and experience. Finally, a few have tried to characterize the prevailing patterns of *social relations*, the fundamental alignments and dynamics of the system of stratification, usually by attempting the reconstruction of interpersonal bonds or by exploring social conflict. These three areas of study are not mutually exclusive, to be sure. An adequate account of the social order would demand that all three be taken into consideration. Nevertheless, each involves a discernible difference of emphasis and focuses attention upon a different dimension of the overall problem. By examining them in turn we can move towards a clearer picture of the current state of knowledge, identify outstanding problems, and detect possible ways forward in both research and interpretation.

Contemporary Perceptions of the Social Order

English historians are singularly fortunate in possessing a variety of sources of information on how sixteenth- and seventeenth-century people viewed the social order. Of these the most accessible, and by far the most frequently discussed, are a variety of formal, often literary, descriptions of society; ranging from the social categories of sixteenth-century sumptuary legislation through the accounts of such writers as William Harrison, Sir Thomas Smith, Sir Thomas Wilson and Edward Chamberlayne, to the work of early social statisticians, notably Gregory

King.[1] These social descriptions vary in their purposes and in the degree of detail which they provide. Each has its own idiosyncracies. They do, however, describe what is recognizably the same society, and their minor differences (like the evidence of eyewitnesses) tend to give more, rather than less, credibility to the general picture which emerges. The principal characteristics of that picture are familiar enough, but deserve brief re-emphasis.

In the first place, contemporaries described society not in terms of the three functional 'orders' or 'estates' of medieval social theory, but as a single hierarchy of status and occupational groups.[2] While traces of older classificatory conventions certainly remained, notably in the separate discussion sometimes accorded the clergy, the writers of the sixteenth and seventeenth centuries had their own distinctive conventions in the 'classical' hierarchy of the titular nobility, knights, esquires and 'mere' gentlemen, the professions, citizens and burgesses, yeomen, husbandmen, artisans, labourers and servants. Within this conventional scheme some, of course, provided greater detail than others.

The origins of this 'classical' hierarchy of social ranks (which is itself a simplification of the complexities of reality) are uncertain, and its evolution would repay further investigation. The standardized titular categories may have owed something to the Statute of Additions of 1413, which first required defendants in legal actions to state their 'Estate or Degree or Mystery', or to the proclamation of sumptuary regulations. Their hierarchical arrangement may have been influenced by conceptions of the heavenly hierarchy and the 'chain of being', by classical models adopted by humanist writers, or simply by a shuffling of the various ranks within each of the medieval 'orders' into a single order of precedence (much as in the rituals of court life or in public

1 The most useful general accounts of such sources are N.B. Harte, 'State control of dress and social change in pre-industrial England', in D.C. Coleman and A.H. John (eds), *Trade, government and economy in pre-industrial England. Essays presented to F.J. Fisher* (London, 1976); and D. Cressy, 'Describing the social order of Elizabethan and Stuart England', *Literature and History*, 3 (1976).

2 Latin and French examples of the 'literature of the three estates' were known in England from at least the twelfth century. From the fourteenth century English language examples of the genre are extant. By the fifteenth century, however, the 'estates' or 'degrees' catalogued in such works had been considerably elaborated in response to changing social realities. When Caxton wrote of the three estates of 'clergye, chevalrye and labourers', or 'clerkes, knyghtes and labourers', his simple tripartite classification was already markedly conservative and anachronistic (probably influenced by a thirteenth-century model). Most writers had abandoned the three estates or orders in favour of a much more complex catalogue of 'estates or degrees' arranged in an order of precedence. The medieval emphasis on the god-given duties of each 'estate or degree' and their functional interdependence, of course, remained very much alive. For a discussion of the development of the moralistic 'literature of the estates of the world' in England (though one which is less sensitive than it could be to change), see R. Mohl, *The three estates in medieval and Renaissance literature* (New York, 1933), chapters 4–5.

processions).[3] What is certain is that whatever its origins it was never rigidly defined, and this is a matter of sufficient significance to deserve emphasis as a second characteristic of contemporary social descriptions. A degree of hesitancy and ambiguity remained concerning the correct placing of certain occupational and social groups, notably the members of what Lawrence Stone has termed 'semi-independent occupational hierarchies': the lesser clergy, merchants, doctors, lawyers and office-holders.[4] Nor were the lines separating social ranks other than perme-able membranes, for a third feature of contemporary social descriptions was that frank, if sometimes grudging, recognition was given to the constant reality of individual social mobility.[5]

Both uncertainty about the precise position of particular groups and acknowledgement of the existence of opportunities for social mobility can be said to have derived from a fourth characteristic of these accounts of the social order: the complexity of the criteria of social estimation and evaluation. The social order was presented as a hierar-chy of status but, as those who sought to describe it were forced to recognize with varying degrees of clarity, rank and degree were not autonomous conditions. Nor could they easily be defined, for they were *compound* qualities which might involve birth, inherited or conferred title, wealth and the nature of that wealth, occupation, mode of land tenure, legal status, lifestyle and tenure of positions of authority.[6] Clearly this was not a system of stratification based upon unambi-guous, well-defined, formal positions. It was not a legally constituted

3 Statute, 1 Henry V c. 5 (1413); R.H. Hilton, *Bond men made free. Medieval peasant movements and the English rising of 1381* (London, 1973), pp. 178–9; F.R.H. Du Boulay, *An age of ambition. English society in the late Middle Ages* (London, 1970), p. 70; Harte, 'State control of dress', p. 136; E.M.W. Tillyard, *The Elizabethan world picture* (London, 1943), especially chapters 2 and 4. For the relationship between urban ceremonial and the social hierarchy see C. Phythian-Adams, 'Ceremony and the citizen: the communal year at Coventry 1450–1550', in P. Clark and P. Slack (eds), *Crisis and order in English towns 1500–1700* (London, 1972), and M. James, 'Ritual, drama and the social body in the late medieval English town', *Past and Present* 98 (1983). For a discussion of early works concerned with precedence, see Mohl, *The three estates*, pp. 129ff.

4 L. Stone, 'Social mobility in England, 1500–1700', *Past and Present* 33 (1966), pp. 18ff.

5 Social mobility was usually discussed in the context of achieving the status of gentility. See e.g. F.J. Furnivall (ed.), *Harrison's description of England*, New Shakespeare Society, 6th series, no. 1 (London, 1877), pp. 128–9, 133; F.J. Fisher (ed.), *The state of England Anno Dom. 1600 by Thomas Wilson*, in *Camden Miscellany XVI*, Camden Society, 3rd series, 52 (1936), p. 19.

6 See the discussion of the criteria of social rank in K. Wrightson, *English society 1580–1680* (London, 1982), pp. 19–22. The Sumptuary Act of 1533, described in Harte, 'State control of dress', p. 136 provides an earlier example of the 'complicated interlocking correlations of rank, income, position and wealth'. In this instance the categories defined were based on birth, title, income level, occupation, landholding and wage labour. The outstanding examples of contemporary confusion over the criteria of status are to be found in their efforts to define gentility. See R. Kelso, *The doctrine of the English gentleman in the sixteenth century* (Urbana, 1929), chapter 2.

'estate' system. The conventional social hierarchy was less an institution in itself than a byproduct of other social institutions.[7] The distinctions which were recognized emerged from the interplay of numerous variables. In this complex process particular individuals might be seen as achieving a certain overall score in a largely informal process of social assessment which subsumed a multiplicity of criteria, and for this very reason a degree of inconsistency in the ascription of status could be expected and undoubtedly occurred.[8] We can certainly detect a single essential determinant of rank in the wealth without which no aspirant to superior standing could hope to establish and maintain his claims.[9] Nevertheless, it would be to caricature the realities of the period to maintain that other criteria, some of them apparently archaic, were of no more than passing significance.[10] The system of social evaluation and the complex constructions to which it gave rise could not be reduced to a single, consistent, yardstick. It involved, like the popular beliefs of the period, both a mental accommodation to the socio-economic realities of the day and 'the debris of many different systems of thought'.[11]

The examination of contemporary social descriptions, then, can reveal much about how certain educated people of the time perceived their own society and serves to underline the complexity and occasional

7 This distinction is derived from T.H. Marshall's classification of stratification systems, quoted in J. Littlejohn, *Social stratification* (London, 1972), p. 10.

8 Inconsistency in the ascription of status to individuals is a familiar phenomenon to historians working at the level of the locality. The problem is discussed in detail in G.A. Kerby, 'Inequality in a pre-industrial society; a study of wealth, status, office and taxation in Tudor and Stuart England with particular reference to Cheshire (unpublished Ph.D. thesis, University of Cambridge, 1983), chapter 7. At the level of the parish, disputes over the relative standing of individuals are revealed in quarrels over seating in church. See S.D. Amussen, 'Governors and governed: class and gender relations in English villages, 1590–1725', (unpublished Ph.D. thesis, Brown University, 1982), pp. 290ff. for an illuminating discussion of such evidence.

9 This reality could be bluntly enough recognized, as when Lord Burghley advised his son: 'That gentleman that selles an Acre of land, looseth an ounce of credite, for Gentilitie is nothing but ancient Riches: So that if the Foundation doe sinke, the Building must needes consequently fall.' Quoted in Kelso, *Doctrine of the English gentleman*, p. 28.

10 One John Hardinge of Whickham in County Durham, for example, was able to continue to describe himself as 'gentleman', and was so described by his neighbours, despite extremely faded economic circumstances. He was in fact a small farmer and poorer than many of his 'yeoman' neighbours. However, he was also a scion of an ancient gentry family which held a small manor in the parish. Moreover, he dressed something like a gentleman: his 'apparrell' was of unusually high valuation compared with that of his neighbours. Clearly he clung to his claim to superior status and his neighbours were prepared to accord him his gentility: University of Durham, Dept of Palaeography and Diplomatic, will and inventory of John Hardinge, 1593.

11 The phrase quoted is from K. Thomas, *Religion and the decline of magic. Studies in popular beliefs in sixteenth and seventeenth century England* (London, 1971), p. 185.

ambiguity of that perception. It is a familiar and fruitful approach to
the social order. Yet it has its problems and its limitations.

In the first place there is the general problem of the extent to which
reliance can be placed on essentially literary sources in the absence of
independent evidence of their accuracy as accounts of social reality.
Secondly, there are a number of specific issues which remain unresolved. The most immediate of these is the fact that contemporary
descriptions of the social hierarchy rarely provide information on the
relative proportions of the population placed in particular categories.
The actual profile of stratification remains obscure, and this precludes
not only comparison with other societies but also the detection of
significant regional and local differences within England.[12] Again, these
sources provide what are essentially views from above. In the case of
the best-known examples of the sixteenth and early seventeenth centuries, their authors were primarily concerned with describing the 'political nation'. They tended to minimize or deal cursorily with social
distinctions below the level of the yeomanry of the countryside and the
full citizens of the towns. If we are to explore social inequality among
the mass of the population for the greater part of this period we need to
proceed beyond the evidence provided by the majority of contemporary
social descriptions.[13]

Even more serious is the problem that these accounts of society
cannot be accepted as a fully reliable guide to contemporary perceptions of the social order. They tell us nothing of how members of the
middling and lower ranks of society may have viewed their social world
– and it remains a live possibility that their perceptions may have been
different from those of highly educated social commentators. They
provide a static, conventionalized, picture of the social order which
implies a fixity and consistency which may well be misleading. Above
all, it should never be forgotten that the graduated hierarchy described
by educated contemporaries in works intended for publication or circulation was very much a *formal* exercise in social classification. In less
formal discourse a very much simpler terminology could be adopted.
The informal language of social classification which can be gleaned
from such sources as letters, court depositions, pamphlets or petitions

---

12 Some contemporary social descriptions did, of course, include estimates of the size of
particular social groups, the outstanding example being Gregory King's frequently reprinted
'Scheme of the income and expense of the several families of England calculated for the year
1688': see J. Thirsk and J.P. Cooper, *Seventeenth-century economic documents* (Oxford, 1972), pp.
780–1. Even if they can be accepted as reliable, however, such figures provide only national
estimates. For recent discussions of the questionable reliability of King see G.S. Holmes,
'Gregory King and the social structure of pre-industrial England', *Transactions of the Royal
Historical Society* 5th Series, 27 (1977), and P.H. Lindert and J.G. Williamson, 'Revising
England's social tables, 1688–1812', *Explorations in Economic History* 19 (1982).
13 Cressy, 'Describing the social order', p. 31.

might distinguish, for example, only 'gentlemen', 'the middling sort of people', and the 'lower sort' or 'the poor', while in the context of social conflict still blunter categories could be readily enough employed.

All this implies the widespread existence of simpler, cruder, perceptions of the principal social groups. A survey of the contemporary terminology quoted in a recent study of fenland riots in the early seventeenth century, for example, yields us 'rich men', 'great men', 'a man of quality', 'sufficient men', 'the better sort', 'able persons of good estates', 'the meaner sort', 'the ruder sort', 'poor labouring men' and the 'common sort'.[14] These are but some of the classifications employed, and they reveal a world of social meanings untapped by most of the formal social descriptions of the period. Historians of early modern England are well aware, I think, of the existence of such alternative languages of social description, and yet their implications are insufficiently grasped. Generations of students have become familiar with the classical hierarchy of formal social analysis, yet the *informal* language employed so frequently and forcefully by contemporaries still awaits examination of a disciplined kind. Until such work is done, it cannot be argued with any real confidence that we have arrived at a satisfactory understanding of either the ways in which the people of the time apprehended their society or the manner in which their perception may have been changing over time. What we can say is that if there was one approved, conventional manner of describing the social order, there were also alternatives. Moreover, there is reason to believe that the cruder perceptions embodied in what can be called the language of 'sorts' was of more practical significance in daily life and that it was gaining in currency. By the early eighteenth century, indeed, this alternative language had become the conventional mode of social description.[15]

14 The examples quoted are drawn from K. Lindley, *Fenland riots and the English Revolution* (London, 1982).

15 Peter Laslett has suggested that the term 'the middling sort of people' emerged in the seventeenth century and was originally of urban provenance: *The world we have lost, further explored* (London, 1983), p. 46. This may be so, though the term was certainly in wide use from very early in the seventeenth century and I suspect that it originated earlier. Certainly examples of the language of 'sorts' can be found all over England from the turn of the sixteenth and seventeenth centuries. The whole problem needs disciplined examination. What is clearer is that by the late seventeenth and early eighteenth centuries such language was much employed even in *formal* social description: see e.g. R.W. Malcolmson, *Life and labour in England 1700–1780* (London, 1981), pp. 11–12; W.A. Speck, *Stability and strife, England 1714–1760* (London, 1977), pp. 31–2. The naturalized Swiss, Guy Miège, who wrote one of the most popular accounts of English society of the early eighteenth century, began by writing of 'orders and degrees', but once he passed below the gentry he adopted the terms 'middle sort', 'common sort', 'inferior sort' and 'meaner sort': reprinted in D.A. Baugh (ed.), *Aristocratic government and society in eighteenth-century England. The foundations of stability* (New York, 1975), pp. 42, 45, 47, 48.

For all these reasons we should exercise considerable caution before we accept formal accounts of the social hierarchy at face value or accord them primary significance. They must be tested and amplified by independent evidence if we are to avoid the risk of becoming trapped within the limitations imposed by partial and arguably misleading images of the past. The accumulation of such evidence has been the particular contribution of what I have labelled the 'social-distributional approach' to the analysis of the social order.

The Social-distributional Approach

In the last two decades studies of this kind have added significantly to our knowledge of the realities of social stratification by the exploration of independent evidence, often in a quantitative and comparative manner. There would be little point, in a short survey of this kind, in rehearsing the detailed findings of such studies, scattered as they are over a now extensive literature and involving as they do complex problems of source criticism. It is more useful, for the purposes of this essay, to emphasize some of the ways in which they have served to confirm, to clarify, or to expand upon the accounts of society presented in the literary sources.

First, social-distributional studies have demonstrated that the conventional ranking of status and occupational groups encompassed real and indeed statistically demonstrable differences in the distributions of land and income, in living standards and in access to positions of power and authority – the very points of differentiation most frequently stressed by contemporary authors. The supreme position of the nobility and gentry and the internal differentiation of 'gentle' society have been abundantly confirmed.[16] So too has the 'certain preheminance and more estimation among the common people' accorded to the yeomanry.[17] In rural society, we have acquired a clearer understanding of the reality of social distinctions below the yeoman level: between yeoman and husbandman, husbandman and cottager, cottager and

16 The best general studies of the nobility and gentry are L. Stone, *The crisis of the aristocracy 1558–1641* (Oxford, 1965), and G.E. Mingay, *The gentry: the rise and fall of a ruling class* (London, 1976). For an excellent recent account of the debate over changing patterns of landownership, see C.G.A. Clay, *Economic expansion and social change: England 1500–1700*, 2 vols (Cambridge, 1984), vol. 1, chapter 5. Of the numerous studies of the landed elites of particular counties, two of the most valuable for their detailed analysis are J.T. Cliffe, *The Yorkshire gentry from the Reformation to the Civil War* (London, 1969) and B.G. Blackwood, *The Lancashire gentry and the Great Rebellion*, Chetham Society, 3rd series, vol. 25 (1978). For some problems of source use and comparability in studies of this kind, see J.S. Morrill, 'The northern gentry and the Great Rebellion', *Northern History* 15 (1979).

17 The phrase quoted is William Harrison's: see Furnivall, *Harrison's description of England*, p. 133. The fullest account of the yeomen remains M. Campbell, *The English yeoman under Elizabeth and the early Stuarts* (New Haven, 1942).

landless labourer.[18] In urban society, explorations of the social origins of leading merchants, tradesmen and professional men have helped to explain and resolve the uncertainties of contemporary writers as to the precise social position of these groups, notably by demonstrating the closeness of the ties which linked the leaders of urban and rural society.[19] Though the nature of stratification in urban society remains in some respects more obscure than that of the countryside, some successful efforts have been made not only to examine the distribution of wealth, but also to establish the ranking of particular trades and occupations in the cities. We have a growing awareness of the distinctions of wealth, status and participation in the *cursus honorum* of civic life which existed between mercantile and manual trades, independent masters and journeymen, freemen and the still scarcely explored ranks of day labourers and the urban poor.[20]

In all these ways social-distributional studies have enhanced understanding of the profile of stratification in Tudor and Stuart society. In

18 For studies of particular communities which bring out these distinctions, see e.g. W.G. Hoskins, *The Midland peasant. The economic and social history of a Leicestershire village* (London, 1957), especially chapters 6–7; M. Spufford, *Contrasting communities. English villages in the sixteenth and seventeenth centuries* (Cambridge, 1974), especially part 1; D.G. Hey, *An English rural community. Myddle under the Tudors and Stuarts* (Leicester, 1974), especially chapters 3–5. For broader explorations of differentials in wealth and living standards among these groups, see D. Cressy, *Literacy and the social order. Reading and writing in Tudor and Stuart England* (Cambridge, 1980), pp. 137–9; A. Everitt, 'Farm labourers', in J. Thirsk (ed.), *The agrarian history of England and Wales vol. IV 1500–1640* (Cambridge, 1967); P. Bowden, 'Agricultural prices, farm profits and rents, in Thirsk, *Agrarian history*, especially section C; M.W. Barley, 'Rural housing in England', in Thirsk, *Agrarian history*, especially sections E–G. See also Wrightson, *English society*, pp. 31–6.

19 P. Clark and P. Slack, *English towns in transition 1500–1700* (Oxford, 1976), pp. 120–1; R. Grassby, 'Social mobility and business enterprise in seventeenth-century England', in D. Pennington and K. Thomas (eds), *Puritans and revolutionaries. Essays in seventeenth-century history presented to Christopher Hill* (Oxford, 1978); W.R. Prest, *The Inns of Court under Elizabeth I and the early Stuarts: 1590–1640* (London, 1972), pp. 26–31; B.P. Levack, *The civil lawyers in England, 1603–1641* (Oxford, 1973), pp. 10–11; P. Clark, 'The civic leaders of Gloucester, 1580–1800', in P. Clark (ed.), *The transformation of English provincial towns 1600–1800* (London, 1984).

20 Clark and Slack, *English towns in transition*, chapters 8–9; J. Patten, *English towns, 1500–1700* (Folkestone and Hamden, Conn., 1978), chapters 4 and 6; W.G. Hoskins, *Provincial England. Essays in social and economic history* (London, 1965), chapter 4; J. Cornwall, 'English country towns in the fifteen twenties', *Economic History Review* 2nd series, 15 (1962), pp. 61ff.; A.D. Dyer, *The city of Worcester in the sixteenth century* (Leicester, 1973), chapter 14; C. Phythian-Adams, *Desolation of a city. Coventry and the urban crisis of the late Middle Ages* (Cambridge, 1979), chapter 10; D.M. Palliser, *Tudor York* (Oxford, 1979), chapters 4–6; T.S. Willan, *Elizabethan Manchester*, Chetham Society, 3rd series, 27 (1980), chapter 6; V. B. Elliott, 'Mobility and marriage in pre-industrial England' (unpublished Ph.D. thesis, University of Cambridge, 1978), part I; S. Rappaport, 'Social structure and mobility in sixteenth-century London: part I', *London Journal* 9 (1983); J.P. Boulton, 'The social and economic structure of early-seventeenth-century Southwark' (unpublished Ph.D. thesis, University of Cambridge, 1983), chapters 2–3; D.V. Glass, 'Socio-economic status and occupations in the City of London at the end of the seventeenth century', in P. Clark (ed.), *The early modern town. A reader* (London, 1976).

addition, recent students have expanded far beyond the initial concern with wealth, status and office to explore further dimensions of social differentiation. Significant and on occasion previously unexpected variations between the conventional status and occupational groups have been detected: in such demographic characteristics as age at first marriage;[21] in household structure and geographical mobility;[22] in family behaviour and attitudes;[23] in educational opportunity and literacy;[24] in patterns of criminal prosecution;[25] and in attitudes, manners and customs and participation in religious and political movements.[26]

21 R.B. Outhwaite, 'Age at marriage in England from the late seventeenth to the nineteenth century', *Transactions of the Royal Historical Society* 5th series, vol. 23 (1973); V.B. Elliott, 'Single women in the London marriage market: age, status and mobility, 1598–1619' in R.B. Outhwaite (ed.), *Marriage and society, Studies in the social history of marriage* (London, 1981). For an attempt at distinguishing between the demographic rates of 'landed' and 'landless' families, see V. Skipp, *Crisis and development. An ecological case study of the Forest of Arden 1570–1674* (Cambridge, 1978), chapter 4.

22 P. Laslett, 'Mean household size in England since the sixteenth century', in P. Laslett and R. Wall (eds), *Household and family in past time* (Cambridge, 1972), p. 154; N. Goose, 'Household size and structure in early Stuart Cambridge', *Social History* 5 (1980); Hey, *An English rural community*, pp. 117, 141–2, 170, 173–6; K. Wrightson and D. Levine, *Poverty and piety in an English village: Terling, 1525–1700* (New York, San Francisco, London, 1979), pp. 81–2; P. Clark, 'Migration in England during the late seventeenth and early eighteenth centuries', *Past and Present* 83 (1979).

23 Social differentials in family life are repeatedly stressed in L. Stone, *The family, sex and marriage in England 1500–1800* (London, 1977); Wrightson, *English society*, chapters 3 and 4; R.A. Houlbrooke, *The English family, 1450–1700* (London and New York, 1984).

24 D. Cressy, 'Educational opportunity in Tudor and Stuart England', *History of Education Quarterly* 16 (1976); Cressy, *Literacy and the social order*, especially chapter 6. See also Spufford, *Contrasting communities*, part 2; Wrightson and Levine, *Poverty and piety*, pp. 146–52; R.A. Houston, 'The development of literacy: Northern England, 1640–1750', *Economic History Review* 35 (1982).

25 Exploration of the connections between social status, crime, prosecution and punishment in this period was pioneered by J. Samaha, *Law and order in historical perspective. The case of Elizabethan Essex* (New York and London, 1974). Since the publication of J.S. Cockburn's 'Early-modern assize records as historical evidence', *Journal of the Society of Archivists* 5 (1975), students of crime have exercised much greater caution in accepting the stated social status of indicted persons. Nevertheless the existence of social differentials in prosecution and punishment has been demonstrated in a number of close local studies and is generally borne out by broader studies of crime. See e.g. J.S. Cockburn, 'The nature and incidence of crime in England 1559–1625: a preliminary survey', in J.S. Cockburn, *Crime in England, 1550–1800* (London, 1977), pp. 61–4; M.J. Ingram, 'Communities and courts: law and disorder in early-seventeenth century Wiltshire', in Cockburn, *Crime in England*, pp. 129–34; Wrightson and Levine, *Poverty and piety*, chapter 5; J.A. Sharpe, *Crime in early modern England 1550–1750* (London and New York, 1984).

26 The theme of cultural differentiation emerges strongly in such works as C. Hill, *Society and puritanism in pre-Revolutionary England* (London, 1964); Thomas, *Religion and the decline of magic*; K. Thomas, *Man and the natural world. Changing attitudes in England 1500–1800* (London, 1983); K. Wrightson, 'Alehouses, order and Reformation in rural England 1590–1660', in E. and S. Yeo (eds), *Popular culture and class conflict 1590–1914: explorations in the history of labour and leisure* (Brighton, 1981); K. Wrightson, 'Two concepts of order: justices, constables and

Such work has abundantly demonstrated the pervasive influence of relative social position on the life experiences and opportunities of individuals. And it has done more. It has revealed the existence of regional and local variations in both the structure of stratification and the complexity of the distinctions between social groups – differences which can be linked to varying economic and occupational structures, the influence of distinctive local customs (such as inheritance), and differential incorporation in processes of economic, social and cultural change. Moreover, it has contributed massively to our appreciation of change. This was no static, traditional social order, but a dynamic society in which both the profile of stratification and the experience of particular groups were subject to variation over time. The investigation of such changes has made us familiar with long-term processes of development of which contemporaries themselves were sometimes only confusedly aware: shifts in the social distributions of land and wealth; the numerical expansion or contraction of particular groups, notably the gentry, the professional and trading 'middling sort', small farmers, artisans and the labouring poor; the accentuation or diminution of differentials in living standards; and the emergence of new distinctions in education, attitudes and manners.[27]

For all this we have every reason to be grateful to the authors of social-distributional studies. 'Socially-specific' analysis has been central to the success of recent social history in reconstructing the structures and dynamics of English society in the sixteenth and seventeenth centuries. Yet for this very reason it is important to remember that it takes us only so far. Even where quantification is possible, the enthusiastic production of neat tabular hierarchies of gentlemen, yeomen, tradesmen and craftsmen, husbandmen and so forth for a wide range of 'stratifica-

---

jurymen in seventeenth-century England', in J. Brewer and J. Styles (eds), *An ungovernable people. The English and their law in the seventeenth and eighteenth centuries* (London, 1980). Studies of these issues can rarely be given a quantitative basis, though some efforts have been made to quantify social variations in behaviour and participation in religious Nonconformity. See e.g. Spufford, *Contrasting communities*, pp. 298–306; J.J. Hurwich, 'Dissent and catholicism in English society: a study of Warwickshire, 1660–1720', *Journal of British Studies* 16 (1976); Wrightson and Levine, *Poverty and piety*, pp. 124–33, 154–72 and chapter 7; R.T. Vann, *The social development of English Quakerism 1655–1755* (Cambridge, Mass., 1969), chapter 2; B. Reay, 'The social origins of early Quakerism', *Journal of Interdisciplinary History* 11 (1980); B.S. Capp, *The fifth monarchy men. A study in seventeenth-century English millennarianism* (London, 1972)·, chapter 4; J.F. McGregor and B. Reay (eds), *Radical religion in the English Revolution* (Oxford, 1984), pp. 18–19, 29, 35–9, 143–4, 173. For discussions of political participation below the level of the gentry and civic elites, see D. Hirst, *The representative of the people? Voters and voting in England under the early Stuarts* (Cambridge, 1975); B. Manning, *The English people and the English Revolution 1640–49* (London, 1976); D. Underdown, 'The problem of popular allegiance in the English Civil War', *Transactions of the Royal Historical Society* 5th series, 31 (1981).

27 Fuller discussion of these issues, together with supporting references, can be found in Wrightson, *English society*, especially chapters 2, 5–7.

tion variables' provides at best an imperfect guide to the essential realities of the social order of this period. Indeed, taken too literally such analytical constructions can actually distract attention from some of the complexities and ambiguities of the social structure.

In aggregate terms it seems clear enough that the conventional titular categories employed by contemporaries and adopted in social-distributional studies provide a fair guide to the relative wealth, standing and opportunities open to individuals. Nevertheless it must be stressed that such neat patterns can break down, or at least fray at the edges, when examined in detail. Social distributions based upon these categories invariably reveal that while there are clearly discernible differences on average, there is also a very considerable degree of overlap between adjacent social categories – between gentlemen and yeomen, yeomen and husbandmen, etc.[28] This in itself should be enough to remind us that the 'ranks' and 'degrees' distinguished by contemporaries were far from being rigorously defined, discrete, or homogeneous social groups.[29] Tabulation can suggest a spurious rigour in social differentiation which masks the complex, compound, nature of the process of status evaluation.

Secondly, the employment of conventional titular categories proves virtually useless when we come to deal with the experience of certain occupational groups of uncertain status in contemporary social descriptions. Merchants and tradesmen, lawyers, clergymen, rural craftsmen and artisans, cannot easily be slotted into place in the standard hierarchy for the simple reason that these were not homogeneous groupings. A social distribution which employs the single category 'crafts and trades', for example, is likely to conceal much more than it reveals. There were undoubtedly distinct rankings of trades and crafts within particular towns, while in the countryside craftsmen and tradesmen were also markedly differentiated. Some enjoyed lifestyles and positions comparable with those of substantial farmers. Others were more akin to agricultural labourers. Many lived by dual or multiple employments, which render such distinctions meaningless.[30]

28 For overlap in the social distribution of wealth, see e.g. M. Brigg, 'The Forest of Pendle in the seventeenth century', *Transactions of the Historic Society of Lancashire and Cheshire* 115 (1962); P. Tyler, 'The status of the Elizabethan parochial clergy', in G.J. Cuming (ed.), *Studies in Church history IV: the province of York* (Leiden, 1967), pp. 96–7; Spufford, *Contrasting communities*, pp. 36–41. Such overlap is equally clear in, for example, the social distribution of illiteracy, or involvement in religious Nonconformity.

29 This point is very forcibly made in Kerby, 'Inequality in a pre-industrial society', chapter 9.

30 For the towns, see note 19 in this chapter. For the countryside, see e.g. Hoskins, *Midland peasant*, pp. 166–7; Wrightson and Levine, *Poverty and piety*, pp. 22–3; Brigg, 'The Forest of Pendle', pp. 88–90; D. Hey, *The rural metalworkers of the Sheffield region: a study of rural industry before the Industrial Revolution*, Occasional Papers of the Department of Local History, 2nd series, no. 5 (Leicester, 1972), pp. 19–31, 34; G.D. Ramsay, *The Wiltshire woollen industry in the sixteenth and seventeenth centuries*, 2nd end (London, 1965), chapter 2–3; J. Thirsk, 'Industries in

Thirdly, too literal a reading of social-distributional studies can blunt awareness of the constant process of individual social mobility in English society. Contemporaries were ready to acknowledge such opportunities and individual case studies have confirmed their existence, though most studies of social mobility remain rudimentary and impressionistic and the implications of life-cycle social mobility have yet to be deeply explored.[31] And finally, there is the problem that the *meaning* of conventional status terms could vary locally and could change over time. In comparing a gentleman or a yeoman of one time or place with a gentleman or a yeoman of another, we may not be comparing like with like. In the north-east of England, for example, the term 'yeoman' was used indiscriminately throughout this period to describe small landholders. It did not carry the implication of relative superiority common in the south. Again, though the issue of change in status designations has not been fully explored, it is well enough known that by 1700 the term 'gentleman' was much more broadly applied than in the sixteenth century, while some more traditional terms (such as yeoman or husbandman) were becoming redundant.[32]

In short, attempts to relate the conventional hierarchy of rank in Tudor and Stuart England to social distributions of wealth, office, demographic characteristics, literacy and the rest undoubtedly succeed in demonstrating the very real content of some of the distinctions recognized by contemporaries. But in considering the invaluable evidence generated by such studies we must pay more attention than has been usual to the implications of the minorities, the exceptions, the cases which do not fit

---

the countryside', in F.J. Fisher (ed.), *Essays in the economic and social history of Tudor and Stuart England* (Cambridge, 1961); M. Rowlands, *Masters and men in the west midland metalware trades before the Industrial Revolution* (Manchester, 1975), chapters 1–3, 6.

31 For general discussions of the problem of social mobility, see Stone, 'Social mobility in England'; A. Everitt, 'Social mobility in early modern England', *Past and Present* 33 (1966); Laslett, *The world we have lost, further explored*, pp. 238ff. Attempts to establish the actual extent and range of social mobility are all too few, largely as a result of the problems of keeping a sample of individuals in observation. See e.g. Cliffe, *The Yorkshire gentry*, p. 16; Blackwood, *The Lancashire gentry*, pp. 18ff. and appendix I; Elliott, 'Mobility and marriage', part III, chapter 3; Wrightson and Levine, *Poverty and piety*, pp. 106–8; L. Stone and J.C.F. Stone, *An open elite? England 1540–1880* (Oxford, 1984). Aspects of life-cycle related social mobility have been highlighted in Hoskins, *Midland peasant*, p. 147; Brigg, 'The Forest of Pendle', pp. 74–5; Hey, *An English rural community*, pp. 170ff; P. Slack, 'Social problems and social policies', in *The traditional community under stress*, Open University Course A322, English Urban History 1500–1780, block III (Milton Keynes, 1977), p. 84. See also, for poverty and the life cycle, the recent contributions by W.N. Brown and T.C. Wales to R.M. Smith (ed.), *Land, kinship and lifecycle* (Cambridge, 1984).

32 Cressy, *Literacy and the social order*, p. 125; A. Everitt, *Change in the provinces: the seventeenth century*, Occasional Papers of the Department of Local History, 2nd series, no. 1 (Leicester, 1970), pp. 43ff; P. Styles, 'The social structure of Kineton Hundred in the reign of Charles II', in *Essays in honour of Philip B. Chatwin, Transactions and Proceedings of the Birmingham Archaeological Society* 78 (1962), pp. 102–3; G. Holmes, *Augustan England. Professions, state and society, 1680–1730* (London, 1982), pp. 9, 11; Speck, *Stability and strife*, pp. 37, 40–1, 47–8.

and the categories which disintegrate on closer examination, are blurred by social mobility opportunities, or are modified in meaning between places and over time. The familiar titular categories and the hierarchy in which they were customarily arranged were valid up to a point. Doubtless we will continue to use them, for we have little choice. But they should be employed with care, preferably in a known local context within which records can be linked in such a way as to cast light upon one another and reveal otherwise concealed significances. And we must remain constantly aware of the fact that these categories were ill defined and that the membranes which separated them were permeable.

This serves to introduce a final point on the subject of social-distributional studies. As has already been argued, there were at least two ways of perceiving the social order of early modern England: as the finely grained hierarchy of formal convention, or in terms of a cruder distinction between two or three broad groups. One of the most valuable indirect contributions made by social-distributional studies has been the light cast upon this dual or multiple perception. For if they have demonstrated that the conventional hierarchy was reproduced in many spheres of life, they also suggest, first, that the discontinuities which can be detected in the profile of stratification cannot simply be tied to the usual status and occupational categories, and second, that these discontinuities varied in their social significance and in their depth.

The implication is that certain status and occupational groups can be said to have formed 'clusters' or 'constellations' in which the social distance between their members, though real, was less deep and less significant than that which separated them from other social groups. Thus the leading merchants of the cities and the higher ranks of the professions were closely akin to landed gentlemen in their birth, education, incomes, lifestyles and tenure of positions of authority. To take another example, smallholding 'husbandmen' in the villages might stand closer to cottagers in their living standards, manners, illiteracy and household structure than to their wealthier, office-holding, servant-keeping, frequently literate, 'yeoman' neighbours. Yeomen in turn might have a good deal in common with the lesser 'parish' gentry.

Such affinities or clusterings are strongly implied by the gradually accumulating evidence of social differentiation and social mobility chances. They have recently been confirmed strikingly by Vivien Brodsky Elliott. In work of notable originality she has demonstrated the possibility of measuring the relative social distance between status and occupational groups by examining systematically the choices exercised by individuals and families in the selection of marriage partners and the apprenticeship of sons. Her results reveal, not an evenly graded hierarchy, but a series of clusters of status and occupational groups whose closeness to one another is discernible in their willingness to intermarry and the similarities of their preferences and opportunities in placing their sons in trades.[33]

What all this suggests is that within the complex hierarchy of formal social description there existed a smaller number of what might be termed social and cultural milieux. It was perhaps just such constellations of social groups that contemporaries were seeking to identify when they employed such broad terms as 'gentlemen', 'the quality', 'the people', 'the best inhabitants', 'the middling sort', 'the meaner sort', 'the inferior sort', 'the poor', and many another imprecise but socially resonant categorization. This was an alternative way of viewing the structure of society, which was by no means incompatible with the finer distinctions of the full social hierarchy but which focused less upon static, formal, classification than upon the basic alignments demonstrated in the dynamics of social relations. Moreover if, as I have suggested, this was becoming the dominant form of perception, then its increasing significance may well have been closely linked to the social changes of the later sixteenth and earlier seventeenth centuries: the expansion of the lesser gentry; the emergence of the urban 'pseudo-gentry'; the diversification of the prosperous 'middling sort'; the whittling away of the husbandmen of fielden England; the massive growth of the labouring poor; and the complex processes of economic, administrative and cultural change which produced both a more integrated national society and a more diversified and differentiated local society.[34]

Taken together, then, the two approaches to the social order which I have examined so far begin to produce a fairly clear picture. This was a society which was highly differentiated but which was far from uniform, rigid, or unchanging in its patterns of inequality. The criteria of social evaluation were complex and ill defined. Local patterns of stratification varied considerably. Individual social mobility was constant and frankly recognized. The sixteenth and seventeenth centuries saw considerable shifts in both the relative size of particular social groups and the nature and degree of their differentiation. Finally, the conventional image of the social hierarchy was resolved in everyday speech and practice into a simpler, less formal, classification, in which relative social distance on a variety of criteria produced a series of clusterings which constituted distinctive social and cultural milieux. There were at least two ways of perceiving the structure of society, expressing equally valid but alternative perceptions of a complex reality, and one of these appears to have been gradually supplanting the other. The language of 'degrees' was becoming archaic, a vocabulary of social conservatism. The language of 'sorts' was increasingly resonant.

33 Elliott, 'Mobility and marriage', part I, chapters 2–4.
34 These developments are fully discussed in Wrightson, *English society*, chapters 5–7.

Social Relations

All in all, recent research has put us in a much better position to *describe* English society in the sixteenth and seventeenth centuries. This does not mean, however, that we *understand* the social order of the time. Accumulating empirical knowledge carries us only so far. The ultimately more significant problem of the nature of social relations and the attitudes and meanings with which they were infused remains open – and it is fair to say that this issue is rarely approached in any very critical way by students of sixteenth- and seventeenth-century England. Instead, the tendency has been to borrow models ready-made from other historical periods, from the historiography of other countries (notably France), or from the theoretical stock-in-trade of sociology, and to impose them in an essentially assertive manner.

But it is easy to criticize: far harder to answer the question of how we should characterize the relations between people occupying different positions in the hierarchies of wealth, status and power in Tudor and Stuart England. Was this, as some would argue, a society characterized by vertical alignments of patronage and clientage, paternalism and deference, in which social conflict was primarily between rival individuals and their networks of interest and connection?[35] Was it, as others would maintain, a society in which manifest or latent animosity between broadly defined classes was already the dominant reality in social relations?[36] On

35 For forthright statements of this view, see P. Zagorin, *The court and the country. The beginnings of the English Revolution* (London, 1969), chapter 2 and P. Zagorin *Rebels and rulers, 1500–1660*, 2 vols (Cambridge, 1982), vol. I, chapter 3. In *The court and the country*, p. 22, n. 2, and in *Rebels and rulers*, pp. 62–3, Zagorin cites his sociological influences. He is also influenced by the French scholar R. Mousnier. For a discussion of the sociological influences on Mousnier's conception of the 'society of orders or estates', see A. Arriaza, 'Mousnier and Barker: the theoretical underpinning of the "Society of Orders" in early modern Europe', *Past and Present* 89 (1980). M. James outlines his concept of a 'Lineage society' in *Family, lineage and civil society. A study of society, politics and mentality in the Durham region 1500–1640* (Oxford, 1974), chapter 1 and conclusion, acknowledging his theoretical debt to the French medievalist G. Duby. James argues, however, that the 'lineage society' was in decay in the course of the period covered by his study. Perhaps the most influential English account of the pre-industrial 'classless hierarchy' is that of H. Perkin, *The origins of modern English society, 1780–1880* (London, 1969), chapter 2 'The Old Society'. Perkin's work has greatly influenced historians attempting to 'place' the early modern period with regard to the subsequent developments of the Industrial Revolution era.

36 Such interpretations tend to focus upon the central problem of the contribution of social change and class conflict to the origins and course of the English Revolution. See e.g. C. Hill, *Reformation to Industrial Revolution*, Pelican edn (Harmondsworth, 1969), pp. 127–34; C. Hill, 'A bourgeois revolution?', in J.G.A. Pocock (ed.), *Three British revolutions: 1641, 1688, 1776* (Princeton, 1980); B. Manning, 'Religion and politics: the godly people', in B. Manning (ed.), *Politics, religion and the English Civil War* (London, 1973); Manning, *The English people and the English Revolution*; W. Hunt, *The Puritan movement: the coming of revolution in an English county* (Cambridge, Mass., 1983). For two useful reviews of class in the English Revolution, see D.

this issue contemporary literary accounts are of limited help. Those contemporaries who concerned themselves with the problem more commonly offered prescriptions for an idealized, organic harmony in social relations, coupled with laments over individual deviations from the ideal, than careful attempts to analyse everyday reality.[37] Nor are these matters readily quantifiable, though the findings of social-distributional studies may certainly help to shape interpretative preferences. If we are to approach them, we have to rely ultimately upon the evaluation of qualitative evidence, the considered weighing of example and counter-example. In this realm, firm and incontrovertible proof of any contention is hardly to be expected. Proof, to borrow Raymond Chandler's apt phrase, becomes 'a relative thing ... an overwhelming balance of probabilities. And that's a matter of how they strike you.'[38] Nevertheless, we are obliged to attempt a reasoned approach to the evidence. And in reviewing the available evidence, what strikes me most forcibly is its ambiguity.

There is no doubt, for example, of the importance of relationships of lordship and service, patronage and clientage, paternalism and deference in sixteenth- and seventeenth-century society. If we choose to emphasize these ties, taking our cue from contemporary social descriptions and moral prescriptions, then society can indeed be represented as 'a graduated ladder of dominance and subordination', a hierarchy incorporating 'gradations of privilege and disability, authority and subordination, deference and disesteem', bound together by personalized ties of patronage and dependence.[39] Does the documented existence of such bonds, however, necessarily imply that English society in this period can be neatly summed up as a vertically integrated deference society, 'a world of personal dependency', a 'classless hierarchy' based on 'property and patronage' of the type eloquently described by Perkin in his account of the 'Old Society' which passed away at the turn of the eighteenth and nineteenth centuries?[40]

Patronage and clientage, paternalism and deference, should never be abstracted from the essential context of the realities of power in society. Given those realities, the deference accorded to superiors might be little

Underdown, 'Community and class: theories of local politics in the English Revolution', in B.C. Malament (ed.), *After the Reformation. Essays in honour of J.II. Hexter* (Manchester, 1980), and M. Fulbrook, 'The English Revolution and the revisionist revolt', *Social History* 7 (1982). It should be emphasized that the use of the concept of class by historians of early modern England is not confined to this context. Nor is it peculiar to avowedly Marxist historians.

37 W.R.D. Jones, *The Tudor Commonwealth 1529–1559* (London, 1970), *passim*.

38 R. Chandler, *Farewell my lovely*, in *Raymond Chandler*, Heineman/Octopus collected edition (London, 1977), p. 856.

39 James, *Family, lineage and civil society*, p. 27; Zagorin, *The court and the country*, p. 25.

40 Perkin, *Origins of modern English society*, pp. 17, 37. Perkin's account of vertical social alignments is particularly trenchant. See e.g. pp. 49–50. Although his account of the 'Old Society' is focused on the eighteenth century, the implication is that these alignments were characteristic of the early modern period.

more than a form of demeanour, a recognition of the imperatives of the particular social situation, and a willingness to adopt a conventional posture of subordination in return for assistance, favour or protection. It did not necessarily involve, as is so often assumed, a full and unconditional subscription to a moral order which endorsed and legitimized the social and material subordination of the inferior.[41] We must be careful not to overestimate the effectiveness of what has been called the 'political socialization' of the common people – the subordination, obedience, humility and patience inculcated by catechism, homily and sermon.[42] Indeed, there is clear enough evidence that all these could dissolve when the terms of the relationship between superiors and inferiors became too exploitative, or when expectations of proper conduct were betrayed – just as lords and patrons themselves could neglect their conventional social obligations when the pressure of their own interests persuaded them to do so.[43]

Again, not every member of society was equally involved, let alone enveloped, in such relationships. Areas of relative independence existed, both socially and geographically. The erosion of the formal obligations of feudal lordship and serfdom, which themselves had never been so all-pervasive as was once assumed, had left behind a situation in which there could be considerable flexibility in the relationships between superiors and subordinates, a state of affairs further enhanced as formal retaining declined at the turn of the sixteenth and seventeenth centuries. At all social levels there were individuals whose effective independence permitted them to accord or withhold their loyalty and deference with

41 For a stimulating discussion of the realities of deference, located in a broad historical context, see H. Newby, *The deferential worker. A study of farm workers in East Anglia*, Penguin edn (Harmondsworth, 1979). A number of recent works have explicitly questioned the binding force of 'vertical' relationships and loyalties. See e.g. E.P. Thompson, 'Eighteenth-century English society: class struggle without class?', *Social History* 3 (1978); R.S. Neale, *Class in English history 1680–1850* (Oxford, 1981), pp. 83–93.

42 The phrase quoted is from G.J. Schochet, 'Patriarchialism, politics and mass attitudes in Stuart England', *Historical Journal* 12 (1969), p. 413. For the Tudor 'Homily on obedience', see G.R. Elton (ed.), *The Tudor constitution. Documents and commentary* (Cambridge, 1962), pp. 15–16. Sermons exhorting the people to patience were particularly common in years of economic crisis and were sometimes preached on the order of the authorities. See e.g. J. Walter and K. Wrightson, 'Dearth and the social order in early modern England', *Past and Present* 71 (1976), pp. 29, 34.

43 These realities are vividly illustrated in the now extensive literature on popular protest and riot in early modern England. The work of John Walter provides particularly sensitive analysis of the equivocal nature of the relationship between the people and their governors: see e.g. Walter and Wrightson, 'Dearth and the social order'; J. Walter, 'Grain riots and popular attitudes to the law: Maldon and the crisis of 1629', in Brewer and Styles, *An ungovernable people*; J. Walter, 'A "rising of the people"? The Oxfordshire Rising of 1596', *Past and Present* 107 (1985). For recent surveys of this field, see Wrightson, *English society*, pp. 173–9; P. Slack (ed.), *Rebellion, popular protest and the social order in early modern England* (Cambridge, 1984).

relative freedom.[44] Moreover, there were also whole communities in which the absence of resident gentlemen or clergymen, the relatively muted nature of social differentiation and the opportunities afforded by the local economy for an independent subsistence of sorts, meant that their inhabitants were less habituated to the daily display of subordination and deference than might be the case in settlements dominated by landlords, parsons, or tight oligarchies of local notables. The truculent independence of woodlanders and fen people, for example, was proverbial throughout this period, and not without reason.[45]

Vertical ties of patronage and subordination, then, were far from being ubiquitous or formally binding relationships in English society, whatever their nature may have been elsewhere. They were flexible relationships which expressed particular accommodations to the realities of social and economic inequality. Their restraining force varied and it was far from unconditional. Nor were they the only forms of relationship between individuals and groups occupying different places in the hierarchies of wealth, status and power.

To come at the problem from the other side: there is no doubt of the existence of tensions and conflicts between landlords and tenants, poor consumers and middlemen, urban oligarchs and the freemen and commons of the cities, village notables and the village poor.[46] Such evidence

---

44 For lord and tenant relationships, see e.g. R.H. Hilton, *The decline of serfdom in mediaeval England* (London, 1969); R.H. Hilton, *The English peasantry in the later Middle Ages* (Oxford, 1975), pp. 18–19; C. Dyer, *Lords and peasants in a changing society. The estates of the Bishopric of Worcester, 680–1540* (Cambridge, 1980), chapters 12–13. For what R.B. Smith has termed the 'emancipation' of the gentry from ties of lordship, see e.g. Stone, *Crisis of the aristocracy*, chapter 5; R.B. Smith, *Land and politics in the England of Henry VIII. The West Riding of Yorkshire: 1530–46* (Oxford, 1970), pp. 43–9, 124, 133, 161, 255–8, 261–2; M.E. James, *Change and continuity in the Tudor North*, Borthwick Papers, no. 27 (York, 1965), pp. 11–12; James, *Family, lineage and civil society*, chapter 2 and conclusion; A. Fletcher, *A county community in peace and war: Sussex 1600–1640* (London, 1975), pp. 23–4. On yeoman independence, see Campbell, *The English yeoman*, pp. 366–9, and for the 'middle sort of people' generally, Hirst, *Representative of the people?*, chapter 6 and Manning, *The English people and the English Revolution*, pp. 152–62.

45 J. Thirsk, 'The farming regions of England', in Thirsk, *Agrarian history*, pp. 111–12; Lindley, *Fenland riots*, p. 2. Industrial communities were also frequently regarded as potentially unruly, as were some upland areas: Wrightson, *English society*, pp. 171–2, 182.

46 For agrarian conflict and food riots see C.S.L. Davis, 'Peasant revolt in France and England: a comparison', *Agricultural History Review* 21 (1973); R.B. Manning, 'Violence and social conflict in mid-Tudor rebellions', *Journal of British Studies* 16 (1977); R.B. Manning, 'Patterns of violence in early Tudor enclosure riots', *Albion* 5 (1974); J. Cornwall, *Revolt of the peasantry 1549* (London, 1977); B. Sharp, *In contempt of all authority. Rural artisans and riots in the west of England, 1586–1640* (Berkeley, 1980); Lindley, *Fenland riots*; and the works cited in note 42 in this chapter. For urban conflict, see Clark and Slack, *English towns in transition*, pp. 56, 69–70, 125, 132–4; Phythian-Adams, *Desolation of a city*, pp. 253–4; Palliser, *Tudor York*, pp. 49–50, and the examples of the conflict underlying borough franchise disputes provided in Hirst, *Representative of the people?*, pp. 197ff. For social conflict at the village level, see Wrightson and Levine, *Poverty and piety*, chapters 5 and 7; Wrightson, 'Two concepts of

can be highlighted and marshalled to justify an interpretation of social conflict in terms of class hostilities and solidarities. But does all this really add up to a society in which social relations were dominated by class alignments?

Clearly, a great deal depends upon the particular definition of 'class' or 'class society' which we choose to employ. On this crucial issue, however, historians of Tudor and Stuart England can be peculiarly slippery and evasive. Very few define their terms at all. As a result, discussion is obscured by a mist of nuance and implication through which we wander while attempting to home in on often weak or impenetrably coded signals of one another's positions.

No useful purpose would be served here by embarking on a discussion of the myriad competing definitions of the concept of class.[47] It will be more helpful to state a position briefly. If we use a fairly eclectic definition of social class to describe a loose aggregate of individuals of varied though comparable economic position, who are linked by similarities of status, power, lifestyle and opportunities, by shared cultural characteristics and bonds of interaction, then I would argue that social classes, so defined, can be discerned in early modern England.[48] Their existence is certainly implied by contemporary terminology, as I have indicated, though they spoke not of classes but of 'sorts'. Such a conception of class informs the work of the many historians of the period who, though otherwise reticent in their use of the term, are willing to describe the gentry as a class. It also seems to me implicit in the work of those who find 'the middling sort of people', 'the meaner sort', 'the labouring poor' or other such contemporary terms meaningful and valuable in discussing this society – however cautiously they avoid the word 'class' on the valid grounds that the term was unknown to the people of the time.[49]

---

order', pp. 40–6; Hunt, *The Puritan moment*, chapter 6; Sharpe, *Crime in early modern England*, pp. 83–93; M. Ingram, 'Religion, communities and moral discipline in late-sixteenth- and early-seventeenth-century England: case studies', in K. von Greyerz (ed.), *Religion and society in early modern Europe, 1500–1800* (London, 1984).

47 For discussions of the sociological literature, see Littlejohn, *Social stratification*; A. Giddens, *The class structure of the advanced societies*, 2nd edn (London, 1981). For the concepts of class and class consciousness in English historiography, see Neale, *Class in English history*; R.J. Morris, *Class and class consciousness in the Industrial Revolution 1780–1850* (London, 1979).

48 This definition is close to Weber's concept of 'social class', as discussed in Giddens, *Class structure of the advanced societies*, pp. 48–9, 105–6.

49 For the emergence of the language of class in social description, see A. Briggs, 'The language of "class" in early-nineteenth-century England', in A. Briggs and J. Saville (eds), *Essays in labour history. In memory of G.D.H. Cole* (London, 1960). An intriguing early use of the language of class is to be found in Gregory King's 1697 reply to Robert Harley's criticisms. King, in a single paragraph, refers to 'the several degrees', 'the poorest sort', 'the middle sort' and 'the better sort' and his distribution of the people 'into classes'. See Thirsk and Cooper, *Seventeenth-century economic documents*, p. 795. (I am grateful to Tom Arkell of Warwick University for bringing this example to my attention.)

The concept of class can thus be used in a descriptive sense, provided always that historians define their terms and avoid the casual importation into early modern studies of the class terminology of nineteenth- or twentieth-century Britain. However, the stumbling block to those who might otherwise go on to discuss the development of early modern England in class terms, who would see classes not simply as descriptive categories but as historical agents and ascribe a major role to class conflict in explicating the social and political dynamics of the period, is clearly the problem of class consciousness. To Marxist and non-Marxist historians alike, to Peter Laslett reconstructing the world we have lost, to E.P. Thompson, H.J. Perkin, R.S. Neale or R.J. Morris charting the social changes of the eighteenth and early nineteenth centuries, a *sine qua non* of a real class society is the presence of class consciousness – a sense of identification among those within a particular class and of differentiation from, and ultimately conflict of interest with, other classes.[50] Some would add that class identities must be national in scope, stabilized and perpetuated in class-based institutions, and rendered articulate in various 'class ideals', before a society can truly be characterized as a 'class society'.[51]

On such exacting criteria there is indeed considerable difficulty in characterizing sixteenth- and seventeenth-century England as a 'class society'. It seems generally accepted that the gentry were conscious of a common social identity as 'gentlemen' which outweighed their internal differentiation and political rivalries, that they detected broad groupings among their social inferiors, and that they were conscious of a latent and sometimes open antagonism between their interests and those of the 'rude multitude'.[52] The social consciousness of other groups, however, is much more difficult to establish and it certainly cannot simply be assumed. They generally lacked the institutions which might encourage a common sense of identity beyond the bounds of parishes, towns or local 'social areas'. They could certainly express solidarities as ratepayers and 'principal inhabitants', or as tenants, freemen, commoners, or industrial

---

50 Laslett, *The world we have lost, further explored*, pp. 22–3; E.P. Thompson, *The making of the English working class*, Pelican edn. (Harmondsworth, 1968), pp. 9–10; E.P. Thompson, 'The peculiarities of the English', in *The poverty of theory and other essays* (London, 1978), pp. 51, 85; Perkin, *Origins of modern English society*, p. 176; Neale; *Class in English history*, pp. 131–3; Morris, *Class and class consciousness*, p. 37. Definitions of 'class consciousness', of course, vary.

51 Laslett, *The world we have lost, further explored*, pp. 22–3; Perkin, *Origins of modern English society*, pp. 177, 209, 219ff.

52 The most influential discussion of the class identity of the gentry is Peter Laslett's in *The world we have lost* (London, 1965), chapter 2. For vivid examples of the intermingling of contempt, hostility and fear which often coloured gentry attitudes to the 'multitude', see C. Hill, *Change and continuity in seventeenth-century England* (London, 1974), chapter 8; Jones, *The Tudor Commonwealth*, p. 50; B. Capp, *Astrology and the popular press. English almanacs 1500–1800* (London, 1979), p. 111; K. Thomas, *Man and the natural world. Changing attitudes in England 1500–1800* (London, 1983), pp. 43–4.

workers, when engaged in conflict. Yet such group identities seem often to have been highly localized, or unstable and negative in form; quickened into temporary existence by a common enemy or grievance, rather than expressing a broader, more enduring, consciousness of collective interest.

Given all these problems, it becomes difficult to describe English society in this period as either a vertically aligned hierarchy or a class society.[53] One solution would be to choose whatever model appears to carry the most conviction and then to admit the outstanding problems as minor qualifications. Thus we might speak of a hierarchical society which was experiencing the early stirrings of class formation, or of an immature class society which retained residual vestiges of earlier social formations. A more positive response, however, would be to recognize the inadequacies of both conventional models and to confront the fact that we are dealing with an altogether distinctive situation.

Doing so would seem to require the jettisoning of several questionable assumptions which have seeded themselves in the minds of historians and struck deep roots. One is the notion that the forms of social alignment that we label hierarchy and class are somehow mutually exclusive and that they are necessarily characteristic of successive stages of social development. Another is the requirement that class identities must be national in scope before their existence can be admitted. A third is the demand that class consciousness must be highly developed, stable, consistent, articulate or even politically aligned before it can be accorded historical recognition. To insist upon such demanding theoretical criteria and to erect them into universal standards of judgement, may well be to blinker ourselves to the extent that we fail to deal adequately with the complex and contradictory realities of actual historical experience. And it is with a satisfactory approach to that experience that we are concerned, not the neat theoretical pigeon-holing of past societies.

If we put aside such inhibiting and question-begging assumptions, then it becomes easier to recognize that English society in the sixteenth and seventeenth centuries exhibited elements of *both* models of social relations. The relevant question becomes not the presence or absence of hierarchical or class alignments but rather the level and degree of their significance. For hierarchy and class can be coexisting dimensions of both individual consciousness and social relations. They may coexist in time in different places and different circumstances. They may even coexist in single minds as alternative responses. To some people in some places society may well have appeared primarily as a localized hierarchy in which they identified themselves with reference to their personal superiors and inferiors. To

53 This point has been forcibly put by R.S. Neale, who describes English society in the period 1650–1750 as 'neither pre-industrial nor industrial, neither feudal nor industrial-capitalist, neither classless nor multi-class, neither order based nor class based, neither one thing nor the other': *Class in English history*, p. 99.

others it may have appeared as being structured into dichotomous groups with conflicting interests. To yet others both views may have appeared appropriate, depending on the particular context and circumstances with which they were dealing: in the home parish or in the broader society; in times of relative stability or in times of divergent interests and conflict. In what was for the most part a relatively small-scale, localized, society much must have depended on local circumstances: on particular patterns of economic and social structure, local events and their perception, historically developed variants in the quality of social relations. Doubtless particular social situations were locally defined and a range of variation is only to be expected. As a general point, however, it can be suggested that local patterns of social relations would emerge from a particular accommodation between the forces of social *identification* – as kinsmen, friends, neighbours, patron and client, co-religionists, fellow countrymen – and the forces of social *differentiation* – as landlord and tenant, master and man, governor and governed, rich and poor. Both dimensions of social relations would be constantly present as everyday realities. The particular balance between them, however, would vary.

Such an approach has the advantage of resolving the contradictions of the commonly employed theoretical models, while at the same time encompassing the complexity, diversity and dynamism of historical reality. It has enough flexibility to allow us to recognize that 'vertical' and 'horizontal' social alignments are not mutually exclusive. Indeed, not only did they coexist, but arguably they were interdependent. The conventions of paternalism and deference can be viewed as one of the means of handling the constant threat of conflict in such a highly stratified society.[54] Manifestations of class conflict can be seen as part and parcel of the process of defining the terms of the relationship between superiors and inferiors in a society in which no practical alternative to the existing social order was envisaged.[55]

The principal deficiency of such an approach, perhaps, is that it runs the risk of flattening the contours of the past. There is no need, however,

---

54 This was fully recognized by contemporaries. In 1570, for example, the northern landowner Leonard Dacre was advised 'See that ye keep a noble house for beef and beer. ... Ride always with a noble company of servants. ... Bid your tenants come to you if wronged by your officers and they will not think much of their rent doubling' (quoted in James, *Change and continuity in the Tudor north*, pp. 8–9). In 1599 the lord keeper urged gentlemen to return to their estates 'there to maynteyne hospitalitie, and releive their poure neighboures, and to see good order kept, whereby natural Love will growe, and be continued between Landlordes and their Tenants and the gentlemen and those of the poorer and meaner sorte which is a matter of noe small movement, for the goode and quiett of the Common Weale' (quoted in Walter, 'A "rising of the people"?', p. 141).

55 Recent studies of riot and popular protest have emphasized the extent to which disorder was a last resort in the defence of popular rights. In 'A "rising of the people"?', p. 143, John Walter writes of 'the roll-call of remembered disorder that continued to play a part in the relationship between rich and poor'.

to fudge the problem of change if we recognize that the relative power of what I have called the forces of identification and of differentiation would vary with the changing economic, cultural, legal and institutional realities of different historical periods. My point is simply that we should not expect such change to involve a grand climacteric or fundamental transition introducing entirely new dimensions in social relations. Class was not born at the turn of the eighteenth and nineteenth centuries, any more than hierarchy died.[56] The difference lay rather in the changing social-structural significance of particular patterns of social relations.

Provision of a little context may help to identify the peculiarities of the early modern situation. By the late sixteenth century social stratification and social relations in England differed significantly in nature, degree and complexity from what had been known in the later Middle Ages. Serfdom was gone. Feudal obligations were attenuated. Personal retaining was giving way to a looser patronage. Inequalities of wealth and living standards had been accentuated. Cultural differentials were more developed. At the same time, however, many of the essential elements of the class alignments associated with the nineteenth century had not yet developed: mass industrial employment and factory work; greater urbanization; residential segregation; a large and independent-minded middle class; trade unions, voluntary associations and other institutions which were class based and able to give class interests national organization and expression and to stabilize and perpetuate class identities; and fully developed conceptions of class structure and class conflict and prophesies of class destiny.

So much for what the later sixteenth and the seventeenth centuries did not have. What they did have was a developing tension between on the one hand processes of change which threatened to produce sharp conflicts of interest between social groups, and on the other hand inherited and enduring ideals of a stable, hierarchical, social order. From at least the 1520s there were forces active which served to accentuate inequalities and to enhance social and cultural differentiation, and which overlapped in such a way as to intensify the risk of conflict – between landlords and tenants, the 'better sort' and the 'meaner sort', the 'godly' and the 'ungodly', the 'polite' and the 'vulgar'. Yet at the same time there were factors which worked against such an outcome: the active paternalism of the Tudor and Stuart state and of individuals responsive to traditional social obligations; the ubiquitous ideology of order and obedience; the ambivalent position of the growing 'middling sort' who formed a social-structural buffer between the ruling gentry and the mass of the common

---

56 For a useful critique of the alleged 'classlessness' of the eighteenth century, see Morris, *Class and class consciousness*, pp. 12–20. For studies of the persistence of paternalism and deference in the nineteenth century and beyond see e.g. P. Joyce, *Work, society and politics. The culture of the factory in later Victorian England* (London, 1980), or Newby, *The deferential worker*.

people; the continued vitality of the institution of service; and the growing complexity of the social order, which undermined some traditional group identities without yet creating new ones of a stable nature.

All these forces could be at work within the bounds of diverse small-scale communities. In every parish the paradoxical nature of the social developments of the period was enshrined in the institutions of the Poor Law – providing relief, enforcing discipline, an expression of communal responsibility yet a potent reminder of social distance. The overall result of these trends was perhaps a peculiarly ambiguous situation compared with what had come before and what was to follow; a persistent, unresolved tension between bonds of social identification and the conflicts of interest and ideals produced by intensified differentiation. We need to recognize the variety, flexibility and ambivalence of social relations in this period rather than to explain them away. And we need to recapture more fully their dynamic over time. For the key to the distinctive social experience of early modern England may lie in the developing ambiguity of its social relations, the very lack of an easily predictable pattern. Moreover, that experience passed on to eighteenth-century England a peculiar legacy which was to provide the basis for future developments. That legacy was not a vertically aligned, pre-class, hierarchical 'Old Society', but a society exhibiting contradictory yet coexisting variations in social alignment: deference and resistance; co-operation and conflict; and countless local variations on the contrapuntal themes of differentiation and identification.[57]

If we are to explore further the social order of early modern England, then it seems to me that it is best explored at the vitally important local level. We need to know more about the range of variation in both local structures of stratification and local perceptions of the social order, about varying patterns of social relations and the conditions of their historical development in distinctive contexts. This means not just the analysis of local society (a task at which English historians are increasingly adept), but also the introduction of a firmer element of chronology, even narrative, which alone can trace the lines of development which gave rise to particular social situations and which involved the contributions of individuals.

---

57 The paradoxes of eighteenth-century social relations have long been recognized. Perkin in *Origins of modern English society*, pp. 26ff. writes of 'latent' class feeling in what he regards as a classless society. The ambiguities of the situation have been discussed extensively in recent attempts to conceptualize the social relations of the period. See, in particular, E.P. Thompson, 'Patrician society, plebeian culture', *Journal of Social History* 7 (1974); Thompson, 'Eighteenth-century English society'; P. Borsay, '"All the town's a stage": urban ritual and ceremony 1660–1800', in Clark, *Transformation of English provincial towns*, especially pp. 251ff.; J. Ellis, 'A dynamic society: social relations in Newcastle-upon-Tyne 1660–1760', in Clark, *Transformation of English provincial towns*, especially pp. 214ff. See also the comments of R.S. Neale quoted in note 52 in this chapter.

This is not just to advocate local study for its own sake. The accumulation of detail can never be an end in itself. The thick context of local study, however, can do much to make concrete and accessible the abstractions and generalizations of historical interpretation if it is combined with a readiness to think anew in a manner which is theoretically informed without being imaginatively dependent. Doubtless there will be no final agreement on these matters, for they lead us directly to historians' most basic convictions about the nature of social organization and historical change. But that is why the problems posed by the nature of the social order of early modern England are worth arguing over. 'We do not understand ourselves because we do not yet know what we have been and hence what we may be becoming. This must change, is changing.'[58]

---

58 P. Laslett, 'Introduction: the necessity of a historical sociology', in *Family life and illicit love in earlier generations. Essays in historical sociology* (Cambridge, 1977), p. 5.

8

The Proximate Determinants of Marital Fertility in England 1600–1799

Chris Wilson

Introduction

The historical demography of Europe before the era of modern censuses and vital registration exists as a serious intellectual pursuit because of our ability to exploit sources of information on past societies which were created for purposes quite different from those of the historian and demographer. The techniques which permit this exploitation are few in number and of recent origin. One is the methodology developed by Peter Laslett and others to analyse household and family structure from census-like documents such as nominative listings. Another is the form of reverse survival known as back projection which enabled E.A. Wrigley and Roger Schofield to turn the series of births, marriages and deaths recorded in English parish registers into interpretable demographic statistics.[1] A third method, and arguably the one with the greatest potential for revealing the detailed demography of past populations, is the record-linking procedure of family reconstitution created by Louis Henry and first applied to English parish records by E.A. Wrigley.[2] Many aspects of a population's demographic behaviour can be analysed using family reconstitutions, but none is better suited to this form of data than marital fertility. This essay concentrates on that topic.

Two studies of pre-industrial England using family reconstitutions have recently appeared; both came to three conclusions about marital fertility:[3]

---

1 E.A. Wrigley and R.S. Schofield, *The population history of England 1541–1871: a reconstruction* (London, 1981).

2 See E.A. Wrigley (ed.), *An introduction to English historical demography* (London, 1966), pp. 96–159.

3 E.A. Wrigley and R.S. Schofield, 'English population history from family reconstitution: summary results 1600–1799', *Population Studies* 37 (1983), pp. 157–84; C. Wilson, 'Natural fertility in pre-industrial England, 1600–1799', *Population Studies* 38 (1984), pp. 225–40.

1 Marital fertility was virtually unchanging in the two centuries from 1600 to 1800.
2 Regional variation in marital fertility was modest, identifying England as an area of unusual homogeneity.
3 Family limitation played no significant role in determining fertility patterns.

The first two of these observations are of methodological importance, in addition to their substantive interest. They suggest that it is legitimate to combine data from different parishes and different periods into larger bodies of data, since this will not disguise underlying differences. This is of great value because measures of fertility calculated for small populations are subject to considerable random fluctuations. When larger populations are studied such random errors are minimized. Therefore in this essay, while presenting results for individual parishes where relevant, I shall give most weight in argument to results obtained for an aggregated set of data comprising several thousand fertility histories drawn from 16 family reconstitutions.

The third observation of earlier studies is also of great interest because the overall level of marital fertility in England was considerably lower than the levels seen in many other pre-industrial European societies. If family limitation was not responsible for this difference, what was? This is the question I attempt to answer in this essay. To do so requires an understanding of both the social and biological determinants of fertility. In particular, I make use of methods developed by mathematical demographers and biostatisticians to determine what have come to be known as the proximate determinants of fertility. Though the work of demographic model builders on reproduction may seem arcane and remote from historical studies, in fact it brings us closer to the behavioural realities of earlier societies. For example, while conventional demographic approaches to fertility are based on abstractions such as fertility rates (an attribute of a population but not an individual), analysis using the proximate determinants relates to such features as coital frequency and the duration of breastfeeding undertaken by mothers.

Data

The data analysed here come from 16 family reconstitutions carried out under the direction of the ESRC Cambridge Group for the History of Population and Social Structure, and I am grateful to the directors of the Group for making the computer tapes containing the data available to me.[4] They form part of a larger study of pre-industrial England, and

4 I am grateful to the following persons who carried out the reconstitutions: J.D. Asteraki (Campton and Shefford cum Southill, Bedfordshire); L. Clarke (Gainsborough, Lincoln-

several more reconstitutions have been completed since the analysis presented here was carried out. When the full data set is analysed some differences between the final results and those presented here are bound to arise. For this reason the results given in this essay should be taken as provisional, though it is unlikely that the main conclusions will be overturned. The 16 parishes analysed present a considerable diversity of geographical and socio-economic settings. They range from small market towns to isolated rural communities, and contain several industrial as well as agricultural areas. Given the large amount of time and effort required to complete a reconstitution, the sampling strategy adopted by the Cambridge Group has been to select examples of several *types* of locality. This aims at achieving a measure of representativeness within the context of a necessarily circumscribed data set. A detailed discussion of the parishes is out of place here and has been presented elsewhere. With regard to fertility, however, it is worth recalling the apparent homogeneity of England. This suggests that almost any sample of parishes would be broadly representative of the country. Moreover, such evidence as there is suggests that the parishes studied have levels of marital fertility very similar to those prevailing generally in mid-nineteenth-century England.[5]

The one important exception to this is London. The work of Roger Finlay has shown that women in certain of the richer parishes of London had markedly higher fertility in the late sixteenth and early seventeenth centuries than the population at large.[6] Indeed, it was comparable with the highest fertility ever reliably recorded. He attributes this difference to the practice of sending children out to wetnurses. This led to a very short period of anovulation and hence high fertility. His evidence suggests, however, that the practice was limited to a handful of particularly wealthy parishes, with the rest of London conforming more closely to the general level of fertility seen elsewhere in England. Given this it is unlikely that more than a small proportion

---

shire); P. Ford (Alcester, Warwickshire); J. Hodgkiss (Earsdon, Northumberland); D. Jeeps (Willingham, Cambridgeshire); K. Leonard (Hawkshead, Lancashire); D. Levin (Bottesford and Shepshed, Leicestershire; Terling, Essex); A. Newman (Ash, Kent); W. Newman Brown (Aldenham, Hertfordshire); K. Oosterveen (Hawkshead, Lancashire); M. Spufford (Willingham, Cambridgeshire); S. Stewart (Banbury, Oxfordshire and Hartland, Devon); K. Wrightson (Terling, Essex); E.A. Wrigley (Colyton, Devon); M. Yasumoto (Methley, Yorkshire); J.D. Young (Gedling, Nottinghamshire).

5 M.S. Teitelbaum, *The British fertility decline: demographic transition in the crucible of the Industrial Revolution* (Princeton, N.J., 1984), pp. 128–9, where the level of marital fertility reported for England as a whole in 1851 is very similar to that for the 16 parishes. Moreover, the amount of variation among the parishes is comparable with the county-by-county variation discovered by Teitelbaum. See C. Wilson, 'Marital fertility in pre-industrial England, 1550–1849' (unpublished Ph.D. thesis, University of Cambridge, 1982), p. 22.

6 R.A.P. Finlay, *Population and metropolis: the demography of London 1580–1650* (Cambridge, 1981), pp. 133–46.

of the whole population was involved, and that it remains justifiable to conclude that the 16 parishes here were typical of the country as a whole. In making this sweeping statement, however, it is as well to inject a note of caution. It may indeed be the case that the 16 parishes are an unrepresentative sample of the some 10,000 parishes of England, but no criterion by which they might be so judged is apparent.

The Fertility Background

In an earlier article it was shown that family limitation was not a significant factor in pre-industrial England, or at least in those parishes for which reconstitutions have been carried out.[7] In that discussion a variety of tests were applied to the data, all of which led to this conclusion. As a simple demonstration consider figure 8.1, which graphs age-specific marital fertility rates for the English parishes as well as for four villages in Waldeck in central Germany and Blankenberghe in Flanders. The English rates are distinctly lower than the others but show a similar pattern. In spite of varying in level by up to 50 per cent, the three curves are remarkably alike in shape. This becomes more apparent in figure 8.2 where the rates are expressed as

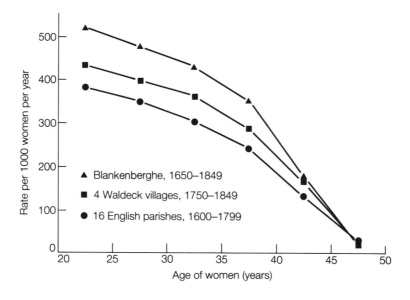

Figure 8.1   Age-specific marital fertility rates
Source: *C. Wilson, 'Natural fertility in pre-industrial England 1600–1799'*, Population Studies *38 (1984), pp. 225–40*

7 Wilson, 'Natural fertility in pre-industrial England'.

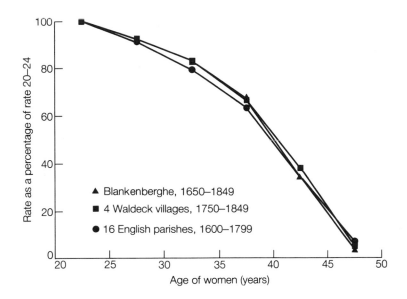

Figure 8.2   Age-specific rates indexed (20–24 = 100)
Source: *C. Wilson, 'Natural fertility in pre-industrial England 1600–1799'*, Population Studies *38*
(1984), pp. 225–40

percentages of the peak value (for women 20–24). In this case the
similarity is such that the three lines are virtually indistinguishable, all
demonstrating a slow decline up to age 35 and falling rapidly thereafter. This feature of many populations was first pointed out by Louis
Henry, who proposed the term 'natural fertility' to describe a pattern of
marital fertility where the behaviour of couples does not depend on the
number of children already born.[8] The opposite situation is family
limitation, where couples make efforts to reduce or cease childbearing
after reaching a certain family size or parity. For this reason fertility
rates fall more rapidly as age, and thus parity, increases than is true for
populations with natural fertility. As figure 8.1 shows, the overall level
of fertility can vary greatly among populations with natural fertility,
but all retain the characteristic age profile. This similarity of pattern is
not due to chance; it is the result of powerful physiological constraints
on reproduction which are apparent because confounding effects such
as contraception and induced abortion are absent. It is through examining these physiological factors that we can gain a deeper understanding of the determinants of marital fertility.

8 L. Henry, 'Some data on natural fertility', *Eugenics Quarterly* 8 (1961), pp. 81–91.

The Proximate Determinants

The analysis of fertility in terms of its proximate determinants, or intermediate fertility variables as they are sometimes called, is one of the most fruitful developments of recent demographic analysis. The great improvement over earlier conceptual frameworks is that they allow the historian to move closer to the behavioural realities of the population being studied. As their name indicates, proximate determinants have a direct effect on fertility; background factors, such as cultural or socio-economic variables, can only influence fertility by altering one or more of the proximate determinants. In terms of figure 8.3 there is no short-cut from left to right; contact is only possible through the proximate determinants.

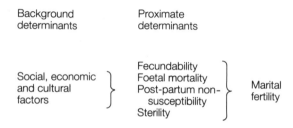

Figure 8.3   The determinants of natural fertility

The process of human reproduction is far from being simple, and early mathematical or conceptual models of it reflected this complexity. For example, Davis and Blake in a seminal article listed eleven different variables, some of which were further subdivided.[9] However, as more information on the biostatistics of reproduction became available it emerged that some factors were largely invariant between populations (though often highly variable among women in each population). Moreover, theoretical model builders were able to demonstrate that fertility was not greatly affected by changes in some of the variables. Finally, since in this discussion marital fertility is being considered, and only in the context of natural fertility, no account need be taken of two of the most powerful determinants of fertility – marriage and contraception. This means that only four components of fertility need consideration: physiological sterility, fecundability (the probability that a woman conceives in one menstrual cycle when at risk to do so), foetal mortal-

9 K. Davis and J. Blake, 'Social structure and fertility: an analytic framework', *Economic Development and Cultural Change* 4 (1956), pp. 211–35.

ity, and the duration of the non-susceptible period (NSP) which follows a birth and during which the mother cannot conceive again.

Only three of these four factors can be analysed using family reconstitutions; foetal mortality cannot because only information on births is recorded. There is no alternative, therefore, to assuming that the chance of a pregnancy miscarrying was the same in all the populations analysed here. This is obviously unlikely to have been true. However, studies of spontaneous abortion in contemporary countries suggest that the level of foetal mortality does not vary greatly among populations. Since most foetal deaths occur early in pregnancy, when environmental considerations usually have only a limited influence, genetic factors probably play a major role.[10] Moreover, Bongaarts, using a mathematical model of reproduction, has suggested that fertility is rather insensitive to variation in intra-uterine mortality, and that very large differences in this component would be needed to produce significant fertility differentials.[11] In short, the assumption which we are forced to make is probably reasonable.

Physiological Sterility

The physiological ability to conceive and bring to term a pregnancy successfully is, perhaps, the most fundamental of all the proximate determinants; without this ability any other considerations remain strictly academic. Sterility provides, therefore, the obvious place with which to begin this study.

In any population of reasonable size at least a small proportion of couples are unable to bear any children because of physiological impairments to either or both spouses. Demographers distinguish between primary sterility, which is attributable to ageing and its effects on the male and female reproductive systems, and secondary sterility, which occurs as the consequence of a birth or, more generally, of a pregnancy. Primary sterility is straightforward to assess and is the principal component of the overall proportion of couples unable to have children in the populations under consideration here. Since it has also been reported for several other historical populations which provide comparative results, I shall concentrate on primary sterility. A more detailed and wider consideration of sterility in pre-industrial England is presented elsewhere.[12]

If we assume that voluntary childlessness was negligible in our sample of parishes, then the extent of primary sterility can be approxi-

10 H. Leridon, *Human fertility: the basic components* (Chicago, 1977).

11 J. Bongaarts, 'Intermediate fertility variables and marital fertility rates', *Population Studies* 30 (1976), pp. 227–41.

12 J. Trussell and C. Wilson, 'Sterility in a population with natural fertility', *Population Studies* 39 (1985), pp. 269–86.

mated by the proportion of married women who remain childless at the
end of their reproductive age span. The age pattern of the proportion
childless is given in figure 8.4, and the numerical values for several
populations in table 8.1. All the data show the same characteristic
profile of a slow increase in sterility up to about age 35 and a more
rapid rise thereafter. There are no significant differences between the
English parishes and the populations with markedly higher fertility.
Clearly the lower marital fertility seen in England was not caused by
high proportions of couples being unable to start a family. Elsewhere, it
has been shown that the age at which mothers had their last child was
also similar in England and the higher-fertility societies.[13]

Given these two observations, it is apparent that the origin of the
lower English fertility must lie in factors which caused the intervals
between births to be longer in England than elsewhere. The two
principal factors of this type are fecundability and the duration of the
post-partum non-susceptible period.

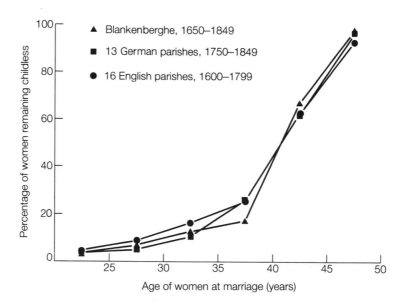

Figure 8.4   Permanent sterility by age at marriage
Sources: *Blankenberghe and English parishes, Cambridge Group reconstitutions. German parishes, J.
Knodel, personal communication*

---

13 Wilson, 'Natural fertility in pre-industrial England', pp. 234–6.

Table 8.1 Percentage of women who remain childless at age 50 by age at marriage

	Age at marriage						
	15–19	20–24	25–29	30–34	35–39	40–44	45–49
16 English parishes (1600–1799)	6.6	4.6	9.1	16.6	25.4	62.2	92.9
13 German parishes (pre–1850)	–	3.6	5.3	10.4	25.9	61.8	96.7
Blankenberghe, Belgium (1650–1849)	–	3.7	7.1	13.1	17.2	66.7	97.6
Norway c.1898	3.5	6	11	19	33	58	–
England (1861–70)	3.5	5	8	13	24	50	–

All data refer to marriages which remain intact up to age 50.
Sources: 16 English parishes and Blankenberghe: Cambridge Group reconstitutions. German parishes: John Knodel, personal communication. Norway and England: H. Leridon, 'Sur l'estimation de la sterilité', Population (special number, 1977), pp. 231–45.

Fecundability

The concept of fecundability was introduced by Gini as long ago as 1924 as the probability of a married woman conceiving during a menstrual cycle (or in one month) in the absence of any deliberate attempt to limit procreation. However, it is only through the work of Louis Henry and others in the 1950s and 1960s that the concept gained currency, and only in the 1970s that straightforward and easily applicable methods of estimating it were developed. The methods used in this chapter are based on the work of John Bongaarts, though the precise specification is slightly different from his proposals.[14]

While certain physiological considerations, for example sperm count and the proportion of fertile cycles, play a role in determining fecundability, the main determinant is believed to be behavioural: coital frequency. For a woman to conceive an act of intercourse must occur during her fertile period (about two days around the middle of the cycle). Clearly, the more frequent is coitus, the higher the chance of one act occurring in this two-day period, and hence the higher the probability of conception. However, since the crucial point is for there to be at least one coitus within the two days the relationship is asymptotic; beyond a certain frequency extra acts have a reduced effect in raising fecundability. A number of models expressing this relationship have been proposed, and figure 8.5 illustrates one of the most plausible.[15] Clearly, coital rate, which is likely to be greatly influenced by social and cultural mores, is of central importance in determining fecundability.

Demographers distinguish three types of fecundability according to the duration of pregnancy at which it is measured. *Total fecundability* relates to all conceptions. This remains something of an abstraction, even in the most thorough medical studies, since a high proportion of pregnancies abort spontaneously in the first month. Thus the woman is often not aware that conception has occurred. The second form is *recognizable fecundability*, which is taken to be the probability of conceiving and the foetus surviving beyond the first cycle, i.e. beyond the point where it delays a menstrual period and is, theoretically at least, detectable. Whether all, some or any women in the past would have recognized the pregnancy at this point is debatable. However, it is this definition which is most widely used in studies of the subject, and, where fecundability is used without further qualification, recognizable fecundability is implied. The final definition, *effective fecundability*, relates only to conceptions which result in a live birth.

14 J. Bongaarts, 'A method for the estimation of fecundability', *Demography* 12 (1975), pp. 645–60.

15 The model is specified in Bongaarts, 'Intermediate fertility variables and marital fertility rates'.

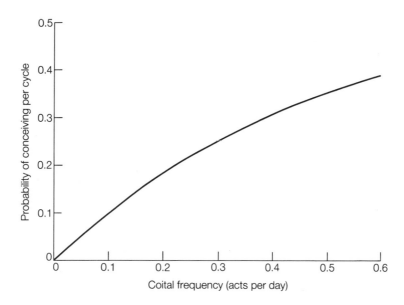

Figure 8.5   Conception probability by coital rate
Source: *model defined in J. Bongaarts, 'Intermediate fertility variables and marital fertility rates',*
Population Studies *30 (1976), p. 235*

Since the only information we have is on births, it is necessary to assume something about the level of foetal mortality if recognizable fecundability is to be estimated. The assumptions made are outlined in the appendix, where the specification of a complete mathematical model of fecundability is given. This model is used to create hypothetical distributions of the interval between becoming at risk to conceive and giving birth for all required combinations of the mean and the variance of fecundability. These model schedules can be compared with observed distributions of intervals between marriage and the birth of a first child in order to assess fecundability.

Bongaarts has proposed two ways of making this assessment.[16] The first is to use a computer to calculate which distribution most closely fits the observed pattern. It is possible in this way to identify both the average fecundability and the amount of variability in it among women. The second method involves the calculation of a simple statistic, namely the proportion of first births that occur in the ninth, tenth and eleventh completed months after marriage, excluding those women who conceived their first child before marriage. When fecundability is

16 Bongaarts, 'A method for the estimation of fecundability'.

high many women conceive quickly and have births within a year of marriage, producing a high ratio. When fecundability is low fewer conceive immediately after marrying and the ratio is lower. The ratio can also be calculated after each model schedule. Bongaarts discovered that the mean and variance of fecundability seemed to be related, a point confirmed by other studies.[17] This enables each mean fecundability to be assigned an appropriate variance, and a single set of ratios to be produced. When this is done estimation of fecundability simply involves finding which mean fecundability has the same ratio of birth in months nine, ten and eleven as the observed population. A table of ratios for each fecundability is given in the appendix.

The application of these methods to real data is complicated by deficiencies in the data and distortions created by certain social customs. The first question arises over pre-marital conceptions which were a feature of pre-industrial England; about one bride in four was pregnant at the time of her marriage. Clearly it is necessary to exclude women who conceived before marriage from the estimation of fecundability. However, the choice of a cut-off point is not always obvious. In some studies of historical data only those births taking place before eight or even seven months of marriage are excluded, while in others all births before nine months are ignored. The problem arises because the time from conception to delivery is not identical in all pregnancies. Leridon has suggested the following distribution as a suitable approximation: 2 per cent of births in the seventh completed month after conception, 23 per cent in the eighth completed month, 66 per cent in the ninth, and 9 per cent in the tenth.[18] For this reason some births are likely to occur in the seventh and eighth months even in the absence of pre-marital sexual activity. With historical data it is impossible to distinguish short post-maritally conceived pregnancies from pre-marital conceptions. To avoid ambiguity, therefore, I excluded all births occurring within 270 days of marriage.

A second potential problem is caused by the fact that the parish registers record baptisms, not births. If a noticeable gap occurred between the two events the estimation of fecundability could be seriously biased. Berry and Schofield have analysed the registers of 43 parishes in which the dates of both birth and baptism were commonly recorded.[19] They found that, in general in England, the average delay from birth to baptism increased from a few days around 1600 to about a month by 1800. They also discovered a great deal of local variation; in some places the average gap remained a few days throughout, while

17 Confirmed, for instance, in Wilson, 'Marital fertility in pre-industrial England', pp. 122–3.

18 Leridon, *Human fertility*, pp. 28–9.

19 B.M. Berry and R.S. Schofield, 'Age at baptism in pre-industrial England', *Population Studies* 25 (1971), pp. 453–63.

in others delays of several months were common. From the point of view of this paper it is unfortunate that few of the 16 parishes studied have registers in which both dates were consistently recorded. Such evidence as exists only relates to a small proportion of births and is limited to short durations during which particularly zealous clergymen or parish clerks recorded more than the normal details.

Some indirect evidence, however, can be seen in examining the proportion of births which occur in the six months from nine to 14 months after marriage, when the largest number of first births occur. In the absence of any delay between birth and baptism these proportions should follow a smoothly declining curve with a peak at nine and each subsequent proportion lower than that of the previous month. The existence of a significant delay between birth and baptism is indicated by distortions in this pattern. The proportion in month ten will increase at the expense of month nine, month eleven at the expense of ten, and so on. Thus the whole distribution is shifted on to longer durations. This distribution was examined for each 50-year marriage cohort in each parish in an attempt to identify parishes affected in this way. No significant lags were apparent down to the 1700–49 cohorts, but in three places (Aldenham, Herts.; Banbury, Oxon.; and Hawkshead, Lancs.) the 1750–99 marriage cohort seemed to be distorted in this way. For these three parishes, therefore, analysis of fecundability was halted with marriages of 1749 and they are not included in the combined set of data for 1750–99.

A further problem arises from the under-registration of first births. If a woman's marriage is registered but her first birth is not, for whatever reason, and then a subsequent birth is registered, the records will appear to indicate a very long interval between marriage and first birth. It will in fact be the interval between marriage and a second or higher-order birth. The effect of this is to change the shape of the distribution of birth intervals and to reduce the proportion occurring in months nine, ten and eleven. Thus both the fitting procedure and the ratio calculation will be distorted and give incorrect estimates of fecundability. Just such a problem is apparent in analysing the English registers, though those for continental Europe seem to have been unaffected.

Several factors may have been responsible. The generally high level of local migration in England is one, as is the custom of baptizing a first child in the mother's parish of origin, even if she had established residence in another parish. Whatever the cause, some parishes show very little evidence of suspiciously long birth intervals, while a few have a relatively high proportion of them. For example, in Methley in the West Riding only 3.9 per cent of marriage to first birth intervals were longer than 60 months, whereas in Shepshed in Leicestershire 24 per cent were this long. A further relevant consideration is that the proportion of unusually long intervals is lower among women who were baptized and married in the same parish, i.e. for whom the question of returning home to baptize a first child would not arise. In Shepshed, for example, less than 8 per cent of intervals were longer than five years for these women. Even among this subgroup, however, the proportion of long intervals remains noticeably longer than the 2 to 3 per cent found in other European populations and suggested by model distributions. Some way of overcoming this is still required.

The answer lies in the fact that the under-registration produces a few long intervals, distorting the mean and the reducing the proportion at short durations, but does not fundamentally alter the relative distribution of births in the first two years of marriage (i.e. the number of births at nine months' duration does not change relative to the number at 18 or 24 months). Therefore, we can employ modified forms of Bongaarts's two methods. Rather than fitting a model schedule to the whole distribution of birth intervals, we can fit it to a truncated distribution including only births occurring in the first two years after marriage (again excluding pre-marital conceptions). Similarly, rather than taking the ratio of births at durations nine, ten and eleven months to all births conceived after marriage, we can compare the number in nine, ten and eleven with the number occurring between nine and 24 months of marriage (i.e. at durations from nine to 23 completed months). To distinguish the two ratios I refer in the tables to the original Bongaarts ratio as the 9–11/9 plus ratio and the truncated version as 9–11/9–23. The logic of the estimation remains the same: the curve fitting is now done using truncated distributions and the ratio is related to fecundability by looking up the values in the final column of table 8.10 (in the appendix).

Table 8.2 presents these ratios and the fecundability they imply in the combined set of 16 parishes for two groups of women: those for whom complete information is available (dates of birth, marriage and the end of marriage) and those for whom the registers contain the date of their marriage and of the birth of their first child, but not necessarily anything else. The two categories represent the extremes of data availability in the reconstitutions. The former represents the detailed core of the reconstitutions, while the latter corresponds to virtually the whole population. Several points of interest emerge from table 8.2. The first is that the straightforward application of the 9–11/9 plus ratio method yields much lower estimates of fecundability than the method using a truncated distribution – testimony to the scale of the problems associated with under-registration. A further observation of some significance is that the two categories of women differentiated by data quality show very similar patterns. It has been argued that family reconstitution, by focusing on those individuals and families for whom most information is available, produces statistics unrepresentative of the population as a whole. This is clearly not true for the estimation of fecundability. Since the knowledge of a date of birth is a prerequisite for the calculation of age-specific rates of any kind, women with known date of birth form the core of the

Table 8.2 Proportions of first births occurring in the first year of marriage (excluding pre-marital conceptions), and the estimated fecundability: 16 English parishes, by marriage cohort

Marriage cohort	Proportion A: 9–11/9 plus	Proportion B: 9–11/9–23	Fecundability predicted by A	Fecundability predicted by B
All women				
1600–49	0.3273	0.4630	0.170	0.213
1650–99	0.3502	0.4831	0.186	0.233
1700–49	0.3660	0.5035	0.197	0.253
1750–99	0.3414	0.4978	0.180	0.248
Women with known date of birth, date of marriage and date of end of marriage				
1600–49	0.3284	0.4481	0.171	0.199
1650–99	0.3582	0.4744	0.191	0.224
1700–49	0.3627	0.4776	0.195	0.227
1750–99	0.3722	0.5045	0.202	0.256

Source: Cambridge Group reconstitutions

reconstitution process, and since they are relatively few in number much has been made of their potential unrepresentativeness by critics of reconstitution techniques. The indication here, however, is that such women cannot be distinguished from the female population at large in terms of their fecundability. This increases considerably the confidence we can feel in the generality of the estimates made. It also means that we can use data on all women in the individual parishes without danger of biasing the results. This is important because the individual parishes generally have a small number of women with complete information, and thus a higher chance of random variation.

Table 8.3 presents the estimates of fecundability for each parish made by both the ratio method and the more elaborate curve fitting method. The similarity between the two sets of results is encouraging. The ratio method suggests slightly higher values overall but the difference is small. To see these results in a wider context, table 8.4 gives the estimates made using the curve fitting method on other historical data. It is clear that, except for a few populations with high fecundability (French Canada, Flanders and Blankenberghe) there is a good deal of overlap between the English range and that of the other populations. The lowest English values are about the same as the lowest German examples, and the upper bounds of the English and German ranges are also much the same. It would seem, therefore, on the evidence of studies made to date that the 16 English parishes had levels of fecundability similar to those found in

Table 8.3   Estimates of fecundability using ratio and curve fitting methods: 16 individual
parishes and marriage cohorts in combined data

	9–11/9–23 ratio method Mean	Fitting method		Coefficient of variation
		Mean	Variance	
Alcester	0.225	0.21	0.012	0.61
Aldenham	0.194	0.19	0.014	0.62
Ash	0.232	0.21	0.020	0.67
Banbury	0.238	0.23	0.018	0.59
Bottesford	0.264	0.25	0.025	0.63
Campton	0.207	0.19	0.015	0.64
Colyton	0.262	0.24	0.019	0.57
Earsdon	0.244	0.23	0.018	0.58
Gainsborough	0.245	0.25	0.018	0.59
Gedling	0.241	0.22	0.019	0.62
Hartland	0.229	0.22	0.021	0.66
Hawkshead	0.196	0.18	0.014	0.65
Methley	0.276	0.22	0.015	0.57
Shepshed	0.248	0.18	0.014	0.65
Terling	0.251	0.25	0.023	0.61
Willingham	0.261	0.20	0.016	0.63
Average of 16	0.238	0.216	0.018	0.62
Marriage cohort:				
1600–49	0.213	0.21	0.016	0.61
1650–99	0.233	0.23	0.023	0.66
1700–49	0.253	0.23	0.022	0.65
1750–99	0.248	0.23	0.016	0.55

Source: Cambridge Group reconstitutions

several other historical populations. A place in the low to medium part of
the European range would seem to be indicated. Thus, while lower
fecundability could have played some role in producing the lower marital
fertility of pre-industrial England, its impact was probably modest.

As a final consideration it is possible to estimate the coital frequency
which was associated with these levels of fecundability. Referring to figure
8.5, the fecundability of about 0.23 in England is associated with a coital
rate of approximately 0.25 (or one coitus every four days). In contrast the
highest fecundability seen, 0.31 in French Canada, would be produced by
a rate of close to 0.4, or once every 2.5 days. Discussion of the social and
cultural origins of such differences lies beyond the scope of this essay.

Table 8.4   Estimates of fecundability: other historical populations

	Mean	Variance	Coefficient of variation
German parishes (pre–1850)			
Grafenhausen	0.25	0.017	0.52
Herbolzheim	0.26	0.020	0.55
Kappel	0.26	0.023	0.58
Oeschelbronn	0.24	0.022	0.62
Three Bavarian villages	0.25	0.025	0.63
Four Waldeck villages	0.19	0.011	0.55
Middels	0.18	0.015	0.58
Werdum	0.20	0.015	0.62
Other populations			
Crulai, France	0.18	0.009	0.53
Tourouvre, France	0.21	0.014	0.56
Genevan bourgeoisie	0.23	0.021	0.63
Europeans of Tunis	0.25	0.020	0.57
French Canada	0.31	0.027	0.53
Blankenberghe, Belgium	0.28	0.029	0.61
Rural Flanders	0.29	0.031	0.61

Sources: German data: John Knodel, personal communication. Blankenberghe: Cambridge Group reconstitutions. Rural Flanders: C. Vandenbroucke, personal communication. Others: J. Bongaarts, 'A method for the estimation of fecundability', *Demography* 12 (1975), pp. 645–60

Post-partum Non-susceptible Period

The last major component of marital fertility amenable to analysis with family reconstitution data is the non-susceptible period (NSP) which follows a birth and during which a woman does not ovulate and thus is not at risk to conceive again. Although there is still some debate on the role of nutritional factors in determining the duration of this period, it is now widely accepted that differences in breastfeeding practices have a major part to play in any explanation of differences. The mechanism linking the two is believed to be a neurally mediated hormonal reflex initiated by the suckling stimulus, whereby increases in the pituitary hormone prolactin act either upon the hypothalamus or directly on the ovaries to prevent ovulation.[20]

One simple way to estimate the mean duration of the non-susceptible period from reproduction histories is to compare the interval between marriage and the birth of a first child (excluding intervals involving

20 See A.S. McNeilly, P.W. Howne and M.J. Houston, 'Relationship of feeding patterns, prolactin and resumption of post-partum ovulation' in G.I. Zatuchni, M.H. Lahboek and J.J. Sciarra (eds), *Research frontiers in fertility regulation* (New York, 1980).

pre-marital conceptions) with the subsequent interval between first and second births. Since breastfeeding only occurs in the latter, the difference between the two intervals reflects the extent to which the birth interval is lengthened by non-susceptibility. The estimate cannot be regarded as a precise measurement, however, since several other factors intrude. First, if fecundability declines with the duration of marriage, as is generally assumed, this will lengthen the time women on average have to wait before becoming pregnant. Thus a part of any increase in mean interval will be caused by lower fecundability after some years of marriage. Moreover, there is some evidence that slight differences in the risk of foetal death exist between first and second pregnancies. Both these factors will tend to bias the estimates of the NSP, as would any attempts to postpone either the first or second birth. In sum, while the method is probably sensitive enough to detect major differences between populations, great precision cannot be expected.

A further potential drawback with a simple comparison is that the interval before a woman's last birth tends to be distinctly longer than other intervals, even in the absence of family limitation. Where a woman has only two children, this interval may yield a poor estimate of the NSP. To control for this, as well as looking at all pairs of intervals, we can consider only women with at least three births, thus ensuring that none of the intervals used in the comparison represents the end of a woman's reproductive experience.[21]

Table 8.5 gives the estimated NSP for each 50-year marriage cohort of the combined set of 16 parishes and for each individual data set. Given the approximate nature of the estimation, great accuracy cannot be expected and the minor differences and fluctuations in the results probably reflect stochastic rather than substantive differences. Nevertheless, a relatively clear picture does emerge. The combined data indicate a period of non-susceptibility of around twelve months, or ten and a half months if only women with three children or more are considered. The individual parishes show a spread around this average, though most lie no more than two months away from the central values.

A second way of estimating the length of the non-susceptible period and hence the impact of breastfeeding practices is to examine the relationship between the length of birth intervals and the age at death of the child born at the beginning of the interval. An interval following the birth of a child who survived beyond the age of weaning will reflect the full influence of breastfeeding, while an interval in which the child dies before being weaned will, on average, be shorter. The strength of this relationship in the aggregate depends on the proportion of infants breastfed and the average duration and intensity of breastfeeding.

---

21 A further consideration is that restricting attention to women with more than two children introduces a bias in the direction of high fertility (i.e. short birth intervals). This could produce a shorter estimate of the NSP than actually pertained.

Table 8.5 The mean duration of the post-partum non-susceptible period (NSP) estimated from the difference between first and second birth intervals: 16 individual parishes and 50-year marriage cohorts for combined data

	Women with at least two births		Women with at least three births	
	NSP (months)	No. of cases	NSP (months)	No. of cases
Marriage cohort				
1600–49	12.17	972	10.72	808
1650–99	13.35	939	11.21	753
1700–49	11.53	1183	10.48	987
1750–99	12.07	1425	10.26	1201
Individual parishes				
Alcester	10.34	212	9.28	128
Aldenham	9.73	149	8.82	136
Ash	9.96	173	7.25	147
Banbury	11.43	579	10.57	473
Bottesford	11.78	262	10.86	227
Campton	11.14	293	10.74	244
Colyton	16.20	300	13.42	236
Earsdon	10.88	342	9.04	279
Gainsborough	11.14	916	9.65	748
Gedling	13.00	383	11.15	318
Hartland	14.92	346	13.29	279
Hawkshead	13.24	249	10.71	204
Methley	13.66	233	11.43	175
Shepshed	12.98	353	11.46	293
Terling	13.57	140	11.25	107
Willingham	13.37	108	12.23	97

Several caveats are worth mentioning. First, the problem raised by last birth intervals in the previous method of estimation is even more important here since all intervals will be used, not only those between first and second births. Secondly, factors other than infant-feeding practices can exert an influence on the relationship between the age at which a child dies and the subsequent birth interval. For example, the sooner the next child arrives, the sooner the previously born child will face competition for attention and care from the parents. The survival of a child might also influence the frequency with which the parents had intercourse. The concern with 'overlaying', or smothering an infant while sleeping, in much of Europe during the eighteenth century suggests that infants often shared their parents' bed. Their presence could have acted as a deterrent to intercourse, while their early death would have removed this constraint. Or the additional burden of work created by the presence of an infant or young child could have reduced the desire for sex. It is also possible that a volitional factor was involved. Parents might have deliberately attempted to postpone the next birth as long as the previous child survived, but given up these efforts when it died. The available data do not permit the disentangling of the many possible influences, but their existence should be borne in mind.

The mean length of the birth interval is presented in figure 8.6 according to the age at death of the child whose birth opens the interval. The increase in the mean with the survival of this child is readily apparent. An almost linear trend exists up to 17 months, after which point the intervals fluctutate with little further increase. Table 8.6 provides a more detailed quantitative picture. There the ages at death are categorized, the groups increasing from zero months (babies who die in the first month of life) to those who survive two years or more. There is also a category 'unknown' which gives the length of the interval in those cases where no burial record of the individual in question was found. Interestingly the mean for these 'unknown' cases is very similar to the value in the '24 months plus' category, suggesting that the persons for whom no

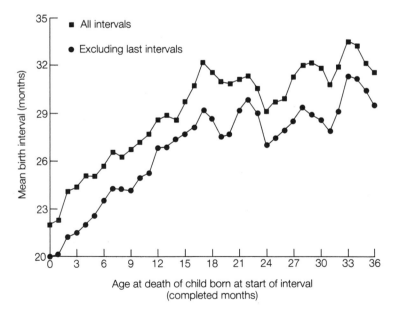

Figure 8.6   Birth interval by child survival
Cases where infant died in the first week of life excluded (see text). Values from one month on are three-month moving averages.
Source: *Cambridge Group reconstitutions*

Table 8.6　Mean birth interval according to the age at death of the child born at the beginning of the interval, and the mean non-susceptible period (NSP)

	All intervals	Excluding intervals before last birth
Age at death of child (completed months)		
0	23.90	21.55
1–2	22.48	20.26
3–5	25.25	22.07
6–11	26.72	23.50
12–33	30.30	27.94
24 +	33.32	30.57
Unknown	33.02	30.55
All 12 +	33.01	30.37
Deaths in first month		
0–6 days	24.77	22.35
1–3 weeks	22.07	20.08
Non-susceptible period (months)		
Including deaths 0–6 days	9.11	8.82
Excluding deaths 0–6 days	10.94	10.29

Includes a small number of cases from the cohorts married 1550–99 and 1800–49. Both show the general pattern.

burial record exists did not die in infancy. The most plausible explanation is that they survived childhood and migrated to another parish where they died, and where their burial was registered. The last values in the first part of the table give the mean for all intervals where the previous child survived at least a year. The 'unknown' intervals are included here since they add greatly to the number of cases, thus providing a less volatile estimate.

In general, the results in table 8.6 conform to the expected pattern, with longer intervals being associated with surviving children, presumably indicating the effect of prolonged breastfeeding. There is, however, one striking exception to this. The intervals following a death in the first month of life are longer on average than those when the previous child survived for a month and then died. Such a pattern runs counter to expectations. Interestingly, the second part of table 8.6 shows that this feature of unexpectedly long intervals is confined to cases in which the infant died in the first week. When infants survived the first seven days the interval that followed falls more in line with the pattern seen for older ages at death. Considering all intervals, those which followed a death in the first week were on average 2.7 months longer than intervals following a death in the remainder of the child's first month of life. If last intervals are excluded the difference is 2.27 months. The causes of this unexpected finding are uncertain, but one possibility is that early neonatal mortality (deaths in the first seven days of life) was associated with complicated deliveries which affected maternal health as well. This could have produced long intervals if poor health led to a later resumption of intercourse, or if it was associated with a general reduction in the mother's physiological capacity to bear children (fecundity).

Whatever the origins of these unusually long intervals after an early death, their effect here is potentially to bias our estimate of the non-susceptible period. If they are included the difference between intervals where the child survives and those where a death occurs will be reduced, and the estimate of the NSP will be correspondingly too low. To overcome this I excluded intervals following an early neonatal death from the comparison of intervals, comparing instead only those where the previous child died at an age between seven days and one month, with intervals in which the infant survived to celebrate its first birthday. The difference between the two is taken as an estimate of the NSP. The estimates produced in this way are 10.94 and 10.29 months, depending on whether or not last intervals are included. The results are, thus, reassuringly similar to those obtained by the comparison of first and second birth intervals. Table 8.7 presents the estimates for each 50-year marriage cohort and for each parish. As before, it is probably unwise to pay too much attention to the results from any one parish, but the range of estimates is broadly similar to that derived from the earlier estimation procedure.

The overall picture, therefore, is of about a year of post-partum non-susceptibility, the exact value depending on the method used in estimation. The duration of breastfeeding that would produce this duration of the NSP cannot be specified precisely. The physiological relationship varies according to the frequency of suckling and the amount of supplementary food given to infants. However, in studies of contemporary societies where lactation is prolonged, an NSP of this length would usually be associated with 14 to 18 months of breastfeeding. This is consistent with the month-by-month results seen in figure 8.6, which show a steadily increasing effect of child survival up to 17 months of age. While an exact value for the average length of breastfeeding cannot be given with confidence, it is unlikely to have been less than a year, and was probably somewhat longer.

To see the results from the English parishes in their proper context it is necessary to look at similar results for other historical populations, given in table 8.8. Clearly there is a similarity between the English results and those for certain other populations – several of the German parishes as well as Crulai and Tourouvre. These parishes also had levels of marital fertility similar to pre-industrial England. There is a marked contrast,

Table 8.7 Non-susceptible period estimated by comparing intervals following infant death and infant survival: 16 individual parishes and by marriage cohort for combined data

	All intervals	Excluding intervals before last birth
Marriage cohort		
1600–49	14.62	14.01
1650–99	10.53	9.52
1700–49	10.63	9.60
1750–99	9.65	8.40
Individual parishes		
Alcester	17.42	17.07
Aldenham	4.86	9.31
Ash	11.35	6.37
Banbury	7.87	10.32
Bottesford	13.45	10.43
Campton	8.30	8.52
Colyton	16.42	13.38
Earsdon	8.43	7.76
Gainsborough	8.99	7.32
Gedling	13.01	9.92
Hartland	13.30	13.76
Hawkshead	10.10	9.45
Methley	16.81	15.52
Shepshed	12.00	12.39
Terling	10.68	10.60
Willingham	11.57	13.36

Source: Cambridge Group reconstitutions

however, between the English results and those for Blankenberghe in Flanders, French Canada and the Bavarian villages, all of which have much shorter durations of non-susceptibility. This conforms with what is known about the infant-feeding practices in these areas, since long-standing traditions proscribing or limiting lactation are believed to have existed in them. The short breastfeeding had two important consequences in these areas. Firstly, it produced short birth intervals and thus high fertility rates. Secondly, given the lack of hygienic and nutritious alternatives to breast milk, it led to very high rates of infant mortality. In Blankenberghe, for example, about one new-born infant in three died before reaching its first birthday. A quite different situation seems to have applied in pre-industrial England, where prolonged lactation kept both infant mortality and marital fertility at much lower levels. The social and economic consequences of these profound differences in the demographic bases of the various European societies is clearly a subject for further consideration, but lies beyond the scope of this introductory essay.

Table 8.8 Non-susceptible period estimated for other historical populations using a comparison of first and second intervals and a comparison of intervals following child death and child survival

	Method of estimation	
Population	Comparison of first and second intervals	Comparison of child death and survival
French Canada (1700–30)	5.2	6.2
Crulai, France (1674–1742)	10.2	8.9
Île de France (18th century)	8.6	6.6
Tunis (19th century)	–	9.1
Tourouvre, France (18th century)	7.2	9.3
Blankenberghe, Belgium (1650–1849)	5.2	–
German parishes (1800–49)		
Grafenhausen	–	7.9
Herbolzheim	–	9.8
Kappel	–	9.5
Oeschelbronn	–	9.4
Three Bavarian villages	–	4.1
Four Waldeck villages	–	14.8
Werdum	–	14.3
Middels	–	15.8

Sources: German data: J. Knodel, 'Demographic transitions in German villages', in A. J. Coale and S. Watkins (eds), *The Decline of European fertility* (Princeton, NJ, forthcoming). Blankenberghe: Cambridge Group reconstitutions. Others: H. Leridon, *Human fertility: the basic components* (Chicago, 1977)

Conclusion

As an illustration of the crucial role played by post-partum non-susceptibility (and hence breastfeeding) we can consider the way in which the various proximate determinants jointly control the level of fertility. Bongaarts has proposed a straightforward model which facilities this.[22] Using this model I calculated the marital fertility rate that would be

22 The model is defined in Bongaarts, 'Intermediate fertility variables and marital fertility rates', as follows:

$$MFR = \frac{12000\ (1-s)}{9 + NSP + (a/1-a)\,Ia + 1/\,(f\,(1-a))}$$

where *MFR* is the marital fertility rate per 1000 women per year; *S* is the proportion sterile; *a* is the risk of spontaneous abortion; *Ia* is the mean post-abortum non-susceptible period; *f* is fecundability; and *NSP* is the post-partum non-susceptible period.

produced by four combinations of fecundability and the non-susceptible period. Since sterility variation was slight and foetal mortality unknown, these two factors are the principal influences on fertility amenable to study. The combinations represent the estimates of these determinants for the 16 English parishes and the values which would produce the highest fertility (highest fecundability and the shortest NSP). The way in which English fecundability and breastfeeding patterns lead to reductions in this maximum value indicates the relative importance of the two in producing the low fertility characteristic of pre-industrial England. Looking at table 8.9, the maximum rate generated is 538 births per 1000 women per year – a value close to that observed for the high-fertility populations of Quebec, Bavaria and Flanders. Lowering fecundability to English levels reduces the rate to 499, a fall of just over 7 per cent. In contrast, increasing the NSP from four months to twelve reduces the rate by almost one-third. The introduction of lower fecundability only serves to make a small additional reduction of 3.6 per cent.

Demonstrating the primary role played by lactation in pre-industrial Europe sets new tasks for social historians, giving a more precise focus to attempts to explain fertility differentials. What now needs to be explained is why different European societies adopted the varying patterns of breastfeeding which led to such dramatic differences in fertility and infant mortality. What caused mothers in England to undertake prolonged

Table 8.9 Marital fertility rate estimated from combinations of fecundability and non-susceptibility

| | | | Fecundability | |
			English parishes 0.23	Highest 0.31
			Rates per 1000 woman-years	
NSP (months)	Shortest	4	499	538
	English parishes	12	351	370
			Index numbers (maximum rate = 100)	
NSP (months)	Shortest	4	92.8	100.0
	English parishes	12	65.2	68.8

Sterility is held at 10 per cent of women in all four examples.

breastfeeding while those in Bavaria and Flanders did not? Such a question cannot be answered by the quantitative methods of the historical demographer, but the quantification outlined here sets the framework within which the answer must lie.

Appendix
Detailed Description of the Model of Fecundability

At numerous points during the discussion of fecundability reference is made to a particular model of fecundability based on one proposed by John Bongaarts. The fundamentals of the model are the same as those suggested by him; however, certain differences in definition were made and a much wider range of statistics of special relevance to the English historical case were produced.

The definition of the model was as follows:

1 Fecundability is distributed according to a beta distribution, the parameters of which are defined by the mean and variance of fecundability. To achieve this, 20 homogeneous sub-populations are estimated and the results from these amalgamated.
2 The population is homogeneous with respect to the risk of spontaneous abortion, which is fixed at 0.162, and with respect to the length of the non-susceptible period following a foetal death. This was defined by a geometric distribution with a mean of 2.5 months.
3 The duration of pregnancy follows a distribution suggested by Leridon, where 2 per cent of births occur in the seventh completed month after conception, 23 per cent in the eighth, 66 per cent in the ninth and 9 per cent in the tenth.

Only in one respect does the model here deviate from the proposals of Bongaarts. He assumed a beta distribution in total fecundability, and defined total fecundability as recognizable fecundability divided by 0.65, since he assumed a risk of spontaneous abortion in the first month of 0.35. At most values of fecundability this is acceptable, but at high values of mean fecundability there are drawbacks in defining the variation in fecundability in terms of total fecundability. This is because at high values of recognizable fecundability (above 0.33) total fecundability exceeds 0.5. Given this, and a plausible figure for the coefficient of variation of fecundability, the two parameters of the beta distribution, a and b, both drop below unity. This produces a shallow U-shaped distribution with high proportions of women with either very high or very low fecundability. The effect of this is to make mean waiting times to conception stop decreasing with higher fecundability and instead increase.

For example, holding the coefficient of variation of fecundability constant at 0.56 as suggested by Bongaarts, and varying mean fecundability, produced the following results:

| Recognizable Fecundability | | Total Fecundability | | Parameters | | Mean |
Mean	Variance	Mean	Variance	a	b	interval
0.21	0.014	0.32	0.033	1.84	3.85	17.8
0.26	0.021	0.40	0.050	1.51	2.27	16.6
0.31	0.030	0.47	0.071	1.19	1.31	16.0
0.36	0.040	0.55	0.096	0.87	0.70	16.1

The mean interval in the final column is the interval from marriage to first birth predicted given the defined values.

To circumvent this undesired effect, the variance of fecundability was defined in terms of recognizable fecundability. Although this involves the unrealistic assumption that some women have fecundability close to one, this was felt to be a less serious problem than the illogicality concerning the mean interval.

With this modification, a wide range of statistics was generated for a combination of 21 values of mean fecundability (0.15 to 0.35) and 16 values of the coefficient of variation of fecundability (0.52 to 0.67). For the model fitting mentioned in the text, expected proportions of women giving birth in each month after marriage were produced for all 336 combinations of mean and coefficient of variation, and the one most closely resembling each observed schedule identified by means of a Kolmogorov-Smirnov test.

In addition to preparing model schedules of first birth intervals, however, the model was also used to estimate a number of other statistics which could be used to estimate fecundability more simply. The means for all intervals and for various truncated distributions were produced, together with the proportion of first births occurring in months nine, ten and eleven after marriage, again for all births and for various truncations. After considerable experimentation it was found that the values related to a distribution curtailed at two years of marriage were particularly suited to data from English family reconstitutions. These, therefore, are presented for a single value of the coefficient of variation of fecundability, 0.56, in table 8.10 and are used extensively in the text.

When the age profile of fecundability is estimated, the fact that the risk of intra-uterine mortality varies with age must be taken into account. This is done by multiplying the proportion of births in months nine to eleven by a correction factor before comparing it with table 8.10. This correction factor is given by $(1-0.162)/(1-a)$, where 0.162 is the value of the probability used in the construction of table 8.10, and a is the value for a particular age group.

Table 8.10 Predicted values for mean and truncated mean intervals from marriage to first birth and for the ratio of first births in months nine to eleven after marriage over all first births after nine months, and over births in months nine to 23 only – by mean fecundability

Fecundability		Mean interval All 9 months		Ratios	
Mean	Variance	plus	9–23 only	9–11/9 plus	9–11/9–23
0.10	0.003	26.32	14.81	0.2087	0.3289
0.11	0.004	24.92	14.67	0.2275	0.3418
0.12	0.005	23.73	14.54	0.2455	0.3545
0.13	0.005	22.72	14.41	0.2630	0.3670
0.14	0.006	21.85	14.29	0.2798	0.3793
0.15	0.007	21.09	14.17	0.2961	0.3915
0.16	0.008	20.43	14.06	0.3119	0.4034
0.17	0.009	19.84	13.95	0.3271	0.4151
0.18	0.010	19.32	13.84	0.3419	0.4265
0.19	0.011	18.85	13.74	0.3562	0.4378
0.20	0.013	18.43	13.64	0.3700	0.4488
0.21	0.014	18.06	13.55	0.3834	0.4596
0.22	0.015	17.72	13.46	0.3964	0.4701
0.23	0.017	17.41	13.37	0.4089	0.4804
0.24	0.018	17.13	13.29	0.4210	0.4904
0.25	0.020	16.87	13.21	0.4328	0.5002
0.26	0.021	16.64	13.13	0.4441	0.5098
0.27	0.023	16.42	13.06	0.4551	0.5191
0.28	0.025	16.23	12.98	0.4656	0.5282
0.29	0.026	16.05	12.92	0.4759	0.5370
0.30	0.028	15.88	12.85	0.4857	0.5457
0.31	0.030	15.73	12.78	0.4952	0.5540
0.32	0.032	15.59	12.72	0.5044	0.5622
0.33	0.034	15.47	12.66	0.5132	0.5701
0.34	0.036	15.35	12.60	0.5218	0.5778
0.35	0.038	15.25	12.55	0.5300	0.5853

Coefficient of variation of fecundability held constant at 0.56. A beta distribution is assumed for the distribution of fecundability among women.

9

Did the Mothers Really Die? Three Centuries of Maternal Mortality in 'The World We Have Lost'

Roger Schofield

Today the risk of death associated with giving birth to a child is very low indeed: in England and Wales in 1980 it was only 0.1 per 1000 live births. Yet 50 years ago, in the early 1930s, the risk was between 40 and 50 times higher, at about 4.5 per 1000. The dramatic improvement that has occurred between the mid 1930s and the present day has been due to sulphonamides and antibiotics, which have almost eliminated deaths from puerperal fever, and to an improved detection and obstetrical management of problem cases. Maternal deaths are an eminent example of preventable deaths; their frequency indicates not only the general level of medical skill and knowledge in a society, but also how far it is applied in everyday life.[1]

In this respect women in the early 1930s were little better off than in the mid nineteenth century: in the quinquennium 1856–60 the maternal mortality rate was 4.6 per 1000 live births, the same as in 1934, and apart from a few exceptional years the rate remained between 4 and 5 per 1000 throughout the intervening period. Continuous data are available on the risk of dying in childbed since 1847, thanks to the Registrar General's office, which collected and tabulated information on cause of death, and to William Farr who analysed and commented on it in the Registrar General's *Annual Reports*. Farr was outraged by the level of maternal mortality indicated by the data. He referred to it as 'a deep, dark and continuous stream of mortality', and asked 'how long is this sacrifice of lives to go on?'[2]

1 For recent maternal mortality rates, see United Nations, Department of Economic and Social Affairs, *Demographic Year Book (1982)* (New York, 1984), pp. 340–3 and J. Tomkinson et al., *Report on confidential enquiries into maternal deaths in England and Wales, 1973–75* (HMSO, London, 1979). For the 1930s, see J. Winter, 'Infant mortality, maternal mortality and public health in Britain in the 1930s', *Journal of European Economic History* 8 (1979), pp. 439–62.

2 *Annual Report of the Registrar General of England and Wales*, 1838–, (London, 1839–). Two of Farr's more extensive commentaries are in the *17th Annual Report* (1854), pp. 72–4 and the

If, therefore, we are to transport ourselves back into the mental and emotional 'world we have lost', one feature that we must take into account is a risk of dying in childbed that is very much higher than that of the world we inhabit. In England, in the past, about nine out of ten people married and, before the 1870s at least, there are almost no signs that fertility was restricted after marriage.[3] Thus all but a small percentage of women were exposed to the risk of childbearing, and death in childbed, on average from their mid twenties to about age 40. During this formative phase of the family life cycle husbands also risked losing their wives, and children their mother. To a far greater extent than today, family life was lived under the shadow of imminent death.

But how deep was that shadow? Was the risk of death in childbed much higher in the distant past? Or was it as unchanging in the centuries before 1850 as it was in the 80 years after that date? Some historians have given the impression that maternal mortality was, indeed, very high in the distant past. For example, Lawrence Stone has no doubts: 'For women, childbirth was a very dangerous experience, for midwives were ignorant and ill trained, and often horribly botched the job, while the lack of hygienic precautions meant that puerperal fever was a frequent sequel'.[4] And Alan Macfarlane, commenting on the entries in Ralph Josselin's diary concerning his wife's deliveries, concludes that 'the actual delivery was a time of fear, amounting to dread on Mrs Josselin's part'.[5] Unfortunately, diaries as detailed as Josselin's are rare, so we shall never know whether Mrs Josselin's apprehensions of the dangers of childbirth were typical or not. But can we, none the less, find a way of estimating the magnitude of those dangers?

Before the national vital registration system began in 1837, there is only one English source which consistently recorded causes of death: the London Bills of Mortality. Though the attribution of deaths to specific causes was probably imperfect as far as most infectious diseases were concerned, 'childbed' was a fairly obvious state, and so the numbers of burials recorded under this head are likely to be reasonably close to the mark. The number of burials in childbed per 1000 baptisms recorded in the printed bills have been calculated for four 'half-centuries': 1657–99, 1700–49, 1750–99, 1800–1830. According to the

---

39th Annual Report (1876), pp. 241–51. The quotations come from the last cited source, p. 242, and the *38th Annual Report* (1875), p. 234.

3 Age at marriage and celibacy are discussed in R. Schofield, 'English marriage patterns revisited', *Journal of Family History* 10 (1985), pp. 2–20. For patterns of marital fertility see C. Wilson, 'Natural fertility in pre-industrial England', *Population Studies* 38 (1984), pp. 225–40.

4 L. Stone, *The family, sex and marriage in England 1500–1800* (New York, 1977), p. 79.

5 A.D. Macfarlane, *The family life of Ralph Josselin, a seventeenth century clergyman*, (Cambridge, 1970), p. 84.

bills the maternal mortality rates in these four periods were 21.0, 14.5, 11.4 and 9.2.[6]

Unfortunately, there are few data with which the first of these figures can be compared; but the maternal mortality rate in one London parish in the late sixteenth century (St Botolph without Aldgate, 1583–99) was close to the late-seventeenth-century London level, at 23.5 per 1000 baptisms.[7] In the early nineteenth century the maternal mortality rate of 9.2, calculated from the bills, is reasonably close to the London rates recorded in the early years of vital registration (e.g. 7.5 in 1847). However, in these years maternal mortality in London was 25 per cent higher than the national rate.[8] Consequently, although London has the most promising data for estimating maternal mortality at earlier dates, the resulting figures are likely to exaggerate the risk of dying in childbed in the country at large.

In the absence of any widespread and systematic recording of causes of death any attempt to estimate maternal mortality outside the metropolis must be based on another approach. In fact there are two distinct methods of calculating maternal mortality. One is based on explicitly attributed deaths, such as the 'childbed' deaths in the bills of mortality and the deaths ascribed to 'accidents of childbirth' and 'metria' (puerperal fever) in the nineteenth-century vital registers. The other method involves an implicit attribution to childbirth of all deaths occurring within a specified number of days after the termination of pregnancy. For example, the International Federation of Gynaecology and Obstetrics defines maternal mortality as comprising 'the death of a woman while pregnant or within 42 days of termination of pregnancy irrespective of duration and site of pregnancy'.[9]

---

6 J. Marshall, *Mortality in the metropolis*, (London, 1832), pp. 70–1, 73 (baptisms); unpaginated tables after p. 82 (deaths in childbed). The numbers of baptisms in each period were 540,472; 822,361; 844,262; and 703,696. The first and last periods are truncated because of data deficiencies. Under-recording of births and deaths in the baptism and burial statistics will offset each other, so that the maternal mortality rate will only be affected by any difference in the level of under-recording in the two series. The burial series includes 'abortive' and stillborn children.

7 T.R. Forbes, *Chronicle from Aldgate* (New Haven and London, 1971), p. 106.

8 1847 is the first year in which deaths are attributed to 'metria' (puerperal fever) as well as 'childbirth'. London rates: *10th Annual Report of the Registrar General* (1847), pp. 33, 309; *11th Annual Report* (1898), pp. 35, 291, 293; *12th Annual Report* (1899), pp. 3, 255, 257. National rates for 1847–54 are conveniently summarized in *17th Annual Report* (1854), p. 72. By 1851 maternal mortality in London was the same as the national rate, and by 1875 it was 21 per cent lower than the national rate: *14th Annual Report* (1851), pp. 28, 126, 128; *38th Annual Report* (1875), pp. 30, 149, 155, 159, 161.

9 This definition is also adopted by the World Health Organization. It is qualified by the clause 'from any cause related to, or aggravated by, the pregnancy or its management, but not from accidental or incidental causes'. *Manual of the international statistical classification of disease, injuries, and causes of death*, vol. 1 (WHO, Geneva, 1977), p. 772.

The second approach, therefore, includes what might be termed 'indirect' maternal mortality, on the grounds that pregnancy and child-birth may increase the chance of dying from other causes, such as infectious disease. Although pregnancy is not recorded in historical sources such as parish registers, childbirth is, so a maternal mortality rate can be calculated based on all deaths occurring within a specified number of days after the birth of a child. Once the individual register entries have been linked by family reconstitution, the calculation of a maternal mortality rate is a simple matter: a woman enters observation at the recording of the birth of a child, and the maternal mortality rate is taken to be the proportion of women who fail to survive the specified number of days. This simplicity, however, is deceptive: there are some severe problems both with the calculation of the rate and with its interpretation.

First, there is no agreement among scholars on the length of the measurement period. Imhof, for example, follows the IFGO standard of 42 days, while most French scholars adopt a period of 60 days, and Perrenoud bases his Genevan maternal mortality rates on a period of 30 days.[10] Unfortunately, there are disadvantages with both short and long periods of observation: the former will exclude some maternal deaths, while the latter will include deaths which have nothing to do with maternity, especially when applied to historical populations in which the chance of dying as a young adult was much higher than it is today.

Second, English parish registers record church ceremonies, not vital events. While the burial registers appear to have recorded most deaths, the baptism registers do not provide an ideal record of the entry into observation for the risk of maternal mortality.[11] After 1600 most children were baptized some days after they were born, and some died before they could be baptized. Fortunately, the registers generally recorded the burial of unbaptized children, and the rules of family reconstitution ensure that these maternities are included on the family forms.[12] However, in the case of children who survived, the interval

10 A.E. Imhof, 'La surmortalité des femmes mariées en age de procréation: un indice de la condition féminine au XIXe siècle', *Annales de démographie historique* (1981), pp. 81–7. A. Perrenoud, 'Surmortalité féminine et condition de la femme (XVIIe et XIXe siècles). Une vérification empirique', *Annales de démographie historique* (1981), pp. 89–104. A. Bideau, 'Accouchement naturel et accouchement à haut risque. Châtellerie de Thoissey-en-Dombes, 1660–1814', *Annales de démographie historique* (1981), pp. 49–66. J.-P. Bardet et al., 'La mortalité maternelle autrefois; une étude comparée (de la France de l'Ouest à l'Utah)', *Annales de démographie historique* (1981), pp. 89–104. H. Gutierrez and J. Houdaille, 'La mortalité maternelle en France au XVIIIe siècle', *Population* 6 (1983), pp. 974–94.

11 The adequacy of baptism and burial registration is discussed extensively in E.A. Wrigley and R. S. Schofield, *The population history of England, 1541–1871: a reconstruction* (London, 1981), chapters 1, 3–5.

12 Procedures for reconstituting families from English parish registers are specified in detail in E.A. Wrigley, *An introduction to English historical demography* (London, 1966), chapter 4.

between birth and baptism means that a period of observation for maternal mortality calculated from the date of baptism will extend longer than if it had been calculated from the date of birth. Moreover, since the interval between birth and baptism varied greatly from parish to parish, it is difficult to know by how much the observational period will be over-extended in any particular case. In the late sixteenth century children appear to have been baptized very soon after birth, but the interval had lengthened to an average of eight days in the late seventeenth century, and 26 days in the late eighteenth century.[13]

The most serious difficulty, however, lies in the failure of English parish registers to record stillbirths in a systematic manner, thereby concealing the existence of maternities which did not issue in a live-born child. As Audrey Eccles pointed out many years ago, the art of midwifery was very undeveloped in England in the past. Midwives may have provided a reassuring social setting for childbirth, but few possessed the knowledge to intervene effectively in a difficult labour. The use of forceps, or of manipulations such as podalic version, to remove children which could not be delivered naturally, date only from the late seventeenth century, and seem to have remained confined to some medical practitioners and very few midwives until well into the nineteenth century. Thus a whole variety of conditions, such as haemorrhage, pelvic deformity, disproportion between the sizes of the child's head and the pelvis, severe abnormal presentations such as transverse lies, eclampsia and uterine inertia early in labour, are likely to have posed problems which were beyond the capacities of those attending the birth to alleviate. In these circumstances a child was likely to have been stillborn, or to have died in the womb. Furthermore, attempts to remove a dead child, especially by the old-fashioned hooks and crotchets in general use before the eighteenth century, probably severely threatened the mother's life.[14]

Thus the English baptismal registers omit precisely those maternities in which the mothers life was most at risk. Consequently, maternal mortality rates based upon them will undoubtedly be too low, though whether they are 'much too low' or 'misleadingly low', as has been alleged, is matter which needs careful investigation.[15] In order to evaluate and correct estimates based on live births alone, we need to dis-

13 The figures cited in the text are for the median birth–baptism interval in the median parish for 1650–99 and 1771–89. B.M. Berry and R.S. Schofield, 'Age at baptism in pre-industrial England', *Population Studies* 25 (1971), pp. 453–63.

14 A. Eccles, 'Obstetrics in the 17th and 18th centuries and its implications for maternal and infant mortality', *Society for the History of Medicine Bulletin*, 20 (June 1977), pp. 8–11. A.F. Wilson, 'Childbirth in seventeenth- and eighteenth-century England' (unpublished Ph.D. thesis, University of Sussex, 1982).

15 The quotations are from B.M.W. Dobbie, 'An attempt to estimate the true rate of maternal mortality, sixteenth to eighteenth centuries', *Medical History* 26 (1982), p. 90; and Eccles, 'Obstetrics in the 17th and 18th centuries', p. 9.

cover the proportion of all maternal deaths associated with stillbirths and undelivered pregnancies.

Unfortunately, very few English registers systematically recorded stillbirths, but even from this limited evidence it is clear that maternal mortality rates associated with stillbirths are at least five times higher than rates based on live births alone. For example, Eccles has reported maternal mortality rates for stillbirths in three Northern parishes (1629–1750) of 57, 64 and 137 per 1000 baptisms, compared with rates of 10–15 per 1000 generally found in family reconstitution studies in the same period.[16] However, before we can correct the latter appropriately, we need to confirm that these stillbirth rates are typical, and we need to discover the relative frequency of stillbirths in the past. Neither of these points can be established using English parish registers; so a study has been undertaken using Swedish sources, which are more detailed and more reliable.

In Sweden, as in England, the church was a branch of the state, and from 1686 its ministers were required to maintain registers listing everyone in the parish by household, in addition to the usual registers of baptisms, burials and marriages. From 1749 each minister was also required to make an annual return tabulating the numbers of marriages, baptisms and burials (from 1773, births and deaths). The returns were made on printed forms, and the totals were cross-classified by factors such as sex, month, legitimacy, age of mother and cause of death. Moreover, every three (from 1775, every five) years the ministers had to fill out a parish census, cross-classified by age, sex, marital status and occupation. The parish tabulations were forwarded to the local deans, who prepared deanery summaries. The latter were forwarded to the local county administrator and to the bishop, who prepared county and diocesan summaries which, in turn were forwarded to the central statistical office in Stockholm for aggregation at the national level. In making their annual returns the ministers had to distinguish between stillbirths and live births and, in assigning causes of death, one of the standard categories they were required to use was death in childbed (*barnsbörd*). Consequently, from 1749 in Sweden there are summary statistics, at several levels of geographical aggregation, from which one can calculate the percentage of all births that were stillborn, and the number of deaths that were attributed to 'childbed' per 1000 birth events of all kinds.[17]

---

16 Ibid., pp. 8, 10.

17 A convenient summary in English of the history of vital registration in Sweden is contained in Erland Hofsten and Hans Lundström, *Swedish population history: main trends from 1750 to 1970*, Urval VIII (Stockholm, 1976), appendix 1. This volume also contains valuable statistics supplementing the basic tabulations of national data in Gustav Sundbärg, *Bevölkerungsstatistik Schwedens, 1750–1900* (Stockholm, 1907), reprinted with preface and vocabulary in English, Urval III (Stockholm, 1970).

If information is to be drawn from Sweden and used in an English context, it must first be established that demographic conditions in the two countries were comparable. Fortunately, in the late eighteenth century, when national comparisons can first be made, both mortality and marital fertility in Sweden were close to English levels.[18] And in the mid nineteenth century, when reliable data are first available for England, the national maternal mortality rate was 5.3 per 1000 (1851–60), while the Swedish rate in the same period was not much lower at 4.4 per 1000.[19] In view of the similarity of the Swedish and English demographic regimes in the decades when they can first be compared, it would seem reasonable to use the superior Swedish data to investigate those aspects of death in childbed that are hidden from view in England in the past.

The first advantage of the Swedish data is that they make it possible to trace the course of maternal mortality over a period of almost a century before data are available for England. Maternal mortality rates, based on deaths 'in childbed', have been calculated on a quinquennial basis, and are presented in table 9.1. For some of the early years the national aggregate tabulations are missing, but it has proved possible to reconstruct figures for most of the years concerned from intermediate manuscript calculations preserved in the Tabulation Office archives in Stockholm. The table shows that maternal mortality rates were about 11 per 1000 around 1760 and then settled at 8–9 per 1000 until 1815. During the next 30 years the rates fell regularly. By 1841 they were half their late-eighteenth-century level and on a par with contemporary English rates.

Second, the national Swedish data establish that in the period from 1751 to 1850 stillbirths comprised 2.8 per cent of all birth events.[20] Thus for maternal mortality associated with stillbirths to have had

18 For mortality, see Wrigley and Schofield, *Population history of England*, figure 7.13, p. 246. The total marital fertility ratio (TMFR) (ages 20–49) in Sweden in the period 1756–1800 was 7.66, while in a group of 13 English parishes (1750–99) it was 7.30. The Swedish TMFR was calculated from data in Hofsten and Lundström, *Swedish population history*, p. 30, omitting anomalously high figures for the first quinquennium (1751–5). For the English TMFR, see E.A. Wrigley and R.S. Schofield, 'English population history from family reconstitution: summary results, 1600–1799', *Population Studies* 37 (1983), p. 169.

19 The English rates from 1847 to 1854 are conveniently summarized in the *17th Annual Report of the Registrar General* (1854), p. 72, and the rates for 1855 to 1876 are summarized in the *39th Annual Report* (1876), p. 279. For the Swedish data see table 9.1, sources. The English rates were calculated per 1000 live births, while the Swedish rates were calculated per 1000 birth events, including stillbirths. The difference between the two bases for the rates is only of the order of 1.53 per cent, which is too small to be worth troubling about. Accordingly maternal mortality rates calculated from English and Swedish data later in this paper will use the base appropriate to the registration system, without attempting to translate between them.

20 On a quinquennial basis the proportion of stillbirths fluctuated within the range 2.5 to 3.2 per cent. Sundbärg, *Bevölkerungsstatistik Schwedens*, p. 129.

Table 9.1   Maternal mortality in Sweden 1756–1855

Quinquennium	Birth events	Childbed deaths	Rate/1000 birth events
1751–55	342,486	a	–
1756–60	328,479	3 376	10.9
1761–65	341,254	3 733[b]	10.9
1766–70	343,073	2 984[b]	8.7
1771–75	319,545	a	–
1776–80	362,020	3 235	8.9
1781–85	343,338	2 864	8.3
1786–90	353,413	3 297	9.3
1791–95	383,556	3 885	10.1
1796–00	385,393	3 289	8.5
1801–05	376,332	2 923	7.8
1806–10	370,757	3 294	8.9
1811–15	402,223	3 181	7.9
1816–20	430,261	3 170	7.4
1821–25	483,835	3 226	6.7
1826–30	480,223	3 184	6.6
1831–35	483,616	2 739	5.7
1836–40	479,386	2 438	5.1
1841–45	513,291	2 289	4.4
1846–50	533,594	2 343	4.5
1851–55	576,689	2 529	4.4
1856–60	639,639	–	4.5

[a]   Defective data for several years in 'Wargentins beräkningar'.
[b]   Data for Jönköping, Kristianstad, and Östergötland counties missing in 1764, 1765, and 1769–70, respectively. The totals for these years have been increased proportionately to each county's share of the total in other years.
Sources:
Birth events
Sundbärg, *Bevölkerungsstatistik Schwedens*, p. 127
Childbed deaths
1756–70: National totals, less Finland, from 'Wargentins beräkningar', Statistiska Centralbyrån, Stockholm: Tabell–kommissionens Arkiv, no. 29, BIIIb:1
1776–1855: *Tabell-kommissions underdåniga berättelse för åren 1851 med 1855, första afdelningen* (Stockholm, 1857), pp. liv–lvii
1856–60: *Bidrag till Sveriges officiella Statistik* (A) Befolkningsstatistik, 1856–60 (Stockholm, 1863), p. xxix.

more than a marginal impact on the overall rate it would have to have been very high indeed. Unfortunately, the tabulated data cannot throw any light on this issue because they do not distinguish live births and stillbirths when presenting the numbers of deaths in childbed. Accordingly, it is necessary to search for stillbirth entries in the original registers, and discover the proportion of mothers who died in childbed. The task is made easier because the need to return annual tables of the frequency and sex of stillborn children encouraged ministers to make entries relating to stillbirths easily recognizable in the registers, and even provoked some into keeping separate registers for stillbirths. Furthermore, the need to cross-classify events by characteristics such as the age of mothers and the cause of death encouraged ministers to keep their registers in a standard format, with information arranged in columns.

Five parishes in southern Sweden were selected for study, in which the layout of the registers expedited the identification of stillbirths and deaths in childbed. One parish (Ivetofta) was situated on an arable plain and contained large commercial farming estates, while three parishes (Bräkne Hoby, Osby and Tving) were scattered settlements situated in a forest pasture region with varying, but small, quantities of arable land. By way of contrast, the fifth parish (Landskrona) was a port town, located on an arable plain on the south-west coast.[21] In order to secure a sufficient number of events the registers were searched from the earliest practicable date up to 1859, when the maternal mortality rate was still 4.5 per 1000. The study was not continued past 1860 because, although the English maternal mortality rates remained stable in the late nineteenth century, the Swedish rate fell to a very low level indeed.[22] In 1820, when all the parishes were contributing data, three (Ivetofta, Osby and Landskrona town) contained about 2000 inhabitants, while Tving and Bräkne Hoby comprised 3700 and 4400 inhabitants respectively. All five parishes were growing rapidly, at between 0.8 and 1.1 per cent per annum over the period studied.[23]

Table 9.2 summarizes the incidence of stillbirths and maternal mortality in the parishes, calculated from the parish tabulations. In most parishes the percentages of all birth events that were stillbirths were a little higher than, though still reasonably close to, the national figure of 2.8 per cent, though in Landskrona town the figure was substantially greater, at 4.4 per cent. The maternal mortality rates in the individual parishes were sometimes above, and sometimes below, the national average figures in table 9.1 for the periods in question. For the group of parishes as a whole, the rate was 7.8 per 1000, fairly close to the average national figure of 7.1 for the quinquennia covered by the parish data.[24] The five parishes, therefore, seem likely to provide a reasonably

21 I am grateful to the chief archivist of the Lund archive, Anna Christina Ulfsparre, for assistance in identifying suitable registers, for information about the parishes, and for help in interpreting the sources.

22 See the annual statistical reports published from 1861 in the series *Bidrag till Sveriges officiella statistik: (A) Befolkningsstatistik* (Stockholm, 1862–). Around 1900 the maternal mortality rate had fallen as low as 2.3 per 100 birth events.

23 The population figures were taken from the triennial (quinquennial) statistical tables, copies of which were retained in the parishes.

24 In calculating the average national rate for the period 1751 to 1860, the figures for the constituent quinquennia were weighted according to the number of parishes contributing data in that quinquennium.

Table 9.2 Overall maternal mortality and stillbirth frequency in five southern
Swedish parishes

| Parish | Period | Birth events | | Rate (2)/(1)×100 | Deaths in childbed | Rate (4)/(1)×1000 |
		All (1)	Stillborn (2)	(3)	(4)	(5)
Bräkne Hoby	1749–1844	13,848	474	3.4	118	8.5
Ivetofta	1749–1839	4,870	148	3.0	34	7.0
Landskrona	1841–1859	4,488	199	4.4	27	6.0
Osby	1816–1859	4,033	103	2.6	19	4.7
Tving	1753–1859 [a]	7,564	232	3.1	75	9.9
All		38,803	1,156	3.3	273	7.8

[a] Data lacking for 1758–1773, 1797, 1801–18, 1821, 1831–4, and 1851–9.
Sources: Statistical tables ('statistiska tabeller') in the parish archives ('kyrkoarkiv') in the Landsarkiv
in Lund, Sweden: Bräkne Hoby (G:1); Ivetofta (GIII:1–3); Landskrona stadsförsamling (G:1), Osby
(G:2); Tving (G:1)

representative set of data for the calculation of maternal mortality
associated with the delivery of a stillborn child.

The study proceeded by identifying mothers of stillbirths in the birth
register and searching the death register for a period of three months
after the delivery. The task was made easier by the fact that the
ministers of each of the five parishes annotated the birth register with
the date on which the mother was churched.[25] According to the Swedish Church Law of 1686 mothers should remain at home about six
weeks after the birth, and then be received back into the church
again.[26] In practice, in Tving in the 1790s, 10 per cent of women had
come to be churched in the fifth week after giving birth, and a further
67 per cent in the sixth to the eighth weeks.[27] Since most maternal

25 English canon law also required women to be churched, but it is very rare to find any
record of the ceremony in the parish registers.
26 Kyrkolagen av år 1686, kap. 5 'Om barnakvinnors kyrkogång', s.l., in G. Lizell and E.
Leufvén, *Sveriges kyrkolag av år 1686* (Stockholm, 1928). Swedish regulations regarding the
interval before the churching of women were based on the Old Testament prescription of 40
days uncleanliness following birth. For a discussion of the development of the law on this
matter, see A. Gustavsson, *Kyrktagningsseden i Sverige* (Lund, 1972), pp. 22–7.
27 Landsarkivet in Lund, Tvings kyrkoarkiv, C:41. One rare example of the recording of
the dates of churchings in England can be found in the notebook of the parish clerk of St
Saviour's, Southwark covering the years 1619–25. A comparison with the baptism register
established that 93 per cent of the mothers were churched, and 90 per cent of them attended
the ceremony in the fourth or fifth week (21–34 days) after the child was baptized. J.P.
Boulton, 'The social and economic structure of Southwark in the early seventeenth century'
(unpublished Ph.D. thesis, Cambridge, 1983), pp. 335–7. The distribution of intervals in

deaths occurred within four weeks of birth, as will be detailed later, possible maternal deaths were easily spotted by looking for blanks, or the annotation 'dead' in the churching column in the register, and then checking the entries in the death register.

The results of this investigation into the fate of the mothers of stillborn children are contained in table 9.3. The maternal mortality rates associated with stillbirths (column 3) were indeed much higher than the overall rates for the parishes reported in table 9.2 (column 5), ranging from 30.6 per 1000 in Tving to 58.3 in Osby. Taking the five parishes together, 43 of the 1125 mothers of stillborn children died shortly after childbirth, producing a maternal mortality rate of 38.2. Although these figures are not quite as high as the rates previously cited for three English parishes about a century earlier, they do confirm that the chance of dying while giving birth to a stillborn child was about five times higher than in the case of a live-born child. But because stillbirths were relatively rare events, the impact of this high maternal mortality rate was much attenuated. For example, for the group of five parishes as a whole, the product of a stillbirth maternal mortality rate of 38.2 (table 9.3, column 3) and a stillbirth rate of 3.3 per cent (table 9.2, column 3) produces a contribution of only 1.26 per 1000 birth events to the overall maternal mortality rate. Since the latter was 7.8 per 1000 (table 9.2, column 5), omitting stillbirths underestimates the overall rate by the relatively modest amount of 16 per cent.

However, the English parish registers not only failed to record stillbirths, but also provided no means of identifying a maternal death

Table 9.3   Maternal mortality rates for stillbirths in five southern Swedish parishes

Parish		Stillbirth events (1)	Deaths in childbed (2)	Rate (2)/(1)×1000 (3)
Bräkne Hoby	1749–1849	471	16	34.0
Ivetofta	1786–1839	92	4	43.5
Landskrona	1814–1859	165	8	48.5
Osby	1816–1859	103	6	58.3
Tving	1790–1859	294	9	30.6
All		1,125	43	38.2

Sources: Parish archives, as cited in table 9.2: Bräkne Hoby (C:5–7, 9–10); Ivetofta (CI:3–4); Landskrona Stadsförsamling (C:7,9); Osby (C:5,7–8); Tving (C:4–5,7)

Southwark is in accordance with English canon law, which considered one month a reasonable time to elapse between birth and the ceremony. R. Burn, *The ecclesiastical law* 8th edn, vol. 1 (London, 1824), p. 319.

when the child died in the womb without being delivered. But such events can be identified in the Swedish registers by noting when a death 'in childbed' has no corresponding entry of either a live-born or a stillborn child. In such circumstances the ministers occasionally explicitly noted that a woman had died in childbed, but undelivered. The Swedish registers, therefore, can also be used to estimate the frequency of this further, and even more elusive, element of maternal mortality missing from the English registers.

In this investigation the parish statistical tables were used to identify the years in which deaths in childbed occurred. Then a search was made in the death registers to find details of the date of death and the age of the mother, and in the birth registers to discover whether the maternal death occurred as the result of a live birth, a stillbirth or an undelivered pregnancy.[28] If a birth entry was found, the interval between delivery and death could be calculated. The Swedish registers, therefore, made it possible to apportion maternal mortality between live births, stillbirths, and no-birth events, and to investigate the timing of maternal deaths for mothers of different ages.

Nine parishes were used for this study, three of which also contributed to the investigation of stillbirth maternal mortality reported earlier. Osby and Landskrona town were dropped, because the documents were defective in the eighteenth century. They were replaced by a group of three adjacent parishes situated on a rich arable plain, not far from Landskrona; two adjacent parishes in a pastoral region on the west coast 100 kilometres further north; and an urban parish in the ancient chartered borough and port of Ystad, situated on the south coast.[29]

The patterns of maternal deaths in the nine parishes are summarized in table 9.4. The first part of the table reports the percentage distribution of intervals to death following a delivery of live-born and stillborn children. Taking all ages together, 29 per cent of the 279 maternal deaths in these circumstances occurred on the day of birth, and a further 19 per cent in the next three days. Nearly half the maternal deaths, therefore, occurred within four days of delivery, and almost 80 per cent within two weeks. The age of the mother seems to have had little effect on the interval to death, apart from a tendency for the proportion of deaths occurring on the day of birth to increase with age. But the numbers of cases are too small to establish this point conclusively.

28 Since both the birth and the death registers recorded the mother's age, this information could be used, together with her name, to ensure that the entries in the two registers referred to the same person.

29 The group of three adjacent parishes comprised Gårdstånga, Holmby, and Skarhult; the group of two adjacent parishes comprised Alfshög and Ljungby; and the Ystad parish was Sankta Maria.

Table 9.4 Maternal deaths; interval from delivery and undelivered, by age

Interval to death from delivery (days)	Live births and stillbirths: age						Illegiti-mate	Multiple	Stillborn	Live births
	under 25	25–29	30–34	35–39	40–49	All				
	Percentage distribution of intervals to death									
0	24	26	27	30	34	29[a]	39	33	53	23
1–3	18	28	20	14	11	19	22	8	14	20
4–6	15	2	12	14	14	11	11	8	14	11
7–14	21	16	22	19	23	20	17	8	12	21
15–30	9	19	12	13	14	14	6	25	2	16
31+	12	9	7	10	5	8	6	17	6	9
0–30	88	91	93	90	95	92	94	83	94	91
0–42	94	98	96	93	98	96	94	83	100	95
0–60	100	100	99	96	98	98	100	92	100	98
N =	33	57	74	70	44	279[a]	18	12	51	228
	Percent dying undelivered									
	13	17	28	19	41	27	14	–	–	–
	All deaths									
N =	38	69	103	87	75	381[b]	21	12	51	–

[a] Includes one case with age not stated.
[b] Includes nine cases with age not stated.

Sources: Parish archives as cited in table 9.2. Alfshög (C:2–3,G:1); Bräkne Hoby (C:5–7, 10; G:1–3); Gårdstånga (C:1–2; G:1:3); Holmby (C:1–2; G:1:3); Ivetofta (C:2–4; GIII:1–3); Ljungby (C:2–4; DII:1; G:1–2); Skarhult (C:1–2; G:1–3); Tving (C:4–5, 7; G:1); Ystad, Sankta Maria (F:1–7; G:1–2).

The numbers of maternal deaths associated with illegitimate and multiple births are even smaller, so the somewhat shorter intervals of the former, and the longer intervals of the latter, may merely be random effects. In the case of stillbirths, however, a much higher proportion of maternal deaths (53 per cent) occurred on the day of delivery, and this is probably a genuine reflection of a set of obstetrical conditions which not only killed the child but brought about the immediate death of the mother. In contrast, the distribution of intervals to death following a live birth was more evenly spread over the first month, only 23 per cent of the maternal deaths occurring on the day of birth.

The second part of table 9.4 summarizes the number of maternal deaths occurring up to 30, 42 and 60 days from delivery. No less than 92 per cent took place within a month. If the period is extended to 42 days, as recommended by the IFGO, 96 per cent are included, and the 60-day limit adopted by most French historical demographers encompasses 98 per cent of maternal deaths. The Swedish data, therefore, suggest that a period as short as a calendar month would be sufficient to capture almost all maternal deaths. On the other hand, a period as long as 60 days brings in only another 6 per cent of maternal deaths, and inflates maternal mortality rates by including the deaths of mothers in the second month arising from other causes.[30]

In the third part of table 9.4 the focus is widened to include maternal deaths when no child was delivered. No less than 27 per cent of all maternal deaths occurred in these circumstances: this hidden dimension of maternal mortality was far from negligible.[31] Although the figures of the percentages by the age of the mother are uneven, there does seem to be an indication that a higher proportion of maternal deaths among mothers aged 40 and above involved no birth at all, than was the case at other ages. If the Swedish data can be taken as typical, they suggest that registers of birth events which include live births and stillbirths will encompass 73 per cent of maternal deaths (279/381), while parish registers which record only live-birth events, as was the case in England, will capture only 60 per cent (228/381).

However, it is possible that the proportional division of maternal deaths between live births, stillbirths and undelivered pregnancies may

30 The inclusion of all deaths up to 60 days after birth also skews the distribution of intervals to death. For example in the INED study of French data 13 per cent of the intervals were longer than 30 days, compared with 8 per cent in the Swedish data based only on known 'childbed' deaths. Gutierrez et Houdaille, 'La mortalité maternelle en France', p. 985.

31 An analysis of the registers of Sankta Klara, a rich central parish in Stockholm, for the years 1780–1820 found a very low maternal mortality rate of 2.1 per 1000, 60 per cent of which was contributed by unmarried servant girls, all of whom died undelivered. This was so unlike the experience of illegitimate mothers in the country parishes that it suggests the practice of lethal methods of abortion.

have varied with the overall level of maternal mortality, reflecting a differential impact of the level of obstetrical skill on each of the three categories. Fortunately, this point can be tested with the parish data since, as is clear from tables 9.1 and 9.3, the level of maternal mortality not only varied between the parishes, but also fell by 50 per cent at the national level during the period being studied. To make the test, the parish data were divided into two periods, at 1800, and in order to obtain sufficient numbers of maternal deaths in each 50-year parish-period the two sets of adjacent parishes were each aggregated into a single composite parish.

The resulting total maternal mortality rates for the 12 parish-periods ranged from 4.0 per 1000 birth events in the town parish of Sankta Maria, Ystad in 1800–55 to 14.3 per 1000 in Tving in 1753–99. When the total rates were compared with those based on live-birth events alone it was evident that the higher the total rate the greater was the fraction comprised by the rate based on live births. Thus the figure of 60 per cent of all maternal deaths contributed by live-birth events that was obtained for the combined group of nine parishes was dependent on the average level of maternal mortality in the group. It would, therefore, appear to be inappropriate to inflate all levels of maternal mortality based on live births by the ratio of 1/0.60.

When the total rates in the 12 parish-periods were plotted against the corresponding live-birth rates, all the points except two lay close to a diagonal line, indicating that the two rates varied together in a systematic manner. Regression analysis was used to measure the relationship, after omitting the two outlying results.[32] On the basis of the remaining ten observations it was found that the total maternal mortality rate (MM_T) could be predicted from the live-birth maternal rate (MM_{LB}) by the following expression:

$$MM_T = 1.07 MM_{LB} + 2.73$$

That is, a maternal mortality rate based on live births alone can be corrected upwards to yield a total rate by adding in a further 7 per cent, and then adding a constant 'base minimum' of unobserved maternal mortality of 2.73 per 1000 birth events. Thus, for example, a live-birth maternal mortality rate of 10 per 1000 would be corrected upward to 13.43 ($(1.07 \times 10) + 2.73$). In this example the rate is

32 The two omitted observations were the eighteenth-century values for the two composite parishes. The regression coefficients were estimated using ordinary least squares. Because total numbers of births could not be obtained for some of the parishes, the live-birth and overall maternal mortality rates were calculated per 1000 average population of each parish in each period. The figures were then converted to rates per 1000 births by dividing by a crude birth rate of 33.61, the average of the crude birth rates for the counties of Blekinge, Halland, Kristianstad and Malmö for the periods 1751–70 and 1796–1850. Hofsten and Lundström, *Swedish population history*, p. 96.

raised by 34.3 per cent. However, a low live-birth maternal mortality rate is raised proportionately more than this, and a high rate proportionately less. For example, a live-birth maternal mortality rate of 5 per 1000 is corrected upwards to 8.08, a rise of 62 per cent, and a rate of 20 per 1000 is corrected to 24.13, an increase of 20 per cent. This is because the constant 'base minimum' rate of unobserved maternal mortality comprises a more significant element when the live-birth rate is low than when it is high.[33]

Although the formula given above 'predicts' the total maternal mortality rates in the Swedish data from the rates based on live births alone with considerable precision (adjusted $R^2 = 0.95$), it should be remembered that it is based on only ten observations. The small number of observations means that the 95 per cent confidence intervals of the two parameters in the formula are wide. The confidence bounds of the coefficient of 1.07 are 0.89 and 1.25; and the bounds of the constant 'base minimum' rate of 2.73 are 1.69 and 3.76. The lower confidence bounds are unlikely to be plausible alternatives, especially since applying them to live-birth maternal mortality rates of 25 and above actually produces a lower total rate. On the other hand, the upper confidence bounds might be taken to represent the highest inflation of live-birth-based maternal mortality rates that could plausibly be claimed to be consistent with the Swedish data. Applying them raises a rate of 5 per 1000 to 12.21, a rate of 10 per 1000 to 20.66, and a rate of 20 per 1000 to 37.56, increases of 144, 107 and 88 per cent respectively. In fact, using the upper bound values of the coefficients produces total maternal mortality rates which are implausibly high by the standards of the Swedish data, but they serve to emphasize the point that the narrow empirical basis of the 'best' correction coefficients given above means that the latter are questionable. Moreover, it also needs to be borne in mind that the correction coefficients were estimated over a range of total maternal mortality rates from 4.0 to 14.3 per 1000, and may not necessarily be appropriate when the rates lie outside that range.

Despite these uncertainties, the unusually full Swedish data do provide an empirical, rather than a wholly speculative, basis for correcting

---

33 This argument assumes that changes in maternal mortality rates do not entail significant changes in the *relative* efficacy of obstetrical practice for live-birth deliveries on the one hand, compared with stillbirths and undelivered pregnancies on the other hand. Data from England and Wales in 1935 confirm the propriety of the assumption, since 57 per cent of maternal deaths were still associated with live births, a figure quite close to the figure of 60 per cent obtained from the historical Swedish data. However, the distribution between maternal deaths associated with stillbirths and undelivered pregnancies was very different from the Swedish data, with 30 per cent of maternal deaths being associated with stillbirths, and only 13 per cent with undelivered pregnancies. P. Stocks, 'Maternal mortality according to the number of previous confinements. Effects of social grade, twin pregnancy and the declining birth rate', *Report of an investigation into maternal mortality* (Ministry of Health: Command Papers, session 1936–7, 5422), p. 105.

the English maternal mortality rates derived from live births alone. In the present study the latter have been based on a set of family reconstitution studies of 13 parishes, selected so as to maximize variation in geographical and economic circumstances. Although the characteristics of the parishes have been described elsewhere, there are two features which are relevant to their suitability as a basis for national estimates of maternal mortality reaching back into the distant past.[34] On the one hand, the remarkable similarity in marital fertility rates that has been found in individual parishes in England in the past suggests that marital fertility was probably uniform throughout the countryside.[35] Consequently, the data from the 13 parishes are likely to give a representative picture of the intensity of exposure to the risk of maternal mortality of married women. Unfortunately the maternal mortality of unmarried women cannot be studied from family reconstitution data, but the omission is unlikely to cause a serious bias. Before 1750, illegitimate births comprised only between 1 and 3 per cent of all births, and between 4 and 5 per cent from 1750 to 1839.[36] Moreover, in one parish in Sweden where the maternal mortality rate of the mothers of illegitimate children could be studied, it was actually lower than that of married women.[37]

On the other hand, the set of 13 parishes is probably not perfectly representative of the level of mortality in the country as a whole. It does not include any parishes from London, or any other large urban centre, and it appears to underestimate levels of infant and child mortality in non-metropolitan England by about 10 per cent.[38] In so far as maternal mortality rates were to some extent influenced by the level of exposure to infectious disease, and evidence is presented later to suggest that this may have been the case, the rates based on the 13 parishes may also be similarly biased below the true national rate. However, there may well have been other factors, such as the availability of skilled obstetrical help, in which the 13 parishes were relatively deficient, and which may produce an upward bias in the estimates of maternal mortality. In the present state of knowledge it is probably better to refrain from any *a priori* judgement about the representative-

---

34 For a description of the parishes and an evaluation of their representativeness, see Wrigley and Schofield, 'English population history from family reconstitution', pp. 158–61.

35 Wilson, 'Natural fertility in pre-industrial England', pp. 226–7.

36 P. Laslett, 'Introduction: comparing illegitimacy over time and between cultures', in P. Laslett, K. Oosterveen and R.M. Smith (eds), *Bastardy and its comparative history* (London, 1980), pp. 14–15.

37 In Bräkne Hoby in the period 1749–1849 the maternal mortality rate for illegitimate mothers was 6.2 per 1000 ($n = 963$), as against 8.7 for married women($n = 13,885$). Landsarkivet in Lund, Bräkne Hobys kyrkoarkiv, C:5–7,10.

38 Wrigley and Schofield, 'English population history from family reconstitution', pp. 160–1.

ness of maternal mortality estimates based on the set of 13 parishes, and evaluate their plausibility in the context of other evidence.

As a first step in estimating maternal mortality, the proportion of women who died less than 61 days after the baptism of their child was calculated from the reconstitution forms of the 13 parishes for each 50-year period from 1550 to 1849. The resulting rates per 1000 baptisms are presented in the first row of table 9.5. They overestimate maternal mortality associated with live births for two reasons. First, and less seriously, the interval between birth and baptism means that deaths occurring a few days after 60 days from birth were counted as maternal deaths.[39] More importantly, as was discussed earlier, it is clear from the Swedish data that a period of observation as long as 60 days includes many deaths of married women that are unrelated to childbirth. Accordingly, the second row of the table contains an estimate of the number of deaths that would have occurred to women from other causes, so that they can be subtracted from the 60-day rate.

The estimates have been derived from the Princeton model North life tables, which are based on life tables of Swedish, Norwegian and

Table 9.5   Maternal mortality rates in 13 English parishes

| | Rate per 1000 births | | | | | |
	1550–99[a]	1600–49	1650–99	1700–49	1750–99	1800–49[a]
60 days after live birth	8.0	10.1	14.2	10.0	6.5	4.3
Less background	1.9	1.8	2.1	2.0	1.9	1.7
Net	6.1	8.3	12.1	8.0	4.6	2.6
Plus stillbirth and no birth:[a]						
Best estimate	3.2	3.3	3.6	3.3	3.1	2.9
Fixed ratio	4.1	5.6	8.1	5.4	3.1	1.7
Maximal	8.0	9.5	12.1	9.3	6.9	5.6
Total:						
Best estimate	9.3	11.6	15.7	11.3	7.7	5.5
Fixed ratio	10.2	13.9	20.2	13.4	7.7	4.3
Maximal	14.1	17.8	24.2	17.3	11.5	8.2
N(birth events)=	18,470	28,880	27,601	32,511	45,816	24,391

[a]   For methods of estimation, see text.
Sources:
Live-birth maternal mortality rates: family reconstitution records as described in the text.
Background mortality: A. J. Coale and P. Demeny, *Regional model life tables* (Princeton, 1966), model North, levels interpolated to match average expectation of life (both sexes) calculated from Wrigley and Schofield, *Population history of England*, pp. 528–9.

39 See note 13 in this chapter.

Icelandic populations in the late nineteenth and mid twentieth centuries.[40] In these populations maternal mortality rates were very much lower than in the more distant past. Indeed, female death rates during the reproductive ages in the model North life tables are lower than the male rates, while in England even as late as the mid nineteenth century, when maternal mortality rates were quite moderate, the reverse was the case.[41] Since in other respects the North pattern of mortality by age fits the English data well, the tables can be used to estimate the 'background' level of mortality for women of reproductive age in the absence of significant levels of maternal mortality. For simplicity the calculation was made for the age group 30–34, which encompasses the mean age at maternity.[42] The model life tables were used to find the age-specific annual death rate (m_x) for that age group corresponding to the average expectation of life at birth in each of the 50-year periods being studied, and from the m_x figure a death rate for a period of 60 days was derived.[43]

The third row of table 9.5, therefore, contains estimates of maternal mortality over a 60-day period after a live birth, net of 'background' mortality from other causes. The amount of maternal mortality associated with stillbirths and undelivered pregnancies is then estimated using the formula derived from the Swedish data, and added to the live-birth mortality to produce a total maternal mortality rate for each of the 50-year periods. For reference, two alternative estimates of the hidden maternal mortality are presented, together with the associated estimates of total maternal mortality. The first (fixed ratio) is obtained by applying to the maternal mortality rate based on live births alone the constant inflation factor of 1.67 (1/0.60) derived from the Swedish data summarized in table 9.4. This alternative mistrusts the applicability of the regression results to England, and assumes that maternal deaths associated with stillbirths and undelivered pregnancies comprised a constant proportion of all maternal deaths, regardless of the level of maternal mortality. The second alternative (maximal) accepts that the proportion may have varied with the level in England as in Sweden,

40 Sweden (1851–90), Norway (1856–80, 1946–55), Iceland (1941–50), A.J. Coale and P. Demeny, *Regional model life tables*, (Princeton, 1966), p. 14. For a comparison between English mortality in the nineteenth century and the Princeton model North table, see Wrigley and Schofield, *Population history of England*, pp. 708–9.

41 A mean of maternity of 32 years is a reasonable average for pre-industrial England. Wrigley and Schofield, *Population history of England*, p. 233. The m_x value for the age group 30–34 is, in fact, very close to an average of the individual m_x values of the five-year age groups comprising a maternity schedule with a mean age of 32 years, weighted proportionately to the contribution of each five-year age group to total marital fertility.

42 Ibid., pp. 528–9.

43 In the periods 1550–9 and 1800–49 not all parishes were in observation all the time. Accordingly, for these periods the parish data were not simply pooled, but the maternal mortality rates for the individual parishes were combined in the proportions that the parishes contributed to the pooled data in the adjacent periods (viz. 1660–49, and 1750–99).

but aims for the maximum plausible estimate of maternal mortality by taking the values of the regression coefficients at the top bound of the 95 per cent confidence intervals.

The resulting estimates of total maternal mortality rates in each 50-year period are plotted on figure 9.1. The 'best' estimates, based on the central values of the regression coefficients, are shown as heavy horizontal bars stretching across each period, with the centre marked as a circle. At each end of the bars the vertical lines indicate the range of the 95 per cent confidence intervals for the estimated 50-year maternal mortality rates.[44] If the vertical bars of any pair of periods do not overlap, then it is likely that the maternal mortality rates in those periods are genuinely different. The 'best' estimates suggest that the maternal mortality rate was just under 10 per 1000 in the late sixteenth century, and just over that figure in the first half of the seventeenth century. The rate then jumps sharply upward to just under 16 per 1000 in the later seventeenth century, to fall back to just over 10 per 1000 again in the first half of the eighteenth century. After 1750 the maternal mortality rate falls, first to just under 8 per 1000 in the later eighteenth century, and then to between 5 and 6 per 1000 in the early nineteenth century.

Since so many uncertainties and approximations were involved in devising the methods by which the original figures were corrected, the so-called 'best' estimates must be taken as indicative rather than precise. From 1750 they can be compared with similar estimates based on a set of French parishes and with the Swedish national maternal mortality rates, presented in table 9.1. The French rates have been recalculated so that they are on an equal footing with the English rates by subtracting an estimate of 'background' mortality and adding maternal mortality associated with stillbirths and undelivered pregnancies, using the 'best estimate' coefficients.[45] The resulting rates for three periods (1700–49, 1750–89, and 1790–1829) are plotted on figure 9.1 as dotted horizontal bars with a diamond at the centre, and with dotted vertical bars indicating the 95 per cent confidence intervals.

In the first half of the eighteenth century the French and English estimates are very close, but thereafter maternal mortality in England appears to have fallen rather faster than in France, the rate in France

44 These confidence intervals are associated with the precision of the original estimates of the maternal mortality rate based on live births, and are mainly a function of the number of birth events observed in each period (see the last row of table 9.5).

45 The 'observed' French data were used as a basis for the recalculation rather than the 'corrected' rates. Gutierrez and Houdaille, 'La mortalité maternelle en France', table 1, p. 978. The correction for background mortality was made in the same way as the correction for England, based on average expectation of life, as indicated by Y. Blayo, 'La mortalité en France de 1740 à 1829', *Population* 30 (1975), p. 141. For the period 1700–49, mortality at level 4 of the North model tables was assumed.

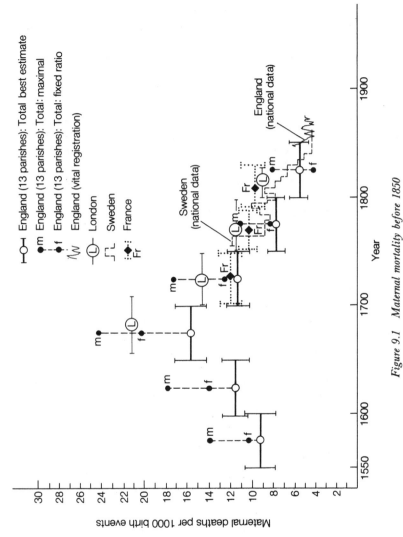

Figure 9.1 Maternal mortality before 1850

Sources: *England, 13 parishes: table 9.5. England, vital registration: note 19 in this chapter. London: note 6 in this chapter. Sweden: table 9.1. France: note 45 in this chapter*

in the early decades of the nineteenth century being just under 10 per 1000, while the rate in England was just over 5. In the circumstances it is reassuring that Sweden, with incomparably the best data (dashed line in figure 9.1), also recorded a similarly steep decline in maternal mortality in the late eighteenth and early nineteenth centuries. Indeed the English estimates of maternal mortality are quite close to the Swedish figures in this period, just as the overall levels of mortality were similar in the two countries.

Furthermore, the estimate of maternal mortality based on the 13 parishes for the early nineteenth century would seem to be reasonably in line with the maternal mortality rates recorded during the early years of vital registration, which are also shown on figure 9.1. If anything, the parish estimate would appear a little low, but it does not include London and, in any case, the national rates are probably about 5 per cent too high because of an under-enumeration of births.[46]

Before 1700 the English data can only be compared with rates estimated for two towns. In the later seventeenth century maternal mortality rates in Geneva lay between 15 and 19 per 1000, and in Rouen the rate was about 12 per 1000.[47] The estimated English rate of 15.7 per 1000 seems reasonably close, considering it is based on rural as well as small urban communities. For comparison the London rates, calculated from the bills of mortality, have been included on figure 9.1 as lighter bars marked with an 'L', and it is apparent that maternal mortality in the capital since the late seventeenth century was between 30 and 50 per cent higher than in the 13 parishes. In the early years of vital registration maternal mortality was 50–70 per cent higher than in the country at large.

The present estimates, therefore, do not appear to be out of line with levels of maternal mortality found in London, and in other countries, at several dates in the past. Nor do they seem to be unreasonable, even in the context of a generally low level of obstetrical knowledge and skill. For example, a report based on 1897 home deliveries among the London poor in the years 1774–81 noted that 94.5 per cent 'had natural labours, not attended with any particular danger', 3.3 per cent had 'preternatural or laborious births, or suffered in consequence of labour' but 'recovered with little more than the common assistance', and only 2.2 per cent had deliveries which were 'attended with particular dif-

---

46 Under-registration of births has been estimated at about 7 per cent in the late 1840s, 5 per cent in the 1850s, and 3 per cent in the 1860s. Deaths were probably under-registered by only 1 per cent in the late 1840s, and appear to have been accurately recorded from the 1850s. Wrigley and Schofield, *Population history of England*, pp. 635–7.

47 Perrenoud, 'Surmortalité féminine', p. 99. Bardet et al., 'La mortalité maternelle autrefois', p. 45. Background mortality was subtracted from the original maternal mortality estimates at the rate of 1 per 1000 per 30 days, and the resulting net maternal mortality rates were corrected using the 'best estimate' regression coefficients.

ficulty or danger'.[48] If these figures can be generalized to the population at large, only 22 per 1000 mothers would have been seriously at risk of dying in childbed. Consequently, a maternal mortality rate of 8 per 1000 (as estimated for 1750–99) would imply a case fatality rate among the 22 per 1000 seriously at risk of 36 per cent, which does not seem to be implausibly low.[49]

It is, perhaps, ironical that the present estimates of maternal mortality before 1750, even after correction for maternal deaths missing from the English registers, should still lie in a range of values which scholars have declared *a priori* to be 'much too low'.[50] The reasons for this outcome are evident from the figures in table 9.5. First, the events which gave rise to the hidden component in maternal mortality, although much more lethal than those which were observed, turned out to have been sufficiently rare that correcting for their absence in the English data only raised maternal mortality rates by about 3 per 1000. Second, about two-thirds of this addition was already improperly included in the maternal mortality estimates based on live births, since the 60-day rates included deaths from non-maternal causes.

The corrected levels of maternal mortality graphed in figure 9.1 depend entirely on the validity of the 'best estimate' coefficients derived from the Swedish data. In order to investigate how far they are sensitive to alternative correction procedures, the 'fixed ratio' and 'maximum plausible' regression estimates presented in table 9.5 are also shown on figure 9.1, labelled with the letters 'f' and 'm', respectively.

Briefly, if it is believed that a constant, rather than a variable, proportion of maternal mortality was missing from the English parish registers, the corrected rates are generally only 1 or 2 per 1000 higher than the 'best estimate' rates in the period before 1750, though in the late seventeenth century the 'fixed ratio' rate is 4.5 per 1000 higher. In the late eighteenth century the two methods of correction produce the same result, and in the early nineteenth century the 'fixed ratio' approach yields a figure which is about 1 per 1000 lower than the 'best estimate' rate. If the 'maximum plausible' inflation consistent with the Swedish data is made to the rates observed in the English parish registers, the corrected rates generally lie between 14 and 18 per 1000 in the period before 1750, except in the late seventeenth century, when they rise to 24 per 1000. They then fall to 11 and 8 per 1000 in the two

48 R. Bland, 'Some calculations on the number of accidents or deaths which happen in consequence of parturition', *Philosophical Transactions of the Royal Society* 71 part I (1781), p. 355. I owe this reference to Irvine Loudon of the Wellcome Institute for the History of Medicine, Oxford.

49 Interestingly, on the same basis a maternal mortality rate of 16 per 1000, as estimated for the late seventeenth century, would imply a much higher case fatality rate of 73 per 1000, but the proportion of deliveries 'attended with particular difficulty or danger' may have been higher then.

50 See note 15 in this chapter.

subsequent 50-year periods. Before 1750 these figures are even higher than those obtained from the bills of mortality for London, and in the early nineteenth century they imply a level of maternal mortality which is too high to be reconciled easily with the vital registration data. Thus the 'fixed ratio' alternative scarcely alters the picture, except to produce an improbably low figure for the early nineteenth century, and the 'maximum plausible' alternative produces estimates which are implausible in the context of other, more secure, data based on stated causes of death.

A salient feature of all the English estimates presented in figure 9.1 is an increase in the maternal mortality rate from the late sixteenth to the late seventeenth century, followed by an uninterrupted decline until the mid nineteenth century. Thus the long period of stability in the maternal mortality rate from the late 1850s until the 1930s was preceded by three centuries in which the rate both rose and fell. The early rise in the rate is, perhaps, the more difficult to explain, since there seems no good reason to suppose that obstetrical practice deteriorated between the late sixteenth and the late seventeenth centuries. However, the general rise in mortality that occurred in this period may well have entailed an increase in exposure to infectious diseases, to which women in the final stages of pregnancy may have been particularly vulnerable.[51] Recent research has established that women in their third trimester of pregnancy, or newly delivered, are several times more likely than others of the same age to become infected by, and die of, diseases which were common in England in the past, such as tuberculosis, smallpox and influenza. This is because **pregnancy suppresses cell-mediated immunity, in a way which permits** foetal retention but interferes with resistance to specific pathogens.[52]

A 'pregnancy-associated immune deficiency syndrome' (PAIDS), therefore, might help to account not only for the rise in maternal mortality rates before 1700, but also for the higher rates in large cities, such as London, where exposure to disease was greater. If a mechanism such as PAIDS lay behind the seventeenth-century rise in maternal mortality, then not all of the subsequent decline in the eighteenth century can be attributed to improvements in obstetrical practice, since this was a period in which general mortality rates fell and the incidence of infectious disease diminished.[53] However, the fall in maternal mortality was greater than the fall in general mortality, and by the early nineteenth century maternal mortality rates had reached an unprecedentedly low level. Consequently, it is likely that some part of the fall in maternal mortality rates after 1700 was due to improvements in obstetrical practice.

51 For the increase in mortality in the seventeenth century, see Wrigley and Schofield, *Population history of England*, pp. 234–6, 249–53, 528–9.
52 E.D. Weinberg, 'Pregnancy and resistance to infectious disease', *Reviews of Infectious Diseases* 6 (1984), pp. 814–31.
53 See note 51 in this chapter.

So far, maternal mortality in England in the past has been discussed as an undifferentiated risk of dying in childbed. However, maternal mortality rates have generally been found to vary according to the age of the mother and the parity of the birth.[54] The first birth is usually the most dangerous: for example in England and Wales in 1935 the risk of dying in giving birth to a first child was 24 per cent higher than the overall risk of dying in childbed.[55] Over the whole period studied here the maternal mortality rate for first births was 39 per cent higher than the overall rate, a figure which is very close to the 38 per cent penalty for first births found for France in the period 1700–1829.[56]

Apart from first births, it is usually only high-parity births which carry a significantly increased risk of maternal mortality, but by very different amounts in different populations. For example, in England and Wales in 1935 the first-birth maternal death rate was exceeded at parities of seven and above, while in a part of Bangladesh in the late 1960s even at parities ten and above maternal mortality was still not as high as it had been for the first birth.[57] The problem with measuring mortality at high parities is that in these cases the mother is much older than average and so there is risk of imputing to parity a maternal mortality effect which may be due to age. A recent study of maternal mortality in England and Wales in the 1970s, which separated the two effects, found that parity played almost no role up to ages 25–29, and then increased in effect, with first births and parities of five and above being especially dangerous for mothers over age 40.[58]

Unfortunately the calculation of maternal mortality associated with higher-order parities from English parish registers poses some severe problems, and the task will not be attempted here. However, some indication of the effect of age on maternal mortality can be obtained by correcting the live-birth data in the English registers by the age-specific omission ratios for hidden mortality derived from the Swedish registers.

54 Patterns of maternal mortality in the developing, and the developed, world today are conveniently summarized, with a comprehensive bibliography, in 'Healthier mothers and children through family planning', *Population Reports* series J, 12 (1984), pp. 661, 673–9, 689–96. For historical populations, see the references cited in note 10 in this chapter.

55 Stocks, 'Maternal mortality according to the number of previous confinements', p. 107.

56 Calculated from data in Gutierrez and Houdaille, 'La mortalité maternelle en France', table 13, p. 987. Maternal mortality for first births in Mogneneins (1660–1814) was also 36 per cent higher than the overall rate. Calculated from data in Bideau, 'Accouchement naturel et accouchement à haut risque', p. 58. However, maternal mortality for first births in Rouen (1650–1792) was only 17 per cent higher than the overall rate. Calculated from data in Bardet et al., 'La mortalité maternelle autrefois', table VII, p. 44.

57 For England, see note 55 in this chapter. The Matlab, Bangladesh data is graphed in 'Healthier mothers and children through family planning', p. 674. The original data are reported in L.C. Chen et al., 'Maternal mortality in rural Bangladesh', *Studies in Family Planning* (1974), pp. 334–41.

58 The data, from Tomkinson et al., *Report on confidential enquiries into maternal deaths*, are graphed in 'Healthier mothers and children through family planning', p. 675.

The first line of table 9.6 contains for each age group over the whole period studied the maternal mortality rate associated with live births, reduced by 2 per 1000 so as to remove 'background' mortality. In the investigation of the Swedish registers it was evident from the data underlying table 9.4 that the proportion of total maternal mortality associated with stillbirths and undelivered pregnancies increased with the age of the mother. But since the age-specific inflation ratios implied by the data were somewhat disorderly, they were smoothed to the regular progression shown in the second row of table 9.6.[59]

Table 9.6   Relative maternal mortality rates, by age, 13 English parishes 1550–1849

	Age					
	15–19	*20–24*	*25–29*	*30–34*	*35–39*	*40–49*
(1) Per 1000 live births[a]	7.8	6.0	7.6	8.4	9.8	7.9
(2) Inflation factor[b]	1.3	1.4	1.5	1.6	1.6	2.0
(3) Total rate	10.4	8.4	11.4	13.4	15.7	15.8
(4) Index (100=av.=12.4)	83	68	92	108	127	127
N	1538	9636	13,609	11,905	8510	4450

[a]   Less 2.00 per 1000 subtracted as 'background' mortality.
[b]   Based on Swedish data; see text.
Source: Family reconstitution data, mortality within 60 days of live birth events

The resulting index numbers, presented in the fourth row of the table, represent a stylized attempt to correct for the deficiencies of the English registers and should only be taken as approximate estimates of the effect of age on maternal mortality. Nevertheless they suggest that, with the exception of teenage mothers, the risk of dying in childbed did indeed increase with age. The least-dangerous age group was 20–24, where the risk was about two-thirds the average; and for teenage mothers it was 83 per cent of the average. Youth would certainly seem to have been associated with lower maternal mortality, since these age groups had a greater than average proportion of higher-risk first births. After age 25, while each age group experienced a greater probability of dying in childbed, it was only those who gave birth after age 35 who were exposed to a significantly increased risk, about 27 per cent higher than average.

59 Despite the stylized smoothing of the age-specific inflation ratios, a weighted average of the age-specific rates in table 9.6 produces an overall maternal mortality rate for all ages of 12.4 per 1000 birth events, close to the figure of 12.0 per 1000 obtained by applying the 'best estimate' regression coefficients to the live-birth maternal mortality rate for all women at all dates.

Most other studies of maternal mortality in pre-industrial Europe have reported similar patterns by age, but usually with a sharper increase in maternal mortality over age 40, with death rates 40 to 70 per cent above average.[60]

Although historical demographers today may calculate differences in the *risk* of dying in childbed by age and by birth parity, it is more debatable whether these differences were large enough for women in the past to have noticed them, and so have, for example, been more apprehensive of their first birth or of giving birth when over age 35. However, women may well have observed that the *numbers* of maternal deaths varied markedly by age, and so gained a rather different, and erroneous, impression of the relative chances of dying in childbirth at different ages. The main reason why maternal deaths were distributed so unevenly by age was that late marriage and a cumulative risk of sterility meant that at some ages a far higher proportion of women were producing children and so were exposed to the risk of death in childbed than at other ages. Combined with the age-specific differences in the risk of death, discussed above, these differences in exposure will have produced large variations in the proportion of all women alive at different ages who died in childbed. And since the chances of dying from other causes also varied by age, the relative importance of maternal mortality will have appeared to have been more severe at some ages than at others.

Table 9.7 presents the results of a stylized calculation, which is intended to reconstruct how the pattern of maternal deaths by age may have appeared to English women in the past. For simplicity, a group of 1000 women in each age group is assumed to have experienced demographic rates which are broadly typical of pre-industrial England, though not necessarily of any one period. The calculation begins with the proportions married in the age groups 15–19, 20–24, 25–34, 35–44, and 45–49 as recorded in the 1851 census (table 9.7, row 1). These figures reflect a situation in which the average age of marriage was about 25 years and about 12 per cent never married – fairly average figures for the timing and incidence of marriage in pre-industrial England.[61] The married women in each age group then experience the average age-specific fertility rates recorded in the set of 13 parishes during the period 1600–1799

60 See Gutierrez and Houdaille, 'La mortalité maternelle en France', pp. 982–3, where results for Mogneneins and Rouen are also cited. Maternal mortality over age 40 was about 40 per cent above the overall rate in the 39 French parishes, and about 50 per cent in Mogneneins. However in Rouen maternal mortality rates did not vary significantly by age. An index of differences in age-specific maternal mortality rates was also estimated indirectly for the nine parishes in southern Sweden by comparing the distribution of maternal deaths by age with the age distribution of birth events given in the parish statistical tables. The implied maternal mortality rate over age 40 was 70 per cent higher than the overall rate. See the sources listed under table 9.4.

61 Schofield, 'English marriage patterns revisited', table 2, p. 10.

Table 9.7 A model of maternal mortality and 'background' mortality, by age

	15–19	20–24	25–34	35–44	45–49
	Per 1000 women per annum				
(1) Married[a]	25	308	643	757	735
(2) Marital fertility rate	0.411	0.413	0.332	0.187	0.028
(3) Birth events (1)×(2)	10	127	213	142	21
(4) Maternal mortality rate[b]	0.0104	0.0084	0.0124	0.0158	0.0158
(5) Maternal deaths (3)×(4)	0.10	1.07	2.64	2.24	0.33
(6) Background deaths	7.41	8.51	10.76	13.96	15.70
(7) 'Total' mortality (5)+(6)	7.51	9.58	13.40	16.20	16.03
(8) Percentage maternal (5)/(7)×100	1	11	20	14	2

[a] The value for the age group 45–49 was interpolated between the values for the age groups 35–44 and 45–54.
[b] The rates for the age groups 25–34 and 35–44 are averages of the values for the constituent age groups in table 9.6.
Sources
(1) Proportions married in 1851 census: B. R. Mitchell and P. Deane, *Abstract of British historical statistics* (Cambridge, 1962), p. 16
(2) Marital fertility rates (1600–1799): E. A. Wrigley and R. Schofield, 'English population history from family reconstitution: summary results, 1600–1799', *Population Studies* 37, (1983), p. 169.
(4) Table 9.6, 'total' rate
(6) A. J. Coale and P. Demeny, *Regional model life tables* (Princeton, 1966), North, level 8, $R=0$

(row 2).[62] For the approximate purposes of the calculation illegitimate fertility is ignored, since it was such a small component of total fertility.[63]

The third row of the table contains the product of the first two rows: that is, the number of birth events experienced each year by the 1000 women in each age group. These are the numbers of women exposed to the risk of maternal mortality, and it is already apparent that very few women aged under 20, or over 40, are in that position. Few of the former have begun their procreative career; almost all of the latter have already ended it. These figures are now multiplied by the appropriate age-specific maternal death rates to derive the number of deaths in childbed each year. The numbers are not large. Maternal mortality will have been most visible in the 25–34 age group, in which just under three maternal deaths occurred annually for every 1000 women of that age. In contrast, among those under 20 and over 45 maternal deaths were rare events, occurring every ten and three years respectively. Averaged over all age groups there were 1.3 deaths per year per 1000 women of reproductive age. Since a

62 Wrigley and Schofield, 'English population history from family reconstitution', p. 169.
63 See note 36 in this chapter.

large English village of say 1000 inhabitants contained about 250 women aged 15 to 49, the death of a fellow villager in childbed would occur on average only every third year.[64]

Moreover, death in childbed was far from being the only cause of death for women of reproductive age, and the dangers of childbirth are likely to have been evaluated not in isolation but relative to the chance of dying from other causes. The sixth row of the table gives the annual numbers of deaths that 1000 women in each age group would have experienced from non-maternal causes on the assumption that women had an expectation of life at birth of 37.5 years.[65] The maternal deaths in row 5 are added to these figures to arrive at the total annual number of deaths in each age group, which are presented in row 7. From the final row of the table it can be seen that maternal deaths were an insignificant fraction of all deaths occurring among women aged under 20 and over 45 years. At those ages death in childbed would have appeared to have been an insignificant cause of death, even though mothers over age 40 in fact ran the greatest risk of all. Among women aged 20–24 and 35–44, 11–14 per cent of the deaths (say one in eight) would have been caused by childbearing, while among the 25–34 age group the proportion would have been 20 per cent, or one in five. Thus it was only among women aged between their mid twenties and mid thirties that childbirth would have been seen as a significant, though still minor, cause of death.

The figures in table 9.7 suggest that it is doubtful that English women in the past would have had a clear and accurate appreciation of the different risks of dying in childbed run by women of different ages. Nevertheless, the larger question remains of whether the general level of maternal mortality in the past was sufficiently high for childbearing to be an occasion of fear. On the one hand, it needs to be remembered that a woman ran the risk of death each time she came to term, which on averge would have been six or seven times in the course of her reproductive career. Thus, with a maternal mortality rate of 10 per 1000 (1 per cent), as it was for much of the period before 1750, a woman on average would have run a 6 to 7 per cent risk of dying in childbed at some time in her procreative career.

On the other hand it is doubtful whether people in the past thought in terms of probabilities cumulated over a span of years; it is more likely that

---

64 The calculation assumes an equal number of males and females, hence 500 women. The proportion of women aged 14–49 (50 per cent) is taken from Coale and Demeny, *Regional model life tables*, model North, assuming mortality at level 8 (e_0 (female) = 37.5; e_0 (male + female) = 36.2), and population growth in the range 0 to 1.0 per cent per annum. Both assumptions seem reasonably representative of pre-industrial England; see Wrigley and Schofield, *Population history of England*, pp. 528–9. Because the model North tables underestimate female mortality in the reproductive age groups, the implied age structure will be somewhat inappropriate for pre-industrial England, but the inaccuracy is small.

65 For the mortality assumption, see note 64 in this chapter.

the dangers of childbirth were evaluated afresh towards the end of each pregnancy. In trying to reconstruct that evaluation in our imagination we need to remember that it was made against a much higher chance of dying from other causes than is the case today. During each of the two to three years which on average separated birth events in the past a woman would have faced a risk of dying outside childbed of between 7 and 16 per 1000, depending on her age (see table 9.7, row 6). That is, the risk of dying in childbed was no greater than the risk she ran every year of dying from infectious disease and a whole variety of other causes.

It is probably impossible for us to gauge how women in the past would have regarded the additional risk involved in childbearing in a world in which life was so much more uncertain than in our own. However, we can, perhaps, gain some subjective appreciation of the meaning of risks of this magnitude in our own world by recalling that a rate of 10 per 1000 is approximately the risk that a mother runs today of seeing her newborn child die before reaching the age of one year.[66] While most people know of cases of infant deaths, the incidence is so low that I suspect that most parents do not consider that their child is seriously at risk of dying in infancy. Similarly, in the distant past women will have known of others who died giving birth to a child; but they may also have considered it such a rare event that there was little risk that the tragedy would befall them.

When Peter Laslett entitled a chapter in *The World We Have Lost* with the provocative and rhetorical question: 'Did the peasants really starve?', he stimulated a stream of research which showed that although the risk of starving was much greater than is the case today, the incidence of starvation was lower than many historians had imagined it to have been. If we were to ask an analogous question 'Did the mothers really die?', the evidence presented in this paper suggests that the answer should be couched in similar terms. Undoubtedly the risk of dying in childbed was much higher than it is today, and many women died needlessly because of the inadequate obstetrical skill of those who attended them. But childbearing in 'the world we have lost' turns out to have been a rather less mortal occasion than we may have been inclined to believe.

66 United Nations, *Demographic Yearbook 1982*, p. 14.

10
Work, Welfare and the Family: An Illustration of the Adaptive Family Economy

Richard Wall

The Changing English Household

Certain historians of the English family, working mainly with evidence on upper-class families, have had very little difficulty in identifying particular family types with particular periods, even if these eras were inclined to overlap. Thus Lawrence Stone argued that there was an open lineage family from 1450 to 1630, a restricted patriarchal nuclear family from 1550 to 1700, and a closed domesticated nuclear family from 1640 to 1800.[1] Historians of the residential group or household have not found the identification of trends so simple. Indeed one of the very first discoveries by Peter Laslett was the near stability over time both in the size of household and in the principle that marriage entailed the formation of a new household.[2] More recently fresh evidence has been assembled enabling us to chart the development of the English household in much greater detail.[3] This is not to say that certain difficulties do not remain – difficulties occasioned by a shortage

This study was originally conceived as part of a broader comparison of household forms in England and Flanders, published in German as a contribution to M. Mitterauer and J. Ehmer (eds), *Familienstruktur und Arbeitsorganisation in Landlichen Gesellschaften* (Vienna, 1986). My thanks are due to these two editors and the editors of the present volume for their valuable advice offered in connection with the various drafts.

1 L. Stone, *The family, sex and marriage in England 1500–1800* (London, 1977).

2 P. Laslett, 'Mean household size in England since the sixteenth century', in P. Laslett and R. Wall (eds), *Household and family in past time* (Cambridge, 1972). The best-known exceptions in England to the principle of an independent household on marriage come from the post-industrial era. See M. Anderson, *Family structure in nineteenth century Lancashire* (Cambridge, 1971); M. Young and P. Willmott, *Family and kinship in East London* (London, 1957).

3 See R. Wall, 'Regional and temporal variations in the structure of the British household since 1851', in T. Barker and M. Drake (eds), *Population and society in Britain 1850–1980* (London, 1982); R. Wall, 'The household, demographic and economic change in England, 1650–1970', in R. Wall, J. Robin and P. Laslett (eds), *Family forms in historic Europe* (Cambridge, 1983).

of census-type evidence (listings) for the period before 1650, the absence of information on the ages of the inhabitants from all but a dozen of listings prior to 1821, and the near impossibility (before the nineteenth century) of marshalling information on the same community as that covered by an earlier enumeration.[4] In many cases the sources for other countries are superior,[5] and it is rather ironic therefore that the study of the household should have originated, and perhaps been carried furthest, in England.

Nevertheless, although it is not possible to produce a fine measure of the changes that have occurred, the main outlines of the English household since the seventeenth century are now clear. For this purpose we must look at the household not just in terms of size but in terms of membership, that is the number and proportion of persons within it classed as head, offspring, kin, servants and attached lodgers.[6] Thus the first phase (seventeenth to eighteenth centuries) involved a decline in the number of servants in the household, but this was more than offset by a rise in the number of kin and, more particularly, in the number of offspring; the result was that by the late eighteenth century households were, on average, some 8 per cent larger than had been the case in the late seventeenth century. During the second phase (up to 1851) there was a much sharper fall in the number of servants and a further rise in the number of kin. A much more fundamental transformation followed during the course of a long third phase (it is 1947 before a detailed breakdown of the membership of the household again becomes available at national level). It was this phase that saw marked falls in the number of offspring, servants and attached lodgers, though not, it now appears, in the number of resident kin.[7]

There is, therefore, a considerable amount of change to be explained and plausible explanations are certainly not lacking. It seems likely, for example, that the decline in the number of servants in the household between the late seventeenth and mid nineteenth centuries reflects the restructuring in the agricultural labour market as farmers, particularly in arable areas, came to prefer 'living-out' agricultural labourers to

4 A brief description of the information provided by each list can be found in the journal *Local Population Studies* beginning with issue 24 (Spring 1980).

5 Although even where the material is more abundant similar problems can arise; see T. Held, 'Rural retirement arrangements in seventeenth century to nineteenth century Austria: a cross-community analysis', *Journal of Family History* 7 (1982).

6 Lodgers are considered as being attached to rather than within the household, because their position in relation to the household is ambiguous. In some cases it may be true that they were employees of the household head and their status close to that of servants, but the more usual pattern seems to be one where lodgings were taken by persons lacking the wherewithal to establish independent households, either because of poverty or because of the temporary nature of their residence.

7 These trends and further changes after 1947 are documented in Wall, 'The household, demographic and economic change'.

'living-in' agricultural servants. This was their response to the rise in
the population and the fall in real wages during the eighteenth century,
which made labour relatively abundant and cheap at the same time as
they made feeding the labourer in one's home relatively expensive. In
such circumstances a natural reaction on the part of the farmers might
well be to switch from living-in farm servants to day labourers who had
to fend for themselves. Associated with this went a change in attitudes.
Farmers, more conscious of the social distance that separated them
from their employees, acquired a taste for privacy that required the
exclusion from their homes of resident sevants.[8]

Demographic factors can also be advanced to account for the rise in
the number of offspring and kin in English households between the
later seventeenth and late eighteenth centuries. During this period the
age structure became more youthful, as the fall in the age at marriage,
and an increase in the proportions of the population ever marrying and
in illegitimate fertility, combined to produced a marked rise in fertility.[9]
Since the type of households in which an individual lives and his
relationship to the household head is very much conditioned by age, it
is to be expected, on the basis of these figures alone, that households of
the late eighteenth century would differ from those of the late seventeenth and, most obviously, that there would be a rise in the number of
children in the household. This is, as we have seen, exactly what is
recorded in the listings evidence. In addition, the increase in the
number of kin in the household is in part a result of the alteration in
the age structure, which increased the number of persons in the young
age groups and therefore the number of persons at risk to become
grandchildren, nephews and nieces, while the greater tendency (with
lower marriage ages) for generations to overlap added to the number of
relatives with whom they might live. Attempts to offset the effects of
demographic expansion only added to the number of kin as parents
placed one of their children with their own parents, took in a daughter's illegitimate child, or were forced into various sharing arrangements as the demand for independent household units outstripped the
expansion of the housing stock.[10]

The Adaptive Family Economy

In the above account of the evolution of the English household the
relationship between family, household and the great economic and

8 See summaries to Question 38 of the Poor Law Report of 1834 summarized by A.
Kussmaul, *Servants in husbandry in early modern England* (Cambridge, 1981), pp. 128–9.

9 For the relative importance of these factors see E.A. Wrigley and R.S. Schofield, *The
population history of England* (London, 1981), p. 267, table 7.29.

10 Wall, 'The household, demographic and economic change', p. 507; and see later in this
chapter.

social changes of the nineteenth century seems at best indirect. There is, for example, the influence of the level of the real wage on age at marriage, and, through marriage, to the pace of household formation and the composition of the household. Occasionally the link between economic change and household forms seems not to exist at all. In this connection one might cite the fact that almost all social groups, from gentry and yeomen at the top of the social pyramid to labourers at the bottom, were more likely to have kin in their households in 1851 than had been the case in the later eighteenth century.[11] However, if we are interested in the relationship between household and family forms and the economy it is impossible to let the argument rest here. It is known that there was considerable variation between one English community and another both in average household size and in composition[12] – a variation that could be linked to the importance attached to access to land, or to the nature of the labour market, or to both in a variety of different combinations. It is also known that there were considerable differences according to the occupation of the household head in the number of children, servants and kin in the household.[13]

However, it is impossible to say, for example, why there were so few servants in one community or so many lodgers in another, unless one understands something of the process by which children left the parental home and eventually established their own households. Few censuses, unfortunately, provide details of non-resident members of the family, but the linking of information in the parish register with that on the same families in the census can reveal the number of children of each age who were away from the parental home on census night.[14] Certain types of household membership are also more revealing than others concerning the motives that led people to leave and join households of particular types. The age, sex and number of offspring residing with the household head is one such group. Kin constitute another in that opportunities as well as need influenced the range and type of kin present. It is particularly important to extend the investigation beyond the relational, age and marital status characteristics of the members of the household to include the work patterns of these persons. This is a topic justly considered important in relation to an understanding of household forms, yet surprisingly little detailed work has been done. The present study is, therefore, intended as a first attempt to test Peter

11 Ibid., table 16.5.

12 As an illustration of this variation one might cite the proportion of households consisting of three or more generations. In a quarter of settlements enumerated between 1750 and 1821 under 4 per cent of households spanned three generations while in another quarter 10 per cent did so. R. Wall, 'Regional and temporal variations in English household structure from 1650', in J. Hobcraft and P. Rees (eds), *Regional demographic development* (London, 1977).

13 See Laslett, 'Mean household size', p. 154.

14 R. Wall, 'The age at leaving home', *Journal of Family History* 3 (1978); and see figure 10.2.

Laslett's argument concerning the frequent failure of household and family to function as work groups.[15]

In order to explore such patterns in the requisite detail, however, it is prudent to limit both the aspects of the household and the number of communities to be investigated. It was decided to concentrate in the first instance on one nineteenth-century community. The nineteenth century, it is claimed, saw a change from the *family economy* to the *family wage economy*.[16] Under the family economy, the family was the unit of production and consumption and the household the locus of work and residence. Family members were retained in the household to fulfil its labour requirements, while those whose labour was not needed left to find work elsewhere. By contrast one of the cardinal tenets of the family wage economy is that there was no limit to the number of wage-earners that a wage-earning family could use and hence no limit to the number of children who could live at home.[17]

In practice, neither the family economy nor the family wage economy, in these particular formulations, corresponds very well with reality. A major weakness with the model of the family wage economy is the failure to take account of the social and economic divisions within society which gave employers the power to direct not only what labour should be employed but where that labour should reside. The family economy, on the other hand, appears to exclude the very possibility of wage labour. In its place we would like to reformulate the model of the family economy to take due account of the wide range of employment on offer and the varied responses of those persons who had to survive on the proceeds of their labour. To emphasize the key characteristic – flexibility – our preferred term for the new model would be the *adaptive family economy*. It would function in a way that would avoid any simple dichotomy between families needing household labourers and families needing cash. On the contrary, it would be expected that families would attempt to maximize their economic well-being by diversifying the employments of family members.

This, then, would be our sketch of the adaptive family economy. It is our contention that the notion of the adaptive family economy will help particularly in the interpretation of societies at the point of transition, where proto-industrial, household-based labour coexisted with a wage economy. In terms of specific occupational groups within a population

15 P. Laslett, 'Family and household as work group and kin group: areas of traditional Europe compared', in Wall et al., *Family forms in historic Europe*.
16 The following account is based principally on L.A. Tilly and J.W. Scott, *Women, work and the family* (New York, 1978), pp. 12, 14.
17 Ibid., p. 141. Exceptions are made for areas without adequate employment opportunities. Daughters in particular might have had to leave for positions as domestic servants. These important qualifications appear to be missing from the recent summary by J. Quadagno, *Ageing in early industrial society* (New York and London, 1982), p. 62.

it seems likely that the adaptive family economy will bear a close affinity to the circumstances faced by the members of craftsmen's or artisans' families without being the exclusive property of this group. Even farmers and labourers could participate in the adaptive family economy when presented, respectively, with opportunities for employment outside the parental home and the growth in proto-industrial activities within the home. The extent to which the adaptive family economy was realized in the chosen nineteenth-century community will be the focus of the present study.

The Farmers, Craftsmen and Labourers of Colyton

Colyton, a parish in the south-west of England, makes a good choice for study in that it comprises a small market town with an extensive agricultural hinterland. It is possible therefore to study the households of the craftsmen and the small tradesmen that congregated in a small town as well as the households of farmers and agricultural labourers. The main advantage of working on Colyton, however, is that it has already been studied intensively in connection with its demographic history.[18]

Admittedly, there is a danger in working on the social structure of one parish in that it may turn out to be atypical of its region or its period, let alone of the country in general, in ways that may be difficult to foresee. Were the objective to find a typical English parish (if such exists), this would indeed be a serious objection. It matters less when, as in the present case, the intention is to describe the relationship between the social structure and a particular economic structure. Any special features appertaining to the latter should become clear as we proceed.

In Colyton farms were small and were rented rather than owner-occupied, and the land was worked by a combination of family labour, resident servants and day labourers (see table 10.11). Unlike the situation that seems to have prevailed in many of the rural areas of central Europe, the farmers did not contribute the most stable element within the community. Whereas two-thirds of the craftsmen resident in Colyton in 1851 had been born there, more than half of the men farming in Colyton in 1851 were natives of other parishes. Some of this mobility may have been occasioned by the need to find suitable farms, although

18 E.A. Wrigley, 'Family limitation in pre-industrial England', *Economic History Review* 19 (1966), pp. 82–109; E.A. Wrigley, 'Mortality in pre-industrial England: the example of Colyton, Devon, over three centuries', *Daedalus* (1968), pp. 546–80; E.A. Wrigley, 'The changing occupational structure of Colyton over two centuries', *Local Population Studies* 18 (1977), pp. 9–21.

it is surprising in how many cases a tenanted farm could pass from one member of the family to another.[19]

The situation is therefore that, as measured by the proportion born outside the parish, the craftsmen of Colyton appear a more stable group than the farmers. However, the distinction between parishioners and non-parishioners, while a relevant one for parochial authorities in that it granted certain rights in the community, may not have been the factor that the inhabitants used to distinguish 'natives' from 'strangers'. The craftsmen were generally to be found in the town of Colyton, while the farmers were in the outlying parts of the parish and many had not migrated far even though they had crossed a parish boundary.[20]

Another problem with occupation groups is the social divisions within them. In the case of the farmers these are fairly easy to identify through the information in the census on farm size. The craftsmen present more difficulties because so few were accorded the title either of 'master' or of 'journeyman'.[21] Most of the others may have worked on a casual basis for a number of employers, or they may have been self-employed, or have alternated between the two. They constitute a group that is difficult to place within the traditional hierarchy of master, journeyman and apprentice – a hierarchy that could in any case be said to be weakening, with a number of journeymen (although no apprentices) heading their own households. In terms of Frederick Le Play's categorization of workers they straddle the three groups of day workers, taskers and the self-employed.[22]

Even with labourers there are some problems of this sort. Certainly they formed their own households, but it is not known whether they worked for one employer or for a succession of employers on a more casual basis. The juxtaposition of some cottages and farms implies that some may have been 'tied' to a particular farmer, in the sense that if they left his service they would have to quit their cottage. However,

19 Twenty-nine farms listed in the 1851 census can be identified as tenanted farms in the Poor Rate Assessment of 1835. Of these, 12 were still occupied by the same farmer in 1851, and a further nine by another member of his family. Eight farms were occupied by persons with no known relationship to the previous tenant. Other farms referred to in 1851 comprised three that were owner-occupied and 14 that could not be traced under that name in the Poor Rate Assessment.

20 A provisional estimate supplied by Jean Robin indicates that, although 52 per cent of the farmers could be described as 'migrants', only about a fifth had not been born either in Colyton itself or in an immediately adjacent parish.

21 Of the 36 craftsmen household heads in the first of the Colyton enumeration districts (where occupation is well recorded; see p. 275) three were styled 'masters' and a further five were recorded as employing either apprentices or journeymen. Nine household heads were specified as journeymen, leaving just over half the group described simply in terms of their craft without any indication as to their standing in it.

22 *Ouvriers-journaliers, ouvriers-tacherons* and *ouvriers chefs de métier*; see F. le Play, *Les ouvriers Européens* vol. I, 2nd edn (Tours, 1878), pp. 230–3.

there were insufficient cottages available in the vicinity of the farms for all the labourers, and many lived within the town of Colyton. Other factors being equal, they should have found it easier than their colleagues in the tied cottages to move from one employer to another.[23] Although it is customary to class labouring as an unskilled or at best a semi-skilled occupation,[24] within the ranks of labourers a number could be found with special skills (hedging, for example) for which farmers might have an occasional rather than a permanent need. Few of these skills, however, were to be recorded in the enumerators' books. One individual is described as a farmer's carter (perhaps to distinguish him from a general carter), and thatchers[25] and dairymen were separately specified. The latter frequently employed a dairymaid and would appear to have occupied a position in the social hierarchy intermediate between that of labourer and farmer. Indeed, a dairyman may have been an English example of Le Play's *ouvrier-tenancier*, leasing from a farmer a part at least of the means of production (cowshed, appurtenances, and perhaps the stock) which he was unable or disinclined to use on his own account.[26] This type of arrangement has been documented for other dairying areas in the west of England and is likely to have applied to Colyton.[27] Thatchers and dairymen, because of their special characteristics, are therefore classed separately from other agricultural occupations in what follows.[28]

23 One of the reasons why the workings of the labour market remain shrouded in so much obscurity is that the census noted only the number and not the names of the farmers' non-resident employees. In other words, it is not possible to discover who employed a particular labourer.

24 See W.A. Armstrong, 'The use of information about occupation', appendix A in E.A. Wrigley (ed.), *Nineteenth century society* (Cambridge, 1972). In the censuses of 1921 and 1951 agricultural labourers were classed as semi-skilled and other labourers as unskilled. No such distinction is attempted in the present paper. A few labourers within the town part of Colyton were employed in the local tannery, but these were too few for separate categorization in the tables to follow.

25 Thatchers have not been classed as craftsmen, alongside carpenters, builders etc., since it is likely that thatchers were as much involved with the thatching of hayricks as the thatching of houses.

26 Le Play, *Les ouvriers*, vol. I, pp. 231–2.

27 S.G. Kendall, *Farming memories of a West Country yeoman* (London, 1944), p. 15. I would like to thank Jean Robin for drawing my attention to this reference.

28 In tables 10.1, 10.2 and 10.4 they are classed with other miscellaneous occupations as 'others', as there are insufficient cases to justify separate analysis. The same problem of ensuring that there is an adequate number of cases in observation also means that for some of the finer analysis of the social structure (see table 10.5) it would be pointless including any but the largest occupational groups. On the other hand, for the less refined measures – the number of households with offspring or relatives – it is possible to extend the analysis to cover six occupational categories (see tables 10.1 and 10.2). Whenever possible, households headed by women are analysed separately from those headed by men to allow for the investigation of the independent influence of gender on the composition of the household.

Occupation and Household Composition

Table 10.1 shows the frequency of households of particular types. In Colyton no more than seven out of ten households contained offspring of the household head. Relatives and servants were found in approximately one in five and inmates in one in eight. There was considerable variation according to the sex and occupation of the head of the household. Female-headed households were less likely to contain offspring but more likely to contain relatives and have attached inmates than were households headed by men. Farmers and the professionals, as might be expected, were the most likely to have servants living with them. Of greater significance is the fact that not all were in this position, since it is an indication of both varying income levels within the groups[29] and the existence of other sources of labour, the latter being particularly important in the case of farmers (see table 10.11).

Other results are not so easy to anticipate or explain, as for example the fact that farmers and the poor were much more likely than other

Table 10.1　Proportion of households with offspring, relatives, servants and attached inmates

			Percentage of households with:			
Sex of head	*Occupational group of head*	*No.*	*Offspring*	*Relatives*	*Servants*	*Attached inmates*
M	Commerce	42	76	18	29	17
	Craftsmen	122	81	21	15	10
	Farmers	43	67	32	74	2
	Labourers	148	81	17	0	14
	Professional[a]	32	41	28	53	9
	Poor	14	79	36	0	14
	Others	47	47	21	23	15
	All	448	73	22	20	12
F	All	67	63	27	22	24
M+F	All	515	71	22	20	13

[a]　Includes persons with unearned income, e.g. annuitants.

29　It would appear that a number of farmers returned themselves as such when they held little more than a smallholding (see table 10.11). The position in regard to the professional group is different in that the category is our own construction, not that of the census-makers, and in its inclusion of annuitants and a range of professions is likely to encompass people in different economic circumstances.

groups in the Colyton population to have relatives living with them. One should, however, be wary of assuming that it was the occupation of the household head (or his lack of occupation) that was instrumental in shaping the form of his household. Age and marital status (neither represented in table 10.1) were important intervening variables, and there can be no doubt that it was the presence of so many elderly and non-married household heads among the professional group that resulted in such a low proportion of their households containing offspring.[30]

The Life Cycle

An essential preliminary to a study of age on entry into the workforce or age at leaving home is an understanding of the overall life cycle of the individual. We have therefore attempted to illustrate the life cycle by setting out the census population according to age, sex and relationship to the household head. For each age group figure 10.1 shows what proportion of the population were heads of household, or occupied other positions within the household such as offspring, relatives and servants, or were classed as inmates.[31] The range of options, however, is not so great as to obscure the main features of the individual's life cycle.

In Colyton only a small minority of men came to head a household during their early twenties.[32] Between the ages of 30 and 60, nine out of ten men headed their own household. After the age of 60, however, the proportion fell slightly, indicating a limited degree of 'retirement' from headship. Evidence is now available to suggest that this was quite a characteristic feature of English populations.[33] The hiatus between leaving the parental household and forming a new household was occupied by a number of transitional roles of which that of servant remained clearly the most important, even for males.

A conceivable alternative, though never very popular, was lodging, the rise of which is somewhat masked in figure 10.1 by the inclusion in younger age groups of a number of boys boarding at two small schools in the town. In sharp contrast the variation over the life cycle in the proportion of the male population comprising relatives of the household head looks almost random.

---

30 Households headed by women had the highest proportion of attached inmates, no doubt because the subletting of house room was one of the chief ways in which a woman might hope to generate additional income to compensate in part for the absence of the chief breadwinner. Very few households were headed by spinsters. On the household position of never-married women in pre-industrial England, see R. Wall, 'Women alone in English society', *Annales de démographie historique* (1981), pp. 303–17.

31 See note 6 in this chapter.

32 With a larger population it would have been feasible (see the role of children, figure 10.3) to examine the movement into headship by single year. As it is, it is impossible to determine whether the marked rise in the headship rate began at age 23 or 24 rather than 25.

33 R. Wall, 'Introduction', in Wall et al., *Family forms in historic Europe*, p. 37, figure 1.1

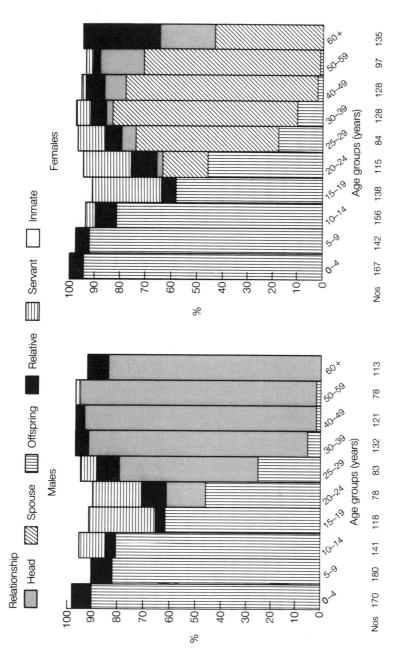

Figure 10.1   Population by age, sex and relationship to household head

Many of the same elements show up in the female life cycle. Just under half of all women in their early twenties were still living with their parents, as was the case with men of the same age. Service, though starting later and lasting somewhat longer than was the case for males, was again a feature of adolescence and early adulthood. Lodging was minimal. By their late twenties more than half of the women had married and were running their own households, as were three-quarters of all women aged 30–59. In addition a few women headed their own households, some even when still in their twenties, although the majority of such women were considerably older. The chief difference from the life cycle of the male arises from the greater number of relatives of the head, particularly among the elderly. More women over the age of 60 entered the household of a relative (usually that of a son or daughter: see table 10.9) than moved into lodgings or headed their own households. In Michael Anderson's now famous portrayal of a nineteenth-century textile town (Preston), this presence of the head's mother or mother-in-law freed the younger woman for employment outside the home.[34] However, we can see that the employment patterns of married women were not such as to require such support.[35]

Further variation in the individual life cycle is to be expected according to the social status of the individual concerned or that of the family from which he or she originated. Fortunately, as far as children are concerned a considerable amount can be inferred by measuring any variation with the occupation of the head in the number and sex ratio of offspring of different ages. In the present case the emphasis will be on the sex ratio of resident offspring over the age of ten, in order to discover whether particular occupational groups, notably farmers and artisans, were inclined to retain sons at home rather than daughters because of the higher labour value placed on their labour. A sex ratio of much over 100 would indicate a preference for sons, of much under 100 a similar preference for daughters, and close or slightly below 100 (to allow for higher male than female infant and child mortality) that the sex of the child was largely irrelevant in the determination of residence patterns. The reality in Colyton was that rather more sons than daughters would leave the parental home but with considerable variation between one occupational group and another (table 10.2). The movement out of sons was most pronounced in the case of those least likely to be able to offer those sons work at home and whose economic need was greatest (labourers and the smaller occupational

34 Anderson, *Family structure in nineteenth century Lancashire*, p. 142.

35 The first of Colyton's enumeration districts contained 57 craftsmen's or labourers' wives said to be employed (see table 10.6). Of these, 14 at most may have been working outside the home. This maximum estimate can only be produced by assuming first that washerwomen, laundresses and the one charwoman worked in the homes of their employers, and secondly that what the census termed 'domestic' represented a non-residential servant and was not a synonym for housewife.

Table 10.2   Sex ratio of offspring by occupation and sex of family head

Sex of head	Occupational group of head	No.	Offspring aged:				
			10–14	*15–19*	*20–24*	*≥25*	*≥10*
M	Commerce	43	175	(100)	(100)	(50)	126
	Craftsmen	149	94	113	53	(200)	96
	Farmers	80	93	(129)	122	(143)	116
	Labourers	148	84	74	50	(60)	74
	Others	67	69	82	(60)	(71)	72
	All	487	92	96	69	108	90
F	All	63	(89)	57	(43)	(180)	80

Brackets indicate ratios based on fewer than 20 cases.
The sex ratio is calculated as the number of males per 100 females in each category.

groups classed as 'other'). Only farmers and tradesmen showed any tendency to keep sons at home in preference to daughters. In an intermediate position, contrary to what we had anticipated, were the craftsmen with slightly more sons than daughters away from home.

Table 10.2 is also laid out to allow for comparison of the sex ratios of different age groups of children. Leaving the parental home would not be, in the past, a sudden, once and for all affair. The reasons for this are not hard to seek. A number of jobs were tailored to persons of a particular age and employers would not automatically re-employ individuals at the end of the hiring year, given that a more demanding position (and higher rate of pay) was now their due.[36] Children might, therefore, leave and then return to the parental home because they found themselves temporarily out of a service position as well as because their parents required assistance. In addition some older sons may have returned in anticipation of their inheritance. It is more likely than not, therefore, that the sex ratio of the child group will not be the same over the child's life cycle, although some of this volatility may well be the product of random variation. On the other hand, there are occasions on which the trends seem reasonably clear. The first concerns the children of labourers for whom the sex ratio declines steadily with the age of the child, indicating an ever more marked exodus of sons; the reverse was true in the case of farmers' offspring.

36 This is well documented for domestic servants. See, for example, T. McBride, *The domestic revolution* (London, 1976), p. 75. For farm servants, see Kussmaul, *Servants in husbandry*, pp. 37–8.

Although not all the sons of labourers would have become servants in the households of farmers, there is some connection between the two trends represented in the redistribution of labour to where it could most usefully be employed.

Table 10.2 also makes clear the rise in the sex ratio for offspring over the age of 25. The rise is most marked when the head of the household was a craftsman or a widow and might suggest that a residual number of sons were remaining in, or returning to, the parental home, in advance of their inheritance. It would be unwise, however, to draw too close an association between staying on in the parental home and an inheritance, either actual or prospective. This becomes clearer if we examine in more detail the composition of the group of coresident offspring aged 25 and over. Not only were there very few, as might be expected from the need to identify such households at a particular point of the head's life cycle, but there were as many households with daughters over the age of 25 as sons (table 10.3). On the assumption that these families would be looking for a male heir when they had the possibility, this must suggest that inheritance, as a factor persuading offspring to remain in the parental home, was outweighed by other considerations.

Table 10.3   Households with offspring aged 25 and over

Composition of Offspring group ≥25	no.
Son, no daughters	19
≥2 sons, no daughter	3
Son and daughter	7
Daughter, no son	19
≥2 daughters, no son	3
Other combinations	1
Total[a]	52
Total households	515

[a]   There are four households with two or more sons and four with two or more daughters.

Home, School and Work

An analysis of the number of sons and daughters resident with their parents as a proportion of all offspring born and surviving at the time of the census can throw further light on why some remained at home longer than others. Earlier work established the importance in this regard of the occupation and marital status of the parent.[37] However, a further variable

37 Wall, 'The age at leaving home' pp. 196–9.

ought to be taken into account: the ability of the child to find suitable employment while continuing to reside in the parental home. This type of exercise requires both thorough recording of children's occupations and an intricate linking of parish register and census to establish the proportion of children living away from home at the time of the census. The exercise is limited in this instance to the offspring of families living in the first of the five enumeration districts into which Colyton was divided. Extension of the analysis to cover the other enumeration districts and the question of the relationship between child employment, leaving home and the occupation of the head of the household had to be omitted for practical reasons.[38] Nevertheless the results of this exercise (displayed in figure 10.2) reveal some important aspects of the early part of the life cycle, which may be summarized in the following way. Although girls entered school earlier than boys, fewer attended thereafter. Girls also entered the workforce earlier. A quarter of daughters aged between five and nine and living at home were employed (all as lace-makers) compared with only 5 per cent of similarly situated sons. Only very rarely was a girl at home over the age of ten and apparently unemployed, although a number of boys (almost a quarter of the entire age group 10–14) were in this position. On the other hand, boys left the parental home earlier. It seems likely, in fact, that these two facets of the male's life cycle were correlated in that the sons' earlier movement out of the parental home was precipitated by their failure to find suitable employment that permitted continued residence with their parents. In such ways the character of the local labour market set limits on the amount of time either a boy or a girl would be able to spend at home or in school.

Some modification in the general pattern is only to be expected, however, depending on the ability (or indeed the need) of the parent to have a child at home. This can be seen in figure 10.3, which shows for labourers and craftsmen how many of their sons and daughters were at home (and unemployed), attending school or working. The breakdown by single year (as opposed to the five-year age blocks of figure 10.2) also emphasizes the extent to which these various phases in the life cycle could

38 Extension to some of the other enumeration districts would be possible, although in the first district (covering approximately half of the town of Colyton) the recording of occupations was more thorough. Only here is the occupation of the wife of the household head reported regularly; even very young children are returned in the column for occupations as being 'at home', leaving little room for doubt that they lacked an occupation. A study of the variation with the occupation of the household head in the proportion of children at home with their parents is impractical because on its own the first enumeration district yields an insufficient number of cases. No detailed results will therefore be presented, although it can be said that the figures do confirm that the sons and daughters of labourers left the parental home at an earlier age than the sons and daughters of craftsmen. For school and employment patterns a larger population can be used (as no linkage with the parish registers is involved), and information on school attendance and work patterns of the offspring of labourers and craftsmen will be presented in figure 10.3.

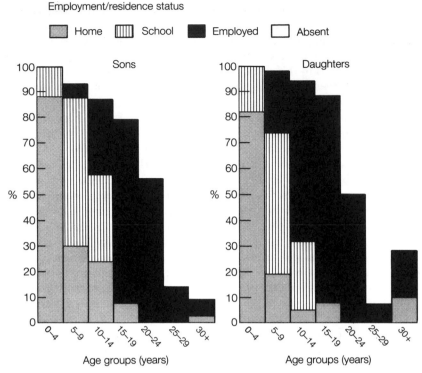

Figure 10.2 School, work and leaving home
Population in observation: offspring whose fathers were still alive in 1851 and resident in the town of Colyton, first enumeration district.

overlap. There was no set age for entering school or beginning work. Boys, for example, were at home from birth until age nine, at school between the ages of three and 13 and at work from the age of nine. Girls were at home until the age of six, at school from three to 11, and at work from the age of seven. Apart from this variability the most notable features of this life cycle profile were the curtailment of girls' schooling, and their earlier appearance in the labour force. Whether their father was a craftsman or a labourer made some difference to the length of their schooling, but did not alter the basic pattern. Nevertheless any interpretation of the life cycle of the individual needs to take account of parental occupation. Sons of labourers were in the labour force at age nine, sons of craftsmen only at age 14. No labourer's son was kept at school beyond the age of 11, while some craftsmen's sons were still at school at the age of 12 or 13.[39]

39 It has to be borne in mind that these figures refer to the earliest and latest ages at which children were at school and are not to be taken as implying a period of continuous schooling. There was also considerable variance around the mean in regard to both school attendance and age at entry into the labour force.

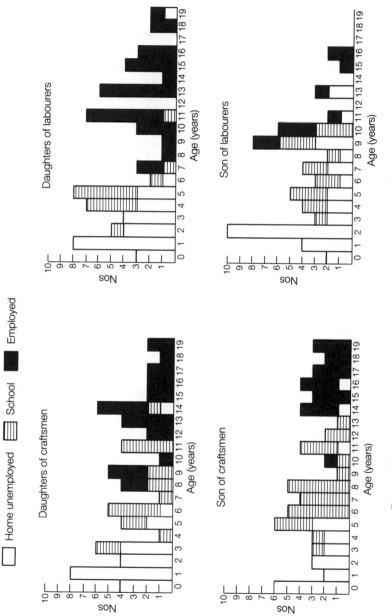

Employment status

☐ Home unemployed ▥ School ■ Employed

Daughters of craftsmen

Son of craftsmen

Daughters of labourers

Son of labourers

Age (years)

Nos

Figure 10.3 Employment of offspring by age, sex and occupational group of father
Population in observation: offspring of craftsmen and labourers in the town of Colyton, first
enumeration district

Similar differences applied in regard to girls' schooling. Brought to an end at the age of seven for the daughters of labourers, schooling could be extended up to the age of 11 for a craftsman's daughter. There was, however, rather less variation in the age at which these girls commenced work (labourers' daughters from the age of seven; craftsmen's daughters from the age of eight). This indicates the way in which lace-making encouraged labour on to the market from families in quite different economic circumstances. In this case the need of these families (as measured in absolute not relative terms) to make full use of their children's labour was not the decisive influence on their work patterns.

A further question that now arises is how many of the children still at home, and in employment, were actually employed by or working alongside their parents. Matching the child's occupation with that of the parent (father or mother) does allow an approximate answer, although there is always the danger of overstating the numbers because not all the practitioners of the commoner trades such as thatchers or masons were necessarily working for their fathers.[40] Nevertheless, at most 28 per cent of employed sons under the age of 20 and 47 per cent of employed daughters can possibly have been employed by their parents.[41] A glance at the range of occupations pursued by the youth of Colyton is sufficient to reveal why these percentages are so low. A number of boys were apprenticed to a trade that was not that of their father, yet were continuing to reside at home. Others were employed as ploughboys, errand boys or labourers. Girls had a much narrower range of occupations open to them, and it is perhaps for this reason that a higher proportion shared the occupation of their mother than did boys that of their father. Of those girls in employment under the age of 20, more than nine out of ten were employed as lace-makers, and lace-making accounted for all but two of those working with their mothers.[42] On the other hand, almost half of all child lace-makers were to be found in families where the mother pursued a different occupation or had withdrawn from the labour market. Clearly, many families were not functioning as integrated work units even when allowance is made for the subdivision of the labour force following the attribution of occupations according to gender.

Enough evidence has now been assembled to raise some wider issues concerning the relationship between the family, the household and the structuring of the economy. The number of sons resident in the parental home but employed outside it establishes that Colyton does not exhibit the full set of characteristics associated with a society organized on the

40 Assumed to be working for their fathers were four thatchers, two masons, two mason's labourers, one apprentice brazier, one glover, one harness-maker and one journeyman paper-maker.

41 Allowance for children away from the parental home (see figure 10.2) would reduce these percentages further to 22 per cent (sons) and 45 per cent (daughters).

42 The exceptions were one shoebinder assisting her father and one school assistant.

basis of a family economy. Neither, however, does Colyton sit happily within its successor, the family wage economy. In particular, a not negligible proportion of offspring in Colyton were employed elsewhere as apprentices or servants.[43] The variety of employments held by members of the same household is indicative rather of a diversified, more flexible attitude to employment by both employer and worker, characteristic of what was earlier termed the adaptive family economy.

Working Wives

The analysis of the household as a work group, however, would be incomplete without some reference to the proportion of married women in the labour force. According to the theory of the family wage economy the work patterns of women took on a classic life-cycle pattern. Women worked[44] when young and unmarried, then withdrew from the labour market until necessity, occasioned by the unemployment of the husband, widowhood or old age, drew them back in.[45] Women's work patterns under the family economy are less clear cut. They may have worked fewer days in the year than men, but taking one year with another it is customary to assume that their productive role was exercised continuously.[46] The whole issue is further complicated by the lack of adequate statistics on the employment of women, arising no doubt both from the part-time nature of some tasks and from the association of others with the main employment of the husband (for example the role of farmer's wife). The result is that it is very easy to understate the extent of the involvement of women in the labour force. In the present case considerable care has been taken to select only that section of the enumeration of Colyton where the occupations of married women were regularly reported. Since this produces a rate of labour force participation by all married women of 56 per cent (table 10.4), a figure in excess of that which David Levine has identified as sufficiently high to encourage early marriage by proto-industrial workers,[47] the question arises of whether the

43 See figures 10.1 and 10.2. It is difficult to discover the actual occupations of children who had left the parental home because so many migrated to neighbouring parishes. An examination of the occupations of in-migrating young people, however, signals the importance of service and apprenticeship.

44 The definition of 'work' is that of involvement in cash-raising activities. Most women would also have had to devote a certain amount of time to housework regardless of any other commitments.

45 Quadagno, *Ageing in early industrial society*, p. 143 again makes the more extreme statement. Tilly and Scott, however, had again recognized that patterns might vary considerably from city to city: Tilly and Scott, *Women, work and the family*, p. 136.

46 Cf. Tilly and Scott, *Women, work and the family*, pp. 50, 136.

47 D. Levine, *Family formation in an age of nascent capitalism* (London, 1977), p. 51. Yet if farmers' wives are added to the number of Colyton women in the labour force, the married women's employment rate rises to 61 per cent.

Table 10.4   Employment status of married women by husband's occupation[a]

Husband's occupational group	Married women	
	Employed	Total
Commerce	6	15
Craftsmen	26	43
Farmers	0	4
Labourers	31	41
Poor	4	6
Professional[b]	0	5
Others	4	8
Total	71	122

[a] Analysis restricted to the first of the five enumeration districts into which Colyton was divided in 1851.
[b] Includes husbands with unearned income, e.g. annuitants.

proportion of married women in employment has been artificially inflated by the selection of one particular enumeration district. However, this seems unlikely for two reasons. First, there is nothing in the occupational structure of the various enumeration districts to indicate that the female labour force might have been recruited almost exclusively from a particular part of Colyton town. There are differences in the social and economic complexion of the various districts, but these chiefly involve a major division between the three outlying districts and the two town districts. The former contained fewer craftsmen but a higher proportion of farmers. The proportion of married women in the labour force is therefore unlikely to have been much lower than that recorded for a town district, given that farmers' wives should be considered as employed.

The second reason why one should consider a labour force participation rate of 56 per cent as no over-statement is that the variation in the rate according to husband's occupation is entirely plausible. Three-quarters of those most likely to be in need – the wives of labourers – were in the labour force compared with six out of ten of the women married to craftsmen, and four out of ten of the women whose husbands were tradesmen.

It is more difficult, however, to identify any clear trend in the rate of labour force participation over the life cycle (table 10.5). Wives of craftsmen would appear to have withdrawn gradually from the labour force, with women aged under 30 registering the highest rates of employment and women over 60 the lowest. On the other hand, the employment rates of labourers' wives remain at a high level subject only to what on these small numbers are probably random fluctuations.

Consideration of the type of work undertaken by married women (table 10.6) adds another dimension to our concept of the adaptive family

Table 10.5 Wives of craftsmen and labourers by employment status and age

	Husband's occupational group[a]			
	Craftsmen		Labourers	
Age of wife	Employed	Total	Employed	Total
20–24	–	–	2	4
25–29	4	5	6	8
30–39	8	13	12	13
40–49	8	11	7	10
50–59	4	9	2	3
⩾60	2	5	2	3
Total	26	43	31	41

[a] Selected occupational groups from enumeration district 1.

Table 10.6 Wives of craftsmen and labourers by occupational group

	Husband's occupational group[a]			
	Craftsmen		Labourers	
Occupational group	Colyton born	Others	Colyton born	Others
Domestic	4	4	1	6
Lace-makers	10	5	13	10
Other	2	1	0	1
Total employed	16	10	14	17
No occupation[b]	5	11	4	6
Total	21	21	18	23

[a] Selected occupational groups from enumeration district 1.
[b] Excludes one case where there was no information as to place of birth.

economy. Very few were primarily involved with their husband's employment,[48] even though it is probable that the majority were able to find work without leaving their homes. Lace-making was undoubtedly the key factor here. However, it was not the dominant employment that it was for girls under the age of 20, being supplemented by a variety of domestic

48 Only four (two grocers, two milliners) out of the total of 71 married women in the labour force.

employments probably performed outside the home.[49] Even wives of
craftsmen might sometimes be found working as laundresses and washerwomen. One reason for this may be that 'craftsmen' under the present
definition span a broad section of society (see p. 267). However, it would
be as well to bear in mind that although domestic work is now almost
invariably regarded as low-status employment, it was not necessarily
always so in the past. Moreover, no information is available on the
relative amount that might be earned for a morning's lace-making in
comparison with a morning's domestic work.[50] What is clear from table
10.6 is that those women working as lace-makers were more likely than
others to have resided in the parish since birth. Locally born wives of
labourers in particular showed a marked reluctance to undertake any
work other than the making of lace. This points to the importance of
tradition as a determinant of employment patterns. Yet it was a tradition
that, even if handed down from mother to daughter, did not necessarily
require the mother and daughter to be employed at the same time (see
p. 278). Nor did it predetermine immobility. The lace-making area
covered more than one parish and a number of lace-makers moved into
Colyton from other parishes. On the other hand, for those women without
the necessary skills in lace-making, domestic work provided one means by
which they could support their families regardless of where the migration
current might lead them.

To complete the picture, a brief comment is required on those married
women who remained outside the labour force (table 10.6, last but one
row). One interpretation of the association among craftsmen's wives of the
lack of an occupation and movement into the parish would be that it was
produced by the inclusion in the category of craftsmen of a number of
wealthier individuals whose wives did not need to enter the labour force.
This presupposes a distinct pattern of migration on the part of this group
of craftsmen which would need to be the subject of further investigation.
As far as labourers' wives are concerned, however, it seems clear that
there was no association between exclusion from the labour force and
migration.

The Role of Relatives within the Household

The small number of relatives to be found in English households renders it
unlikely that they could have made as significant a contribution towards

49 Occupations classed as domestic with the numbers of women involved are as follows:
washerwomen (five), laundresses (four), domestic (four), charwoman (one) and nurse (one),
although there is a problem over the appearance in the census of the term 'domestic' since it
might indicate the role of housewife rather than any additional employment.
50 There may be some significance in the fact that four of the five washerwomen had
husbands who were labourers, whereas six of the eight domestics and laundresses were
married to craftsmen, but with so few cases on which to draw it is impossible to be sure.

the economic well-being of the household as would wives and offspring. As will be demonstrated, relatives had only a minor role to play in this regard and one must look elsewhere to account for their presence. One may begin by noting that two sets of factors could be involved. The first arose from the circumstances of the host family that made possible or even desirable the receipt of kin. The second reflected the need of the individual relative for employment or care. The requirements of the host family are not easy to assess from the information at our disposal. The census indicates occupations, not wealth, and the small number of cases precludes effective use even of occupation. However, a start can be made on inferring some of the possible needs of the host household using information on the sex, marital status and age of the household head. The type of relative present can be inferred in a similar manner by the use of a combination of criteria: age, relationship, marital status and shared occupation with the household head. Given a larger number of cases, a more complete analysis of the presence of relatives according to the life-cycle stage of the household might have been desirable. However, it is our view that the concept of the life cycle has been overvalued, too simply defined in many conventional studies by sole reference to the age of the household head, or by the imposition of arbitrary categories that may not reflect reality in the population in question.[51]

Certainly in Colyton the age and marital status of the household head would seem to have little influence on the presence of relatives in the household. In tables 10.7 and 10.8 all the households containing relatives have been divided according to whether the head was male or female, above or below 60, married or non-married and, if married, whether childless. The elderly, the widowed and the childless were, it was considered, among the groups most likely to need the support of a relative, although not always with the advantage of the largest circle of relatives from which to draw.[52] Yet as the final columns of table 10.7 and 10.8 show, over a third of all relatives in Colyton were to be found in other types of household. This would seem to indicate that many kin did not perform a specific service role. However, the categories of households in need may be too crude for the purpose. Where one can refer to the reconstitution, it is sometimes possible to deduce what the role of kin

51 The latter approach is represented by the too-casual adoption of the life-cycle categories in Anderson, *Family structure in nineteenth century society*, p. 202, n. 46.

52 The unmarried seem likely to have the smallest pool of relatives. The variation in the number of relatives according to the age of the head is one of the results which should be forthcoming from the simulations of family and household composition currently being undertaken by James Smith, visiting fellow at the ESRC Cambridge Group for the History of Population and Social Structure, 1982–3. At the time of writing it is still unclear whether the increase in the number of grandchildren with the age of the head will wholly compensate for the loss due to mortality at older ages of many of the relatives of the head's own generation. Simulations of some of the specific kin types included in tables 10.7 and 10.8, particularly those involving servants, are as yet unspecified.

Table 10.7 Male relatives by role in household and nature of host family

Host family		Category of relative								
		Children with parents		Children without parents[b]	Servants		Elderly (≥60)	Single/widowed parent <60	Other relatives	Total relatives
Sex of head	Category	Married offspring of head[a]	Other		Apprentice[c]	Other				
M	Married, age ≥60	2	1	9	1	0	1	2	0	16
	Non-married, age ≥60	1	4	0	0	0	0	0	0	5
	Non-married, age <60	1	7	1	4	0	0	0	0	13
	Married, childless, age <60	0	0	3	0	0	2	1	1	7
	Other	1	2	3	3	0	4	1	4	18
	All	5	14	16	8	0	7	4	5	59
F	Age ≥60	0	0	1	0	0	0	0	0	1
	Childless, age <60	0	1	0	0	0	0	0	1	1
	Other	1	1	0	0	0	1	0	0	3
	All	1	1	1	0	0	1	0	1	5

a Includes four in-laws.
b Males, other than servants, aged <15 and no coresident parent.
c Also includes persons sharing the occupation of the household head when it seems likely that the household head was the employer. Labourers related to a household head who was a labourer are not included.

Table 10.8 Female relatives by role in household and nature of host family

Host family		Category of relative								
		Children with parents		Children without parents[b]	Servants		Elderly (≥60)	Single/widowed parent <60	Other relatives	Total relatives
Sex of head	Category	Married offspring of head[a]	Other		Apprentice[c]	Other[d]				
M	Married, age ≥60	2	4	5	0	0	1	6	1	19
	Non-married, age ≥60	1	1	0	0	2	1	1	0	6
	Non-married, age <60	1	1	2	2	4	5	3	6	24
	Married, childless, age <60	0	0	2	0	1	2	0	0	5
	Other	1	1	6	1	2	16	3	6	36
	All	5	7	15	3	9	25	13	13	90
F	Age ≥60	0	0	0	0	0	5	0	0	5
	Childless, age <60	0	0	4	0	0	3	0	2	9
	Other	1	0	2	0	0	2	0	1	6
	All	1	0	6	0	0	10	0	3	20

[a] Includes two in-laws.
[b] Females, other than servants, aged <15 and no coresident parent.
[c] Also includes persons sharing the occupation of the household head when it seems likely that the household head was the employer. Lace-makers related to a household head who was also a lace-maker are not included.
[d] Includes nurses and housekeepers as well as house servants.

might have been from the fact that census night was to be followed shortly by a birth or death in the family. Such inferences, however, can be made too seldom to merit incorporation in the categorization scheme, and it has to be accepted that the census, even combined with evidence from the parish registers, will inevitably fail to explain every detail of residence patterns.

Some of the reasons why it is so difficult to trace clear-cut patterns emerge when account is taken of the wide range of kin to be found in the household. Seven separate categories of kin were identified in all: three types of child and two types of servants, besides the elderly and lone parents under the age of 60. Most of the classification is self-explanatory, but some terms require elaboration. First, children identified as relatives and living with a parent were divided into married offspring of the household head and 'others' (mainly grandchildren). There were also a number of grandsons and granddaughters among the child relatives present without their parents, a particularly important proportion of the total kin group in Colyton households.[53] Secondly, the category of single or widowed parents includes persons temporarily separated from their spouses and mothers with illegitimate children,[54] as well as the younger widowed.

Further examination of these kin types reveals some variation with the age, sex and marital status of the household head. Not surprisingly, almost all married offspring were from households where the head had passed the age of 60 and there were no relatives acting as servants in female-headed households. Other variations, for example the more even sex ratio of the kin group in the households with older heads, can be attributed to the greater share of the total kin group occupied by grandchildren with or without their parents. Less easy to anticipate is the finding that female-headed households would contain an above average proportion of elderly female relatives and female children without their parents, but no widowed offspring and mothers with illegitimate children. How significant these associations are for an interpretation of the social structure is uncertain. Some are supported by a small number of cases[55] and need confirmation from further studies. It also remains to be

53 There is an unavoidable inconsistency in the definition of 'child', in that for children living apart from their parents an arbitrary cut-off point of 15 was adopted to separate children from adults, whereas elsewhere 'child' is defined as a relationship (i.e. son, daughter) rather than as an age category.

54 The children themselves, with others, are classified as living with a parent (column 2 of tables 10.7 and 10.8). The numbers are based on mothers living with their illegitimate children rather than the mothers of illegitimate children, as the latter are hard to trace if all the children had died or left home prior to the census. No illegitimate children were living with their fathers.

55 Also to be placed in this category is the fact that grandsons constituted a much larger proportion of the kin group in households headed by a married male over 60 than did granddaughters.

determined whether these particular combinations of people arose because they provided female-headed households with the best economic base,[56] or whether it is simply a reflection of the availability of certain types of kin.

The principal characteristics of the kin group are clear, however. In Colyton, in common with English experience, the majority of relatives within the household were female.[57] Many of these female relatives were elderly or, if younger, lone parents. Their presence largely accounts for the surplus of females in the Colyton kin group and, together with parentless children,[58] for the larger part of the kin group in Colyton. Very few relatives were recorded as servants or shared the occupation of the head of the household. Employment of a relative by the head of the household is therefore somewhat unusual, in contrast with the situation in some communities on the Continent.[59]

The final tables in this section consider some of the channels of kin recruitment; first through the husband or wife (table 10.9) and secondly through married (and some unmarried) sons and daughters (table 10.10).[60] In Colyton servants were recruited exclusively from the husband's relatives. On the other hand, a head of household was as likely to take his mother-in-law as his mother into his household (table 10.9).

Table 10.9   Relatives of married couples

Category	Husband's relatives		Wife's relatives		Unknown	
	Male	Female	Male	Female	Male	Female
Apprentice and servant	3	4	0	0	1	0
Parent[a]	2	10	3	10	0	0
Other relative aged <60	3	6	5	4	1	5
Other relative aged ≥60	2	0	0	1	1	1
Total	10	20	8	15	3	6

[a]   With one exception all aged ≥60.

56 See R. Wall, 'The composition of households in a population of 6 men to 10 women: south-east Bruges in 1814', in Wall et al., *Family forms in historic Europe*, especially pp. 473–4.
57 Wall, 'Regional and temporal variations', pp. 112–13.
58 The term 'parentless children' is from Michael Anderson, 'Household structure and the Industrial Revolution; mid-nineteenth-century Preston in comparative perspective, in Laslett and Wall, *Household and family in past time*, pp. 223–4, 227–8. The definition of a parentless child, however, is not identical with Anderson's, since the reconstitution permits the identification of some coresident parents, particularly the mothers of illegitimate children who would escape detection in a purely census-based study (see table 10.10 and Anderson).
59 See R. Wall, 'Does owning real property influence the form of household formation?', in Wall et al., *Family forms in historic Europe*, p. 390.
60 This exercise would normally be impossible on an English community, particularly with the wife taking her husband's surname on marriage, and it has been necessary to rely on the reconstitution to identify the specific kin link.

Table 10.10, on grandchildren, reveals that the illegitimate offspring of daughters constituted almost a third of all grandchildren and that there was a large category of grandchildren present without their parents.

To conclude this section of the study we will now try to judge the role of kin within a broader context. The very diversity in the composition of the kin group within the household, particularly in Colyton, marks it out as a significant feature of the social structure. Its strengths, however, are all too easily overvalued. In order to assess its true place in society it is necessary to consider whether there were any alternative ways of fulfilling the social and economic roles performed by particular relatives. We may begin by considering the question of the coresidence of parents and married offspring. The vast majority of the young married avoided both residing with their parents and living in lodgings. They established their own households, and even those who were living with a parent would soon move away.[61] Secondly, one might cite the number of elderly female relatives. Reference to figure 10.1 indicates, admittedly for only one point in time, that 40 per cent of the women aged over 60 were still married to a head of household, while a further 20 per cent headed their own household. Thirdly, other relatives, as we have seen, fulfilled the role of servant. However, as they represented only a tiny proportion of the total number of servants, it is clear that servant recruitment proceeded by other means than directly through the kinship system.

Table 10.10 Grandchildren of the household head

Parent's relationship to household head	Parent co-resident	Parent absent	Unclear
Ever-married son	3	6	–
Ever-married daughter	4	5	–
Daughter and illegitimate child(ren)	7	3	–
Unknown	0	5	4
Total	14	19	4

Finally, we may consider the situation of the mothers with illegitimate children. Here the family did have an important role to play. A number of mothers and children might have been removed, by those responsible for administering the Poor Law, to the local workhouse situated in the next

61 In figures 10.1 and 10.2 married offspring are included in the total of relatives. The prediction about the shortness of the period of coresidence with a parent is based on the fact that such households contain on average only one grandchild. A search for other married couples in Colyton who were not household heads produced a total of five, with a further four forming a household themselves but sharing a house with another household.

market town. Within the community, however, economic and possibly social pressures appear to have left daughters with illegitimate children with just two alternatives: living at home with their parents, or leaving the child with them while finding work elsewhere. Only one clear instance had been identified of an independent household formed by a mother and an illegitimate child. This case was exceptional in that the 'child' has already reached the age of 42 and was probably the chief supporter of her elderly mother who was said to be in receipt of alms.

Parentless children were something of an enigma when Michael Anderson first identified this class of person in the 1851 census of Preston.[62] Thanks to the reconstitution of Colyton, absences from the parental home can sometimes be linked to the mother's recent confinement with, for example, a grandparent stepping in to relieve the younger family of a temporarily unwanted body. Only a small proportion of parentless children would appear to have been illegitimate grandchildren (compare tables 10.7, 10.8 and 10.10).

The Farm Labour Force

An alternative perspective on the adaptive family economy comes from considering the situation of those persons who were both employers and utilizers of family labour. As noted earlier, farmers had the option of using family labour, or employing servants or labourers. The 1851 census offers much information on these points, but little use has been made of it by historians, principally because it is difficult to be certain precisely who was included in the totals of persons that farmers reported as being in their employ. Some farmers followed the instruction to include in their total of employees both resident servants and their adult sons. Other farmers, however, recorded only that part of the labour force that was non-resident.[63] One possible solution to the problem is to prepare alternative estimates of the labour force. The total labour force can first be calculated by adding together the number of male servants, family members aged 15 and over and registered employees, and then recalculated by assuming that family members (excluding the farmer himself) and the resident servants have already been included in the total of registered employees. The first calculation gives a maximal estimate of the size of the labour force, and the recalculation a minimal one. Nevertheless, this procedure is justified by the fact that even on such basic issues as the relationship between farm size and the constitution of the labour force,

62 Anderson places some stress on the economic role of parentless children (Anderson, 'Household structure and the Industrial Revolution', pp. 227–8), but this seems less relevant in the case of Colyton where few of such children were given an occupation in the census.

63 This seems to have been a fairly common failing. There is some evidence of its occurrence in Colyton. See also P.M. Tillott, 'Sources of inaccuracy in the 1851 and 1861 censuses', in Wrigley, *Nineteenth century society*, p. 119.

very little research has been completed. One obviously expects the size of the labour force to increase with the size of the farm, though not perhaps in the same proportion. At a certain point economies of scale might come into operation, so that on the large farms the mean number of acres per worker might well be somewhat higher than on the smaller farms. In Colyton this point seems to have been reached with farms of 200 acres.[64] A similar break occurs at 40 acres, but may in this case be an artefact of the data, derived from the fact that not all the workers credited to the smaller farms were engaged full time on their holdings.[65] The overriding impression, however, is one of the variability of the size of the workforce for a given acreage. For example, the maximal estimate of the size of the farm labour force suggested that farms of 30–80 acres could have between one and five workers and farms of 200 acres or more between five and 13. Models of peasant economies such as those developed by A.K. Chayanov tend to assume a strict relation between land and labour. Precisely how this might translate into the economies of opportunity in western Europe has never been entirely clear, but in Colyton the mere amount of land held would not appear to be a useful guide to the size of the enterprise. The varying quality of land is a factor that is more difficult to measure in the case of historical populations, but this, in combination with the ability (or otherwise) of the farmer to tune his activities to the market, would appear to have given certain of them an advantage over their neighbours which they were not slow to use.

The question of the composition of the farm workforce, relying in this case on the minimal estimate of the size of the workforce, is considered in table 10.11. Clearly it was difficult for the farmer's own family to supply all the labour that was required. Only 18 of the 46 farmers had another adult male family member resident with them, and many farmers were forced to hire outside assistance, either servants or labourers, and usually both.[66] Nevertheless, one of the surprises of table 10.11 is that there is so little evidence of the 'family farm', that is the farm relying purely on family labour power. Even at the bottom end of the farm range, where the 'family farm' is most likely to be encountered, we find approximately a fifth of the farmers employing outside labour and one in ten a resident male servant aged 15 or over. Small family farms (on our definition) numbered just five, yet fell into that category of farms that might not have sufficed to give full-time employment to the family members present.

The other point to note is the variation in the nature of the labour force according to the size of the farm. Generally speaking the larger farms had

64 The maximal and minimal estimates of the workforce yield comparable results.

65 It is not possible to determine more precisely which of the resident members of the family worked on a particular farm because, although the enumerators diligently asked for details of farm servants and employees, the members of farmers' families were not given occupations, perhaps because their position was felt to be self-evident.

66 For example, even on the minimal estimate of labour force, 15 of the 22 farmers with resident male servants aged 15 and over also used outside labour.

Table 10.11   Labour characteristics of farms

Farms employing[a]	Acreage				
	<50	55–99	100–199	≥200	Total
≥2 male family members, age ≥15	3	7	5	3	18
≥1 male servant, age < 15	3	5	7	1	16
≥1 male servant, age ≥15	1	5	10	6	22
≥1 female servant	2	5	9	5	21
Family labour only[b]	5	3	1	0	9
≥1 non-resident[b]	2	5	13	5	25
No. of farms	10	14	16	6	46

[a]   Farmers frequently relied on more than one category of employed, with the result that the numbers in the columns do not add up to the total numbers of farms in each size category.
[b]   Minimal estimates of the labour force (see text).

a more varied as well as a larger labour force; that is, they were more likely than smaller farms to have male servants aged 15 and over, female servants and outside employees.[67] On the other hand, the very largest farms made very little use of male servants under the age of 15, and no more use than some of the smaller farms of adult male members of the family. The absence of a relationship between farm size and the presence of male family members emphasizes the point that the family was not the primary means of labour recruitment. Indeed, taken in conjunction with the other evidence on servants and outside employees, the indications are that the family lacked the flexibility to respond to the extent that was required.

So far, the emphasis has been on servants, family members and employees as independent members of the workforce, but the farmers may have seen them as alternatives. However, this can only have been true up to a certain point. First, servants were predominantly young and unmarried.[68] Their tasks were allotted to them as befitted their age and experience. They lacked both the strength and the skill to undertake the full range of tasks that a labourer would be expected to perform and were far from being a perfect substitute for labourers. Secondly, although as figure 10.1 shows there were still some male servants in their twenties, i.e. at an age when they might be considered as the 'equals' in skill or strength of the labourers, the fact that the farmer had not made the substitution would suggest that he found the arrangement to his advantage. In short, labourer and servant were not exact equivalents. If the labour market was

67 Again this holds whether maximal or minimal estimates of the labour force are considered.
68 Kussmaul, *Servants in husbandry*, provides the authoritative interpretation of the nature of farm service in England.

underdeveloped, or the supply of labour at a premium, the situation might be different, but it is difficult to believe that the farmers of Colyton were not in a position to find sufficient labourers or servants had they so wished. Indeed, as far as the latter are concerned, there are some indications that supply exceeded demand in that there were certain boys at the younger end of the age range at home and unemployed (see figure 10.2).

If servants and labourers were not easily interchangeable, a farmer might well need to employ both. Such would seem to have been the case in Colyton. On the other hand, an interchange between servants and family members and family members and employees seems more feasible because of the greater chance of an overlap of age and hence of potential function. The substitution of the labour of sons and daughters for the labour of servants has usually been studied in the context of the life cycle of the household. Berkner's classic study of the peasant household in eighteenth-century Austria revealed, for example, that the more offspring there were resident in the household, the lower the proportion of households with servants; the younger the eldest son, the higher the proportion of households with servants.[69] Such a fine analysis is impractical here given the number of cases at our disposal, but even the crude cross-sectional data suffice to show that the presence of two or more male family members over 15 substantially reduced the proportion of farmers employing servants and, less certainly, the proportion employing labourers.[70]

Proving an association between variables is not the same as establishing the nature of the processes involved. It is possible that farmers kept some of their adult children at home in order to avoid employing servants. It is equally possible that they stayed on for quite other reasons, for example because of an inability to establish their own households until their parents retired and the assets of the parental generation could be dispersed or transferred. Not all sons and daughters of farmers, though, remained continuously in the parental home. As an earlier study of Colyton showed, 21 per cent of farmers' sons and 36 per cent of farmers' daughters aged between 10 and 19 were absent on census night in 1841, while some farmers with surviving adult offspring had no adult son or daughter present.[71] In 1851 there were again some children of farmers not at home,

69 L.K. Berkner, 'The stem family and the developmental cycle of the peasant household', *American Historical Review* 77 (1972), table 4.

70 The uncertainty arises because the two measures of the labour force point in different directions. Counting all the registered employees as outside employees gives 89 per cent of the 2+ male family member farms with outside employees, against only 70 per cent of the single male adult farms.

71 R. Wall, 'Real property, marriage and children: the evidence from four pre-industrial communities', in R.M. Smith (ed.), *Land, kinship and life cycle* (Cambridge, 1984), pp. 457–8, tables 14.6, 14.8.

but it is difficult to relate this movement to the employment or otherwise of servants and outside employees. The farmers' own mobility means that we cannot hope to identify all the older offspring. Nevertheless, it must be significant that it is only possible to cite one instance of the hiring of a male servant in the absence from the parental home of adult sons. The farmers hiring servants were those without sons or with sons who were still young.

We may draw the conclusion, therefore, that the family, either by accident (the survival to adulthood of several sons) or by design (keeping adult sons at home), could in certain circumstances modify the shape of the workforce even when the family itself was not the primary means of labour recruitment. In certain respects, too, it has to be admitted that our analysis of the role of the family in providing labour is incomplete. With more cases at our disposal, for example, we could have taken greater account of the age structure of employment, to discover for example whether the boundaries between age groups were so rigid as to prevent somewhat younger children substituting for the labour of somewhat older servants. The role of women in the rural workforce is also somewhat obscure. No one would question that some share of the work on the farm was allotted to farmers' wives, daughters and female servants. In this work they may have been joined by a number of the wives of the agricultural labourers, although it is interesting that their occupations when recorded were almost without exception either domestic or textile (see table 10.6).[72] The point at issue, however, is whether the work of the female members of the family and female employees ever sufficed to replace better-paid, and hence more costly, male labour. The rigidity in the allocation of occupational tasks according to gender may have made such substitutions difficult, and it is here that the uncertainty arises. There were certainly some women farmers (three of the 46 farmers in 1851, all widows). However, only one had no son to assist and she had three hired male servants. Another pointer to the rigidity of gender roles is that so many of the dairymen to whom reference was made earlier found it necessary to hire a dairymaid. Between family members on the larger farms a more flexible approach to daily tasks may have applied, but this has yet to be proven.

Conclusion

It would be rash to make generalized claims about the nature of English society on the basis of an analysis, however detailed, of the social structure of a particular place. Indeed, it would be surprising if work and family patterns were identical with those in other communities where, for

72 It is possible that agricultural employment went unrecorded because of its seasonal nature. For this suggestion I am grateful to Dr. K. Snell of the University of Leicester.

example, women and girls were not employed in domestic industry to the same extent as in Colyton, where farms were of a different size, or where the relationships between skill, status and occupation were of a different nature. It also may be said that certain conclusions have been hazarded here on the basis of a small number of cases, particularly in examining the composition of the group of relatives within the household. This was a deliberate choice, intended to generate a number of hypotheses to be tested by further research, but in any case there is no realistic alternative. Only by focusing, at least initially, on a small population is one able to see how individual and familial occupational opportunities and social responsibilities framed the process by which some children left the parental home, became servants in the households of others, moved on to form their own households, and were occasionally absorbed into the small kin groups that characterized households in north-west Europe.

Considerable attention has been focused on the process of recruitment into the labour force, the different patterns of work for boys and girls, and the way in which these patterns could be modified according to the standard of living enjoyed by individual families. The proportion of married women in the labour force in the nineteenth century, it was suggested, has frequently been underestimated through reliance on censuses which provide an incomplete record of women's work. The primary intention, however, has been not to establish how many relatives 'doubled' as servants or at precisely what age children left the parental home, or even how many were in the labour force at particular ages, but to demonstrate that all these matters are interrelated. Current theorizing about the family economy and the family wage economy proving inadequate for the conceptualization of these complex realities, it was proposed that the concept of an *adaptive family economy* might prove a more appropriate model for societies where wage labour blended with proto-industrial activity and where some employers had the power to determine not only the place of work but also the residence of the employee. The families of mid-nineteenth-century Colyton were faced with more than the simple choice between all their members working in home industries, or all leaving to follow the dictates of their employers. Their economic activities were diversified against the prospects of bad times and to make the most of the good, and it was precisely in order to encapsulate such diversity that the concept of the adaptive family economy was formulated.

11

Men on the Land and Men in the Countryside: Employment in Agriculture in Early-Nineteenth-Century England

E. A. Wrigley

The main purpose of this chapter is to re-examine the census evidence about the size of the agricultural labour force in England in the first half of the nineteenth century. Because of the limitations of the census data, the review is conducted chiefly in terms of the totals of adult males engaged in agriculture. It reinforces the conclusions of others who have considered the same evidence – that there was very little expansion of employment on the farm in this period.[1] Indeed, taken in conjunction with the more conjectural estimates of agricultural employment over the period 1520 to 1800 which I recently attempted, it seems reasonable to suggest that in the quarter-millennium between 1600 and 1850 employment on the land rose by less than 50 per cent, although the population of England rose more than fourfold and remained very largely home fed.[2]

However, there is a subsidiary theme to this chapter, as the title suggests. Although employment in agriculture rose so modestly, by perhaps a tenth between 1811 and 1851 (table 11.12), the population of rural England continued to grow vigorously during most of the first half of the century. It was only after 1850 that stagnation set in. Men on the land may have increased very little, but the number of men in the countryside grew by roughly a half between 1811 and 1851, and

I am grateful to the editors, and especially to Richard Smith, for advice about how to improve the organization of this essay: also to Keith Snell, who drew upon his exceptional knowledge of many matters related to the lives of the labouring poor to provide me with much helpful comment and information.

1 Notably P. Deane and W.A. Cole, *British economic growth 1688–1959: trends and structure* (Cambridge, 1962), table 31, p. 143.

2 See table 11.12 for estimates of the male agricultural labour force in the first half of the nineteenth century, and p. 335 below for an estimate of its size in 1600. The population of England rose from 4.110 to 16.736 million between 1601 and 1851. E.A. Wrigley and R.S. Schofield, *The population history of England 1541–1871. A reconstruction* (London, 1981), table 7.8, pp. 208–9.

employment outside agriculture but in rural areas therefore grew faster still.

It has occasionally been supposed that the rapidly rising English labour force of the period, no longer able to find work on the land, turned principally to industrial employment as a means of support, whether in the new form of the factory or in the older form of domestic industry. In either case those concerned are pictured as making products sold mainly in distant markets, serving either national or international demand; they are seen as wage-paid proletarians, or moving rapidly towards that state.[3] Even a cursory examination of the census material, however, shows vividly how mistaken it would be to give credence to the view that factory or domestic industry of this type was the chief source of new employment in the first half of the nineteenth century. It also reveals some features of comparative occupational change in rural and non-rural England that are thought provoking. Since these aspects of the subsidiary theme serve to complement the absence of significant growth in agricultural employment, it is convenient to begin by briefly treating the wider issue.

The English Male Labour Force 1811–1851

English population growth rates reached their highest level ever in the early decades of the nineteenth century, and labour force growth rates followed suit.[4] Between 1811 and 1851 the adult male labour force rose by 77 per cent, or by 1.4 per cent annually. The number of adult males employed in agriculture, however, grew by only 11 per cent over the same period, representing an annual growth rate of only 0.26 per cent. In 1811 agriculture employed 39 per cent of the total adult male labour force; by 1851 only 25 per cent. Employment outside agriculture, of course, expanded dramatically, rising from 1,405,000 to 3,090,000 in the 40-year period, or by 120 per cent. Non-agricultural male employment was expanding by 2.0 per cent per annum, a rate significantly

---

3 For example, in the course of an exposition of the contrast between peasant and proletarian demographic systems, Levine argues that between 1700 and 1850 'the proletariat mushroomed from about 2.5 million to nearly 14 million. Both the agricultural and industrial sectors and the rural and urban areas grew. Clearly, however, the dramatic gains were in the proto-industrial, industrial and urban spheres. ... The crucial point is that wage work in agriculture had a limited scope for growth, whereas proto-industry and factory industry had practically insatiable appetites for new recruits'. D. Levine, 'Production, reproduction and the proletarian family in England 1500–1851', in D. Levine (ed.), *Proletarianization and family history* (London, 1984), p. 114.

4 In the three quinquennia between 1811 and 1826 the English population was rising by more than 1.5 per cent annually, and over the first 50 years of the century the average annual growth rate was 1.33 per cent, an appreciably higher rate than in the preceding or succeeding period. Wrigley and Schofield, *Population history of England*, table 7.9, p. 213.

higher than the comparable rate in the second half of the century.[5] In the early censuses there is little information of value in identifying the relative rates of growth in different types of employment outside agriculture. But the 1831 census contains much of value in this regard, and over the next two decades some interesting trends may be sketched in with fair confidence.

When Rickman made provision for more extensive occupational returns of males over 20 in the 1831 census, the distinction which he drew between manufacturing on the one hand, and retail trade and handicraft on the other, corresponded closely with the distinction between the production of goods for a large, dispersed, national or international market and the production of goods or the provision of services for a local market. For the retail trade and handicraft category, though not for any other group, detailed returns were required from each overseer.[6] An additional form was distributed listing what Rickman believed to be the 100 largest occupations within the retail trade and handicraft category, and overseers were instructed to add as many additional occupations as might be necessary to cover any other local occupations not on the printed list. As a result the occupations in this category which afforded most employment can be specified; and the claim that those recorded within the retail trade and handicraft category were serving a local market almost exclusively can be substantiated. Analysis of the geographical dispersion of employment in retail trade and handicraft and of its near constant share of total employment, down often to the level of the individual hundred, further underlines it.[7]

In 1831 adult male employment in manufacturing constituted only 10 per cent of total adult male employment, whereas retail trade and handicraft comprised 32 per cent (or 15 and 47 per cent of non-agricultural employment).[8] Manufacturing employment was very heavily concentrated still in two counties, Lancashire and the West Riding of Yorkshire, which jointly provided 55 per cent of all such jobs. If they are excluded, in the rest of England the proportion of adult males

---

5 For the data underlying these calculations, see table 11.12. The male labour force figures are taken from column 2 of the table. Employment outside agriculture was taken as the difference between the totals in columns 1 and 2 at a given date.

6 The parish was the basic unit used for census purposes, and the overseers of the poor in each parish were responsible for making up the returns.

7 I hope to provide fuller information on this point in a forthcoming essay, 'England in 1831'.

8 There were 314,106 males over 20 employed in manufacture, compared with 964,177 in retail trade or handicraft. The total of males over 20 was taken as 3,010,595 (that is, 'other males' were excluded as being predominantly out of the active labour force: see next section). Those in the army, navy and merchant marine were also excluded (see notes to table 11.12). *1831 Census*, enumeration abstract, I, *Parliamentary Papers* 1833, XXXVI, preface, pp. xii–xiii.

employed in manufacture falls to just under 6 per cent.[9] Since manufacturing included employment both in the new factory industry and in
those types of domestic manufacture, such as framework knitting or
nailing, which were dependent on mass markets at a distance, the
census provides striking evidence of the predominantly 'traditional'
nature of employment outside agriculture at this date.

The sheer scale of the contrast in employment totals in 'new' and
'old' forms of employment outside agriculture is revealing. Although
space constraints prohibit further inquiry into most related aspects of
the phenomenon as a whole, a consideration of two points may serve to
illustrate the nature of the developments in train.

The first concerns rates of growth, as opposed to the absolute scale of
employment, in manufacturing and in retail trade and handicraft. The
radical redesign of the categorization of employment in 1851 makes for
difficulties in comparing the general categories of the 1831 census with
those for 1851 or any later census. The relative rates of growth in
manufacturing and retail trade and handicraft between 1831 and 1841,
however, can be established approximately from an *ad hoc* tabulation
made in the 1841 census, in which an attempt appears to have been
made to mirror the same two general categories used in 1831. For
England and Wales combined, including islands in the British seas (no
other breakdown was published), employment in manufacturing rose
from 320,743 to 479,774; in retail trade and handicraft from 1,015,092
to 1,282,128.[10] The totals refer to males aged 20 or more. Predictably
the annual rate of growth was substantially higher in the former than
the latter category, 4.1 per cent compared with 2.4 per cent; but of the
overall growth in employment in the two categories combined, 63 per
cent was in retail trade and handicraft. In absolute terms many more
additional jobs were still being found in 'traditional' forms of employment meeting the needs of local markets.

The second point extends the first by examining some of the trades
within the retail trade and handicraft sector which were providing so
many new jobs, and at the same time serves to show how rural
England was faring in comparison with the rest of the country in this
respect. In these trades comparison between 1831 and 1851 is feasible.
To provide a setting for the comparison between rural England and the
rest, table 11.1 provides summary population data for 17 rural counties
and for the country as a whole (England is defined as including
Monmouth, following the convention observed in the first five censuses:

9 *1831 Census*, enumeration abstract, II, *Parliamentary Papers*, 1833, XXXVI, pp. 832–3.
Excluding Lancashire and the West Riding, manufacturing employed only 141,920 out of
2,487,427 (calculated on the same basis as the figures quoted in note 8 in this chapter).

10 *1841 Census*, occupation abstract, *Parliamentary Papers*, 1844, XXVII, preface, p. 26. The
1831 totals were obtained from *1831 Census* (reference as in note 9 in this chapter), pp. 925
and 1059.

Table 11.1 Population totals and growth rates in the rural counties of England (totals in '000s)

				Annual growth rates (per cent per annum)	
	Rural countries (1)	England (2)	(1) as percentage of (2) (3)	Rural counties (4)	England (5)
1811	2,628	9,553	27.51	1.49	1.68
1821	3,046	11,282	27.00	1.08	1.50
1831	3,391	13,090	25.91	0.80	1.37
1841	3,671	15,003	24.47	0.62	1.21
1851	3,904	16,922	23.07	0.28	1.22
1891	4,362	27,484	15.87		

The 17 rural counties are Bedfordshire, Berkshire, Buckinghamshire, Cambridgeshire, Cumberland, Devon, Dorset, Hereford, Huntingdonshire, Lincolnshire, Norfolk, Oxfordshire, Rutland, Somerset, Suffolk, Westmorland and Wiltshire. Industrial counties and those most affected by rapid urban growth were excluded.
The growth rates in columns 4 and 5 each refer to the period between the date on the line in question and the date on the next line: thus the rate of 1.49 on the first line in column 4 refers to 1811–21; that of 0.28 on the fifth line to 1851–91.
Source: B. R. Mitchell and P. Deane, *Abstract of British historical statistics* (Cambridge, 1962), chapter 1, tables 2 and 7

this definition is used throughout this essay). Between 1811 and 1851 population in rural England grew by 49 per cent; in England as a whole by 77 per cent; while in non-rural England, that is in the remaining 25 counties, population rose by 88 per cent.[11] In the next 40 years, between 1851 and 1891, the comparable percentages were 12, 62 and 78 respectively. The two final columns of the table show that in the first decade 1811–1821, there was little difference in growth rates between the rural counties and the whole country, though thereafter growth rates fell away steadily and quickly in the former until after 1851 there was little further growth, whereas in the latter the fall in growth rates was modest; indeed by the mid century it had ceased.

Given that farming took on very few new hands between 1811 and 1851 (table 11.12), it is obvious that other forms of adult male employment must have grown rapidly in the rural counties down to the mid century. Table 11.2 provides some details of the fortunes over a 20-year period of the ten types of occupation within the retail trade and handicraft category which employed the largest number of men in

11 If the three ridings of Yorkshire are treated as separate counties, there were 42 English counties at this date.

Table 11.2 Employment in ten major retail and handicraft employments 1831–1851 (males aged 20 and over)

	In the ten trades			Male population 20–64				Percentage of male population 20–64 in the ten trades			Ratio of employment in ten trades 1851/1831	Ratio of population 1851/1831
	1831	1841	1851	1831	1841	1851	1851/1831	1831	1841	1851		
Rural counties	134,189	151,525	164,418	779,000	842,000	906,527		17.2	18.0	18.1	1.225	1.164
Rest of England	382,790	495,149	555,907	2,246,000	2,805,000	3,193,158		17.0	17.7	17.4	1.452	1.422
England	516,979	646,674	720,325	3,025,000	3,647,000	4,099,685		17.1	17.7	17.6	1.393	1.355

The ten trades

	Rural counties				Rest of England				England			
	1831	1841	1851	1851/1831	1831	1841	1851	1851/1831	1831	1841	1851	1851/1831
Baker	6,603	7,413	8,627	1.307	17,127	21,327	25,629	1.496	23,730	28,740	34,256	1.444
Blacksmith	13,233	15,966	16,436	1.242	32,172	47,524	50,132	1.558	45,405	63,490	66,568	1.466
Bricklayer	6,468	7,674	10,114	1.564	22,471	27,746	44,579	1.984	28,939	35,420	54,693	1.890
Butcher	7,811	8,946	9,752	1.248	23,215	29,287	34,926	1.504	31,026	38,233	44,678	1.440
Carpenter	23,847	30,325	29,731	1.247	59,963	82,547	86,374	1.440	83,810	112,872	116,105	1.385
Mason	9,983	14,584	15,134	1.516	21,648	34,954	41,190	1.903	31,631	49,538	56,324	1.781
Publican	13,869	11,628	11,370	0.820	38,752	33,147	36,866	0.951	52,621	44,775	48,236	0.917
Shoemaker	27,671	29,866	34,489	1.246	82,451	114,735	118,843	1.441	110,122	144,601	153,332	1.392
Shopkeeper	11,405	7,487	11,414	1.001	38,124	39,942	48,767	1.279	49,529	47,429	60,181	1.215
Tailor	13,299	17,636	17,351	1.305	46,867	63,940	68,601	1.464	60,166	81,576	85,952	1.429
Total	134,189	151,525	164,418	1.225	382,790	495,149	555,907	1.452	516,979	646,674	720,325	1.393

The ten trades: employment per 10,000 of the adult male labour force

	Rural counties			Rest of England			England		
	1831	1841	1851	1831	1841	1851	1831	1841	1851
Baker	85	88	95	76	76	80	78	79	84
Blacksmith	170	190	181	143	169	157	150	174	162
Bricklayer	83	91	112	100	99	140	96	97	133
Butcher	100	106	108	103	104	109	103	105	109
Carpenter	306	360	328	267	294	270	277	309	283
Mason	128	173	167	96	125	129	105	136	137
Publican	178	138	125	173	118	115	174	123	118
Shoemaker	355	355	380	367	409	372	364	396	374
Shopkeeper	146	89	126	170	142	153	164	130	147
Tailor	171	209	191	209	228	215	199	224	210
Total	1723	1800	1814	1704	1765	1741	1709	1773	1757

The rural counties were taken to be the following: Bedfordshire, Berkshire, Buckinghamshire, Cambridgeshire, Cumberland, Devon, Dorset, Herefordshire, Huntingdonshire, Lincolnshire, Norfolk, Oxfordshire, Rutland, Somerset, Suffolk, Westmorland and Wiltshire.

Most of the occupational totals were taken directly from the census returns but the census categories and definitions varied from census to census in two cases, making some amalgamation of groups necessary. The term shopkeeper was taken to comprise the following groups. In 1831: grocer, greengrocer, shopkeeper. In 1841: greengrocer and fruiterer: grocer and tea dealer; shopkeeper and general dealer. In 1851: shopkeeper; greengrocer; grocer. For the elements combined under the term publican at the three censuses, see note 14 in this chapter.

The totals in each occupational group were all males over 20 in 1831 and 1841 when the census included categories for the infirm, the 'superannuated' etc., but males aged 20–64 in 1851 when there was no such provision. For the derivation of the totals of men aged 20–64 at the three census dates, see the notes to table 11.12.

Sources: 1831 Census, enumeration abstract, I, Parliamentary Papers 1833, XXXVI,; 1841 Census, occupation abstract, part I, Parliamentary Papers, 1844, XXVII, p. 287; 1851 Census, population tables, II, ages, civil condition, occupations and birth place of the people, vols I and II, Parliamentary Papers 1852–3, LXXXVIII, parts 1 and 2

1831. Between them in 1831 the ten trades provided a livelihood for 17 per cent of all males aged 20–64 (for reasons explained later, having to do with the treatment of those too old for regular employment, it is appropriate to relate totals of adult males in employment to the population aged 20–64).[12] They accounted for 25.5 per cent of all non-agricultural employment, and these ten occupations alone engaged five men for every three in the whole of the manufacturing category. The ten trades comprised an almost identical fraction of the adult male labour force in both the rural counties and the rest of the country.

In the two classes of employment where the changing of categories from census to census introduces special difficulties in making comparisons over time (publicans and shopkeepers: see notes to table 11.2), there was apparently either a slight fall in employment (publicans) or a more modest rise than in other occupations (shopkeepers). This may be a function of 'leakage' into other occupational heads, though if so it is not immediately obvious from the census. Equally, there may be similar distortions concealed within some of the other eight occupations which appear less vulnerable to this difficulty. Nevertheless, the overall impression of vigorous expansion in the group as a whole is not misleading: nor is the differentially rapid growth in the two major building categories, bricklayers and masons, whose numbers came close to doubling nationally in the 20-year period.

It is striking how similar a fraction of total adult male employment was to be found in the ten occupations in both the rural counties and elsewhere, and, equally, how little the relevant percentages changed over the three censuses. If anything, employment in the ten was growing slightly faster than the population of working age (though the differences are too slight to be significant), yet these were all occupations in which there had been little if any change from earlier generations in work methods or organization. And a large proportion of all the men employed in these trades, probably a majority overall, were independent small masters rather than wage-paid proletarians. Table 11.2 strongly underlines the falsity of the belief that manufacturing employment related to distant markets, whether in the home or the factory, was the dominant source of new jobs for the rising generations of young men in these decades.[13]

12 See next section.
13 Failure to appreciate the relatively modest size of total employment in all the newer forms of employment has led at times to the posing of false problems. Pollard, for example, noting that there was 'plentiful labour supply or labour surplus', especially in the period c.1814–50, went on to ask: 'How could this easy labour supply be maintained at a time when new industries and occupations were voraciously absorbing labour at unprecedented rates? How did the Industrial Revolution manage to have its cake and eat it too?' Industries which have only 10 per cent of the labour force, however voracious their appetites, can have only a limited impact on the overall labour market. S. Pollard, 'Labour in Great Britain', in P. Mathias and M.M. Postan (eds), The Cambridge economic history of Europe, vol. vii, part I (Cambridge, 1978), p. 148.

The absence of employment growth in agriculture proved no bar to employment gains elsewhere in the local rural communities. The number of men aged 20–64 grew by 127,000 in the rural counties between 1831 and 1851, while employment in the ten trades alone rose by 30,000. Since the ten formed only 59 per cent of the employment in retail trade and handicraft generally in 1831, it is likely that further investigation would reveal that employment in this occupational category was providing two-fifths or more of all new employment in the countryside in the second quarter of the century.

When the proportionate shares of the individual trades are examined (final part of table 11.2), the similarity between rural England and the rest of the country is as striking as in the case of the ten trades combined. Everywhere, for example, about 1 per cent of the adult male labour force were butchers, 3 per cent carpenters, 3.5 per cent shoemakers. Such similarities are suggestive. The remarkably even spread of butchers across the country, for example, does not appear to be consonant with great differences in this important aspect of diet between rural England and the rest. Often the evidence of the table raises questions as well as suggesting conclusions. The apparent ebbing of employment in the drink trade is an instance of this. It may possibly be a misleading result of the long list of synonyms for publican used in the successive censuses rather than evidence of a declining enthusiasm for drink, but there are also grounds for supposing it to be genuine.[14] It is one of several issues which would warrant further attention.

Tables 11.1 and 11.2 clearly show that rural England retained sufficient economic momentum in the first half of the nineteenth century to permit notable increases in employment in many classes of occupation which could only flourish if the local economy were healthy since they depended on a local market. Yet employment in agriculture, the prime industry of rural England, was almost at a standstill. It is time to turn first to the question of the evidence for near stagnation in

14 In 1831 there was a single category: publican, hotel or innkeeper, retailer of beer. In 1841 under the general heading of tavern-keeper there were subheads for beershop-keeper; hotel and innkeeper; publican and victualler; and spirit merchant (of these the last was excluded from the total in table 11.2 since both spirit merchant and wine dealer were separate categories in 1831). In 1851 innkeeper; licensed victualler; beershop-keeper; and wine and spirit merchant were distinct categories. The first was in class VI; the other two in class XIII. In this case the first two were included but the third was not. It would not be surprising, however, if there were a fall in the number of publicans. Pressure from the magistrates against small front-room beershops; high taxes on malt and hops; and the spread of tea-drinking may all have played a part. Some contemporaries much regretted the decline in beer drinking. See, for example, W. Cobbett, *Cottage economy*, first published 1822 (Oxford, 1979), pp. 20, 22, 42. Per caput consumption of beer fell substantially over the period. In the successive decades 1820–9 to 1850–9 the totals run (in gallons per annum) 28.70, 22.40, 19.45 and 21.55 (the first figure refers to England and Wales, the others to the UK). Consumption of spirits changed little. The comparable data are (in gallons) 0.89, 1.14, 0.93 and 1.04 (all UK). But tea consumption rose sharply: (in pounds) 1.29, 1.37, 1.55 and 2.25 (all UK). P. Mathias, *The first industrial nation*, 2nd edn (London, 1983), table V, p. 200.

agricultural employment, which has so far been asserted rather than demonstrated; and, in a final section, to the place of agriculture in the wider changes going forward in the English economy at the time.

Agricultural Employment 1831–1851

In 1851 there was a radical overhaul of the system of occupational classification in the English census, which thereafter changed little during the rest of the century. After 1851 the total number of men employed in agriculture fell. The total stood at 1,129,841 in 1851; by 1861 it had fallen to 1,120,310, a minor change, but one which was to herald uninterrupted decline.[15] Before 1851 the census occupational data were both less detailed and given in a form which varied substantially. It is not therefore possible to say whether 1851 represented a peak of agricultural employment, the edge of a plateau, or part of a downward slope, without probing the available data with some care.

In attempting to survey the first half of the nineteenth century it is convenient to move backwards in time from 1851 and to pay particular attention to the 1831 census, since it is both a notably informative source in itself and a bridge into the tabulations published in still earlier censuses. In some respects indeed, it is reasonable to claim that the 1831 census was the most valuable of all nineteenth-century censuses from the point of view of economic history. Its special value is discussed in detail elsewhere,[16] so that here only three points need be noted initially: that the 1831 census was the last to be based on returns made by the overseers in each parish, rather than on individual household schedules; that the data refer almost exclusively to males aged 20 years and over; and that, in addition to six main employment categories for adult males, there was a seventh category for the elderly and infirm and those not included elsewhere under other heads.[17]

Table 11.3 shows the census totals of agricultural employment in 1831 and 1851. They relate to males over 20 in both cases. At first sight it seems evident there had been a growth in employment in agriculture over the 20-year period, even though the increase, at 15 per cent, is only about half the overall population growth of the period (the total population of males aged 20–64 rose from 3,025,000 to 4,099,685

15 The totals relate to England only (including Monmouth) and refer to men aged 20 years or over. The apparent small drop in numbers from 1851 to 1861 may well not be significant because of the changing treatment of the subcategories within agriculture. For example, the male relatives of farmers resident on the farm were treated differently. See p. 307.

16 See note 7 in this chapter.

17 The question put to the overseers were phrased as follows: 'How many other males upwards of twenty years old ... have not been included in any of the foregoing classes? Including, therefore, in answer to this question, retired tradesmen, superannuated labourers, and males diseased or disabled in body or mind.' *1831 Census* (reference as in note 8 in this chapter), p. vi.

Table 11.3   Agricultural employment in England in 1831 and 1851: males
aged 20 and over

1831	
Occupiers employing one or more labourers or farm servants	141,460
Occupiers employing no labour other than their own family	94,883
Labourers and farm servants employed by the first class of occupiers	774,407
Total	980,750

1851	
Landed proprietors	16,098
Farmers and graziers	192,968
Farmers' and graziers' sons, grandsons, brothers and nephews residing on the farm	60,971
Bailiffs	9,966
Agricultural labourers (outdoors)	693,925
Shepherds	9,926
Farm servants (indoors)	72,982
Others (in agriculture)	3,103
Woodmen	6,774
Gardeners, nurserymen	63,128
Total	1,129,841

The totals refer to England including Monmouth. The 1831 data are for ancient counties: those for 1851 are for registration counties, and the national totals are therefore not exactly comparable as Monmouth was not the same entity on the two occasions.
Overseers in 1831 were instructed to include in their returns for agriculture graziers, cowkeepers, shepherds and other farm servants, gardeners (other than those taxable as servants) and nurserymen. In 1851 farmers and graziers were separately tabulated but the latter were few in number and have not been separately distinguished. Similarly, gardeners and nurserymen were separately stated but have amalgamated. The full occupational breakdown also included returns for 'others' in arboriculture and horticulture, but the totals involved were very small and they have in each case been included with the related main category.
Sources: see sources to table 11.2.

over the period, or by 36 per cent).[18] On further consideration, however, the difference between the two totals narrows sharply.

First, the scope of the 1851 total is broader in that landed proprietors· were included in agriculture. In 1831 there was a category covering capitalists and professional men. This was defined to include the following: 'wholesale merchants, bankers, capitalists, professional persons, artists, architects, teachers, clerks, surveyors and other educated men'. In addition, the overseers were told: 'You will include generally persons maintaining themselves otherwise than by manufacture, trade or bodily

18 See table 11.12.

labour.'[19] Landed proprietors should therefore be excluded from the 1851 total for purposes of comparison.

Second, some adjustment is called for to reflect the fact that the later census placed those who were no longer able to work, or who were out of work, in the same category as those currently in work, whereas in 1831 there was a separate, if vaguely defined, category for such men. This category of 'other males' comprised 189,389 men, or 5.92 per cent of the total of males over 20 (3,199,984).[20] If it is assumed that agriculture was affected in the same way as other industries by decrepitude and disease among its workforce, the 1851 total should be reduced proportionately to facilitate comparison with 1831. The following exercise gauges its effect:

1851 total in agriculture (table 11.3)	1,129,841
deduct landed proprietors	16,098
	1,113,743
deduct 5.92 per cent	65,934
	1,047,809

Alternatively, the issue may be approached more directly. For example, assuming that in 1831 occupiers of land continued to be included in the total for agriculture, however advanced their age, but that farm labourers incapacitated by age, injury or illness were counted among 'other males', a plausible correction for the 1851 census might be made in the following way, taking advantage of the existence of cross-tabulations by occupation and age: retain all farmers and graziers irrespective of age, on the ground that they would probably have been counted within the agricultural total in 1831, but for all other subdivisions used in 1851 exclude those aged 65 years or more.[21] If this is done, and landed proprietors are again excluded, as in the first exercise, the resulting total is 1,039,101.

Third, there is the category consisting of the male relatives of farmers, living on the farm and not known to have been otherwise employed. All sons and grandsons, brothers and nephews of farmers were required to be placed in this category in the process of census tabulation, unless

19 *1831 Census* (reference as in note 8 in this chapter), p. vi.

20 The total of males over 20 excludes those in the army, navy and merchant marine. For a discussion of the problems of estimating the number of men missed for this reason, see notes to table 11.12.

21 Tranter, in a recent survey of labour supply in early-nineteenth-century England, after noting the difficulty of making any generalizations about the age at which people normally ceased work, concluded that 'adult males normally expected to retire around the ages of 60 or 65'. N.L. Tranter, 'The labour supply 1780–1860', in R. Floud and D. McCloskey (eds), *The economic history of Britain since 1700*, vol. i (Cambridge, 1981), p. 222.

specifically returned on the householder's schedule as otherwise employed. Proceeding in this fashion was an arbitrary way of dealing with a difficult problem, since it meant that a census official rather than the individual concerned determined occupation. It must tend to maximize apparent agricultural occupation. Farmers' male relatives were numerous, comprising, 60,971 individuals in 1851. It is interesting to note that the comparable totals in the next two censuses declined sharply to 49,489 and 38,994 respectively. Since the number of farmers was virtually constant (table 11.4), and therefore the number of resident male relatives is very unlikely to have changed other than marginally, it is evident that attribution of employment by census officials was carried out with greater discretion after the first introduction of the practice. The *Reports* of the censuses of 1861 and 1871 do not comment on the sharp contraction in the size of this group, but the regional patterning of change suggests that the original blanket instruction to include all male relatives was interpreted with increasing care.[22] In a group of contiguous counties in the west midlands the total of relatives either rose between 1851 and 1861 (Shropshire and Hereford) or did not materially alter (Worcestershire and

Table 11.4   Occupiers of land in England 1831 to 1871: males aged 20 and over

	1831
Occupiers employing one or more labourers or farm servants	141,460
Occupiers employing no labour other than their own family	94,883
All occupiers	236,343

	1841	1851	1861	1871
Farmers and graziers	194,596	192,968	193,355	191,947
Gardeners, nurserymen	42,364	63,128	69,104	87,506
Farmers' and graziers' sons, grandsons, brothers and nephews		60,971	49,489	38,994

For definition of England see notes to table 11.3. In 1841 florists were included with gardeners and nurserymen.
Sources: for 1831 and 1851 see source notes to table 11.2. *1841 Census*, occupation abstract, part I, *Parliamentary Papers*, 1844, XXVII, p. 287; *1861 Census*, population tables, II, ages, civil condition, occupations and birthplaces of the people, *Parliamentary Papers*, 1863, LIII, parts I and II; *1871 Census*, vol. III, civil condition, occupations and birthplaces of the people, *Parliamentary Papers*, 1873, LXXI, part I

22 In the 1851 census the strictness of the procedure followed in allocating male relatives of farmers to agriculture as an occupation is suggested by the insertion of a footnote in each county tabulation specifying that 'the "sons", "grandsons", "brothers", and "nephews" (not otherwise described) of farmers and graziers, being 15 years of age and upwards, and resident on the farm, etc., are separately returned in Class IX in connection with agriculture, as they are usually engaged in the business of the farm.'

Warwickshire), whereas in a band of counties in the south-east the fall was precipitate (in Suffolk, Essex, Kent and Sussex the percentage fall in the totals in this subgroup was 39, 26, 26 and 24 respectively). While any adjustment to assist comparability between 1831 and 1851 must be arbitrary, the evidence of later censuses suggests that the 1851 total in agriculture should be reduced by, say, 15,000 if the number of men engaged in agriculture is not to be exaggerated.

Fourth and finally, the existence of a considerable discrepancy between the total of occupiers of land in 1831 and the total of farmers and graziers in 1851 calls for examination. There were 236,343 of the former but only 192,968 of the latter, yet there can be no reasonable doubt that the number of farmers in 1831 was almost the same as later in view of the stability in the size of the group over the next four censuses (table 11.4). Given the very limited breakdown of total agricultural employment made in 1831, it might seem at first sight difficult to determine whether the reasons for the discrepancy can be identified, or even whether it is a 'real' problem related to changes in classification or simply a result of hapha-zard and unreliable estimation. Fortunately, however, the use of county-level data discloses patterns which appear to resolve the problem of reconciling the totals in question.

There are two possibilities to be investigated. As will be clear from table 11.4, the number of gardeners in 1841, when added to the total of farmers, results in a figure very similar to the total of occupiers in 1831. In the 1831 census only those gardeners who were not taxable as male servants were to be included in the return for agriculture. It is conceivable, therefore, that many were occupiers of land and would be included in the 1831 returns in that category. The alternative possibility is that the adult male relatives of farmers who were resident on the farm were returned within the 'occupiers of land' category, though they were placed in a separate category in 1851 and later. Again, the numbers involved are of the right order of magnitude to account for the difference. The alternative possibili-ties are not, of course, mutually exclusive, though the latter is inherently more likely. None of the other categories used in 1851 contains men who might have been classified as occupiers using the 1831 divisions.

That the returns of 1831 and 1851 bear an intelligible and consistent relationship to each other is strongly suggested by the information set out in table 11.5. The division between occupiers employing labour and those using only family labour in 1831 is shown for each county together with a wider range of information from the 1851 census: the number of farms which employed men, the number employing no men (or failing to specify the number employed), the number of farmers and graziers, the number of gardeners and nurserymen, the number of farmers' resident male relatives (the totals here refer to 1861, not 1851) and, finally, a derived total. It should be noted that the number of farms making a return of the number of men employed (column 6) does not equal the number of farmers (column 7). The lack of agreement arises from several causes, as is made clear by the notes to the tables in the census volumes. On the one hand, some farmers made no return of acreage and numbers employed, and the census category of farmers included many who had retired and no longer occupied a farm. On the other hand, some returns were obtained from men who engaged in farming but whose principal occupation lay outside farming and who were not therefore included in the main census tabulations as farmers. Further, it should be remembered that there was a tiny number of farmers under 20 years of age (709 in all), whereas the totals relating to farms (columns 4 to 6) make no distinction as to the age of the farmer.

Perhaps the first point to note is the generally excellent accord between the totals in columns 1 and 2 on the one hand and those in columns 4 and 5 on the other. In the country as a whole there were about four-fifths as many farms employing labour in 1851 as occupiers employing labour in 1831 (columns 4 and 1), and the same holds good for farms employing no labour and occupiers employing no labour (columns 5 and 2). The ratio between farms employing labour and those employing none in 1851, however, varied enormously from county to county. In some eastern counties where farms were large there were seven or eight times as many of the former as of the latter, while at the other extreme there were four counties where farms employing no labour were in a majority.[23] The totals in columns 1 and 4, and 2 and 5, can be compared for the 42 counties, making 84 comparisons in all; in only three instances are the 1851 totals larger than the 1831 equivalents, in each case by a tiny margin.[24] Given the great variations in the proportions of employing to non-employing units, and the fact that the overall totals in 1851 were roughly four-fifths of those in 1831, this is impressive testimony to the consistency with which the two sets of returns were collected and compiled. It is equally clear that some factor or combinations of factors was at work to cause the earlier sets of totals to exceed the later. What does the county evidence suggest about the relative importance of farmers' male relatives and gardeners in causing the observed differences?

Undoubtedly many of the male relatives of farmers resident on the farm were engaged in farming; nor is there any reasonable doubt that the overseers in 1831 would have included such men among the occupiers of land rather than as farm labourers. There is persuasive indirect evidence that in 1851, when male relatives of farmers were separately disting-uished, they were initially over-counted, and that the totals in later censuses were probably more accurate.[25] It is for this reason that the totals in the category in column 9 are taken from the 1861 rather than the

23 Derbyshire, Lancashire, Westmorland, and the West Riding of Yorkshire.
24 Durham (columns 2 and 5); Hertfordshire (columns 1 and 4); West Riding, Yorkshire (columns 2 and 5).
25 See p. 307.

Table 11.5 Testing the consistency of the 1831 and 1851 county totals for farmers and related categories

	1831			1851						
	Occupiers with labour (1)	Occupiers without labour (2)	Total (1) + (2) (3)	Farms with labour (4)	Farms without labour or not stated (5)	Total (4) + (5) (6)	Farmers and graziers (7)	Gardeners and nurserymen (8)	Farmers' male relatives (1851) (9)	Derived total (10)
Bedfordshire	1,330	474	1,804	1,228	161	1,449	1,409	797	330	1,698
Berkshire	1,711	458	2,169	1,655	184	1,839	1,994	1,327	472	2,408
Buckinghamshire	2,152	453	2,605	1,598	212	1,810	1,868	788	399	2,218
Cambridgeshire	2,421	1,266	3,687	2,220	1,071	3,291	3,409	790	680	4,005
Cheshire	4,374	4,059	8,433	3,357	3,326	6,683	6,372	1,517	2,157	8,263
Cornwall	4,608	3,613	8,221	4,063	3,154	7,217	7,523	736	1,784	9,087
Cumberland	3,617	2,839	6,456	2,517	2,444	4,961	4,687	363	2,151	6,572
Derbyshire	3,320	4,257	7,577	1,834	2,955	4,789	5,051	747	1,367	6,249
Devonshire	9,328	3,356	12,684	7,414	3,013	10,427	11,413	1,990	3,354	14,353
Dorsetshire	2,243	967	3,210	1,860	471	2,331	2,842	658	677	3,435
Durham	2,229	1,544	3,773	1,839	1,586	3,425	3,705	820	1,097	4,166
Essex	4,561	888	5,449	3,670	446	4,116	4,025	2,026	788	4,716
Gloucestershire	3,675	1,846	5,521	2,640	946	3,586	3,883	2,305	989	4,750
Hampshire	2,774	1,234	4,008	2,485	595	3,080	3,117	2,246	692	3,724
Herefordshire	2,505	1,679	4,184	1,684	850	2,534	2,623	41	651	3,194
Hertfordshire	1,518	399	1,917	1,561	182	1,743	1,660	1,164	403	2,013
Huntingdonshire	857	397	1,254	764	189	953	1,001	278	204	1,180

Kent	4,361	2,152	6,513	3,767	954	4,721	4,938	3,597	1,106	5,907
Lancashire	6,658	9,714	16,372	5,865	9,585	15,450	15,959	3,690	4,938	20,287
Leicestershire	2,656	2,145	4,801	2,507	1,237	3,744	3,462	793	654	4,035
Lincolnshire	6,901	6,204	13,105	5,922	5,095	11,017	10,225	1,152	2,046	12,018
Middlesex	1,050	490	1,540	836	168	1,004	1,300	6,878	164	1,444
Monmouthshire	1,648	1,143	2,791	1,276	1,118	2,394	2,418	461	666	3,002
Norfolk	5,229	2,718	7,947	4,868	1,664†	6,532	6,463	1,894	1,069	7,400
Northamptonshire	3,015	1,117	4,132	2,438	382	2,820	2,761	780	591	3,279
Northumberland	2,376	1,268	3,644	1,875	946	2,821	2,935	834	1,210	3,996
Nottinghamshire	2,643	2,414	5,057	2,526	1,867	4,393	3,871	909	816	4,586
Oxfordshire	2,054	458	2,512	1,939	295	2,234	2,249	712	594	2,770
Rutland	429	424	853	412	314	726	677	102	150	808
Shropshire	3,832	2,139	5,971	3,357	1,578	4,935	4,797	963	1,503	6,114
Somerset	6,032	3,731	9,763	5,254	1,936	7,190	7,988	2,098	1,995	9,737
Staffordshire	3,781	3,649	7,430	3,128	2,898	6,026	5,856	1,559	1,370	7,057
Suffolk	4,526	1,121	5,647	4,353	749	5,092	5,180	1,409	784	5,867
Surrey	1,873	727	2,600	1,563	376	1,939	1,955	5,452	502	2,395
Sussex	3,160	1,330	4,490	3,153	719	3,872	3,961	1,752	853	4,709
Warwickshire	2,838	1,142	3,980	2,467	949	3,416	3,611	1,583	906	4,405
Westmorland	1,435	1,685	3,120	939	1,425	2,364	2,328	175	823	3,049
Wiltshire	3,387	1,239	4,626	2,563	517	3,080	3,176	1,202	791	3,869
Worcestershire	2,636	1,260	3,896	1,985	859	2,844	2,810	1,586	655	3,384
Yorkshire, East Riding	3,671	1,914	5,585	2,683	1,451	4,134	4,252	1,059	1,109	5,224
Yorkshire, North Riding	4,950	4,334	9,284	3,535	3,272	6,807	6,710	566	2,045	8,502
Yorkshire, West Riding	7,096	10,636	17,732	6,602	10,783	17,385	16,504	2,959	3,954	19,970
England	141,460	94,883	236,343	118,232	72,922	191,154	192,968	63,128	49,489	236,343

The data for 1831 relate to ancient counties, other data relate to registration counties. For the importance of the changed basis of tabulation, see note 27 in this chapter. In 1851 and thereafter parts of the counties of Kent, Surrey and Middlesex were included in the county of London. The county totals for the three counties in columns 7 and 8 are none the less accurate because the breakdown by registration district within London enables the county totals to be reconstructed. Those in columns 4, 5, 6 and 9 were estimated on the assumption that the totals in question for London were split between the three counties in the same proportion as the London total of farmers in 1851 was split between them. For derivation of column 10 totals, see main text.
Sources: See sources to table 11.2

1851 census. The pattern of relationship between the totals in columns 1 and 2 and those in columns 4 and 5, already noted, strongly suggests that the former exceed the latter by a fairly stable ratio. This creates a strong presumption that male relatives represented the bulk of the difference since they varied only moderately as a proportion of farmers (columns 7 and 9), whereas the totals of gardeners fluctuated widely in this respect, ranging from under 10 per cent in Cornwall, Cumberland, Herefordshire, Westmorland and the North Riding of Yorkshire, to over 70 per cent in Hampshire, Hertfordshire and Kent (ignoring the special cases of Middlesex and Surrey).

A simple test can be made of the hypothesis that men who would have been classed as farmers or male relatives of farmers in 1851 and later censuses constituted the two classes of occupiers of land in 1831, and that gardeners were either never included among them or, if so, in numbers so small as to make only a negligible difference. If we assume that the number of farmers in 1831 was identical to the number in 1851 and that all others in the 'occupiers' class were their male relatives, the number of such relatives is easily calculated (43,375 = 236,343–192,968). They comprised a smaller number than in 1861 (49,489), though the discrepancy is not large. If the county totals of male relatives in column 9 of the table are in each case reduced in the ratio 43,375/49,489, and the resulting totals are added to the totals of farmers in 1851, the sum of the resulting county totals (column 10) is constrained by the method adopted to equal the national total in the two classes of occupiers in 1831. Comparison of the county totals at the two dates (columns 3 and 10) then affords a test of the propriety of the assumption that those who were not themselves farmers in the 1831 occupiers' totals were their male relatives. If other elements, such as gardeners, were contributing significantly to the 1831 county totals, there would be a poor correspondence between the 1831 and 1851 totals for many counties. The mean difference is 9.5 per cent (that is, if the 1831 figure is taken to be 100, the 1851 figure differs on average by 9.5). It is some indication of the generally satisfactory closeness of the two series that if comparison is made between the county totals of farmers in 1851 and 1871, another interval of 20 years, the mean difference is 6.5 per cent.[26] Since this is a simpler comparison involving only one category rather than two, and avoids the substantial distortions involved in the earlier comparison in moving from ancient to registration counties, it seems fair to regard the comparison of 1831 and 1851 as broadly confirming the assumptions made and as suggesting also that the underlying operations undertaken at the two censuses were consistent with each other.[27]

26 The overall totals of farmers in 1851 and 1871 were almost identical.

27 The goodness of fit between the county totals in 1831 and 1851 is considerably better than appears in the calculation above, and probably as good as that between 1851 and 1871. The mean difference of 9.5 per cent exaggerates the 'true' position because the 1831 data

It is time to take stock. To make a fair comparison between the numbers engaged in agriculture in 1831 and 1851, the gross total at the latter date must be reduced because it includes landed proprietors, because both those currently employed in the industry and those formerly employed but now retired or incapacitated were included, and because there is strong evidence to suggest that the number of those returned in 1851 as farmers' male relatives engaged in agriculture was substantially exaggerated. The successive corrections made to offset these sources of discrepancy reduced the original total of 1.130 million by roughly 16,000, 75,000 and 15,000 respectively, leaving a revised total of 1.024 million, a figure only 4.4 per cent larger than the 1831 total of 0.981 million. Investigation of the apparent differences between the 1831 total of occupiers of land and the 1851 total of farmers proved on examination to be reassuring rather than otherwise as to the accuracy of the two censuses.

If the revised total for 1851 was accurate there would remain an increase of just over 40,000 between 1831 and 1851 in the labour force engaged in agriculture. The increase is more likely to be overstated than the reverse. Men engaged in silviculture were included in agriculture in 1851, but in 1831 they were not specifically mentioned by Rickman in his instructions to overseers, and it is quite likely that some or all of them were placed in the 'other labourers' group, as fishermen, for example, were required to be. In 1851 woodmen numbered some 7000 (table 11.3). Again it is possible that some elderly, retired farmers in 1831 were not included in the total for agriculture as has been assumed. Farmers were in general an elderly body of men. In 1851 35,308 out of a total of 192,968 were over 65, and 10,923 were over 75, or 18.3 and 5.7 per cent respectively (the comparable national percentages for all males were 7.9 and 2.3). The 1861 census report remarked: 'It should be borne in mind ... that many of the farmers by profession are superannuated, or have given up their farms.'[28] It is possible that a further element in the remaining difference between the census totals would disappear if this point were capable of testing.

Notwithstanding these additional considerations, which might reduce any increase in agricultural employment between 1831 and 1851 almost to vanishing point, there was clearly a marked rise in one element within the

---

refer to ancient counties while those for 1851 refer to the new registration counties. Since the differences were sometimes pronounced, the effect is important. For example, there were 17 counties whose 1831 and 1851 totals differed by more than 10 per cent. Of these, three – Lancashire, Warwickshire and the West Riding of Yorkshire – experienced a major expansion in agriculture during the period so that their totals 'should' have risen sharply (see pp. 314–15). In the remaining 14 counties the mean difference between the 1831 and 1851 totals was 14.7 per cent. If the 1851 totals of farmers and their male relatives in each of these counties is adjusted in the ratio of the population of the ancient county to that of the registration county in 1851, the mean figure drops quite sharply to 9.6 per cent.

28 *1861 Census*, general report, *Parliamentary Papers* 1863, LIII, part 1, p. 29.

agricultural labour force between 1831 and 1851 which is both intriguing and instructive. Elsewhere in England farm employment was probably at best static and may even have been in slight decline, but in the neighbourhood of great cities and near the areas of greatest industrial expansion it grew precipitately. The data set out in table 11.6 show both the scale of the growth and the contrast between the metropolitan and industrial counties and the rest of England. The 1831 totals represent the straightforward division between occupiers of land and labourers already described in connection with table 11.3. Those for 1851 require more explanation. To assist comparability with occupiers in 1831, and for reasons discussed earlier, the total for farmers is supplemented by that for male relatives in 1861. For the same reason males over 65 have been deleted from the totals in the columns for gardeners and for others. The last category (others in agriculture) includes all who formed part of the return for agriculture in 1851, excluding farmers and their relatives, landed proprietors and gardeners, and therefore consists principally of labourers.

The difference between the 1831 and 1851 national totals comes to about 42,000. Of this over 30,000 relates to the industrial and metropolitan counties. The increase taking place elsewhere in England was no larger than the several uncertainties involved in comparing 1831 and 1851, but the growth in the industrial and metropolitan counties was far too great to be accounted for in this way (the percentage rises in the former and the latter were 1.3 and 23.3 respectively). So far from the high level of wages in the urban and industrial areas of England drawing labour out of agriculture in their vicinity, the strength of their demand for food stimulated more intensive agricultural activity. Von Thunen's model concerning the intensity of land use is strongly vindicated.[29]

The most spectacular growth took place in Lancashire and the West Riding of Yorkshire, where the overall growth in agricultural employment was 39 per cent and 19 per cent respectively. In the London metropolitan counties the rise was 18 per cent and in Warwickshire 13 per cent. The bulk of the expansion was in small-scale farming and in market gardening. The metropolitan and industrial counties in 1851 contained 13 per cent of all English farm labourers (treating column 13 totals as consisting essentially of labourers), 20 per cent of all farmers, and 33 per cent of all gardeners, which immediately suggests the prominence of small farms and market gardening in the agriculture of these counties. The percentage figure for gardening is especially striking. However, it should not be overlooked that even in the metropolitan and industrial counties gardeners formed only 11 per cent of the total employed in agriculture. In the London metropolitan counties alone the figure was much higher at 30 per

29 J.H. von Thünen, *The isolated state*, English edn of *Der isolierte Staat in Beziehung auf Landwirtschaft und Nationalökonomie*, ed. P. Hall (Oxford, 1966).

cent; in the industrial counties as a group (Lancashire, the West Riding and Warwickshire) 6 per cent; in the rest of England only 4 per cent. Though only a small element in the agricultural total even in some of the counties most likely to attract expansion in market gardening, the number of market gardeners had risen rapidly. The 1841 census material in table 11.6 suggests that during the 1840s gardening employment rose by 32 per cent.

General comparisons between 1841 and either 1831 or 1851 require caution because farmers' male relatives appear to have been 'lost'. On the face of it the returns suggest a simple pattern of change. The number of farmers and labourers changed only marginally, but the number of gardeners increased substantially, rising by much the same proportion in the country as a whole as in the industrial and metropolitan counties, but affecting the latter more since market gardening was so heavily concentrated near the big cities and new industrial areas. Farmers' male relatives, however, were not separately tabulated, nor were they clearly subsumed in another category, as with occupiers of land in 1831. Most were probably excluded altogether from the census totals.[30] A few may have been included among the labourers; others may have ended in the category listed as the 'residue of the population'. It is unlikely, however, that this complication affects the total of gardeners other than marginally. Moreover, the strong rise in the number of gardeners after 1851 (table 11.4) encourages the view that the apparent rise in the 1840s is genuine. In 1841, as in 1831, the existence of categories for the 'superannuated' and infirm makes it reasonable to compare the totals for gardeners and labourers with the 1851 totals shown in the table, from which men aged 65 or more were excluded.

Agricultural growth in the urban and industrial counties was not confined to market gardening, however. Indeed, only in the vicinity of London does it appear to have been the dominant element in the expansion. In Surrey and Middlesex, if it is safe to assume that the number of gardeners grew as fast in the 1830s as in the 1840s, almost all the gross rise in agricultural employment could be attributed to market gardening. In the industrial counties, in contrast, where overall agricultural employment rose by about 25,000 men, the same assumption would cover less than a sixth of the increase. Small farming by men employing no labour accounted for the bulk of the growth. Comparison of the percentages at the foot of columns 1,2, 15 and 16 shows this very clearly. In the

30 The enumerators' books of the 1841 census afford innumerable instances of, say, farmers' sons whose occupation is indicated in the book as agriculture, but the instructions to enumerators state: 'The profession, etc., of wives, or of sons or daughters living with their husbands or parents, and assisting them, but not apprenticed or receiving wages, need not be set down.' It is possible that at some point in the processing of the returns this instruction was interpreted in a way which eliminated farmers' resident male relatives from the occupational count. *1841 Census*, enumeration abstract, *Parliamentary Papers* 1843, XXII, p. 3.

Table 11.6 Agricultural growth in the metropolitan and industrial counties 1831–1851

| | 1831 | | | | | 1841 | | | |
	Occupiers with labour (1)	Occupiers without labour (2)	All occupiers (3)	Labourers (4)	Total (5)	Farmers (6)	Gardeners (7)	Labourers (8)	Total (9)
Surrey	1,873	727	2,600	16,761	19,361	1,892	3,734	15,865	21,491
Middlesex	1,050	490	1,540	11,376	12,916	1,118	4,761	9,627	15,506
Metropolitan counties	2,923	1,217	4,140	28,137	32,277	3,010	8,495	25,492	36,997
Lancashire	6,658	9,714	16,372	20,949	37,321	14,740	2,195	24,761	41,696
Yorkshire, West Riding	7,096	10,636	17,732	24,502	42,234	15,327	2,038	24,615	41,980
Warwickshire	2,838	1,142	3,980	15,644	19,624	3,461	1,105	15,914	20,480
Industrial counties	16,592	21,492	38,084	61,095	99,179	33,528	5,338	65,290	104,156
All metropolitan and industrial counties (A)	19,515	22,709	42,224	89,232	131,456	36,538	13,833	90,782	141,153
England (B)	141,460	94,883	236,343	744,407	980,750	194,596	42,364	724,625	961,585
England less the metropolitan and industrial counties	121,945	72,174	194,119	655,175	849,294	158,058	28,531	633,843	820,432
Total line (A) as percentage of total of line (B)	13.8	23.9	17.9	12.0	13.4	18.8	32.7	12.5	14.7

1851

	Farmers (10)	Farmers' male relatives (1861) (11)	Gardeners (12)	Others in agriculture (13)	Total (14)	Farms with labour (15)	Farms without labour (16)	Total farms (17)
Surrey	1,955	502	4,980	15,039	22,476	1,563	376	1,939
Middlesex	1,300	164	6,254	7,860	15,578	836	168	1,004
Metropolitan counties	3,255	666	11,234	22,899	38,054	2,399	544	2,943
Lancashire	15,959	4,938	3,287	27,602	51,786	5,865	9,585	15,450
Yorkshire, West Riding	16,504	3,954	2,614	26,993	50,065	6,602	10,783	17,385
Warwickshire	3,611	906	1,404	16,205	22,126	2,467	949	3,416
Industrial counties	36,074	9,798	7,305	70,800	123,977	14,934	21,317	36,251
All metropolitan and industrial counties (A)	39,329	10,464	18,539	93,699	162,031	17,333	21,861	39,194
England (B)	192,968	49,489	55,822	724,355	1,022,634	118,232	72,922	191,154
England less the metropolitan and industrial counties	153,639	39,025	37,283	630,656	860,603	100,899	51,061	151,960
Total line (A) as percentage of total of line (B)	20.4	21.1	33.2	12.9	15.8	14.7	30.0	25.8

Sources: See sources to table 11.2

20 years betwen 1831 and 1851, the proportion of farms employing labour found in the industrial and metropolitan counties rose from 13.8 to 14.7 per cent of the national total. This is a substantial rise, but it was dwarfed by the massive rise in the comparable percentage share for farms employing no labour, which rose from 23.9 to 30.0. Both the scale of the rise and the fact that the absolute percentage for the small farm category was so much higher than for larger farms are eloquent testimony to the history of farming in these counties. In the industrial counties alone the shares for large farms were 11.7 and 12.6 per cent in 1831 and 1851; and for small farms 22.7 and 29.2 per cent.

Absolute totals in these categories for the two dates cannot be calculated on a basis which affords an accurate comparison, because in 1831 the two categories of occupiers included many resident male relatives of the farmers concerned. However, making a crude allowance for this, it is reasonable to suppose that the number of farms in the three industrial counties rose by 11 and 23 per cent respectively for the two categories of those which did and those which did not employ labour. In the rest of England, as we have seen, there are no grounds for supposing that the number of farms increased at all over the same period. In the metropolitan counties there was a very sharp drop in the number of small farms (columns 2 and 16), and it seems possible that in these counties, if not elsewhere, there was some transposition into the category of gardeners to account for so marked a change. The same tendency to transposition into the gardening category probably lies behind most of the drop in the number of labourers in these counties (columns 4 and 13). Both nationally and in the industrial counties the number of labourers showed little change between 1831 and 1851.

Agricultural Employment 1811–1831

Before 1831 the problems involved in making estimates of the trend in agricultural employment change in nature. The first three censuses asked only very general questions about occupation, dividing the population as a whole into those engaged in agriculture; those in trade, manufacture and handicraft; and the rest. In 1801 the information was requested for individuals but, since this gave rise to much confusion, in 1811 and 1821 it was requested for families. When Rickman greatly expanded the scope of his enquiries about occupation in 1831, he reverted to individuals as the basis for the returns to be made, concentrating principally, as we have seen, on men aged 20 or over. However, he also asked word for word the same questions about occupation by families as had been asked 10 years earlier, expecting that the result would enable sufficiently accurate comparisons to be made with earlier censuses for the trend in the three very broad categories used to be identified with confidence.[31] Rickman's expectation was disappointed, as is clear from table 11.7. Between 1821 and 1831 there was a slight fall in the total of agricultural families, only a marginal increase in those engaged in trade, manufacture and handicraft, but a massive rise in the total of families engaged in other occupations. It was clear to him that, though the wording of the questions had been unchanged, the overseers had interpreted them differently.

Rickman gave the following explanation of the altered interpretation of the questions: 'The overseer in England, who knew that many industrious labourers in his parish were employed in mines, or in road-making, and otherwise during the larger proportion of the twelvemonth, but were occasionally employed in harvest, or in the cultivation of their gardens, was heretofore induced to class these as agricultural rather than in the column which *seemed* to denote idleness or no employment at all; but when (as in 1831) a distinct column was assigned to useful labour of whatever kind, he placed them in it, and having so classed them, he could not consistently class their families in the agricultural column, which was thereby lessened in amount, and the seemingly non-productive column of families proportionally increased.'[32] He believed a parallel set of considerations had also influenced overseers in ways which caused the total in trade, manufacture and handicraft to be similarly reduced relative to earlier censuses.

Rickman's explanation, though plausible, was misconceived, as may be seen in figures 11.1 and 11.2. In order to grasp the implications of the figures it is first necessary to note that in the 1831 census there was a marked asymmetry between the total of males over 20 years old employed

Table 11.7 Occupational distribution of families in England 1811–1831

	Agriculture		Trade, manufacture, handicraft		Other		Total	
	(no.)	(%)	(no.)	(%)	(no.)	(%)	(no.)	(%)
1811	697,353	34.7	923,588	45.9	319,450	19.5	2,012,391	100.0
1821	773,732	30.0	1,118,295	47.7	454,690	19.4	2,346,717	100.0
1831	761,348	27.7	1,182,912	43.1	801,076	29.2	2,745,336	100.0

Sources: *1811 Census*, enumeration abstract, *Parliamentary Papers* 1812, XI, p. 427
1821 Census, enumeration abstract, *Parliamentary Papers* 1822, XV, p. 427
1831 Census, enumeration abstract, vol. II, *Parliamentary Papers* 1833, XXXVII, p. 832

31 The question ran, 'What number of families in your parish, township, or place are chiefly employed in and maintained by agriculture; or by trade, manufacture, or handicraft; and how many families are not comprised in either of the two preceding classes?'
32 *1831 Census* (reference as in note 8 in this chapter), p. xii.

in the three great occupational subdivisions of the early censuses and the totals of families in the three categories. Table 11.8 sets out the totals in question. The ratio of the former total to the latter was far higher in agriculture than in either of the other two categories.

A priori there seems no reason why the ratio for agriculture should have been much higher than in the other groups. The high ratio suggests that in the case of agriculture either the numerator was too high, the denominator too low, or both distorting influences were present. Moreover, the existence of such large variations in the ratio counts against Rickman's view that overseers in 1831 were induced in 1831 to make the old-style returns by families consistent with the new-style returns by the occupation of males over 20. If they had been consistent, the ratios would have been less widely spread.

Table 11.8 Adult males and families in major occupational categories in 1831

	Men aged 20 and over (1)	Families (2)	(1)/(2) (3)
Agriculture	980,750	761,348	1.288
Trade, manufacture, handicraft	1,278,283	1,182,912	1.081
Other	940,951	801,076	1.175
Total	3,199,984	2,745,336	1.166

Sources: See sources to tables 11.2 and 11.7

Figures 11.1 and 11.2 provide a strong hint about the source of the distortion in the ratio for agriculture. Figure 11.1 shows that when the ratio of all males over 20 engaged in agriculture to all agricultural families is plotted for each county against the ratio of occupiers employing labour (the larger farmers) to the total agricultural labour force of males over 20, a distinct pattern is visible. Where one ratio was low the others tended to be low also, and high ratios were similarly associated with each other. However, if the larger farmers are removed from the total of males over 20 in agriculture in the numerator of the ratio plotted on the horizontal scale, leaving all the other totals unchanged, the relationship disappears (figure 11.2).[33] Of course, in the latter case the ratios plotted on the horizontal axis are all lower because some individuals are lost from the numerator in every county, but the reduction is naturally far greater where the larger

33 It may be worth noting that in both figures three of the four 'outliers' in the 'south-east' corner of the figure were the metropolitan counties of Middlesex, Surrey and Kent, where the circumstances of agriculture in the period were unusual (see pp. 314–18). If these are disregarded the uniformity of pattern is in both cases enhanced.

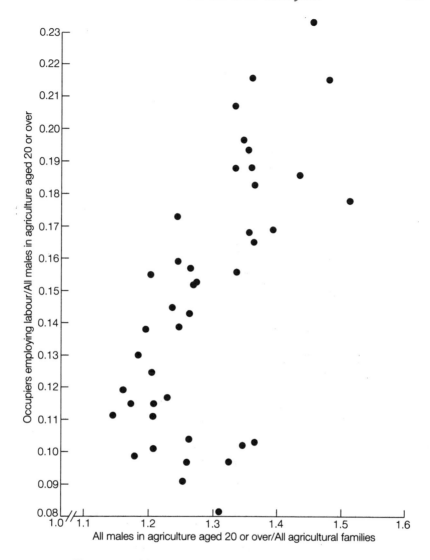

Figure 11.1 Males in agriculture and agricultural families: I
Source: 1831 Census, *enumeration abstract, vols I and II*, Parliamentary Papers *1833, XXXVI and XXXVII*

farmers were a substantial element in the agricultural labour force as a whole than where they were only a small minority, This suggests that the families of the big farmers employing hired labour were not included in the totals of families in agriculture even though they were counted in agriculture in the new-style individual occupational count in 1831. If such

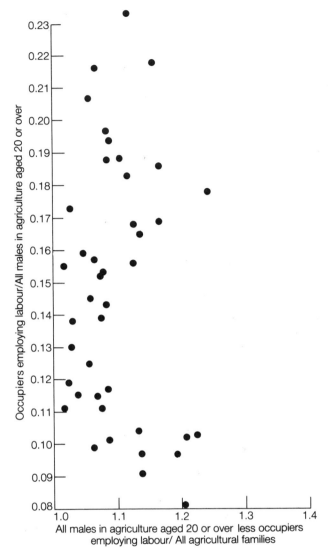

Figure 11.2   Males in agriculture and agricultural families: II
Source: 1831 Census, *enumeration abstract, vols I and II*, Parliamentary Papers *1833, XXXVI and*
XXXVII

families had been included it would be natural to expect no relationship
between the ratios represented on the horizontal axis to those on the
vertical axis in figure 11.1. The disappearance of a relationship between
the variables plotted in figure 11.2 leaves little doubt that this is the
explanation of the change between the two figures.

This explanation rests on the assumption that the denominator of the ratio represented on the horizontal axis is artificially depressed by the exclusion of farmers who employed labour, and that removing this group from the numerator as well brings down the ratio to a level close to the overall average, thus destroying the previous positive relationship between this ratio and the proportion of big farmers in the agricultural total.[34] It amounts to assuming that the overseers normally did not choose to regard the larger farmers as 'chiefly employed and maintained by agriculture' when classifying families, even though they were happy to include them as 'occupiers of land who constantly employ and pay one or more labourer or farm servant in husbandry' when classifying them as individuals. The apparent inconsistency is less quixotic than might appear, given that it might seem odd to classify a man as simultaneously employed and an employer, even though the imprecisions of English usage do not prohibit such an interpretation.[35] The same difficulty does not of course arise, at least with the same acuteness, with occupiers employing no labour. The ratios plotted against the horizontal axis of figure 11.2 suggest that they were normally included among agricultural families. Otherwise in counties where they were relatively numerous the ratios would have been aberrantly high. In fact, however, in the 16 counties where farmers employing no labour formed 10 per cent or more of the total male agricultural labour force, the average of the ratio was virtually identical to the average in the other counties (1.100 and 1.098 respectively). In these 16 counties small farmers were 18.2 per cent of the total of males in agriculture aged 20 or more: in the remaining 26 counties they were only 5.3 per cent, so that the similarity in the ratio in the two

34 The same effect might be found if it were not the denominator which was artificially depressed but the enumerator which was artificially raised. This possibility deserves to be considered but proves to be hard to entertain. The notion that the presence of resident servants in the households of the larger farmers might explain the high ratios can be dismissed. Such men were required to be included with farm labourers. An alternative explanation may also warrant brief attention. If farmers' male relatives were included in the case of the larger farmers but not in the case of others employed in agriculture, then conceivably this might produce an inflation in the numerator; their removal as part of the total for occupiers employing labour might be sufficient to produce the change visible between the two figures. This is intrinsically improbable since the households of labourers and small farmers must have contained equivalent members who would have been included in the occupational totals, and thus render it unlikely that the removal of the larger farmers from the ratio calculation would produce the relative changes observed. Moreover, experimental calculation shows that if a notional allowance is made for the male relatives of the larger farmers and they are removed from the overall agricultural total, the pattern found in figure 11.1 still appears in a slightly muted form.

35 Rickman showed himself to be aware of the ambiguous position of the larger farmers In wrestling with the problem of reconciling the returns for families with those relating to men aged 20 or more, he noted: 'Strictly speaking a large number of occupiers of land who employ labourers may be said not to subsist by *manual* labour; but they are so nearly allied to it and in such various degrees, that no computation of the exempted number can be hazarded.' *1831 Census* (reference as in note 8 in this chapter), p. xi, footnote.

categories is probably meaningful. Finally, the absolute level of the ratio is significant. At 1.102 for England as a whole it was slightly higher than that found in trade, manufacture and handicraft, and only a little below the national average (table 11.8). This further strengthens the view that the larger farmers were missing from the returns for families in agriculture. Had any significant number been included, the denominator would have been higher and the resulting ratio lower.

It follows from this train of argument that the total of families in agriculture needs to be increased if a 'true' figure is to be obtained for comparison with earlier censuses (though it does not follow, of course, that the totals in 1821 or earlier were free from distortions and therefore directly comparable with any revised figure for 1831).

Precision is beyond reach. If, however, one were to assume that the families of the larger farmers were indeed usually excluded from the count of farming families, then one might further assume that the relationship between the number of adult males per family in this category was the same as the national average (1.166) and that therefore the total of such families was 121,321 (141,460/1.166) – a total very close to the total of farms employing labour returned as part of the 1851 census (118,232). This in turn would increase the total of families engaged in agriculture from the census total of 761,348 to 882,669. In 1821 the total of farming families recorded in the census was 773,732, suggesting a substantial rise in agricultural employment in the 1820s. Indeed, if the 1821 census total were directly comparable with the revised figure for 1831, the 1820s would be the last decade in English agricultural history in which employment in the industry was still rising quickly. It transpires, however, that it would be very rash to accept this supposition. It is entirely possible, even likely, that stagnation in male employment had already set in by the 1820s.

In order to understand the problems involved in using occupation data relating to families, it is essential to note that at least 15 and possibly 20 per cent of all families were headed by women. Such families presented special difficulties to the overseers seeking to classify them into one of the three census categories. They could not ignore them because the total of families divided by occupation was required to equal the total number of families in the parish, and it is clear that this total included all families whether headed by men or women, since the mean family size calculated from census date corresponds so closely to mean household size derived from listings of inhabitants. It is the existence of such listings which enables the frequency of households headed by women to be established. They also show that very few female-headed households contained an adult male.[36] Many, of course, were well known to the overseers because

36 Laslett published data derived from 100 English community listings over the period 1574 to 1821. In them, 20.5 per cent of all households were female headed (16.7 per cent by widows, 1.3 per cent by single women, and 2.5 per cent by women whose marital status was unclear). P. Laslett, 'Introduction: the history of the family', in P. Laslett and R. Wall (eds),

they were in receipt of relief. Some, such as those consisting solely of an elderly widow, earned little or nothing from participation in economic activity.[37]

The decisions made by the overseers about the categorization of families headed by women, given their large number, must make a significant difference to the way in which the 1821 census returns are interpreted. Rickman dealt with the matter summarily in his preliminary observations to the 1821 census. After describing some of the difficulties encountered in relation to miners and fishermen, and over the definition of agriculture (which he believed to have been largely overcome in correspondence with the overseers), he continued: 'The subject of classification may be dismissed by stating, that the third or negative class appears to consist chiefly of superannuated labourers, and widows resident in small tenements; this may serve to show that scarcely any information can be drawn from the numbers which appear in the third or negative class.'[38]

Broadly speaking, Rickman's judgement is borne out by the pattern observable in the county data in table 11.9. Of the 42 percentage figures relating to the proportion of families in the 'other' category, 24 lie in the range between 10 and 17.5 per cent, a range within which it is likely that a large majority of the families were female headed. A further four were under 10 per cent. High percentages were largely confined to London (Middlesex and Surrey) and mining counties, notably Cornwall, Durham and Northumberland. Comparatively high percentages elsewhere are almost invariably due to the presence of large urban centres with concentrations of service employment.

If, however, it is safe to suppose that all families with women as head were placed in Rickman's 'negative' class, then the distribution of male employment is clearly likely to be seriously distorted if the published totals of families in the three great divisions are used without adjustment, especially if the argument is couched in terms of the percentage distribution of employment. For example, the middle panel of table 11.10 shows how the implied proportion of the male-headed families employed in

---

Household and family in past time (Cambridge, 1972), table 1.8, p. 78. Listings which detail age are rare, so that information about the proportion of female-headed households containing an adult male is much more narrowly based. As an example, however, in the Yorkshire settlement of Wetherby in 1776 there were only eight adult males (over 21) in the 39 households headed by a woman. On the excellent fit between household sizes calculated from pre-census listings and those derived from the nineteenth-century censuses, see P. Laslett, 'Size and structure of the household in England over three centuries', *Population Studies*, 23 (1969), table 3, p. 210.

37 That solitaries were treated as forming households is suggested not only by continuities in mean household size, but more directly in Rickman's remark in relation to the 1821 census: 'One single person inhabiting a house cannot but be returned as a family, though the word *family* usually denotes more than one person.' *1821 Census*, preliminary observations, *Parliamentary Papers* 1822, XV, p. vii.

38 *1821 Census* (reference as in note 37 in this chapter), p. vii.

Table 11.9 Percentage distribution of occupation by family for English counties 1821

	Agriculture	Trade, manufacture, handicraft	Other
Bedfordshire	61.9	27.8	10.3
Berkshire	53.3	31.7	15.0
Buckinghamshire	57.6	28.8	13.5
Cambridgeshire	60.7	27.2	12.1
Cheshire	34.8	52.1	13.1
Cornwall	37.7	30.4	31.9
Cumberland	35.5	41.3	23.1
Derbyshire	34.4	48.4	17.3
Devonshire	40.8	37.5	21.7
Dorsetshire	48.9	35.7	15.4
Durham	20.5	44.0	35.5
Essex	55.7	28.8	15.5
Gloucestershire	32.1	49.8	18.1
Hampshire	41.9	34.2	23.9
Herefordshire	61.9	25.7	12.4
Hertfordshire	51.5	30.3	18.2
Huntingdonshire	61.9	28.2	9.9
Kent	35.9	35.1	29.0
Lancashire	11.2	74.9	13.9
Leicestershire	35.4	55.1	9.5
Lincolnshire	59.4	27.0	13.6
Middlesex	3.6	61.6	34.8
Monmouth	42.6	43.5	13.8
Norfolk	48.8	35.2	16.0
Northamptonshire	53.4	32.9	13.7
Northumberland	26.8	47.7	25.5
Nottinghamshire	35.4	56.6	8.0
Oxfordshire	55.4	31.1	13.5
Rutland	61.2	26.3	12.5
Shropshire	44.2	42.0	13.8
Somerset	42.8	36.9	20.3
Staffordshire	26.6	61.7	11.7
Suffolk	55.9	31.6	12.4
Surrey	16.8	52.7	30.5
Sussex	50.3	35.5	14.2
Warwickshire	27.9	65.2	6.9
Westmoreland	48.8	36.4	14.8
Wiltshire	52.4	35.6	12.0
Worcestershire	38.3	47.6	14.1
Yorkshire, East Riding	38.2	41.1	20.7
Yorkshire, North Riding	43.2	29.9	26.9
Yorkshire, West Riding	19.6	67.4	13.0
England	33.0	47.7	19.4

Source: 1821 Census, enumeration abstract, *Parliamentary Papers* 1822, XV

Table 11.10   Occupational distribution of families in 1821

	Agriculture		Trade, manufacture, handicraft		Other		Total	
	(no.)	(%)	(no.)	(%)	(no.)	(%)	(no.)	(%)
Census totals	773,732	32.97	1,118,295	47.65	454,690	19.38	2,346,717	100.0
Assuming 10 per cent of all families are female-headed and were placed in the 'other' category:								
Revised totals	773,732	36.63	1,118,295	52,95	220,018	10.42	2,112,045	100.0
Assuming 15 per cent of all families are female-headed and were placed in the 'other' category:								
Revised totals	773,732	38.79	1,118,295	56.06	102,682	5.15	1,994,710	100.0

Source: table 11.7

agriculture would change on the conservative assumption that 10 per cent of the overall total of families were both headed by women and placed in the third category. If we further suppose that the revised distribution of male-headed families is exactly reflected in the distribution of adult male employment, the total of males over 20 engaged in agriculture can be simply calculated. The total male population aged 20–64 may be estimated as 2,608,000, and the total in agriculture as 955,310 (2,608,000 × 0.3663).[39] If the calculation is based on men aged 20–69, the total rises to 991,208, while if it is assumed that 15 rather than 10 per cent of the overall total of families were female headed and placed in the 'negative' class, the two comparable implied totals of male adult employment in agriculture rise to 1,011,643 and 1,049,657.

It will be recalled (table 11.3) that the total adult male employment in agriculture in 1831 was 980,750, and it is therefore clear that it would be unwise to conclude that agriculture was employing significantly more men at the end of the 1820s than at the beginning of the decade. A 'best guess', based on the lowest of the four figures just quoted, might be a rise of about 3 per cent. The additional complications involved in the estimation of the totals of men in the army, navy and merchant marine and their relative

39 For the population totals, see table 11.12; for the multipliers see table 11.10.

importance at the two census dates suggest that the most modest of the four estimates is to be preferred (see notes to table 11.12).[40]

To complete the comparison of 1821 and 1831 we may revert to the question originally posed about the changing total of families recorded as engaged in agriculture at the two censuses. It will be recalled that the published total fell from 773,732 to 761,348 but that a revised figure for 1831 is calculable, making allowance for the apparent reluctance of the overseers to include occupiers of land who employed labour on their farms in the totals of agricultural families. The revised figure was 882,669, suggesting a large increase in agricultural employment.

The problem of reconciling the evidence of family totals with that drawn from a consideration of probable totals of adult male employment, however, is more apparent than real. In 1831 as in 1821 15 per cent or more of all families were headed by women, and once again very few such families included an adult male. However, it is unlikely that the overseers were so apt to consign all such families to the third category, 'all other families not comprised in the two preceding classes', because of the influence of the new set of questions regarding the employment of men aged 20 or more. If they had done so it would have tended to cause the ratio shown in table 11.8 to be exceptionally low in the 'other' category since it would have greatly increased the number of families in the second column without affecting the total in the first column. But the ratio for the 'other' category was actually higher than the national average in spite of the presence of the families of the larger farmers in column 2, not offset by a corresponding boost to the total in column 1. Adjusting for this factor must, of course, increase the ratio significantly, and virtually rules out the possibility that all female-headed families were allotted to the 'other' class in 1831.

Rickman offered no comment on the placing of female-headed families in 1831, though he had done so ten years earlier. The most reasonable assumption to make is that such families were distributed between the three classes in much the same proportion as male-headed families. A further consideration which underwrites this conclusion is that the total number of men over 20 in the three categories of male adult employment that would certainly have caused their families to be placed in the 'other' category (capitalists, bankers, professional and other educated men; labourers not employed in agricultural labour; other males over 20) represent 27.8 per cent of the total of males aged 20 or more,[41] compared

40 This view is reinforced by taking note of the lack of consistency in the treatment of the 'negative' class at the parish level, evident in the 1821 census. If all female-headed households, for example, had been consistently placed in that category, there would be few parishes of any size in which there were no families in the 'negative' class. But instances are easily found.

41 In the calculation of this percentage, servants were excluded from the numerator and the denominator since they were seldom married. Their number was small (70,629) in

with a figure of 29.2 per cent for the total of families in the 'other' category. If the larger farmers (occupiers employing labour) are included in the range of occupations to be related to families in the 'other' category, the proportion of males over 20 whose occupation would have caused their family to be placed in the 'other' category rises to 32.3 per cent. Once more, there appear to be no grounds for supposing that female-headed families were disproportionately represented in the 'other' class in 1831, though there is good reason to think that this had happened in the previous census. But, if they were distributed evenly among the three classes, then for the purpose of comparing 1821 and 1831 the revised 1831 total for agricultural families would need to be reduced by removing its 10–15 per cent share of female-headed households, which restores rough parity to the totals at the two dates.

The 'plateau' in male agricultural employment therefore probably covered the whole period from 1821 to 1851. It is conceivable that employment may have risen from, say, 900,000 to 1,000,000 over the period, but more likely that the scale of growth was closer to 50,000, and it would be unwise to rule out the possibility that there was no growth at all.

The first two censuses also contained some occupational data. What was collected in 1801 is worthless. Even the most cursory inspection and analysis reveals massive and haphazard inconsistencies in the way the questions were interpreted by the overseers.[42] In 1811, on the other hand, the questions were the same as in 1821, and there appears to be no complication affecting the comparison of these two censuses of the sort which entails such marked difficulties in comparing 1821 and 1831. As might be expected the 'other' category was an unchanging fraction of the whole, comprising, as it seems to have done, chiefly families headed by women. There was both absolute and proportional growth in trade, manufacture and handicraft, while agriculture grew in absolute numbers but declined as a fraction of the labour force (table 11.7). The total number of families in agriculture grew by just under 11 per cent.

It is tempting to interpret these data in a straightforward way, and to conclude that in the 1810s the agricultural labour force was in its last period of rapid increase, to be followed by only the most muted growth thereafter. Once again, however, first impressions may be misleading, for there is evidence that the apparent scale of expansion overstates the true position. There are two reasons for caution. First, as may be seen in table 11.11, the number of agricultural families in the most rapidly industrializ-

---

relation to either the numerator (870,322) or the denominator (3,129,355). It should be noted that military personnel and sailors were also excluded since their number is so hard to establish (see notes to table 11.12).

42 Rickman was most positive on the point, writing in 1811: 'Hence the question regarding occupations may be said to have produced no result in 1801, if indeed an incorrect result be not worse than none, as giving colour to unfounded speculations.' *1811 Census*, preliminary observations, *Parliamentary Papers* 1812, XI, p. x.

Table 11.11 Agricultural growth in the industrial counties 1811–1821

	1811				1821			
	Agriculture	Trade, manufacture, handicraft	Other	Total	Agriculture	Trade, manufacture, handicraft	Other	Total
Derby	14,283	15,825	7,332	37,440	14,582	20,505	7,317	42,404
Durham	10,288	17,094	11,906	39,288	9,427	20,212	16,301	45,940
Lancashire	23,305	114,522	24,072	161,899	22,723	152,271	28,179	203,173
Monmouth	5,815	4,812	1,916	12,543	6,020	6,147	1,955	14,122
Northumberland	10,945	16,547	10,251	37,743	11,567	20,565	10,996	43,128
Staffordshire	18,361	34,011	10,165	62,537	18,265	42,435	8,060	68,780
Warwickshire	15,131	29,775	4,160	49,066	16,779	39,189	4,155	60,123
Yorkshire, West Riding	30,868	86,522	16,211	133,601	31,613	108,841	21,012	161,466
Industrial counties	128,996	319,108	86,013	534,117	130,996	410,165	97,975	639,136
England	697,353	923,588	391,450	2,012,391	773,732	1,118,295	454,690	2,346,717
England less industrial counties	568,357	604,480	305,437	1,478,274	642,736	708,130	356,715	1,707,581
Percentages								
Industrial counties	24.2	59.7	16.1	100.0	20.5	64.2	15.2	100.0
England	34.7	45.9	19.5	100.0	33.0	47.7	19.4	100.0
England less industrial counties	38.4	40.9	20.7	100.0	37.6	41.5	20.9	100.0

Source: 1811 *Census*, enumeration abstract, *Parliamentary Papers* 1812, XI, p. 427

ing counties showed no growth. In view of the evidence that a quarter of a century later agriculture was expanding in such counties, though not elsewhere,[43] this means that there was a striking change in the nature of agricultural growth between the 1810s and the 1830s and 1840s; or, if this was not the case, that there may have been other influences at work causing distortion of the returns from the more rural counties.

This suspicion is strengthened by detailed examination of the returns for counties in which the rise in agricultural employment appeared swiftest. Individual hundreds within the same county often show a suspiciously wide range of percentage rises. The returns for Buckinghamshire, for example, show a sharp rise in the total of families in agriculture over the decade (19.4 per cent), but this was especially marked in the hundreds of Newport and Cottesloe where the rises were 43 and 45 per cent respectively. Elsewhere in the county the overall rise was only 11 per cent. When individual parishes within the hundreds are studied in turn the large overall rise proves to be disproportionately concentrated in a few parishes, such as Ivinghoe in Cottesloe or Hanslope and North Crowley in Newport. In Ivinghoe, for example, the total of agricultural families rose from 27 to 261. Clearly increases on such a scale must be due to faulty returns. In most cases, consulting the returns for 1831, where there is much additional information about the agricultural employment of adult males, settles the question of which of the two earlier returns is the more reliable. Scattered but unsystematic checks of a number of hundreds with very rapid apparent growth in agricultural employment, such as Tendring in Essex or the Lathe of Scray in Kent, suggest that it is much more common to find a serious undercount in 1811 than exaggeration in 1821. More extensive testing would be required to substantiate this impression, but there is enough initial evidence to lend weight to the view that the number of men on the land was not rising as rapidly as the censuses appear to show at first blush.

Rickman was aware that the number of families in agriculture might be understated in 1811. He wrote of these data that they were 'a remarkable proof ... of the difficulty of putting any question which shall be universally understood. In some places *occupiers* of land, but not *labourers* in agriculture, are supposed to belong to that class; in other places exactly the contrary.'[44] He believed such mistakes were usually evident and had been corrected, but in this he was probably too sanguine.[45]

43 See pp. 314–18.

44 *1811 Census* (reference as in note 42 in this chapter), p. x.

45 The phrase quoted was repeated in the preliminary observations to the 1821 census, but this was very common in the compiling of the introductions to the early censuses and it may well have had less point on the second occasion. The 1811 census was not free from substantial numerical errors. For example, the population of the North Riding of Yorkshire was given as 152,445 when the 'true' figure was 165,506. The mistake arose because the total for the Liberty of Langbaugh East was given as 2418 when it should have been 15,479. The printed total is that for the parishes of Ormsby, Skelton, Upleatham, Westerdale and Whitby only.

In summary, therefore, the totals set out in table 11.12 represent reasonable estimates of the changes taking place in the male labour force actively engaged in agriculture between 1811 and 1851. After 1851 the course of change is easier to follow because the census returns, though not without inconsistencies which demand caution in constructing a time

Table 11.12   The adult male labour force in agriculture in England 1811–1851

	Males employed in agriculture (aged 20 or more) (1)	Male population (aged 20–64) (2)	Male population (aged 20–69) (3)	(1) as percentage of (2) (4)	(1) as percentage of (3) (5)
1811	910,000	2,315,000	2,407,000	39.3	37.8
1821	955,000	2,608,000	2,706,000	36.6	35.3
1831	981,000	3,025,000	3,141,000	32.4	31.2
1841	996,000	3,647,000	3,771,000	27.3	26.4
1851	1,010,000	4,099,685	4,241,827	24.6	23.8

All figures given in column 1, except those for 1831 and 1841, were arrived at after making a series of assumptions about the changes needed to make the totals comparable with each other, and to offset various sources of distortion detected in the returns. Details will be found in the main text. The 1831 total was taken directly from the census. That for 1841 is simply an interpolation between the 1831 and 1851 figures. The census total was 962,000 (table 11.6) but there seems reason to fear that the number of male relatives of farmers, living and working on the farm, were undercounted relative to either 1831 or 1851 censuses (see text).

The totals in columns 2 and 3 were derived as follows:

1821: the census provides age data for 88 per cent of the male population. It was assumed that the male population as a whole corresponded in age structure to that part of it whose ages were known. Since the age group 60–69 was undivided, a split between those aged 60–64 and those age 65–69 was made on the assumption that their relative size was the same as was the case in 1851.

1811: the census provides no age data. It was assumed that men aged 20–64 and 20–69 formed the same proportion of the total male population over 20 as in 1821.

1831: the census provides a total for all males aged 20 or more. The totals for 20–64 and 20–69 were obtained on the assumption that they formed the same proportion of the male population over 20 as in 1821.

1841: as in 1821, though the number who failed to declare an age was tiny.

1851: directly from the census returns. In every census except 1851 a further adjustment was necessary because men in the armed forces and the merchant marine were reported separately without even division between English, Welsh, Scottish or Irish men. The totals in question in the four censuses 1811 to 1841 were 640,500; 319,300; 277,017; and 188,453. Rickman drew attention to the high proportion of foreigners on British vessels when commenting on the 1811 return, suggesting that 100,000 men were involved. He implied that the figure had fallen sharply after the end of the war period. It is essential to make some allowance for these men since they formed a widely changing fraction of the adult male population. The following arbitrary adjustments were made to the raw figures. First, deduct 100,000 from the 1811 total; 25,000 from that for 1821; and 20,000 from those of 1831 and 1841. Next, reduce the resulting totals on the assumption that the English share of the total was equal to the English share of the combined populations of England, Wales, Scotland and Ireland (at the four successive dates the factors used for multiplication were 0.539, 0.540, 0.545 and 0.562). Finally, multiply the resulting totals by 0.88. In 1851, of the total of men in the army, navy or working in the merchant navy, 88 per cent of those under 65 years of age were in the age range 20–64. The totals yielded by this series of operations for 1811 to 1841 were 256,000; 140,000; 123,000; and 83,000 respectively. In 1851 when all such men were returned like those in any other occupation, the comparable total was 145,000.

Sources: see sources to tables 11.2, 11.9 and 11.11. The census totals for Ireland and earlier estimates of the Irish population totals were taken from W. E. Vaughan and A. J. Fitzpatrick (eds), *Irish historical statistics. Population, 1821–1971* (Dublin, 1978), pp. 1–3

series, were collected on a broadly uniform basis. Moreover, after 1851 there is no reason to doubt that employment in the industry was beginning to ebb, though only very slowly for a further quarter-century. The table also shows the total of the male population aged 20–64 at each date to enable the adult male agricultural labour force to be expressed as a percentage of the total adult male labour force.

The totals given in column 1, especially for the two earlier dates, are less accurate than might be wished. It is a reasonable guess, but no more, that the figures for 1811 and 1821 are unlikely to be out by more than plus or minus 5 and 3 per cent respectively. The 1831 and 1851 totals are probably more accurate – if not in an absolute sense, then in the sense that their size relative to each other is unlikely to be seriously inaccurate. Further work on the censuses themselves might narrow the margins of uncertainty further, and it would also be possible to strengthen all estimates of occupational structure considerably by work based on the occupational data available under the provisions of Rose's Act in the baptism registers from 1813 onwards.[46] But the estimates presented in table 11.12 permit some tentative conclusions to be drawn both about other characteristics of the male labour force, and about some wider issues.

Reflections

First, it appears that agriculture at the beginning of the nineteenth century employed a much higher proportion of the adult male labour force than of the labour force as a whole. Deane and Cole, for example, estimated that agriculture, forestry and fishing comprised the following percentages of the total occupied population in 1811, 1821, 1831, 1841 and 1851 (table 11.12 percentages for males relative to the male population 20–64 shown in brackets): 33.0 (39.3), 28.4 (36.6), 24.6 (32.4), 22.2 (27.3), 21.7 (24.6).[47] Their estimates refer to Britain rather than England and, since agriculture was probably relatively more important in Britain as a whole than in England, the true contrast is even more marked than the percentages suggest. The differences are not irreconcilable, of course, given the marked variance between male and female employment patterns. More difficult to reconcile, however, is the contrast in growth rates over time. Deane and Cole's estimate of the total British labour force in agriculture, forestry and fishing remains unchanged at 1.8 million from 1811 to 1831 before rising sharply to 2.1 million in 1851.[48] Since they

46 Under the Act the occupation of the father was to be recorded on registrtion forms printed as books. Similarly the occupation of the deceased was to be set down in the burial register. Initial experimentation suggests that they would prove a very informative source if a sufficient number of registers were analysed using an appropriate sampling frame.

47 Deane and Cole, *British economic growth*, table 30, p. 142.

48 They remarked, indeed, that 'the results are little more than guesses': ibid., table 31, p. 143.

included women and children in their estimates and they were probably a declining fraction of the agricultural labour force, the true contrast is understated by these totals.[49] Their estimates were explicitly rough and ready,[50] and it is difficult to pinpoint the cause of the differences between the trends in the two series. It is highly probable, however, that the principal reason was their belief that 'up to and including 1871, persons described as "retired" from any stated occupation were classified by that occupation'.[51] As was noted earlier, this procedure was new to the 1851 census. Before then some or all of the 'superannuated' were classified separately. The rise in agricultural employment in the 1840s, which is a striking feature of Deane and Cole's figures and to which they themselves drew attention, was probably therefore the spurious effect of a failure to make allowance for changes in census practice.[52] If this is taken into account, the trends in the two series are closely similar.

Second, if agricultural employment scarcely rose in the early nineteenth century, output per man must have risen substantially. This was the age of Ricardo. Both he and Malthus were concerned about the danger of declining marginal returns to factor inputs in agriculture. Both believed that it would prove very difficult if not impossible to avoid the problem in practice, just as they considered it appeared unavoidable in theory. Yet English agriculture in this period was clearly well able to overcome such pressures. It is true that the proportion of food needs covered by home agriculture declined steadily though slowly, but the physical output of agriculture must have expanded considerably. A simple calculation demonstrates the point. Between 1811 and 1851 the population rose by 77 per cent (table 11.1). Over the same period the number of adult males employed in agriculture rose by about 11 per cent (table 11.12), and total labour inputs must have risen less because of the declining extent of female participation in field work. Assuming, as an illustration of possibilities, that in 1811 the country met 90 per cent of its food needs, and in 1851 80 per cent, and that food consumption per head did not change significantly, output per man engaged in agriculture would have risen by 42 per cent.

There is room for argument about scale of growth in productivity per man, but no reason to doubt that it was considerable. Most of the improvement must reflect success in intensifying production on land already in farm use since, by the early nineteenth century, little land

---

49 K.D.M. Snell, 'Agricultural seasonal unemployment, the standard of living, and women's work in the south and east, 1690–1860', *Economic History Review*, 2nd series, 34 (1981), pp. 407–37.

50 Deane and Cole, *British economic growth*, note to table 30, p. 142.

51 Ibid., pp. 142–3.

52 They had sufficient confidence in their estimates of agricultural employment to identify the 1840s as the only period in the nineteenth century in which the steady decline in the proportion of the labour force engaged in agriculture was interrupted. Ibid., p. 141.

capable of arable or pastoral use remained to be broken in. Nor did the first half of the nineteenth century represent a new departure in this respect. The share of agriculture in total employment had been falling steadily for the preceding 200 years. Indeed a comparatively static agricultural labour force in absolute terms was a striking feature of English history from 1600 onwards. The population of England in 1600 was about 4.0 million and, on the assumption that agriculture then employed 70 per cent of the male labour force, the implied scale of employment in the industry would be 700,000.[53] Calculations similar to that made above imply a very handsome long-term rise in output per man in agriculture over the whole period 1600–1850.

Estimates made in this way are apt to be misleading, of course, if taken in isolation. The steady, rapid growth in employment in the industries listed in table 11.2, all of which were principally engaged in providing goods and services to the local market, is in part a reflection of the boost to local demand arising from the prosperity produced by increasing efficiency in agriculture. In part, however, it may be regarded as an element in the process by which rising productivity was achieved. To the degree that the farmer called upon carters or builders to provide goods and services which his father or grandfather might have provided for himself, a part of the proliferation of employment outside agriculture but in the countryside represents an element in the increasing specialization of function which played so large a part in raising output per head generally in early-nineteenth-century England. Similarly, farming and labouring households created additional employment in trades such as tailoring, baking, butchering and shopkeeping as they turned to an external market to perform what would earlier have been done at home to a greater extent. Nevertheless the productivity gains in agriculture must have been substantial. Each man at work on the land in the 1850s was capable of meeting the food needs of significantly more people engaged in other work than his predecessor in the 1800s had been able to do. Changes in techniques and organization had more than offset the influences tending to cause declining marginal returns as land use intensified.

The third reflection is a general one. There were industries in which both productivity per head and employment were rising rapidly in the first half of the century. Cotton and iron manufacture fall into this

---

53 The population total is taken from Wrigley and Schofield, *The population history of England*, table A3.3, p. 532. For the basis of the estimate of the percentage of employment in agriculture, see E.A. Wrigley, 'Urban growth and agricultural change: England and the continent in the early modern period', *Journal of Interdisciplinary History* 15 (1985), table 4, pp. 700–1, columns 1 and 5. The percentage figure for employment was converted into an estimate of the total employed on the crude assumption that males aged 20–64 were a quarter of the total population. Experimentation with model life tables with values of e_0 and r at the levels prevailing about 1600 suggests that this figure must be approximately correct. In 1851 under a somewhat different demographic regime the comparable percentage was 24.2 (tables 11.1 and 11.12).

category. There was one great industry, agriculture, in which output per head rose markedly but in which employment grew very little in absolute terms, and fell sharply as a fraction of the workforce. But there was also a host of industries, of which those represented in table 11.2 are typical, which collectively employed a very large proportion of adult men, and in which employment was fully keeping pace with the increase in the labour force, yet where it is improbable that there were any major changes in productivity per man in this period. The tools and methods of work of tailors, butchers, blacksmiths, carpenters and bricklayers changed very little. Nor were they caught up in a process of specialization of function akin to Adam Smith's pinmakers which might have allowed large gains in · the quantity or quality of output per man. They were scattered over the country, working for the most part as isolated individuals or in tiny production units very much as in earlier generations, serving only a local market. They were beneficiaries of greatly enhanced productivity elsewhere in the economy rather than contributors to it.

Conclusion

Between 1800 and 1850 there were striking changes in the English male labour force. It grew at an unprecedented pace. Agriculture lost ground rapidly relative to other forms of employment. When the century began two men in five still worked on the land: by the mid century fewer than one in four. The adult male labour force grew by 1.8 million between 1811 and 1851 but agriculture provided only about 100,000 new jobs. It is not possible over the whole period 1811 to 1851 to quantify the relative contribution of manufacturing on the one hand and retail and handicraft employment on the other to the provision of work for the balance of the much enlarged labour force, but even the limited data presented in the first main section of this essay leave no doubt that the latter was much more important than the former in this regard. Retail trade and handicraft were forms of employment in which there were few changes in work practices or output per head, and where small independent masters were common and wage-paid proletarians rare; and output from such industries and service trades was principally for local markets. Thus this finding is not only significant in relation to the better appreciation of the course of economic change in the period, but needs to be taken into account when considering the history of social structure, of the development of classes, and of political allegiances. Further work on the history of English occupational structure may prove to have surprisingly far-reaching implications.

12

The First Scientific Social Structure of Modern Britain 1875–1883

S. R. S. Szreter

I

Just over a century ago a long-forgotten episode occurred in the prehistory of British social science. In 1875 the British Association appointed an Anthropometric Committee, which sat until 1883 and produced what could be described as the first 'scientific' formulation of modern Britain's social structure.[1]

Social structure is used here in the sense of differential and unequal lifechances and experiences.[2] It is significant that this has been identified as the medical demographic sense which is implied by the current Registrar-General's system of social classification, since it is suggested that the scheme discussed here can be seen as the ancestor of that system.[3] One could inevitably point to earlier formulations of Britain's

This paper benefitted from the comments offered by the members of the King's College Cambridge Social History Seminar, at which an earlier version was delivered in May 1985.

1 The original committee members appointed at the Bristol meeting of 1875 were: Dr John Beddoe; Lord Aberdare; Dr William Farr (Chairman); Sir H. Rawlinson; Colonel Lane Fox (after 1880 known as Pitt-Rivers); Sir Rawson Rawson; J. Heywood; Dr J. Mouat; Professor G. Rolleston; P. Hallet; F. Fellows: Professor Leone Levi; and Francis Galton was the secretary. The final report was written by Charles Roberts and Sir Rawson Rawson and was presented at the Southport meeting of 1883. Their fellow committee members by this time were: Galton (Chairman since 1880); E. Brabrook (secretary since 1880); Fellows; Heywood; Levi; Lt-General Pitt-Rivers; Dr F. Mahomed; and J. Price. There were also four associates named: Dr T. Balfour; Dr J. Gladstone; Dr Lawson (Inspector-General of Hospitals); and Dr William Ogle (who succeeded Farr as Superintendent of Statistics at the General Register Office (GRO) on the latter's retirement through ill-health in 1880). Various other figures were temporary members of the committee between 1876 and 1882: Captain Dillon; A. Redgrave; Dr W Bain; Sir G. Campbell; Earl of Ducie; Professor Flower; Distant; Park Harrison; G Shaw Lefevre; Dr W. Lewis; Dr Muirhead; F. Rudler. Many of the committee members seem to have played no direct part in the compiling of the reports but were instrumental in the provision of data sets for analysis.

2 Of course, this is only one of several possible meanings. For a review of various other empirical formulations, see J.H. Goldthorpe and P. Bevan, 'The study of social stratification in Great Britain 1946–76', *Social Science Information* 16 (1977), pp. 279–334.

3 Ibid., section 6. See also J.A. Banks, 'The social structure of nineteenth century England as seen through the census', in R. Lawton (ed.), *The census and social structure* (London, 1978), p. 181.

social structure in this sense; however, it is maintained that this was
the first explicitly scientific product, albeit of the naïve empiricism of
high Victorian naturalistic social science.[4]

Of course Charles Roberts, the principal architect of the scheme to
be discussed here, was not actually engaged in the study of social
structure *per se*.[5] He was primarily interested in providing a scientific
explanation for the phenomenon of physical and mental variation between individuals of the British 'race'. However, it was this preoccupation with what was in effect the issue of social inequality, despite the
biological and individualistic formulation, which inevitably led him to
construct the first 'scientific' model of social structure, in the sense
defined above.

II

It was the ubiquitous Francis Galton who first proposed that a national
anthropometric survey be conducted.[6] His desire to establish whether
'the general physique of the nation' was deteriorating or improving,
both absolutely and comparatively with that of other nations, was
prompted by his social interpretation of the Darwinist theory of natural
selection through survival of the fittest. He claimed that since 'Civilization is a new condition imposed upon man', 'the needs of centraliza-
tion, communication and culture call for more brains and mental
stamina than the average of our race possess.'[8] In the competitive
struggle with other nations and races, imperial mastery would be won
by the nation breeding these desirable characteristics most efficiently.[9]

4 For instance, J.A. Banks mentions both Rickman's classification of occupations from the
1831 census (subsequently abandoned at the following census of 1841) and also William
Farr's classification scheme, which was in use at the GRO during the second half of the
nineteenth century. However, the former was not based on explicitly scientific principles,
while the latter did not incorporate a notion of unequal life chances. Ibid., pp. 185–9.

5 Charles Roberts qualified at St George's Medical School, London in 1859 and then
practised in York as a prison surgeon. He returned to the metropolis in 1871 when he was
elected Fellow of the Royal College of Surgeons, taking up employment as Surgeon to the
Outpatients Department at the Victoria hospital for children. Although he was possessed of
ample private means, his date of birth does not appear to be known. He died on 31 December
1901 after a year's illness. For some further details, see J.M. Tanner, *A history of the study of
human growth* (Cambridge, 1981), pp. 172–80.

6 F. Galton, 'Proposal to apply for anthropological statistics from schools' *Journal of the
Anthropological Institute* 3 (1873–4), pp. 308–11.

7 F. Galton, *Hereditary genius* (London, 1869), p. 344.

8 Ibid., p. 345.

9 Galton's increasing involvement in the late 1860s with these issues of imperial
supremacy was part of a general sense of unease which the Victorians experienced at this
time, following the less than impressive military performance in the Crimea and the new
unifications of Germany and the USA. With the defeat of the Austrians at Sadowa in 1866,
and then the French in 1871, the sense of growing Prussian strength and menace heightened
sensitivities further. See G.R. Searle, *The quest for national efficiency: a study in British politics and
thought 1899–1914* (Oxford, 1971), chapter 4.

Galton was especially concerned that far from a desirable raising of the nation's average abilities, blind social conditions seemed to be conspiring to exert the opposite effect. A paper which Galton delivered to the Statistical Society of London (later the Royal Statistical Society) in January 1873 lamented that 'the more energetic of our race, and therefore those whose breed is the most valuable to our nation, are attracted from the country to our towns.'[10] This was worrying from the eugenic viewpoint, because a series of demographic calculations based on the differences between the GRO's urban (Manchester) and 'healthy districts' lifetables then purported to show that the pernicious effects of the urban, high-mortality environment meant that 'the adult grandchildren of artisan townsfolk are little more than half as numerous as those of labouring people who live in healthy country districts.'[11] Thus, Galton feared that dysgenic rather than eugenic social selection was in fact occurring and that the average ability of each generation was actually declining.

As the above illustrates, Galton's analysis was suffused with an entirely meritocratic understanding of British society and an associated belief in an actual, empirically visible social hierarchy. In order to study the problem of national deterioration he went on to propose a methodology entirely premised on this model of society. He reasoned that since 'different grades of school represent different grades of the community' the anthropometric data sets which he proposed to collect from various schools could be categorized according to the type of school.[12] Galton was here merely following the conventional wisdom of educationalists — exactly that section of the nation who believed most strongly in the same meritocratic principles as himself![13] This is confirmed in the views of the famous contemporary Taunton Commission 1864–7: that each grade of school catered for a distinct, graded social constituency within the nation. These social gradings were conventionally defined in terms of a vague reference group of adult male occupations.[14]

10 F. Galton, 'The relative supplies from town and country families to the population of future generations', *Journal of the Statistical Society* 36 (March 1873), p. 19.

11 Ibid., p. 23.

12 Galton, 'Proposal to apply for anthropometric statistics', p. 309.

13 On the historical origins of this ideology, see K. Hope, 'The political conception of merit' (unpublished typescript, Oxford, 1977).

14 The Commission recognized four grades of educational establishment. The first three grades were all categories of secondary school, commencing with the public boarding school for the upper class, the future gentlemen and their ladies. Second-grade schools were for the middle class, those with a white-collar life in commerce and industry ahead of them. The third grade was for 'commerce of the shop and town', including higher craft trades. The fourth grade was the elementary school only, for the children of the labouring poor. See G. Sutherland, *Ability, merit and measurement* (Oxford, 1984), pp. 101–9 for these descriptions of the categories.

Galton therefore suggested that these broad groupings of occupations could be precisely defined and organized into an exhaustive set of discrete classes, which could then be identified in the occupational returns of the 1871 census. This would show what proportion of the national population each social class constituted, and therefore what proportion of the nation each equivalent grade of school represented. These proportions would then provide appropriate weightings for the calculation of the overall national average from the data collected in each of the four grades of school. The anthropometric data, which was collected from an unstratified sample of schools, could then be grouped and averaged according to the type of school from which it came. Then the grouped results for each category of school could be appropriately weighted to reflect the proportion of the nation which each grade of school served, so as to arrive at an estimate of the overall national average physique of schoolchildren at each successive year of age.

III

At the same time that Galton was coming to the conclusion that an anthropometric survey was required, as a result of his social Darwinist speculations, Charles Roberts was already engaging in such an inquiry, but for quite separate purposes: those of practical administration of the state's protective factory legislation. He was one of five doctors appointed to take anthropometric surveys of factory children for the Parliamentary Commission of 1872, which reported in 1876 on the working of the Factory and Workshop Act.[15]

As a result of this work, Roberts became fascinated with anthropometrics, and was inspired by reading the latest publication of the veteran Belgian statistician, Adolphe Quetelet, to proceed towards a general study of the dimensions of the British peoples.[16] However, he never completed this project and his only major publication on the subject remains *A Manual of Anthropometry* (1878). In this, he justified his proposed exercise on a host of pragmatic grounds, concerning the advantages such knowledge would bring to the individual and to the

15 The administrative problem in question was that of devising a procedure for factory surgeons to enable them to certify whether or not a child or young person was physically capable of work, within the age limits set by Parliament. It was recognized that birth certificates, even if produced, were insufficient evidence of an individual's physical fitness for factory work, since there was such wide variation in individuals' physical development at given ages. Hence arose the project of determining empirically the typical proportions of children of the labouring class, so as to fix uniform minimum standards of age-specific physique to facilitate enforcement of the laws. The collection of anthropometric data by the Commission was in keeping with the precedent set by Edwin Chadwick's 1833 Commission and also a subsequent inquiry by Leonard Horner in 1837. See Tanner, *Human growth*, pp. 147–61.

16 L.A.J. Quetelet, *Anthropométrie ou mesure des différentes facultés de l'homme* (Brussels, 1870).

state for maintenance of personal health and longevity, efficiency of occupational and military recruitment and so on.[17] What he conspicuously did *not* find it necessary to discuss at all throughout the *Manual* was the relationship of his work on the proportions of the British race to the theory of evolution.

This does not, however, mean that contemporary developments in social Darwinism were unimportant to Roberts's work. It is vital for a proper understanding of what follows – the machinations which produced the first scientific social structure of Britain – that we try to follow the author's changing (but unfortunately only implicit) interpretation of evolutionary theory. The reason for Roberts's lack of any detailed discussion of these issues in 1878 was probably the conventionality of his views, which comprised a very gradualist, broadly Lamarckian and environmentalist understanding of evolution.[18] He believed that each of the 'races' of mankind was a relatively fundamental and unchanging unit produced by a process of very long-term adaptation to a characteristic set of environmental conditions prevailing during the prehistoric past. By contrast the current observable variations between individuals of the same race, for instance those found between the representatives of the middle and of the working classes of 'the British race', were conceptualized as due to relatively superficial environmental influences which could not alter the long-established characteristics of the race, but merely lead to their under- or over-expression in individual specimens.[19] Thus Roberts stated that 'the permanent and constant elements which modify the development of the human body are age, sex and race, and some of the secondary and temporary ones are disease, occupation, social habits, nurture, food, exercise, rest, etc.'[20] Hence his initial goal was formulated as 'fixing the typical forms of man for each age as they exist at present'.[21] He warned that:

It is necessary to bear in mind that the typical form ... is not necessarily the most perfect form of man, but represents the equilibrium, as it were, of many contending forces which may be disturbed by the future predominance of any one of them; hence the typical form is not the same for the working and the

17 C. Roberts, *A manual of anthropometry* (London, 1878), introduction.
18 See note 35 in this chapter.
19 Of course, race was itself a very imprecise notion at this time. Roberts seems to have envisaged three historical racial groupings – Celtic, Scandinavian and Teutonic – as constituting 'the British race'. On the complexities of the notion of race at this time, see: M. Banton, *The idea of race* (London, 1977); D.A. Lorimer, *Colour, class and the Victorians. English attitudes to the negro in the mid nineteenth century* (Leicester, 1978); N. Stepan, *The idea of race in science: Great Britain 1800–1960* (London, 1982). J.W. Burrow, *Evolution and society* (Cambridge, 1966) is excellent for a more general coverage.
20 Roberts, *Manual*, p. 95.
21 C. Roberts, 'The physical development and the proportion of the human body', *St George's Hospital Reports* 8 (1874–6), p. 16.

non-working man, for the man living in towns and the man living in the rural districts.[22]

During the account that follows it is important to remember this distinction which Roberts had himself so carefully made, between the neutral *descriptive* notion of the typical or average form and the *prescriptive* notion of the most perfect form.

Roberts was soon able to compare the large data set of measurements generated by the Parliamentary Commission, relating predominantly to children in factory towns, with a growing miscellany relating to public and secondary school children. These were collected mainly by members and correspondents of the British Association, especially after the appointment of the Anthropometric Committee following Galton's call for a survey. The classification scheme which Roberts originally devised to present these data was not necessarily premised on the meritocratic image of the nation's class structure, as Galton's initial proposals were. It testifies more to his strongly environmentalist interpretation of the causes of the variation exhibited.[23] His primary distinction was between urban and rural populations. The rural category was then subdivided into factory districts and agricultural districts. The urban category was also subdivided into factory (additionally distinguishing cotton from woollen mills) and non-factory children (further distinguishing those residing in factory towns from those in country towns). As well as confirming the strong influence of urban conditions, this early work seemed to show that the children of the 'non-labouring' class completed their growth at younger ages and finished taller and heavier than those of the 'labouring class'.[24]

A Manual of Anthropometry subsequently established Roberts as the foremost practitioner of the new science in Britain, and he was co-opted on to the British Association Committee, where he became its most active member. Before summarizing his work to date, Roberts explained in his first contribution to the British Association that:

To obtain the typical proportions of the British race it would be necessary to measure a proportionate number of individuals of each class. ... If we take the census of 1871 we shall find that such a model community would consist of 14.82 per cent of the non-labouring class, 47.46 per cent of the labouring class, and 37.72 per cent of the artisan and operative classes.[25]

22 Ibid., pp. 16–17. (Repeated verbatim in Roberts, *Manual*, p. 24).

23 C. Roberts, 'The physical requirements of factory children', *Journal of the Statistical Society* (December 1876), p. 683.

24 Roberts 'The physical development', table I.

25 Report of the Anthropometric Committee, *British Association Reports* (1879), pp. 202–3. These figures were based on a calculation which Roberts had made in the *Manual*, pp. 42–3. The method itself, which was effectively that of taking a stratified sample, was of course that which had originally been suggested by Galton, 'Proposal to apply for anthropological statistics', pp. 308–9.

However, he contrasted with this his own methods so far:

As the statistics which I have collected in England represent various classes rather than the general population, I have arranged them in a double series – a most favoured class and a least favoured class – and I have adopted the average of the two extremes as typical of the English nation.[26]

Roberts had not initially pursued Galton's methodological proposals himself because his environmentalism had predisposed him to examine the effects of urbanism rather than social class membership. It is quite clear, furthermore, that at this stage the goal of his empirical work and the associated classification of occupations which he had now developed was still the elucidation of the descriptive average or typical form of 'the English nation' and not the prescriptive 'most perfect form', which he had distinguished at the outset of his work as a separate concept.

However, within a year this had all changed. It was announced at the beginning of the next annual report of the Committee that 'the scheme of classification' prepared by Mr Roberts

is based on the principle of collecting into a standard class as large a number of cases as possible which imply the most favourable conditions of existence in respect to fresh air, exercise and wholesome and sufficient food – in one word, nurture – and specializing into classes which may be compared with this standard, those which depart more or less from the most favourable condition.[27]

As recently as 1878 he had written in the *Manual* that the difference in growth rates between

the non-labouring and the artisan class ... shows the marked effect of social surroundings on the development of the body; the one class being retarded and depressed by laborious occupations and insanitary influences, the other *expanded and probably exaggerated* by the prevalence of circumstances favourable to growth.[28] (my italics)

In other words, those individuals exhibiting characteristics which were more developed than the national average were to be considered as much a deviation from the true national type as those showing relative under-development. That those subject to the 'most favourable conditions' could now be used as a standard from which all else was to be considered a deviation or departure, was clearly a radical change from Roberts's earlier emphasis on the average or modal type of the nation as a whole as the fundamental reference point for measuring variation or deviation.

26 Report of the Anthropometric Committee, *British Association Reports* (1879), p. 203.
27 Report of the Anthropometric Committee, *British Association Reports* (1880), p. 121.
28 Roberts, *Manual*, p. 99.

IV

The new scheme first appeared as table III of the 1880 report of the Anthropometric Committee, which is reproduced here. This classification was confirmed virtually unchanged in the final report of the committee three years later.[29] As can be seen, the collected data were to be divided *a priori* into a series of bifurcating classifications so as to arrive at a rank order corresponding to groupings of the male occupations which were distinguished at the decennial census, commencing with the most 'favoured' and ending with the least 'favoured'.

The primary division was that between the 'non-labouring classes' and the 'labouring classes' of the nation according to 'social condition', by which was meant 'influences of leisure, mental and manual labour'. This, then, was clearly felt to be the most fundamental and determinative criterion for a scale measuring achieved physical development of individuals. A modern student might be excused for supposing that this was done because that part of the nation engaged in physical labour would be much more physically developed; the reasoning was the reverse, of course! The assumption locked within this procedure was that 'social condition' in this sense of achieved social status, as reflected by the prestige of the (male) parental occupation, was most strongly and reliably correlated with some kind of inherited, natural differential in physique between the individuals who were their children.[30] Social position, then, was the sign by which the elect and the reprobate of nature could be most unequivocally identified.

Next, these two primary conditions of existence were subdivided according to the secondary influence of 'nurture', which was defined as 'the influences of food, clothing, nursing, domestic surroundings etc'. The children of the non-labouring classes were judged to have received 'very good' nurture if the head of household's occupation was 'professional'. This subdivision formed the standard class, class I (including under this heading only bankers and wholesale merchants from the entire business community). The remainder of the non-labouring classes were judged to experience only 'good' nurturing; this applied to the commercial class of occupations, who were assigned to class II. For the labouring classes, their children's nurturing was judged to be either 'imperfect' or plain 'bad'. The former applied to class IV, all artisan and skilled trades, but also to class III – all types of labourers whose working conditions were considered to be 'outdoor' or 'country'. Presumably miners were included

29 Table XII of the final report of the Anthropometric Committee, *British Association Reports* (1883).
30 Whether or not this inherited differential was seen as *ultimately* due to environmental factors, as in Roberts's interpretation, or solely to heredity, as Galton believed. See next section.

TABLE III.—Classification of the British Population according to *Media*, or the conditions of life.

Social Condition.*—Non-labouring Classes			Labouring Classes			Selected Classes
Nurture.† Very Good		Good	Imperfect		Bad	
Professional Classes ‡ (Upper and Upper Middle Classes) 4·46 per cent.		Commercial Class (Lower Mid. Classes) 10·80 per cent.	Labourers 47·46 per cent.	Artisans 26·82 per cent.	Industrial Classes (Sedentary Trades) 10·90 per cent.	
Out-door Country §	In-door Towns	In-door Towns	Out-door Country	In-door Towns	In-door Towns	
CLASS I. Country-gentlemen. Gentlemen-farmers. Officers of Army and Navy. Auxiliary Forces. Clergymen. Lawyers. Doctors. Civil Engineers. Architects. Dentists. Civil Servants. Authors. Artists. Teachers. Musicians. Actors. Bankers. Merchants (Wholesale).		CLASS II. Teachers in Elementary Schools. Clerks. Shopkeepers. Shopmen. Dealers in Drugs. „ Books. „ Wool. „ Silk. „ Cotton. „ Foods. „ Drinks. „ Furniture. „ Metals. „ Glass. „ Earthenware. „ Fuel, &c.	CLASS III. Labourers and Workers on Agriculture. „ Gardens. „ Roads. „ Railways. „ Quarries. Navvies. Porters. Guards. Woodmen. Brickmakers. Labourers, &c., on Water. „ Sailors. „ Fishermen. „ Watermen. Labourers, &c., in Mines. „ Coal. „ Minerals.	CLASS IV. Workers in Wood. „ Metal. „ Stone. „ Leather. „ Paper. &c. Engravers. Photographers. Printers. &c.	CLASS V. Factory Operatives. Tailors. Shoemakers. &c.	CLASS VI. Policemen. Fire Brigade. Soldiers. Recruits. Messengers ? Industrial-Schools. Criminals. Idiots. Lunatics.

* Social Condition ; (influences of leisure, mental and manual labour).
† Nurture ; (influences of food, clothing, nursing, domestic surroundings, &c.).
‡ Occupation ; (influences of external physical conditions, exercise, &c.) Percentage of male population, including male children (Census of 1871).
§ Climatic and sanitary surroundings.

under the latter head not because of the father's occupational environment but because of the likely environment of his growing children. 'Bad' was then reserved for the sedentary trades and factory operatives of class V (although it is not clear why the conditions entailed by the working practices of these adults should directly influence their children's nurturing when those of the miners presumably were not supposed to do so). Thus, this process of a two-stage *a priori* division of the data, firstly by social condition and then by nurture, had produced an ordinal scale of four hypothesized subdivisions of the population (one of which contained two classs, III and IV), each synonymous with certain groupings of male occupations.

Finally, a distinction was made within the third of these four nurture categories to account for differences in 'climate and sanitary surroundings', by which was meant a rural–urban dichotomy of the environment. This enabled class III (labourers) to be divided off from class IV (artisans) on the grounds that the former were outdoor rural and the latter indoor urban occupations. Additionally within class I, the professional classes of the 'very good' nurture category, there was an attempt to grade the occupations into an ordinal scale of three zones: entirely rural, entirely urban and intermediate.[31] Notice that the vector which Roberts had used as the primary discriminant in his first classification of 1876, the rural–urban dimension, was now relegated to the status of a third-order scale of effect, while pride of place was assigned to 'social condition', i.e. social position according to occupational status.

Thus, the following extract from the report illustrates a number of pertinent points. In particular, the classes – groupings of paternal occupations – had now come to be viewed as concrete social units, or phenomena in their own right. They were therefore generating their own derivative procedures for scientific study. We find that the classes are being invoked as basic analytical units and the anthropometric data to be employed were now fashioned to expose most effectively the differences between these classes:

The classification has been constructed on the physiological and hygienic laws which are familiar to the students of sanitary science, and on a careful comparison of the measurements of different classes of the people, and especially of school children of the age from eleven to twelve years. This age has been selected as particularly suited to the study of the media or conditions of life which influence the development of the human body, as it is subject to the wide and more powerful agencies which surround and divide class from class but it is yet free from the disturbing elements of puberty and the numerous minor modifying influences such as occupation, personal habits, etc. which in a

31 In addition to these five graded classes, there was a residual one for anomalous 'selected classes', by which was meant data sets which the Committee had acquired, which were evidently biased in their composition through selection of individuals on physical or mental criteria: such as policemen, military recruits, lunatics.

measure shape the physique of older boys and adults. The data on which the classification has been based are given below. The most obvious facts which the figures disclose are the check which growth receives as we descend lower and lower in the social scale: a difference of five inches exists between the average statures of the best and worst nurtured classes of children of corresponding ages, and of three and a half inches in adults.[32]

It had now become a primary aim of the whole exercise simply to measure the anthropometric properties of these artificially created classes, rather than those of the nation as a whole, as an empirical aid to expounding the causes of the differences between them.

The 'national standard' had therefore come to be defined *prescriptively* as that of the 'best' indentifiable 'class' of individuals – those who could be isolated by controlling for various influences which were considered in some sense prejudicial to the human organism obtaining its most complete, i.e. physically largest, development.[33] The process whereby this particular abstract and ideologically loaded construct, referring only to a particular section of society, became the objective of analysis, rather than the more neutral descriptive concept of the national average or mode with which the project was begun, is an important moment in the development of the 'scientific' study of social structure in modern Britain. The episode is also a near-perfect historical example of the insidious manner in which the initial *ad hoc* introduction of a model – reflecting a hierarchic image of society in this case – for a specific methodological purpose can subsequently subvert the entire investigative procedure by becoming the principal subject of investigation in and for itself.

V

It seems most probable from the published writings available that this new methodology was not adopted autonomously by Roberts in 1880 but was a change which was initially foisted upon him by other(s) on the Committee, Galton's influence being strongly indicated.[34]

By the later 1870s Galton had succeeded to his own satisfaction in discrediting the weak Lamarckianism which had become generally accepted since Darwin's endorsement of it in 1871.[35] Galton now

32 Final report of the Anthropometric Committee, *British Association Reports* (1883), paragraph 53.

33 Ibid., paragraph 52.

34 Galton's considerable involvement with the work of the Committee at this time is signified by his assumption of the chairmanship during 1880 (on the retirement of William Farr, due to ill-health) and his major contribution to the report of the following year.

35 The Lamarckian notion of use inheritance, which Roberts implicitly endorsed in the *Manual* (see section III in this chapter), emphasized the importance of the social environment in selecting, over the long term, only those variations which were 'useful' or 'fitted' to society from among the many mutations which nature spontaneously generated. With

gained confidence in his own strongly hereditarian predilections for a theory of natural selection and inheritance. As he put it in his memoirs: 'I had long tried to gain some insight into the relative power of Nature and Nurture, in order that due allowance might be made for Environment, neither too much nor too little.'[36] He claimed of a study of human twins (in fact little more than a highly selective and small-scale accumulation of primarily anecdotal material) which he published in 1875 that 'the evidence was overwhelming that the power of Nature was far stronger than that of Nurture'.[37] Galton now conceived of naturally inherited characteristics as a finite number of discrete and fixed elements each determining correspondent observable mental and physical properties. This led him to an exclusive interest in that section of the nation which supposedly 'possessed' the most valuable sets of these elemental units of inheritance. Such well-endowed individuals would be instantly recognizable by their highly developed mental and physical abilities. Only they could pass on these desirable qualities to future generations. A further corollary, then, was his increased emphasis on breeding alone as the correct eugenic strategy, since the overall average abilities of the nation could only be improved or raised – always Galton's ultimate motivating aim – by this elite segment of the nation increasing itself as a proportion of subsequent generations, through out-breeding the more feeble sections.

Thus, for Galton, by the later 1870s the most important aspect of any exploratory survey of the current range of human faculties in Britain would be the clear delineation of the nature and extent of the elite section of the population, so as to establish the 'standard' which it could be hoped that the British nation would approximate to in the future, given the implementation of the appropriate eugenic breeding policies. Simultaneously this would provide the yardstick to judge the scale of deterioration among the remainder of the nation. It is possible, therefore, that Galton, after being introduced to Roberts's proposed scheme in 1879, somehow prevailed upon its author to alter the focus to conform more closely with his own designs.

Darwin's adoption of this mode of argument in *The descent of man*, published in 1871, the early 1870s seems to have been a brief period of consensus among evolutionary social theorists, during which this view held sway. See Greta Jones, *Social Darwinism and English thought* (Brighton, 1980), pp. 78–82.

36 F. Galton, *Memories of my life* (London, 1908), p. 294.

37 Ibid., p. 295. It seems likely that Galton may have been encouraged to exaggerate the value of his rather flimsy positive evidence in favour of his hereditarian theory, owing to the more robust work of demolition of Darwin's pro-Lamarckian 'provisional hypothesis of pangenesis', which he carried out in a separate study completed at the same time in 1875. For an account of this episode, see the excellent D.A. Mackenzie, *Statistics in Britain 1865–1930* (Edinburgh, 1981), p. 60. Mackenzie, perhaps a little whiggishly, does not mention the twins study, which represents something of an embarrassment to Galton's reputation as a statistician.

However, it can also be shown that – at the latest by 1883 – Roberts had subsequently developed his own reasons, independent of Galton's, for presenting the classification in this way. By then he had moved in quite the opposite direction from Galton, to an extreme form of environmental determinism (but it can also be shown that he does not appear to have subscribed to these more extreme views in 1880 when the scheme was first presented).

The principal evidence to support this contention is a bizarre paragraph and accompanying footnote in the final report of the Anthropometric Committee, submitted in 1883.[38] Firstly, a table of statistics of height and weight of liveborn infants at birth was presented as 'one of great interest to the student examining the physical development and the physical improvement of a race, as it presents the materials with which he has to deal in its earliest and simplest form'.[39] It was noted that this table confirmed the slightly larger average size of viable male babies and also suggested a tendency to their greater variation about the mean than female babies. Next, the established fact of a higher rate of stillbirths among male babies in Britain was invoked. Finally the astounding inference was offered that:

As the largest surviving infants are those of males, it would appear, therefore, that the physical (and most probably the mental) proportion of a race, and their uniformity within certain limits, are largely dependent on the size of the female pelvis, which acts as a gauge, as it were, of the race, and eliminates the largest infants especially those with large heads (and presumably more brains), by preventing their survival at birth. (sic)[40]

This may seem a little over-imaginative, but there was much worse to follow in the appended footnote. All pretensions to scientific rigour were abandoned as a handful of skeletons from the Museum of the Royal College of Surgeons were pressed into service by Roberts 'to ascertain if there is any difference between the circumference of the skull as compared with that of the pelvis in adults of very different races of man'.[41] As D.J. Cunningham, a Professor of Anatomy at Edinburgh University, was to point out many years later, not only was Roberts's comparison of European and Andaman Islanders' skeletons based on a statistically meaningless sample (only a single European

---

38 This report was co-authored by Charles Roberts and Sir Rawson W. Rawson (a career civil servant who had been Governor of the Bahamas and the Windward Islands before his retirement in 1875; he was President of the International Statistical Institute 1885–98). But it is clear from internal evidence that the relevant part of the report referred to here was the work of Roberts alone.

39 Final report of the Anthropometric Committee, *British Association Reports* (1883), paragraph 55 (p. 285).

40 Ibid.

41 Ibid., footnote, p. 285.

female pelvis was used), but furthermore the female pelvic ring was compared with adult skull circumferences, not infant ones![42]

The conclusion drawn by Roberts from this exercise was that 'it is not improbable that the relatively small pelvis of the female Andamanese has been instrumental, in some measure, in differentiating that diminutive race.'[43] But the real *pièce de résistance* was the next sentence, concluding this section of the report:

> It is probably in this direction we must look for an explanation of the degenerating influences of town life and sedentary occupations, as they, together with the new movement for the higher education of women, favour the production of large heads and imperfectly developed bodies of women in this and other civilized countries, and a corresponding disproportion between the size of the head and the circumference of the pelvis.[44]

It seems certain that Roberts did not hold this specific set of views in 1880, since it was quite deliberately pointed out in his original specification of the Committee's classification scheme that 'at birth children are of the same average size in all classes',[45] a statement that would be inconsistent with the implications of the above passages, and which was omitted from the 1883 report, where the remainder of the paragraph from which it was drawn was reproduced verbatim. Formerly Roberts had only attributed to environmental forces the status of secondary effects after 'age, sex and race', owing to his gradualist Lamarckianism. He was now, through this extreme form of environmentalism, prepared to grant such short-term influences as those acting over the lifetime of a single individual the power to modify the dimensions of the female pelvis and thereby to exert a determining influence over the average physical size – and supposedly correlated mental abilities – of future generations. Furthermore, not only was the environment supposed to be able to exert a profound and rapid influence, but also it was now assumed that in the increasingly urban and industrial British context this influence was an entirely negative and degrading one. It followed that the most common human form found in Britain would simply reflect the prevalence of these degenerating urban conditions rather than the true national type. Therefore only among 'the most favoured' class of the population could the true national type be discovered.

The reasons why Roberts should have so significantly shifted his position between 1880 and 1883 are obscure. It seems possible that it

42 Interdepartmental Committee on Physical Deterioration, British *Parliamentary Papers* (1904), XXXIII, Cd 2210 (evidence), paragraph 2241.
43 Final report of the Anthropometric Committee, *British Association Reports* (1883), footnote, p. 287. The intrinsic inferiority of the diminutive Andamanese was, of course, assumed to be self-evidently true!
44 Ibid.
45 Report of the Anthropometric Committee, *British Association Reports* (1880), p. 121.

may partly have been a polarizing reaction precipitated by closer exposure to the strongly hereditarian ideas of Galton. In addition to the more deterministic environmentalism, the attitudes and the assumptions behind the reasoning deployed in the extracts cited have much in common with the pronouncements of certain craniologists such as Carl Vogt, Paul Broca and Gustave Le Bon, who worked within the recapitulationist evolutionary paradigm.[46] However, since we know that Roberts was already familiar with their work by 1878 (witness the bibliography in his *Manual*), there still remains the question of why he should have become so much more attached to this school of thought between 1880 and 1883. Apart from the obvious point that the theory of recapitulation was continually gaining ground during the relevant years,[47] a more specific answer may be that recapitulation appeared to offer an explanation for an apparent anthropometric conundrum which had been increasingly vexing Roberts, something to which his great mentor Quetelet had not given much attention. This was the sex-differential growth pattern, whereby girls achieved their mature adult form earlier and quicker than boys.[48] In support of this suggestion, it seems significant that Roberts retrospectively attached great importance to this aspect of his work.[49]

Thus, we see Roberts in this period passing out from under the spell of Quetelet and the empiricist project of simply discovering and recording the proportions of the human races, and moving on to an attempt to explain his findings in terms of evolutionary theory, and so coming under the influence of the recapitulationists.[50]

The net result was an abandonment by Roberts of the search for the typical member of the British race, defined descriptively as simply the

46 See S.J. Gould, *The mismeasure of man* (Harmondsworth, 1984, first published USA 1981), pp. 100–7. For a more comprehensive treatment of recapitulation theory and its influence, see the same author's *Ontogeny and phylogeny* (Cambridge, Mass., 1977).

47 E. Haeckel's *Generelle morphologie der organismen*, 2 vols, published in Berlin in 1866 was the first coherent formulation of the recapitulationist ideas evident in the earlier work of craniologists such as Broca.

48 Roberts's preoccupation with this matter can be found in the *Manual*, p. 25 and chapters 5, 6; *British Association Reports* of 1879, pp. 206–8, and 1880, pp. 141–7. The theory that the ontogeny of the individual recapitulates a putative phylogenesis of its species, conceived as a linear process of development through all supposedly lower life forms, purported to 'explain' earlier cessation of growth in humans by the smaller sex as being consistent with the assumption that the female was the simpler form of the more developed, larger-bodied and larger-brained male sex.

49 See his letter to the editor in *Nature* 21 August 1890; also his 'Memorandum on the medical inspection of and physical education in secondary schools', pp. 352–74 in the report of the Royal Commission on Secondary Education in England, vol. V, *British Parliamentary Papers* (1895), XLVII, Cd 7862–iv.

50 Quetelet's work was independent of this later school of thought: there is no reference to Haeckel in *Anthropométrie*. For further details regarding Quetelet's project, see P.F. Lazarsfeld, 'Notes on the history of quantification in sociology – trends, sources and problems', *Isis* 52 (1961), pp. 299–311.

most frequently observed combination of dimensions, the modal type. The extreme form of environmentalism adopted by him, because it was asymmetrically determinist (envisaging current environmental influences only as a negative, degrading force), came to focus upon the professional, upper middle class as the only safe repository of the nation's true 'genius'. As a result the derivative representation of social structure paradoxically came to approximate to that expounded by the extreme hereditarian Galton: a hierarchy of grades, defined as groupings of certain occupations which departed increasingly from the prescriptive standard of the professional upper and middle classes at the apex. Thus, we find that deterministic 'scientific' explanations of social inequality tended towards the same simple graded model of society, whether or not they were hereditarian or environmentalist.

VI

The resulting scheme of social classification is not merely a dust-covered Victorian curio. It was the first formal appearance of a genus of model which has since had a particularly long career. In 1901 Francis Galton – infamously – revived and publicized a modified version of this naturalistic model of social structure, in the context of the debate over national efficiency following the reverses of the second Boer War.[51]

It was Roberts's scheme that had originally demonstrated that it was feasible to identify empirically social classes or grades as groupings of male occupations, and that these classes apparently corresponded to differentials in natural endowment within the nation. However, the anthropometric data with which he was concerned did not exhibit a unidimensional pattern following conventional status gradings. As we can see from the reproduction of table IV of the 1880 report, although all three categories of manual worker fell comfortably below the two non-manual categories, it was the lowest-status labourers who recorded the 'best' anthropometric measurements among the manual classes, followed by the artisans of highest manual status, with the medium-status factory operatives coming last. In other words the graded social classes were shown to exhibit differential life chances, as measured by average achieved physical development, but it appeared that this primary association could be modified to a significant degree by other factors associated with the extent to which the occupations within a class entailed an urban existence.

In 1901 Galton reasserted the notion of a naturalistic social structure composed of occupational classes of the nation. Conveniently he forgot

---

51 See B. Norton, 'Psychologists and class', in C. Webster (ed.), *Biology, medicine and society* 1840–1940 (Cambridge, 1981), pp. 289–316, for a discussion of Galton's model and its subsequent influence on the work of Cyril Burt.

TABLE IV.—Table showing the Relative Statures of Boys of the age of 11 to 12 years, under different social and physical conditions of life. The zig-zag line running through the means shows the degradation of stature as the boys are further and further removed from the most favourable conditions of growth. (C. Roberts.)

Height in inches	Total No. of Obs.	Public Schools Country	Public Schools Towns	Middle-class Upper—Towns	Middle-class Lower—Towns	Elem. Agricultl. Labourers—Country	Elem. Artisans—Towns	Factories and Workshops Country	Factories and Workshops Towns	Military Asylums	Pauper Schools ?	Industrial Schools	Total percentages
60 to 61	6	2 1		3 1	3 1	2 1	1						2
59–	16	2 1		9 3	5 1	5 1	2 1			1			5
58–	35	9 6		17 6	8 2	4 2	0 1	2 1		2			15
57–	66	11 8		23 8	13 4	14 4	4 2	5 1	5 1	7 1		1 1	25
56–	118	21 14		35 12	27 7	32 10	4 2	10 3	3 1	15 2			42
55–	230	28 19		53 18	57 14	47 16	15 8	13 6	17 5	33 4		2 3	78
54–	329	33 22		55 19	68 17	47 16	24 13	36 12	20 6	46 6		4 6	113
53–	361	15 10		37 12	58 15	58 19	26 15	34 13	38 11	84 10		6 9	115
52–	441	14 9		25 9	61 15	36 12	36 20	52 17	59 17	118 14		10 15	132
51–	370	6 5		23 7	40 10	32 10	28 15	45 16	57 17	123 14		11 18	113
50–	367	7 4		8 3	27 7	14 5	17 10	46 15	61 18	148 17		11 18	106
49–	252	2 1		3 1	20 5	7 2	12 6	31 10	40 12	114 14		10 15	74
48–	132			3 1	1 1	5 1	4 3	11 4	20 6	76 9		6 9	41
47–	102				4 1	5 1	7 3	5 1	13 3	59 7		3 4	28
46–	22					1 1	1 1	3 1	7 2	7 1		1 1	10
45–	12								1 1	10 1		1 1	3
44–	1									0			1
43–	1									1			
42 to 43	1									1			
Total	2862	160 100		294 100	399 100	304 100	181 100	293 100	341 100	840 100		66 100	90
Average height	52·60	54·98		53·85	53·70	53·01	52·60	52·17	51·56	51·90		50·02	
Mean height	52·5	55·0	54·5	54·0	53·5	53·0	52·5	52·0	51·5	51·0	50·5	50·0	

the non-linearity in the relationship between occupational prestige and natural endowment of individuals which had been found 20 years earlier, while maintaining the principle that occupationally defined social classes exhibited distinctive anthropometric characteristics.[52] Significantly, he chose to transpose his normal distribution of 'civic' worth on to the hierarchy of occupational categories devised rather later than Roberts's work and in a somewhat different – not explicitly scientific – context by Charles Booth, rather than to employ the classification which he had himself been so intimately involved with and which was more directly a product of the natural science of society to which he subscribed.[53] Of course, this was because Roberts's scheme did not unequivocally illustrate the central Galtonian belief. This was the simplistic notion that social inequality merely reflected inherited natural differentials between individuals, which could usefully be conceptualized as a unidimensional grading of society correspondent with the supposed differential status or prestige of the various (male) occupations.

As I have shown elsewhere, Galton's revival of the naturalistic social structure in a modified, hierarchical format led to the adoption of this graded model of society by the General Register Office in a form which has since been retained, essentially unchanged, down to the present day![54] This occurred through a paradoxical process of antagonism and opposition to Galton's hereditarianism on the part of T.H.C. Stevenson, the Superintendent of Statistics at the GRO. Stevenson subscribed to an alternative interpretation which viewed the demographic differences between social classes as evidence of differential life chances due to unequal environmental experiences. This was rather as Roberts had initially, in the 1870s, interpreted the variation in physique which he had found among factory and school children when he began his investigation as a moderate 'environmentalist'. Thus, the episode recounted here can be seen as initiating a protracted and tortuous process whereby the empirical study of British society by social scientists and by social historians has become saddled for many years with a simplistic hierarchical model of social structure derived, ultimately, from within the terms of reference of the social Darwinism of a century ago.

52 Interestingly, Roberts himself suffered a similar form of selective amnesia when referring in 1895 to his earlier work for the British Association. Roberts, 'Memorandum on the medical inspection', pp. 357–9.

53 On Booth's classification, see E.P. Hennock, 'Poverty and social theory in England: the experience of the 1880s', *Social History* 1 (1976), pp. 67–91.

54 S.R.S. Szreter, 'The genesis of the Registrar-General's social classification of occupations', *British Journal of Sociology* 35 (December 1984), pp. 522–46.

13

Welfare and the Historians

David Thomson

I

The question of the community's responsibility for maintaining its weaker members has moved to the forefront of the political stage in Britain. This latest manifestation of a perennial debate has been marked by a number of loose and emotive allusions to the long history of efforts to foster social service in this country. At the prompting of some leaders of the Conservative government the discussion has returned, as it has not done for many years, to the broad issue of the respective roles of family and community in providing for those in need of assistance.[1] As part of this reappraisal, the experiences of the Victorian era in particular have been cited on many occasions in support of a drive to make individuals more responsible for the welfare of themselves and their relatives. The 'principles of 1834', the virtues of independence, thrift and self-reliance, and a presumed willingness of nineteenth century families to shoulder responsibility for their members out of a strong sense of moral duty, have all been referred to in the current dialogue. The aim of the 'reformers' of the 1980s, whether inside government or out, appears to be to 'turn the clock back', to shift the locus of responsibility for the welfare of individuals away from the community and back towards the individuals themselves and their relatives. Appeals to history and to former virtues now lost are therefore a major lever in the campaign for change.

The historical exegesis focuses attention upon the quality of existing research. After all if the past is to be appealed to, it must be reconstructed and analysed. However, despite considerable and sustained interest in the history of social welfare and most especially in the 'rise of the Welfare State', much work is uncritical and limited, providing an incomplete account of the evolution of institutions for the redistribution

---

1 Not all such questioning has come from politicians or from the period of Conservative party government. The emphasis upon the duties of individuals to act rather than upon their rights to receive has been a constant if muted theme in welfare debates throughout the Welfare State era: see, for example, W.A. Robson, *Welfare State and welfare society, illusion and reality* (London, 1976).

of resources within our community.[2] In few fields of intellectual enquiry can the relationship between the ideas of the leading researchers and writers, and those of the proverbial man-in-the-street, be so close, so comfortable and so uncomplicated as it is in this instance. The shared beliefs can be summarized simply: 'in the past' people looked to their own well-being and to that of their immediate family, neighbours and friends, whereas the twentieth century has been distinguished by a rapidly growing dependence upon formal communal mechanisms for the provision of sustenance and the enhancement of life. Historians in general have seen no reason to challenge this popular consensus, and as a consequence have assumed the role of the providers of texts that will reinforce a powerful social myth. The titles of such works speak of their function – *The Coming of the Welfare State, The Rise of the Welfare State, the Evolution of the British Welfare State* or *Before the Welfare State.*[3] Other countries have their companions to these volumes, and Asa Briggs commented very pithily upon this widespread phenomenon some years ago when he dubbed it 'the reorganization of twentieth-century history around the term "Welfare State"'.[4]

The major exception to the pattern of uncritical detailing has been the study of the contemporary period.[5] For at least 20 years a number of competent scholars, most associated in one way or another with Richard Titmuss and the London School of Economics, have been scrutinizing the achievements of social welfare policies after the Second World War.[6] Their emphasis has been upon performance rather than policy or ideology, for they are aware that what may be intended in theory and what actually occurs are often linked only tenuously. Their findings concerning the limited successes of programmes of 'social engineering' in securing significant and lasting redistributions of resources

2 Since this is an essay concerned with general themes, a somewhat loose definition of what is meant by 'social welfare' is perhaps acceptable. The term is used here not to mean every action which may be construed as advancing the well-being of members of the society, but only the most obvious and direct measures taken to alleviate suffering or to ease poverty. Social security, health and welfare expenditures are what interest us here, the core items in any social welfare programme – or history of such.

3 E.g. M. Bruce, *The coming of the Welfare State* (London, 1961 and several subsequent editions); G. Williams, *The coming of the Welfare State* (London, 1967); D. Fraser, *The evolution of the British Welfare State* (London, 1973); M. Bruce (ed.), *The rise of the Welfare State: English social policy 1601–1971* (London, 1973); U. Henriques, *Before the Welfare State* (London, 1979).

4 A. Briggs, 'Social welfare, past and present', in A.H. Halsey (ed.), *Traditions of social policy* (London, 1976), pp. 4–5.

5 One other area of more critical scholarship has been the study of the last years of the Old Poor Law. J.D. Marshall, *The Old Poor Law 1795–1834* (London, 1968), provides a useful brief introduction to this debate.

6 The works of B. Abel-Smith, A.B. Atkinson, and P. Townsend, especially his massive *Poverty in the United Kingdom* (London, 1979), are among the major examples of the genre pioneered by Richard Titmuss.

have sometimes countered and sometimes confirmed the ill-articulated apprehensions of many ordinary citizens. At the very least such studies have raised substantially the intellectual level of discussions of welfare issues.

The study of the longer-term history of social welfare has remained largely unaffected by these recent advances in critical thinking and technique. Writers on contemporary matters seldom do more than include a few prefatory remarks upon the Poor Law or pensions legislation prior to 1945, even when they purport to outline the background to current issues. The effect is to reinforce the sense that 1945 marks an immense watershed in the development of the society, the point at which some quantum leap was made that lifted the society to a new plane of civilization.

The historians of social welfare, that is those whose concern is with many decades or centuries, have for their part done little to bridge the chasm. Their interests remain little affected by the work of the 1960s and 1970s. The concentration is still upon policy, administration and ideology rather than performance and achievement. Legislative enactments, parliamentary debates, press statements, pressure group publications, committee minutes, administrative directives – in short, all the long-accepted resources of the historian – continue as the stock-in-trade of the welfare historians. The concern remains to establish who said what to whom and why, rather than with measuring and assessing who got what from whom, when, how often, and at what cost to giver, receiver or society at large.

A number of unfortunate consequences flow from this unhelpful division within the study of social welfare. Both studies, the contemporary and the historical, are weakened by their mutual exclusiveness. Current analyses of welfare issues – and, by extension, popular debate of them – take place in an historical vacuum. What happens now is viewed in the context of what happened in the 1960s and 1970s. The 1950s and the 1940s are of background interest: the 1930s and earlier belong to the realm of myth. This should be a serious concern. The lack of an historical perspective – the belief that to glance back over 10 or 20 years is to gain a long-term appreciation – impoverishes us all. It leads social researchers to substantive errors and an inability to distinguish short-term fluctuations from long-term trends. It hampers a citizenry that is seeking to understand current developments. Both researchers and citizens are left with little sense that the questions troubling modern society have worried our predecessors. More significantly, our historical ignorance means that we often fail to appreciate that the options facing us now are very similar to those considered, tried and discarded by previous generations which also had to decide how to care for the lonely elderly, the husbandless mother, the parentless child or the unemployed family man.

Thus, current debates are rendered shallow by the lack of historical context. On the one hand we exhibit disbelief when the basic tenets of the 'Welfare State' are questioned, because we have been taught that the story of social welfare is a tale of evolutionary progress, and that the Welfare State of the post-1945 era is our society's crowning achievement. On the other hand, when disillusionment sets in as the limits to the Welfare State's accomplishments are recognized, a simple-minded and misguided nostalgia for a lost past has been able to flourish. An uncritical history of social welfare has for too long abetted the persistence of excessive expectations and disappointments which have bedevilled the Welfare State.

II

Turning to this last point, the question of why too many aspects of the history of social welfare lack intellectual vigour – it was suggested earlier that historians have accepted uncritically the simple-minded premise that families cared for their disadvantaged members. In part, historians have done so because such a system conforms to the thesis that only 'modern' as opposed to 'traditional' societies possess complex forms of social organization that could administer a system of social welfare. Yet they have failed to consider the economic dimension of a family-based system; it would have required large-scale income redistribution between young and old, and present models of wealth transfer suggest that the system would need much larger wealth surpluses on the part of the young than can realistically be imagined.

However, historians' insularity goes much further than merely disdain for economic models, for they have failed to consider the advances in historical sociology pioneered by Peter Laslett. Laslett and others have questioned received wisdom on the character of life in traditional society.[7] Their studies have occasioned a good deal of debate, and their claims as to household size, the propensity of kin to live together, and the effects upon families of migration, desertion or death, have all attracted a number of sometimes spirited ripostes. The specific outcomes of these exchanges need not concern us unduly here. What does matter is that these explorations in historical sociology must alter the history of social welfare. Social welfare is inextricably linked with such things as composition of families, the structure of households, the strength of kin networks, or the expectations of health and life. Research on these issues has called into question, often indirectly it must

7 See, for example, P. Laslett, *Family life and illicit love in earlier generations* (Cambridge, 1977); P. Laslett, K. Oosterveen and R.M. Smith (eds), *Bastardy and its comparative history* (London, 1980); P. Laslett and R. Wall (eds), *Household and family in past time* (Cambridge, 1972).

be admitted, some of the most cherished central assumptions that underpin our histories of social welfare, and the writers of these histories have failed to integrate Laslett's research into their theses.

The consensus view still implicit in our histories of social welfare may be summarized quickly. In 'pre-industrial' or 'pre-modern' societies the family was responsible for the well-being of its members. Those in need of assistance for any number of reasons would look for support to their immediate families in the first instance, to more distant kin if that first recourse was impracticable, or to charitable neighbours if all else failed. In no event could they look to the wider community with any expectation of material assistance, since the larger community was equipped neither administratively nor ideologically for the maintenance of the frail. The corollary of this view is that 'industrial' or 'modern' societies are distinguished by their emphasis upon regular, collective and bureaucratized support for their weaker members. In turn the family has been demoted to a subsidiary role as the provider of emotional support but not of the large and recurrent amounts of hard cash which are essential in the maintenance of the 'unproductive' members of the community.

Such a summary implies that historians will have been concerning themselves with two things: the nature of pre-modern society (meaning, in this context, Britain before the Welfare State), and the steps by which a modern society comes to supersede an older one. In fact welfare historians have, almost without exception, concerned themselves solely with the second of these issues. The nature of pre-modern society is seldom the focus of attention, as it is for historical demographers or historians of the family for example. The reader is left to assume that familial support just somehow worked in the past, and that this truth is so self-evident and so self-explanatory that it needs little comment. How families or neighbours of a century or two ago maintained the old, the young, the pregnant, the sick, the lame, the unemployed or the insane is not discussed: it is sufficient to imply that they must have done so.

This will not do. Scholarly enquiry should not be built upon unvoiced and unacknowledged vital assumptions. This chapter aims to examine critically the plausibility of these assumptions about social welfare arrangements in the past, in the light of the work of historical sociologists.

One premise linked with the assumption that families maintained their disadvantaged is that since no other means of income redistribution have been detected or could be expected, families must have lived together in some extended fashion as the means of maintaining the frail. However, it is now recognized that for many centuries households in England have generally been small, containing very few kin beyond the core family of parents and children. Co-residence by persons who were related to but outside of the central nuclear unit has not been common. How then did families perform their presumed all-encompassing welfare role if not through shared residence? Perhaps family members lived nearby but not with their relatives, a point to which little research attention has been directed, but if so it remains to be shown by what mechanisms the constant, prolonged and expensive transfers of resources took place between separate households.

This question, like so many others to do with welfare issues, is especially pertinent with regard to the elderly, and for this reason the example of the aged will be alluded to frequently during the remainder of this chapter.[8]

In the later twentieth century each elderly person appears to 'cost' the community about 70 per cent as much as does each non-elderly person, in that the resources which the community allots to the average person over 65 years of age are equivalent to a little more than two-thirds of the total resources assigned to the average younger person.[9] The ratio may well have been higher in the past. These costs must, too, be met over a long period. At present the average person reaching 65 years of age can expect to be maintained by the community for the best part of 15 years, and even if the gap between retirement and death was smaller in the past than now there is little to indicate that it has ever been other than substantial. Major transfers of resources must have been effected on a constant basis in the past if the elderly were to survive; how, then, were these made?

The economic premise underlying our assumption that families supported their disadvantaged is that they made enormous redistributions of income between young and old. Families might have done so by living with the elderly, or by paying the rent and food bills of the aged who lived apart from them. Because census and other similar enumerations do not suggest co-residence, the only plausible alternative to public assistance must have been extensive intra-familial transfers. It is

---

8 The discussion here and in the remainder of this essay is based upon my research into the position of the aged in Britain during the past two centuries. Some of the results of this research have appeared in D. Thomson, 'Provision for the elderly in England', 1834–1908', unpublished Ph.D. thesis, University of Cambridge, 1980); and in a number of articles, including 'Workhouse to nursing home: residential care for the elderly in England since 1840', *Ageing and Society* 3 (1983), pp. 43–69; 'I am not my father's keeper: families and the elderly in nineteenth century England' *Law and History Review* 2 (1984), pp. 265–86; and 'The decline of social security: falling state support for the elderly since early Victorian times', *Ageing and Society* 4 (1984), pp. 451–82.

9 The figure is calculated by disregarding entirely the means by which shares in the nation's total resources are allocated. Earnings from paid employment, social security benefits, capital gains, interest on investments, shares in public expenditure on health and welfare and more are all treated alike as means by which the resources of the nation are distributed, and the calculation of shares is concerned solely with the total amounts delivered to persons of different ages. The calculation is discussed in Thomson, 'The decline of social security', pp. 472–6.

difficult for this writer to conceive of regular transfers of resources within families but between separate houscholds such as would suffice to maintain the independence of an elderly relative. Moreover there is no evidence of such major transfers of cash or food between households. The supporters of modernization theory and the writers of welfare histories would, one presumes, find little reason to disagree with these points if pressed to explain the mechanisms by which resources were transferred before the state took over the task since they have always implied that transfers took place through co-residence. But this position now looks untenable in view of the evidence of the predominance of small, nuclear households in the past.

Admittedly, objections can be lodged. One is that the elderly maintained their own employment, income and independence for much longer than they do today, and families therefore would support the old for much shorter periods. This argument fits with another aspect of a vague modernization theory – the belief that industrialization deprives the family in general and the elderly in particular of a useful economic and social role, leaving the majority of the aged as unemployable and dependent.

No significant body of evidence has been assembled to substantiate a claim of continued employment in old age in the past. For many centuries retirement has been a recognized feature of English life. The ages at which retirement has occurred have varied over the years by not more than five years to either side of age 65, and it occurred at all levels of society. Often retirement was a functional necessity in an agrarian economy in which full employment all the year round could not be assured to men with dependants, let alone to everyone, and the removal of ageing workers from the active workforce was one widely accepted response to this. In the rural areas of Bedfordshire, for example, an area of which I have made a special study, the prolonging of paid employment past age 65 was very rare indeed in the nineteenth century.

Further, there is little evidence that the elderly of England before the Welfare State were somehow more capable of sustained hard work than is the case now. One might argue that having survived harsh and dangerous early lives, the elderly of a century or more ago would have been a hardy and healthy lot. A reading of nineteenth century Poor Law and census records, or of the claims made for civil service or military pensions, leaves quite the opposite impression. The evidence is depressing, emphasizing the physical and mental penalties of lives of poverty, poor housing, and heavy and dangerous work in appalling conditions. Rheumatism and failing eyesight are recorded with numbing regularity, along with a host of less specific but crippling and debilitating incapacities. There is little here to suggest that the elderly were more capable of continued employment and independence in old age in the past than now. Old age dependence was clearly a problem that society had to face before 'modernization'.

A second objection to the claim that communal social welfare arrangements must have been substantial in the past might be demographic: populations in the past are thought to have included few from such dependent groups as the aged. This, it could be argued, might explain in turn the paucity of evidence on familial resource redistribution: few elderly persons meant few transactions leaving few records.

Demographic records do not support this position. By 1841, the date of the first national census to incorporate a detailed question as to age, England and Wales were home to 1.15 million persons aged 60 years or more, with close to half a million of them aged 70 or older. These numbers were undoubtedly small in relation to those of the later twentieth century: 9.8 million aged 60 years or more by 1981, 4.8 million of them 70 or above. The numbers were also small by comparison with the numbers of younger persons: in 1841 the elderly formed 7 per cent of the national population, today 20 per cent. But if these mid-nineteenth-century numbers were small by some standards, they represented nevertheless a very substantial body of aged persons to whom the means of life had to be transferred by one mechanism or another. The numbers are not so small as to be dismissible.

In addition, it is likely that the numbers of the elderly were much larger in relation to the numbers of the young prior to 1841. In the early nineteenth century the ratio of elderly to other persons was at an historic low. By 1841 the English population had been undergoing sustained growth for half a century. During periods of population growth a society will be comparatively 'youthful', because populations grow through the injection of new members by either increased fertility or immigration, or through increased life expectancy for infants. In each case the net effects are similar – a large number of the young and a smaller number of the elderly, who are survivors of earlier, smaller cohorts. As a consequence of these developments the population by 1841 included a relatively small elderly component, but this was not a 'normal' condition of the past. Sizeable elderly populations were a feature of past European societies, and their maintenance, its means and the costs cannot be ignored.[10] Twentieth-century populations are not the first to face the question of how to provide for large numbers of the dependent elderly.

Other aspects of the recent advances in the study of demographic history raise additional serious issues for the historians of social welfare.

---

10 P. Laslett, 'The history of ageing and the aged', in *Family life and illicit love in earlier generations*, pp. 192–6. See too the remarks of R.M. Smith, 'The structured dependence of the elderly as a recent development: some sceptical historical thoughts', *Ageing and Society* 4 (1984), pp. 413–15. For another type of evidence on this see the back-projections for the English population reported in E.A. Wrigley and R.S. Schofield, *The population history of England, 1541–1871* (London, 1981).

The assumptions that families could have maintained elderly and other dependants by means of sharing a home with them has been brought into question indirectly by the research which shows that English households were not normally large or multi-generational. We should note at least two further more direct challenges to the view that co-residence might have been the major means by which the elderly were supported. One of these queries is raised by the simulation work of E.A. Wrigley. He has argued that given the probable birth, marriage and death regimes of pre-industrial England, at least 20 per cent of all men and women who married would have had no surviving heirs at the time of death.[11] To this 20 per cent can be added another 10–20 per cent who would approach death childless because they had never married or formed families. Wrigley concerned himself with the childlessness of all those dying, but the proportions without heirs would have been still higher among the elderly, since for those who survived to die in old age the chances increased that their heirs would die before they did.

The implication of such estimates is clear. At least one in every three, and perhaps closer to one in every two, of those living into old age would have had no surviving children with whom they might even conceivably have lived. When it is recalled in addition that many of the elderly would have become separated from their surviving children by physical distance in a society in which migration was a common feature, it becomes apparent that only a minority of the aged would have had a child or two close at hand with whom they might possibly live. These points may well help explain the lack of three-generation households in pre-industrial England, but they leave intact the central question: if many or most of the elderly, of whom there were large numbers, had few or no surviving children with whom they might share a home, how were they provided with the means of life?

More direct evidence of the limited role of families in furnishing the material, as distinct from the moral, support of the aged comes from analyses of census enumerators' books. Studies of household size and shape which show that few households consisted of families extending beyond a nuclear core may not prove conclusively that the aged lived apart from family and kin, but specific analyses of the living arrangements of the elderly themselves do substantiate the claim. Little research on this question has yet been published, in part because the elderly have seldom been of concern to scholars and in part because few relevant historical records bearing on this point date from the pre-nineteenth-century period, the period of greatest interest to students of the family and demography.

---

11 E.A. Wrigley, 'Fertility strategy for the individual and the group', in C. Tilly (ed.), *Historical studies of changing fertility* (Princeton, NJ, 1978), pp. 137–48. It should be noted that the levels decline sharply if demographic growth occurs.

One person who has made some brief comment on this matter is Michael Anderson, who found in his study of Preston in 1851 that about 70 per cent of persons aged 65 years and more were living in a household which included at least one child of the elder.[12] This much-quoted finding stands alone in the published debate on household characteristics, and it is easy to see in it confirmation of the belief that families were the source of support for the old 'before the Welfare State'. My own research into some similar mid-nineteenth century records suggests that Anderson's sample was not typical. Time after time, for place after place, the percentages of the elderly who lived with a child were found not to be above 40, with a few more per cent living with some other kin, especially grandchildren, nieces, or brothers or sisters.[13]

In each instance it was apparent too that, as people approached and advanced into old age, the movement away from living with children was at least as strong if not stronger than the move towards shared residences; a movement incompatible with the proposition that families came together to assist the weak or dependent. The evidence suggests that living with a child was related inversely to age: the older a person the less likely they were to live with a child. The point was revealed much more explicitly in a number of the analyses in which identifiable individuals were traced from one census to the next as they passed from middle age to old age. The number of such successful record matchings over 10 to 20 years were not large, so that the conclusions must remain tentative. Nevertheless, moves to incorporate an ageing parent into the home of a child were not widespread. At least as frequent were the shifts of very young kin – grandchildren or nephews and nieces – into the homes of the elderly.

Counterbalancing this drawing together of family or kin were the many cases of 'abandonment' of parent or parents as they advanced into old age. Substantial portions of the elderly lived alone – though not in Anderson's Preston – even where they were observed not to be alone at the previous census. The implication of at least some of these 'abandonments' was that the elderly had not been drawing sustenance from their children so much as completing a life phase of childrearing. With the continuation of family formation in the nineteenth century into their forties for many men and women, significant portions of those reaching their sixties still had minor or barely adult children in their homes. That some or all of these children should want to leave home in their turn is not surprising, and there appears to have been no strong

12 M. Anderson, *Family structure in nineteenth century Lancashire* (Cambridge, 1971), pp. 139–44.

13 The areas surveyed included the rural village of Puddletown in Dorset (1851–81), a range of rural parishes in Bedfordshire (1851–71), the large and growing parish of Ealing on the fringe of London (1851–61), Bedford borough (1851–71), and Cambridge city (1871).

social prohibition against their doing so, even where this meant leaving elderly parents behind.

One further aspect of this pattern of families drawing sustenance from the aged, rather than the opposite, was the housing of young grandchildren or other kin with the elderly. Such young kin may well have been vital in the running of elderly households, and in this way perhaps essential in maintaining the independence of the ageing, thus avoiding the issue of whether or not they were to be taken into the homes of their adult children. Nevertheless, it seems highly unlikely that such an aged person could have drawn the whole or even part of his or her maintenance from the limited earnings of a teenage grand-daughter or two. The elderly must have been deriving their incomes by some other means.

III

Having argued that the modernization paradigm must be abandoned in the light of recent research, one may consider an alternative thesis. It is simply that, sketched in brief, the history of social welfare in Britain in recent centuries must be seen as a series of shifts to and fro between two loci of responsibility. At one pole is the individual and his or her immediate family; at the other is the wider community of non-kin. Responsibility for the maintenance of the elderly lies at some point between these extremes of total familial responsibility, and the assumption of all charges by the community. The location of the balance of responsibilities between these two poles changes over time, shifting continually according to a multitude of social, economic, demographic, political, religious or ideological pressures.

Locating the balance is complicated further by a number of factors. For one thing, the point of balance need not be fixed similarly for all groups in the community. For example, the rich may assume greater responsibility for the material well-being of relatives than do the poor, perhaps because it is infinitely more practicable for them to do so. Second, regional variations of habit can affect the location of the balance. Third, the point of balance varies greatly according to the particular category of dependant in question. Children have been and remain to a very large extent the responsibility of families, whereas the elderly by contrast have for a very long time been accepted as a charge upon the community rather than relatives. Fourth, we accept different balances of responsibility for varied aspects of the material sustenance which the dependant requires. For instance, we appear to agree now that families bear little duty to supplement the monetary incomes of the aged, let alone supply them with a major portion of their resources. But when those same elderly persons need care because of ill-health, and the community is faced with paying for it in cash or with pressuring families to provide it for free, we require families to invest time and money to save the community from this type of expense.

The history of social welfare in Britain in recent centuries can be seen therefore as one of recurrent experimentation with the various options lying between the extremes. The options that have proven even partially practicable appear to be limited in number, and variations of most of them have already been tried. The situations of human need, and the plausible responses to these which face late twentieth century Britain, are little different in kind if not always in scale to those confronting previous generations. The possible alternatives for a community that has to decide what is to be done with an unmarried mother, an elderly spinster, a widowed family man or the unemployed father of many children are not unlimited, and it is not easy for a society to come up with new ones. The current willingness to allude to Victorian models is but one indirect recognition of the recurring nature of welfare questions and answers: examples from Tudor, Stuart or Hanoverian England might also be drawn into the debate as we contemplate, incredulously for many, the 'post-Welfare State era'.[14]

However, this experimentation with options over a long period has not been random or patternless. One of the more distinctive of these enduring patterns has been the persistent emphasis upon communal rather than familial responsibility for material provision for the elderly. For a couple of centuries now, and perhaps for much longer than that, the tendency has been for the range of acceptable options in respect of the elderly to be grouped at the communal rather than the familial end of the continuum of welfare responsibilities. For other categories of dependants the grouping has been much less tight, the options more widely spaced, the shifts between them more dramatic. The welfare responsibilities accepted by the community should be seen as ranked in a series of orders. At the core of the welfare commitment have been the elderly, a group who have been accepted fairly consistently as dependent by force of circumstances and to whom therefore no sense of blame attaches. (A major recent exception to this, one of immense significance for the history of social welfare, will be remarked upon presently.) To such blameless and harmless dependants the community has been willing to commit its collective resources while expecting little complementary expenditure by families in return.

Further removed from this 'welfare core' lie a number of other more marginal dependent groups. Varying degrees of personal and familial

14 The need to grapple with intractable welfare questions goes well back beyond Tudor times, of course: B. Tierney, *Medieval Poor Law* (Berkeley, California, 1959), provides a fascinating study of earlier societies debating such issues. See too R.M. Smith 'The structured dependence of the elderly', pp. 419–22 and his 'Transfer incomes, risk and security: the roles of the family and the collectivity in recent theories of fertility change', in R. Schofield and D. Coleman (eds), *Forward from Malthus: the state of population theory in 1984* (Oxford, 1985).

responsibility attach to these groups – the physically or mentally handicapped, the sick, the child born out of wedlock, the mother of such a child, children in general or the unemployed. A sense that such needy persons are in some part the architects of their own predicaments, coupled with a belief that it could be dangerous for the community if it were seen to encourage certain forms of behaviour by assuming too much of the responsibility for their consequences, has meant that the community's accepted level of commitment to the welfare of these groups has been more attenuated than in the case of the aged. In some circumstances and for some periods the collective commitment to a few or all of these groups has been quite strong, with pensions and other forms of material assistance being made available. In other instances the commitment has been weak and the dependents have been directed to look to their own resources and to those of their families, the community's responses being those of indifference or repression. However, few of these fluctuations in commitment have affected the elderly, the expensive core of the communal welfare undertaking, and a marked willingness to redistribute resources to the aged through communal rather than familial institutions has been evident in Britain for a long time.

The evidence to support this argument is much stronger than that underlying the existing assumption that families previously provided for their own welfare needs in the way that the State does in the later twentieth century. Evidence of the varying levels of commitment to differing dependent groups is found in a wide range of records relating to the history of social welfare, when these records are reanalysed with an emphasis upon identifying and measuring amounts delivered rather than policies discussed. A large body of data from the pre-Welfare State era lends itself to this type of enquiry. None of it is newly discovered; it consists entirely of previously ignored records. To date, investigations of these records have been confined to the last two centuries, and those of particular interest include: census enumerators' returns; Poor Law registers of relief distributions; workhouse and hospital admissions, discharges and other registers; military and civil pensions lists; surveys of wages and of household incomes and expenditures; and the financial records of charitable, governmental and other organizations.

The example of the elderly, aged 60 years or more, continues to provide our central illustration. During the past two centuries the aged have drawn significant shares of the resources of the community, with little being derived from their families. For men in their early to mid sixties the primary claim to a share of the resources of the community has been exercised by way of paid employment. A large portion of the women of similar age were married either to such men or in many instances to younger men, and thus laid claim to a share of resources through marriage. A minority of elderly women pursued employments of their own, although these were generally of a limited nature. It was – and is –

from about age 65 on, perhaps a little earlier for women, that dependence upon redistributions by means other than paid employment became crucial for the elderly.

Mid-nineteenth-century census enumerators' lists indicate that a substantial minority of the elderly of a century or two ago held property and claimed a maintenance from the community by means of returns on these assets. Such listings of the occupations of persons aged 60 years or more are studded with references to property holding as the means of gaining an income. Examples of the more common entries of this nature are 'landed', 'landed proprietor', 'houses', 'land and houses', 'private means', 'funds', 'dividends' and 'interest'. Most widespread of all such references were 'independent', 'independent means' and 'annuitant'. Some of these people would undoubtedly have been of very modest means. For example, it was noted in more than one area studied that all the elderly persons who receive Poor Law pensions (as revealed by the Poor Law registers) were returned as 'independent' at the census, an interesting affirmation of the nineteenth-century attitude to Poor Law pensions for the old (and to which further comment will be directed later). But in most cases the derivation of some income from the property reported can be assumed with confidence. The shapes of the households of many of the propertied elderly indicate this: 'servants' and 'companions' were found in many such homes, witnesses to at least a modicum of surplus income and comfort.

The numbers of the propertied elderly were not insignificant. At least 20 per cent of the women aged 60 and older in the large Middlesex parish of Ealing were returned at the censuses of 1851 and 1861 with some form of property as their 'occupations'. While the proportions were even higher in Cambridge city, they were lower in all rural areas. A further portion of the elderly, especially of aged men, may have been propertied but were disguised in the census returns behind some other occupational description. It may be assumed with some confidence that 'retired solicitor'. 'former army colonel', 'late manufacturer, employed ten men', 'baronet' and 'gentleman' were all in fact men who lived in old age upon the returns of property. No national estimate is possible at this stage of the property holdings of the aged, now or in the past, but a reading of mid-nineteenth century census schedules suggests that perhaps one in five elderly persons may have derived their maintenance by means of returns on investments.

More elderly men and women drew their sustenance from the community through pensions, superannuations and allowances. A rough estimate, again for the mid-nineteenth century, suggests that a significant minority of elderly men received civil or military pensions. At the beginning of the 1840s, for instance, about 100,000 men were in receipt of regular Chelsea, Greenwich or other military pensions, or civil service superannuations.[15]

15 Brief figures on these are available in a number of parliamentary returns, especially a return of military pensions, and a return of naval pensions, in *Papers of the House of Commons* 1846, vol. XXVI.

A large but unspecified portion of these men would have been over 60; yet even if just one-half of the pensioners were of that age, then at least 10 per cent of all men over 60 would have been receiving State pensions. A less conservative estimate of the ages of pensioners would mean that a still larger percentage of all old men were receiving government allowances.

Unknown numbers of aged men and women would have received pensions, free housing or other forms of allowances from former private employers. Instances of such forms of redistribution to the elderly are reported fairly widely in the literature of the nineteenth century, and we may suspect that among the elderly men and women whose occupations were 'late servant', 'former coachmen', perhaps even 'lady's companion', were those who were being rewarded by private means.[16]

Money distributed by charities, both formal and informal, were significant to the elderly community before the twentieth century, but again there are few means for measuring their importance. From my own reading of the statistics of charities I suspect that prior to the nineteenth century, when most charitable distributions were channelled through almshouse and pension foundations, the elderly were major beneficiaries of the redistribution of society's resources by charitable giving. The proportion of all elderly women in particular who received free housing and perhaps also cash allowances in almshouses could well have been quite high, especially in some of the older cities. As late as the mid-nineteenth century, when the number of almshouses in England were shrinking and the elderly population was swelling, perhaps five per cent or more of all elderly women in England could have been supported in almshouses: in earlier periods and in certain places the proportions were almost certainly greater. Other elderly persons, both men and women, received pensions from charitable foundations but did not receive free housing. During the nineteenth century, when the dominance of philanthropic activity in England was passing from the almshouse foundations to the newer, often national, single-purpose charity organizations, the elderly seem to have become relatively insignificant among the plethora of claimants for attention.[17] This need not surprise us: the society possessed so many alternative means for distributing resources to the aged that the charity option was not really needed.

These various mechanisms of redistribution – paid employment, ownership of property, pensions and charity – could account for the maintenance of a substantial portion of elderly persons alive a century or more ago, without any reference to redistributions within families. The primary

16 An example of the references found in many places to this type of income redistribution is the following recorded in 1830 by William Cobbett of his own treatment of an aged cottager who lived in retirement on Cobbett's estate: 'The old man paid me no rent; when he died ... I gave his widow a shilling a week as long as I was at Botley.' Cited in E.P. Thompson, *The making of the English working class* (London, 1968), p. 835.

17 This switch to new categories of claimant is reflected in D. Owen's discussion of the main forms of philanthropic activity in Britain during the past three centuries: *English philanthropy 1660–1960* (Cambridge, Mass., 1965).

mechanism of redistribution however, was the English Poor Law. Because of its wide range of social functions, including a number of repressive social controls, the Poor Law attracted at all times a good deal of unfavourable comment and attention. Historians have concentrated too much upon this critical commentary, failing to recognize that what contemporary critics were doing in berating the Poor Law may have been very often analogous to what we do today with our own welfare systems, that is to lambast their failings while accepting in silence the enormous benefits. Seen from the perspective of what it could and did deliver to beneficiaries, the Old Poor Law of before 1834, and even the much-reviled New Poor Law that followed the reforms of the 1830s, were remarkably effective mechanisms of income redistribution.

This can be seen most distinctly in the case of the aged. During much of the nineteenth century a clear majority of all women aged 70 or more in England and Wales, married, widowed or single, were regular pensioners of the Poor Law. They received weekly cash allowances of around 2s 6d on average, but sometimes up to 3s 6d or more in special circumstances. Slightly less than one-half of all men aged 70 or more, together with substantial minorities of both men and women in their sixties, were also regular Poor Law pensioners in receipt of weekly allowances. Pensions were paid in the great majority of cases on a regular and uninterrupted basis, from the date of admission to the pension lists to the time of death. Substantial "extras", free or subsidized housing, medical attention, nursing assistance, medicines and diet supplements, were also available to pensioners in addition to cash allowances. In rural communities, where alternative mechanisms for income redistribution were weaker than among the propertied retired persons of towns, and where the expectation that the community would support the aged was shared most strongly, the lists of elderly Poor Law pensioners would often include every elderly person in the district, barring perhaps the local landowner or the vicar. The English Poor Law, financed through a local property rate that was levied on real property, was far from being the minimal, miserly, last-resort form of public assistance which it is still portrayed as having been in most historical works.[18] It constituted instead a formalized institution of income redistribution to which the two-thirds to three-quarters of the population who were non-propertied could look with a near-certain expectation of regular and prolonged assistance in old age.

Moreover, the pension given by the nineteenth-century Poor Law was, relative to the incomes of others in the community, far more generous than anything handed out by the later-twentieth-century Welfare State. The retirement pension of recent decades has been fixed at around 40 per cent

18 A recent writer to repeat this view is Henriques, *Before the Welfare State*. In the first couple of pages of her book the point is made unmistakeably: 'The Poor Law ... was the last resort of ... the old and infirm' and 'The Poor Law relieved only those whom charity had failed.'

of the average resources of non-aged 'working-class' adults. By contrast, the Poor Law pension of 2s 6d or 3s a week gave elderly pensioners in the mid nineteenth century the equivalent of 80 per cent or more of the spending power of their younger relatives and neighbours. The inclusion of other public welfare expenditures in the comparison does not alter the central point: expenditures in the later twentieth century upon the health, welfare, housing and so on of the elderly were more than matched by similar community expenditures a century and more ago.[19]

The accumulating evidence of this extensive 'welfare state' of Victorian and earlier times cannot be reviewed here. What should be noted in passing, however, is that once we drop the belief that families in England performed the welfare functions now taken on by the collectivity, many awkward features of the existing histories of social welfare are removed. A few examples of this will illustrate the point. The persistent lack of evidence that families were doing what the theory told us they must have been doing, that is organizing their affairs so that they might maintain elderly and other relatives, is now readily explicable: families did not have to so arrange their affairs much more than do families today. The failure to detect wide-scale movements of the elderly into the homes of the young, or of adult children into the homes of the ageing, is similarly of little concern. The millions of resource transactions which were necessary annually if an elderly population was to be maintained did not take place through families but through a range of community institutions, most of which have their modern counterparts today.

The existence of this long-standing 'welfare state' helps explain another problem which should have been troubling the historians of social welfare for a long time, although they seem not to have recognized its existence. In a society in which the family was the locus of welfare provision it could have been expected that the law would support the enforcement of familial obligations. Quite the opposite was true in England. Both statute and its legal interpretation have for several centuries been concerned almost entirely with making it all but impossible to force anyone to give material assistance to elderly or any other relatives, apart from wives and children. Instead, elderly persons have enjoyed a legal right to sustenance by the community by way of the Poor Law, and the community in turn has claimed the right – almost never acted upon – to seek from the young some small recompense for the expenses incurred in maintaining their elderly parents. In other words, the legal arrangements of England a century or two before the arrival of the twentieth-century Welfare State were those to be expected as the counterparts of a system of collective provision for the elderly and others, but they are quite incomprehensible if we hold to the strict notion of family-centred welfare systems.[20]

19 This point is developed in some detail in Thomson, 'The decline of social security', pp. 461–7.

20 The question of the nature of legal arrangements is the central issue of Thomson, 'I am not my father's keeper.

This description of the relationship between a large population of elderly persons, their families and the wider community, has allowed for few subtleties in the way of regional or temporal variation. Variations of this nature have been significant, and some brief acquaintance with them is essential if we are to understand something of why it is that historians have been misled in their approaches. One major regional variation appears to have been introduced with rapid industrialization and urbanization from the late eighteenth century, although future research may reveal that these disparities enjoyed lengthier antecedents than this. The pre-twentieth century welfare system that has been outlined in the previous section of this essay belonged most distinctly to rural and small-town England. Concentration upon those areas has not been inappropriate in a historical essay, for until the last decades of the nineteenth century the majority of elderly persons still resided in non-urban areas. Nevertheless the numbers and the proportions of the elderly who did live in the larger urban units grew steadily as the nineteenth century advanced, and the older communal systems of provision for the elderly and others did not transplant readily into urban areas. The reasons for this have yet to be explored adequately, and because of a very poor survival rate for Poor Law and other records from industrial and urban areas the story of these regions may never be known in detail. Despite this a certain amount does survive, and it is evident from this that levels of public assistance to groups such as the elderly were distinctly lower there than in those rural areas in which the bulk of the elderly lived.

The logical corollary of this is that the balance of responsibility for the elderly would have been located in such communities at some point much closer to the family pole of the family–community welfare spectrum. Michael Anderson's evidence of a very high incidence of co-residence between young and old in industrial Lancashire provides a fitting suggestion of how transfers of resources between the generations were effected in communities which functioned at the familial end of the welfare continuum. Anderson's high levels of shared residences were particular to a certain type of society, and he is right to have suggested that, contrary to the expectations of some theorists, industrialization increased rather than diminished the importance of supportive kin networks. Future research might reveal how perfectly or imperfectly the levels of co-residence match in time and place with extensive or attenuated networks of alternative, public mechanisms for the redistribution of income.

The progressive relocation of the population into urban and industrial areas during the nineteenth century would in itself have weakened the English system of public provision for old age and other 'life crises'. This trend was given a further and very powerful push during the quarter-century from the late 1860s on when, for a variety of reasons too complex to be explored here, English society in general took a decided lurch towards the familial pole of the continuum of welfare responsibilities. Both contemporaries and the historians who have followed them were well aware of the outlines of this phenomenon, commenting upon it in their writings under various headings such as 'the reform of charity', 'the reform of the Poor Law', or 'the assault upon outdoor relief'. All have remarked upon the harsher tone that entered debate on welfare issues at the time, and many observed the somewhat strident emphasis placed upon individual self-responsibility and the duties of families towards their more unfortunate kin. In drawing attention to this period now we are not breaking with the outlines of that interpretation.

What is suggested is that, because historians have misconceived important aspects of the welfare relationship between individuals and their communities, they have never really known what to make of this peculiar period in the history of social welfare. It has been axiomatic among such observers that history is concerned with steady progress. A very recent period during which a reversal appears to have occurred, when the emphasis was towards rather than away from familial responsibility, does not make good sense, and for this reason it has been handled uncomfortably or glossed over in many works. An embarrassment is overlooked, and attention focuses instead upon the few faint glimmers of the future which can be detected amid a reactionary darkness. Some writers have got themselves into tangles over this period. Maurice Bruce provides a good illustration of this in a widely used text on welfare history. Within a very few pages Bruce both comments upon the effectiveness of the campaign to cut back public assistance to the elderly and others, and sums up the movement by asserting a progressive interpretation of the period: 'From the [18]70s the policy was increasingly adopted of confining deterrence to the able-bodied and of making more adequate provision for those unable to care for themselves.'[21] Others 'solve' the problem by splitting their works, perhaps unconsciously, into a tale of the Poor Law which breaks off somewhere in the late nineteenth century, and 'the rise of the Welfare State' from the 1870s on in which the emergence of State institutions is traced without reference to the Poor Law past.[22]

This is inadequate. The late-nineteenth-century attempt to shift responsibility for such expensive dependants as the elderly from the community to the family was of major significance, then and for the history of social welfare in the twentieth century. For one thing, that attempt was centred not just upon some marginal welfare group but specifically upon the elderly, the core of the public welfare commitment, in a way not seen before or since. The reforms of the Poor Law in the

21 Bruce, *The coming of the Welfare State*, 4th edn (1968), pp. 117–24.
22 For example, see Fraser, *The evolution of the British Welfare State*, and Henriques, *Before the Welfare State*.

1830s, for example, represent perhaps the most widely remarked instance of a shift towards public irresponsibility during several centuries of Poor Law history. Yet those attempts at reform were explicitly not directed towards the elderly, and they made very little impact on the continuing high levels of public expenditure upon the aged. The attack of the 1870s and 1880s went to the core of the welfare commitment as never before.

Second, the campaign to curtail and to end public assistance to the elderly scored some remarkable successes, despite its inherent impracticability given the history of welfare responsibilities in England. By 1890 the proportion of elderly persons who received some form of public assistance was less than half of what it had been in 1870 or earlier. The value to each individual of the pensions still paid to the shrinking body of beneficiaries was only about half in 1890 of what it had been in the 1860s, relative to the incomes of other persons in the community. The additional supplements that had formerly complemented Poor Law pensions shrank to insignificance, and the pensions still in existence by the 1890s were paid out under a wide variety of new and onerous restrictive conditions. These included in particular repeated inquisitorial investigations of pensioners and their kin which made the application for and the receipt of a pension still less attractive than ever. The last quarter of the nineteenth century saw not some temporary slowing along the road to the Welfare State, but an aggressive and for a time successful attempt to steer society in another direction altogether by effecting a lasting realignment of public and private responsibilities for the welfare of citizens.

The fact that the assault was both fundamental in nature and produced some striking successes had an enormous impact upon the nature of the debate surrounding social welfare in our own century. The first half of this century can be viewed in simple outline as a series of steps in a return to a more normal balance of responsibilities between individual, family and community, a return made slow and tortuous by the powerful legacies bequeathed a century ago. If a people have been taught that dependence upon anyone other than self or relatives is evil, and if history and the language have been commandeered and perverted in the process of making this point, then it will take time to re-establish the view that citizens have a legitimate moral claim upon their community.

A single example may serve as an illustration of the lasting effects of the late Victorian campaign and of the difficulties of re-establishing after it a more normal balance in welfare responsibilities – this process of re-establishment being what we refer to as 'the rise of the Welfare State'. Means-testing of applicants for public assistance had been a standard feature of the administration of welfare for as long as the history of social welfare can be observed. Persons were sorted, judged and graded according to various measures of need, regardless of whether the source of the income being redistributed was the Poor Law, an almshouse foundation, a charity organization or a hospital. Means testing was the way in which redistributions were directed to selected areas of need. In the late nineteenth century, however, means testing of both governmental and 'charitable' assistance was enforced so rigorously, so pryingly and so remorselessly, as a deliberate feature of the campaign to kill the notion of a right to look to the community for assistance, that it became a *sine qua non* of the re-emerging public welfare system of the early twentieth century that means testing should be avoided wherever possible. Universality became the catch-cry, meaning that all should be treated equally, regardless of degree of need.

Progress towards universality was slowed by powerful remnants of late-nineteenth-century thinking, even though the impetus towards it arose from those same experiences. With the ascension of the Labour government in 1945, and the acceptance of similar policies by subsequent Conservative governments, the universality principle gained its fullest implementation. Universality has been perhaps the most marked and historically unusual feature of social welfare arrangements from the 1940s to the 1980s. The social luxury of avoiding having to make choices between claimants for public assistance proved possible for a couple of decades, but mounting general economic difficulties and a recognition of some of the inevitable consequences of undiscriminating welfare policies – continuing poverty, injustice, the redistribution of income to the wealthy, the distorting of government budgets – are increasingly revealing the limits to this option. This society is now having to reconsider universality and to look once again to means testing, repugnant though that still is to many older citizens, just as early generations had to grapple with the unpleasantness of choosing among welfare claimants in the search for an optimum location for the balance of responsibilities.

V

The course of development during the past century seems to have made it peculiarly difficult for historians in the twentieth century to place recent trends in a long-term perspective. For one thing, the experiences of their own and their parents' lifetimes confirm for them in a myriad of subtle and often unconscious ways the sense that the history of social welfare has indeed been all about progress from family-centred to community-centred welfare provisions. If one's view is restricted to the period since about 1890, a very convincing argument can be made that such has been the course of history: the mistake has been to assume that what went before conformed to a similar pattern.

Second, the theories of social development which are available to historians who struggle to understand this development have similarly been coloured by the peculiar experiences of the last 100 years, and they tend to reinforce the faulty long-term view. Modern disciplines such as sociology or social economics took much of their shape around the turn of the century, and it may not be too fanciful to suggest that their concerns with family and kin arose out of the issues of prime interest at that time. Many of the leading figures involved in the seminal studies of welfare issues and of social statistics, for example, were active participants as well as less conscious products of the welfare debates of the late nineteenth century.

Third, reinvestigation of the history of social welfare has been rendered difficult by the peculiar emotional stamp given to many terms and concepts during the campaign to abolish public assistance to the elderly and others. The example of means testing has been mentioned already, but many other words gained emotion-laden connotations during the same period from which they have never been freed. Among the most striking are the derogatory meanings given to 'Poor Law', 'pauper' and 'pauperization'. Consider the term 'Poor Law', for instance. For centuries it had been the legal and the everyday description of the system of public provision for those in need of sustenance. The systems of administration changed over the centuries; debates raged over the role of the Poor Law; its properties were attacked and burned from time to time; and varying groups of claimants joined and dropped out of the lists of approved beneficiaries. Through it all, however, the system and its name survived, providing assistance to large numbers and the assurance of future help to a great many more.

But once the term 'Poor Law' and all it stood for became a centrepiece of the vilification that was the main weapon of the late-nineteenth-century 'reformers', it became all but inevitable that the term 'Poor Law' would never recover its former fuller meaning and would have to be abandoned as the society shook itself free from the peculiar experiences of that period. The formal pronouncement in the very first line of the National Assistance Act of 1948 that 'the existing Poor Law shall cease to have effect' was dramatic but predictable confirmation of this – all significant public welfare developments for 40 years had already been taking place outside the Poor Law. So great was the popular revulsion at the meaning given to the term in the late nineteenth century that a term and a system which had adapted and persisted for hundreds of years was abandoned in the attempt to leave behind bitter memories. Historians have yet to shake off this incubus and to see the language in its varying earlier meanings, and it is perhaps only by pursuing alternative approaches, for example the one adopted here which emphasizes the measurement of achievement, that the subtleties of the concepts may be recaptured.

A fourth and perhaps more sinister reason for historians' failures to rethink long-term trends is that they have fallen victim to some very deliberate deception by the late-nineteenth-century campaigners against public involvement in private welfare. This goes beyond some Orwellian reshaping of language, so that former meanings are lost sight of, and along with them the very concepts to which those terms referred. It extended to deliberate suppression of statistical evidence at a time when the study of social statistics was in its infancy, when its agendas were being set and its spheres of enquiry mapped out. Among those guilty of this were some who were and have since been accredited with fostering a clear-headed approach to social questions and their investigation. Charles Booth was undoubtedly the key figure here, although there were others. Booth believed strongly that public welfare was morally indefensible and that individuals and their families should be responsible for personal well-being, and he threw his considerable prestige behind the campaign to reduce and to eliminate public expenditure through the Poor Law.[23]

In the course of his investigations of London and elsewhere Booth was given access to many sets of Poor Law registers, and to people who had the care of many more sets. These records would have shown to Booth the true effects of the anti-pensions campaign upon which he and others were engaged – that pensions lists which had 10 or 20 years earlier contained the names of hundreds of ageing men and women had by the end of the 1880s shrunk to a few dozen names or to nil in a few extreme cases. Such evidence could have been disturbing if made public and would not have helped the campaigners' cause. What, it might be asked, had happened to all those who were disinherited of their pensions; was this why talk of 'poverty' and 'starvation' in old age were becoming familiar topics of discussion where they had not been before? Even more troubling, it might have been seen that families were unwilling to or incapable of supporting their relatives as the theorists had insisted they would, could and must.

It was better for the purposes of Booth and others that the debate over welfare duties remain at an emotional, moral and non-specific level, so that awkward questions about the actual conditions of ageing and other dependent persons might be avoided. Booth chose to lead the debate away from unhelpful statistics. He did this both by ignoring the records of the past, and by stating on different occasions that records from the past could not be used to throw light on current developments. Booth wrote in 1894, for example, that:

We have, unfortunately, no particulars as to the ages of those in receipt of relief previous to Mr Burt's return of 1889. Consequently we cannot say whether there had been any decrease in old age pauperism on the whole, or under what circumstances any improvement has taken place. It seems to me very doubtful whether there has been any general change for the better, but I am no more able to prove this than the reverse.[24]

By 'any improvement' or 'general change for the better' Booth meant a decrease in Poor Law expenditure, that is a drop in public assistance to

23 Booth did however exhibit the flexibility of mind as the 1890s advanced to recognize the practical hardships and injustices resulting from the policies that he and others had been advocating, and to revise his opinions in favour of communal assistance for the old – under some new state administration other than the Poor Law, of course.

24 C. Booth, *The aged poor in England and Wales* (1894), p. 32.

the elderly who absorbed at least 60 per cent of the average nineteenth century Poor Law budget. Booth considered that the historically low levels of public assistance – and he should have known that they were such – were 'both startling and deplorable' in their magnitude.[25]

Booth was disingenuous in asserting that nothing could be known of the past. No single national return of the ages of pensioners had been published before Burt's of 1890 (why Booth said 1889 is unclear), but there are many ways of investigating the statistical evidence of the past despite this fact. Such pieces of ideologically motivated misinformation as these by Booth served their purpose well, nevertheless. The history of social welfare has been written for almost a century within the limits prescribed by Booth and others, and the time for a fresh approach is long overdue.

25 This comment appears in C. Booth, 'Enumeration and classification of paupers', *Journal of the Royal Statistical Society* 54 (1891), pp. 631–2.

14

Mountains, Rivers and the Family: Comments on a Map from the 1975 French Census

Hervé le Bras and Emmanuel Todd

In the last ten years research on household structure has concentrated on the analysis of old nominative listings of inhabitants, dating mostly from the seventeenth, eighteenth and nineteenth centuries. These documents make it possible to reach and analyse the local communities of the past, at least some of them. They cannot lead to a detailed geography of European family systems. They are too few and scattered over too wide an expanse of territory.

The village-based studies pioneered first by Peter Laslett, and then by people working in association with the Cambridge Group for the History of Population and Social Structure, soon revealed the existence of different national, regional and local patterns of family organization. What we now need is a more systematic inventory of these patterns. Since, because of their patchy survival, such an inventory cannot be produced from historical records, we must turn to the much more comprehensive record of recent European censuses.[1] A majority of those taken during the 1970s contain a simplified but nevertheless reasonable description of household types. Many of them break down that simplified information geographically. Some of them use very small local units of analysis, thus reaching the scale and level of observation considered as typical of social-anthropological enquiry. Such is the case of the 1975 French census, which gives for about 3500 cantons the number of complex households and the total number of households. A canton is in fact a group of villages – eight or nine of them on average – linked by close geographical and historical ties. Drawing from these data a detailed and exhaustive map of complex household forms in France in 1975 is therefore a simple (though time-consuming) operation.

1 See recent attempts along lines proposed here for various parts of Europe, including France, in R. Wall, 'Introduction', R. Wall, P. Laslett and J. Robin (eds), *Family forms in historic Europe* (Cambridge, 1983), pp. 51–60.

We first used the household composition tables of the 1975 French census in a book published four years ago, in which we wanted to test the existence of several possible correlations between family structure on the one hand, and other aspects of social life such as political, religious or demographic behaviour on the other.[2] The map we drew at the time was established for a rather large scale: it gave, for each of the 95 French *départements* (the closest English administrative equivalent is the county) the proportion of complex households. These first results were already very clear: large and coherent anthropological zones appeared, with smooth transitions between them. The map, however, was criticized for its very scale, supposedly too large and thus unable to reach small homogeneous anthropological areas. Given the fact that the statistical indicator used varied from less than 1 per cent to over 20 per cent, the distortion created by the use of the *département* as a mapping unit could only have been very small. Going down to the level of the canton actually takes us below the geographical level defining homogeneous anthropological areas. Traditionally, statistical studies concerned with rural or agricultural phenomena use not the 3500 cantons but 698 homogeneous peasant regions – an already detailed grid when one considers that France only produces 350 different kinds of cheese!

The canton, however, being an electoral as well as an administrative unit, is often chosen by electoral geographers and psephologists as the proper level of observation; this tradition was inaugurated 80 years ago by André Siegfried in his *Tableau politique de la France de l'ouest*.[3] The canton has also been used extensively by the French school of religious sociology, and therefore appears as a basic element in the *Atlas de la pratique religieuse en France*.[4]

The household map presented here could therefore be compared systematically to those contained in these classic works. Correlations and non-correlations, general or partial, could certainly be found and perhaps explained. However, the main purpose of this brief essay is of a different kind. It is concerned with an analysis of the internal structure of the map, and leaves aside possible statistical and geographical relationships between household structure and other sociological variables. The only external factor taken into account is physical geography. Mountains, rivers and their valleys are just as important in defining the real shape of the map as absolute distances and positions.

Complex Households

In the microfiche of the 1975 census, one finds in table P20 a rough classification of households, given for the population as a whole and for

2 H. Le Bras and E. Todd, *L'Invention de la France* (Paris, 1981).
3 A. Siegfried, *Tableau politique de la France de l'ouest* (Paris, 1913).
4 F.-R. Isambert and J.-P. Terrenoire, *Atlas de la pratique réligieuse des catholiques en France* (Paris, 1980).

farmers (*agriculteurs*), which makes it possible to estimate the proportion of non-nuclear households. To get closer to the anthropological origins of the country we have chosen the distribution for farmers as the most significant one. It must however, be pointed out that maps drawn separately for urban, rural and agricultural populations at the level of the 95 French *départements* are extremely similar.[5]

The figures used for the 3500 cantons were taken not from an exhaustive count in the 1975 census but from the 20 per cent sample. Random fluctuations are reasonably moderate, the average number of agricultural households per canton being about 450. Purely urban cantons have of course been left aside and appear as 'empty areas' on the map.[6]

The description of households given in the census is a crude one. We find in table P20 only the total number of households and the number of secondary families. Within a household, a family is the classic nuclear unit, which can take any of its three distinct shapes: a married couple without children, two parents with children, and one parent with children. One must add the restriction that a child over 25 years old is no longer considered as a child by the classification. A secondary family is a nuclear family which does not include the household head. Obviously, the existence of a secondary family presupposes that of a primary one and that of a 'complex' household structure. We can therefore consider the proportion of secondary families to the total number of households (multiplied by 100) as a valid estimate of the degree of complexity of household structure in a given canton. One must, however, bear in mind that, according to French conventions, the existence of a secondary family does not imply that of *two* married couples. A three-generation household containing one married couple, plus the wife's father, will be considered as containing *two* families – a primary and a secondary one – if the wife's husband is the household head.

The concept of complex household used here therefore overlaps the much more precise 'extended' and 'multiple family household' categories of the Laslett typology.[7] Tests carried out at the departmental level nevertheless show that, in France, all possible types of statistical indicators measuring the proportion of households containing more than a nuclear family yield closely correlated series and lead to very similar

5 See Le Bras and Todd, *L'Invention de la France*, pp. 111–19.

6 The administrative map used is that from 1968. Differences between the 1975 and the 1968 maps mainly concern urban cantons. In the case of a non-urban canton subdivided between 1968 and 1975, the index calculated for the part of the canton keeping in 1975 the original name and code number is considered as applying to the whole of the 1968 area. As we are dealing with agricultural households only, this procedure simply increases random fluctuations.

7 P. Laslett, 'Introduction: the history of the family', in P. Laslett and R. Wall (eds), *Household and family in past time* (Cambridge, 1972), pp. 28–32.

maps. From this single statistical index we have deduced a single series
of results for the 3500 or more cantons, but three different maps. The
first map (map 14.1) gives detailed results concerning household complexity; six intensities of complexity are used, with cut-off points at
4,6,9, 15 and 20 per cent. Surfaces darken as household structure
becomes more complex. This treatment of the information tends to
emphasize complex forms, as the eye and the mind give greater importance to black surfaces than to white ones. To achieve a symmetrical

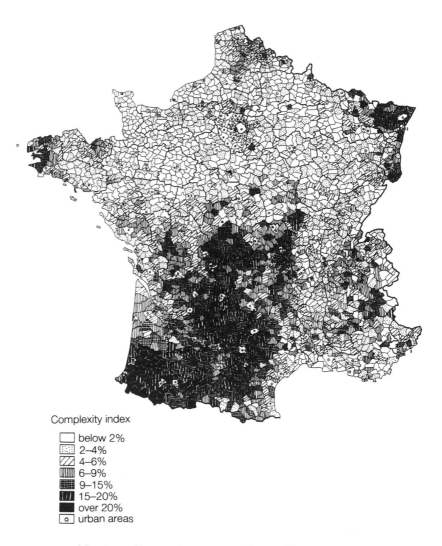

Complexity index

☐ below 2%
▨ 2–4%
▨ 4–6%
▥ 6–9%
▦ 9–15%
▮ 15–20%
■ over 20%
⊙ urban areas

Map 14.1   Household complexity in France, 1975: six intensities

presentation of the complex and nuclear family household types, we
have drawn two additional maps.

On map 14.2 only cantons with a complexity index below 2 per cent
are blackened: a 'nuclearity' map is thus obtained, which shows as
black the regions where household structure is particularly simple. Map
14.3 can be considered as symmetrical: only cantons with an index
above 9 per cent are blackened. This map is in fact a simplified version
of map 14.1, showing only regions of maximum household complexity.

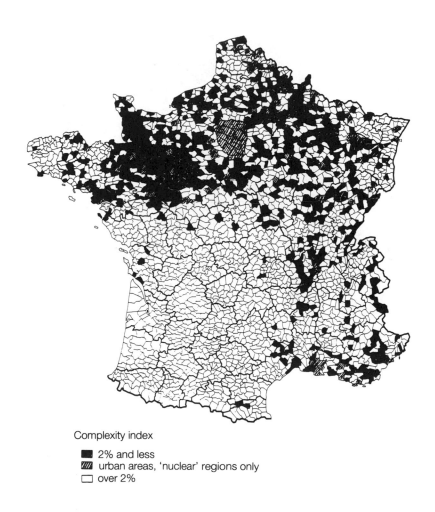

Complexity index

■ 2% and less
▨ urban areas, 'nuclear' regions only
□ over 2%

Map 14.2   Household complexity in France, 1975: nuclearity map, based on 2 per cent index

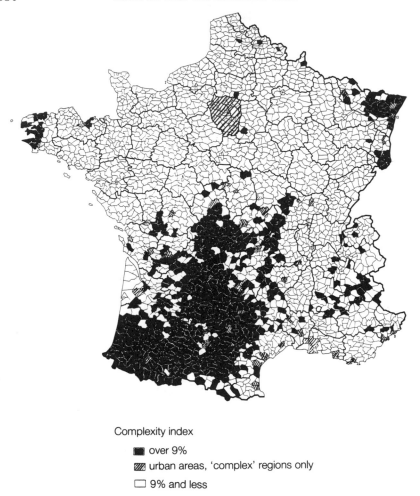

Complexity index

■ over 9%

▨ urban areas, 'complex' regions only

□ 9% and less

Map 14.3 Household complexity in France, 1975: maximum complexity, based on 9 per cent index

Centre and Periphery

The overall structure of map 14.1 is very clear. Complex household forms are mostly located in peripheral regions: Alsace, Brittany, the Alps, most of the south-west and, more surprisingly, the heavily industrialized and urban north. At this stage the obvious (and much too simple) interpretation could be the traditional one which describes complex and ancient family forms as transformed by modernization into simple nuclear ones. We can easily imagine a disintegration process leading to nuclearity, starting from Paris at the centre of the national system, and spreading outwards to the provinces. Unfortunately for such an argument, Paris is by no means at the centre of map 14.2. Although nuclear household forms occupy most of the Paris Basin, what we might call the *epicentre of nuclearity* is clearly situated west of Paris, half-way between the capital city and Brittany.

In the case of Alsace, Brittany, the south-west or the Alps, the statistical analysis of census data only confirms and refines, geographically, well-known ethnological facts. The stem families of these regions were first described as early as the middle of the nineteenth century by Frédéric Le Play. On the other hand, the location of the negative pole in the system, the region where nuclear forms predominate absolutely, is a discovery in the strictest sense.

Traditional ethnological fieldwork makes it relatively easy to identify positive rules concerning the association of several adult generations within the household; it is less well adapted to the identification of negative rules specifying that father and adult son should not live together. However, negative and positive attitudes concerning the coresidence of generations must equally be considered as social or anthropological norms. Statistical analysis considers both attitudes as extreme and will grant no privilege to the positive norm.

Within the French national system, the epicentre of nuclearity must also be considered as lying on the periphery. The 'interior west' as it is called, although not very far from Paris, is in fact rather isolated. Distant from the sea and from the Loire or Seine river systems, it is clearly outside the main communication network. Thus its nuclear family cannot be considered as a product of modernization; on the contrary, it is a primitive form, emerging from an indefinite past. This unexpected result certainly comes as a verification of the Laslett hypothesis concerning the English family. Again, the nuclear household appears, not as a historical variable, but as an anthropological constant.

We are left with at least one major question unanswered: what was the original factor or factors which led to the emergence of different types of household structure in the various French provinces? No ultimate cause can be given at this elementary stage of research. However, the coincidence of the main anthropological frontiers with simple elements of the natural landscape points to a very ancient origin. Differences in family systems were defined and stabilized at a time when population movements and cultural influences could be stopped by rivers and mountains.

The main division of France into two great anthropological areas – a northern one dominated by nuclear family systems, and a southern one occupied by more complex family systems – clearly follows a frontier defined by the river Loire. North of that line, the percentage of complex households falls below 4 per cent. South of it, the percentage is almost always above 4 per cent.[8]

Disintegration of Complex Forms

As remarked above, the geographical distribution of household types in France contradicts the traditional evolutionary model concerning the history of the family, particularly when it is expressed in general and absolute terms: a simple and direct look at the map shows that there is no relationship between nuclearity and modernization. It is in the isolated and rural regions of the interior west that the hardest nuclear systems can be found, and these cannot be the outcome of a disintegration process leading from complex to simple household forms. However, a less general process of disintegration can be observed on the map. The moderate variant of the nuclear type, dominant at the national level, influences and partly destroys complex households in contact regions. Hence the existence, south of the Loire, of intermediate zones where the complex types are not as strong as in the core area of the south-west: along the Tours–Bordeaux axis, in the Alps, in the eastern part of the Massif Central or the eastern half of the Pyrenees. The location of these intermediate zones starts from the national centre in Paris but is a multiple one, with some forces acting from the capital city and its region, and others from the Mediterranean coast and the Rhône valley.

The weakening of the complex family pattern in the eastern part of both the Massif Central and the Pyrenees reveals the existence of an east–west gradient. The orientation of these anthropological forces allows us to indulge in a little guesswork on the historical period during which the disintegration process was most active. To do this we must add the supplementary hypothesis that anthropological influences spread from culturally dominant regions. However, the Mediterranean coast and the Rhône valley could in no way be considered as dominant, within the French system, during the modern or even the medieval period. To find that particular region in a pre-eminent economic and social position we must go further back – to the era of Roman imperial rule. The hypothesis that the Roman settlement in the Narbonnaise province started a disintegration process in the stem-family regions of the Pyrenees, the Massif Central and the Alps is no doubt a very risky and speculative one. We know relatively little about the Roman family. But one thing is certain: its inheritance system was strongly egalitarian,

8 Peter Laslett did in fact call attention to this basic divide in 'Characteristics of the western family considered over time', *Journal of Family History* 2 (1977), pp. 89–115. See, too, F. Mendels, 'La composition du ménage paysan en France au XIXe siècle: une analyse économique du mode de production domestique', *Annales, économies, sociétés, civilisations* (1978), pp. 780–802.

and therefore in strong opposition to that of the upland regions of the south – the Alps, the Massif Central or the Pyrenees.

The association between natural landscape and geographical distribution of household types is not a simple one. There is no general correlation between type of landscape and type of household structure. Mountains in particular cannot be considered as the natural home of the stem family and of complex households. They appear as such in the case of the Alps, of the Pyrenees or of the Massif Central. But the Vosges mountains close to the eastern border are dominated by nuclear households and look very much like a barrier raised against the spread of Germanic complex household systems. The central part of the south-west, Aquitaine, where complex forms predominate, is on the other hand a river basin. The complex household structures in the north are located in regions that can even be described as remarkably flat.

It would be absurd to propose any kind of exhaustive and final interpretation. What we really want to suggest is, first, that much original information on the anthropological structure and social history of Europe can be found in many very recent censuses, and second, that the mapping of the data thus obtained is likely to reveal in most cases the existence of unexpected cultural areas. The striking fact about the detailed description of complex households in France is that it bears no relation at all to the distribution of classic economic variables such as industry, income level or urbanization.

15

The Genesis of Experimental History

Kenneth W. Wachter and Eugene A. Hammel

'Myriadminded' was James Joyce's elegant translation of the Latin *amplius*, the quality, so the passage runs in the Aeolus chapter of *Ulysses*, most necessary in human society to be esteemed among multitudes of friends. The chapters for this volume reflect the esteem of Peter Laslett's multitudes of friends. The myriadminded character of his thought and inspiration is illustrated by all these chapters, and particularly by the story of the computer simulation studies of pre-industrial household kin composition which in the 1970s opened up the approach since called 'experimental history'. This research enterprise combined not only the central themes of historical sociology found in all the Laslett works, but also anthropology, demography, mathematics, computer science and statistics. We were privileged to share with Peter Laslett the seven years of reconceptualizations that led him to begin the foreword to *Statistical Studies of Historical Social Structure* with the sentence 'Statistics makes exacting demands on the imagination.'[1] In this chapter we chronicle those exacting demands and their consequences, not only in celebration of our collaborator and friend, but as an aid to understanding this approach to history.

Statistical Studies, as we shall refer to it, gives the scientific presentation of the first fruits of the research. The enterprise continues to this day, and many later papers carry the scientific presentation forward. 'Experimental history' itself is the title for a subsequent paper by one of the authors of this essay.[2] But science tends to cover its tracks. Scientific books and articles often conceal, as finished products, the whys and wherefores behind the experimental design and inferential edifice. We offer this historical presentation of the early years of the research and of Peter Laslett's role to clarify these whys and wherefores, as well as to emphasize what is too often slighted – the human dimension of scholarly endeavour.

---

1 K.W. Wachter with E.A. Hammel and P. Laslett, *Statistical studies of historical social structure* (London and New York, 1978), p. xi.

2 E.A. Hammel, 'Experimental history', *Journal of Anthropological Research* 35 (1979), pp. 274–91.

The first of the strands that were to be interwoven over years into this research enterprise can be traced back clearly to the 1969 conference on household structure in Cambridge which led to the 1972 volume *Household and Family in Past Time*. It was at this conference, organized by Laslett, that he and Hammel met for the first time. Over the formal sessions and the informal gatherings it became clear how many of Hammel's interests as an anthropologist overlapped Laslett's as a historian.

There was their common interest in early household listings, Laslett's with English and Hammel's with Balkan. There was the formal structure of kinship. As Laslett was beginning the search for appropriate classification of patterns of coresident kin for the tables for *Household and Family in Past Time*, Hammel was publishing on the formal analysis of kinship systems and exploiting analogies with linguistics whereby parsing syntactical trees could be likened to parsing genealogical trees. Furthermore, Hammel's contribution to the conference, 'The zadruga as process', was, together with the contribution of Jack Goody from Cambridge, the main paper to emphasize the household cycle and the different configurations of coresident kin that could all be observed when the same process of household formation, growth and dissolution was viewed at different stages in the lives of the household members.[3] If the 1969 conference was to be a starting point rather than a summing up, here in the tension between composition at a point in time and process over time was the issue for the future. In the months after the conference, Laslett and Hammel corresponded and arranged for Hammel to spend his sabbatical year 1970–71 at Trinity College, Cambridge.

The chief joint work during this year of collaboration, sharing Laslett's rooms on the first floor of Bishop's Hostel, was the classification system for sets of coresident kin published in 1974.[4] But the relationship between household cycles over time and household listings at a single time continuously occupied their attention, and by the spring they began to speculate that methods of simulation on a computer might provide leverage on this relationship. Simulation was an approach with which Hammel already had experience. During his year at the Center for Advanced Study in the Behavioral Sciences at Palo Alto in 1962–3, he had developed a small kinship simulation model with the aid of John Gilbert, the Statistician in Residence at the Center, later at Harvard.

With this model Hammel and Gilbert had studied frequencies of cousin marriage. They showed that patrilocal post-marital residence

3 E.A. Hammel, "The zadruga as process' in P. Laslett and R. Wall (eds), *Household and family in past time* (Cambridge, 1972), pp. 335–73.

4 E.A. Hammel and P. Laslett, 'Comparing household structure over time and between cultures', *Comparative Studies in Society and History* 16 (1974), pp. 73–109.

and a preference for nearby brides could of themselves account for a substantial portion of the high frequencies of patrilateral parallel cousin marriages found in various field studies in the Middle East. Thus the elaborate cultural preferences that might be adduced to explain the high frequencies would only be sufficient and not necessary as explanations.[5] This example, where simulation had showed simple constraints to be capable of accounting for a complicated cultural phenomenon, encouraged the idea that the same might occur for complicated patterns of coresidence. The simulations with Gilbert had also pointed up the importance of a sensible random model. Hammel and Laslett had preliminary discussions with John Barnes and Roger Schofield about how such a model might work, and during the spring of 1971 Laslett and Hammel began looking for someone with statistical and computing experience to join them in specifying and implementing one.

Here a second strand entered the picture, leading toward the fortuitous encounter described in the preface to *Statistical Studies*. Wachter had arrived at Trinity College, Cambridge from the United States in January 1970 as a Keasbey Scholar, and had become a research student in statistics under David Kendall. He was enjoying sitting in occasionally on lectures outside his speciality, and one evening he asked his fellow Trinity student Mark Kaplanoff, later himself a historian at Cambridge, which historians were worth hearing. Kaplanoff replied that his adviser at Yale had told him that the one in England most worth listening to was Laslett, and he was lecturing that term on pre-industrial English society. Thus at 10.00 a.m. on 27 April 1971 Wachter made his way to the History Library basement, introduced himself, and heard a stirring class on English population subgroups of the 1600s and their political participation.

After several classes, Wachter stopped by the Trinity library to consult *The World We Have Lost*, but found no card for it in the catalogue. This omission struck him as bizarre, the author being a Fellow of Trinity. The explanation, as it later turned out, was that the presentation copy had been refused by the college librarian as being 'of too little scholarly interest for the library'. In 1985, in the midst of the worldwide fame of the Cambridge Group and their accomplishments, it is worth remembering how hostile a reception they faced and fought against for more than a decade, especially in Cambridge. The distinguished French historian who, viewing computers as a species of magic, quipped that the Cambridge Group consisted of 'a priest, a prophet, and a mountebank' could have had in mind the lines of Matthew 13:57: 'a prophet is not without honour, save in his own country.'

---

5 J. Gilbert and E.A. Hammel, 'Comparative analysis of problems in kinship and social structure', *American Anthropologist* (1966), pp. 71–93.

One strong supporter of the Cambridge Group inside Cambridge, however, was David Kendall, Professor of Statistics, whose early work had established the probabilistic models for age-dependent population processes in continuous time. As Wachter's research supervisor, Kendall was ready to encourage him in modelling household structure, as an adjunct to the abstract mathematical work on random matrices going into the Ph.D. thesis. The possibility of such modelling was raised by Laslett when, after a class, he invited Wachter to meet himself and Hammel in Bishop's Hostel, before the latter's return to the United States.

The meeting took place at 2.00 p.m. on 8 June 1971. The brown leather bindings of Peter Laslett's rare book collection on long low shelves under the southern window lent the occasion a serious aura, though the discussion was brief and tentative. The idea was a project of a matter of months to design a Monte Carlo simulation programme with demographic events and household choices that could be varied to predict the proportions of complex households that would result from different combinations. Wachter recently wrote:

We who venture into simulation studies all no doubt first harbour a hope of capturing something as it was, is, or will be, of producing a copy as realistic as possible and more realistic than descriptive generalities can offer, of some process as it might happen. The word simulation itself connotes the making of a likeness. But the pursuit of realism through simulation is in fact a chimera. ... What we make when we simulate is not a likeness of the operation of the world but a likeness of some set of our own ideas concerning the operation of the world.[6]

In June 1971 the three participants in the Bishop's Hostel meeting set off in full pursuit of chimerical realism. They planned, rather vaguely, to create in the computer a simulacrum of some particular village; whether immediately or slightly later, the intended village came to be Ealing, outside London, to which the earliest known (1599) English age and household listing pertains. The main labour was to be of algorithm design and computer programming. From the computer outputs, the cross-sectional household structure resulting from rules of post-marital household residence would be read off. As Hammel wrote in the following year in an application for preliminary funds from the Berkeley Institute for International Studies:

We will go on to the problems of post-marital residence and household composition, using the appropriate historical rates to simulate household composition in communities, for which Laslett has not only the vital rates but also household listings or family reconstitutions. If these match, we will feel confident in

6 K. Wachter, 'Microsimulation of household cycles', in J. Bongaarts, T. Burch and K. Wachter (eds), *Family demography: methods and their applications* (Oxford, 1986). See too Wachter's preface to Wachter et al., *Statistical studies*, pp. xv–xxii and N. Howell, *The demography of the Dobe 'Kung* (London and New York, 1979).

estimating either household composition in terms of known vital rates or vital rates in terms of known household composition.

What could be simpler? Laslett put down his diary, in which he was recording essential moments of the discussion. He found a piece of paper, and Hammel started to write down a computer programme flow chart. Wachter offered some ideas about appropriate distributions for the random numbers. Simulations always look straightforward on paper. The computer would prove a great educator. Only by building the model would the researchers be forced to concede that a meaningful simulation requires the specification of far more rates than can be estimated directly from modern data sources, far less historical. Only by trial and error would they learn that some interactions cannot be ignored without affecting key results, while others can. Only by paging through great piles of computer printout would they understand that the random variability that must be allowed to village-sized populations defeats any direct comparison between single villages and single simulation outputs. Once these lessons were learned, the computer work itself would come to seem secondary, and the chief labour would turn out to be the reconceptualization of hypotheses. Had the group in Bishop's Hostel glimpsed not the months but the years ahead, it is open to question whether they would ever have proceeded.

When Hammel returned to Berkeley, he learned of the existence of the POPSIM computer demographic simulation programme. POPSIM was being developed at the Research Triangle Institute in North Carolina by a team headed by Daniel Horvitz. POPSIM had been designed for estimating the impact of different contraceptive adoption scenarios in Third World countries like India. At first it seemed as if the POPSIM computer code might be taken over directly for the demographic component of household simulation. But, in fact, the Research Triangle Institute team had abandoned what was for the demographic project the appropriate model of POPSIM – the 'closed-model' version. In a closed model, individuals in the hypothetical computer population choose spouses from among the already present individuals in accordance with a marriage search algorithm. Instead, the team under Horvitz had turned for reasons of programming convenience to an 'open model'. In an open model, a spouse is invented at time of marriage and assigned characteristics like age, whenever the random numbers decree a marriage for an individual in the computer population.

For the interests of the participants at the Bishop's Hostel meeting, a closed model seemed to be required. The much simpler open model would suffice for aggregate national estimates such as those concerning contraception sought by the POPSIM group. But only in a closed model would the reckoning of kinship relationships through both parents be tractable, if demographic rates were to be permitted to change over time. The added complexity of a closed model over an open model is so great that a decade later, in designing the new CAMSIM simulations, Laslett and Jim Smith would forgo the power to change rates over time and restrict genealogical reckoning to a depth low enough for an open model to be utilized. But the original group, without precedents to chasten them, opted for a closed model.

It was the practicality of genealogical reckoning that swayed the choice of a closed model. Genealogical reckoning was particularly uppermost in Hammel's mind, since he became eager to use the intended simulation programmes to carry on the cousin marriage research he had begun almost a decade earlier with Gilbert and to investigate other anthropological issues like incest as well as to tackle the problem of household cycles. But in fact the choice of a closed model turned out to be crucial to the household studies for a different reason. In small pre-industrial villages, the timing of marriage must depend heavily on the availability of marriageable young people. Any quantities like the generational depth of a household, which ought to depend on the overlap in the married lives of parents and children, would be sensitive to marriage squeezes. Thus marriage partners needed to be drawn from a marriage pool that could shrink or grow with the course of the simulation, as in a closed model. Thus the complexity of a closed model would prove unavoidable.

Horvitz generously provided code and documentation for the closed-model version of POPSIM, as far as it had been carried, and later for the working open model of POPSIM as well. David Hutchinson was hired by Hammel as a programmer on a small budget from the Institute of International Studies at Berkeley. He replicated POPSIM test runs, tried altering POPSIM, and eventually began writing a new closed-model programme to be called SOCSIM (social simulation), based on the POPSIM experience. Fortunately, POPSIM had been written in standard FORTRAN. It was comprehensible and reasonably portable to the Berkeley machines. For the sake of comprehensibility, portability and reliability, the SOCSIM programming proceeded in FORTRAN too.

It never seemed a sensible alternative to use one of the special-purpose 'simulation languages' which have since been recommended by some writers. Most of the effort in writing large socio-demographic simulation programmes like SOCSIM goes into designing and debugging the demographic algorithms and social rules, involving constant interaction between programming decisions and substantive reasoning about the problem at hand. An even higher level of language spares the designer none of this reasoning. It may shorten the time spent coding, but the time spent coding is not a large part of the total effort.

This issue of whether to use simulation languages is one in which it seemed wise to be governed by the same suspicion of black boxes with which most of the world regards simulation in general. Great oaks of seemingly relevant conclusion can grow from the smallest acorns of quirks of programming. SOCSIM was programmed in a language which the researchers and many of their readers and critics all under-stood, a language that had been tested for consistency by many thousands of programmers over many years, rather than in one that merely had convenient handles to turn. It also seemed advantageous to avoid non-standard approaches because of the extra overhead, and the consequent higher expense of production runs, considering the need for many replications to arrive at statistically stable results.

Laslett received the news of progress at Berkeley with great enthu-siasm. A week after the June meeting, Wachter had been elected a Fellow of St Catherine's College, Oxford, in Applied Mathematics, and moved to Oxford in September 1971. He began the practice of coming to Cambridge for the evening seminars in social history in Laslett's rooms. Each morning afterwards they would meet, usually for a walk around the backs of Trinity and St John's along the Cam, to discuss the news from Berkeley and the pitfalls they were encountering in trying to specify demographic rates for a 'replication of Ealing'.

In the winter began a long, ill-fated attempt to run, in England, a version of simulation programmes written in Berkeley. *En route* back from Scottish Hogmanay with the family of his friend McKinnon in Ayrshire, Wachter stopped in Newcastle, where the machine for Cam-bridge Group remote computing was located. He tried to make the rewritten POPSIM code from Hutchinson compile and run. Not even the password would work. Dictated as CAMPOC, it should have been CAMPOP. Making CAMPOC work immediately prevented everyone at the Cambridge Group from logging in, producing unmitigated dis-may in the old Group rooms in Silver Street. There was nothing wrong with the code, but such a host of minor differences in machine conven-tions plagued the attempt, first in Newcastle, later in Oxford, briefly in London, and finally in Cambridge that no 'production runs' of the simulation programmes ever took place in England.

Laslett always placed the highest priority on having the simulation programmes run in England as well as Berkeley. He would put this forward as a matter of national pride, but even in 1972 there was another more pressing reason. A friendly but stubborn tug of war was beginning over the problems to be tackled by the project and the order of tackling them. Hammel decided to try out the capabilities of the new programmes first on anthropological problems with which he had ex-perience from the work with Gilbert. He began with the effects of territorial bias in mate selection on matrilateral cross-cousin marriage, and proceeded to effects of incest taboos on small group viability.[7]

7 E.A. Hammel and D. Hutchinson, 'Two tests of computer microsimulation', in B. Dyke and J. MacCluer (eds), *Simulation of human populations* (London and New York, 1974), pp. 1–14.

Laslett wanted to know, and to know as soon as possible, about the effects of household cycles on the proportions observable in household listings. He began to fear that unless the household simulations were run in England, they would never be run at all.

It must be borne in mind that no one foresaw or admitted they foresaw a large project stretching over many years which would investigate a dozen salient problems in historical, anthropological, mathematical and contemporary demography. The target was one paper on demographic influences on household composition. For Wachter the work specifying demographic rates was being done on 'time out' from his mathematical research on infinite-dimensional matrices. But like so many areas that Laslett initiated, such as the analysis of household listings before or the history of illegitimacy later, the research with simulation grew.

Laslett galvanized the enthusiasm of everyone who worked with him. Wachter found himself being more and more involved. On his regular visits back from Oxford to Cambridge, he found that Jan Laslett went out of her way to welcome him and make him feel at home. Like earlier cohorts of students of Locke under Laslett, he helped on Saturday afternoons to trim and rake in the garden of the home on Clarkson Road, amid the vestiges of 'ridge and furrow' which remain there from the medieval open fields of West Cambridge. Conversation ranged from the graffiti of the French student barricades, which Laslett had experienced first hand in Paris in 1968, to the hotel in Davos, once the asylum in Mann's *Magic Mountain*, which Wachter had sought out over school holidays. In February the Lasletts came together to guest night at St Catherine's in Oxford. A friendship and long-term working relationship was being forged.

By springtime, Wachter was seeing the statistical interest of the simulations in a different light. Recognizing that it is wrong to treat the inhabitants of a village, with all their interrelationships of descent, like an independent sample of a larger population, he tried to find out what was known about the variances of demographic statistics like the numbers in age groups for a closed or semi-closed small population. The models which his supervisor Kendall had studied in the 1960s provided a framework for studying such questions, but the equations for age group variances, for instance, had never been solved in closed form. Most available theory applied only to limiting behaviour over infinite time. The simulations which were being undertaken could provide an opportunity to measure such variances directly as functions of the specified demographic rates, and so to fill in this serious gap in the theory of random population processes.

The randomness of village-sized populations thus came to be a topic of interest in its own right. It became apparent that measures of randomness would be needed before the goodness or the badness of fit of simulated to real populations could be assessed. From this reflection, it was only a small step to realize that such measures were also needed before the similarity or contrast among patterns of household composition from village to village or country to country could be assessed by historians with due regard to the statistical significance of the apparent differences. The contributors to *Household and Family in Past Time* had not been worrying about randomness. But here was an aspect of the subject that could not in the future be ignored.

As demographic rates were being gathered from the family reconstitution studies of Colyton and Aldenham from Tony Wrigley and Roger Schofield at the Cambridge Group, and as the statistical aspects of matching simulation outputs with empirical tables were being pondered, work also began on the specification of a household cycle process for simulation. Laslett focused on the stem family cycle. He was finishing the preface to *Household and Family in Past Time* and tracing for it the pivotal role in the social literature played by the stem family system, hypothesized as one of three historical stages by Frédéric Le Play. The principal challenge to taking the English tables in the volume at face value, with their low levels of coresident kin of any form, came from the suggestion that late marriage and early mortality might make households going through a stem-family succession appear to be simple-family households during much of the time that a single listing might catch them in observation. Its centrality in the household debates made the stem family the natural starting point for simulation.

Exact specification of rules that would constitute stem-family systems in weaker and stronger versions grew into a long and tricky task. In the broad sense, stem-family behaviour need not entail coresidence at all. In the narrower sense relevant to studies of observed household structure, the basic idea involves one marrying child, usually a son, who with his spouse and children coresides with the parents, carrying on the 'stem', while the siblings either remain unmarried or leave the parental home at marriage. In such a system the years during which three generations coreside might be rather sharply circumscribed by ages at marriage of parents and children. Thus a stem-family system is a promising case for finding strong effects of demographic constraints preventing a complex-family cycle from manifesting itself in high proportions of complex-family households at a point in time. It is a good test case for general propositions about the effect of demographic rates on household structure.

On 19 May 1972 Wachter made a presentation at the evening seminar in Cambridge, explaining the current formulation of the stem family hypothesis and the statistical issues involved in testing it by simulation. In the audience, besides members and students working with members of the Cambridge Group, was George Homans, visiting Cambridge for the term, whose work with English medieval manorial court records in the 1930s had established the belief that early English villagers lived or tried to live in complex households.[8] Naturally, the speaker was pleased to have such an influential senior figure present. This pleasure was mitigated, however, when Homans suddenly cried out, 'It's all bunk. I don't believe a word of it. It's all bunk'.

Perhaps Homans meant, as the SOCSIM researchers were indeed proposing, that it was bunk to suppose at all that, under the late marriage and severe mortality of the 1600s and 1700s, English villagers could have been often found living in complex family households, however much they might have wanted to. To some in Cambridge the efficacy of demographic constraints seemed obvious. To others it seemed doubtful. In the published literature, the view that demographic constraints were a principal determinant of household size and structure, moderating differences between east and west and between past and present, had been championed by Marion Levy of Princeton, and was widely accepted.[9] With the question so much in the air, Laslett looked forward to simulation outputs with suspense. The British Social Science Research Council had granted funds to support modest programming and travel, but machine incompatibilities slowed the progress with trial runs at Oxford so much that the English side of the project had no substantive results to present when Wachter travelled to Pennsylvania State University on 12 June 1972 for a conference organized by Bennett Dyke and Jean MacCluer on 'Computer simulation in human population studies'.

Hammel and Hutchinson had in the meantime made progress, using an adaptation of POPSIM, and their paper with preliminary simulation results on matrilateral cross-cousin marriage and on incest taboos became the first chapter in the book edited by Dyke and MacCluer.[10] The conference provided the opportunity for detailed discussions with researchers developing alternative simulation programmes, especially with Jean MacCluer, Nancy Howell and Mark Skolnick, from whose experience with simulation many ideas for the further rewriting of POPSIM into SOCSIM came. At the same time, the conference generated a feeling of impatience with a field in which so much work never went beyond preliminary results and demonstrations of feasibility, and strengthened the resolve to carry at least one computer simulation project beyond provocative suggestions to a full, empirically relevant conclusion.

Wachter proceeded to Princeton to present, at a conference organized by Stephen Thernstrom, a joint paper written with Laslett on extinction rates on English baronetcies, and, as it turned out, to debate with

8 G.C. Homans, *English villagers of the thirteenth century* (Cambridge, Mass., 1940).

9 M.J. Levy, 'Aspects of the analysis of the family structure', in A.J. Coale et al. (eds), *Aspects of the analysis of family structure* (Princeton, NJ, 1965).

10 See note 7 in this chapter.

Lawrence Stone the purpose of statistics in history.[11] From there he flew to Berkeley. Laslett followed, and on 22 June 1972 he, Hammel and Wachter met for the first time together since the Bishop's Hostel meeting.

Laslett at this meeting agreed that all computer work for the immediate future should be done at Berkeley by Hutchinson, with plans for eventual conversion of a completed SOCSIM programme to run in England. Wachter would travel back and forth in term breaks between Oxford and Berkeley, keeping each side in touch with the thinking of the other as strategic programming decisions were made. A two-year grant application to the US National Science Foundation was planned. As finally submitted in December 1972 and funded, the proposal contemplated activity on a greatly expanded scale. A consortium of ten scholars in England and America became loosely affiliated, expressing their interests in using a completed SOCSIM programme for their own problems in anthropology, history and demography. The core SOCSIM group itself proposed to work on no less than nine problems. The list of problems seemed grandiose at the time, and years beyond the expiration of the grant still seemed wishful fancy. But it is interesting in retrospect, 13 years later, to see how many of the nine topics in this initial application eventually bore fruit.

Problem A, 'marriage impediments and population viability', led to the incest studies published in *Science* by Hammel, McDaniel and Wachter in 1979, and an expanded version in a volume on genealogical demography in 1980.[12] Problem B, 'the skewing of consanguineal relationships in marriage', was treated in a paper published by Hammel, Hutchinson and Wachter in 1976.[13] Problem C was the central problem put forward by Laslett, 'household composition and demographic rates', treated in full detail in *Statistical Studies of Historical Social Structure* and now being pursued further in the context of nuclear hardship models by Laslett and Jim Smith. Problem D was 'living kin and demographic rates'; what was contemplated was the estimation of demographic rates from counts of kin. The simulations here eventually demonstrated the unfeasibility rather than the feasibility of such

11 Later published as chapter 7 of Wachter et al., *Statistical studies*.

12 E.A. Hammel, C.K. McDaniel and K.W. Wachter, 'Demographic consequences of incest tabus', *Science* 205 (1979), pp. 972–7; E.A. Hammel, C.K. McDaniel and K.W. Wachter, 'Vice in the Villefranchian: a microsimulation analysis of the demographic effects of incest prohibitions', in B. Dyke and W. Morrill (eds), *Genealogical Demography* (London and New York, 1980), pp. 209–34.

13 E.A. Hammel, D. Hutchinson and K.W. Wachter, 'A stochastic simulation and numerical test of the deterministic model. Appendix to the matrilateral implications of structural cross-cousin marriage', in E. Zubrow (ed), *Demographic anthropology; quantitative approaches* (Albuqerque, 1976), pp. 145–60.

estimation in most practical circumstances.[14] But the problem in reverse – the prediction of proportions of living kin in the future from
assumptions about demographic rates – came to loom much larger,
culminating in essays published in the early 1980s and in work (as yet
largely unpublished) by Laslett and by Laslett and Jim Smith with the
aged in England and in China that continues to the present day.[15]

Problem E, 'the reliability of family reconstitution', was never tackled, partly because Tony Wrigley and Roger Schofield at the Cambridge Group turned their attention away from reconstitution to
aggregative analysis and back projection, reducing the active demand
for reliability studies in the later SOCSIM years. Problem F, the
'sensitivity of analytic models', figured in the studies of living kin, and
continues today in studies at Berkeley of new parity-based measures of
the extent of family limitation. Finally, three policy-relevant topics were
enumerated: G, 'perception of mortality and family planning'; H, 'inheritance laws and family planning'; and I, 'taxation and family planning'. These were never brought to scholarly fruition, perhaps having
served their purpose by stimulating the benevolence of mission-oriented
reviewers.

The next year was a difficult one. Hutchinson successfully rewrote
the computer routines, producing the household version of SOCSIM.
Ruth Deuel wrote for it the complex algorithms for recomputation of
intra-household kinship relationships on changes of membership and
headship, based on Hammel's earlier formal kinship analyses. But as
the marriage choice routines were completed, the difficulties of the
problem of choosing rates became evident. In the closed model, a
marriage event decreed for an individual by the random numbers of the
Monte Carlo routines may fail to take place, since a suitable partner as
determined by the spousal preference criteria may not be found in the
existing population at that time. Therefore, the observed marriage rates
will not agree with the specified marriage rates that govern the Monte
Carlo. Since the observed marriage rates and ages and age differences
between spouses needed to be made to agree with the English pre-
industrial targets, a long elaborate process of hit-and-miss rate tuning
was required. Another long process seemed to be required to give an

14 K.W. Wachter, 'The sister's riddle and the importance of variance when guessing
demographic rates from kin counts', *Demography* 17 (1979), pp. 103–114; C.K. McDaniel and
E.A. Hammel, 'A kin-based measure of *r* and an evaluation of its effectiveness', *Demography*
21 (1984), pp. 41–52.

15 E.A. Hammel, C.K. McDaniel and K.W. Wachter, 'The kin of the aged in 2000 AD', in
J. Morgan, V. Oppenheimer and S. Kiesler (eds), *Ageing, vol. 2: Social change* (London and
New York, 1981), pp. 11–39. See too the preliminary remarks in P. Laslett, 'The significance
of the past in the study of ageing', *Ageing and Society* 4 (1984), pp. 384–88 and the contribution
of J.E. Smith, 'The computer simulation of kin-sets and kin-counts', in Bongaarts et al.,
Family demography.

initial population with which to begin simulating a consistent initial age, kinship and household structure. This problem, however, was solved by the trick of beginning with the age structure of Ealing in 1599 and letting a simulation with stationary demographic rates create the kinship and household structure for later use in further simulations.

The winter passed. It was a time of frustration. *Household and Family in Past Time* was going to press, and no more had been learned about the effect of household cycles than had been known at the beginning. What was the computer simulation project? A mix of grandiose plans and endlessly petty details. Wachter felt himself wrenched away from his mathematical work, with nothing to show for his efforts, and nothing in immediate prospect.

On 22 March 1973 Laslett addressed a faculty colloquium on comparative and historical social structure of the Institute of International Studies at Berkeley, the forerunner of the present-day Stanford-Berkeley Colloquium in Demography. Instead of discussing the speculations of the simulation project, he concentrated on the empirical household evidence which was just now reaching publication in *Household and Family in Past Time*. Hammel and Wachter both heard his presentation after dinner at the Durant Hotel, a presentation arguing that pre-industrial English villagers must not have been trying in any numbers to live in 'traditional' complex kin-connected households. Voices and passions rose as distinguished figures in the audience asserted that the listings proved no such thing, that household listings gave no useful information on kinship relations, and that demographic constraints on the portion of the household cycle during which it would appear complex could just as easily explain the observations. Laslett replied that he and his colleagues were worrying about just these problems, but much of the audience remained unconvinced.

It is worth noting at this point that the central hypothesis of the work discussed at the seminar and later reported by Hammel, Wachter and Laslett was precisely that of the potential importance of demographic constraints.[16] Numerous cautionary remarks about the interpretation of household listings had been made by Laslett in *Household and Family in Past Time*, and were later made with Hammel in their paper of 1974 on household composition, and by Hammel in 1984 in a paper on household form and function.[17]

The following Sunday, taking a break from SOCSIM planning meetings, Peter and Jan Laslett invited Wachter out for a drive down the peninsula between San Francisco and Palo Alto, through stands of

16 E.A. Hammel and K.W. Wachter, 'Primonuptiality and ultimonuptiality; their effects on stem family household formation', in R. Lee (ed.), *Population patterns in the past* (London and New York, 1977), pp. 133–34; and Wachter et al., *Statistical studies*.

17 E.A. Hammel, 'On the XX of investigating household functions', in R. Netting, R.R. Wilk and E.J. Arnould (eds), *Households* (London, 1984).

redwoods and over the hills to the Pacific Coast at Half Moon Bay. They talked about redwoods, about Nietzsche, about the Lasletts' happy year at the Center for Advanced Study; and by the time they left the car to walk in the fog on the sand near Half Moon Bay, they were talking about SOCSIM. It was an uneasy conversation. It had been years, and no results were yet in view. Wachter felt torn between his loyalty to the project and his hesitancy about the long leap into the dark that carrying the household simulations to completion now seemed to demand. How far afield from his primary mathematical interests was he being drawn by the simulation project? How conclusive would the findings be? How important a contribution to long-term knowledge? Finally, listening to all these misgivings, Jan Laslett said, 'You need to give Ken a real chance to back out now.'

The chance was offered, but never taken. Laslett's conviction in the importance of the research was constant, despite his frustration at the slowness of the progress. He had seen similarly arduous and uncertain research initiatives in the early days of the Cambridge Group finally prosper. He managed to communicate his own determination to go forward, and his own conviction of eventual success.

By the summer a few computer runs were ready using the initial population constructed from the Ealing listing and the demographic rates tuned to agree with target rates based on the Colyton and Aldenham family reconstitutions. Laslett arranged for a paper on the classical statistical problem of the variances of numbers of people in age groups in a closed village-sized population to be presented by Wachter at the Conference on Historical Demography at Clare College, Cambridge, organized by the Cambridge Group in July 1973.

In Berkeley the team around Hammel, now funded by NSF, was growing and producing. He and Deuel reduced the Hammel-Laslett system for classifying households to computer algorithms and added other useful routines, published in 1977 as 'Five classy programs'.[18] Laslett often teased Hammel that he had reduced the system not merely to algorithmic form but to unrecognizability. Whenever they met, they always took delight in deciphering with pencil and paper the variety of possible classifications of some new intricate household, empirical or artificial, and the SOCSIM routines occasionally generated households so unforeseen from experience with listings that new refinements of the classification rules were unavoidable. Robert Lundy, a student under Nathan Keyfitz in the old Berkeley Demography Department, wrote programmes for demographic rate calculations and later for generating initial populations. Hutchinson began the long task

---

18 E.A. Hammel and R.Z. Deuel, 'Five classy programs for the classification of households', Institute of International Studies, Research Monograph no. 33, University of California, Berkeley, 1977.

of documenting the SOCSIM code. Wachter spent the second half of the summer of 1973 and the middle of the winter at Berkeley, writing up the mathematical assumptions for the manual and, most important, thrashing out with Hammel an operational version of stem-family household formation rules.

The British Social Science Research Council agreed to sponsor a conference in Cambridge on Mathematics and Historical Sociology in July 1974. Under Peter Laslett's guidance, Ken Wachter undertook the organization of the meeting, with sessions in the basement of the Cambridge History Faculty Library, and accommodation in St John's College for the participants from France, Germany, America and Britain. The morning of 9 July 1974 was reserved for the first SOCSIM results on 'demographic rates and complexity of households'. Five papers were promised. The first gave the 'rationale for the experiment'. In the second, Peter Laslett analysed the empirical evidence on households, setting the context of 'differing views on the importance of stem-family tendencies in European development'. The third and fourth dealt with 'demographic assumptions' and with 'behavioural rules of household formation'. The fifth was titled 'experimental results'. The results arrived in Cambridge with Hammel and Hutchinson on Saturday. On Sunday Wachter hid himself away in the Cambridge Group rooms in Silver Street, eerie and deserted over the weekend, pressing conclusions out of the computer tables and typing them into text.

Here in the tables were answers toward which the SOCSIM team had worked for years. But the task of constructing arguments based on the computer outputs brought home an uncomfortable realization. The answers were provocative, but not conclusive. The household rules had been designed to embody a strong stem-family formation system, with the stem continued by the earliest-marrying son, so as to elevate, if not strictly to maximize, the proportion of observable multi-generational households. These household rules did produce much higher proportions of complex households than those in the 14 English historical listings in the table Laslett had prepared for the second of the SOCSIM papers. But nothing yet ruled out the possibility that weaker versions of stem-family systems might not prove after all compatible with the listings evidence.

The high proportions of stem-family households in the simulations suggested that demographic constraints were not very potent; but a sceptic could easily ask, very potent compared with what? The answers with one set of rates gave no knowledge of how much leverage a difference in demographic rates would exercise over household types. The simulations had indicated extensive randomness in household proportions. Again, a sceptic could ask, extensive randomness compared with what? The 14 cases with which the simulations were being compared had been selected for various characteristics, and by no means did they resemble a random sample. Therefore no strict comparison between the observed variability and the random variability predicted by the simulations could be drawn.

The suggestive results were well received at the conference for the promise they held out, but the writing of the five papers had led Laslett, Hammel and Wachter to confess that the intellectual labour was just beginning, not ending. Several versions of household rule systems needed trying, to give lower bounds, upper bounds, and a measure of central tendency to household proportions. Demographic parameters needed to be varied systematically, to measure their leverage. Features of the simulation model needed to be redesigned, so that the foreseeably important sources of variability were all incorporated. In particular, William Brass had called attention to the importance of giving women heterogeneous levels of fecundability, to create more realistic variances in completed family size. With these changes, all the runs would need to be redone. Most of all, however, the simulations dictated the need for a new kind of empirical research project. A collection of listings must be brought together which were not preselected for the occurrence of particular household forms but which approximated as nearly as possible a random sample of all listings of a quality sufficient to permit household classification.

At the end of the SOCSIM day at the conference, Jan and Peter Laslett gave a party for the participants in the garden at Clarkson Road. Their sons George and Robert, balloonists, launched a great balloon in celebration. To the researchers it seemed that after three years of research the investigation, like some trial balloon, was still in the launching stage.

On 12 July 1974, before parting, Laslett, Hammel and Wachter met for breakfast in the Judge's Room at Trinity College, the guest room below the Master's Lodging where Queen Victoria used to stay when visiting Cambridge, and where the crimson-covered bed is still surmounted by the monogram V&A. In these splendid surroundings the three made a decision – much less portentous than others reached within those walls but ultimately fateful nevertheless – that the research results should not be fragmented into a series of journal articles but should become a book. The five hasty papers presented to the conference would form the core around which, through four years of reworking and rewriting, *Statistical Studies of Historical Social Structure* would condense.

Laslett now set out on the difficult and unprecedented task of going through all the 500 complete household listings for English pre-industrial villages and towns collected over the years in the files of the Cambridge Group. He and his son Robert, then an undergraduate at St John's College, Oxford, set up criteria for selecting listings solely on the basis of quality of recording, without reference to any household characteristics. From the 500, a main sample of 30 highest-quality listings and a reserve sample of 34 high-quality listings were culled and analysed – the first sampling exercise, so far as we know, in the study of historical household structure.

For the revision of the simulation programmes, the central issue was which aspects of historical realism should be insisted upon and which might be forgone. Two fundamental issues govern decisions about realism. The first is whether the addition of some 'realistic' feature can be expected to make an important difference to the outcome of the simulations – important, that is, with respect to the particular problem being investigated. Thus, for example, Brass's intuition about the relationship between heterogeneous fertility and the variance of completed family sizes was persuasive; here was a point of realism that might make a difference in the outputs of an important variable. It was not and is not clear that anything would have been gained by introducing migration into the simulation, because the rates used already reflected ongoing migrational processes in the Aldenham data, and the net effect in a random exchange of population should be nought.

Much clearer was the utility of class- or wealth-specific rates. It may be that the cherished stem family was the behavioural property of only the privileged few but the cultural ideal property of all. But here arises the second issue involved in the achievement of realism – whether one can discover reasonable rates, or probabilities, or logical decision trees that will permit non-trivial and non-arbitrary simulation. Nowhere in the historical literature or even in the voluminous files of the Cambridge Group are there sufficient and sufficiently connected data to permit distinguishing demographic rates for migrants and for non-migrants, for rich and for poor, for owners and for the landless. To guess at such rates would be to hunt unicorns from a flying carpet, deserving of the criticism that we discovered from simulation only what we had put into it.

On 3 August 1974 Wachter embarked for the United States to take up an Assistant Professorship of Statistics at Harvard. In October, Laslett, Hammel and Wachter met again in Philadelphia to present the first simulated contrast between two household formation systems, 'primonuptiality and ultimonuptiality', at the conference organized by Ronald Lee and published subsequently under the latter's editorship.[19] Lee, like Wachter, would later join Hammel in the refounded Graduate Group in Demography at Berkeley.

Back at Berkely struggles with computing continued. A sensitive test of the performance of the routines, comparing outputs to predictions from stable population theory, identified a small persistent bias, finally eliminated by changes in the rounding conventions for dates of birth events. The manual documenting the SOCSIM programmes was painstakingly completed. Chad McDaniel, a new graduate student in anthropology who

19 See note 16 in this chapter.

would collaborate and contribute to all the later SOCSIM investigations, joined the team. Progress also continued in Cambridge. When Wachter returned to take his Ph.D. degree in a congregation in the Senate House in Cambridge, Laslett proudly produced for him the tables from the new household samples, and they began to write the empirical chapters for the book together.

From 5 August to 14 August 1975 the US Mathematical Social Science Board sponsored a working seminar specifically devoted to demographic microsimulation at the Center for Advanced Study in Palo Alto, with participants over a range of disciplines from the United States, Great Britain, Australia and France. The battery of results from SOCSIM, which had been merely suggestive a year before in Cambridge, were now reaching conclusive form. Each piece in an elaborate jigsaw puzzle of inferences was being fitted into place, so that hypotheses could be put forward precisely, tested precisely, and related directly to a relevantly assembled body of empirical data.

The SOCSIM programmes were now available as a documented, general tool for experiments in history, demography and anthropology. One conference participant (Barbara Anderson) specified computer runs for testing a particular demographic hypothesis which were run on the spot at the conference and presented the next day. Part of the conference was methodological. For example Lutz Berkner and others argued strongly for maximum realism, urging the inclusion of simulations of migration. Mark Skolnick and Chris Cannings pressed for what they felt were greater efficiencies of prescheduled sequences of demographic events to persons rather than the almost continuously recomputed probabilities characteristic of SOCSIM. That idea has now been adopted in CAMSIM but continues to be rejected in SOCSIM in order to retain close control of complexly interacting processes, the ability to model closely at the level of microevents rather than at that of aggregate probabilities of their occurrence, and the ability to change rates in the flow of time in response to events in the simulation.

But another part of the conference took up the status of empirical knowledge of household structure in the light of the experimental results. On 13 August Laslett opened the empirical debate with a speech that began 'the greatest friend of the historical sociologist is the busybody.' He traced the making of the lists, the circumstances of various communities that appeared in the new household sample, and the interpretation of levels of complex household membership observed in England compared with continental cases in the light of the simulated stem-family household levels. In his view, the simulations laid to rest the ghost of the stem-family hypothesis as a predominant family form for England. But what of the possibility noted earlier of stem-family inclinations as a minority family form among, for instance, the subgroup of landed villagers? That possibility too could in principle be simulated, and the proponents and opponents of stem-family organization might find their apparently conflicting expectations fulfilled in the aggregate outputs for a heterogeneous population. If only a meeting between more detailed data and refined techniques could be brought about!

It is in just such questions that we see the fruitful marriage of Laslett's kind of history and the technological acrobatics of computer simulation. In the long run it is up to the archaeologists of attics and the watchers of busybodies to discover and interpret the fine-grained social data that will find for us the world lost to time. And it is up to the exercise of the statistical imagination to judge whether the data they bring to light can be regarded as trustworthy evidence about a world that might have existed. It requires, indeed, a priest, a mountebank, and a prophet to regain a world.

Contributors

Jacques Beauroy is Chargé de Recherche au Centre National de la Recherche Scientifique in Paris. He has taught at the Universities of Toronto and Dalhousie in Canada and has served as French cultural attaché in the United States and Morocco. He is author of *Vin et société à Bergerac* (Anma Libri, 1976) and co-editor of *Popular Culture in France* (Anma Libri, 1975). He is currently engaged in a major study of the social structure of north-west Norfolk in the thirteenth and fourteenth centuries.

Lloyd Bonfield is Associate Professor of Law at Tulane University. He was both a research student and research fellow at Trinity College, Cambridge, where he worked closely with Peter Laslett. He is the author of *Marriage Settlements, 1601–1740; the development of the strict settlement* (Cambridge University Press, 1983), formerly edited *Law and History Review* and is co-founder of *Continuity and Change*. He is presently working on a study of peasant inheritance in early modern England.

Vivien Brodsky is Lecturer in History at the University of Adelaide, South Australia. She studied under Peter Laslett's supervision at the Cambridge Group for the History of Population and Social Structure, completing her Cambridge Ph.D. in 1978. She is currently working on a study of marriage and social mobility in pre-industrial England.

Eugene Hammel is Professor of Anthropology and Demography at the University of California, Berkeley, and is the author of many books and articles in both of these fields. He has researched extensively into the family history of south-east Europe and has worked collaboratively with Peter Laslett in deriving a classificatory system for the comparative analysis of domestic group structures and in the application of microsimulation techniques to family history. The latter research resulted in their co-authored publication (with Kenneth Wachter), *Statistical Studies in Historical Social Structure* (Academic Press, 1978).

Hervé Le Bras is a graduate of l'École Polytechnique, Directeur d'Études l'École des Hautes Études en Sciences Sociales and Directeur de Recherche à l'Institut National d'Études Démographiques in Paris. He is author of numerous articles in *Population* of which he is principal editor. He is author of *La Famille et l'enfant dans les pays développés* (OECD, 1979) and co-author (with Emmanuel Todd) of *L'Invention de la France* (Pluriel, 1981).

L.R. Poos is Assistant Professor of History at The Catholic University of America. He was a research student at Trinity College, Cambridge and subsequently a research fellow at Fitzwilliam College, Cambridge. He is currently researching a number of topics in the demography, economy and social structure of later medieval England, and is completing a book on the social and economic history of Essex after the Black Death.

Roger Schofield is the Director of the Cambridge Group for the History of Population and Social Structure and a fellow of Clare College, Cambridge. He is an editor of *Population Studies* and *Local Population Studies* and is currently President of the British Society for Population Studies. He is the author of numerous articles on English demographic history and a co-author (with E.A. Wrigley) of *The Population History of England 1541–1871* (Edward Arnold, 1981). He is preparing a demographic study of early modern England based on the detailed data from a large number of parish family reconstitutions.

Richard Smith is a fellow of All Souls College, Oxford, and University Lecturer in Historical Demography at the University of Oxford. He was formerly Assistant Director of the Cambridge Group for the History of Population and Social Structure and a fellow and tutor of Fitzwilliam College, Cambridge. He has published many articles on the demographic and family history of medieval and early modern Europe and England and was co-editor with Peter Laslett and Karla Oosterveen of *Bastardy and its Comparative History* (Edward Arnold,

1980) and editor of *Land, Kinship and Life-cycle* (Cambridge University Press, 1984). He is author of *The Demography of England and her European Neighbours 1500–1750* (Macmillan, 1986) and is currently preparing a study of the economic and social history of marriage in England from 1100 to 1700.

Simon Szreter is University Assistant Lecturer in History and a research fellow of Gonville and Caius College, Cambridge. He was an undergraduate and a research student at Pembroke College, Cambridge, and did his Ph.D. at the Cambridge Group for the History of Population and Social Structure on 'The decline of marital fertility in England and Wales *c.*1870–1914' (1983). He is currently extending his research into the causes of fertility decline in the later nineteenth and early twentieth centuries.

David Thomson is Lecturer in Social History at Massey University, New Zealand, and is currently a Research Associate at the Rank Xerox Unit on Ageing founded by Peter Laslett at the Cambridge group for the History of Population and Social Structure. He was a research student at the University of Cambridge where he was supervised by Peter Laslett, receiving his Ph.D. on 'Provision for the elderly in England 1830–1908' in 1980.

Emmanuel Todd was a research student at Trinity College, Cambridge, where he studied under Peter Laslett's supervision and obtained his Ph.D. in 1975. He has published many books, some of which, such as that co-authored with Hervé le Bras, *L'Invention de la France* (Pluriel, 1981), *La Troisième Planète* (Seuil, 1982) and *L'Enfance du monde* (Seuil, 1984) have been largely concerned with relations between demographic systems, family forms and political ideologies. *La Troisième Planète* was published in English under the title of *The Explanation of Ideology* (Blackwell, 1985).

Pier Paolo Viazzo received his Ph.D. in social anthropology from the University of London and is now completing a volume entitled *Upland Communities: environment, population and social structure in the Alps* to be published by Cambridge University Press. He has worked collaboratively with Peter Laslett on various aspects of illegitimacy in pre-industrial Europe.

Kenneth Wachter is Professor of Statistics and Demography at the University of California, Berkeley, having taught previously at Harvard and been a research fellow at St Catherine's College, Oxford. He has published many articles in the fields of statistics and demography and was a principal developer of SOCSIM, which formed the basis for his collaborative research with Peter Laslett on household formation processes. He is a co-author (with Peter Laslett and Eugene Hammel) of *Statistical Studies of Historical Social Structure* (Academic Press, 1978) and is co-editor of *Family Demography: Methods and their Application* (Oxford University Press, 1986).

Richard Wall is Senior Research Officer at the Cambridge Group for the History of Population and Social Structure. He has published extensively on family and household patterns in past and contemporary societies and is a co-founder of the journal *Continuity and Change*. He is also an editor of *Local Population Studies* and has co-edited (with Peter Laslett) *Household and Family in Past Time* (Cambridge University Press, 1972) and (with Peter Laslett and Jean Robin) *Family Forms in Historic Europe* (Cambridge University Press, 1983).

Christopher Wilson is Lecturer in Demography at the London School of Economics. He was an undergraduate and research student at Trinity College, Cambridge, completing his Ph.D. in 1981 on 'Marital fertility in pre-industrial England'. He has published papers on various aspects of fertility in pre-industrial England and Europe and is the editor of *The Dictionary of Demography* (Basil Blackwell, 1985).

Keith Wrightson is University Lecturer in History and a Fellow and Tutor of Jesus College, Cambridge. He was an undergraduate, research student and research fellow at Fitzwilliam College, Cambridge. He studied under Peter Laslett's supervision and obtained his Cambridge Ph.D. in 1974. He was also a Lecturer in History at the University of St Andrews from 1975–1984. He is the author of (with David Levine) *Poverty and Piety in an English Village: Terling 1575–1700* (Academic Press, 1979) and *English Society 1580–1680* (Hutchinson, 1982) and has published several articles on the social history of early modern England.

E.A. Wrigley is Professor of Population Studies at the London School of Economics and a director of the Cambridge Group for the History of Population and Social Structure (of which he was a co-founder with Peter Laslett). He is the author of numerous articles, in addition to *Industrial Growth and Population Change* (Cambridge University Press, 1961), *Population and History* (Weidenfeld and Nicolson, 1969) and (with Roger Schofield) *The Population History of England 1541–1871* (Edward Arnold, 1981). He edited *An Introduction to English Historical Demography* (Weidenfeld and Nicolson, 1966), *Nineteenth-century Society* (Cambridge University Press, 1972), *Identifying People in the Past* (Edward Arnold, 1973) and (with Philip Abrams) *Towns in Societies* (Cambridge University Press, 1978).

Index

Abbreviations: *p* passim, scattered references; n note.
Figures in **bold type** indicate whole chapters or sections.
Figures in *italic type* indicate tables.